THE CHILD

THE CHILD

DEVELOPMENT FROM BIRTH
THROUGH ADOLESCENCE

Judith Rich Harris

Robert M. Liebert
State University of New York
at Stony Brook

Prentice-Hall, Inc., Englewood Cliffs, New Jersey 07632

Library of Congress Cataloging in Publication Data

Harris, Judith Rich.
   The child, from birth through adolescence.

   Bibliography.
   Includes index.
   1. Child development. 2. Infants. 3. Adolescence.
I. Liebert, Robert M., (date). II. Title.
HQ767.9.H36 1984   305.2'3   83-24429
ISBN 0-13-130436-4

Production Editor: Jeanne Hoeting
Photo Research: Mira Schachne
Book Design and Page Layout: Kenny Beck
Cover Photo: Thomas Rampy, The Image Bank
Cover Design: Jayne Conte
Manufacturing Buyer: Ron Chapman

(Acknowledgments appear on p. 579, which
constitutes a continuation of the
copyright page.)

ISBN 0-13-130436-4

Prentice-Hall International, Inc., *London*
Prentice-Hall of Australia Pty. Limited, *Sydney*
Editora Prentice-Hall do Brasil, Ltda., *Rio de Janeiro*
Prentice-Hall Canada Inc., *Toronto*
Prentice-Hall of India Private Limited, *New Delhi*
Prentice-Hall of Japan, Inc., *Tokyo*
Prentice-Hall of Southeast Asia Pte. Ltd., *Singapore*
Whitehall Books Limited, *Wellington, New Zealand*

To Sam L. Rich and Frances Lichtman Rich
and to Harry Liebert and Minnie Schorr Liebert

Contents Overview

Contents

PART II INFANCY AND TODDLERHOOD

PART III THE PRESCHOOL YEARS

PART IV MIDDLE CHILDHOOD

PART V ADOLESCENCE

Preface

This is a book for those who wish or need to know about children. It was written for all those who are now or who may someday be responsible for the welfare of children, as well as for those who are interested in their own beginnings and in how they developed. Our goal for this book is to describe the growth and development of the child, beginning at birth (or even before birth, for our story really starts at conception) and continuing through adolescence. Our book is intended to be an introduction to this topic—the reader is not assumed to have had any previous courses in child development or in related fields.

Just in the last quarter-century or so, a great deal has been discovered about children and how they develop. Making discoveries of this sort is a complex and painstaking task, one that requires both talent and effort. Before we describe the discoveries themselves, we want our readers to have some notion of how they are made—of how this kind of knowledge is acquired. Then too, certain basic ideas—especially theoretical ideas—are essential to a full understanding of our subject matter. Thus, to explain what is known about child development we must first say something about the study of child development and about its theoretical underpinnings. We do this is the first section of the book.

From there on, the book is organized chronologically, like a history, beginning with conception and following the developing individual through to the end of adolescence. The focus, by and large, is on the normal development of the normal child. However, it is also necessary to acknowledge that things do not always go so smoothly. In our "Problems in Development" boxes, set apart from the rest of the text, we examine various difficulties that may occur during the course of development. Other boxes—the "Close-Ups"—provide an opportunity to go into more detail on some particular topic of interest, often by means of actual case histories or real-life vignettes. In the last kind of box, labeled "The Child in Society," we look at issues of social importance—for instance, moral or ethical questions and cross-cultural findings.

A vast quantity of prose has been written about children and their development, including much that is biased and political, and much that is simply wrong. In addition, there is far too much interesting and "good" material for any introductory book. So, of course, we have had to be selective. Several criteria guided our selection. One was balance. There are different methods and viewpoints in the study of child development (for example, in answering questions about how children develop their ideas about morality), and we have tried to include all the major current ideas bearing on each important topic. At the same time, agreement was also a primary selection criterion for us, in the sense that we wanted to make sure that we conveyed all the important facts and ideas on which researchers have agreed. Another kind of balance also matters to us, and that is the balance between truly classic studies and very contemporary ones. We want our readers to be aware of the several dozen very famous studies in child development, which have stood the test of time and which illustrate how a science of child development has itself developed. On the other hand, we have sought to identify and describe very recent studies that represent current trends or promise to be the classics of the future.

Throughout, a major concern has been that our book will be easy to learn from. We have tried to write in clear, nontechnical language. We have worked to produce well-thought-out chapter summaries and a complete glossary, in order to provide clarification and to facilitate review of the material. When writing about children in general would seem too vague or abstract, we have looked instead at one particular child (generally a composite drawn from several typical or interesting cases) in order to bring to life the processes and changes we describe.

A good deal of time has been spent on obtaining illustrations that are accurate and informative, rather than merely decorative. We are indebted to Mira Schachne and Anita Duncan for their tireless efforts to find photos to meet our very detailed specifications.

Several reviewers deserve our thanks, both for their helpful criticisms and for their favorable comments. We thank:

Ann L. Bradford, California State University
William Crain, The City University of New York
David Dolfinger, Denver Auraria Community College
Ed Fahmeier, Regional Institute for Children and Adolescence
Larry Fenson, San Diego State University
Allen Frerichs, Northern Illinois University
Bernard Gorman, Nassau Community College
Megan Gunner, University of Minnesota
Paul Hutko, State University of New York at Oswego
Paul S. Kaplan, Suffolk County Community College
David McGrevy, St. Lawrence University
Thomas Moeschl, Broward Community College
Craig Peery, Brigham Young University
Jay B. Pozner, Jackson Community College
J. Randall Price, Richland College
Sidney Rosenblum, University of New Mexico
Martin Schulman, Essex County College
Tirzah Schutzengel, Bergen Community College
Jean Tracy, Elmhurst College
Katherine Van Giffen, California State University, Fullerton
Michael Walraven, Jackson Community College
Diana Woodruff, Stanford University

We also thank Pamela Hilligoss and Addison Woodard, Governor's State University, for preparation of the Study Guide, and Jeffrey Fagen, St. John's University, for preparation of the Instructor's Manual.

We are indebted to many other people whose efforts, patience, and understanding have been essential to making this book a reality. John Isley of Prentice-Hall brought us together as a writing team and provided motivation, encouragement, and counsel throughout the project. Jeanne Hoeting permitted us to make the almost unending succession of final touches that authors are wont to do when deeply involved in a project. Jean Steinberg, Claire Spettell, and John Richters served as research assistants for various aspects of the project. Nomi Harris did an excellent job of typing the manuscript; her astute comments and suggestions (made from the point of view of the student) were also of great value to us. Finally, we thank our spouses for their encouragement and support.

Judith Rich Harris
New Providence, New Jersey

Robert M. Liebert
Port Jefferson, New York

THE CHILD

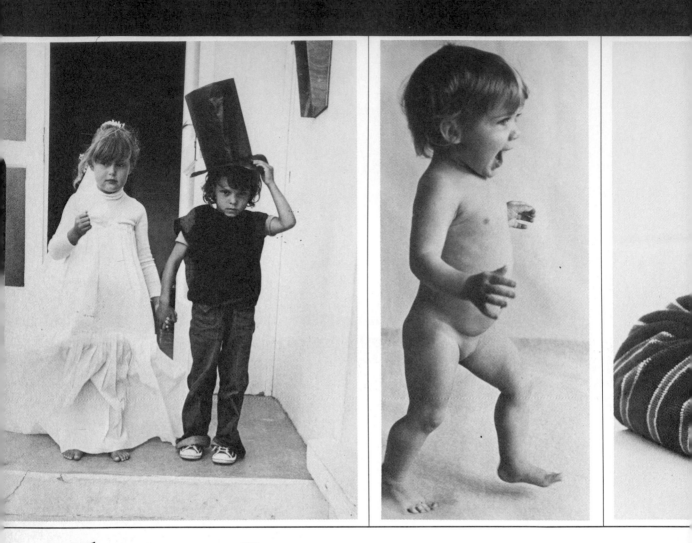

Chapter One

SOME BASIC CONCEPTS

One

You are no longer a child. Childhood is something that is behind you—something that you can look back on in memory. Perhaps your childhood was exceptionally happy and your memories are pleasant ones, tinged with a bit of regret that those days are gone forever. Or perhaps your childhood was not so happy, and you are glad that those days are behind you and you can go forward into the future as an independent adult.

In either case, you can probably remember many things that happened to you, many things that you did, when you were a child. You can remember things that occurred when you were 5 or 6 years old, and perhaps when you were even younger. But there's an odd thing about those memories: when you remember yourself, let's say at age 5, you know it's *you* who experienced the events you're remembering; and yet, in a way, it's almost as though it were someone else. If it weren't for your knowledge that the person you're remembering is yourself, it would be possible to think of that 5-year-old as a different person, not you at all.

In a sense, that 5-year-old *is* a different person. You have changed considerably over the intervening years. You are bigger, stronger, and quite different in appearance. You are wiser. You possess more information. You can do many more things, understand many more things, than you could as a young child. Even so, in that child you once were you can see quite clearly the essential features of the person you have become. And yet, looking at that child, who could have predicted that you would turn out to be exactly the person you are now?

We are talking about **development,** about the process that turns babies into children, children into adolescents, adolescents into young adults, and young adults into old people. It goes on, whether we want it to or not, from the time we are conceived until the moment we die.

In this book we will be concerned primarily with development between birth and late adolescence. We will be telling you about some of the findings that have emerged from the study of child development.

THE STUDY OF CHILD DEVELOPMENT

Research in child development is a fairly new field of endeavor, historically speaking. Whereas the study of the stars and the planets, for example, began in ancient times, the scientific study of childhood dates only from the late nineteenth or early twentieth century. One of the first to do research in this field was G. Stanley Hall, an American psychologist who got his Ph.D. degree at Harvard and later taught at Clark University. In the 1880s, Hall asked a great many questions of a great many children, in an effort to discover how their beliefs changed and their knowledge increased as they grew older. A couple of decades later Alfred Binet, a French psychologist, began to test schoolchildren in Paris in an attempt to distinguish between those of normal intelligence and those who would require special help in school. (This was the beginning of IQ testing.) At about the same time Sigmund Freud, in Vienna, was developing his ideas of the human mind and personality. Childhood plays a very important role in Freud's theories—in fact, Freud felt that what happens during infancy and early childhood is crucial. (We'll discuss Freud and Binet in greater detail later in the book—Freud in Chapter 3 and Binet in Chapter 10.)

G. Stanley Hall and Alfred Binet were psychologists; Freud, if he were alive today, would be considered a psychiatrist (since he had a medical degree). Other fields, too, have contributed to the study of childhood: anthropology, biology, sociology, education, and even philosophy. But today the majority of people who are doing research in this field consider themselves psychologists—developmental psychologists, to be exact.

Who are these people? Many of them are college professors, members of psychology departments in colleges and universities all over the world. Some are their students—graduate students or even undergraduates. Some are associated with other university departments (biology or sociology, for example), or with schools of education, of medicine or nursing, or of home economics. A few are members of private research organizations or of the research divisions of large companies. A few work at mental health clinics or are in private practice.

All of these people are united in their interest in young human beings. They find children fascinating, and they want to find out more about them. Moreover, having found something out, they want to tell others about what they have learned.

The results of research on child development are made public in several different ways. The most common way is to write a report describing the research and its results, and to submit it to one of the journals that publish scientific papers on such topics. There are a number of publications of this type. Much of the work that we will be telling you about in this book originally appeared in one of three journals: *Child Development, Developmental Psychology,* and *Journal of Experimental Child Psychology.* Issues of these journals appear several times a year, and each issue generally contains between 10 and 40 papers on child development. The authors of these papers have carried out a research project, done some statistical analyses of their results, written a concise report (in the style and format demanded by these journals) describing what they did and what they found out, and submitted this report to a journal. The journal editor then sends copies of this paper to two or three reviewers—usually college professors who have done research of a similar nature to that reported in the paper. These reviewers give their

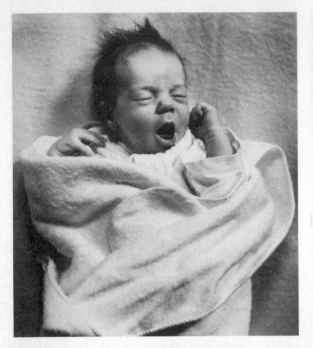

Development from infancy . . .

. . . through adolescence

opinions: that the research reported in the paper is interesting and competently done and that the paper should be published as is; or that the research is of insufficient interest or quality and that the paper should *not* be published; or that the research has merit but the paper needs to be revised in some way before it can be published. The authors must usually wait several months to learn whether their paper will be published; if they are lucky, it will appear in print within a year or so of when they first submitted it. They receive no payment from the journal, no royalties. Their reward consists of the recognition their work receives, and the fact that university positions and research grants are obtained more readily by people whose work is well-known and well-regarded.

Aside from journals, research in child development is also reported in books, in masters' and doctoral dissertations, and in papers spoken aloud at conferences and conventions (for instance, the biennial meetings of the Society for Research in Child Development). In general, we prefer to tell you about work that has been published in journals or books, so that if you are interested you can go to a university library and read the original report, which will of course contain more details than we can give you here. In a few cases, though, we have had to refer to dissertations or oral reports because a published version does not exist (or, if it does, we weren't aware of it).

In any case, whenever we give you some piece of information that comes from a specific source, we will tell you that source. The names and dates in parentheses you'll find scattered throughout the text can be looked up in the reference list at the back of this book. If we make a factual statement and it *doesn't* have a reference after it, it's because we are summarizing results distilled from many sources, not just one or two.

Using the Techniques of Science to Learn More about Childhood

One of the ideas on which this book is based is that it is possible to study child development in a scientific way, using the same research methods that other sciences use. Some people question whether it is possible to do this. They point out that children in particular (and people in general) are complicated and unpredictable. Doing research on children is not going to be like doing research in, say, chemistry. In chemistry you can add substance A to substance B, and inevitably (given a certain temperature, pressure, and so on) you will get substance C. But child A will do one thing under certain conditions, and child B, under what seem to be the same conditions, will do something else. What's worse, child A will do one thing on Monday and something altogether different on Tuesday—again under what seem to be the same conditions. So how can you have a science when the thing you're studying refuses to behave consistently?

The answer is that you can study *anything* in a scientific way. Whether or not a particular endeavor is a science doesn't depend on what's being studied—it depends on *how* it's being studied. It's perfectly possible to do good scientific research on the question of whether the toast *really* tends to fall butter-side-down. It's also perfectly possible to do *non*scientific research on the effects of temperature changes on chemical interactions.

Precisely because children are so complicated and unpredictable, it's not easy doing research on development. That doesn't mean that we *can't* do it, though—just that progress will be a little slower than we would like.

Does Science Dehumanize?   Another worry that people sometimes express is that studying childhood in a scientific way will take the warmth and caring out of it. Nonsense! The people who've been doing research in child development are doing it partly because they *do* care about children. And one of their important motivations is the hope that the knowledge they are so painstakingly acquiring may be used someday to improve children's lives and their futures. Not all that is discovered about child development can be put to immediate use, of course. But much of it can—it can give us some clues about how to deal with certain problems of development, or (better still) how to avoid them. Other findings may not have immediate practical applications, but they might turn out to have some in the long run, or they might just increase our knowledge about children in general.

Look at the great benefits that modern medical science has brought to the world—particularly to the world of childhood. A couple of centuries ago a child had only about a 50–50 chance of living long enough to become an adult. Now nearly every child grows up. Without scientific research, medical science couldn't have accomplished all that.

What's Wrong with Observation and Common Sense?   Another objection that has been raised to doing research on child development is: Why is it necessary? Can't we just observe children and use our common sense? Certainly we can observe children. Observation can be an extremely productive scientific method—look at all we've found out about the stars and the planets, simply by observing them! But in order for observation to be useful, it must be systematic. Careful records have to be kept, and careful provisions made, to avoid being misled by the biases of the observer.

Common sense is another matter altogether. Many people have criticized research on people on the grounds that "it wasn't necessary—common sense could have told us the same thing." That's all very well to say, *after* the fact. The point is, some of the things that people's common sense tells them turn out *not* to be true. And what one person's common sense tells him isn't always the same as what someone *else's* common sense tells *her*. Common sense warns us to Look before you leap, but also that He who hesitates is lost. It tells us that Absence makes the heart grow fonder, but it also says, Out of sight, out of mind.

DIFFERENT WAYS OF STUDYING CHILD DEVELOPMENT

In order to make clearer the kinds of research we will be describing, it will be helpful to have a quick look at some of the methods that are used to study child development.

Descriptive Studies

The first big surge of research in child development came in the 1920s and 30s. Much of this work (and a fair amount of later work, too) was of a sort we call **descriptive.** A good example is the research carried out by Mary Shirley in the early 1930s (Shirley, 1933). Studying 25 infants as they grew to toddlerhood, Shirley recorded their **motor development** (the development of the ability to move and coordinate the parts of the body, as in crawling, walking, and grasping things with the hands). A summary of her findings is shown in Figure 1–1. Clearly, there is a need for this sort of data. People who deal with children—parents, for instance—want to know what to expect from a child and roughly when to expect it.

There are problems, though, with most of the early descriptive reports. First of all, the babies Shirley studied were almost certainly not what we call a **representative sample** of American babies. A representative sample contains individuals from different racial and ethnic groups, different social and economic backgrounds, different geographical locations, and so on, in roughly the same proportions that they occur in the population as a whole. But Shirley's babies were probably all born in Minnesota, probably all were white, and probably most of them were born to parents of Northern European ancestry. Such a sample gives us some idea of what to expect from a baby born in Minnesota to white parents of Northern European ancestry; but what if the baby we're interested in is born in New York City to parents of Italian ancestry, or in Arizona to Mexican-American parents, or in South Carolina to black parents? Can we simply apply Shirley's data to all these babies and hope it will work? No, we can't: we have to test babies of all different backgrounds and ancestries, if we want to draw conclusions about babies in general.

The fact that Shirley didn't do this is one reason that the **norms** (or averages) she gave for the ages of the motor milestones do not agree with more recent figures. Shirley put the average age of walking at 15 months; according to modern figures the average baby walks at about 12 months. One reason for this discrepancy is the absence of black infants in Shirley's sample—black babies walk a little earlier, on the average, than whites. But even for white babies, Shirley's figure of 15 months seems too late. Perhaps babies are walking a little earlier now because of nutritional factors (solid foods are introduced into the diet sooner now than in the past) or other factors (such as the use of walkers). But it is also possible that Shirley's group of 25 babies happened, by chance, to be a little slow in learning to walk. After all, 25 babies

figure 1–1

Motor milestones in the first 15 months of life, according to Shirley (1933).

aren't really very many—not enough even to give you an accurate estimate of what to expect from Minnesotan babies born to white parents of Northern European ancestry!

Nor are 25 babies enough to give us an idea of the **variability** of the measured qualities. Are all babies quite similar, or are there great differences from one to another? The average age of walking in Shirley's sample was 15 months. But what if a child is still not walking at 20 months—can we consider him or her "normal"? What about 24 months, or 30 months? At some point, clearly, we must begin to realize that this child has a problem. But when?

There can be no hard-and-fast answer to this kind of question. If Shirley had studied 250 babies instead of 25, she might have found that 95 percent of them walked between, say, 9 months and 18 months. Then we would know, at least, that a nonwalking 20-month-old is quite unusual and should certainly be given a careful examination by a pediatrician.

The Normal Curve. Variability is an inevitable feature of any set of measurements, large or small. But to get a good estimate of just how unusual a measurement is, we need a fair amount of data. We now have a good deal of data for many aspects of child development. Consider physical growth, for example. We have ample quantities of data on children's heights, collected from hundreds of children of all different ages.

Figure 1–2 shows a portion of this data in a somewhat idealized form—how it might look if thousands of children, rather than hundreds, had been measured. This graph represents heights of 8-year-old American girls. The different heights are arranged along the horizontal axis, and the height of each bar shows the percentages of 8-year-old girls that we would expect to find in each half-inch interval. (For example, 2.5 percent would be expected to measure between 46 and 46½ inches, 3.4 percent between 46½ and 47 inches, and so on.)

The outline of the bars in this graph form what is called a **normal curve,** bell-shaped in appearance. Height measurements, like a great many other kinds of measurements, are usually found to be **normally distributed,** which means that the data fall into a curve similar in shape to the one in the figure. The highest point of a normal curve is in the center. The average measurement, which is also called the **mean,** is also in the center. In this case the mean is 50 inches. The average 8-year-old American girl is 50 inches (127 cm) tall.

In normally distributed data, measurements at or close to the mean are by far the most common. More than two-thirds of all 8-year-old girls are found in the 5-inch interval between 47½ and 52½ inches. As we get farther from the mean in either direction, the percentage of girls with those heights drops

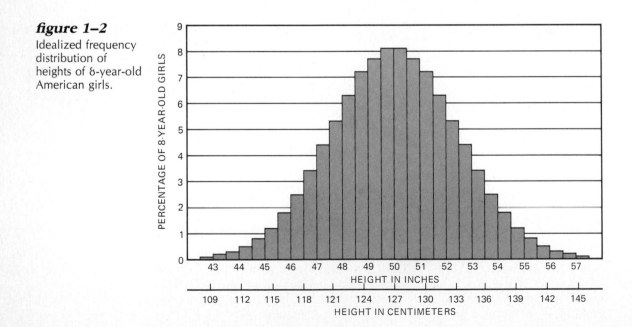

figure 1–2

Idealized frequency distribution of heights of 8-year-old American girls.

off sharply. Fewer than 5 percent are found to be shorter than 45 or taller than 55 inches.

What all this implies is that we don't have to measure a very large number of 8-year-old girls in order to get a good idea of the mean, because most of the girls we measure will be fairly near the mean. But if we want an estimate of the proportion that measures between, say, 55½ and 56 inches, we have to do a lot of measuring. According to Figure 1–2, only half of one percent of 8-year-old girls fall into that interval. If we measure 100 girls of this age, we might find no girls this tall, or one girl, or perhaps even two or three. Random factors—the tallest girl in the class gets sick and stays home on the day we do our measuring—are going to make a lot of difference in estimating the frequency of the rarer heights. They make less of a difference the more girls we measure.

Bear in mind that the "normal" in "normal curve" doesn't mean the kind of "normal" that's the opposite of "abnormal." It's just a term applied to a curve of a certain shape and mathematical description. The normal curve actually doesn't tell us anything about what is "normal" and what is "abnormal." Normally distributed data tell us only what is average and common, and what is unusual. Any further distinctions are arbitrary—a question of where to draw the line. One child might be labeled "mentally retarded" because his or her IQ score falls a point below an arbitrary cutoff, whereas another child—not noticeably different at all—might score a point or two higher and be classified as "low normal." This is not to imply that there's no use trying to make distinctions. We distinguish between night and day, and there, too, it's hard to say where one ends and the other begins.

Finally, we said that "the average 8-year-old American girl is 50 inches (127 cm) tall." Obviously, we were talking about an 8-year-old girl who is average in *height*. Any given 8-year-old girl who is average in height might be very far from average in weight, or strength, or intelligence, or musical ability, or in countless other ways. In fact, it would probably be impossible to find a child who is average in *everything*. Thus, when we speak of an "average child" we are referring to a theoretical child who measures at the mean in one particular characteristic—the characteristic we are interested in at the moment.

Cross-Sectional and Longitudinal Studies. What if we wanted to know about children's heights not just at age 8 but at every age from birth to age 18? In other words, we want a growth chart that shows how height increases as children mature.

We could do this in either of two ways. The easy way is to measure, say, 500 newborns, 500 1-year-olds, 500 2-year-olds, and so on, up to 500 18-year-olds. That, in fact, is how growth data are usually collected—in what we call a **cross-sectional study.**

The second way of charting changes over time is to do what is called a **longitudinal study**—a group of, say, 500 children are measured yearly from birth to age 18. Individual growth charts can then be made for each child; there are various ways of combining the data. One disadvantage of this

In parts of the world where food is often in short supply, children growing up in times of famine will not be as tall as those growing up when food is more plentiful.

method is immediately obvious: it will take us 18 years to accumulate the data we want, whereas the other method might take only a few months. Another disadvantage is that, of the original 500 children, we'll be lucky if 350 of them remain in the study for the full 18 years. Some children or their parents will decide to withdraw from the study, some will move away. In order to be sure of ending up with 500 children, we will have to start off with considerably more than that. There is also the question of whether the children who remain in the study are a representative sample of the whole group. What if very short or very tall children are particularly reluctant to come back and be measured again?

The disadvantages of the longitudinal method are plain to see. Less obvious are the disadvantages of the cross-sectional procedure. Let's say we're measuring growth not in North America or Europe, but in some country where food is often in short supply and there are occasional periods of real famine. Imagine that there was a severe famine in this country 10 years ago. More recently there was a big improvement in children's lives here: 3 years ago, other countries began sending nutritional supplements, vitamins, and medical supplies.

The 9- and 10-year-olds we now find in this country were born in the hungry years. They were undernourished in infancy, and their mothers were probably undernourished before they were born. As a result they are a little smaller, on the average, than they would have been if they'd been born in more fortunate times. The 2- and 3-year-olds, on the other hand, have been reasonably well-nourished and healthy all their lives. A child who is now an average 2-year-old might be as large as the average 3-year-old of 8 or 9 years ago. So when we do our cross-sectional study we'll be ending up with a growth curve based on relatively large 2- and 3-year olds, and relatively small 9- and 10-year-olds. Consequently, the curve will be distorted—it will show too little growth between age 3 and 9.

This may seem like a rather remote example, but it serves to illustrate the point. Whenever we want to make comparisons between children of different ages, we have a choice between using different children for the different age groups, or using the same children and examining them at different points in their lives. The first, the cross-sectional method, is quicker, but it means that the comparisons involve children born in different years. Sometimes this doesn't matter, but sometimes it does. Say that we're interested, not in the growth of the body, but in the way some mental process or ability develops as children get older. A cross-sectional study done on this topic 30 years ago might have involved a comparison between young children who spent their early years watching television and older children who grew up without TV. More recent studies might involve young children who spent their early years watching Sesame Street and older children who grew up watching Bugs Bunny, or young children who spent their early years playing with computers and older children who grew up without computers. Any of these things could make the results misleading—differences that appear to be due to differences in age might be due instead to differences in experiences or in opportunities for learning.

The chances of being misled are greater, of course, when we try to compare people born a great many years apart. It used to be thought that intelligence declines steadily as people grow older, starting at about the age of 20. This belief was based on cross-sectional studies which showed that 40-year-olds score lower on IQ tests than 20-year-olds, and 60-year-olds score lower than 40-year-olds. The trouble is that a 60-year-old grew up at a time when educational and cultural opportunities were quite different from what they were 40 or 20 years ago. Longitudinal studies give more optimistic results: they show that if particular individuals are examined over a span of many years, they decline only slightly in intelligence (Schaie, Labouvie, and Buech, 1973).

Children's IQ tests, unlike those given to adults, are scored on the basis of age, with 100 being the mean score at every age. Thus, a 3-year-old with an IQ score of 100 has scored at the mean for 3-year-olds, and a 10-year-old with an IQ score of 100 has scored at the mean for 10-year-olds. When IQ tests first came into use, it was assumed that a child's IQ would remain pretty much the same all through childhood. But it is possible for a child who scored below most of his agemates at age 3 to score *above* most of them at age 10, in which case the child's IQ score would increase dramatically. Do IQ scores remain stable in most children, or are they very likely to change over time? Longitudinal studies are the *only* way to answer such questions.

The same is true for questions like "Is a very active baby likely to become a very active child?" or "Can an irritable baby turn into a cheerful adult?" (The question of stability of IQ will be dealt with in Chapters 7 and 10. Stability of temperament will come up in Chapter 2.)

The distinction between the cross-sectional and longitudinal methods applies not only to descriptive studies but also to the more complex kind of studies that we'll discuss later in this chapter. Note, too, that it's possible to combine the cross-sectional and longitudinal methods in a single research project. If 2-year-olds, 5-year-olds, and 7-year-olds are all studied longitudinally for 5 years, then the study has spanned the ages from 2 to 12 and done it in 5 years instead of 10.

Other Kinds of Descriptive Studies.   Child development research need not involve comparisons between children of different ages. It doesn't even necessarily involve measurement. Sometimes it just involves observation and description.

A good example is a recent study on social relationships among nursery school children (Corsaro, 1981). The investigator was William Corsaro, a sociologist from Indiana University. Corsaro simply observed the children in a nursery school for several months, taking notes or videotaping their interactions with one another. He paid special attention to the ways that individual children gained entry into a group of children who were already playing together, and to the ways children who were playing together accepted or resisted the entry of a new child. He also recorded how long social interactions lasted (the majority lasted less than 10 minutes) and how they ended (generally one child simply walked away, often without even saying goodbye).

A special kind of descriptive report is the **case study.** A case study generally involves only a single child—often one who is unusual in some way. Some period of the child's life, or at least certain aspects of it, are described in detail, along with something of the child's previous history (if it is known). Freud used case studies to show how psychoanalysis uncovered what he felt were the hidden motivations of his patients. An example is the case of "little Hans," a 5-year-old boy who was terrified of horses.

Other case studies involve children who grew up in uniquely unfavorable circumstances. There is the shocking case of Genie, for instance. Genie spent most of the first 13 years of her life tied to a potty seat by day and to her crib at night. No one talked to her. When she was discovered she knew no language. The efforts to turn Genie into a normal person and to teach her to speak were only partially successful (Curtiss, 1977).

Fortunately, cases like Genie's are extremely rare. But for that reason they're also very important, because they're usually our only way of finding out answers to certain questions. That is why developmental psychologists have studied the reports on Genie with great interest, even though findings involving a single child are ordinarily felt to be of little value.

By the way, the three examples we used in this section—Genie, little Hans, and the social interactions of nursery school children—will be discussed in more detail in later chapters of the book.

Correlational Studies

A **correlation** is a relationship between two sets of measurements. **Correlational studies** are designed to investigate that relationship. Let's say we wanted to see if there is a relationship between how much milk children drink and how fast they grow. We would measure some children's milk consumption over a period of months and record their height at the beginning and end of that period. Then the relationship between the two factors—how much milk each child drank and how much that child grew—would be examined. We'll assume that our study involved five children and yielded the following results:

Meredith drank 50 gallons, grew 2.00 inches
Robert drank 45 gallons, grew 1.75 inches
Benjamin drank 35 gallons, grew 1.25 inches
Alice drank 30 gallons, grew 1.00 inches
Chris drank 20 gallons, grew .50 inches

Clearly, these numbers show a relationship between amount of milk consumed and amount of growth: the more milk a child drank, the more he or she grew. In other words, there is a correlation between the two things. In this case it's a **positive correlation.** If we had made up the opposite results—that the more milk children drank the *less* they grew—that would have been a **negative correlation.**

Figure 1–3 shows how our imaginary results would look if we put them on a graph. Obviously, it is extremely unlikely that we would ever find such a clear-cut relationship in the real world. Correlations can be given a numerical value that ranges from just above zero to 1.00 for positive correlations,

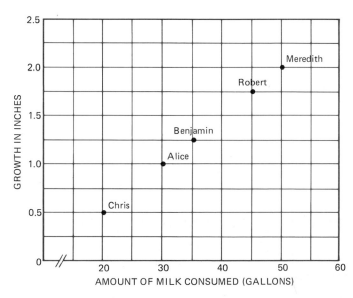

figure 1–3
Relationship between amount of milk consumed and amount of growth (imaginary data).

and from just below zero to −1.00 for negative ones. (If the numerical value turns out to be zero or very close to zero, the two sets of measurements aren't correlated at all.) The correlation shown in Figure 1−3 is 1.00, the highest possible value. That's because all the points are right on the diagonal line.

Real correlational studies almost always involve many more than five children and virtually never produce correlations of 1.00. An unusually high real-life correlation is, for example, that between the heights of identical twins, which is .94 (Tanner, 1978). Figure 1−4 shows how the data might look if we measured 25 pairs of identical twins—let's say, all 8-year-old girls. Each point on this graph represents one pair of twins: the height of one twin is shown on the horizontal axis and the height of her twin sister on the vertical axis. (It doesn't matter which twin you put on which axis.) If each twin had been exactly the same height as her sister, all the points would have fallen along the diagonal line and the correlation would have been 1.00. But there usually are small differences from one twin to another, so the points are close to the diagonal line but not all *on* it, and the correlation is .94, not 1.00.

Ordinary sisters are less similar to each other in size than identical twins, and the correlation is lower: only about .57 (Tanner, 1978). If we examined 25 pairs of sisters, measuring each girl when she is 8 years old, the data might look like the graph shown in Figure 1−5.

What if we measured pairs of 8-year-old girls who, instead of being related to each other, are best friends? As far as we know, this hasn't actually been done, but we might expect there to be *some* correlation, because two children who are good friends tend to be more similar to each other than two children picked at random from a schoolyard. So if we measured 25 pairs of

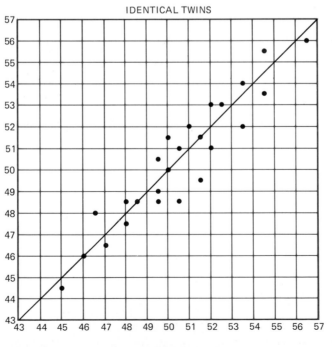

IDENTICAL TWINS

figure 1−4
Pairs of identical twin girls, all 8 years old (imaginary data). There is a correlation of .94 between the heights of the twins.

CHAPTER 1 / Some Basic Concepts

friends, the results might look something like the graph in Figure 1–6, which shows a correlation of .20—hardly any correlation at all.

Finally, if we measured pairs of 8-year-old girls picked at random from a schoolyard, the correlation would probably be close to zero. (We say "close

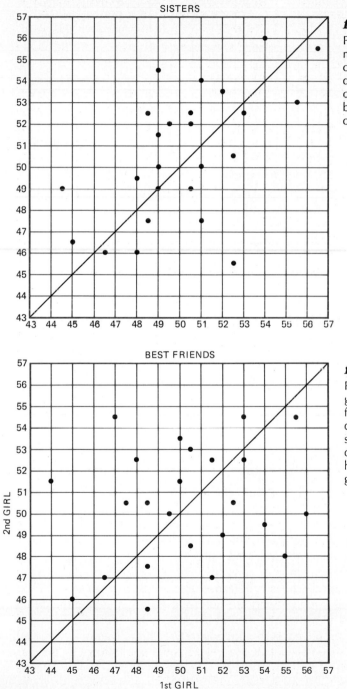

figure 1–5

Pairs of sisters, each measured at the age of 8 (imaginary data). There is a correlation of .57 between the heights of the two girls.

figure 1–6

Pairs of 8-year-old girls who are best friends (imaginary data). This graph shows a correlation of .20 between the heights of the two girls.

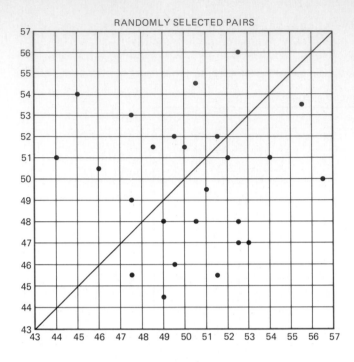

RANDOMLY SELECTED PAIRS

figure 1–7
Pairs of 8-year-old girls selected at random (imaginary data). This is a zero correlation—the girls' heights are uncorrelated.

to'' because correlations of *exactly* zero are extremely rare, though not as rare as correlations of 1.00 or −1.00.) Figure 1–7 shows what a zero correlation looks like.

The Direction of Causality. What does a correlation tell us? Only that there's a certain relationship between two sets of measurements. It's very important to remember that it tells us nothing about what *caused* that relationship. Consider the imaginary data for milk consumption and growth—the correlation showed that the children who drank the most milk grew the fastest. If this correlation were based on real data, would it prove that drinking lots of milk makes children grow faster? No, it wouldn't. It's just as possible, given only that correlation, that children who are growing rapidly are hungrier and thirstier than children who are growing slowly, and consequently they drink more milk.

A correlation tells us nothing about the direction of causality, about which is the cause and which is the effect. The reason that's so important to remember is that developmental psychologists have occasionally made some rash assumptions about the direction of causality. For instance, it has been noted many times that children who are punished frequently and severely misbehave more often than children who are punished mildly and seldom. In the past it was assumed that the punishments produced the misbehavior—that too many spankings produce a surly, uncooperative child. That may very well be true. But it is *also* possible that the *child's* behavior influences the *par-*

ents—that parents who punish their children harshly may be reacting to their children's behavior, rather than (or in addition to) producing it. Twenty or 30 years ago the direction of causality was always assumed to be *from* the parent *to* the child—the child's characteristics were invariably seen as a result, never as a cause. Now we recognize that children have effects on their parents, just as parents have effects on their children. This is an issue to which we will return many times in the next 14 chapters.

There is one way to get around the problem of the direction of causality, and that is to do correlations between measurements taken at different times. For instance, it's been found that children who spend a lot of time watching violent television shows are more aggressive than ones who seldom watch those shows. But what causes what? Are aggressive children more likely to enjoy watching violence, or are children who watch violence more likely to become aggressive? The results of a 10-year longitudinal study support the second view, that watching the violent shows causes the child to become more aggressive. The investigators got ratings of boys' aggressiveness at age 9 and at age 19, and they recorded the boys' TV-watching habits at the same ages. They found a positive correlation (it was .31, which is fairly high for correlations of this sort) between watching violent TV shows at age 9 and aggressiveness at age 19. Now, it *can't* be the case that aggressiveness at age 19 *causes* a child to watch violent TV shows at 9, because, logically, causes must come before effects. Moreover, aggressiveness at age 9 was *not* correlated with watching violent TV shows at age 19 (the correlation was .01, which means the two things were essentially unrelated). Thus, these results imply a one-way direction of causality: watching violent TV shows causes aggressiveness, whereas being aggressive doesn't necessarily lead to watching violent TV shows (Eron, Lefkowitz, Huesmann, and Walder, 1972).

One more thing to note about correlations is that sometimes *neither* of two correlated measurements is the causal factor. For example, we might find that the number of hours of homework children do each week is correlated with the number of permanent teeth they have. Doing homework doesn't cause teeth to grow; nor do permanent teeth cause a child to do homework. Rather, both are a function of age: older children do more homework than younger children, and they also have a greater number of permanent teeth. So neither of the correlated measurements (homework or teeth) is the causal factor— both result from a third factor, age. In this example the causal factor is something fairly obvious and easily measurable, but in real-life cases that might not be true.

It is also good to remember that, in the real world, we seldom have clear-cut "causes" and clear-cut "effects." There are many situations in which the effects work in both directions at once, as in the case of punishment and misbehavior. In such cases we might find "vicious circles"—the child misbehaves, the parents punish, the punishment produces more misbehavior, and so on. And finally, in the real world there is seldom a *single* cause for any given kind of behavior. Children's behavior generally results from many factors—some inherited, some environmental—all working at once.

The Experimental Method

The correlational method looks for relationships that already exist—the investigator's task is to make measurements and see how they're related. With the experimental method, on the other hand, the investigator does something and sees what happens.

To illustrate, we'll consider an experiment that was reported in the journal *Child Development* in 1979. The investigators were two Canadian developmental psychologists, Darwin Muir and Jeffrey Field. The subject of their inquiry was whether newborn babies turn their heads in the direction of a sound. This question is part of a topic on which there has been a considerable amount of research in recent years: the previously unsuspected abilities of newborn babies. In this case, the investigators were interested in the ability of newborn babies to localize sounds—in other words, to act as though they know what direction a sound is coming from. It used to be assumed that babies have to learn this, but in 1961 a psychologist found some indication of sound localization in a baby only 3 or 4 minutes old. That experiment, however, had involved only a single baby, and a couple of later experiments—using more babies—had failed to find any evidence for sound localization. Thus, the issue was not settled. Muir and Field felt that the later experiments may have failed because those investigators used sounds that were too loud.

The experimenters started out with 12 babies from the newborn nursery in a Canadian hospital. The experiment was performed in a quiet room next to the nursery. (It was necessary, of course, to have the hospital's permission to carry out this research. Presumably, the permission of the babies' parents was also obtained.) The babies—six boys, six girls—were all healthy and normal in size and weight, and all were less than a week old. In order to perform the experiment it was essential for the babies to be in an alert, receptive state, neither sleeping nor crying. Getting a newborn into such a state is not easy. In fact, the experimenters completely failed to accomplish this with three of the babies, and those babies weren't tested any further. The other nine were tested one at a time. Each baby was held in an experimenter's hands, face upwards, in an almost horizontal position. The other experimenter was holding two opaque medicine bottles, one in each hand, and the baby's head was placed between the two medicine bottles. Both medicine bottles were then shaken. One bottle was empty and made no noise, but the other was half filled with hard corn and made a rattling sound. The bottles were shaken for 20 seconds or until the baby turned her head to one side or the other and held it there for at least 5 seconds. If the baby tended to turn her head to the side with the corn-filled bottle, it couldn't have been that she was attracted by the *sight* of the moving bottle, because there was a moving bottle on *both* sides of her head.

The test was given from five to eight times to each baby, depending on how long the baby remained cooperative. The corn-filled bottle was sometimes on the right, sometimes on the left, in a random order. Two people—one experimenter and one other person—wrote down which way the baby had moved her head on each trial. (If a baby turned her head in both directions during the course of a trial, they wrote down the direction in which her head had turned the farthest.) The two observers almost always agreed in their judgments.

The results seemed to indicate that the babies *could* tell which direction the sound was coming from: they turned their heads in the direction of the rattling sound on a total of 52 of the 60 trials. Their movements, according to the experimenters,

> [suggested] that they were making a deliberate attempt to investigate the locus of the shaking rattle; they hunched their shoulders, actively pulled their heads up, turned to the side of the stimulus, and then seemed to inspect the sound source visually. (Muir and Field, 1979, p. 432)

But the experimenters—or perhaps their colleagues, or perhaps the reviewers for a journal to which the experimenters might have sent an earlier version of their paper—were not satisfied. The experiment we've just described has a flaw: both the person holding the baby and the people recording her responses *knew which way the sound was coming from*. It's possible that the experimenter who was holding the baby would involuntarily look in the direction of the rattling sound himself, and that the baby was responding to his eye movements. Or perhaps the way he was holding the baby was affected by his expectation that she would be turning her head in a certain direction, and the baby was responding to the way she was being held rather than to the sound. And the people recording the responses may also have been biased by their expectations. If the baby moved her head once in one direction and once in the other within a given trial, they were supposed to record the direction of the larger head movement. But what if the two head movements were equal, or almost equal—wouldn't they be more likely to write down the response they were expecting (or hoping) to get?

To answer these objections, the experimenters did a second experiment. This time the rattling sound was recorded in advance and played through one of two stationary loudspeakers, one located on each side of the baby's head. This time the experimenter holding the baby couldn't tell which side the sound was coming from: he was wearing earphones that piped a continuous rattling sound into both his ears, and the sound that the baby heard was controlled by someone else. And this time the people who recorded the babies' responses also didn't know which side the sound was coming from: instead of watching the experiment itself, they viewed a silent videotape that showed the babies' movements during each trial. The observers viewed the videotapes, decided which way the babies turned their heads, and recorded their judgments; afterwards these judgments were compared with records indicating which side the sound had come from on each trial.

The results of this second experiment are shown in Table 1–1. This table shows how many times each baby turned his or her head in the direction of the sound. (Some of the babies didn't turn their heads at all on a few of the trials. The experimenters provided that information, but we've omitted it.)

Now it's pretty clear-cut. Of the 12 babies, 11 turned in the direction of the sound more often than in the opposite direction. (The twelfth turned in

TABLE 1–1 Results of the Second Sound-Localization Experiment

Baby	Head-Turns Toward Sound	Head-Turns Away from Sound
1	7	1
2	7	1
3	8	0
4	7	1
5	7	1
6	5	2
7	7	1
8	3	3
9	6	2
10	5	1
11	3	2
12	7	1

(Adapted from Muir and Field, 1979, p. 433.)

the two directions equally often.) Altogether, 82 percent of the head-turns were in the direction of the sound. If the babies had just been turning their heads at random we would expect roughly 50 percent of the head-turns to be in that direction, but 82 percent is considerably more than 50 percent. Such a sizable effect is unlikely to be a mere coincidence. Nor can these results be due to the babies having a preference for turning their heads in a particular direction, because the sound came equally often from the left and from the right. (In fact, babies *do* have a preference for turning their heads in a particular direction. The experimenters also ran some "control trials" in which there was no sound at all. On these trials the babies often didn't turn their heads at all, but when a head-turn did occur it was to the right side 72 percent of the time.)

We've said that results that are this clear-cut—11 out of 12 babies responding in a particular way—aren't likely to have been a coincidence. That statement deserves a closer look. Note that we didn't say it *couldn't* be a coincidence. Improbable things sometimes do happen just by chance: you can flip an ordinary coin high into the air 10 times in a row, and it's possible for it to turn up heads all 10 times—possible, but highly unlikely. We can say exactly how unlikely: by the laws of mathematical probability, the chances are one in 1024, or roughly .001, of having an unweighted, fairly tossed coin turn up heads 10 times out of 10. Even 9 heads out of 10 tosses is pretty unlikely: the chances are 10 in 1024, or roughly .01. When a result is this unlikely to have occurred purely by chance, statisticians say that that result is **significant.**

With regard to the babies the situation is similar. It's possible that 11 of the 12 babies turned their heads toward the sound purely by chance, but the probability of that result being a coincidence is only .006. Statisticians will generally use the label "significant" for any result that has less than a .05 probability (less than one chance in 20) of being a coincidence. By this criterion—or even by the stricter criterion of requiring the probability to be less than .01—the results of the sound localization experiment are significant. If only 10 babies out of 12 had responded in the correct direction, the results would still have been significant by the more lenient criterion (less than .05 probability of being a coincidence) but not by the stricter criterion (less than .01 probability). And if only 9 babies had responded that way the results would not have been significant by *any* criterion, because the probability of that result occurring by chance is about .15.

Note that the "significance" of a given result doesn't depend only on the proportion of the results that are in the correct direction—it also depends on the number of times you flip the coin or the number of babies you test. If you flip a coin 10 times you have to get at least 9 of them—90 percent—turning up heads in order for your result to be significant. But if you flip it 20 times you need only 15 heads—75 percent—to reach significance. The more times you flip it, the smaller the proportion of heads you need for your results to be significantly above the chance expectation (which, in the long run, is 50 percent heads). Thus, if Muir and Field's babies had had only a slight tendency to turn their heads toward a sound, the experimenters still could have ended up with significant results. However, in this case they might have had to test 50 or 100 babies, rather than just a dozen.

The Significance of Differences.   We've been talking about the significance of a particular kind of result, in this case the responses of one group of babies. More often, however, the term **significant** is used to describe a **difference.** Let's say Muir and Field decide to test the theory that newborn babies will turn toward a fairly soft sound but not toward a loud one. Then the investigators would have to test *two* groups of babies: one group with a loud sound, the other with a softer one. The procedure would have to be identical in every other way—otherwise, if the two groups behaved differently, you couldn't be sure that this was due to the difference in sounds. Ideally, the babies should be identical too, so that you could be sure it wasn't a difference between the two groups of babies. For instance, what if you tested baby girls with the softer sounds and baby boys with the louder ones? If you found that the girls turned toward the sound but the boys didn't, this could be due to a difference in sounds, or it could be due to a difference between girls and boys. For this reason, experimenters who use two groups of subjects usually try to have an equal number of boys and girls in the two groups. Sometimes the groups are matched in other ways, too: for example, two groups of babies might be matched in weight, to make sure that one group doesn't end up with larger babies than the other group. More often, the subjects in an experiment are simply divided up at random. In the long run this method works to produce two reasonably even groups.

It's also possible to use the *same* babies in the two groups. We can test a baby with soft sounds and then later test the same baby with loud sounds.

The trouble with this procedure is that we're not testing exactly the same baby both times—the first time we're testing a "brand-new" baby, but the second time we're testing a baby who has already had certain experiences. We can't be sure that the experiences he had while being tested the first time won't affect his responses in the second test. What we have to do in this case is to test one group of babies with loud sounds first, then soft ones; and another group of babies in the opposite order. Even this is not a perfect solution—maybe the experience of having heard loud sounds isn't the same as the experience of having heard soft ones!

In the type of experiment we've just described, the goal is to find out if two different treatments (or two different stimuli) have different effects on similar groups of babies. It's just as common—perhaps even *more* common—for an experiment to involve two groups of subjects that are given the *same* treatment. The different groups might be boys versus girls, or older children versus younger ones, or very active children versus quieter ones, or firstborn children versus later-born ones. The experiment is designed to find out whether the two groups will respond in different ways to a certain situation. Sometimes the experiment is more complicated than that: there may be *two* tests. The first one is used to divide the subjects into the two groups (good readers versus poor ones, for example), and the second one is to see whether the children in these two groups will also perform differently in *another* kind of test.

In any of these cases, the investigators end up with two sets of measurements and must then ask, Do these two sets of measurements differ significantly, or are differences of this magnitude likely to have occurred just by chance? The methods used to answer such questions rely on the same kind of reasoning that we applied to the coin-flipping and head-turning examples. These methods are a little more complex, though, because they must take into account not only the size of the difference and the number of subjects, but also the variability of the measurement. For instance, children's weights are more variable than their heights. It's easier to show that 10-year-olds differ significantly from 9-year-olds in *height* than it is to show that they differ significantly in *weight*.

In these examples, we have talked about experiments with two groups. It's possible, of course, to use three groups, or four, or even more. The groups, if they differ in age, can be part of a cross-sectional study or a longitudinal one. And the distinction between the correlational method and the experimental method is not as sharp as we've made it seem. The different methods of research overlap a great deal.

We have tried to give you some feeling for what research in child development is like. We've also tried to give you a glimpse of the kinds of problems that researchers are up against, and the kinds of questions that readers of research reports have to keep in mind. A tremendous amount of research in child development has been reported in the past 25 years. Out of all this research, we have tried to distill for you an accurate and reasonably complete picture of the developing infant, child, and adolescent.

The Ethics of Child Development Research

In 1939, Dr. Myrtle McGraw of Briarcliff College reported on her research on "Swimming Behavior in the Human Infant" (McGraw, 1939/1967). Her paper described the results of experiments performed on a total of 42 babies, ranging in age from 11 days to 2½ years. Most of these babies were tested a number of times over a period of months.

McGraw was interested in the question of whether human babies have any inborn ability to swim. Her method of testing them was straightforward:

At each examination the baby was placed in three different positions: (1) With the hands of the experimenter placed under his chin and on the crown of his head, he was supported in such a way that his body and extremities could move freely while his nose and mouth were protected above the water level; (2) he was submerged in a prone [face-down] position without any support whatsoever; and (3) he was submerged without support in a supine [face-up] position. (1939/1967, p. 128)

McGraw reports that very young babies *do* have some swimming ability. They lose it, however, when they get a little older.

The movements of the infant only a few weeks old are striking when he is placed in water in a prone position. . . . [The baby remains in face-down position and makes rhythmic movements of his arms, legs, and body.] These movements are ordinarily sufficiently forceful to propel the baby a short distance through the water. . . . Another outstanding feature of the infant's behavior during the newborn phase is breath control. Apparently a reflex inhibits his breathing while he is submerged, since he does not cough or show disturbances common among the older babies after they have been submerged. . . .

After the baby is 4 months of age or older, the rhythmicity and pattern of the early behavior become disorganized. Often the babies are quite inactive when supported under the chin, and when submerged prone they usually rotate into a dorsal [face-up] position, and the movements of the extremities are of the struggling order. They clutch at the experimenter's hand, try to wipe the water from the face, or they may sink deeper into the water without marked manifestations of motor activity. . . . It was apparent during this phase that the baby had more noticeable difficulty with respiration, or controlling respiration, when he was submerged. Often the ingestion of fluid was considerable, and the infant would cough or otherwise show respiratory disturbance when he was taken out of the water. (pp. 128–131)

McGraw doesn't tell us whether any of these babies suffered serious ill effects as a result of their unwilling participation in her experiment. Nor does she tell us where and how she obtained these babies. We can safely assume, however, that she did not seek or obtain the permission of the babies' parents: what parent would allow an 11-day-old infant to be "submerged in a prone position without any support whatsoever"?

Nowadays, research of this nature could not be carried out in the United States. It is very unlikely that it would even be proposed. In 1973, a special committee of the American Psychological Association drew up guidelines for research with human subjects. Among their recommendations was a question that must be asked of every research project in child development: "whether there is a negative effect upon the dignity and welfare of the participants that the importance of the research does not warrant" (APA, 1973, p. 11). McGraw's experiment clearly fails this test. It *did* involve "a negative effect upon the dignity and welfare of the participants,'' and the importance of the research was *not* great enough to justify inflicting that effect on them.

The American Psychological Association's guidelines also listed a number of specific points that an experimenter must consider. For instance, when children are used as subjects, the experimenter is expected to obtain their parents' *informed* consent. This means that the parents must be told about any aspects of the experiment that might influence their decision to let their children participate. Experimenters are also expected to avoid the use of deception, except where deception is necessary to the purpose of the experiment; in this case they are supposed to *un*deceive the participants (''debrief'' them) when the experiment is over.

These guidelines are not always easy—or even possible—to put into practice. In some experiments, it's necessary that the participants not know that they are subjects in an experiment. An example might be an experiment in which a ''lost'' wallet is left in a school corridor and the investigator watches to see what the finder does. The use of deception or concealment is also necessary in some cases. Investigators of the development of moral behavior might give children the impression that they are being left alone in a room and then watch them through a pane of one-way glass to see how well they can resist temptation. Afterwards they would be expected to tell the children of this deception, and also to relieve them of any feelings of guilt that might follow from a failure to resist temptation. But if the children are participants in a longitudinal study, it wouldn't be possible to tell them about the one-way glass—it would affect their behavior the next time they were tested.

Another case in which deception may be required is in the study of the children of convicted criminals or mentally ill patients. If such

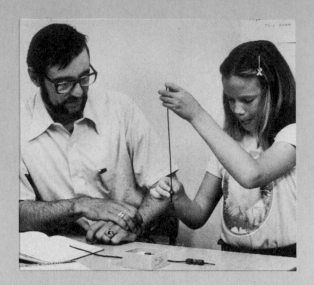

Ethical considerations are particularly important when research involves children.

a study required that these children be observed in a school setting, it would be necessary to conceal from the children's classmates and teachers the reason for studying those particular children. It might even be necessary to conceal *which* particular children were being studied. And in this case—in order to keep these children's backgrounds from becoming public knowledge—the deception would have to be permanent.

These examples show that ethical considerations are not always easy to apply—often, it's a matter of weighing the importance of one principle against the importance of another. Many universities now have committees that review proposed research in advance and decide whether it is ethical.

In order to learn about human beings we must study human beings. Given the present-day standards of ethics in research, the risks to the subjects are usually negligible. The potential benefits—for all of us—are vast. ∎

summary

1. **Development** is the general name for the process that turns babies into children, children into adults, and adults into old people. Child development includes changes in size and shape, in knowledge and reasoning ability, in physical and social skills, and so on.

2. Research in child development is carried out by developmental psychologists and by scientists in other fields. Child development can be studied in a scientific way despite the fact that children seem to be complicated and unpredictable.

3. One type of research in child development is the **descriptive study.** A descriptive study based on a **representative sample** of adequate size can tell us about the **mean** (the average) and about **variability.**

4. Many kinds of measurements are **normally distributed**—in other words, they form a **normal curve.** A normal curve is simply a curve of a particular shape; it tells us nothing about what is "normal" and what is "abnormal." In a normal curve, most measurements fall near the mean, which is located in the center of the curve.

5. There are two basic ways to study the changes that occur as children grow older. In a **cross-sectional study,** this is done by testing children of different ages. In a **longitudinal study,** a group of children are repeatedly tested over a period of time, as they grow older.

6. An IQ score tells us how well an individual child has done on an IQ test, relative to other children of the same age. An IQ score of 100 indicates that the child's performance was at the mean for children of that age.

7. A **case study** is a descriptive report that is generally based on only a single child.

8. **Correlational studies** are designed to investigate the relationship between two (or more) sets of measurements. A **correlation** is a numerical description of such a relationship. **Positive** correlations range from just above zero to 1.00; **negative** ones from just below zero to −1.00. A zero correlation means that the two sets of mea-

surements are unrelated.

9. A correlation between A and B tells us nothing about which is the cause and which is the effect. A could have caused B, B could have caused A, or both could be the result of a third factor, C. More likely, both A and B are produced by many factors, some environmental and some hereditary.

10. When parental behavior and child behavior are correlated, it used to be assumed that the parental behavior was the cause of the child behavior. Now we recognize that children have effects on their parents, just as parents have effects on their children.

11. One way to decide about direction of causality is to examine correlations over time. A 10-year longitudinal study showed that watching violent TV shows produces aggressiveness, rather than the other way around.

12. With the **experimental method,** the researcher does something and sees what happens. If the people carrying out the experiments or making the measurements know how they're supposed to come out, this might bias the results. There are ways of doing experiments that minimize the danger of bias.

13. Any result can be a coincidence (due to chance). A **significant difference** is a difference between two (or more) sets of measurements that is unlikely to be due to chance. The measurements may be from two groups of subjects, or they may be two sets of measurements taken from a single group.

14. Research with human subjects must take ethical considerations into account. Researchers are expected to avoid producing negative effects on their subjects' dignity or welfare that are not justified by the importance of the research. Another guideline is that children cannot be used as subjects without the informed consent of their parents. Experimenters are expected to avoid the use of deception unless it is necessary to carry out the purpose of the research or to protect the rights of the subjects.

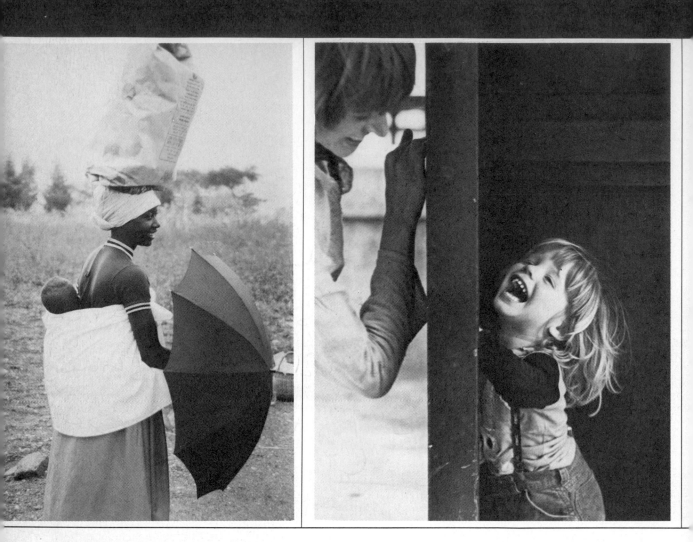

Chapter Two

HEREDITY AND ENVIRONMENT

TWO

Look at a group of young children in a kindergarten classroom. Each one is different, both in appearance and in behavior. Karen is shy and quiet, John is talkative and bold. Malcolm acts silly and moves around a lot, Doug is serious and remains in his seat. Jane is absorbed in what she's doing, Paula is easily distracted.

Why? What makes people turn out the way they do? The answer psychologists give is that children are shaped by two forces: their heredity and their environment. But, you'll say, everyone knows that. True. Everyone has known it for thousands of years. Sayings such as The apple doesn't fall far from the tree, and Like father, like son, acknowledge the obvious fact that people inherit many of their characteristics from their parents and grandparents. The importance of the environment—of what happens to people during

Children differ from one another in so many ways. What are the sources of these differences?

their childhood—is recognized too. The Bible says, "Train up a child in the way he should go, and when he is old he will not depart from it" (Proverbs 22:6).

Although everyone already knows the importance of heredity and environment, it's not so easy to use that knowledge to account for people's behavior. For example, why is Karen shy and quiet? Heredity? But both of her parents are friendly and outgoing. Well, maybe it's environment. Maybe outgoing parents tend to overwhelm their children, so the children react by withdrawing from people. But then why is Karen's younger brother jolly and sociable? Well, maybe the parents only act that way with their first child . . .

You see the problem. It's all very well to say *in theory* that children are a product of their heredity and their environment. But when we get down to individual children and particular characteristics, those generalities don't help very much. Children differ in many ways—in size, in strength, in shape and color; in intelligence and talent; in how sociable or talkative or helpful they are; in how active or aggressive or emotional they are; and so on. It's usually not clear whether a certain characteristic is inherited, or is due to environmental influences, or results from a combination of the two. The answer almost always turns out to be, "results from a combination of the two," but that still leaves plenty of room for debate. Psychologists have debated for decades over whether various qualities are *primarily* inherited or *primarily* a result of the environment. This debate is sometimes called the **nature-nurture issue.**

NATURE VERSUS NURTURE

Because the two words go together so well, the terms *nature* and *nurture* are sometimes used instead of heredity and environment. **Nature,** or **heredity,** refers to inherited characteristics, also called **genetic** characteristics. These characteristics, or **traits,** are carried by the genes. Later in this chapter we will describe how genes transmit various inherited traits.

Nurture refers to the way a child is reared. The term **environment** actually includes a lot more than that. Everything that a person sees, hears, feels, smells, tastes, eats, drinks, breathes, or experiences—from the time of conception to the time of death—is that person's environment. Notice that this includes things that happen even before birth, to a developing fetus in its mother's uterus (womb). Is she well-nourished during pregnancy? Does she smoke, drink, or take drugs? Is she exposed to radiation, or to polluted air or water? Is she under stress? All these factors can affect the environment of the unborn child.

Once a child is born the environment expands tremendously. Undoubtedly, the most important aspect of the environment is the family. What are the parents like? How forceful, how kind, how emotional, how intelligent, how well-educated are they? How much time do they spend with their child, and how do they act? What are their views on discipline, on toilet training, on showing affection? Are there siblings (brothers or sisters)? How many, and how old are they? What is the family's social and financial status, its religious affiliation (if any), its race?

This is only the beginning. The environment includes many, many other factors—from the mobile hanging over the crib to the very air the child breathes—the apartment or house the child grows up in, the neighborhood, the school, the teachers, the playmates, and so on.

Over the past 50 years, psychologists have devoted considerable time and effort to finding out what effects various environmental influences have on children. Until recently, heredity has gotten much less attention. There was a good reason for the emphasis on environment: discoveries about environmental effects have a practical value. If we find out that something in the environment has a good effect or a bad effect on children, we can put that knowledge to use—we can try to increase the good influences and decrease the bad influences. The emphasis on environment came from an optimistic view of the human race: humans do not come "ready made"—they are flexible, they can change in response to changes in the environment. The ability to change implies the ability to improve.

On this optimistic note, we'll begin our discussion of heredity and environment. We'll start with a quick look at the major environmental influences on children. (Later chapters will deal with some of these influences in greater detail.)

BASIC ENVIRONMENTAL INFLUENCES

If we look at the world as a whole, and back into history as well as in the present, we see that children's environments vary over a tremendous range. Ancient Greeks and contemporary Americans, Sri Lankans and Samoans, the Masai of Africa and the Inuit of northern Canada—all have very different views on how children should be treated. In some countries, at some times, children are coddled and given lots of attention and affection. In others, children are ignored or treated harshly. Children may be expected to start acting like adults when they're still quite young, or they may be permitted to remain dependent on their parents until their twenties. These widely different attitudes toward children reflect basic differences among cultures.

Cultural Differences

A group of people who share common traditions, activities, beliefs, behaviors, and values, and who speak the same language, share a common **culture.** The ways that adults act toward children differ widely from culture to culture. Consider the following interaction between a 4-year-old girl and her aunt (Briggs, quoted in Kagan, 1979, p. 888). Here's the aunt talking to her niece:

> What a beautiful new shirt you have. Why don't you die so I can have it? Don't you want to die? Don't you want to die? Do die, then I can have the shirt.

Did you see your new baby brother? Do you love him? Did you carry him on your back? You love him? I don't love him. Why don't you tip him out of your parka and kill him?

If you overheard an adult speaking in this way to a child, you would probably assume that the adult was mentally unbalanced. You would also expect the child to be a little upset, and to need some explanation of her aunt's bizarre behavior. But in this case you'd be wrong. The child recognized that her aunt was just teasing her, and was smiling happily while her aunt was speaking. This kind of teasing is common and perfectly acceptable in Inuit society. The little girl and her aunt are members of the Inuit, who live on Baffin Island in the north of Canada.

Jerome Kagan, the Harvard psychologist who quoted the interchange just described, used it to illustrate an important point. One cannot look at an isolated bit of behavior out of context. What effect a given sample of adult behavior will have on a child depends partly on the child's previous experiences. The child's experiences depend, to a large extent, on her culture.

A **society** is a group of people with a common culture. One of the jobs of a society is to teach its children to become acceptable members of that society. In order for that to happen, the children must acquire not only the knowledge and skills, but also the beliefs and attitudes of that society. Because cultures differ, methods of childrearing must differ too. A method of childrearing that produces an acceptable American would probably produce a very *unacceptable* Inuit.

People tend to take their own society's methods of childrearing for granted—it's hard for them to realize that the methods they use are not the

The experiences of a child reared in one culture may be very different from those of a child reared in another. This Balinese mother is teaching her children the prayer gesture used in Bali (an island of Indonesia).

only ones that are possible. We can understand American childrearing practices better if we contrast them with some of those used in other cultures.

The Hutterites.   The childrearing methods of a society serve to adapt the child to the needs of that society. This is beautifully illustrated by the childrearing practices of a group of people called the Hutterites. The 230 Hutterite colonies in Canada and the northern United States contain a total of about 24,000 people. These people live communally, sharing their farmlands, buildings, and equipment, and eating together in community dining halls. They share a common religion which calls for adult baptism and total pacifism. The rules of the religion are very strict and demand complete conformity. For example, the women must wear long-sleeved, full-length dresses that button to the neck, even when working outdoors in hot weather. Their heads are always kept covered, first with a cap that buttons under the chin, and on top of that a black, polka-dotted scarf. Girls must dress in this way from the time they reach school age.

An anthropologist named Gertrude Enders Huntington lived with a Hutterite colony in Canada for many months. She brought along her three children (ranging in age from 2 to 9), her husband, and her mother. In a fascinating article Huntington (1981) describes the Hutterite methods of childrearing.

A Hutterite baby is regarded as a gift from God. When a baby is born, the

These Hutterite kindergarten girls are ready for their nap.

mother (who has worked hard throughout her pregnancy) is relieved of all responsibility other than the care of the newborn. The grandmother or another woman of the community takes over all her other chores. Three months after the birth, the baby's mother resumes her community duties. From that time on the baby will be fed, played with, or left alone according to the community's schedule. When it's time for the adults to go to church or dining hall, the baby is put in a crib and left.

When out of the crib, however, the Hutterite baby is the center of attention. Everyone in a Hutterite colony wants to hold a baby, and the infant is passed from hand to hand—spoken to, played with, tickled.

By toddlerhood the children are already under pressure to belong to the community rather than to their parents. A Hutterite 3-year-old might be whipped for refusing to go to a person other than his parents. He might also be whipped for quarreling with other children, for refusing to share, or for being noisy. After the punishment the crying child is immediately comforted.

From age 3 to 6 Hutterite children spend their days in the "kindergarten." Kindergarten children are held in very low esteem—no one wants them around. They are kept in one small building under the care of a woman called the "kindergarten mother." They are taught obedience, and they memorize prayers that they cannot yet understand. The idea of kindergarten is to break the "stubborn will" of the child, to make him or her a passive, conforming member of the group. Quiet, cooperative behavior is praised. Bad behavior is prevented with threats ("If you go outside a bear will get you!") or punished impartially by means of a willow switch. But the children are not made to feel guilty for their misbehavior, since "it is only natural for a child to sin" (Huntington, 1981, p. 42).

At age 6 Hutterite children enter the community school, where they learn to read and write English and German, and to do arithmetic. They study religion and Hutterite history. They're praised for working hard, but a fast learner is not given any special attention.

At 15 the Hutterite joins the adult work force and is allowed to eat in the adult dining hall. Physical punishment is no longer given. Young people must do their work and speak respectfully to their elders, but the community tolerates a certain amount of disregard for its rules. They are allowed to yield to some of the temptations of the outside world, as long as they do it in private. Boys of this age sometimes smoke secretly; girls might use nail polish on their toenails—which they then must hide under their thick black shoes. Teenagers of both sexes often own transistor radios, on which they secretly listen to popular songs. The community permits these little indulgences, because it knows that in another couple of years the young Hutterite will turn away from them and back to the community. He or she will humbly request baptism and will willingly become a full-fledged member of the Hutterite colony. The years of training and discipline will have accomplished their purpose.

Childrearing in the Soviet Union.   One classic study of cultural differences in childrearing contrasted American methods with those used in the Soviet Union. A psychologist from Cornell named Urie Bronfenbrenner made sev-

Children in the Soviet Union are expected to conform to group standards.

eral trips to Russia during the 60s. Later he wrote a detailed report of what he found there (Bronfenbrenner, 1970).

Most cultures use methods of childrearing that have gradually evolved along with the culture itself. What's interesting about the Russian method is that it didn't just evolve—it was purposely and consciously developed, over a rather short period of time. Its goal is clearly understood—to prepare children to live in a communist society.

Like the Hutterites, the Russians want their children to be polite and obedient and to work for the good of the group. But the methods they use to accomplish these aims are quite different. Instead of physical punishment, a Russian mother is told to use a technique called *withdrawal of affection* to control her children. Here's a sample from a Russian book on childcare quoted by Bronfenbrenner:

> For example, a mother says to her son: "once again you disobeyed me by not coming home on time. Now I no longer wish to finish the chess match we began yesterday. It is even unpleasant for me to look at you." For the rest of the evening, she confines herself only to cold responses to her son's questions. (p. 13)

The most important influence on Russian children comes, not from the family, but from their **agemates** or **peers**—other children of about the same age. Children in a Russian school are encouraged to compete with one another, not as individuals but as members of a group—one row in a classroom against the other rows, for example. Instead of telling young children to "sit up straight," a teacher will say, "Let's see which row can sit the straightest" (Bronfenbrenner, 1970, p. 55). The same technique is used for good behavior, for cleanliness and neatness, and for school performance. The group is scored on the performance of all of its members and is praised and rewarded only if all do well. A child who *doesn't* do well drags down the status of her entire group, so the other members of the group are very motivated to improve her performance. They will publicly criticize a child who misbehaves, or give assistance to one who needs help with his school work. Eventually, the child's group becomes the main source of reward and punishment. Adult supervision is no longer needed.

American Childrearing Methods.   The American child, in contrast to the Russian or the Hutterite, tends to be independent and assertive, rather than obedient or passive. An American toddler is usually encouraged to explore, to use initiative. The Russian toddler's movements are a lot more restricted. Soviet parents worry about cold drafts and other possible dangers, and don't let their children do much exploring.

In the United States individual achievement is stressed, rather than conformity to the group. American children are more competitive, less cooperative.

Of course, it is an oversimplification to talk of "American childrearing methods." American culture is divided into many subcultures, shared by groups of people who have a common national origin, a common religion, a common race, or even a common social class. Class differences do exist in American society. For example, upper-middle-class childrearing practices clearly differ in some ways from lower-middle-class practices. Psychologists and sociologists call these groups **socioeconomic classes.**

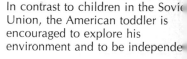
In contrast to children in the Soviet Union, the American toddler is encouraged to explore his environment and to be independent.

The Effects of Socioeconomic Level

A family's **socioeconomic level** depends on the income, profession, education, and social status of its members. A family that includes a doctor, a judge, or the president of a big company is at a high socioeconomic level. A family whose chief wage-earner is a farm laborer or a domestic worker or is frequently unemployed is at a low socioeconomic level. Such a family is sometimes described as **disadvantaged.**

Americans pride themselves on the fact that a child from a humble background—one raised in a log cabin, for instance—can grow up to be president. But, in fact, presidents of governments and of companies, doctors and lawyers, teachers and scientists, are much more likely to come from middle-class or upper-class homes than from disadvantaged homes. Conversely, children from disadvantaged homes are much more likely to become farm hands, construction workers, or unskilled laborers than are children from higher socioeconomic levels.

There are a number of possible reasons for this. Certainly there are clear differences between growing up in a disadvantaged home and growing up in an advantaged one. Parents who are engaged in a constant, wearying struggle for survival may be less able to give their children the attention that they need—especially when, as is often the case, there are many children in the family. The children in disadvantaged homes are more likely to be ignored or even abused, more likely to have health problems that are neglected. They are less likely to receive adequate nutrition, both before birth and after. Babies from disadvantaged homes run a greater risk of weighing under 5 pounds at birth, and a greater risk of dying within the first month. In fact, death rates at every age are higher for the disadvantaged. So are the rates of illegitimacy, divorce, or desertion—so the disadvantaged child is far more likely than the middle-class child to grow up in a fatherless home. Housing is also likely to be poorer—noisier and more crowded.

Children from disadvantaged homes are also deprived, to some extent, of the intellectual stimulation that more fortunate children receive. For example, middle-class mothers tend to provide their children with a greater number and variety of suitable toys. They also talk to their infants more than lower-class mothers, especially if the baby has just made a sound. That doesn't mean, however, that their babies get more affection. Babies in disadvantaged homes are loved just as much as middle-class babies. They are held, touched, and smiled at no less than middle-class babies (Clarke-Stewart, 1977; Tulkin, 1977). If anything, development in the first 6 or 8 months of life is *faster* in the baby from the disadvantaged home. The unfavorable differences show up later, particularly when the children enter school.

One study of class differences in childrearing (Hess and Shipman, 1969) compared mothers from four socioeconomic classes. (All the mothers were black.) One question the mothers were asked was what they would tell their children to prepare them for their first day of school. Here's how an upper-middle-class mother replied:

> First of all, I would take him to see his new school, we would talk about the building, and after seeing the school I would tell him that he should meet new children who would be his friends; he would work and play with them. I would explain to him that the teacher would be his friend and would help him and guide him in school, and that he should do as she tells him to.

Here's a lower-class mother:

> Well, I would tell him he going to school and he have to sit down and mind the teacher and be a good boy, and I show him how when they give him milk, you know, how he's supposed to take his straw and do, and not put nothing on the floor when he get through. (Hess and Shipman, 1968, p. 96)

What's important about these two replies is not the difference in language but the difference in tone. The first mother emphasizes the good things about school, and explains to her son why he should listen to what the teacher says. The second mother makes school sound rather unpleasant, and simply *tells* her son that he must obey the teacher. It wouldn't be surprising if these two children started out with very different attitudes toward school. These different attitudes may be one reason (there are many others) why disadvantaged children tend to do poorly in school. Of course, if they do poorly their attitude becomes still more negative. And when they grow up, what will they tell *their* children about school?

The Family

The previous section was supposed to be about socioeconomic levels, but we seem to have ended up talking mainly about families. That's because a culture (or a subculture, such as a socioeconomic class) doesn't usually act on the young child *directly*. It acts *indirectly*, through the family. The family is responsible for preparing the young child to live in society—for teaching the child the language, the attitudes, and some of the basic skills he or she will need.

But the most important function of the family isn't teaching. It isn't even providing food and shelter. The most important thing the family provides for the baby or the young child is *love*.

There is a story—perhaps untrue—told about Frederick II, ruler of Sicily in the thirteenth century. He believed that babies are born knowing a language, and he wanted to find out what that language was. So he took a group of newborn babies and had them cared for by foster mothers, who were told never to utter a single word to the babies. Alas, instead of speaking spontaneously in the native tongue of mankind (Hebrew, perhaps), the babies all died.

The same sad ending has befallen many other babies in similar situations. It was noticed in the 1700s that children in orphanages and foundling homes had a very high rate of mortality. As recently as the 1940s, more than a third of the infants in foundling homes in the United States and Canada died, most before they were a year old (Gardner, 1972).

Babies who survived the cold, barren, and restrictive environment of the old-style institutions were likely to be retarded in every way—intellectually, verbally, emotionally, socially, and in **motor development** (sitting up, crawling, walking, reaching for objects, and so on). They were also likely to be smaller than average (Gardner, 1972). These differences did not show up in early infancy. Babies who are reared in institutions progress normally for the first 3 months, as long as the physical care is adequate. After that the institution-reared babies begin to fall behind the home-reared ones—they are slower to walk and to talk, they smile later and less often. Young children who remain institutionalized for long periods never catch up with their home-reared agemates. Their IQs may be lowered by as much as 30 or 40 points (Clarke-Stewart, 1977). Forty IQ points is a big difference—it can mean the difference between an IQ of 100 (average) and an IQ of 60 (mentally retarded), or an IQ of 100 and an IQ of 140 (exceptionally bright). What is it that the babies who grew up in old-style institutions lacked? They lacked interesting things to look at and play with, they lacked the freedom to crawl around and explore their environment. Most important, they lacked someone who cared about them—someone who came when they cried, who smiled when they smiled, who cuddled them when they needed cuddling. In other words, they lacked what used to be called "mothering," but which can be given by any caring person—not necessarily a mother, not necessarily a woman, not necessarily even an adult.

This is vividly illustrated by a story told by Harold Skeels (1966), about a group of toddlers from an orphanage who were transferred to an institution for the mentally retarded. You wouldn't have much hope for these youngsters, would you? But, in fact, most of them did quite well—considerably better than other children who had remained in the orphanage. It turned out that the children who went to the institution were well cared for by the older girls and women there, whose mental ages ranged from 5 to 12 years. Only one or two toddlers were assigned to each ward, and they received a lot of love and attention from the residents of these wards. In most cases, some older girl or woman would become very attached to a particular child and would become that child's unoffical "adoptive mother."

Clearly, it's very important for older babies and toddlers to become attached to particular people—a few people who take care of them and whom they see again and again. A child who is not able to form emotional attachments of this kind—whose caretakers are "here today, gone tomorrow"—may grow up with normal intelligence, if the environment is stimulating enough. But he or she may be permanently retarded in social and emotional development, unable to relate well to other people or to care deeply about anyone (Rutter, 1979).

A baby monkey hugs its terrycloth "surrogate mother."

Something similar happens to baby monkeys that are raised in isolation, away from their mothers and from other monkeys. A psychologist named Harry Harlow raised some baby monkeys with "surrogate mothers" made of wire covered with terrycloth. The monkeys appeared to be normal enough when they were young—they clung to their terrycloth mothers just the way baby monkeys usually cling to their monkey mothers. But when these monkeys grew up and were put in with other monkeys, they were clearly abnormal. They were never able to interact peacefully with other monkeys—they lacked the "social skills" possessed by monkeys reared in the ordinary way. When a few of these isolated monkeys became mothers themselves, they behaved in a very abnormal way toward their own offspring. They wouldn't let their babies nurse, and they abused and neglected them (Harlow, 1971). Although we know from later studies by Harlow and others that some of the effects of isolation can eventually be reversed by special care, there is little doubt that the effects of early social isolation are serious and long-lasting.

Working Mothers. Human babies do need people who care about them, but does that mean they need full-time mothers? No, not necessarily. Whether it's bad for a child to have a working mother depends on the circumstances and on her reasons for working. In general, if a mother is working

Child Abuse

How bad can an environment be? Ask Warren, whose father picked him up and threw him against a wall, breaking several bones, when the child's whining got on his nerves. Or ask Louise, who will be scarred for life from the burns she suffered when her mother dumped a pot of scalding water on her, as punishment for wetting her pants. You won't be able to ask Freddie. He died as the result of a beating administered by his mother and his stepfather, designed to "teach him to behave himself."

Child abuse is nothing new—it has probably been around throughout human history. But until relatively recently, the problem was seldom mentioned. In former times it was felt that children "belonged" to their parents, and therefore that the parents were entitled to punish them however they wished. And as for those punishments that proved fatal, they were seldom recognized for what they were. It was only in 1961, when the American Academy of Pediatrics held a symposium on the plight of the battered child, that the problem became a subject of public discussion. The publicity it has received since then, and the laws that have been passed as a consequence, have greatly increased the likelihood that cases will be reported. In Michigan, for example, the number of reported cases went from 721 in 1968 to 30,000 in 1972; in California it went from 4,000 to 40,000 in the same period of time. That a single state would have 30,000 to 40,000 reported cases within a year gives us some idea of the prevalence of child abuse (Kempe and Kempe, 1978).

You may have read statements claiming that child abuse is found in well-to-do homes as well as disadvantaged ones, and in educated families as well as uneducated ones. That is true, as far

as it goes. The fact is, however, that child abuse is much more common in certain kinds of homes than in others. Because family stress is a critical factor in child abuse, anything that increases family stress is associated with an increased risk of a battered child. These factors include unemployment, lack of education, inadequate housing, marital difficulties, and large family size. Abusing parents also tend to be younger than nonabusing ones, and to have conceived their first child before they were married.

Other characteristics of abusing parents have been noted as well. Mothers are more likely to be responsible than fathers, which is not surprising since mothers generally spend more time with their children than fathers do. Stepparents are more likely to injure a child than are the child's original parents. Abusing parents are often socially isolated people who have little contact with people outside their immediate family—and, thus, no one to turn to in times of stress. They are also likely to have unrealistic ideas of what can be expected from a child of a given age. And finally, most abusing parents were themselves abused, or at least treated with unusual harshness, when they were children (Isaacs, 1981; Kempe and Kempe, 1978).

Abused children may also have some distinctive characteristics. In a large family, one particular child might be singled out for mistreatment, while the other children are treated reasonably well. When such a child is removed from that family and placed in a foster home, he or she sometimes becomes the target of further abuse in the foster home (Vasta, 1981). It has been noted that children with any sort of abnormality—mental, physical, or behavioral—run a greater risk of being battered (Frodi, 1981).

Child abuse often begins in infancy—in fact, babies and toddlers are the most frequent victims. What can a baby do that would make someone angry enough to injure him? The answer is obvious: he can cry. There is some evidence that the victims of child abuse tend to be babies and toddlers who cry or whine a lot (Vasta and Copitch, 1981). Couple a baby who cries incessantly with a mother under stress—a mother who was herself treated harshly as a child and who has few friends or relatives who can help her—and there may be trouble:

> Kathy made this poignant statement: "I have never felt really loved all my life. When the baby was born, I thought he would love me; but when he cried all the time, it meant he didn't love me, so I hit him." (Steele and Pollack, 1974, p. 96)

Kathy's infant son, age 3 weeks, was hospitalized with head injuries.

Crying is the most common stimulus for child abuse; toilet accidents are probably second on the list. In both cases the parent may be upset because he or she is unable to control the child's behavior. Abusing parents often seem to want to be in complete control of everything their child does. When the child doesn't do what they want him to, they punish him. In punishing, they may lose control, perhaps not even realizing that they are using enough force to do injury:

> Henry J., in speaking of his sixteen month old son, Johnny, said, "he knows what I mean and understands it when I say 'come here.' If he doesn't come immediately, I go and give him a gentle tug on the ear to remind him of what he's supposed to do." In the hospital it was found that Johnny's ear was lacerated and partially torn away from his head. (Steele and Pollack, 1974, p. 96)

Battered children need help. If nothing is done to help them, many of them will be per-

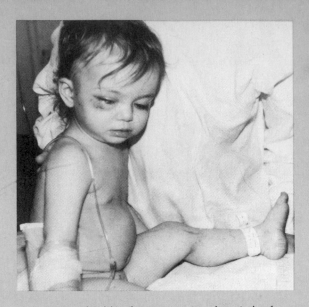

Fifteen-month-old Jody recovers in a hospital, after a court order removed her from the home in which she had been abused.

manently disabled by their injuries (brain damage is common); some of them will die. Most states now have laws requiring doctors to report suspicious-looking injuries. If there's good evidence of child abuse, the child is generally removed from the home—often to his parents' relief, because they, too, are likely to be aware that the child is in danger. Counseling and therapy can help an estimated 80 percent of abusing parents to learn how to deal with their children in a more humane way (Kempe and Kempe, 1978). For the remaining 20 percent, finding a new permanent home for the child may be the best solution.

Perhaps the most important thing that counseling does for abusing parents is to make them feel less isolated, by giving them someone to turn to in times of crisis. Even a child-abuse hotline, a number they can phone when they feel unable to cope, may serve that function. A little thing like a phone number—and yet it may be enough to save a child's life. ■

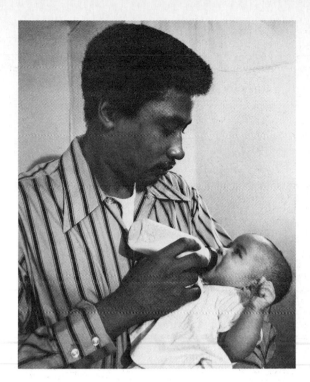

There is no reason to believe that fathers are less capable of taking care of babies than mothers are.

because she wants to, there is no evidence of ill effects on the child. If she is working because she must, for financial reasons, there are more likely to be problems. It's interesting that *not* working may be more harmful for a mother-child relationship than working—if the mother is dissatisfied with her role as a housewife (Clarke-Stewart, 1977).

What about day-care centers? Assuming that the center is a reasonably good one, they do not appear to have any unfavorable effects on development. Studies have found no intellectual differences between young children raised at home and those who attend day-care centers. The day-care children are just as attached to their mothers as the home-reared ones—they overwhelmingly prefer their mothers to the caregivers at the center. The only noteworthy difference seems to be in sociability: day-care children tend to interact more with their peers, even when their day-care years are over (Belsky and Sternberg, 1978; Kagan, Kearsley, and Zelazo, 1978).

School-age children of working mothers are generally *superior* to their classmates with stay-at-home mothers, both in achievement and in adjustment. This is especially true of girls (Hoffman, 1979).

Fathers as Caregivers. Throughout history and in most of the societies across the globe, fathers have usually played no more than a minor role in childrearing. In apes and monkeys too, the male has little or nothing to do with his offspring. Does this mean that fathers *can't* care for young infants—that they're biologically unsuited for the job? This question is of particular importance now that more than 40 percent of mothers with preschool children are working (Hoffman, 1979), and now that divorced fathers are more often given custody of their children.

The evidence suggests that fathers are quite capable of taking care of babies. When fathers were left with their 3-day-old infants, they looked at, touched, spoke to, and kissed their babies as often as mothers did. They were just as sensitive to the little sounds or movements the infants made. Other studies have shown that most toddlers are just as attached to their fathers as they are to their mothers (Parke, 1979).

Brothers and Sisters. Among the important influences on children's early years are their siblings. Whether a child is born first, last, or in the middle—an only child or one of many—has a lot to do with the way he or she will develop. Firstborns tend to be high achievers, especially in school. They are likely to be more verbal and to have slightly higher IQs. But, on the average, they are less sociable and less popular with their peers than their younger siblings. As preschoolers, firstborns tend to be less self-confident and more dependent than later-born children.

One reason for these differences is that parents tend to treat firstborn and later-born children in different ways. They are likely to be more strict with their first child, more demanding, less consistent. They spend more time with the firstborn, until the second child is born. (After that, the younger child or children get more attention.) Parents are more relaxed with later-born children. The greater sociability and self-confidence of later-borns seems to be due partly to this more relaxed attitude of the parents, and partly to the experience of interacting with other children right from the start. Younger children also tend to imitate the behavior of their older siblings. For example, a girl or a boy with brothers tends to act more masculine (or less feminine) than a girl or a boy with sisters (Clarke-Stewart, 1977).

The *number* of siblings also makes a difference. In large families, parents can't give as much individual attention to each child. On the average, children from large families score a little lower on IQ tests than children from small families—the larger the family, the lower the score (Zajonc and Markus, 1975). Spacing of children matters, too. Children born one or two years apart have slightly lower IQs, on the average, than those born three or four years apart. The children born closest together in time are those in multiple births—twins, triplets, and so on. Twins have IQs that average 4 or 5 points lower than children born singly, and this difference seems to be related to the fact that they must almost always share their parents' attention. It isn't just due to crowding or poorer nutrition in the uterus, because a child who has a twin that dies at birth tends to have an IQ nearly as high as a child born singly (Zajonc, 1976).

From what we've told you so far, it would seem obvious that the highest IQ of all would be found in the only child. Oddly enough, that is not the case. The first child in a family of two, three, or even four comes out ahead of the only child. Robert Zajonc and Gregory Markus (1975) have a possible explanation for this. They point out that only children, unlike first children, never have the opportunity to serve as "teacher" for their younger siblings.

But a child without any brothers or sisters is not to be pitied. Only children do just fine. There's no evidence that they are more spoiled or selfish than children with siblings. When they grow up, "onlies" are just as satisfied with their lives as "non-onlies." On the average, they are as happily married, they are as good at parenting, and they spend as much time socializing with friends. They do differ, however, in achievement. Onlies are even more likely to have college or graduate degrees than firstborns—and firstborns are better educated than later-borns. Onlies are also more likely to have highly paid, prestigious occupations (Polit, Nuttall, and Nuttall, 1980).

Changes in the American Family

The American family is currently in a state of flux. Attitudes toward marriage and childrearing have changed drastically in the last decade. If current trends continue, about 40 percent of present marriages will end in divorce. Due to divorce and to unmarried parenthood, it is estimated that close to 50 percent of American children will spend some time in a single-parent home. The great majority of these homes are headed by a woman. Although more divorced fathers are getting custody of their children than ever before, this still happens in only 10 percent of cases.

The Effects of Divorce on Children.   Mavis Hetherington of the University of Virginia has done a considerable amount of research on the effects of divorce on children (Hetherington, 1979; Hetherington and Martin, 1979). Her findings are summarized here.

It has long been known that the children of divorced parents tend to have higher rates of behavior problems. This is particularly true with boys—in general, girls seem to be better insulated against unfavorable environmental influences. The male behavior problems associated with divorce tend to be of the variety known as **antisocial behavior**—lying, stealing, truancy, drug use, vandalism, and aggressiveness toward people.

One reason for this increase in antisocial behavior is the family conflict and stress that accompany divorce. The period before a divorce or separation is painful for parents and children alike. When a husband and wife are getting along poorly, they are less able to be attentive and affectionate parents. There are quarrels, tensions, and attempts to turn a child against the other parent. A two-parent home that is full of this sort of conflict is more stressful for a child than a well-run single-parent home. The more poorly the parents are getting along, the more antisocial behavior the children are likely to show.

But divorce itself brings no immediate relief for a child. In the first year after a divorce, family conflicts and children's behavior problems increase, not decrease. Children react to a divorce with grief, and often with feelings of self-blame. Divorce is particularly damaging when it results in a move to a new residence, and the children must lose their home, their neighborhood, and their friends, as well as their two-parent family.

For a mother who has custody of her children, the first year after a divorce is rough going. She generally has no help with household or childrearing tasks, which often seem overwhelming. As one divorced mother put it, "There's no time-outs in the parenting game in one-parent families" (Hetherington and Martin, 1979, p. 270). She tends to feel socially isolated. Her financial situation has probably worsened considerably. And to top it off, her children are giving her a hard time. Sons are negative and disobedient, daughters tend to whine and complain.

This kind of behavior gradually declines as the mother learns to cope with the demands of single parenthood. By the end of the *second* year after a divorce, children are experiencing fewer difficulties than they were in the period just before the divorce. However, behavior problems remain more common in the children of divorced parents than in children living in an average two-parent family, and this appears to be true for both girls and boys (Wallerstein and Kelly, 1980).

The Fatherless Home. How much of the antisocial behavior of boys in mother-headed homes is due simply to the absence of the father? Quite a bit, it seems. Boys in two-parent homes are more obedient to their fathers than to their mothers, so it is not surprising that the father's absence leads to problems with discipline. There are other problems, too. Children from fatherless

For the mother in a single-parent home, parenthood is a job with "no time-outs." It is estimated that nearly 50 percent of American children will have the experience of living in a single-parent home.

homes tend to do less well in school and on IQ tests, particularly on tests of mathematical skills (Shinn, 1978). They also have more psychological problems, whether the father's absence is due to divorce or to death. However, the kinds of problems differ, depending on the reason for the father's absence: divorce is more likely to lead to antisocial behavior, death is more likely to lead to depression. In girls the father's absence may produce problems when they start to date. Again, the nature of the problems depends on the cause of the father's absence. According to one study, a girl whose father died is likely to be shy with boys and to be inhibited about sex. If her parents were divorced, the girl is more likely to be overly bold and sexually active at an early age (Hetherington and Martin, 1979).

Mother-headed homes don't necessarily lead to problems. Many of the ill effects of divorce can be prevented if the father remains in close contact with his children. A father's role may also be filled by a stepfather, a grandfather, or other male relatives or friends. And there is some evidence that genius may actually flourish in one-parent homes. Of 700 famous men whose biographies appeared in the *Encyclopaedia Britannica,* 25 percent had lost one parent by the age of 10 (Eisenstadt, 1978). An unusually high rate of father absence was also found in a group of 19 children with IQs over 180 (Albert, 1971).

Stepparents.   Children of divorced parents are usually better off if their parents find other partners. But the initial period of adjustment to a parent's remarriage, like the initial period of adjustment to divorce, is difficult. The total or partial loss of a parent through death or divorce is a painful blow. Children need to have a period to mourn, to come to terms with their feelings of loss and grief. Usually it takes them longer to do this than it takes an adult (Visher and Visher, 1979). Thus the parent may get over the loss of a mate before the child has gotten over the loss of a parent. If the parent's remarriage occurs at this stage, the child is unlikely to accept the stepparent gracefully. The remarriage is seen as disloyalty to the other parent. The newly married parent is also likely to be engrossed in his or her new romance and to pay much less attention to the child. Then the child feels that she's lost *both* parents instead of one. And finally, the parent's remarriage puts an end to the child's dream that someday her parents will reunite and live happily ever after.

Remarriage after a period of time may cause problems, too—especially if there are teenage children. A boy who is used to being the "man of the house" is not likely to be pleased if a new stepfather puts him back into the role of a child. Similarly, a girl who was helping her father to run the home may bitterly resent the intrusion of a new stepmother.

With divorce so common now, most stepfamilies are the result of divorce rather than death. Yet most present-day stepparents grew up in nuclear families and had no **role models** for stepparenthood—no older person performing that role whose behavior could serve as a model. Thus it's often difficult to know just how to act as a stepparent. Many stepparents make the mistake of expecting too much, too soon. They are unrealistic if they expect instant affection from their new stepchildren. And if they try to pretend instant affection *for* their new stepchildren (or even if they really feel it), the children are likely to mistrust it, to assume it's phony. Things work out better if allowed to proceed slowly (Kompara, 1980).

In the end, stepparents and stepchildren usually do adjust to each other. One study found that 64 percent of stepfamilies have "excellent" relationships (Duberman, 1973).

THE WORKINGS OF HEREDITY

We've come rather far afield in our sampling of environmental influences. But we've tried to touch on the many ways that one child's environment might differ from another child's, and on the many ways these differences might affect children. Now, in the next section, we confront the fact that children themselves differ, right from the start—they differ genetically.

Inherited characteristics, also called genetic characteristics, are transmitted by the **genes.** As you probably know if you've ever taken a biology course, genes are located in the nucleus of every cell that makes up a human, an animal, or a plant. They are composed of long, twisted molecules of DNA (deoxyribonucleic acid) and are so small that even with an electron microscope they cannot be seen clearly.

Chromosomes

Chromosomes, however, show up quite well through the microscope (see photograph on p. 49). Chromosomes are large collections of genes strung together in a particular order.

The number of chromosomes in a cell depends on what kind of plant or animal the cell belongs to. But all the normal members of a species have the same number of chromosomes. In humans that number is 46. Chromosomes come in pairs, so that means 23 pairs; but the two chromosomes in a pair are not identical. A human has 46 *different* chromosomes.

However, the egg cells (or ova) in a woman's ovaries have only 23 chromosomes, one from each pair. During the formation of an egg cell the chromosomes separate randomly into two halves, so each egg gets only half the usual number. The same thing happens when sperm cells are formed in a man's testicles—each one has 23 chromosomes. When conception occurs an egg and a sperm unite, and the result is a fertilized egg containing the normal number of 46 chromosomes. Half of these chromosomes come from the mother, half from the father.

Since the 23 chromosomes in an egg or a sperm are chosen at random, one from each pair, it is theoretically possible for one person to produce 2^{23}, or 8,388,608, genetically different eggs or sperm, each containing a slightly

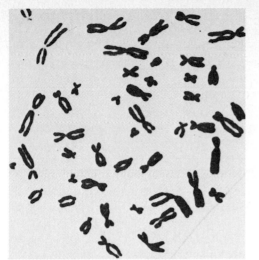

Human chromosomes.

different assortment of chromosomes. That means that a given couple is theoretically capable of producing 70,368,744,177,664 genetically different offspring. To look at it another way, your chances of being conceived were less than one in 70 trillion!

The Sex Chromosomes. These 23 pairs of chromosomes that are contained in a fertilized egg include one pair known as the **sex chromosomes.** These chromosomes determine whether the fertilized egg will develop into a girl or a boy. Sex chromosomes are of two kinds, called X and Y because their shapes look like those letters. People normally have two sex chromosomes in each of their cells: females have two Xs, males have one X and one Y. An unfertilized egg cell in a woman's body contains only one of the woman's sex chromosomes, and this is always an X (since women have only X chromosomes). But men have one X and one Y, so when sperm are formed some sperm get an X chromosome and some get a Y. When a baby is conceived, its sex depends on which kind of sperm fertilized the egg. If the sperm contained a Y, the fertilized egg has an X and a Y: a boy. If a sperm with an X wins, the result is two Xs: a girl. So, oddly enough, a girl has actually inherited her femaleness from her father!

Genes and Heredity

Here's the fertilized human egg with its 46 chromosomes, each made up of a large number of genes. This cell divides, and divides again, and eventually turns into a baby. It's the genes that are responsible for this remarkable transformation of a microscopic cell into a kicking, screaming human being. The genes trigger the formation of specific body chemicals (proteins) in particular places and particular times during development. In this way they determine whether the new creature will be tall or short, male or female, dark or fair—or, for that matter, human or frog. Genes are responsible not just for the *differences* among people. They are also in charge of all the things that people have in common: head on the top, feet at the bottom, bones on the inside, skin on the outside, muscles and nerves, intestines and hair—the works.

Bear in mind that genes don't *directly* make a person. They just provide the instructions, the recipes for making a number of different proteins. They also determine where and when the different proteins are made. Timing is a very important aspect of the job. The same set of genes has to produce a small baby with hardly any hair, then a young boy (let's say) with blond hair, then a young man with brown hair and a brown beard, and finally an old man with a gray beard and hardly any hair.

Usually we don't think of genes as producing a batch of chemicals: we think of them as carrying certain characteristics or traits, such as blue eyes or freckles. It's strange to think that the rules of the inheritance of simple traits were not known until 1866, when Gregor Mendel (an Austrian monk) published his theories. Even then, these rules were not generally accepted by scientists until after the turn of the century.

What made it so difficult to work out the laws of genetics? The problem was the seemingly unpredictable way that traits have of showing up or not showing up. A family may contain one child who looks just like the mother, another who looks just like the father, and another who doesn't look much like either parent. Yet we know that all three of these children have inherited half of their genes from their mother and half from their father. What's particularly puzzling is when a child has some trait that neither parent has. Mendel explained how this can happen with his idea of *dominant* and *recessive* traits.

Dominant and Recessive Traits. Mendel worked out several of the basic laws of inheritance in experiments with pea plants. In peas, a single pair of genes—each located in the same place on the two chromosomes of a pair—determine whether the seeds will be smooth or wrinkled when they are dried. A plant that has two genes for the smooth-seed trait will have smooth seeds. A plant that has two genes for the wrinkled-seed trait will have wrinkled seeds. But what happens when one gene says "smooth" and one says "wrinkled"? As Mendel found, all plants with this combination of genes will have smooth seeds, because the smooth trait is **dominant** and the wrinkled trait is **recessive.** When the two genes in a pair don't match, the dominant gene wins.

But the recessive gene doesn't just go away—it remains hidden in the chromosomes of the pea plant. A smooth-seeded plant that has a hidden chromosome for wrinkled seeds is called a **carrier** of the wrinkled-seed trait, because it is capable of passing that trait on to its descendants.

In humans, very few common characteristics are determined in a simple dominant-recessive manner: almost all normal human traits are controlled by two or more pairs of genes, and so the rules of inheritance are more complicated. Eye color, for instance, was once considered to be a simple dominant-recessive trait, with brown dominant over blue. But eyes don't come in just blue or brown—they can be any shade from lightest blue to nearly black, including gray, green, and hazel. Geneticists now believe that eye color is determined by two or more pairs of genes (Moody, 1975).

One human trait that probably does depend on a single pair of genes is red hair. Red hair is recessive to blond or brown, so a redhead must have *two* red-hair genes—one inherited from the mother, one from the father. A person who inherits only one red-hair gene will not have red hair but will be a carrier of the trait. What happens when two carriers marry and have children? On the average, one-fourth of their children will have red hair. This is because each child has a 50–50 chance of getting the chromosome that contains the mother's red-hair gene, and a 50–50 chance of getting the chromosome that contains the father's. So there's one chance in four that the child will luck out and get *both* red-hair genes.

Genetic Abnormalities

Unfortunately, getting a double dose of a recessive gene isn't always lucky. A number of uncommon genetic defects are inherited in this manner. Some of them are very serious, others are relatively harmless. One of the milder kinds is albinism. You may know a person with yellowish-white hair, pinkish or pale blue eyes, and very fair skin that won't tan. Such a person is called an *albino*. Albinos lack the normal coloring in their skin, hair, and eyes because a genetic defect prevents their bodies from forming the necessary pigment.

Since albinism is a recessive trait, a couple with normal coloring who have an albino child must both be carriers of the trait. If they have another child, that child too has a 1-in-4 chance of being an albino. The chances work separately for each child, so it is possible for this couple to have four albino children in a row, just as it is for a card player to pick four clubs in a row from a freshly shuffled deck.

Other abnormalities that are carried by recessive genes are the Tay-Sachs disease (see the box on Genetic Counseling), cystic fibrosis, and various metabolic disorders. Several of these lead to mental retardation.

When defects are carried by a single pair of recessive genes, what has usually happened is that these defective genes lack the correct instructions for making a crucial kind of protein called an **enzyme.** It takes dozens of genes to determine a person's eye color, hair color, and skin color; but it takes only a single pair of albino genes to wreck the plans of the other genes. The result is a person without any coloring at all. The other genes are still there—the genes that perhaps would have produced a brown-eyed person with black hair and medium skin—but these traits are not expressed. An enzyme is missing, because the gene that should be carrying the recipe for making that enzyme has lost it. Without that enzyme the necessary pigment can't be formed.

Defective genes of this sort are generally recessive and thus can be hidden in the chromosomes of normal people, carried from generation to generation with no one the wiser. It's only when a mating occurs between two people with the same recessive gene that the abnormality may show up. The possibility that this will happen is much greater if the people are related to each other. Marriages between first cousins are illegal in some places for this reason. Cousins have one set of grandparents in common, so they may both have inherited the same defective gene from their grandmother or grandfather. This is not just a theory—studies have shown that the children of marriages between cousins are almost twice as likely as the children of nonrelatives to have major defects or to die in infancy (Moody, 1975).

Disorders Carried by Dominant Genes. A disorder that is carried by a dominant gene shows up in everyone who inherits that gene—a child has to inherit only one gene, not two, in order to have the disorder. And the parent from whom the gene is inherited must have that disorder too. For example, abnormally short fingers (brachydactyly) is carried as a dominant trait. A person who has a single short-finger gene has short fingers. When that person has children, half of her eggs—or half of his sperm—will contain the chromosome with the short-finger gene. So each child has a 50–50 chance of having short fingers. The unaffected children do not have the gene and therefore cannot be carriers of the trait.

Because everyone who has the gene has the trait, very serious disorders are unlikely to be transmitted by dominant genes. The exception is when the disorder doesn't show up until late in life—after the person has perhaps had children and passed the gene on to half of them. An example of this sort of trait is Huntington's chorea. Huntington's chorea is a brain disease that generally appears in middle age. The victims' movements become jerky and their mental processes begin to deteriorate. The deterioration leads eventually to paralysis and finally to death. Woody Guthrie, a folk singer and songwriter of the 1950s (he was the composer of "This Land Is Your Land"), died of Huntington's chorea. His five children have had to live with the knowledge that each of them has a 50–50 chance of coming down with the disease.

Occasionally, a child may be born with a dominant-gene disorder that neither parent has. When this happens, we know it's due to a **mutation.** Sometimes a gene will change into some other kind of gene, perhaps because of exposure to radiation (X-rays, cosmic rays) or to some chemical—or perhaps for no particular reason at all. Certain genes seem to be more prone to mutate than others. A spontaneous mutation of this sort is responsible for a growth disorder called *achondroplasia*. People with this disorder have normal-sized heads and bodies, but very short arms and legs. Once the gene has mutated it stays that way. Achondroplasia is a dominant trait, so the child of a person with this disorder has a 50–50 chance of inheriting it. If *two* achondroplastic people marry, their children have only one chance in four of growing to normal size.

Sex-Linked Traits.   Another mutated gene is responsible for a blood disorder called hemophilia ("bleeder's disease"). Hemophilia is not carried as a dominant trait, but as a **sex-linked** trait. Color-blindness is another, more common trait that is inherited in the same way.

The gene for a sex-linked trait such as color-blindness is located on one of the sex chromosomes, the X chromosome. Girls have two X chromosomes, and if only one of them contains a gene for color-blindness they will have normal color vision. A girl has to inherit color-blindness from *both* her parents in order to be color-blind. But a boy has only *one* X chromosome—a boy's other sex chromosome is a Y, which is much smaller than the X and contains no genes for color vision. That means that a boy who has inherited one gene for color-blindness has no normal gene to oppose it, so he is born color-blind.

Now suppose that this color-blind boy grows up and marries a woman who has no genes for color-blindness. When his wife conceives a child, it will be a boy if it receives the father's Y chromosome, a girl if it receives the father's X. The father's Y chromosome doesn't contain his color-blindness gene, so his sons will have normal color vision. But the father's X chromosome *does* have the defective gene, so he will pass it on to all of his daughters. Because they have another X chromosome they will have normal color vision, but they will all be carriers of the trait. When they grow up and get married, half of their eggs will contain that X with the color-blindness gene. That means that each of their sons will have a 50–50 chance of being color-blind, and each of their daughters will have a 50–50 chance of being another carrier of the color-blindness gene.

Because a sex-linked trait is located on the X chromosome, it can never be passed from a father to a son. A boy who is color-blind has always inherited his defective gene from his mother, who probably has normal color vision.

Problems Involving Chromosomes.   There is another class of disorders that are genetic—caused by the genes—but that are not necessarily inherited. A man and a woman with entirely normal chromosomes can have a child with a disorder caused by a chromosomal abnormality. What has happened is that something went wrong with an egg or a sperm, so that instead of having the normal complement of 23 chromosomes, it has too many or too few. Then the fertilized egg ends up with 45 or 47 chromosomes, instead of the normal 46.

What happens next depends on which chromosome is missing or extra. In most cases, the fertilized egg will be unable to develop properly and it will die—either right away or after a few weeks. A good proportion of early miscarriages are believed to result from chromosomal abnormalities. In other instances, a baby will be born with multiple defects and will die soon after birth.

In two cases, however, babies who are born with chromosomal abnormalities are likely to survive. The first is when the extra or missing chromosome is a sex chromosome. Extra or missing sex chromosomes have relatively mild

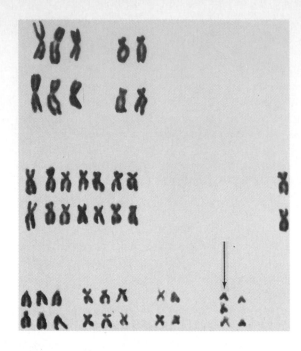

Human chromosomes sorted out by the process known as *karyotyping*. The arrow is pointing to the chromosomal abnormality that produces Down's syndrome: three of the twenty-first chromosome. The two large chromosomes on the right side are X chromosomes, indicating that the sex of this fetus is female.

consequences, although there are often defects of the internal and external sex organs. There is also an increased risk of mental retardation.

The other case involves an extra chromosome in the twenty-first set—one of the smallest human chromosomes. The result of this extra twenty-first chromosome is a child born with **Down's syndrome,** which produces a wide variety of mental and physical problems. A child with Down's syndrome is mentally retarded, has a short neck, small head, stubby fingers, thin hair, and a large tongue. Heart defects are often present. The face has a distinctive appearance, especially around the eyes. It was the odd shape of the eyes that led Langdon Down, a British physician of the 1800s, to name the disorder *Mongolism* (after Mongolia, a country in Asia). Down's syndrome children used to be called "Mongoloids," but this inaccurate term is used less frequently now.

Down's syndrome is a fairly common disorder: about 1 in 700 children is affected. The chances of having a child with Down's syndrome increase as the mother gets older. It is 1 in 1,500 for mothers under 30 and gradually rises to 1 in 60 for mothers over 45. However, it is possible to test for the presence of Down's syndrome early in pregnancy, and many doctors recommend that this be done if the pregnant woman is over 35. The test involves a procedure called **amniocentesis.** A needle is carefully inserted into the pregnant woman's uterus and some fluid is withdrawn. This fluid contains some of the cells of the developing fetus. Checking the chromosomes of these cells is done by a technique called **karyotyping** (see photograph above): a cell nucleus is photographed under a microscope, and the pictures of the individual chromosomes are cut out of the photograph and sorted out. If the kary-

A Down's syndrome child.

otype shows three of the twenty-first chromosome, the child will invariably be born with Down's syndrome. (See box.)

Polygenic Inheritance

So far, our discussion of the basic mechanisms of heredity seems to have concentrated on all the things that can go wrong. Don't be misled—things usually *don't* go wrong. But in order to explain how individual genes (and individual chromosomes) work, it was easier to consider what happens when a mistake occurs.

Inheritance of *normal* human traits, as we said earlier, generally involves many genes, not just a single pair. A trait that depends on more than one pair of genes is called **polygenic.** Inheritance of polygenic traits is more complicated than single-gene traits because there are so many more possible combinations of genes and, therefore, so many possible variations of the trait. A pea plant has only two kinds of seeds, smooth or wrinkled; a baby has or doesn't have Tay-Sachs disease, is or isn't an albino. But when it comes to polygenic traits such as size, coloring, strength, or musical ability, there is a tremendous range of possibilities. A person's adult height can be anywhere from over 8 feet to under 2. Musical ability can range from genius to zilch.

It's typical of polygenic traits that the two extremes are very rare. Most people fall somewhere in the middle.

It's also typical of polygenic traits that they're more flexible, more capable of being influenced by environmental factors, than single-gene traits. This is true of skin color, which depends mostly on heredity but also on the amount of exposure to the sun. It is certainly true of accomplishment in music, which depends as much on training as on inherited qualities. And it is true even of height, which depends mostly on genetic factors but also on environmental factors such as diet and health care during childhood. For example, over the past 100 years children in many countries have been growing taller with each generation, so that the typical American child born today will be two or three inches taller as an adult than a child of similar parentage born in 1890. Improved nutrition and health care are believed to be the major causes of this trend (Roche, 1979).

CLOSE-UP

Genetic Counseling

Bob and Marlene Lippman had been married 10 years when Evelyn, their first child, was born. Understandably, they were delighted with her. Evelyn was a lovely baby, with doll-like features and big, long-lashed eyes. "She was so beautiful," says Marlene, "that people used to stop me on the street to exclaim over her." Even Evelyn's pediatrician was impressed. At her 1-month checkup he told Marlene, "I can't fault your baby. She's perfect."

At 6 months Evelyn was smiling and alert, just starting to reach for toys. She wasn't sitting up yet, but Bob and Marlene figured that she "just wasn't in any hurry."

Four months later Evelyn still wasn't sitting, and Marlene mentioned it to her doctor. He told her not to be concerned. "My daughter didn't sit up till 10 months, either."

By 11 months Marlene and Bob were starting to worry. They brought Evelyn to the doctor again, and this time he examined her more closely. He saw that her movements were "floppy," and that her eyes were no longer following moving objects. He recommended that the Lippmans take Evelyn to a pediatric neurologist—a children's doctor who specializes in problems of the brain and spinal cord.

The Lippmans live in a pleasant, suburban town in New Jersey. On Evelyn's first birthday they drove to New York City and brought her to the pediatric wing of a major medical center. The neurologist spent only ten minutes examining Evelyn. He pulled no punches when he gave them the diagnosis. "Your daughter has Tay-Sachs disease. She will die, probably within two years. Before that she will become blind, deaf, and paralyzed. She'll lose the ability to suck, the ability to swallow. You'll have to put her in an institution."

The neurologist explained that Tay-Sachs disease is an inherited metabolic disorder carried by recessive genes. Babies who inherit two Tay-Sachs genes lack an enzyme that is necessary for metabolizing a certain kind of fat molecule. Without that enzyme the molecule gradually builds up in the brain, eventually destroying it.

Stunned and grief-stricken, Bob and Marlene took their baby home. In the next month they

With a polygenic trait such as height, something is inherited, but it isn't a certain number of inches or centimeters. One inherits a *range* of possible heights. Within this range, the final height is determined by environmental factors. If everything goes well and nutritional needs are met in abundance, a person will end up at the tall end of his or her potential range. If nutrition is just barely enough to keep the person alive and health is poor throughout the growth period, final height will be at the short end of the range. Generally neither of these extremes occurs and people end up somewhere in the middle of their potential range of heights.

Since the inherited range sets limits to potential height, once the upper limit is reached, further improvements in nutrition will have no effect. There are indications that the gradual increase in height of American men and women is finally coming to an end. Future generations will probably be no taller than their parents.

came to two decisions. First, they *wouldn't* put Evelyn in an institution. They'd keep her at home, love her and care for her, and give her whatever happiness she was capable of experiencing in her short life-span. Second, they still wanted children—normal, healthy children. But they'd never have another child if there was any chance of having another Tay-Sachs baby.

The hospital where Evelyn's disease had been diagnosed, like most large medical centers, contains a genetics clinic. The Lippmans made an appointment to see a genetic counselor at that clinic. Genetic counselors are trained in the medical aspects of genetics and can give advice to people like the Lippmans—people who want children but who have reason to fear that their children might not be normal. Many couples who seek genetic counseling, like the Lippmans, have already had one abnormal child. Others have a close relative who bore a child with a serious defect.

The genetic counselor explained to the Lippmans that if they conceived another child, that child too would have a 1-in-4 chance of inheriting two Tay-Sachs genes and getting the disease. But, she told them, it is possible to test a fetus for Tay-Sachs less than four months after conception, by the process of amniocentesis. If the test showed that the fetus had Tay-Sachs, what would the Lippmans do? There was no

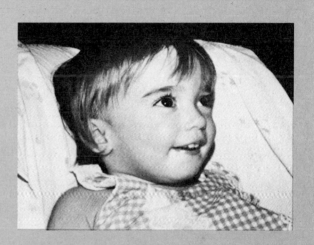

Evelyn Lippman at age 17 months.

question in their minds. Marlene would have an abortion. Neither she nor Bob could see any point in letting a pregnancy continue if it would result in a baby like Evelyn—a baby doomed to die, slowly and horribly.

Marlene became pregnant a few months later. Amniocentesis showed the fetus to be normal. Julia Lippman is 3 now, a lively, talkative youngster with hazel eyes and dark-blond hair. Her older sister is 5 years, 4 months old—one of the oldest Tay-Sachs children in the country. Evelyn still breathes, her strong heart keeps

All the interesting characteristics of children, if they have any hereditary basis at all (and they usually do), are inherited polygenically. That means that these traits depend not just on the genes, but on the interaction between the genes and the environment. In the next section we will discuss what is known about these interactions.

INTERACTIONS BETWEEN HEREDITY AND ENVIRONMENT

The modern view of the nature-nurture issue is quite different from the view that prevailed in the 1950s and 60s. The earlier view was that a child is born with certain characteristics—genetic characteristics—and the environment

Marlene, Julia, and Bob Lippman.

acts on these characteristics to modify them. The child was seen as something passive, like a block of wood. The wood has a certain shape to begin with, and then the sculptor modifies the shape by sawing or chiseling away at it.

Now we recognize, more and more, that the environment doesn't just act on the child: the child acts on the environment too. The shape of the block of wood has an effect on the sculptor, so that the same sculptor will do certain things with one block of wood and quite different things with another. And even if the *same* things are done to two blocks, they will not turn out exactly alike.

People react differently to different children. They respond in one way to a lively child, another way to a quiet one. Their behavior with a girl is not the same as their behavior with a boy. A child who learns things quickly is treated in a different way from a child who learns things slowly.

But suppose children were cared for by robots, instead of by human

beating. But most of her brain died long ago. She smiled for the last time at 17 months. She has not been able to see or hear for more than two years. Bob and Marlene have to feed her through a plastic tube that goes from her nostril to her stomach. They lift her out of her crib several times a day; they handle her with affection. She doesn't move. She is unable to respond in any way.*

An estimated 1 out of every 350 Americans is a carrier of the Tay-Sachs gene. But the proportion of carriers is 10 times higher in one population group: Jews whose ancestors came from Russia or Poland. Marlene and Bob are both Jewish by birth, but they had never heard of Tay-Sachs until Evelyn's neurologist told them about it. A simple blood test (developed in 1969) can detect a carrier of the Tay-Sachs gene. In the mid–1970s there was a concerted effort among Jews in the New York City area to inform young people about the problem and urge them to be tested. At that time Bob and Marlene were in Thailand, serving in the Peace Corps.

Several other genetic defects are more common in certain population groups. For example,

many black people (perhaps 1 in 10) are carriers of the gene for sickle-cell anemia. This is a painful, crippling blood disease that kills half its victims before the age of 30. Another blood disease, thalassemia, is prevalent among Italians and Greeks. Tests are available to detect carriers of both diseases. If two carriers marry, amniocentesis can tell them whether their unborn child is normal.

Almost 50 genetic diseases and chromosomal abnormalities can now be detected by amniocentesis, before the fourth month of pregnancy. These include the Lesch-Nyhan syndrome, Hurler's syndrome, Hunter's syndrome, and Down's syndrome, all of which lead to severe mental retardation.

A severely retarded or permanently ill child is a terrible burden for a family, both emotionally and financially. The goal of genetic counseling is to enable people to have children without fear of this kind of burden. More often than not, amniocentesis tells them that their child will be okay. When a serious genetic defect is detected, most couples choose the alternative of having an abortion and trying again. People who are firmly opposed to abortion for philosophical or religious reasons, and who have learned that they run a sizable risk of having an abnormal child, may decide to try for another alternative: adoption. ∎

*Evelyn Lippman died on January 2, 1983, at the age of 5 years, 10 months. She was one of the longest-lived Tay-Sachs children on record.

beings, so we could be sure that they were all treated alike. Would they all turn out the same? Of course not. Each child is a unique individual. Each child reacts in a unique way to his or her environment.

The point is that the interactions between heredity and environment are extremely complicated. It's not that the effects of environment are simply added to the effects of heredity, the way flowers are added to a bouquet.

The new view of the interaction between heredity and environment means that many of the older studies on environmental effects must be reinterpreted—their findings can no longer be taken at face value. For example, one study (Caldwell, Bradley, and Elardo, 1975) was designed to discover factors in the home environment that increase the intelligence of young children. The researchers found that the most intelligent children tended to come from homes in which mothers were warm and responsive, bought their children suitable toys, and played with them a lot. In other words, there was a positive correlation between maternal behavior of this sort and the IQ of the child. But does that mean that the behavior of the mothers *caused* their children to be more intelligent? Not necessarily. A correlation only shows that two things tend to go together—not that one causes the other. It is possible (as the researchers themselves pointed out) that some or all of the correlation could be due to an effect in the opposite direction—an effect of the child on the mother's behavior. Perhaps some children are more intelligent than others for genetic reasons. Perhaps they are more rewarding or more interesting to be with than less intelligent children, so their mothers play with them more and are more responsive to them. Perhaps their mothers buy them better toys because these children are more capable of expressing their desire for certain toys, or more sensible in their choice of which toy to ask for, or better at influencing a parent's decision to buy or not to buy. And so on.

We assume that children's characteristics *do* affect adult behavior. But adult behavior affects children, too—parents who are responsive to their children and spend a lot of time with them undoubtedly *do* produce some increase in their children's intelligence. If intelligent children bring out certain behaviors in parents, and these very behaviors increase the children's intelligence, you can see that we have a sort of "vicious circle," which in this case is anything but vicious. The circle *is* vicious in the opposite case, though. Less intelligent children may be less fun to be with, and parents may not play with them as much. This would lead to a further drop in the children's intelligence.

In this example, children's intelligence was the characteristic under study. As it happens, intelligence has probably been the subject of more research than any other characteristic of children. One reason for this is that we have a way of measuring it—we have IQ tests. Of course, an IQ score is not a *perfect* measurement of intelligence—in some cases it might be quite inaccurate. But at least there is a certain amount of agreement among psychologists about what is meant by "intelligence." IQ tests are the best way we have at present to express that quality (or those qualities) as a number. Having a number to work with has made it very much easier to do research on intelligence. The situation is quite different for other psychological characteristics.

When we talk about "persistence" or "sociability" or "enthusiasm," we first have to come to an agreement on what is meant by the term. Then we have the much trickier problem of how to measure that quality. Although there *are* tests designed to measure various personality traits, they haven't been nearly as successful as IQ tests.

There is another reason why investigators have concentrated so often on IQ: intelligence has become the focus of the nature-nurture debate. People seem to be much more concerned about inheritance of intelligence than they are, say, about inheritance of artistic ability. Perhaps this is because the question has practical, even political implications. It has long been recognized that people in different socioeconomic classes differ in mean IQ. The average unskilled laborer has an IQ of about 90, the average accountant or engineer has an IQ of about 125 (Harrell and Harrell, 1945). Similarly, the children of unskilled laborers have lower IQs than the children of professional people. Are these differences in the children primarily genetic, inherited from their parents, or are they primarily due to the considerable differences in the children's environments? Most people who believe that the differences are mostly environmental hope that environmental differences will eventually be eliminated. Their idea is that if you can give all children the same advantages, then each one will have an equal chance to grow up to be a doctor or a judge or a president. On the other hand, many people who believe that intelligence is mostly inherited think that eliminating environmental differences will have little effect on IQ differences: decreasing the importance of the environment will only *increase* the importance of heredity (Herrnstein, 1973).

We hope you will agree with us in believing that no possible outcome of the nature-nurture debate could be used to justify a policy that forces children to grow up in unfavorable environments. We should work to improve children's environments because *all* children ought to have a good environment—whether or not it improves their intelligence.

In the next section we'll discuss some of the evidence for environmental and genetic influences on intelligence. We'll start by describing some of the techniques that psychologists have used in their attempts to separate the effects of environment from those of heredity.

Studying Genetic and Environmental Influences

It makes little sense to ask whether human intelligence is inherited or is the result of environmental influences. If your parents had been mice instead of people, no environment in the world could have enabled you to read this book! Obviously, you can only have human intelligence if you have human genes.

What we really want to know is whether *differences* in human intelligence are due to genetic differences or environmental differences. If Doug is brighter than Paula, is it because he inherited brighter genes, or because he developed in a brighter environment?

Experiments with Rats. Even rats differ in something that could conceivably be called intelligence. Some rats learn their way through mazes, for example, more quickly than others. These differences show up even if all the rats have exactly the same environment—the same cages, the same food, and so forth. When the effects of environment are **controlled** in this fashion (by being held constant), any differences among the rats are probably genetic. That they *are* genetic is proved by the fact that they can be passed on—the offspring of the bright rats are brighter than the offspring of the dull rats (Thompson, 1954).

It is also possible to control rats' heredity and vary their environment. The rats that are usually used for laboratory experiments have been purposely **inbred** for many generations. Inbreeding means mating close relatives to each other—fathers to daughters, brothers to sisters, and so on. Generation after generation of inbreeding produces groups of animals that show hardly any variation from one individual to another. They all have practically the same genes.

Now we can take some of these carbon-copy animals and divide them randomly into two groups. One group can be raised in an "enriched" environment—a big pen with all sorts of interesting toys to play with and mazes to explore. The other group can be raised in an "impoverished" environment—separate cages with bare walls and no frills.

Experiments of this sort have been done many times. What is found is that the rats reared in the enriched environment turn out brighter (Rosenzweig, 1966). They do better than the impoverished rats on several different tests. And they even have bigger, heavier brains!

Studies of Human Families. With rats, we can control both heredity and environment. When it comes to humans the situation is quite different. We obviously can't tamper with people's heredity. We can't even do much to change their environments, except in small ways or for short periods of time. The problem in trying to find out anything about humans is that their heredity and environment tend to vary together. We usually can't hold one factor constant in order to see what effect the other has.

Several reports published early in this century claimed to show that certain groups of people are genetically inferior. Perhaps the most famous of these was written in 1912 by Henry Goddard, director of a New Jersey institution for retarded children. Goddard's report concerned the descendants of a man named Martin Kallikak. Kallikak, a Revolutionary War soldier, was said to be the father of a child born to a mentally retarded girl who worked in a tavern. He later married a woman from a respectable family and fathered other children. Goddard traced the families, and found that Kallikak had almost a thousand descendants by 1912. About half could be traced back to the tavern girl's child, half to the children of his marriage. Goddard interviewed people who knew these descendants or had heard of them from others, and reported that there was a striking difference between Kallikak's legitimate descendants and the descendants of the tavern girl. According to Goddard, the legitimate descendants consisted mainly of fine, upstanding citizens; the other group contained many mentally deficient people, as well as criminals, alcoholics, prostitutes, and the like.

Goddard blamed the differences between the two groups on heredity. But it's clear that they must have had different environments, too. There's no way of knowing which mattered more—the differences in heredity or the differences in environment.

Twin Studies.   Although it is never possible to give two people exactly the same environments, nature does occasionally provide us with two people who have exactly the same heredity: **identical twins.** Identical twins are formed when a fertilized egg splits in two at some early stage of development. The two halves, each containing an identical set of 46 chromosomes, grow into two babies. These babies are always the same sex, and generally look so much alike that it is difficult to tell them apart. Their bodies are composed of exactly the same proteins; their blood type is always the same.

Only about a third of twins are identical. The rest are **fraternal**—born of two different egg cells that have been fertilized by two different sperm. Fraternal twins happen to be born at the same time, but they are no more alike than any other pair of brothers or sisters. They are not necessarily the same sex. Like siblings born at different times, fraternal twins have, on the average, 50 percent of their genes in common.

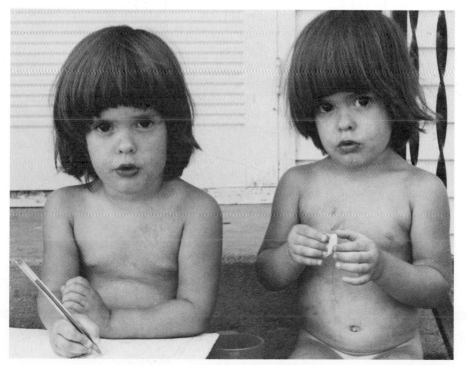

Identical twins develop from a single fertilized egg, so they have exactly the same genes.

Notice that we said "on the average." Since every fertilized egg gets a random selection of 50 percent of its father's genes and 50 percent of its mother's, it is theoretically possible for any two siblings (born at the same time or at different times) to have *no* genes in common: child 1 gets a certain selection of half of the parent's chromosomes, and child 2 happens to get exactly the opposite half. Of course, that is extremely unlikely. Equally possible—and equally unlikely—is the chance that child 1 and child 2 will get the *same* selection of genes. (You already know how improbable that is: less than one chance in 70 trillion!) So although two siblings can actually have from 0 to 100 percent of their genes be the same, the low and high percentages occur very rarely. A percentage around 50 is by far the most likely.

In contrast, identical twins have 100 percent of their genes in common. That is, they have exactly the same genes.

Since identical twins have the same genetic makeup and—assuming they are raised together—very similar environments, they should be very much alike. Fraternal twins being raised together also have very similar environments. However, only about half of their genes are the same, so they will be less alike than identical twins. One kind of twin study makes use of this difference. The assumption is that if a particular trait is very similar in identical twins and noticeably *less* similar in fraternal twins, that trait must be at least partly genetic. For example, eye color is nearly always the same in identical twins, but sometimes differs in fraternal twins, because eye color is genetic. On the other hand, whether or not a child gets chicken pox is primarily environmental. Identical twins are likely to get chicken pox at about the same time—but so are fraternal twins.

In twin studies there are two ways of saying how similar or how different the two children are. The first is **correlation,** which we talked about in Chapter 1. Researchers have given IQ tests to many pairs of twins. They've found that the correlation in IQ scores for identical twins raised together is quite high, about .86. (Remember that 1.00 is the highest possible correlation.) The correlation in IQ for fraternal twins is much lower, about .60 (Bouchard and McGue, 1981; Plomin and DeFries, 1980).

The other way of describing the similarity or difference of twins is **concordance.** This way is used when the trait in question can't be measured. The experimenter simply records whether a pair of twins is the same or different in a particular trait. If they are the same they are said to be *concordant.* Many pairs of twins are examined, and the results are expressed as the percentage of pairs that are concordant. Concordance of eye color in identical twins is 99.6 percent (sometimes expressed as a proportion, .996). This means that if one twin has brown eyes, there's a 99.6 percent chance that the other has brown eyes, too (Strickberger, 1968).

Even with identical twins raised in the same home, concordances are hardly ever 100 percent, and correlations are never 1.00. There are two reasons for the minor differences that are always found. One is that genes have a certain amount of randomness or variability in their actions. Fingerprints are never exactly the same, and identical twins with freckles don't have them in exactly the same places. When a person has one gene for brown eyes and one for blue eyes, the brown gene is usually dominant, but on rare occasions the blue gene wins. That's why identical twins can differ in eye color 0.4 percent of the time, and why every so often you find a person with one blue eye and one brown.

The other reason that identical twins are never exactly the same is that they don't have precisely the same environments. Even before birth, the environments of twins can differ. One fetus may be in a better position in the uterus and may grow bigger and heavier than its twin. After they're born, the twins may have different experiences, different accidents or illnesses.

Any small differences between identical twins, whether they're present at birth or appear later, are likely to be exaggerated by environmental influences. For example, the baby that weighs more may be a little more alert, or cry a little less. This twin might be typecast by its family as "the bright one" or "the tough one" or "the cheerful one." Then the differences in the family's behavior to the two children may increase the differences between them. This is called the **contrast effect,** and it works on fraternal twins (and on nontwin siblings) too.

Fraternal twins, being less alike to begin with, are even more likely to be treated differently. It is very difficult for an outside investigator to detect subtle differences in parents' attitudes toward their children, but the children themselves can detect them. In one study, twins were asked to rate their mothers and fathers according to how "accepting" or "rejecting" they were. Identical twins tended to agree in their ratings, fraternal twins frequently disagreed (Rowe, 1981). Evidently a parent of identical twins was equally accepting or rejecting of both children, whereas a parent of fraternal twins might be more accepting of one than of the other. Psychologists have also noted that fraternal twins are more likely than identical twins to have different friends and do different things (Loehlin and Nichols, 1976; Rowe, 1981).

It's important to bear in mind the possibility that the environments of fraternal twins may differ more than the environments of identical twins. The kind of twin study we've just described is based on the idea that their environments *don't* differ more. The assumption is that fraternal twins are less concordant than identical twins because of genetic differences. But if there are also greater environmental differences, then concordance measurements aren't as meaningful. If fraternal twins are not concordant, we can't tell if it's due to their genes or to their different roles in the family.

There's another kind of twin study that gets around this objection, but it's very difficult to do. This kind of study examines identical twins who have been raised apart, in different homes. The problem is that cases of separated identical twins are quite rare. When identical twins are adopted, most adoption agencies prefer that they be kept together. Nevertheless, such cases do occur (see box), and they are naturally of great interest to psychologists.

Adoption Studies. Identical twins raised apart are pretty hard to find. But in any group of 20 or 30 American children, the chances are good that one or two of them are adopted. Psychologists are interested in adopted children

Identical Twins and Triplets Raised Apart

You may have read of cases of identical twins who were reunited as adults and discovered that they looked amazingly alike and had many characteristics in common, despite the fact that they were brought up in different homes. Not long ago an even more remarkable case came to light—remarkable because identical *triplets* were involved.

Identical triplets, all from the same fertilized egg, are produced when the developing cells split twice: first one cell (or group of cells) splits into two parts, and then one of these parts splits into two *more* parts. If the splitting occurs once or twice more, identical quadruplets or even quintuplets might be produced. The famous Dionne quintuplets (born in Canada in 1934) are believed to have developed from a single fertilized egg. It's also possible for multiple births to be a mixture of identical and fraternal. Triplets sometimes consist of an identical pair plus a fraternal sibling.

The story of the identical triplets (Battelle, 1981) begins in September, 1980, when 19-year-old Bobby Shafran enrolled in a community college in upstate New York. Always a sociable fellow, Bobby wasn't surprised when his fellow students seemed very glad to see him, but he *was* a little puzzled about why everyone kept calling him "Eddy." He found out why when someone showed him a photo of Eddy Galland. "It was like looking in a mirror," Bobby said. "It was unmistakably *me*. I didn't know what to say or do."

Eddy Galland had attended the same community college the year before, and then had transferred to another college on Long Island, nearer to his home. He was at home one evening at 9:00 when the phone rang. It was Bobby, who said, "Eddy, I think you're my twin brother."

The two boys wasted no time getting together and comparing notes. They had been born in the same Long Island hospital on the same day: June 12, 1961. Both had been adopted in infancy.

The story of the reunited identical "twins" made the local newspapers. A day or two later, the phone rang again at the Galland home. Eddy wasn't home this time and Mrs. Galland answered the phone. The caller said, "You're not going to believe this, Mrs. Galland, but my name is David Kellman and I think I'm the third."

It was true: there were three of them, all so much alike that it's hard to tell them apart. All three had been adopted from the same adoption agency; none of the adoptive families had been informed of the multiple birth.

Bobby, Eddy, and David are alike in many ways besides their looks. All have high IQs but have trouble with math. They are all outgoing, lively young men who excel in wrestling and have similar tastes in food, music, and women.

These reunited triplets found that they had much in common. But don't jump to the conclusion that all their similarities were inherited. Bobby, Eddy, and David, though growing up in different homes, actually had rather similar environments. All three were raised in upper-middle-class homes in the New York City area, all three had older adoptive sisters, and in each case both of the adoptive parents were business or professional people. So what this story shows is that when people who are genetically identical are placed in similar environments, they turn out very much alike, both in personality and intelligence.

The environments of identical twins raised in separate homes are always going to differ more than the environments of fraternal twins raised

Robert Shafran (left)
David Kellman (center)
and Eddy Galland

together. So if separated identical twins are more similar in some trait than *un*separated fraternals, that is strong evidence for a genetic influence on that trait. Intelligence, as estimated from performance on IQ tests, is more similar in identical twins raised apart (.72) than in fraternal twins raised together (.60) (Bouchard and McGue, 1981).

IQ correlations are lower for identical twins raised apart (.72) than for those raised together (.86). But when it comes to personality, twins reared in separate homes may be *more* similar than unseparated twins. A psychologist named Susan Farber has collected all the data on separated twins and weeded out the questionable cases—for example, "separated" twins who were actually not separated until after the age of 4. She was left with 95 pairs of identical twins who had spent all or part of their childhoods in different homes. Although a few pairs were fairly dissimilar (generally those whose environments had been extremely different), many were incredibly alike. They had similar styles of talking, very similar voices and laughs, and used similar

gestures. They walked in the same way, sat in the same positions, and had many of the same mannerisms. They laughed at the same things and often had similar interests.

Farber found that the twins who had spent the least amount of time with each other seemed to be the most alike. She thinks there are two reasons why twins raised together may differ. The first is the tendency of the family to see them as separate individuals. The second is the efforts of the twins themselves to carve out distinct personalities for themselves. For twins raised apart neither tendency comes into play, so "genetic predispositions can show themselves more forcefully." (A **predisposition** is an inborn tendency to develop a certain trait, given environmental conditions that favor that trait.)

Farber also believes that separated twins, because of their biological similarity, may *experience* their separate environments in similar ways. As she puts it, "Whatever treatment they get may seem alike to both twins because of their similar, genetically determined response patterns" (Farber, 1981, p. 80). ■

because they provide another way to separate the effects of heredity and environment. When children who were *not* adopted turn out to be similar to their parents, we don't know if it's their genes or their environments—their parents supply both. But with adopted children, one set of parents supplies the heredity, another the environment. We can ask, Which set of parents does the child resemble more?

Before we say any more on this subject, we should clarify some terminology. Despite the fact that adoption is so common in this country, many people (even some psychologists) still confuse terms such as **adopted child** and **foster child.**

Adoption is a legal procedure that makes a child a permanent member of the adoptive family. An adopted child has the same legal rights as a child born into that family.

A woman who has adopted a child is that child's **adoptive mother,** a man is the child's **adoptive father.** These people are legally, financially, and emotionally the child's "real" parents. Adoptive parents are sensitive about this. They don't like to hear anyone refer to the woman who gave birth to their child as the child's "real mother" or "natural mother." (Are the adoptive parents *un*natural?) Accepted terms for the woman and man whose genes the child carries are the **biological parents,** or the **genetic parents,** or the **birth parents.**

Foster children, on the other hand, often have "real" (legal) parents but are not living with them. They are living temporarily in someone else's home—the home of their **foster parents.** Generally, a small salary is paid to foster parents to cover the expenses of caring for foster children.

Children who are in foster care are there for one of two reasons: their biological parents are unable to care for them but have not "given them up" for adoption, or the children *are* available for adoption but a permanent adoptive home has not been found. In the first category are many children who grow up in temporary homes (often, a series of temporary homes) because their biological parents go on hoping, from year to year, that they will someday be able to provide a permanent home for them. The second category, nowadays, consists primarily of older children (age 10 and up), children with serious physical or mental handicaps, and black children. There are usually more black children waiting for adoptive homes than there are black men and women interested in adopting a child. For that reason, black children are sometimes adopted into white families.

The question we started out with was whether adopted children are more like their adoptive parents or more like their biological parents. When it comes to intelligence, it turns out that the children are about equally similar to both sets of parents. Thomas Bouchard and Matthew McGue, of the University of Minnesota, put together all the data they could find—111 studies from all over the world—on IQ resemblances between parents and children (Bouchard and McGue, 1981). The average correlation between the IQs of adopted children and their adoptive parents was .19, between adopted children and their biological parents was .22.

Although the correlation between adopted children and their adoptive parents is not high, the environment of these children has clearly had an important effect on them. Their biological parents tended to have IQs slightly below 100. The children's IQs generally average 10 or 15 points higher than their biological parents—closer to that of their adoptive parents, who tend to have IQs considerably above 100. (Remember that adoptive parents are a highly selected group—selected both by their own high motivation to adopt a child and by the adoption agencies' filtering process.)

The Heritability of IQ

In 1969 an article by a psychologist named Arthur Jensen appeared in the *Harvard Educational Review*. Jensen summarized all the previous data about IQ—data from studies on twins, relatives, and adopted children. He claimed that these studies showed that the **heritability** of IQ is about .80.

Heritability is a concept originated by geneticists and useful to plant and animal breeders. A field of wheat will contain individual plants that vary in many ways—height, for example. A plant breeder might want to know how much of the variation in this particular kind of wheat is due to differences in the genetic makeup of the plants, and how much to environmental differences such as soil quality, fertilizer, and amount of sunshine. A heritability of .80 for height would mean that 80 percent of the variation in this type of wheat was due to genetic causes, implying that only 20 percent was the result of differences in environment.

So Jensen's estimate of .80 for the heritability of IQ was really quite a strong statement. If Jensen's estimate were right, it would mean that controlling the environment—giving every human being exactly the same environment—would leave most of the variation in human IQ unchanged. Jensen went on to conclude that there is no point trying to boost the IQs of children in lower socioeconomic classes by means of enrichment programs. This conclusion follows naturally from his belief that IQ differences are mostly genetic.

Jensen's paper provoked an enormous response. Many psychologists attacked his conclusions, giving a number of reasons why they thought that his estimate of IQ heritability was much too high. The strongest arguments came from Leon Kamin, of Princeton University.

Jensen had assumed that the environments of identical twins and fraternal twins were equally similar. Kamin (1974) pointed out that this assumption is unjustified, since identical twins tend to be treated more alike than fraternal twins. Furthermore, the identical twins who were raised apart often ended up in rather similar homes. In fact, in many of Jensen's "identical twins raised apart" cases, the twins were not separated right away or were not really separated at all—they were raised by relatives and saw each other frequently. Kamin also questioned the value of studies showing that IQ correlations are higher for close relatives than for distant relatives. Close relatives are likely to have more similar environments than distant relatives, as well as more genes in common.

But the most telling blow against Jensen was the exposure of the British psychologist, Sir Cyril Burt, as a fraud. Jensen had placed a lot of emphasis on the IQ studies reported by Burt, especially on Burt's 1966 paper about separated identical twins. Careful investigation revealed that Burt had simply made up most of the data he reported—the separated twins were imaginary, or if they were real, he hadn't tested them. Burt even invented two "assistants" who had supposedly helped him with his research. No one has been able to find any evidence that these two people ever existed.

The Burt affair is a sad episode in the history of psychology. Science, by its very nature, tends to attract people who are devoted to finding out the truth. But in every science there are a few people who are more devoted to winning fame or fortune, or who are so sure they are right that they are willing to invent the data to prove it. Burt seems to have been one of the second type. Unfortunately, he got the fame and fortune too. He was the first British psychologist to be knighted.

Burt's so-called data have now been thrown out, and a lot of new studies have been completed since Jensen's 1969 paper. Current estimates of the heritability of IQ are in the neighborhood of .50 (Plomin and DeFries, 1980; Scarr and Weinberg, 1978). If that estimate stands up, it means that heredity and environment are about equally important in determining IQ. Thus, it seems possible that the nature-nurture debate may not have a winner.

Genetic and Environmental Influences on Personality

So far in this chapter we have said a lot about intelligence and not very much about other psychological characteristics of human beings. This was not because we consider intelligence to be the most important human quality. It *is* important, but so are many other psychological qualities: persistence, enthusiasm, honesty, sociability, and so on.

Much of our evidence on genetic and environmental influences on personality comes from twin studies. One extensive study involved 850 pairs of identical and fraternal twins who had not been separated. All were high school juniors. The twins were given personality tests and were scored on 18 different traits: dominance, responsibility, flexibility, tolerance, self-control, and so on. The investigators found that the identical twins correlated about .50 on the personality traits. The correlations were rather similar for all 18 traits. Fraternal twins correlated about .32 overall, and again the individual correlations didn't vary much (Loehlin and Nichols, 1976).

Could the greater similarity in the personalities of identical twins be due to their very similar environments, rather than to their identical genes? It doesn't seem so. For one thing, as we mentioned earlier, identical twins who are reared apart often seem to have more similar personalities than those reared in the same home. For another thing, the investigators found no relationship between how similarly twins were treated and how much alike their personalities were. Twins who dressed differently and slept in separate rooms were just as similar as twins who dressed alike and shared a bedroom.

So identical twins are more similar in personality than fraternal twins, and the greater similarity doesn't appear to be due to the environment. This implies that many personality traits are partly inherited. The correlations for these traits are lower, though, than the correlations for intelligence—perhaps because of the factors we mentioned earlier that tend to increase personality differences between twins.

Sociability. A human characteristic that has long been recognized to have a genetic component is **sociability.** Some children tend to be **introverts**—they withdraw from people (especially unfamiliar people) and like to be by themselves a lot. Other children tend to be **extroverts**—outgoing, at ease with people, generally preferring to be in the company of others. We have already mentioned one factor that affects sociability: birth order. First children are a little more likely to be introverts, later-borns are more often extroverts. Now we see that genetic makeup also affects sociability. Several twin studies, using several different ways of measuring sociability, provide evidence for its heritability (Freedman and Keller, 1963; Loehlin and Nichols, 1976; Plomin and Rowe, 1979; Scarr, 1969).

Twin studies are one way to get at inborn aspects of personality. Another way is with longitudinal studies. Individual children have been observed over long periods of time—many years. If a personality characteristic appears very early in life and persists for a long time, it seems likely that some genetic component is involved. Sociability follows this pattern. Outgoing infants tend to become outgoing teenagers (Schaefer and Bayley, 1963).

Temperament. Unfortunately, it's rather hard to measure many personality traits in very young infants, simply because there is so little they can do. We can't measure "dominance" or "tolerance" or "self-control" in a brand-new baby. By the time such traits *can* be measured, it's no longer clear how much is genetic, how much environmental.

Despite these difficulties it is clear that newborn infants *do* differ in many ways, and that some of these differences remain throughout development. We use the term **temperament** for these persistent aspects of personality. Temperament includes the tendency to be active or inactive, emotional or "cool," cheerful or irritable, and so on.

An important study on temperament was carried out by Alexander Thomas and Stella Chess, both psychiatrists at the New York University Medical Center. In this study infants were rated on a number of temperament traits over a period of many years. Ratings were made every three months in infancy, less often as the children grew older. The rated traits included activity level, usual reaction to new things (favorable or negative), usual mood (cheerful or "fussy"), distractibility, regularity (the tendency to eat or sleep at the same times each day), sensitivity to visual stimuli and to sounds, and intensity of emotional reactions (mild or strong). The investigators found that children differ in these ways quite early in life, and that some of these differences persist throughout childhood. (Thomas and Chess, 1977; Thomas, Chess, and Birch, 1968).

"Easy" and "Difficult" Children.   Thomas and Chess describe how children's temperaments affect their relationships with their parents. For instance, some babies are "easy," right from the start. They are cheerful rather than fussy, they easily fall into regular patterns of eating, sleeping, and toileting, and they adapt readily to new foods, new experiences, and new people. Parents of "easy" babies understandably take much pleasure in their infants. The mother of such a baby might assume that her child is "easy" because of her excellence in childrearing, and this might make her feel superior to other mothers who have "difficult" babies. She may be in for a rough time if her child later turns out to be less than perfect, or if her next baby is more difficult. Another possible problem with "easy" babies is that they fuss so seldom that busy parents might tend to give them too little attention.

"Difficult" children, on the other hand, tend to demand and to receive a lot of attention, but not all of it is favorable. A "difficult" baby is one who adapts slowly to change, whose eating and sleeping patterns are irregular, and who is unhappy more often than happy. Parents of such a child are likely to blame themselves for their child's behavior—they may end up doubting their ability to be good parents. Worse still, they may blame the child. In either case they tend to do things that make the situation worse, not better. A psychologist who sees such a family at a later stage in this "vicious circle" might think, "It's not surprising that this child has problems. Look at how his parents treat him!" Yet these people might have been very capable parents with a child of a different temperament.

Thomas and Chess run a clinic in which they attempt to prevent the sort of "vicious circle" we have just described. They give advice to parents with "difficult" children, or children whose temperaments mesh poorly with their parents' expectations. They describe what happens, for example, with a child who is "slow to warm up." Such a child tends to have negative reactions to new things and takes a while to get used to them. In infancy these tendencies are not a problem—a baby who doesn't like a new food or a new person is likely to be allowed to get used to them gradually. But the same child also tends to react negatively to her introduction to nursery school or kindergarten, and that worries the parents a lot more. When the parents come to realize (through counseling) that the tendency to be "slow to warm up" is part of their child's temperament, they are able to be more patient with her.

Activity Level.   A child with a high activity level presents problems that are more difficult to cope with. A very active toddler must be watched constantly because he is more likely than other children to get into trouble. If parents interpret their child's activity as sheer disobedience, it may lead to problems with discipline. Understanding that neither they nor their child is at fault relieves some of the tension. There is good evidence that activity level has a genetic basis. The parents of a very active child are likely to have been active children themselves. Environmental factors—such as the parents' attitudes toward childrearing—seem to have relatively little effect on activity level (Willerman and Plomin, 1973).

Parent-child Interactions.   Earlier generations of psychologists attributed differences in childrearing styles to the parents' attitudes and personalities. Now it is recognized that the children themselves have an important influence on the parents' behavior. For example, a classic study (Sears, Maccoby, and Levin, 1957) found that harsh punishment and badly behaved children tended to go together—the worst-behaved children came from the homes where the most severe punishments were given. But recent evidence indicates that parents' methods of discipline are influenced both by the nature of the child's misbehavior and by the child's reaction to discipline (Grusec and Kuczynski, 1980; Mullhern and Passman, 1981). Even how much a mother smiles at her baby is determined as much by the baby's behavior as by the mother's attitudes or personality. As developmental psychologist Alison Clarke-Stewart puts it,

> . . . The frequency of the child's positive social behavior to the mother (looking, smiling, vocalizing) seems to affect how much time mother and child spend together and how responsive the mother is . . . . The child's smile elicits the mother's—not just immediately, but over a period of months. . . . Children who smiled a lot at their mothers at 11 months, for example, were observed to have mothers who smiled at them more often at 16 months. (Clarke-Stewart, 1977, p. 31)

Sibling Interactions.   The success of a parent-child interaction hinges partly on how well the parent's temperament meshes with that of the child. Temperaments also affect interactions between *children*—particularly between siblings. Most siblings fight with each other—some more, some less. It makes as little sense to attribute all sibling fights to "sibling rivalry" as to attribute all divorces to "sexual incompatibility." *Any* two people, forced to live in close and continuous contact, will irritate each other at times. The strains of living together account for many sibling disagreements, as well as for many husband-wife disagreements. And siblings, like husbands and wives or parents and children, may be well or poorly matched. Studies have shown that husbands and wives with very different personalities are less likely to stay married than couples with similar personalities (Willerman, 1977). We know of no studies of "compatibility" of sibling personalities. Nevertheless, it seems clear there will be problems when a sensitive, inactive child is followed by a noisy, active sibling. A child whose moods are mostly negative will probably get along poorly with either an older or younger sibling. And a child who is dismayed by *anything* new is unlikely to greet a new baby brother or sister with wild enthusiasm!

Interactions between siblings, like interactions between any two people, will depend in part on how well their temperaments mesh.

The Outcome of Interactions with the Environment

We've seen how babies are born with certain characteristics, and how these characteristics interact with the environment in unique and complex ways. Babies differ from one another to begin with; the environment may either decrease these differences or increase them. Differences in activity level, for example, are likely to be decreased. Parents and teachers put pressure on a highly active child to "keep still," whereas they may prod an inactive one to "do something—don't just sit there!"

Differences are *increased* when a "vicious circle" gets going. This can have a good effect, as in the case of an intelligent baby who gets played with and talked to a lot. Moreover, adults are likely to talk to her in a way that they wouldn't use with a slower child—using bigger words, supplying more information. Later this child may seek out an intellectually stimulating environment for herself, by going to museums, libraries, and so forth. So she really grows up in a very different environment from the one she would have had if she'd been born with less intellectual potential (Scarr and McCartney, 1983).

A "vicious circle" that *is* vicious might work to lower the IQ of a child born with a limited mental capacity. Or, a child born with a "difficult" temperament may become more difficult—may even develop serious behavior problems—if the parents react to their child's temperament in ways that make things worse. Some kinds of child behavior are extremely likely to provoke unfavorable reactions from parents. These unfavorable reactions (such as punishment or criticism) are a source of stress for the child—a source of anxiety, unhappiness, tension. One of the many ways that children differ is in their ability to handle stress. Certain children appear to be especially vulnerable to the effects of environmental stress. Unfortunately, these are often the very same children whose behavior is likely to *produce* stress, in the form of unfavorable parental reactions (Graham, Rutter, and George, 1973).

Richard Bell, a psychologist who was one of the first to state clearly the "new view" of parent-child interactions (Bell, 1968), has recently commented on the unhappy results that grew out of the older view. The Freudian theory of childhood (which we'll discuss in the next chapter), plus the strong environmental bias that was so prevalent in the 50s and 60s, made parents feel that their behavior was entirely responsible for how their child turned out. As a result, parents were so nervous about doing the wrong thing that they sometimes did nothing at all. Bell (1979) believes that parents should have the self-confidence to provide guidance for their children and should realize that many other factors—both inborn and environmental—influence their children's development.

PROBLEMS IN DEVELOPMENT

Childhood Schizophrenia: Heredity or Environment?

The psychological problems of children fall into two categories. The first includes such relatively mild problems as fearfulness, nervousness, irritability, bedwetting, and difficulties in making friends. For the children in this category the long-term outlook is good. Whether or not they receive counseling or therapy, most of them grow up to be reasonably normal adults.

The situation is quite different for those unfortunate children who suffer from **childhood schizophrenia:** the majority of these children will never completely recover from their disor-

der. Schizophrenia is the most common form of **psychosis** (serious mental illness)—an estimated 1 percent of Americans (of all ages) are schizophrenic. People with this disorder have serious difficulties in interacting with reality. There are disturbances of perception, thought, emotion, and social relationships. Hallucinations are common.

Schizophrenia most often makes its first appearance in adolescence; it is quite rare in young children. Whether schizophrenia that appears in early childhood is the same disorder as schizophrenia that appears in adolescence or adulthood is not certain. Children diagnosed as schizophrenic show a variety of abnormal behaviors, such as strange mannerisms and movements, disordered speech or no speech at all, self-destructiveness, a lack of awareness of time and place, and inappropriate emotional responses. Symptoms may make their appearance at any time during childhood.

For many years, a child with a serious mental disorder was believed to be the product of a seriously disordered environment. This belief fit in well with the environmental bias of the 1950s and 60s, and also with the failure to find anything physically wrong with these children. Also, schizophrenic children usually develop normally for a while. This makes it look as though their troubles are environmental and that they are "born all right." The assumption was made, therefore, that a childhood psychosis must be due to the way the parents (particularly the mother) acted toward the child. The mother was supposed to have been cold or cruel, unresponsive or inconsistent. It didn't matter that she might have other children, older or younger, who were normal.

We know more now. The role of genetic factors in schizophrenia is beyond dispute. Schizophrenia "runs in families," just as diabetes or heart disease does. The child of one schizophrenic parent has almost a 15 percent chance of developing schizophrenia, either in childhood or in adulthood. With two schizophrenic parents the risk is closer to 50 percent. In an adopted child the risk depends on the biological parents, not the adoptive ones. A child with a schizophrenic adoptive parent does not have an increased risk of becoming schizophrenic (Hanson and Gottesman, 1976).

Schizophrenia is clearly a polygenic trait. That means that the chances of getting it depend partly on how many unfavorable genes are inherited, and partly on the environment. The identical twin of a schizophrenic person doesn't have a 100 percent chance of also becoming schizophrenic—only a 50 or 60 percent chance. It takes a certain combination of inherited predisposition plus environmental stress to produce a schizophrenic. But exactly what that environmental stress consists of, we still don't know. ■

Experiencing the Environment

The child's environment is the context for the child's development—what he or she becomes is partly determined by the environment. But in another sense the child is the context for the environment, because the effect of a given environmental influence depends on the child. Unlike genetic messages, messages from the environment must be interpreted. How a child interprets an environmental message depends on many factors. It depends on the child's past experiences: an Inuit child and an American child will have very different reactions to an aunt who says, "Why don't you die?" It depends on temporary states such as fatigue or hunger. And it depends on the characteristics of the individual child. The death of a parent may cause one child to become a delinquent, whereas another may triumph over adversity and become outstandingly successful. Because human beings receive so many different kinds of messages, and because they can respond in so many different ways, we can never predict human behavior with 100 percent accuracy.

Children do not only receive messages—they send them, as well. A child's behavior has an important effect on the behavior of parents and other adults. Recognition of this two-way interaction makes it necessary to interpret many experimental results with caution. Correlations between certain kinds of adult behavior and certain kinds of children's behavior can be due to many causes. We hope you will keep this point in mind as you read the rest of the book.

summary

1. Psychologists agree that children are shaped by their heredity *and* their environment. But in accounting for the specific characteristics and behavior of individual children, it's seldom clear how much is inherited and how much results from environmental influences.

2. **Environment** refers to everything a person sees, hears, feels, smells, tastes, eats, drinks, or experiences, from the time of conception to the time of death.

3. Childrearing practices differ widely from one society to another. The fact that the child-rearing practices of one society produce an acceptable member of that society doesn't mean that they would produce an acceptable member of a different society.

4. The Hutterites of northern North America live communally and in strict adherence to the rules of their religion. Though Hutterite babies are coddled, older children are punished for disobedience and are under pressure to become conforming, cooperative members of the group. Even if Hutterite children rebel in adolescence, they generally end up accepting the restrictions of the community.

5. Russian childrearing methods also are designed to produce obedient children who will work for the good of the group. In contrast, American childrearing methods tend to put more emphasis on individual achievement and independence.

6. A family's **socioeconomic level** depends on the income, profession, education, and social status of its members. Children from homes of low socioeconomic level, also called **disadvantaged** homes, are likely to have environments that are unfavorable in a number of respects: for example, they are likely to receive less intellectual stimulation and poorer nutrition and health care than children in middle-class homes. However, the amount of affection given to children does not seem to depend on socioeconomic level.

7. Without the kind of warm, personal attention that has been called "mothering" but that can be given by any caring person, babies do not thrive. Their physical, intellectual, and emotional development may all be affected.

8. Child abuse becomes more likely when a family is under stress or when it's socially isolated. A child with any abnormality, or one who cries a lot, runs a higher risk of being battered; abusing parents tend to have unrealistic expectations for their children and to have been abused themselves when they were young.

9. Having a working mother appears to produce no unfavorable effects on a young child, as long as the mother is working because she wants to. No intellectual differences have been found between children who spend their days in day-care centers and children cared for at home, and they are equally attached to their mothers. For a school-age child, having a working mother may actually be beneficial.

10. Although fathers have traditionally played a minor role in childrearing, they appear to be quite capable of doing a good job at it—even in caring for very young infants.

11. Children with older siblings tend to be more sociable than firstborn children, but firstborns tend to have slightly higher IQs and to do better in school. Children from large families tend to have somewhat lower IQs than children from small families, especially if the children are close together in age. There's no evidence that only children are more spoiled or selfish than children with siblings.

12. The children of divorced parents, particularly the boys, have a higher rate of behavior problems. Though a well-run single-parent

home is probably better for children than a home with two quarreling parents, family conflicts tend to increase, rather than decrease, in the first year after a divorce.

13. Children from fatherless homes tend to do less well in school and on IQ tests, and to have more psychological difficulties. These effects can be prevented if a divorced father remains in close contact with his children or if the father's role is filled by a male relative or a stepfather. Though adjusting to a parent's remarriage is difficult at first, most stepchildren and stepparents do end up making a good adjustment to each other.

14. Inherited characteristics are transmitted by the **genes,** located within the **chromosomes** in each cell of a living thing. Humans have 46 chromosomes, 23 from the mother and 23 from the father.

15. One pair of chromosomes, the **sex chromosomes,** determine whether a fertilized egg will become a girl or a boy. Each fertilized egg has one X chromosome from the mother. If the sperm that fertilized it also contained an X chromosome, the child will be a girl. If the sperm contained a Y chromosome, the child will be a boy.

16. Genes provide the instructions for making a large number of different proteins, each in a certain place and at a certain time.

17. When a characteristic is controlled by a single pair of genes, a **dominant** characteristic will win out over a **recessive** one. The recessive characteristic remains hidden in the genes, capable of being passed on to the next generation. It will show up in a child who inherits two genes for the recessive characteristic, one from the mother and one from the father. Some genetic defects are transmitted in this way.

18. If a serious genetic defect is inherited as a dominant characteristic, it's likely to be either a defect that doesn't show up until relatively late in a person's life, or one that is due to a **mutation.**

19. The gene for a **sex-linked trait** is located on the X chromosome. Sex-linked defects such as hemophilia and color-blindness are far more common in boys than in girls. A boy with such a defect has inherited his defective gene from his mother.

20. Chromosomal abnormalities occur when a fertilized egg has too many or too few chromosomes. Missing or extra sex chromosomes have relatively mild consequences, though there is an increased risk of mental retardation. An extra twenty-first chromosome leads to **Down's syndrome,** which produces mental retardation and a variety of distinctive physical characteristics. The risk of having a baby with Down's syndrome increases as the mother gets older.

21. Many genetic and chromosomal abnormalities, including Down's syndrome and Tay-Sachs disease, can be detected before birth by the process of **amniocentesis.**

22. Most human characteristics are **polygenic**—controlled by more than one pair of genes. Polygenic traits tend to vary over a wide range, with the majority of cases falling in the middle of the range. Most polygenic traits are influenced by the environment.

23. The environment doesn't just act on the child—the child acts on the environment, too. People react differently to different children. For example, intelligent children might be more rewarding or more interesting to be with, so their parents might give them more time and attention. The extra time and attention might cause them to become still more intelligent, thus producing a favorable type of "vicious circle."

24. IQ has become the focus of the **nature-nurture** (or heredity-environment) debate. Do the children of unskilled laborers tend to have lower IQs than the children of professional people because of differences in heredity or because of differences in environment? For many reasons, the question is a difficult one to answer.

25. With rats, it is possible to control both heredity and environment. When environment is held constant, some rats still learn mazes faster than other rats, and these differences are passed on to their offspring. When heredity is held fairly constant (by **inbreeding**), rats reared in enriched environments have bigger brains and are better at mazes than rats raised in bare cages.

26. With humans, we can control neither heredity nor environment. Since heredity and environment tend to vary together, it is usually impossible to say whether differences among people are due primarily to differences in their environments or primarily to genetic differences.

27. **Identical twins** provide us with an opportunity to distinguish the effects of heredity and environment, because identical twins have exactly the same genes. **Fraternal twins** like separately born siblings, have only about 50 percent of their genes in common. If a given characteristic is almost always the same in identical twins but sometimes differs in fraternal twins, that characteristic is probably at least partly genetic.

28. Even identical twins reared together will usually differ in some ways. One reason is that genes operate with a certain amount of randomness—thus, fingerprints and the locations of freckles will differ. Another reason is the **contrast effect**—the twins' family will tend to notice any little differences between them and then act in a way that will increase these differences. The twins themselves may also attempt to carve out distinct personalities for themselves.

29. Although many twin studies are based on the assumption that the environments of fraternal twins are as similar as the environments of identical twins, that is probably not the case. However, the environments of fraternal twins reared in the same home are certainly more similar than those of identical twins reared apart. The finding that IQ correlations are higher in identical twins reared apart than in fraternal twins reared together supports the view that IQ has a sizable genetic component.

30. The IQs of adopted children correlate about as much with their adoptive parents' IQs as with their biological parents' IQs. However, their IQs tend to be considerably higher than those of their biological parents.

31. A paper published in 1969 claimed that IQ is 80 percent inherited. Current estimates place the **heritability** of IQ in the vicinity of 50 percent.

32. The heritability of personality traits appears to be lower than that of IQ. Nonetheless, most personality traits do seem to have a genetic component.

33. Children are born with differences in **temperament,** and some of these differences may persist throughout development. For instance, some babies are "easy"—cheerful, adaptable, and regular in their habits. Others are "difficult"—they dislike new things and they're often unhappy. The parents of "difficult" babies can be helped through counseling to accept their children's characteristics and to realize that they're not to blame for them.

34. Children vary in how active they are. These differences appear to be primarily genetic in origin.

35. Parenting styles do not result solely from parents' attitudes or personalities. Children's behavior definitely influences how their parents act toward them.

36. Children's interactions with their siblings, like their interactions with their parents, will be affected by how well their temperaments mesh.

37. Children differ from each other at birth; the environment may increase these differences (by means of a "vicious circle"), or it may decrease them.

38. Childhood schizophrenia is a serious mental disorder. Fortunately, it is quite rare. In the past the child's environment was held to be responsible; now it's clear that genetic factors play an important role in this illness.

39. How a child will interpret a given environmental "message" will depend on the child's individual characteristics and on his or her past experiences.

Chapter Three

IMPORTANT THEORIES OF DEVELOPMENT

Early Views of Development
Locke's Tabula Rasa
Back to Nature with Jean-Jacques Rousseau
Darwin on Instinct

The Psychoanalytic Viewpoint
Sigmund Freud
The Freudian View of Development
  Stages of Development

_____ Three

What do we need theories for, anyway? Instead of constructing theories about child development, why can't we just _look_ at children and report what we see?

First of all, what would we look at? A child does a lot of things just within the course of a day. But children do not develop within a day—it takes thousands of days. And there are millions of children, all different. So what do we notice? What do we write down?

One thing a theory does is tell us where to direct our attention. It tells us what matters and what doesn't. A new theory may direct our attention to something that was previously considered unimportant. Toilet training was considered merely an unpleasant chore, until Freudian theory put it in the spotlight. The grammatical errors children make when they're learning to speak were thought to be cute but of no consequence, before linguists used them to analyze the ways that children learn a language.

Secondly, a theory gives us a way of organizing our observations, of summarizing what we see. A good theory makes some sense out of what would otherwise be a random collection of data.

EARLY VIEWS OF DEVELOPMENT

People have always had theories of child development, although for a long time they weren't recognized as such. In ancient times childhood was not viewed as a special time of life, or as different from adulthood in any important way. Children were seen simply as undersized adults, differing from grownups only in quantitative ways such as size, strength, and wisdom. Ancient people didn't even realize that children have different bodily proportions from adults. Until late in the Middle Ages, pictures and statues of children didn't look like children at all, because the artists depicted them simply as miniature adults.

The microscope wasn't invented until the 1600s, Mendel's laws of genetics were not generally known until 1900, the structure of DNA was only unraveled in 1953. How did ancient peoples explain the miracle of prenatal development, of development from conception to birth? Very simply. Just as a baby was considered a miniature adult, a developing fetus was considered a miniature baby. In fact, the prevailing idea in the ancient world was that an infinitesimally small grownup was contained in the egg or the sperm (take your pick), and this tiny but perfect creature just grew and grew—first into a baby, then into a child, and finally into the adult it was destined to become.

Laocoön and his sons being attacked by a serpent. This Greek sculpture, now in the Vatican Museum, was made about 2100 years ago. The two smaller figures were meant to be little boys.

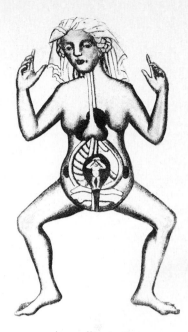

According to the ancient doctrine of *preformationism,* the womb of a pregnant woman contains a miniature creature that differs only in size from the adult it will someday become.

This belief is called **preformationism,** and it remained popular right up to the 1800s. Even the invention of the microscope didn't put an end to preformationism. When no one could detect the tiny person through the microscope, preformationists claimed that it was too tiny and too transparent to see, even under the finest lens (Crain, 1980).

Preformationism *is* a theory of child development, but it isn't a very good one—not because it explains too little, but because it explains too much. The idea is that *everything*—Miriam's curly hair, Harry's pot belly, Claudius's stutter—is present from the start, within the seed. All it has to do is grow. By explaining everything, preformationism ended up explaining nothing.

Locke's Tabula Rasa

An idea that went along with preformationism was the **doctrine of innate ideas.** Most people who lived before the modern era believed that certain ideas are inborn—that the mind comes already furnished with the knowledge of such things as Truth, Beauty, and God. But this time-honored doctrine was called into question by a paper published in 1690, entitled *An Essay Concerning Human Understanding.* Its author was a British philosopher named John Locke.

Locke maintained that the mind of a newborn baby is a **tabula rasa**—an "empty slate," with nothing written on it. What gets written on this slate is

John Locke.

what the baby experiences—what he or she sees, hears, tastes, smells, or feels. All that we know, says Locke, comes to us through these five senses. No knowledge or ideas are built in.

John Locke had a conventional boyhood; he got on well with his father, who was a lawyer and property owner. Locke attended Oxford University. He stayed on as a tutor, giving lectures on Greek, rhetoric, and philosophy, experimenting in chemistry, and dabbling in medicine. Later he served as private secretary and confidant to the Earl of Shaftesbury, a British nobleman. During this period he got into a conversation with five or six friends, and when a philosophical disagreement arose, he offered to jot down some of his ideas on the "limits of human understanding." He figured that one sheet of paper would be enough. The essay took 20 years, and reams of paper, to complete.

Locke never married, never had children. Yet he had definite ideas about children—what they're like, how they should be educated. Some of his thoughts on education seem very modern. Unlike most others of his time, Locke believed that children should never be whipped, but should be rewarded with praise for good behavior. They should be taught how to think rather than be forced to memorize facts.

Although psychology didn't even exist in his day, in the long run Locke had as much influence on psychology as he had on philosophy. His view of the mind—an empty room until it is furnished by experiences provided by the environment—makes him the first important environmentalist, the first to take the side of nurture rather than nature.

Back to Nature with Jean-Jacques Rousseau

The pendulum soon swung back to nature again, but nature in a different sense—nature meaning "natural," the opposite of "civilized" or "artificial." In 1749 the Academy of Dijon (France) offered a prize to the person who submitted the winning essay on the subject of whether the progress being made in the arts and sciences was good or bad for the human race. "Bad!" shouted the winning essay, submitted by an uneducated Swiss named Jean-Jacques Rousseau.

Jean-Jacques Rousseau.

Rousseau was born in 1712, in Geneva. He was a strange fellow, and he lived a strange, troubled life. His troubles began the day he was born: his mother died in childbirth. He was raised by his father, a watchmaker, who was kind to Jean-Jacques except when he was reminding his son of his responsibility for his mother's death. But when the boy was 8, his father injured a man in a fight and had to leave Geneva in order to avoid imprisonment. For the next eight years, Jean-Jacques was tossed around from relative to relative and was unsuccessfully apprenticed out to various tradesmen, who treated him badly—or so Rousseau later claimed. But Rousseau usually ended up thinking that *everyone* treated him badly.

At any rate, Rousseau ran away from Geneva at the age of 16 and began a life of wandering—of fleeing, really, from one place after another. He lived in France, Italy, Switzerland, and England, and everywhere he went he made influential friends, then quarreled with them. He got along best with women—especially older women. For a while he lived in the home of a wealthy widow whom he addressed as "Mama" and who became his mistress. The chief love of his life, however, was a poor, illiterate woman who worked as a servant at an inn. He lived with Thérèse for many years, on and off. According to Rousseau's own account, she bore him five children. But Rousseau refused to play the role of father, and each child was delivered, soon after its birth, to an orphanage!

Thus Rousseau, like Locke, never reared a child of his own. Yet, like Locke, he had very clear ideas about how *other* people's children should be reared. He believed that children are born good and should be left alone to develop naturally. It is civilized society, claimed Rousseau, that is responsible for corrupting people. Rousseau believed that "savages," such as the natives of North America, live noble, healthy lives. They need no laws (or so Rousseau believed); they are happy and self-sufficient.

In one of his books, Rousseau described how he would educate a fictional boy named Émile. Émile would pretty much educate himself, by exploring his environment with no more than some subtle encouragement from his teacher. There would be no rules, no commands—the child would simply progress as his nature intended him to.

The "back-to-nature" theme keeps recurring from time to time; it was very big in the 1970s. The idea that anything natural is good, and anything artificial is bad, forms part of the theme. Another part of it—more relevant to our interests—is a certain view of childhood. Children are seen as capable individuals, right from the start—capable of determining the course of their own development, their own education. Rousseau influenced educational philosophy by introducing the theme of the self-directed child. The "open classroom" is one product of this kind of philosophy.

Whether this attitude is right or wrong is not the issue here. The important thing is to recognize it for what it is—one way, out of many possible ways, to view development.

Darwin on Instinct

A major event in the history of science was the publication in 1859 of Charles Darwin's *The Origin of Species*. Darwin was a member of a distinguished British family that gave rise to many prominent scientists, physicians, philosophers, and poets. When he was a child, his parents thought him to be destined for failure; at Cambridge University (where he studied for the ministry) he did not distinguish himself. But his leanings toward science finally emerged, and at the age of 22 he was selected to accompany the expedition of the *Beagle* as the ship's biologist. During this voyage, which took him to exotic places like the Galapagos Islands, Tahiti, and New Zealand, Darwin collected the data that led to his famous theory of evolution by means of natural selection.

Darwin is important to psychology for two reasons. Before 1859 the human species was considered to be unique, exempt from the "laws of nature" that were acknowledged to control the responses of animals. By convincing the scientific world that humans are a kind of animal, Darwin made human behavior a proper subject for a natural science. In a way, Darwin made experimental psychology possible.

The second reason for Darwin's importance is what he had to say about **instincts** (such as nest-building). Earlier thinkers spoke of inborn ideas, but instincts are inborn *patterns of behavior*. Darwin believed that such patterns are inherited in the same way as physical features, and that they evolve in the same way. Different members of a species would inherit slightly different patterns of instinctive behavior (just as they would inherit slightly different shapes of nose, or colors of hair). The individuals with the most successful variations would survive and pass on these behavior patterns (or noses or colors) to their descendants.

The existence of built-in patterns of response—now called **species-specific behavior**—was recognized in animals long before Darwin's time. Darwin said that people, too, are born with instincts—many instincts. That was the prevailing view for the next half a century.

THE PSYCHOANALYTIC VIEWPOINT

Now we come to the most famous name in all psychology, Sigmund Freud. From Darwin, Freud got his idea of the human baby as a little animal, full of instincts and primitive desires. Like Rousseau, Freud saw this baby in an unavoidable conflict with society. But there the similarities end. Freud's view of the development of the child's mind was very different from Darwin's, very different from Rousseau's. Freud's view was entirely original—not because every one of his ideas was original, but because of the new way he brought these ideas together.

Sigmund Freud

Sigmund Freud.

Born in 1856, Freud lived almost all of his life in Vienna. He was his mother's first and favorite child; she was only 20 when he was born. His father, who had children from a previous marriage, was 40.

A brilliant student throughout his school years, Freud was attracted to all the sciences. He settled on medicine, specializing in neurology. He soon became interested in patients who had a certain kind of problem, called a **hysterical** symptom. A patient who had hysterical blindness had nothing wrong with her eyes. A patient who had hysterical numbness of the hand—no sensation from the wrist down—had nothing wrong with the nerves in her hand. Such symptoms, which in those inhibited Victorian times were much more common than they are today, were psychological in origin.

To get at the source of hysterical symptoms, Freud first tried hypnotizing his patients. Under hypnosis, patients were sometimes able to connect the appearance of their symptoms with some **traumatic** (highly upsetting) event in their lives—an event they were unable to remember in a nonhypnotic state. Knowing the cause of their symptom was sometimes sufficient to make it go away.

But hypnosis didn't really work that well. The symptom usually came back, and some patients couldn't be hypnotized at all. So Freud devised a new technique, which he called **free association,** to get at what was bothering his patients. In free association the patient just says whatever comes into her head.

Freud named his new method for analyzing the mind **psychoanalysis.** Through psychoanalysis of his patients, and through careful self-analysis, Freud arrived at a new view of the human mind. He believed that most of the psychological problems of adults had their origins in childhood experiences—making childhood a much more important time of life than was previously believed. Furthermore, he felt that most of these problems were sexual in origin.

Now, by "sexual," Freud really meant a lot more than we usually understand the term to mean. He meant *all* kinds of pleasure, including eating, being stroked, urinating and defecating, and so on. But the greatest emphasis was placed on the sorts of things that the word *sexual* usually refers to.

It's hard to imagine, now, the courage it took to talk about such matters at a time when "nice" people didn't even use the word *leg* in public. For a while Freud was shunned, ignored. But the times were changing, and by the early years of this century he had a few followers, including Carl Jung and Alfred Adler. In 1909 he visited the United States, where he gave a series of lectures (in German) at Clark University and received an honorary degree. In America he acquired new adherents to his theories, and gradually his fame spread. In the long run his American followers proved more faithful than the European ones. Some members of his original circle—including Jung and Adler—later developed their own theories (basically variations on the Freudian view). In his old age, Freud spoke with great bitterness about those who had willfully turned away from what he perceived as Truth (Freud, 1938).

The Freudian View of Development

According to Freud, the human mind consists of three different "agencies" or aspects: the id, the ego, and the superego. They develop in that order. The **id,** present from birth, is the home of powerful instinctive desires or **drives,** such as hunger, thirst, and (especially) the sexual urge. The aggressive urge also forms part of the id. The mind of a baby at first contains nothing besides these inborn drives—no concept of self, no idea that anyone else exists. The id is interested only in the instant gratification of its desires.

The baby's conflict with society, represented by the parents, is immediate and inevitable. The baby wants to be fed the minute she feels hungry; the parents may not be able (or willing) to drop everything and run. When the child is older she may want to grab food from others, bite or kick, urinate and defecate when and where she wishes. All of these urges must eventually be brought under control. Freud does not see the baby as innocent and virtuous, the way Rousseau did. His view is closer to the opposite—the baby as a greedy, self-centered creature whose fierce desires must be curbed, if she is to become a decent, responsible person.

The experiences the young baby has with reality—that she *can't* have everything she wants the moment she wants it—produce the **ego.** The ego is the "thinking" mind, the part that "stands for reason and good sense" (Freud, 1933/1965, p. 76). It directs the child's actions in a rational way, trying to fulfill the id's desires and at the same time keep the child from getting into trouble. Freud used the analogy of a powerful horse controlled by its rider—the id is the horse, the ego the rider.

Later, between the ages of 3 and 5½, the **superego** develops. It's similar to a conscience. The superego is in favor of what society regards as "good" behavior; it's opposed to "bad" behavior. A child's ego might keep her from doing something because it knows she won't be successful, but her superego stops her for a different reason: Don't do it because it's *wrong.* If the child goes ahead and does it anyway, the superego is what makes her feel guilty. When she's a little older her superego will make her feel guilty even for having forbidden thoughts. Such thoughts may eventually become **repressed,** or driven down into the unconscious mind. There they remain, likely to cause trouble later, until rooted out by psychoanalysis.

Freud made a clear distinction between the conscious mind (mostly ego) and the unconscious (mostly id). The unconscious is depicted as a seething pool of desires and impulses, repressed thoughts and "forgotten" memories. Some of these things leak out in the form of dreams or slips of the tongue ("Freudian slips"). Some are **displaced.** For example, an unacceptable aggressive urge against a parent or teacher might be repressed, but it will emerge in another form. This **displaced aggression** might be directed toward a younger sibling, a classmate, or even an animal. In other cases a repressed impulse might be transformed into its exact opposite—instead of hitting her little brother, the child kisses him. This is called **reaction formation.**

Stages of Development.   Freud was the first important psychologist who saw development as a series of **stages,** rather than as a smooth, continuous process. The path from birth to adulthood can be viewed either as an inclined plane, like a wheelchair ramp, or as a set of stairs. Freud (and many later psychologists) chose the staircase model. Each step in the staircase represents a stage of development.

The important feature of stage theories of development is that what goes on in one stage is *qualitatively different* from what went on in the stage before. It's not just bigger or better. A small grasshopper just grows into a larger grasshopper, but a caterpillar turns into something qualitatively different—a butterfly.

Another assumption is that the stages have to come in a certain order—you can't get to step 3 unless you've been on step 1 and step 2 first. However, the *rate* at which these stages are achieved may vary considerably. Thus, stage theorists don't say that stage X *always* comes at age Y, but that

that's the *typical* time. Some children may reach a given stage sooner, some later. And some may never reach it at all. A retarded child, or one from a severely deprived environment, may never progress to the highest stages of development. Stage theories allow for that possibility.

Finally, the transition from one stage to another is not assumed to be as clear-cut and sharp as our staircase and butterfly analogies would suggest. Transitional periods, and periods in which a child may fluctuate between two stages, are permitted.

The Five Freudian Stages.   According to Freudian theory, the first stage lasts from birth to around 1½ years. This is called the **oral stage,** because it focuses on the mouth. The important sources of pleasure are sucking, biting, and (later) chewing.

When the child is weaned he progresses to the **anal stage.** Here the pleasurable sensations involve the bowel—withholding feces (bowel movements) or letting go. During the anal phase there is a struggle between the child (who wants to choose when and where he will defecate) and his parents (who want him toilet-trained).

A lot depends on the outcome of this stage. According to the Freudian view, if things don't go well a person may be **fixated** at a certain stage of development. A child fixated at the oral stage will suck his thumb, an adult may be a habitual smoker or pencil-chewer. Fixation at the anal stage produces one of two possible results. A child who fights toilet training by defecating when and where he pleases may become an impulsive, messy adult. One who reacts to harsh training by withholding feces may become an *overly controlled* adult—compulsively neat and clean, inhibited and stingy.

The anal stage normally ends at about age 3, and the **phallic stage** follows. During this stage attention is focused on the pleasurable sensations produced by the genitals. Masturbation is discovered as a way of achieving these sensations. The child is also greatly interested in *other* people's genitals, and notices the difference between males and females. A boy becomes sexually interested in his mother, a girl in her father.

The phallic stage is really what all the fuss was about. Freud was saying that little children have sexual feelings, and most people found that notion unacceptable. Even more unacceptable was that these feelings should be directed, incestuously, toward the parents. But Freud's depiction of what happens during this period (especially what happens with boys) forms the very center of his theory.

The boy in the phallic stage (*phallus* means penis) wants to be near his mother, wants to touch her, wants her all to himself. But he must share her with his father. This causes him to have aggressive feelings toward his father, and these feelings, in turn, cause him anxiety. He imagines that his father is aware of his feelings, and fears that punishment may result. The punishment he fears, according to Freud, is **castration**—he fears that his penis will be cut off! He sees that women and girls lack that organ, and assumes that *they* had suffered that punishment. You must remember that in those days a little boy who was caught masturbating was threatened with dire consequences: that his penis would "drop off," or even that someone would cut it off. Indeed, it is probably due to Freud's influence that such threats are no longer used.

Freud named the struggle he claimed was taking place in the boy's mind the **Oedipal conflict** (after Oedipus, a character in a Greek myth, who killed his father and married his mother). He said that a girl goes through a parallel ordeal, the **Electra conflict.** The girl, though, thinks her penis was *already* cut off. The result is **penis envy,** which Freud thought was eventually transformed into a desire for a baby—particularly a boy baby. Again, this belief must be seen in the context of its time. In those days boys were considered superior beings who would grow up and become famous. Girls were seen as inferior creatures who would grow up and become mothers. A girl might well have envied a boy, though not necessarily for his penis!

The Oedipal and Electra conflicts are resolved when the child faces the fact that he cannot have his mother, she cannot have her father. Instead the child begins to **identify** with the parent of the same sex—the boy tries to be like his father, the girl like her mother. It is this identification that gives rise to the superego. By the time the phallic stage ends, at age 5 or 6, the child's personality is assumed to be almost completely formed. This assumption—that nothing really important happens after age 6—is one of the most controversial parts of Freudian theory.

After the phallic stage comes the **latency stage.** All sexual feelings are repressed; girls play only with girls and boys play only with boys. The child concentrates on other matters, such as acquiring skills and knowledge.

The final stage is the **genital stage,** which begins at adolescence. Due to biological maturation the submerged sexual feelings become too powerful to suppress, and they reappear. This time, if all goes well, they find a proper outlet—a love relationship with a suitable person of the opposite sex.

Freud's Place in History. Freud's view of development is highly complex, extraordinarily rich and subtle. It gives both heredity and environment their due. The child is seen as being born with certain characteristics, individual traits as well as universal drives and instincts. These characteristics are modified by, and interact with, the environment. Freud's work has had a tremendous impact on psychology, though not all of it has stood the test of time. The parts that have fared least well were those that were based on life as he knew it, in nineteenth-century Vienna. For example, he assumed that a little boy would inevitably go through a stage of feeling aggressive toward his father, because he was competing with his father for his mother's attentions. But an anthropologist studied a society (the Trobriand Islanders) in which boys were taught and disciplined by their mother's brothers, not their fathers. A Trobriand Island boy evidently directs his aggressive feelings toward his *uncle* instead of his father, even though it's his father who shares his mother's bed (Malinowski, 1927).

Freud erred in being too absolute, in making claims that were supposed to apply to *all* people, *all* the time. For instance, he thought that *every* slip of the tongue resulted from a repressed desire trying to emerge. Human behavior is more complicated than that. At this point we must be satisfied if a psychological theory works for *some* of the people, *some* of the time.

Freud's daughter Anna followed in his footsteps, continuing his work and extending some of his ideas. She is particularly known for her work with children and adolescents. One of Anna Freud's students was Erik Erikson.

Erikson's Psychosocial Theory

Erik Erikson.

Erikson was born in Germany of Danish parents. He was never much of a scholar, and he didn't go to college. For a while he considered becoming an artist. Later he moved to Vienna and began his association with Anna Freud. In 1933, when Erikson was 31, the rise of Hitler made him decide to leave Europe. He settled in the United States. Despite his lack of a formal degree he eventually became a professor at Harvard.

Erikson Compared with Freud.   Erikson's theories are extensions and modifications of those of Freud. His view of development is similar to Freud's in that it involves stages; moreover, most of Erikson's stages parallel the Freudian stages. But Erikson differs from Freud in what he believes goes on *within* these stages. Erikson places more emphasis on social interactions—interactions between child and family, between child and society. There is less stress on sexual matters. Thus, Erikson speaks of **psychosocial** stages of development, whereas Freud's are called **psychosexual.**

Another difference is that the Freudian stages end at adolescence. Erikson believes that development continues throughout life, and he defines three further stages that encompass adulthood. Erikson places less stress on events that happen in infancy and early childhood. He doesn't believe, for example, that traumatic experiences occurring in childhood necessarily lead to trouble. "There is little," he says, "that cannot be remedied later" (1963, p. 104). In other words, good experiences at a later stage can make up for bad ones at an early stage. It's a more cheerful outlook than Freud's.

Erikson's Eight Stages of Development.   According to Erikson's view, each stage revolves around a different theme or conflict. In stage 1, which corresponds to Freud's oral stage (see Table 3–1), the basic theme is **trust versus mistrust.** The focus is on the way the new baby interacts with his parents. If the parents are reliable, consistent in their handling of the child, he comes to feel that he can rely on them, *trust* them.

In the second stage, toddlerhood, the major issue is **autonomy**—the ability to do as one pleases, not to be pushed around by others. This is the famous "No!" stage, in which the child must show that he is an individual in his own right. At the same time he worries, **doubts,** that he is capable of doing the things he wants to do. He also feels **shame** for the first time—he wants people to think he is "good," and fears that they won't.

The third stage, which takes place during the preschool period, involves

TABLE 3–1   The Psychoanalytic Stages of Development

Approximate Age	Freud's 5 Stages (and the Conflicts Involved)		Erikson's 8 Stages
Birth to age 1½	Oral	(Weaning)	Basic trust versus mistrust
Age 1½ to 3	Anal	(Toilet training)	Autonomy versus shame and doubt
Age 3 to 5½	Phallic	(Oedipal and Electra)	Initiative versus guilt
Age 5½ to 12	Latency	—	Industry versus inferiority
Adolescence	Genital	—	Identity versus role confusion
Young adulthood	—	—	Intimacy versus isolation
Middle adulthood	—	—	Generativity versus stagnation
Late adulthood	—	—	Ego integrity versus despair

the development of **initiative**—the child's ability to work toward a goal, to make plans. One of his ambitions, as in Freud's phallic stage, is to win his mother away from his father—a goal he can never attain. He comes to feel that he was wrong to wish to possess his mother. He develops a superego, and experiences **guilt.**

In the next stage, from 5 or 6 to 11 or 12, the conflict is between **industry** and **inferiority.** Children industriously apply themselves to learning the skills that society requires of them. It is a period of **ego growth,** as they become more sure of their abilities. But it is also a period in which feelings of inferiority are common, because the price of failing (socially or scholastically) is so high.

Puberty comes next, with what Erikson calls the **identity crisis**—the "Who am I?" stage. Adolescents must develop an identity of their own, apart from their family identity. At the same time they are faced with a rapidly changing physical appearance, and with the necessity to start making decisions that will determine the course of their lives.

By early adulthood, the psychologically healthy person has established his or her identity. When that happens—and not before—the person becomes capable of mature, unselfish relationships with other people (such as a husband or wife). This stage leads naturally to the next one, in which the emphasis is on creating something: children, works of art, scientific discoveries, or the like. Finally, in old age, people look back and ask, "Has it been worthwhile?" If they can answer yes, they have achieved **ego integrity.**

Evaluating Erikson.   Erikson, like Freud, began as a clinician. Thus, they both started off thinking of people as patients, not as subjects. Later, both men became interested in discovering things about humans in general—in other words, they became more like experimental psychologists and less like clinical psychologists. But the methods they used were clinical methods, not experimental methods. The evidence they used to support their theories was gained from individual patients in one-to-one sessions. In that kind of situation, patients probably have a tendency to say what they feel they are expected to say; psychologists may have a tendency to hear what they expect to hear. The clinical situation does not produce objective data, the way a controlled experiment can.

Much of what Erikson says about human development is convincing—it rings true. But it's hard to think of *any* kind of evidence that would disprove his theories, evidence that couldn't be explained away. A theory that can't be proved wrong can't be proved right, either. It's closer to art than to science. Nevertheless, such a theory may contain some important insights about human development.

THE COGNITIVE-DEVELOPMENTAL APPROACH

The stage theories of Freud and Erikson deal with the emotional development of the child, and with the changing relationships between children and other people (primarily parents). In this section we will discuss a different kind of stage theory, one that deals with **cognitive development**—the development of the capacity to think, to reason, to understand. The originator of this

Jean Piaget and one of his colleagues, engaged in the study of cognitive development.

theory, Jean Piaget, has had an enormous influence on child psychologists all over the world.

Piaget, like Rousseau, was born in Switzerland and spent part of his early life in France. But there the resemblance ends. Piaget was a highly educated man, and a dedicated scientist right from the start. At the age of 10 he published his first scholarly article; by 21 he had earned a doctorate in science! Piaget and his wife had three children. Unlike many European fathers of the 1920s, he found his children fascinating. He spent long hours observing them and recording their behavior. Jacqueline, Lucienne, and Laurent Piaget were Jean Piaget's best subjects.

What interested Piaget was the development of intelligence, the growth of knowledge and understanding. In his view, children do not simply receive information from the environment—they actively seek it, they achieve knowledge through their own efforts. Their drive to do this is built in; it's one of the characteristics of the human species. Piaget sees cognitive development from the point of view of a biologist—as a kind of biological **adaptation.** All living species have ways of adapting to their environment: plants send down longer roots in dry climates, animals search for food in a wider area if food is scarce. Humans are the most adaptable of all. They adapt by using their intelligence, by the active process of gaining understanding of their environment.

Piaget's Theory of Cognitive Development

Piaget divides childhood into four major periods (see Table 3–2). However, development is seen as a continuous process, and transitions from one period to another are gradual rather than abrupt. Is this a stage theory, then? Yes, because there are assumed to be *qualitative* differences between one period and another—qualitative differences in the way children think, the way they understand the world.

TABLE 3–2   Piaget's Stages of Cognitive Development

Approximate Age	Stage	Characteristics
Birth to age 2	Sensorimotor period	Infant develops concept of permanent objects.
Age 2 to 7	Preoperational period	Egocentric thought; child centers on one aspect of situation.
Age 7 to 11	Period of concrete operations	Child can decenter but cannot reason abstractly.
Age 11 on	Period of formal operations	Abstract reasoning and systematic experimentation are now possible.

The Sensorimotor Period.   The first period of development begins at birth and lasts until age 1½ or 2. Even at birth, babies are not entirely helpless. For example, they can suck—they are born with a sucking reflex. Within a few hours after birth they are capable of looking at a stationary object; within a few days they can track a slowly moving object with their eyes. Later they learn to grasp objects—first with the entire hand, eventually with thumb and forefinger. Piaget calls such patterns of action **schemes.** Schemes can be inborn, like sucking, or acquired later, like grasping. They can also be modified—a baby learns to grasp a stuffed animal in one way, a small piece of food in another way. And schemes can be extended or combined, forming ever more complicated schemes.

The most important thing the baby develops during the sensorimotor period is the concept of **object permanence.** According to Piaget, babies start out with no conception of the permanence of objects or people—they are aware of the existence of things only when they can see them or feel them. When the object disappears, the baby instantly forgets it: out of sight, out of mind. Here is Piaget's description of his daughter Jacqueline, at 9 months, 21 days:

> Jacqueline is seated and I place on her lap a rubber eraser which she has just held in her hand. Just as she is about to grasp it again I put my hand between her eyes and the eraser; she immediately gives up, as though the object no longer existed. (Piaget, 1954, pp. 21–22)

Lucienne at about the same age watches her father hide a doll under a piece of cloth. "She does not react." Then:

> I let the doll's feet emerge: Lucienne grabs them at once and pulls the doll out. (p.48)

After several more trials, Lucienne learns to find the doll, even when it is completely hidden by the cloth. But then Piaget hides the toy in a different place, under a coverlet, "Lucienne searches only under the cloth and never under the coverlet" (p. 49). She does this even though she has *seen* her father put the doll under the coverlet!

By the end of the sensorimotor period, objects have a permanent existence. Toddlers can think of a toy as being in a place *other* than where they last saw it. At age 1½,

> Jacqueline throws a ball under a sofa. But instead of bending down at once and searching for it on the floor she looks at the place, realizes that the ball must have crossed under the sofa, and sets out to go behind it. (p. 205)

Jacqueline must make a detour around a table in order to get behind the sofa. Her ability to do this shows that she has an overall idea of the locations of various objects (such as furniture) in the room. Her ability to go to a certain place by an indirect route also shows that she is capable of making a plan, of thinking ahead. All of these new abilities require the use of what Piaget called **representations**—mental images (or, later on, arbitrary symbols such as words) used to represent real actions or things.

By the end of the sensorimotor period children are also capable of **deferred imitation**—they can imitate an action they saw previously. Jacqueline at 16 months saw a little boy having a tantrum, and watched him with interest. The next day she screamed and stamped her feet on the floor of her playpen, just as the little boy had done the day before (Piaget, 1962).

The Preoperational Period.   From around age 2 to age 7, the child is in the second of Piaget's developmental stages. This period is marked by the increasing use of representational thought—words and other symbols are used as substitutes for actual objects or actions, in solving problems and in recalling past events. Their growing skill with language also enables preschoolers to communicate their thoughts to others.

What are the characteristics of preoperational thought? For one thing, according to Piaget, it's **egocentric.** By this term Piaget doesn't mean selfishness or conceit—he means the inability to see a situation from the point of view of another person. For instance, a preschool child is shown a model of three mountains, constructed out of cardboard. A doll is also in the room, "looking" at the mountains. The child is asked, "What does the doll see?"

> The child describes what he himself sees from his own position, without taking into account the obstacles which prevent the doll from seeing the same view. When he is shown several pictures from among which he is to choose the one which corresponds to the doll's perspective, he chooses the one which represents his own. (Piaget, 1954, p. 365)

Piaget's most famous experiment reveals another limitation of preoperational thought. A child is shown two identical glasses, each filled to the same level with a liquid such as juice. The child is asked, "Which glass has more juice?" "That's easy—they both have the same amount," is the reply. Now, as the child watches, the juice from one glass is poured into a tall, narrow beaker. The same question is asked again—which has more? Most children see that the level of juice in the beaker is way above that in the glass, and say that the beaker has more. Some children notice that the glass is wider than the beaker, and say that the *glass* has more. In neither case will the child agree that the two containers still have the same amount of fluid! The same results are found in other, similar situations: for example, the young child believes that a ball of clay contains more clay when it is flattened out into a pancake, or divided up into several smaller pieces.

Why are these children unable to see that the quantity of liquid or clay remains the same? Because, according to Piaget, they can **center** on only one aspect of the situation at a time—the height of the liquid, or the width. They can't **decenter**—they can't consider both aspects at the same time. Later, by the end of the preoperational period, they will be able to do that (Piaget and Inhelder, 1941).

Piaget's experiment produced a lot of controversy. Psychologists and nonpsychologists alike were skeptical at first, but most now feel that Piaget's findings were substantially correct. One mother, sure that *her* son would an-

Which glass holds more? By the time a child is 7 or 8 she is likely to understand that the amount of liquid stays the same, whether it's poured into a tall, narrow container or a wide, flat one.

swer correctly, instead found herself arguing with him: "But they *have* to have the same amount!" "Well, they *don't!*"

On the other hand, Piaget's belief that 2- to 6-year-olds are only capable of egocentric thought has been challenged successfully. Young children *are* capable of taking another's point of view in some simple situations. For example, 4-year-olds were asked to pick out toys for another 4-year-old, or for a 2-year-old. They picked toys that were suitable for the age of the other child, not necessarily the toys they themselves would want. Other studies have shown that preschoolers are capable of realizing that other people don't know everything that *they* know—that another child doesn't know what went on while she was out of the room, or while her eyes were blindfolded (Gelman, 1978).

The Period of Concrete Operations.   By age 7 or 8 children understand that the amount of liquid stays the same, whether it's poured into a tall, narrow container or a wide, flat one. They can consider several aspects of a situation at once. But their understanding is tied to real events, real (concrete) objects. They cannot, according to Piaget, abstract a general principle from particular examples. Nor can they disregard reality and temporarily put aside what they believe to be true, for the sake of argument. Piaget asked some 8- to 10-year-olds whether a rapidly swinging object would still make a breeze if the room were empty of air. "Yes," was the reply, "because there is always air in the room." "But in a room where all the air had been taken away would it make any?" "Yes...because there would be some air left" (Piaget, 1928, p. 68).

The Period of Formal Operations. At around age 11 or 12, children begin to reason logically and abstractly. They can now draw conclusions even from impossible suppositions—they are no longer troubled by a question such as "If dogs had six heads, how many heads would 15 dogs have?" (Piaget, 1928). Given a scientific problem to solve, such as what determines the amount of time it takes for a pendulum to complete its swing, they can carry

THE CHILD IN SOCIETY

The Development of Moral Reasoning

One of the aspects of cognitive development that Piaget studied was the development of **moral** concepts—ideas of good and bad, right and wrong, moral and immoral. Piaget (1932) asked children of various ages to make moral judgments about fictional children, characters in stories he told them. For instance, one story was about a boy who broke a teacup while trying to steal some jam. Another boy broke a whole trayful of teacups, but he wasn't doing anything wrong—it was just an accident. Piaget asked his subjects, "Which boy is naughtier?" He found that preschool children thought the second boy was naughtier, simply because he had broken more cups. The children took into account only the magnitude of the damage and not the boy's intentions. This finding is in line with Piaget's belief that young children can't decenter—they can focus on only one aspect of a situation at a time.

An American psychologist named Lawrence Kohlberg has extended Piaget's work on moral reasoning. His method, which he used in his Ph.D. thesis in 1958 and has used ever since, is similar to Piaget's: tell children stories, then ask them questions. Here is one of Kohlberg's stories:

In Europe, a woman was near death from cancer. One drug might save her, a form of radium that a druggist in the same town had recently discovered. The druggist was charging $2,000, ten times what the drug cost him to make. The sick woman's husband, Heinz, went to everyone he knew to borrow the money, but he could only get together about half of what it cost. He told the druggist that his wife was dying and asked him to sell it cheaper or let him pay later. But the druggist said, "No." The husband got desperate and broke into the man's store to steal the drug for his wife. Should the husband have done that? Why? (Kohlberg, 1969, p. 379).

Kohlberg isn't particularly interested in whether the child answers yes or no to the first question. The important part is the answer to the second question, "Why?" On the basis of children's answers to questions about this story and other similar stories, Kohlberg constructed his theory of moral reasoning.

According to this theory there are three levels of moral reasoning, which Kohlberg calls **preconventional, conventional,** and **postconventional.** Preconventional moral reasoning is concerned only with the possibility of success or failure, where failure consists of "getting caught." A preconventional response to the Heinz story would be, "No, Heinz shouldn't have stolen the drug. He'll probably get caught and sent to jail."

Conventional moral reasoning focuses on upholding society's rules: "No, Heinz shouldn't

out systematic operations to find out the answer. In a study done in Piaget's laboratory, children of different ages were asked to try to solve the pendulum problem. They could vary the length of the string, the weight of the object swung by the string, or the height at which the object was released. Concrete-operational children couldn't solve the problem, because they didn't know how to test the possibilities systematically. Formal-operational children, how-

have stolen the drug. It's wrong to steal.'' Post-conventional moral reasoning admits the possibility that some principles might be more important than upholding society's rules—the principle of saving a human life, for instance: "Stealing is wrong, but it would be worse to let a person die if there's a way to save her.''

Kohlberg believes that all children start at level 1; most children below the age of 9 are at this level. But some never progress beyond level 1—criminals, for example, tend to be stuck at the first level. Normally, development goes on to level 2. But admission to level 3 is restricted to a select few. The majority of Americans, according to Kohlberg, remain at level 2 all their lives. In fact, studies of other societies (Kohlberg, 1968) have revealed some societies in which no level 3 individuals were discovered. That finding calls into question Kohlberg's claim that his levels of moral reasoning are universal—that all people, all over the world, progress through the same stages.

Kohlberg also believes that the levels are always climbed in the same order—no skipping, no backwards steps allowed. But longitudinal data, based on following individual subjects over a period of years, failed to support that prediction. Some people do seem to regress from a higher level to a lower level (Holstein, 1976; Kohlberg and Kramer, 1969).

The most questionable part of Kohlberg's theory is the clear implication that some kinds of moral reasoning are better than others. Value judgments of that sort belong in the realm of philosophy or religion, not psychology. And even philosophers and religious leaders, arguing the question for almost 3000 years, have failed to agree on a set of universal standards of right and wrong.

Moral reasoning versus moral behavior. Kohlberg's theory is entirely based on what children and adolescents *say*. But what do they *do*? On the basis of what children say in an interview, can we predict how they will act when forced to make a moral decision? The evidence is that we *can't*. In a classic study (Hartshorne and May, 1928), the investigators observed thousands of children in many situations—at home, at school, and at play—in which there are temptations to lie, cheat, or steal. They found, first of all, that children are not consistent even in their actions—a child who cheats in one situation will not necessarily do so in another; a child who lies is not necessarily a child who steals. Secondly, there was little or no connection between children's moral (or immoral) behavior and what they *said* when they were asked questions about morality. Children who cheated expressed just as much disapproval of cheating as those who didn't. (Later research by Burton, 1976, supported Hartshorne and May's findings.) Evidently what Kohlberg has been studying is not the development of morality, but the development of a certain way of *talking* about morality.

As for moral *behavior*, we'll have more to say about that in later chapters of the book. ■

ever, realized that they must vary only one factor at a time (holding the others constant) in order to test its effects. One 15-year-old girl first tried two different lengths of string with a 100-gram weight, and then the same two strings with a 200-gram weight. "It's the length of the string that makes it go faster or slower," she correctly concluded. "The weight doesn't play any role" (Inhelder and Piaget, 1958, p. 75).

BEHAVIORISM

Piaget and Kohlberg were interested primarily in the thoughts and beliefs of the children who were their subjects. Behaviorists, on the other hand, aren't particularly interested in what their subjects think, or what they feel, dream, wish, or worry about. They're only interested in what their subjects *do*—as a behaviorist would put it, in their **responses.** Responses are assumed to depend on external events, such as **visual** and **auditory stimuli** (sights and sounds); how long it's been since the subjects ate, drank, or slept; and the past history of the subjects—what they did in the past and what happened to them when they did it. Internal events, such as thoughts and ideas, are not considered important. Nor are hereditary factors. Behaviorism takes no official notice of individual differences among members of a species. Even genetic differences *between* species are pretty much ignored. Subjects are called **organisms,** a word that can be applied equally well to people and to animals.

In the previous chapter we discussed the nature-nurture debate and we said that there is currently a move back to the heredity side, after a long period in which the environmental view was dominant. Yet so far in this chapter we have mentioned only one environmentalist: John Locke. The other theories we've discussed, with the possible exception of Freud's, have all been slanted more to nature than to nurture. So where did that dominant environmental view come from? It came from behaviorism. Behaviorism has had a very strong influence on American psychology, even among those who did not hold to all of its assumptions.

Give Me the Baby

The most famous quote in all of behaviorism is this one, from the pen of John B. Watson:

> Given me a dozen healthy infants, well-formed, and my own specified world to bring them up in and I'll guarantee to take any one at random and train him to become any type of specialist I might select—doctor, lawyer, artist, merchant-chief, and, yes, even beggar-man and thief, regardless of his talents, penchants, tendencies, abilities, vocations, and race of his ancestors. (Watson, 1924, p. 104)

Watson was not really the founder of behaviorism (that honor belongs to a psychologist named Thorndike, who did experiments with cats). Rather, he was its first popularizer. That statement we just quoted shows his style, his boldness. Watson was willing to go out on a limb.

He showed some of the same traits in his personal life. In 1929 Watson was accused of becoming romantically involved with a young woman who was his research associate. (He was 51 at the time.) His wife divorced him, and the resulting scandal lost him his position at Johns Hopkins University. He ended up working for an advertising agency.

Although he was an experimental psychologist, Watson is remembered for only one important experiment—and that experiment was not very good and not at all ethical, by present standards. It involved a single subject: an 11-month-old child called "little Albert." Watson had read about the experiments of the Russian psychologist Pavlov, who **conditioned** a dog to salivate at the sound of a bell, by **pairing** food with the sound of the bell—in other words, by feeding it whenever the bell rang. Watson decided to produce **conditioned fear** in little Albert, by pairing a loud noise with the sight of a harmless white rat. Albert was afraid of the loud noise; he wasn't afraid of the rat. But after the experimenter had several times made the loud noise behind Albert's back while he was looking at the rat, Albert became afraid of the rat. Moreover, he became afraid of *other* white, furry things, such as a toy rabbit and a Santa Claus beard (Watson and Rayner, 1920).

Watson had planned to *decondition* little Albert and get him to like white rats again. But before he got around to doing so, the child was removed from the hospital where the experiment had taken place. Albert was allowed to go out into the world with his experimentally produced fear of white, furry objects! We'll have more to say about little Albert later in the chapter, in the Problems in Development box, Phobias.

B. F. Skinner

In 1929, the year that Watson's career in psychology came to an abrupt end, the career of another psychologist was just beginning. B. F. Skinner was a first-year graduate student in Harvard's psychology department, having spent the previous couple of years in an unsuccessful attempt to become a writer. (He ended up writing anyway, with countless journal articles and more than a dozen books, including one novel, to his credit.) The young Skinner was a man of many talents. He was a fine musician (who once played saxophone in a jazz band) and adept at languages (he could read German, French, and Italian). He also possessed unusual mechanical ability—he was a tinkerer. In one of the old Cambridge houses where he lived as a graduate student, he rigged up a device that automatically opened the damper of the furnace every morning (Skinner, 1979). Later, when his second daughter was born, he used his mechanical talent to build her a special enclosed area, provided with warm, filtered air, where she could play or sleep without the restrictions of clothing. (It was called an "air-crib.") Skinner had always been fond of children, and was a devoted father.

B. F. Skinner.

It was Skinner's love of tinkering that led him to invent, in 1930, the device for which he became famous: the **Skinner box,** as it's now called. This is simply an animal cage, built originally for a rat (but later used for other animals, such as pigeons). In the cage is a movable piece of metal, called a *lever.* When the rat pushes the lever an electrical circuit closes, causing a pellet of food to drop into a feeding tray. With this simple device Skinner worked out his theories of behavior. Skinner's position is that the behavior of humans and animals is lawful—that it follows rigid laws of cause and effect, just the way the ricocheting balls on a billiard table do. If we knew all the laws, and if we could completely control the environment, then human behavior would be perfectly predictable.

Skinner's Laws of Learning.   Skinner made a clear distinction between **classical conditioning,** as in Pavlov's experiments, and what he called **operant conditioning.** Classical conditioning involves the conditioning of a simple, automatic, inborn response called a **reflex**—salivating or becoming afraid are two examples. To condition the response a stimulus that normally produces it is repeatedly paired with a neutral stimulus—food (which produces salivation) is paired with the sound of a bell, or a loud noise (which produces fear) is paired with the sight of something white and furry. Eventually the neutral stimulus alone is able to produce the response.

Operant conditioning, on the other hand, is capable of producing a brand-new response. A nonpsychologist would just call it "learning." For example, a rat learns to press a lever, a pigeon learns to peck at a lighted plastic disk. Both animals are rewarded with food for their responses. But Skinner doesn't call the food a reward, he calls it a **reinforcer** (because it reinforces the tendency to press or peck). Anything an animal or a person is willing to work for is a reinforcer—food or water to a hungry or thirsty organism, a kind word or a pat on the head to a child or a dog.

In Skinner's terms, a hungry rat is **reinforced** with food when it presses the lever, and that **reinforcement** keeps it pressing the lever. The first lever-press was accidental, but the fact that it immediately produced food increased the likelihood that the rat would press again. If we *stop* giving the rat food when it presses the lever (and feed it in some other way instead), it will eventually stop pressing the lever. This is called the process of **extinction.** The response has been **extinguished** by the absence of reinforcement.

One of Skinner's important findings was that reinforcement does not have to be given consistently in order to work. **Partial reinforcement** works too. For example, we can feed the rat after every 5 lever presses, or every 15, or every 25. Or the number of required presses can vary—the rat may be reinforced after 9 responses on one trial, after 5 on the next, and after 16 on the next. In such situations the rat eventually ends up pressing the lever very rapidly, over and over. You might say that it "knows" that it has to press the lever many times to get food. Skinnerians do not say that—they say that the rat has been reinforced for pressing many times. What the rat "knows" is of no interest to the Skinnerian; and anyway, there's no way of *knowing* what the rat "knows." What we know is what it *does.*

One interesting thing about partial reinforcement is what happens in extinction, when the lever is disconnected from the food dispenser. If reinforcement has been continuous, the rat soon stops pressing the lever when food no longer comes. But if it's been partial, the rat may go on pressing, over and over again, emitting thousands of responses before it stops. That's because, in its past, unreinforced responses were eventually followed by reinforced ones. If your dog whines for food when you're eating, and every now and then you toss him a tidbit, you have put him in a partial reinforcement situation. You have reinforced his whining by giving him food. Now if you decide that he's become a pest and you stop feeding him when he whines, he will go on whining for food day after day—much longer than if you had fed him *every* time he whined!

Shaping. With reinforcement, organisms can eventually learn to perform complicated actions that are quite different from those they would normally perform. The process of teaching them such actions is called **shaping.** A pigeon can be taught to turn around in a circle, for example, by this method. First you reinforce *any* sideways movement. Once this response is learned you gradually increase your requirements—reinforce the bird only for a quarter of a turn, then only for half a turn, and so on. Soon the pigeon is pirouetting like a ballerina. Skinner taught a pair of pigeons to play ping-pong with each other, by the method of shaping.

One important thing to remember about reinforcement is that it primarily affects the *last* response made—the one that occurred just before the reinforcement was given. If a pigeon turns around, then lifts its wing, then stretches its neck, and then is reinforced, it's the neck-stretching that's been reinforced. The same is true of **punishment.** Punishment consists of administering an unpleasant stimulus, such as one that causes pain (or in removing a pleasant stimulus, such as food). Punishment decreases the strength of a response, just as reinforcement increases it. The response that is primarily affected is the last response before the punishment. So if your dog does something wrong and you call him over to you and smack him, what have you done? You've punished him for coming when you call!

Although most behaviorists believe that punishment is an effective way to eliminate an undesirable response, Skinner does not. He believes that the best way to get rid of an unwanted kind of behavior is to extinguish it—to avoid reinforcing it until it goes away. He practiced what he preached. When his older daughter, Julie, was 5 years old he announced to her that she would never be punished again. "For a month or two she tempted us, beginning to act in punishable ways and watching us closely, but it did not last. For one thing, having abandoned punishment, Yvonne [his wife] and I looked for and found better ways of treating her" (Skinner, 1979, p. 279). The "better ways" consisted of using reinforcement to increase desired behavior, rather than punishment to decrease unwanted behavior. (See box on Behavior Modification.)

SOCIAL LEARNING THEORY

Although a baby's crying isn't necessarily increased by parental attention, many other kinds of behavior are affected by reinforcement. But it's a long step to go from saying that reinforcement works to saying that *all* learning depends on reinforcement. Remember Piaget's daughter Jacqueline, screaming and stamping her foot in imitation of a little boy she had seen having a tantrum? Clearly, she had learned something simply by watching the other child. She had learned it without being reinforced. Social learning theorists believe that much of human behavior is acquired in this way: by observing another person's behavior and, in some cases, imitating it. The other person is called a **model,** and what the model does is called **modeling.**

Social learning theory has been around for a while; in the 1940s two Yale psychologists published a book called *Social Learning and Imitation* (Miller and Dollard, 1941). But the name that has been most closely associated with

CLOSE-UP

Behavior Modification

Reinforcement works, there's no question about it. Children and grownups, horses and dogs, rats and pigeons—all are more likely to do something if they've been reinforced for doing it in the past.

One of the earliest experimental uses of reinforcement to modify the behavior of a child took place in 1945. Years later, Skinner described how he was holding his 9-month-old daughter on his lap as dusk fell:

> The room grew dark, and I turned on a table lamp beside the chair. She smiled brightly, and it occurred to me that I could use the light as a reinforcer. I turned it off and waited. When she lifted her left hand slightly, I quickly turned the light on and off. Almost immediately she lifted her hand again, and I turned the light on and off again. In a few moments she was lifting her arm in a wide arc "to turn on the light." (1979, p. 293)

Similar methods, using many different types of reinforcers, have been used to condition a wide variety of behaviors. Skinner toilet-trained his daughter in no time, by building her a potty that played the "Blue Danube" waltz whenever a few drops of urine triggered the mechanism.

Perhaps the most important use of behavior modification techniques has involved children with serious problems that haven't responded to other forms of treatment. Neale and Liebert (1969) taught a mentally ill patient to talk, using the method of shaping. They first reinforced her for making any sounds at all (such as "buh" or "mmm"). Once she was doing that the experimenters began rewarding her only for words ("bread," "milk"), then for short phrases ("milk, please"), and finally for complete sentences ("May I have some milk, please?").

In another experiment, behavior modification was used to improve sibling relationships. A 6-year-old boy named Karl, who had been diagnosed as brain-damaged, fought constantly with his younger brother Jeff. The experimenters visited the boys' home and observed their behav-

this viewpoint is that of Albert Bandura, a psychologist at Stanford University. Bandura has made important contributions both to the development of the theory and to the experimental evidence that supports it.

The best-known of Bandura's experiments (1965) deals with the modeling of aggressive behavior. The subjects were children; they watched an adult model perform in a short TV movie. In the movie the adult was shown attacking a large, inflated plastic toy called a "Bobo doll," which comes back for more each time it's knocked down. The model sat on the doll, punched it, and hit it with a mallet, yelling things like "Pow, right in the nose," and "Sockeroo . . . stay down." Bandura filmed two different endings for the movie. One group of children were shown a version that ended with the model being reinforced for hitting the Bobo doll—the model was praised by another adult, and given rewards of candy and soda. The second group saw a film with a different ending—the model was hit with a rolled-up newspaper by the second adult, who exclaimed, "You big bully!"

ior. The boys hit each other, broke each other's toys, threw things, and yelled insults. Operant conditioning techniques were then put into effect. The experimenters began by rewarding all instances of cooperative behavior (playing together, sharing toys, and so on) with small pieces of candy. Later they switched to "token" reinforcers: checkmarks on a blackboard. The children could exchange these checkmarks for bubble gum, comic books, or toys. Fighting was punished by a "time-out": the guilty child was put in a separate room for five minutes, and he had to be quiet for at least three minutes before he could come out. (The children resisted this punishment at first, but later accepted it without much argument.)

The experiment was carried out over a period of weeks. By the end, more than 90 percent of the boys' behavior was cooperative. In the last four sessions only one time-out had to be given—to Jeff, the younger brother (O'Leary, O'Leary, and Becker, 1969).

Some people are bothered by the thought that using reinforcement to change behavior is "bribery." Aren't we just bribing these children to do what we want? The word "bribe" has acquired

unpleasant connotations because it usually means paying a person to do something they *shouldn't* do—to lie on the witness stand, for instance. If you want to call *any* incentive a bribe, then you've got to say that all working people are being "bribed" by means of their paychecks, and parents are "bribed" to do things for their children by means of the smiles and hugs they get in return. The charge of bribery is not a problem for behaviorism.

What *is* a problem is the tendency for behaviorists to see everything in terms of responses rewarded and responses punished. For example, many behaviorists have viewed the baby as a creature whose behavior is largely determined by rewards and punishments given by the parents. If the baby cries and the parent responds by picking up the child, the parent has reinforced crying. Therefore, the baby should cry more and more. In fact, babies who are picked up or fed when they cry tend to cry less and less (Bell and Ainsworth, 1972). In the long run it's probably better for parents to feel that their baby's cries are due to hunger, pain or unhappiness than for them to think that the baby is crying because he's been reinforced for crying. ∎

After seeing a movie that showed an adult attacking a "Bobo doll" (top), these children (middle and bottom) imitated the model's aggressive behavior.

After the movie the children were brought one at a time into a room containing a Bobo doll, a mallet, and some other toys. Each child was left alone in the room and observed through a one-way screen. The children who had seen the movie with the reward ending were likely to imitate the model's behavior—they sat on the Bobo doll, hit it with the mallet, and so on. The children who had seen the model punished did much less of this kind of thing.

Imitative behavior, then, does depend on reinforcement and punishment. But in this case it is the consequence experienced by the *model* that counts. Bandura calls this **vicarious reinforcement** and **vicarious punishment**—rewards and punishments that we see someone else get. We learn by watching other people and by seeing what happens when they do something. This is considerably more efficient than if we had to try everything out for ourselves. A child who sees another child burned when he touches a hot stove, or scolded by the teacher for speaking out of turn, doesn't have to try it herself. She already knows the consequences.

Thus, learning occurs whether the model is rewarded or punished. In one case the child learns what to do; in the other, what *not* to do. Both groups of children in the Bobo doll experiment could later tell the experimenter exactly what the model had done. The children who saw the film with the punishment ending remembered just as much about the film as the children who saw the reward ending.

On the basis of such results, Bandura has made a distinction between the *acquisition* of new responses and the *performance* of them. Children acquire information from watching a model, but whether they will perform what they learned depends on other factors—on whether they saw the model rewarded or punished, and on what happened when they performed similar acts in the past. So rewards and punishments matter, but they needn't be experienced "in person." This approach is sometimes called **cognitive behaviorism.** What is learned is not a response but an idea.

Modeling of Other Kinds of Behavior

Children not only imitate undesirable behavior such as tantrums or aggression. They imitate more approved kinds of behavior, too, such as sharing and helping. One type of behavior that has been studied by social learning theorists is self-control—for example, how children learn to deny themselves a small reward for the sake of a larger reward later. In an experiment by Bandura and his colleague Walter Mischel (1965), children were offered a choice between a small gift right away or a bigger one in a week. They made their decision, which was recorded. Then the children watched an adult model being offered the same kind of choice. In some cases the adult chose to wait, and said something like "The better one is worth waiting for." In other cases the adult chose to get the smaller gift right away. Afterwards the children were tested again. Their responses had shifted in the direction of the model. Children who had previously picked the immediate gift now decided to wait, after seeing the adult make that choice. If the adult model chose not to wait, the children tended to shift toward *that* decision.

Unquestionably, the behavior of models has a very important influence on what children do. We'll have a lot more to say on this topic in later chapters of the book.

WILL THE RIGHT THEORY PLEASE STEP FORWARD?

We've come to the end of the chapter. We've told you about a number of different approaches to child development. Now, perhaps, you're waiting for us to answer the big question, Which theory is right?

Let's evade that issue for a minute and instead answer an easier question, Which theories are *wrong?*

Preformationism is wrong. There really *isn't* a tiny humanoid inside of the egg and/or sperm, ready to inflate (gradually) to adult size. Locke's basic idea was wrong too. The baby *isn't* born with an empty slate. As we'll see in the next chapter, the newborn baby's slate already has quite a bit written on it. He or she comes with a lot more standard equipment than Locke realized, to say nothing of the custom features.

None of the other theories can be labeled *wrong.* They focus on different aspects of development; thus, they are not necessarily incompatible. It's possible to imagine a child's emotional development progressing along the lines

Phobias: Little Hans Meets Little Albert

Most children have fears. When a fear gets out of hand and starts to interfere with the child's day-to-day activities, we call it a **phobia.** For example, a child may be so afraid of dogs that she is reluctant to go out of the house because she might meet one.

One of Sigmund Freud's most famous cases concerns a 5-year-old boy referred to as "little Hans." Little Hans had a phobia about horses. Since he lived in the days before motor cars—when the streets of Vienna were teeming with horse-drawn vehicles—this was a real problem. His parents sought Freud's aid. The boy was psychoanalyzed. Eventually, Freud decided that little Hans was caught up in an Oedipal conflict. Horses symbolized Hans's big, powerful father. Hans unconsciously feared that his father would discover that they were both in love with the same woman (Hans's mother), and that his father would retaliate by castrating him. Since these fears were unacceptable to Hans's con-

scious mind, they were converted into a fear of horses (Freud, 1909/1950).

Little Hans had long since gotten over his fear of horses by the time little Albert was born. Albert was the child in Watson's experiment, who was taught to fear white rats. Afterwards Albert had a rat phobia. Watson's explanation of little Albert's phobia—a simple matter of classical conditioning—is quite different from Freud's explanation of little Hans's. Yet these children reacted in much the same way to the sight of a feared animal.

Later experimenters tried to repeat Watson's experiment using other stimuli. They found they were unable to condition children to be afraid of such stimuli as curtains or wooden blocks (Bregman, 1934; English, 1929). Why is it so easy to teach a child to fear a white rat, and so difficult to teach him to fear a curtain? Why do phobias so often involve stimuli like animals, or heights, or thunder and lightning—all poten-

of Erikson's theory, while his intellect grows according to Piaget. He may learn to ride a bike by reinforcement of the right responses and punishment of the wrong ones, but he learns to cook by watching his mother. One theory really isn't enough to account for all the things that happen as a child grows up.

What this means is that none of the theories presented here is *completely* right. Each of them represents an extreme position, a radical point of view. Each theory contains some truth, but each overstates its case. Heredity is important, but not as important as Darwin makes it out to be. Sex is important, but not as important as Freud makes it out to be. Imitation and social reinforcement are important, but not as important as the social learning theorists make them out to be. (Social learning theorists don't pay much attention to heredity.)

In this chapter we've sketched out the broad outlines of some important theories of development. Later chapters will fill in additional details. There are other theories, too, that deserve some notice, and that we'll be mentioning from time to time. Here our goal was to introduce you to some of the basic ideas that lie behind modern developmental psychology. These ideas

tially harmful things? Why do *other* potentially harmful things—razor blades, plastic bags, electric outlets—so seldom figure in phobias?

Martin Seligman, of the University of Pennsylvania, has a convincing explanation (Seligman, 1972). His idea is called **preparedness.** According to this theory, people are genetically more **prepared** to become afraid of certain things. These are things that, far back in the history of our species, *were* associated with danger. Seligman doesn't believe that we're actually born with these fears—just that it doesn't take much to bring them out. Albert became afraid of a white rat after a few occasions in which Watson made a startling noise while Albert was looking at the rat. It might have taken only a *single* unpleasant experience to make Albert afraid of snakes or spiders. But to get him to fear a wooden block might take thousands of trials, or perhaps something worse than a loud noise. A child is more prepared to fear an animal than to fear a wooden block. We might speculate that preparedness varies among *children,* too—some children appear to be more prepared to be afraid than others.

What about little Hans? If he was really afraid of horses, not his father, how did his fear start?

Hans himself had the answer. He linked his phobia (which he called "the nonsense") to a single frightening incident involving a horse that was pulling a bus. Hans described how the horse had fallen down and kicked its feet, violently and noisily. "When the horse in the bus fell down, it gave me such a fright, really! That was when I got the nonsense." (Freud, 1909/1950, p. 192).

If phobias are acquired by a kind of learning, then it should be possible to *un*learn them. Behavior modification techniques have, in fact, proved to be highly successful in curing people of their phobias. The first use of this type of treatment was reported by Mary Cover Jones, in 1924. Her subject was a boy named Peter, 2 years and 10 months old. Peter, like Albert, was terrified of small, furry animals. Jones used a combination of two methods to "decondition" Peter: classical conditioning and modeling. She gave Peter good things to eat, while a white rabbit was gradually brought closer and closer to him. She also had Peter watch other children, who had no fear of animals, play with the rabbit. These methods worked. Peter's fear went away, and eventually he was able to play with the rabbit himself. ■

will run through the rest of the book, as threads do through a piece of woven cloth. We hope we can tie them all together for you.

summary

1. Theories of development help us to decide what to observe and how to organize our observations.

2. Until fairly recently, childhood was not viewed as a special time of life. Children were seen simply as undersized adults.

3. Two beliefs popular in former times were **preformationism,** the notion that the egg or the sperm contains a miniature version of the adult it is destined to become, and the **doctrine of innate ideas,** the notion that babies are born with their minds already furnished with certain ideas.

4. Locke denied the doctrine of innate ideas. He believed that the baby's mind is empty—a **tabula rasa**—until it is furnished with experiences provided by the environment.

5. Rousseau believed that children are capable individuals and should be left alone to develop naturally. This view has been a popular one in recent times.

6. Darwin's work persuaded the scientific world that humans are a kind of animals, and hence that humans are subject to the same "laws of nature" that control the responses of animals.

Darwin believed that people, as well as animals, are born with **instincts**—inherited patterns of behavior.

7. Freud was the founder of **psychoanalysis.** He believed that most of the psychological problems of adults have their roots in childhood experiences, and that most of these problems are sexual in origin.

8. According to Freud, the human mind consists of the **id,** the **ego,** and the **superego.** The id is present from birth and is the home of powerful instinctive drives. The ego results from the baby's conflicts with society; it directs the child's actions in a rational way. The superego is similar to a conscience; it develops during the preschool period. Thoughts that are frowned upon by the superego may be **repressed**—driven down into the unconscious mind. Desires or impulses may also be **displaced,** emerging in another form or directed at a different target.

9. Freud offered the first important **stage theory** of development. In a stage theory, what goes on in one stage is qualitatively different from what went on in the stage before. The stages have to come in a certain order, but the speed at which the stages are achieved can vary.

10. Freud's five stages of development are the **oral, anal, phallic, latency,** and **genital** stages. If things don't go well, a person can be **fixated** at a certain stage. It is during the phallic stage (age 3 to 5½) that the **Oedipal conflict** occurs: little boys become sexually interested in their mothers and fear that their fathers will punish them with castration. Girls are presumed to go through a parallel experience, called the **Electra conflict.** The resolution of these conflicts cause children to **identify** with the same-sex parent. This identification gives rise to the superego.

11. Freud based his theories on life as he knew it, in nineteenth-century Vienna, but he claimed that they apply to *all* people, *all* the time.

12. Erikson's stage theory is **psychosocial**—compared to Freud's, there is more emphasis on social interactions, less on sexual matters. De-

velopment does not stop at adolescence, but continues throughout life.

13. In the first of Erikson's eight stages, infancy, the basic issue is **trust versus mistrust**—if the infant's parents are reliable and consistent, he will come to trust them. In toddlerhood, the issue is **autonomy versus shame and doubt**—toddlers want the freedom to determine their own actions, but doubt their capabilities. In the preschool period, the issue is **initiative versus guilt**—the Oedipal conflict plays a role here. In middle childhood, a period of **ego growth,** the issue is **industry versus inferiority.** In adolescence, teenagers go through the **identity crisis.** Erikson's last three stages occur in adulthood.

14. Both Freud and Erikson based their theories on clinical experiences with their patients. Such theories may contain important insights about development, but are unproved and probably unprovable.

15. Piaget awakened interest in **cognitive development**—the development of the ability to think, to reason, and to understand. In his view, children do not simply receive information from the environment—they actively seek it.

16. In Piaget's first stage, the **sensorimotor period** (birth to age 2), babies develop the concept of **object permanence.** Newborn babies are aware of the existence of things only when they can see them or feel them. By the end of this period, objects have a permanent existence, **mental representations** are used, and **deferred imitation** is possible.

17. In the **preoperational period** (age 2 to 7), preschoolers tend to **center** on a single aspect of a problem. According to Piaget, their thought is **egocentric**—they can't see a situation from the point of view of another person. Other psychologists have found evidence that preschoolers *can* sometimes adopt another person's point of view.

18. In Piaget's **period of concrete operations** (age 7 to 11), children can consider several aspects of a situation at once, but their understanding is tied to real (concrete) objects. They cannot temporarily put aside what they believe

to be true for the sake of argument.

19. Piaget's fourth stage is the **period of formal operations** (which starts around age 11). Children now begin to reason logically and abstractly, and to solve problems by systematically testing the possibilities.

20. Kohlberg believes that there are three levels of moral reasoning. In the **preconventional** level, moral reasoning is concerned only with the possibility of success or failure; failure is "getting caught." In the **conventional** level, moral reasoning is based on upholding society's rules. Reasoning in the **postconventional** level admits the possibility that some principles might be more important than upholding society's rules. Kohlberg admits that most people never get to the third level. Other psychologists have found little or no connection between what children *say* about moral issues and what they *do* when faced with a moral decision.

21. Behaviorists are interested in their subjects' responses and not in their thoughts, feelings, or dreams. Responses are assumed to depend on external stimuli and on the past history of the subjects.

22. Watson, the first popularizer of behaviorism, performed only one important experiment: he produced **conditioned fear** of white rats in an 11-month-old boy.

23. Skinner distinguished between **classical conditioning** and **operant conditioning.** In classical conditioning, a neutral stimulus is paired with a stimulus that produces a reflex; eventually the neutral stimulus alone can produce the reflex. In operant conditioning, a response is **reinforced** with a **reinforcer** such as food or praise; such **reinforcement** makes the response more likely to occur again. In **extinction,** reinforcement is no longer given, and the response eventually stops being made. If reinforcement was **partial** rather than continuous, the response takes much longer to **extinguish.** New responses can be **shaped** in operant conditioning by gradually increasing the requirements for reinforcement.

24. Punishment, the administration of an unpleasant stimulus (or the removal of a pleasant one), decreases the tendency to make a response. The response that is affected is the last one that occurred before the punishment. Skinner believes that extinction, rather than punishment, is the most effective way to eliminate undesirable behavior.

25. In **behavior modification**, the principles of operant conditioning have been used successfully to improve children's behavior in a variety of situations.

26. Social learning theorists believe that children can learn without reinforcement, by observing the behavior of other people, called **models.** A child's tendency to imitate a model's behavior will be influenced by the rewards or punishments received by the model. Such **vicarious reinforcement** or **vicarious punishment** has been shown to affect children's tendency to imitate adult models who behave aggressively. Children's behavior is also influenced by adults who model approved behavior, for instance, self-control.

27. The different theories of child development are not necessarily incompatible—they focus on different aspects of development. Each theory contains some truth, but each overstates its case.

28. Freud attributed little Hans's phobia of horses to the Oedipal conflict; Watson used classical conditioning to produce a similar phobia of white rats in little Albert.

29. Attempts to produce phobias of such things as curtains or wooden blocks have failed. This is explained by the concept of **preparedness**—children are genetically more **prepared** to be afraid of certain things. With the help of behavior modification techniques, many phobias can be unlearned.

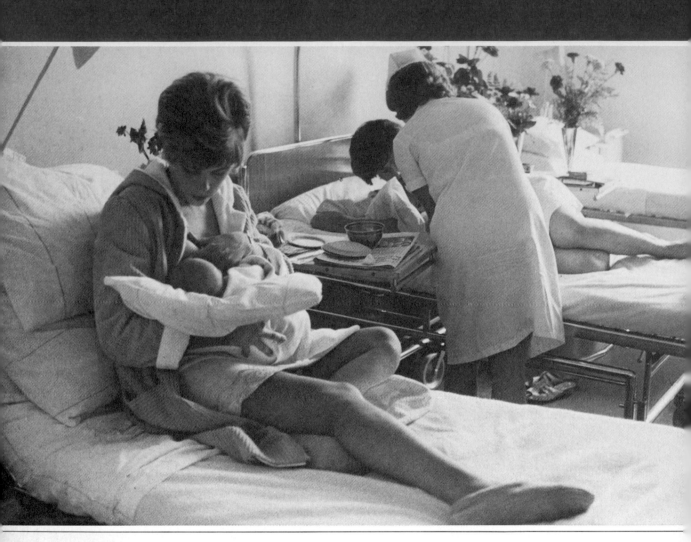

Chapter Four

FROM CONCEPTION TO BIRTH

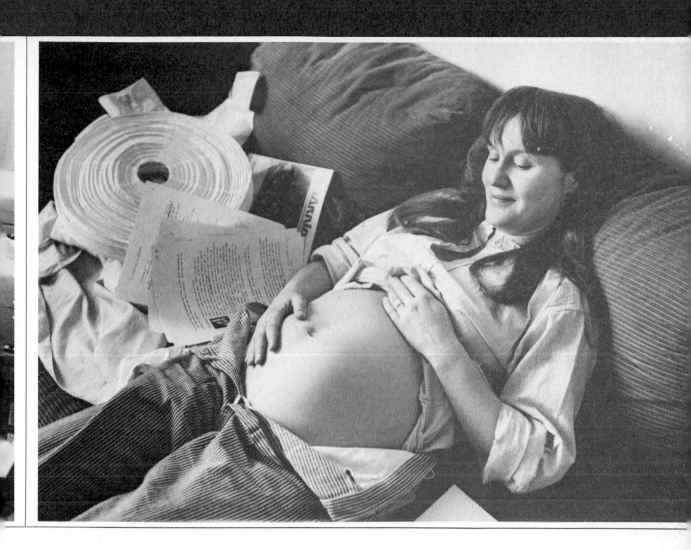

Four

At last, the moment we've been waiting for! Labor started almost twelve hours ago (about average for a first pregnancy), and the doctor has finally said, "Okay, it's time." The woman, now soon to be a mother, is wheeled into the delivery room. She's tired, but excited. Her husband, who accompanied her to the childbirth-preparation classes she took during pregnancy, dons hospital garb and proudly joins her in the delivery room.

The baby's head has now "crowned," and dark, wet hair is visible at the opening of the birth canal. "Push," says the doctor, "Push again." The head emerges, nose down. The doctor turns the baby a little and eases the shoulders out. They emerge sideways, one above the other. The rest of the body slips out easily. "It's a boy," exclaims the doctor, and the parents' first big question is answered. (Slightly more than half of American births—about 51.5 percent—result in a boy.) The second big question quickly follows: "Is he all right?" As in the great majority of cases, the answer is reassuring: "Yes, he's fine." The baby's cries already resound through the delivery room. He's breathing on his own for the first time, though he's still attached to his mother by way of the umbilical cord. The umbilical cord is cut, the baby is wiped off and weighed. His weight, 7½ pounds (3,400 grams) puts him close to the mean for boy babies. (Girls weigh, on the average, slightly less.)

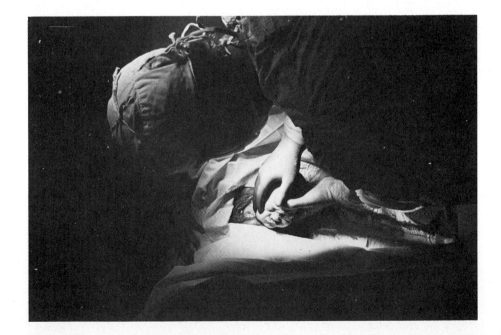

While the baby's needs are being tended to, his mother is completing the birth process by delivering the **placenta** (afterbirth), to which the other end of the umbilical cord is attached. The placenta is a large organ, liverlike in appearance, that was responsible for nourishing the **fetus** (the unborn baby) in the months before his birth.

Now, at last, the baby is placed in his mother's arms. She holds him a little awkwardly—she's new at the job, and he's so very tiny. He's also, frankly, not very handsome. His head is rather pointy, having gotten temporarily out of shape during his passage down the birth canal. His nose is flattened, his chin is virtually nonexistent, and his eyes (what she can see of them) are a cloudy color, more gray than blue. Nonetheless he is that most remarkable of creatures—a newborn human child.

But newborn isn't the same as new. Although this baby has had virtually no environment other than the interior of the uterus, virtually no experiences other than that of being born, he's already been developing for nine months. In this chapter we'll look at what went on during those nine months. We'll return for a closer look at the **neonate**—the newborn infant—in the next chapter.

DEVELOPMENT IN THE PRENATAL PERIOD

Prenatal means before birth. The entire time from the moment of conception to the moment of birth is called the **prenatal period** (or, alternatively, the **period of gestation**). In humans, this period averages 266 days, or 38 weeks—one week short of nine months.

Conception

Conception occurs when a sperm from a man's testicle unites with an egg from a woman's ovary. The ovaries generally put forth a single egg (or *ovum*) each month, about midway through the menstrual cycle. In contrast, there may be as many as 400 million sperm cells released in a woman's vagina during sexual intercourse. Some small proportion of these sperm make their way through the uterus and up the **Fallopian tubes,** which lead from the uterus to the ovaries. It is in one of the Fallopian tubes where conception normally takes place, most often within 24 hours after intercourse. Only a single one of those 400 million sperm can fertilize the egg.

Conception Outside the Body.   In the past, a woman whose Fallopian tubes were permanently blocked or damaged could never bear a child. But in 1978 just such a woman gave birth to Louise Brown, the world's first "test-tube baby." Louise was conceived in a glass dish containing some human egg cells, which had been surgically removed from her mother's body, and some sperm, contributed by her father. About a day after conception the fertilized egg began to divide, forming new cells, and doctors inserted this tiny clump of cells into Mrs. Brown's uterus. From there on her pregnancy progressed in the usual manner. Louise Brown appears to be a normal child in every respect.

Although this advancement in biological science is amazing enough (and, to some people, a little frightening), an even more dramatic step is now possible. The small clump of cells needn't necessarily be inserted back into its "mother." Theoretically, it can just as well be put into some *other* woman's uterus. How would Louise Brown have turned out if she had spent nine months in Mrs. Smith's uterus, instead of Mrs. Brown's? In all probability, she wouldn't be very different. Louise Brown owes her blond curls, her turned-up nose, and all her other inborn characteristics to the genes she received from Mrs. Brown's egg and Mr. Brown's sperm. But the job of the uterus is nonetheless an important one—it must provide a suitable environment for carrying out the instructions contained in the genes.

Louise Brown and her parents.

Stages of Prenatal Development

In the usual case, as we've said, conception takes place in one of the Fallopian tubes. The fertilized human egg (or *zygote*) is a single cell containing 46 chromosomes; like other cells, it multiplies by dividing in two. When a cell splits in half, the chromosomes also split in half, so the two new cells have the same number of chromosomes as the old one. The two cells divide again, becoming four cells, and so on. Only 20 such divisions are needed to put the number of cells over a million.

But cell division doesn't just occur at random—it follows a very precise pattern, regulated by the genes. In the 38 weeks of prenatal development, a single cell becomes a baby. (Occasionally, as we explained in Chapter Two, a single fertilized egg develops into two—or even more—babies; these are identical twins, triplets, and so on. More commonly, multiple births are *fraternal* twins, triplets, and so on. These occur when two or more eggs are released from a woman's ovaries and are fertilized, each by a different sperm.) Prenatal development can be divided into three stages: the **germinal stage,** the stage of the **embryo,** and the stage of the **fetus**.

The Germinal Stage.   During the germinal stage—the first two weeks of prenatal development—the fertilized egg undergoes rapid cell division. In the first three or four days after conception, the small clump of dividing cells (now called the **blastula**) travels down the Fallopian tube and into the uterus. The blastula is a hollow ball of cells, filled with fluid. At first it floats freely in the uterus. Soon, however, the outermost layer of its cells produces threadlike structures that work themselves into the soft lining of the wall of the uterus. This implantation process is difficult and is not always accomplished successfully. When it's unsuccessful, the blastula is expelled during the woman's next menstrual period.

If all goes well, the blastula is firmly implanted in the uterine wall by the tenth or twelfth day after conception. Some of the cells from its outermost layer will develop into the **umbilical cord,** the **placenta** (the organ that nourishes the developing life in the uterus), and the **amnion** (the protective sac, filled with fluid, that encloses the growing baby throughout its prenatal existence).

Soon the inner mass of cells of the blastula separates into layers. The outer layer develops into the cells of the skin and the nervous system. The inner layer forms the cells that will make up some of the internal organs of the baby's body. The remaining organs, plus the muscles and the bones, will come from the cells of the middle layer.

The Stage of the Embryo.   When this **differentiation** of cells has taken place, the developing human is called an **embryo**. The stage of the embryo begins at two weeks and lasts until two months after conception. The embryo grows rapidly, with growth in the upper part of its body going faster than in the lower part, and growth in the central part going faster than in the outer parts. That is, the head, face, and upper arms take shape before the parts below the

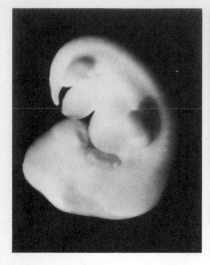

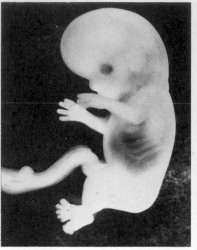

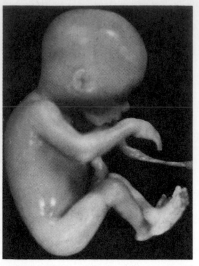

The embryo 1 month after conception.

The fetus 2 months. . .

and 5 months after conception.

waist, and the internal organs and torso develop before the limbs, fingers, and toes.

Two months after conception, the embryo (from now until birth to be called the **fetus**) roughly resembles a human being, though it's only a little over an inch (2.5 cm) long. Its head is disproportionately large and is bent over. Its heart, also disproportionately large, has begun to beat. The fetus floats gently in a watery liquid (the amniotic fluid) within the baglike amnion.

The Stage of the Fetus. The developing human's rate of growth reaches a peak during the early part of the stage of the fetus. Most of the essential organs already exist and now become larger and more complete. Bones start to harden; the external sex organs form. At this point, the fetus can move freely in its watery environment. It can swallow amniotic fluid, clench its fists, move its arms, legs, fingers, and toes, and even turn somersaults (Apgar and Beck, 1972).

During the second **trimester** (three-month period) of pregnancy, the fetus's heartbeat becomes strong enough to be heard through a stethoscope. Fingernails, toenails, hair, eyelashes, and eyebrows appear. Most pregnant women become aware of the fetus's movements for the first time about four months after conception. At this time the first hint of individual differences also appears—some fetuses move around a great deal, while others are relatively quiet. Later in the second trimester comes clear evidence that the fetus's sense of hearing has begun to function. A fetus can hear loud noises in its mother's environment and may react to them with startled movements.

By six months, enough development has occurred to give the fetus a chance, though a slim one, of surviving if it is born prematurely. But usually the fetus remains in the uterus until it is around 38 weeks old, by which time it is ready to make its first public appearance.

Girl or Boy?

About 106 boys are born in the United States for every 100 girls. The proportion of males is believed to be even greater at conception. Evidently, the sperm carrying the boy-producing Y chromosome have a slight edge over those carrying the girl-producing X. It almost seems as though nature permits more males than females to be conceived as a way of compensating for the greater fragility of the male. For all through life—from prenatal development through old age—the male death rate is higher than the female. (This is true not only of deaths from natural causes, but also from accidents, homicides, and suicides.) By age 15, the number of boys and girls is approximately equal. By age 70 there are almost 170 women for every 100 men.

Embryos destined to be male and embryos destined to be female start out exactly alike, inside and out. The sex differences don't appear until the end of the stage of the embryo. The early embryo has a pair of primitive internal glands that can become either ovaries or testes (the male sex glands). Seven or eight weeks after conception these primitive glands begin to develop into ovaries if the embryo has two X chromosomes, into testes if the embryo has an X and a Y. These glands soon start to produce **hormones**—biochemical substances that are present in the blood in very small amounts. It is the hormones that determine what kind of external sex organs the embryo will develop. Testes secrete the male hormone called **androgen**; androgen causes a penis to form. Ovaries secrete the female hormone called **estrogen**; estrogen causes a vagina to form. Actually, the fetus need not produce any hormones at all in order to develop female organs. A female body is invariably formed unless androgen is present, probably because of the influence of the mother's hormones. (In birds, which go through prenatal development *outside* of their mothers' bodies, the situation is just the opposite—the embryo will develop into a male unless its glands secrete estrogen.)

What do we mean by "male" and "female"? Do we judge by the chromosomes, by the sex organs, or by other characteristics such as breasts or beards? In exceptional instances these criteria may not agree. For example, a male athlete can be made to appear womanly by the administration of female hormones, but he will still have the larger bone structure and stronger muscles of the male—and thus an unfair advantage over female athletes in many sports. The Olympic committee defines a person's sex by the chromosomes. When they examine some cells from a female athlete to see if she is "really female," it is genetic sex they are concerned about.

It's the hormones, though, and not the chromosomes, that are responsible for the visible differences between males and females. There's an extremely rare condition in which an XY fetus develops testes and the testes produce androgen, but (probably because of a defective enzyme) the androgen is ineffective—it can't be utilized by the fetus's body. Under the influence of its mother's estrogen, and of the tiny quantities of estrogens that every normal male produces, this fetus develops into a normal-looking baby girl, and later into a normal-looking woman. Except for the fact that she lacks ovaries (so she can't become pregnant), she's female in every respect. Yet the Olympic committee would classify her, on the basis of her XY chromosomes, as a male (Money and Ehrhardt, 1972).

The Development of the Nervous System

The body system that is of most interest to psychologists is the **nervous system**. The nervous system consists of the nerves and the spinal cord, which specialize in transmitting information, and the brain, which specializes in processing and storing information. The brain and the spinal cord together make up the **central nervous system**.

Nerves are of two types, **sensory** and **motor.** Sensory nerves carry messages *to* the central nervous system from the sense organs, the skin, the muscles and joints, and the internal organs. Motor nerves carry messages *from* the central nervous system to the muscles, directing them to contract or relax. Everything you have ever seen, heard, tasted, smelled, or felt has come by way of sensory nerves. Everything you have ever *done* has been accomplished by means of motor nerves.

Like the other parts of the body, the nervous system is composed of cells. The basic cell of the nervous system is the **neuron**. Nerves are made up of bundles of parallel neurons. A nerve's message is carried by the neurons in the form of a very small electrical pulse that moves rapidly down the length of a neuron till it reaches the end. Neurons transmit messages to other neurons at locations called **synapses.** A message from the eye or the toe has to cross a number of synapses before it gets to the brain.

Growth of the Brain.   The nervous system develops from some cells on the outer layer of the early embryo. Twenty-five days after conception these cells have formed a hollow tube. The tube becomes the spinal cord; its front end enlarges to become the brain. The brain develops extremely rapidly. Nine months after conception it contains an estimated 100 billion neurons—as many as there are stars in our galaxy! The rate of brain cell formation during prenatal development averages out to 250,000 a minute (Cowan, 1979). But that average is misleading, because developing cells don't increase in number at an even rate. They increase by dividing in two, doubling in number each time. The increase in the number of cells is slow at the beginning (when 1 becomes 2, 2 becomes 4) and very fast at the end (when 1 billion becomes 2 billion). To get from one cell to 100 billion, it takes only 35 doublings, or one doubling every seven or eight days throughout the pregnancy.

Figure 4–1 shows how the brain changes in size and appearance during prenatal development. The brain of a five-month fetus is smooth, like that of a cat or a rat. Not until seven months after conception does the human brain begin to develop its characteristic wrinkles. These wrinkles are formed because the important outer layer of the brain, the **cortex,** grows faster than the

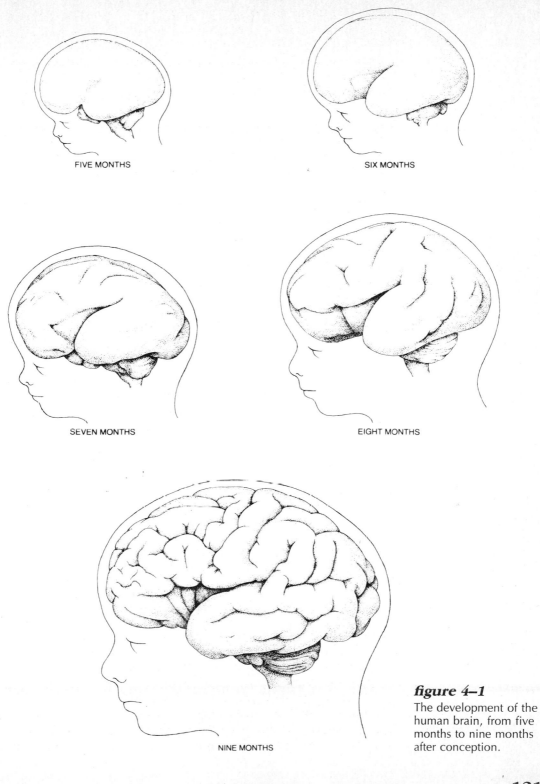

FIVE MONTHS

SIX MONTHS

SEVEN MONTHS

EIGHT MONTHS

NINE MONTHS

figure 4–1
The development of the
human brain, from five
months to nine months
after conception.

inner portions. It is the cortex that enables us to do all the things that differentiate humans from animals—to speak, to think, to plan, and even to laugh.

Making Connections. The nervous system is not just a mass of isolated cells. In order for it to function properly the cells have to be hooked up correctly—they have to form synapses with certain other cells. For example, visual information from the eye has to cross several synapses before it gets to the part of the brain where "seeing" actually occurs. In order for the visual system to function properly, the correct synapses have to be formed, so that a signal from a particular neuron in the eye ends up in exactly the right spot in the brain.

For another example, consider the **reflex.** A reflex is a simple, automatic response to a stimulus. Your leg swings forward when the doctor taps it under the knee (the knee-jerk reflex); the pupil of your eye contracts when a light shines into it (the pupilary reflex). Not many synapses are involved in a reflex—only a small number of neurons (in some cases only one) intervene between the sensory neuron that carries the signal to the brain or spinal cord, and the motor neuron that carries back the order to the muscle. But the synapses have to be the *right* synapses. If the connections are wrong, the reflex won't work: when you're tapped under your knee your *arm* swings up, or when a light shines into your eye you sneeze.

As we will explain in the next chapter, babies are born with reflexes and visual systems that usually work just fine. This means the cells involved have found the right cells to synapse with, out of all the billions of cells in the nervous system. Surely, this is one of the greatest marvels of development!

Yet there is some evidence (Cowan, 1979) that not all the connections made during prenatal development are made correctly. Evidently some cells do grow in the wrong direction, or form the wrong synapses. What seems to happen then is that these wrong cells die or shrink in the first few months after birth. The connections that don't work right are dismantled. The ones that do work, the useful ones, are strengthened. Thus, what happens during the period following birth will determine the final form the nervous system will take.

FACTORS THAT INFLUENCE PRENATAL DEVELOPMENT

What danger can threaten the developing human life that is floating in its watery surroundings, cushioned within the walls of the uterus? Even if its mother suffers a serious accident—a fall down the stairs, for instance—the pregnancy is likely to continue in the usual way. Yet, there may be things in the mother's environment that are potential sources of harm to the child growing within her.

Crossing the Placenta

During prenatal development, oxygen and nutrients from the mother's bloodstream are transmitted to the fetus. At the same time, carbon dioxide and other waste products from the fetus are deposited into the mother's bloodstream for disposal by her body. This exchange takes place in the placenta, to which the fetus is attached by way of the umbilical cord. The placenta is a unique organ: it contains the interwoven blood vessels of the mother and the unborn child. The connection is not direct, though—the two blood supplies never actually mingle. But the mother's blood vessels lie close enough to the fetus's to permit molecules to pass from one to the other. Substances transmitted in this way are said to **cross the placenta.**

Any substance that is dissolved in the mother's blood can cross the placenta and affect the fetus's development or its behavior. For example, antibodies in the mother's bloodstream can cross over to the fetus's. In most cases this is beneficial—it means that the baby is born with at least partial immunity to many diseases. But in one case it is harmful. When the mother's blood type is Rh negative and the fetus's is Rh positive, the mother's body may form antibodies that attack and destroy the fetus's blood cells. This seldom happens in a first pregnancy; usually, it is only after an Rh-negative woman has delivered a Rh-positive child that she becomes sensitized to Rh-positive blood.

In the past many babies died or were left brain-damaged by Rh disease. Nowadays the pregnancies of Rh-negative women are monitored very carefully. If necessary, the baby can be given a complete blood transfusion right after birth, or even *before* birth. But a better solution is to prevent the mother's body from forming those harmful antibodies in the first place. There is now a substance that can be administered to an Rh-negative woman each time she has a child. It will protect her *next* baby, by keeping her from becoming sensitized to Rh-positive blood.

Teratogens

The term **teratogen** refers to any environmental factor that can produce abnormalities in the developing embryo or fetus. Potential teratogens include diseases, drugs, hormones, nicotine, alcohol, radiation, and pollution.

Diseases. Disease-producing microorganisms are a source of possible harm to the unborn child. One infectious organism that is particularly harmful to the developing embryo is the **rubella** virus. Rubella, commonly known as German measles, is a mild illness that produces a fever and a slight rash. When a woman contracts it in early pregnancy, it attacks the embryo, usually causing serious birth defects such as blindness, deafness, and heart abnormalities. But because the mother's symptoms are so mild that they may not even be noticed, the connection between rubella and birth defects was not made until 1941. Now there is a vaccine for rubella. When we inoculate

PROBLEMS IN DEVELOPMENT

Birth Defects

If the first question parents ask about their new baby is "boy or girl?" don't be misled: that's *not* ordinarily their biggest concern. Perhaps they ask that question first just so they'll know what pronoun to use for the crucial second question: "Is she all right?" "Is he all right?" No matter how deeply parents may desire a baby of a particular sex, their first wish is to have a normal, healthy child. In most cases this wish comes true.

But sometimes, unfortunately, it doesn't. Birth defects range in severity from merely annoying (for instance, the dark-red birthmarks that mar the faces of some newborns but fade away as they grow older) to quickly fatal (for instance, anencephaly, the absence of most of the brain). They include problems that are easily correctable by surgery, such as pyloric stenosis (an overdeveloped muscle at the top of the intestine, which prevents the passage of food), and problems that require more delicate surgical techniques, such as cleft lip and cleft palate (where the two sides of the upper lip or the roof of the mouth have failed to join together during early development). Some birth defects, such as deafness and muscular dystrophy, may not be detected until months or years later. With others, such as Down's syndrome (which we discussed in Chapter 2) and spina bifida (a serious malformation of the spine), the parents know almost at once that their child will probably never be able to lead a normal life. Some Down's syndrome babies and many spina bifida babies die in the first days or weeks after birth. The spina bifida survivors are often left partially paralyzed, unable to use their legs or to gain control of bowel and bladder.

Can birth defects be prevented? Some can. In Chapter 2 we described abnormalities that are due to defective genes or chromosomal accidents. A number of tests are now available that can detect carriers of these defects or the presence of an abnormality in the early fetus. The value of many of these tests depends on whether the parents of the fetus are willing and able to consider abortion. Most do choose that alternative when told that they will otherwise have a child born with a serious defect. In the past, many of the children committed to institutions for the mentally retarded have been Down's syndrome children. Now, with amniocentesis and abortion available, the number of Down's syndrome children born each year is steadily decreasing.

Another class of birth defects are those that are only partly genetic—they are inherited in a polygenic fashion, so their appearance depends both on receiving a certain number of unfavorable genes *and* on the presence of unknown environmental factors in the uterus. Spina bifida, anencephaly, cleft lip, and cleft palate are all in this category. The embryo inherits, not the abnormality itself, but rather an increased risk of developing it. Since the abnormality doesn't depend only on heredity, even identical twins may be affected differently. When one identical twin

school-age children against rubella (as is required in many states), we are protecting not them, but the children who have not yet been born.

Several other kinds of infectious organisms can cross the placenta, including those that cause mumps, measles, chicken pox, polio, and the venereal disease **syphilis.** Before the discovery of antibiotics, syphilis was responsible

is born with a cleft lip, 60 percent of the time the other twin is normal (Nyhan, 1976).

Progress in dealing with these polygenic defects has been made. Prenatal detection of anencephaly and spinal bifida is now possible—fairly accurate ways of testing the fetus for these defects currently exist. Modern surgical techniques make cleft lip less disfiguring than it once was, and cleft palate less of a problem.

The birth defects that we have the greatest opportunity to do something about are those due primarily to environmental factors. In some cases, what seems to be a random stroke of fate can be traced to a specific causal factor. That was what happened in the case of the thalidomide tragedy. Occasionally, for no obvious reason, a baby is born missing an arm, or both arms, or both legs. Usually this defect is extremely rare, so when a German geneticist saw several affected babies in a short space of time, he began to investigate. A prescription drug named **thalidomide** was eventually found to be the culprit. Fortunately, thalidomide was never approved for release in the United States, but in Canada, Europe, and England an estimated 8,000 babies were born with missing or deformed arms or legs. Their mothers had taken thalidomide during the first trimester of pregnancy, to quell nausea and vomiting.

Because of the rapid growth of the embryo and fetus in the first trimester of pregnancy, many environmental influences have their greatest impact at this time. Harmful environmental influences during early pregnancy are responsible for nearly all nongenetic birth defects, including structural deformities such as missing limbs and sensory defects such as some forms of deafness and blindness.

The thalidomide disaster illustrates an impor-

This child was born with deformed arms because his mother took thalidomide in early pregnancy.

tant point: prenatal development does not take place in a totally isolated, protected environment. What the pregnant woman eats or doesn't eat, what she smokes, drinks, or injects into her body, the viruses and bacteria to which she is exposed, all are potentially capable of harming the tiny embryo inside her—an embryo that she may not yet even know she is carrying. ∎

for many stillbirths and deformities. Now, tests for syphilis are required in many states, and women who are found to have the disease can be treated with antibiotics even after they become pregnant. (Such treatment is effective because the organism that causes syphilis cannot cross the placenta during the early months of pregnancy.) The combination of better detection of the disease and more effective treatment of it has significantly reduced the number of birth defects due to syphilis.

Today, the venereal disease that worries people most—because it is still incurable—is **genital herpes.** The herpes virus can be transmitted to the baby during its passage through the vagina. A herpes infection in the newborn is often fatal, even though it virtually never kills the adults who carry and transmit it.

Toxoplasmosis is another disease that produces no more than a mild infection in adults but represents a great threat to the fetus. Toxoplasmosis is caused by a parasite sometimes present in uncooked meat and, more frequently, in cat droppings. For this reason, pregnant women should not eat undercooked meat, and they should ask someone else to clean their cat's litter box.

Not all the diseases that threaten the fetus are produced by microorganisms. **Toxemia** is a relatively common disorder of pregnancy. Pregnant women who are still in their teens or who live in disadvantaged homes are particularly likely to be affected. The precise causes of toxemia are still not understood; one theory attributes it to harmful substances produced by the woman's own body during pregnancy. Toxemia almost always strikes during the last trimester of pregnancy. Its symptoms include high blood pressure, excessive water retention, and protein in the urine. Most cases of toxemia can be successfully diagnosed and treated. If it is untreated, it may eventually be fatal to both mother and fetus.

Synthetic Hormones. As we mentioned earlier, hormones secreted by the fetus's body play an important role in the normal development of the reproductive organs. Synthetic hormones, too, can influence prenatal development, but the effects are likely to be unfavorable rather than helpful. How does the fetus come in contact with these potentially harmful synthetic hormones? One way is if the mother continues to use oral contraceptives after she becomes pregnant (but before she realizes she is pregnant). Another possible source of prenatal exposure to synthetic hormones is when they are given to a pregnant woman to prevent a miscarriage. This practice is on the decline, now that research shows that synthetic hormones can influence the physical characteristics, and even the psychological characteristics, of the developing child.

The best-known example of a synthetic hormone that can harm the fetus is diethylstilbestrol, usually called **DES.** DES is a synthetic form of the female hormone estrogen; it was routinely prescribed in the 1950s and 60s to prevent miscarriage in the early months of pregnancy. This practice was stopped when researchers found a relationship between the use of DES and the incidence of certain types of cancer, years later, in the daughters of women who had been given the drug. These young women, who had been exposed to DES months before they were born, run a much greater than normal risk of developing cancer of the vagina. Furthermore, DES daughters are significantly more likely than other women to experience complications during their own pregnancies (Barnes and others, 1980).

The evidence that synthetic hormones can influence the personality of the unborn child is of considerable interest, because it's a clear example of how chemical and biological processes can influence social behavior. One study (Reinisch, 1977) found a relationship between children's personalities and the particular combination of synthetic estrogen and progesterone (another female hormone) that their mothers took while pregnant. When the drug used during pregnancy was primarily progesterone, the children tended to be independent, self-assured, and self-sufficient. The children who had been exposed mostly to estrogen were significantly more group-oriented and group-dependent. These effects were found in both boys and girls.

Prescription Drugs.   The devastating effects of thalidomide on prenatal development have already been described (see the box on Birth Defects). Many other prescription drugs are known to cross the placenta. The dose and duration of drug use, as well as the stage of development during which the embryo or fetus is exposed to the drug, are all factors that determine the amount of risk and the specific effects produced by the drug.

Opiates.   The use of opiates, typically in the form of heroin or methadone, has been associated with delayed prenatal growth. The child of a woman who is an opiate user during pregnancy will also be physically addicted to the substance at birth. After birth the infant will undergo severe withdrawal. The symptoms might include hyperactivity, vomiting, and fever. He or she may cry more than most babies and in a particularly shrill voice, and there may also be muscle tremors (Zelson, 1978).

Alcohol.   It has recently become clear that alcohol poses a definite threat to the fetus. Alcoholic mothers run a sizable risk of giving birth to an infant with **fetal alcohol syndrome.** These infants have certain characteristic abnormalities of the face and head and may also have defects of the limbs and heart. Their mental and physical development tends to be slower than average. Some of these symptoms have shown up in babies of women who drank the equivalent of only three or four cocktails a day (Hanson, Streissguth, and Smith, 1978).

Alcohol seems to have a direct influence on brain development in the fetus. In several studies, mental retardation has been associated with drinking during pregnancy. Alcohol use during the third trimester appears to have the most pronounced effect on brain development, for it is during this period that the brain is growing most rapidly (Stechler and Halton, 1982).

Even moderate amounts of alcohol have been shown to have an immediate effect on the behavior of the fetus. In one experiment (Fox and others, 1978) moderate drinkers in the third trimester of pregnancy were given a mixed drink containing 1 ounce of vodka. A similar group of women received a nonalcoholic drink. The fetuses of the women who had received the nonalcoholic drink continued to make certain rhythmic movements that fetuses normally make. These movements stopped, sometimes for as long as 30 minutes, in the fetuses of the women who had received the vodka. As the blood alcohol level in these women decreased, the movements of the fetuses began again.

Tobacco.   Tobacco is another substance that has been found to have unfavorable influences on prenatal development. Recent figures show that 28 percent of women of childbearing age are cigarette smokers. A woman who smokes gives birth to a baby that weighs, on the average, 200 grams (about half a pound) less than the baby of a nonsmoker (Finnegan and Fehr, 1980). The smoker's baby is small because it has not grown as much as it should have in the uterus, not because it is born too early. The results of several studies reveal that cigarette smoking during pregnancy affects development by depriving the fetus of oxygen (Stechler and Halton, 1982).

Cigarette smoking during pregnancy has also been linked to a higher risk of miscarriage and of abnormalities such as anencephaly, cleft lip and palate, and reduced head size. The risk that the baby will die just before or just after birth is 35 percent greater than for the baby of a nonsmoker (Finnegan and Fehr, 1980). The smoker's child is also more likely to die suddenly in the first few months of life for no apparent reason—the so-called *sudden infant death syndrome*, which we'll discuss in the next chapter.

Environmental Hazards and Other Prenatal Influences

Although a pregnant woman may take care to eat well and to refrain from drug use and smoking, she may still be exposed to environmental influences that could harm the fetus. For example, exposure to radiation can cause death of the fetus, major developmental abnormalities, and mental retardation. Chemicals and pollutants such as methyl mercury and hexachorophene have been found to cause severe birth defects and behavioral abnormalities. Most environmental hazards of this type affect the fetus by crossing the placenta, but some, such as radiation, can act upon it directly.

Emotional Stress.   Although it is difficult to conduct and evaluate research on the effects of a woman's emotions on the prenatal development of her child, several investigators have found a relationship between stressful life events and pre- and post-natal abnormalities. Emotional upset and anxiety in the mother have been associated with mental retardation and behavior problems in the child. Marital discord during pregnancy, anxiety about the marriage, moving to a new home, and an unwanted pregnancy all increase the risk of poor infant health or behavioral disturbances (Stott and Latchford, 1976).

The Expectant Father.   A father can indirectly influence prenatal development by his attitude and behavior, in a way that is either helpful or harmful. It has been noted that a husband's concern for his wife's health can be an important factor in how well the expectant mother takes care of her body. Likewise, an interested and supportive husband can relieve some of the emotional stress his wife experiences during pregnancy.

BIRTH

In the section that introduced this chapter, we described the birth of an infant. Aside from the presence of the father in the delivery room (which is still not permitted in some hospitals), the events we described were those that occur most typically or frequently. It is still the case that most babies in this country are born to married couples and are delivered in a hospital by a physician. Most are born head first and are full-term, healthy infants. Slightly more are male than female.

Stages of Labor

We've already mentioned that for most full-term pregnancies, birth occurs about 38 weeks after conception. The event of birth involves three stages. The first stage, **dilation,** begins with the onset of labor. The involuntary contractions of the uterus that occur during labor serve to widen the opening of the **cervix**—the entrance to the uterus through which the baby will pass. This stage of childbirth takes about twelve hours, on the average, for women delivering their first child, but there are considerable differences from one woman to another. (Compared with her first labor and delivery, a woman's later childbirths are faster and easier.)

As the dilation stage progresses, the contractions become more intense, longer, and more frequent, until they are finally coming as rapidly as one every 60 seconds. At the end of the dilation stage the woman experiences very intense contractions as the cervix is stretched around the baby's head.

Birth occurs during the second stage of labor. Over a period of about an hour, intense and highly coordinated contractions push the baby through the vagina and into the world. During the third and final stage of labor, several minutes after the delivery of the baby, the placenta is expelled.

Complications of Birth

The day of birth is the most hazardous time in a child's life, and until relatively recently it was a hazardous time in the life of the mother as well.

Anoxia. Complications during the birth process can cause the baby to suffer **anoxia,** which means that he or she is not getting enough oxygen. Anoxia may occur prenatally if the mother is anemic, takes certain drugs, smokes cigarettes, or drinks alcohol. It can also result from the placenta or umbilical cord being damaged or defective. Anoxia may occur at birth if the umbilical cord is pinched shut for any reason during the birth process, or if the baby fails to begin breathing immediately.

Severe anoxia can be fatal; milder anoxia can destroy some of the baby's brain cells. The brain damage may later show up as cerebral palsy or mental retardation. However, even for babies who do not breathe on their own and have to be resuscitated, the risk of serious brain damage is still low. The neonatal brain can apparently withstand a much longer period of oxygen deprivation than the brain of an older person.

Nevertheless, even mild or very brief anoxia may have effects that can be detected later, though they are not as severe or as lasting as mental retardation or cerebral palsy. Several studies have found that babies who suffered mild oxygen deprivation at birth tend to cry more than other infants, and later to show higher rates of learning disabilities and behavior difficulties, although the problems appear to lessen with age (Stechler and Halton, 1982).

Unusual Birth Positions.   A common complication of childbirth occurs when the fetus is not in the typical head-first position at the beginning of labor. This condition is more frequently found in premature deliveries than in those that are full-term. Some babies emerge feet or buttocks first; this is known as a **breech birth.** A breech birth is hard on the child, and if there are signs of trouble, most obstetricians will perform a **cesarean.** In this surgical procedure, an incision is made through the woman's abdomen and uterus so that the baby can be removed through the incision, rather than having to pass through the vagina. Cesareans are a matter of necessity when the fetus is positioned sideways in the uterus, or when the mother's pelvis or birth canal are too narrow for the baby's head to pass through.

Forceps Delivery.   A medical procedure that is often used when there are birth complications is **forceps delivery.** Forceps are two metal tongs shaped to fit around the baby's head. The physician may use forceps during the second stage of labor to hasten and ease delivery, or in the case of a breech birth, or when there are signs that the baby is in difficulty. However, the procedure can lead to complications of its own. If forceps are applied too early in labor or too roughly, brain damage is a possible result. Thus, forceps must be used with great care and skill.

Medication During Childbirth.   The use of medication, including pain-killers, sedatives, and stimulants, is quite routine in childbirth. Medication may be used to reduce the pain of labor, to ease the mother's anxiety, or to hasten the birth process by speeding or strengthening the contractions. Although such drugs may benefit the mother and in some cases are necessary, they can cross the placenta and may have unfavorable effects on the fetus. (This is one reason that general anesthetics, which produce unconsciousness, are now seldom used for childbirth.)

Newborns who have been exposed to pain-killing drugs in the hours preceding their birth may be rather sluggish for a few days or even weeks. They may be less alert, less socially responsive, less attentive to visual stimuli, and less active. Of course, these effects will depend on the drug that is used and on its dosage and timing.

PROBLEMS IN DEVELOPMENT

Low-Birthweight Babies

The average weight of an infant at birth is a little over 7 pounds (3,200 grams), with girls weighing slightly less than boys. Traditionally, any baby weighing in at less than 5½ pounds (2,500 grams) has been considered "premature." About 7.5 percent of American babies fall into this category. But this group actually includes two kinds of low-birthweight infants: those who were truly born too soon, and those who are small despite being full-term or nearly full-term. Babies in the second group are called **small-for-dates.** Various disorders of pregnancy may produce small-for-dates babies. A small baby is also more likely if the mother smokes, or if she doesn't get the proper nutrition during pregnancy. "Proper nutrition" doesn't just mean vitamins, minerals, and proteins—it means an adequate intake of calories, too. A woman who eats enough to gain 30 pounds during pregnancy will, on the average, have a bigger baby than one who gains only 15 pounds. In the past, many obstetricians firmly instructed their patients to limit their weight gain to 15 or 18 pounds (7 or 8 kg). Now it is recognized that healthier babies are produced by women who gain 25 to 30 pounds (11 to 14 kg) during pregnancy.

Most cases of low birthweight are simply due to premature birth—properly defined as delivery three weeks or more before the due date. The exact cause of a premature birth is generally impossible to determine, but the problem is more common among teenage mothers and among women from lower socioeconomic classes. Prematurity is the rule, rather than the exception, in multiple births. Twins are born three weeks early, on the average; triplets and quadruplets are usually earlier still. These sharers of a crowded uterus are also apt to be small-for-dates. But weight may vary considerably, even between identical twins developing at the same time in the same uterus. Some locations in the uterus provide a more favorable environment for development than other locations. Identical twins may differ in birthweight by a pound or two. The lighter twin is likely to remain somewhat smaller than his or her sibling all through life. Babies who are born small because they are born early will generally catch up in the long run, but small-for-dates babies tend to remain slightly smaller than their agemates (Tanner, 1978).

In the past, any baby weighing under 2,000 grams (about 4½ pounds) had a relatively poor chance of surviving. But advances in medical techniques have produced a dramatic improvement in survival rates over the past 20 years. Nowadays, a sizable majority of babies over 1,500 grams (3.3 pounds) are saved, and even when the birthweight is under 1,500 grams, the chance of survival is better than 25 percent.

The most common cause of death in premature infants is breathing difficulties, which result from the immaturity of their lungs. Babies born more than five weeks early often exhibit signs of

Alternative Methods of Childbirth

Because of concerns about customary childbirth procedures in the United States, alternative methods of childbirth have gained popularity in recent years. These methods include natural childbirth, the Leboyer method, home delivery, and the use of birthing centers.

respiratory distress—breathing may be irregular or it may even cease entirely. Very premature infants are born without fully developed reflexes and need special medical care. Heated **isolettes** are used to maintain them at a suitable temperature until they are developed enough to regulate their own body temperatures. Isolettes also protect them from infection, which is important because these infants are more susceptible than larger, fully developed newborns.

What happens to the very small premature babies who survive? Are we saving these miniature babies only to have them grow up defective—crippled or retarded? Happily, the answer is no, in most cases. Although problems such as cerebral palsy and mental retardation are definitely more prevalent in children who were extremely small at birth, at least 85 percent of these survivors turn out to be physically and intellectually normal (Hansen, Belmont, and Stein, 1980). ∎

A low-birthweight baby in an isolette.

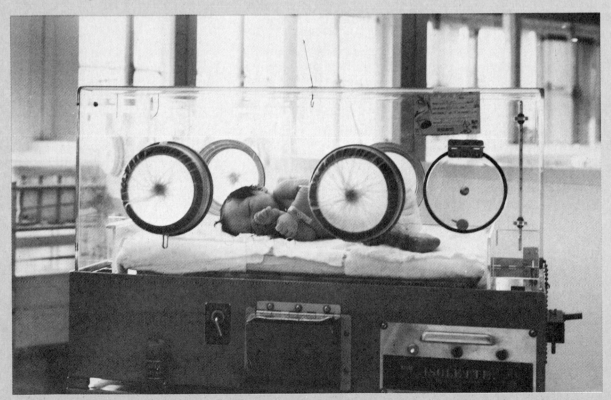

Natural Childbirth.   **Natural childbirth** (sometimes referred to as the Lamaze method) usually means that the mother receives a minimum of drugs—or better still, none at all—during labor and delivery. Expectant parents who opt for natural childbirth often enroll in childbirth-preparation classes during the last months of pregnancy. During pregnancy the expectant mother practices exercises and breathing techniques that will help her cope with the pain of labor contractions. Ideally, the expectant father attends these prenatal classes too, and learns to coach the mother in her exercises. The importance of the father's role in providing comfort and encouragement during labor and delivery should not be underestimated. One study (Sosa, Kennell, and Klaus, 1980) found that the presence of someone who provided emotional support and conversation during labor significantly reduced the length of labor and the probability of complications during labor and delivery. There was also more interaction, immediately after birth, between the mother and the baby.

The Leboyer Method.   Another variation on the theme of childbirth is the **Leboyer method.** Frederick Leboyer is a French obstetrician who has pioneered the concept of "gentle birth." He believes that the way newborns are usually introduced into this world is needlessly cruel and frightening—they emerge from a world of warmth and darkness into a cold noisy room with bright lights shining at them. They're held upside down and possibly slapped. The umbilical cord is cut almost immediately, so babies must learn to breathe on their own at once.

Leboyer's method is quite different. He feels that the newborn should be welcomed to this world with gentleness and compassion. In a Leboyer birth, the room is dimly lit and noise is kept at a minimum. When the baby is born it is placed on the mother's abdomen. The cord is not cut until the blood vessels it contains cease to throb. Then the newborn is placed in a warm bath, to ease the transition from the warmth of the uterus.

Does a baby born by the Leboyer method have a better head start in life than a baby born in the usual American fashion? That's impossible to say at this point. Parents who choose the Leboyer method are likely to differ, as a group, from those who don't choose it. They are likely to be better educated and to provide the kind of home environment that will stimulate intellectual and social development. So if their babies turn out to be better adjusted or more intelligent than average, there's no way of knowing whether this is due to their "gentle" birth or to any of a number of other factors. It should also be mentioned that critics of the gentle-birth method claim that the dim lighting of the birth room may prevent the physician from quickly detecting signs of distress, such as poor color or breathing difficulties, in the newborn.

Other Variations.   There are several other variations in childbirth practices. One, of course, is giving birth at home rather than in a hospital. Another is having a specially trained nurse attend the birth as a midwife instead of using a physician. Finally, **birthing centers** have become popular in recent years. A birthing center may be part of a hospital or it may be a separate facility. A homelike, relaxed atmosphere prevails, and family and friends are welcome.

Childbirth in Other Societies.   We've so far looked at childbirth only as it's likely to occur within our own culture. If you feel, as Leboyer does, that being born in an ordinary American or European hospital is a harsh and frightening experience, consider this description of birth in a primitive society:

> The baby is born on an unsheltered hillside, where the mother and attending women crouch shivering over a tiny fire until finally the baby falls with a soft little thud on a cold, dew-coated leaf—to be left there, perhaps five minutes, while the mother herself cuts and ties the cord, packs up the placenta, and wipes out the baby's eyes and nose. Only then can the squirming, exposed little creature be gathered up and laid against the mother's breast. (Mead, 1955, pp. 54–55)

Perhaps birth is bound to be a shock to a baby, no matter how "gentle" we try to make it. The great differences in childbirth customs and procedures from one culture to another may be insignificant compared to the greater difference between life in the uterus and life outside of it.

> At birth itself, whether the mother kneels squatting holding on to two poles or to a piece of rattan hung from the ceiling—whether she is segregated among females or held around the waist by her husband, sits in the middle of a group of gaming visitors or is strapped on a modern delivery table—the child receives a sharp initial contact with the world as it is pulled, hauled, dropped, pitched, from its perfectly modulated even environment into the outer world, a world where temperature, pressure, and nourishment are all different, and where it must breath to live. (Mead, 1955, p. 54)

summary

1. The **prenatal period** starts at the moment of conception and ends at the moment of birth. In humans, this period averages 266 days (38 weeks) in length.

2. **Conception,** when a man's sperm unites with a woman's egg, normally takes place in one of the **Fallopian tubes.** Recently, however, some human babies have been conceived outside of their mothers' bodies, in a glass dish containing egg cells and sperm. The genetic characteristics of such a baby are determined by the genes in the egg cell and the sperm that were involved in the conception, and not by the uterus in which it develops.

3. Prenatal development can be divided into three stages: the **germinal** stage, the stage of the **embryo,** and the stage of the **fetus.** In the germinal stage, the fertilized egg (a single cell containing 46 chromosomes) divides, forming two cells, then four, and so on. The cells form a hollow ball called a **blastula,** which implants itself in the wall of the uterus. Some of the outer cells of the blastula develop into the **umbilical cord,** the **placenta,** and the **amnion** (a protective sac filled with fluid). The rest of the blastula undergoes **differentiation:** the cells from the outer layer form the skin and the nervous system, those from the inner layer form some of the internal organs, and those from the middle layer form muscles, bones, and the remaining internal organs.

4. About two weeks after conception, the developing organism is called an **embryo.** The embryo grows rapidly. Two months after conception it roughly resembles a human being, though it's only a little over an inch (2.5 cm) in length. Most of its essential organs now exist; its heart has begun to beat. It is now called a **fetus.**

5. The growth rate reaches a peak in the early part of the stage of the fetus. Bones harden, the external sex organs form. The fetus can move nearly every part of its body.

6. In the second **trimester** (three-month period) of pregnancy, the mother can detect the fetus's movements for the first time. The fetus grows hair and nails; it reacts to loud sounds in its mother's environment. By the end of the second trimester, the fetus has a slim chance of surviving if it is born early.

7. Many more boys than girls are conceived, but the death rate for males is higher than that for females from conception through old age. At birth, boys outnumber girls by about 106 to 100.

8. Visible sex differences don't appear until early in the stage of the fetus. The primitive sex glands of the early embryo become the ovaries of a female or the testes of a male. Ovaries secrete **estrogen,** which causes female internal and external sex organs to form. Testes secrete **androgen,** which causes male organs to form. It's these hormones, rather than the chromosomes, that produce the visible differences between males and females.

9. The **nervous system** consists of the brain, the spinal cord, and the nerves. The basic unit of the nervous system is a cell called a **neuron.** At birth, the human brain contains an estimated 100 billion neurons. Brain growth is fastest in the last trimester of pregnancy.

10. Neurons transmit messages to other neurons at locations called **synapses.** The fact that babies are born with many reflexes in working order indicates that most (though probably not all) of their neurons have managed to form the proper synapses with other neurons.

11. In the **placenta,** the mother's blood vessels are interwoven with those of the developing child in such a way that molecules can pass between them. In this way, nourishment from the mother is provided to the embryo or fetus; its waste products are transferred to the mother. Any substance dissolved in the mother's blood can **cross the placenta.** Sometimes this has a beneficial effect, as when the mother's immunities are transmitted to the unborn child. Sometimes this is harmful, as when the body of an Rh-negative mother who has been sensitized to Rh-positive blood sends out antibodies that destroy the blood cells of an Rh-positive fetus. It is

now possible to prevent Rh-negative women from developing such a sensitivity.

12. Birth defects are of three types: abnormalities due to defective genes or chromosomal accidents (many of these can now be detected through amniocentesis), those that are partly genetic and partly environmental, and those due entirely to unfavorable environmental influences. It is the defects in the last category that we have the best opportunity to prevent.

13. A **teratogen** is anything that can produce abnormalities in the developing embryo or fetus. Because growth is most rapid in the first trimester of development, teratogens have their greatest impact at this time. Many women who took thalidomide in the first trimester of their pregnancies gave birth to babies with missing or deformed limbs.

14. Disease-producing microorganisms can cross the placenta and damage the embryo or fetus. The **rubella** virus is particularly harmful—it can cause blindness, deafness, and heart abnormalities. Other diseases that pose a threat to the unborn child are **syphilis, toxoplasmosis,** and a disorder of pregnancy called **toxemia** (which is not caused by an infectious organism). **Genital herpes** can infect a baby during its passage through the vagina, producing a potentially fatal infection.

15. Synthetic hormones taken in order to prevent miscarriage can have harmful effects on the embryo. This is particularly clear in the case of **DES,** a synthetic form of estrogen. Abnormalities of the reproductive system have been found in the daughters of women who were given DES during early pregnancy to prevent miscarriage. Synthetic hormones can even influence the personality of the unborn child.

16. The use of heroin or methadone during pregnancy results in delayed prenatal growth, and the child is born physically addicted to the opiate.

17. Alcoholic mothers run the risk of giving birth to a baby with **fetal alcohol syndrome,** which consists of various physical abnormalities plus retarded mental development. Even moderate amounts of alcohol may affect the fetus.

18. Tobacco has a harmful effect on prenatal development. The baby of a smoker is smaller at birth than that of a nonsmoker, and significantly more likely to die, either before or after birth.

19. Other environmental hazards to the unborn child include pollutants and radiation.

20. Emotional stress and anxiety in a pregnant woman can have harmful effects on the development of her child. A husband can be of benefit by providing emotional support and by showing concern for his wife's health.

21. In the first stage of labor, **dilation,** contractions of the uterus widen the opening of the cervix. In the second stage, the baby is delivered. In the third stage, the placenta is expelled.

22. **Anoxia,** a failure to get enough oxygen, is a threat to the baby during and immediately after birth. Anoxia can destroy some of the baby's brain cells, producing mental retardation or cerebral palsy; in extreme cases it can be fatal. Even mild anoxia may have noticeable effects.

23. A **breech birth,** in which the feet or buttocks are delivered first, is harder on the baby than the normal head-first delivery. If a normal birth is difficult or impossible, or if the baby is in trouble, a **cesarean** may be performed. For less serious complications, a **forceps delivery** may be used.

24. Medication (for instance, pain-killers) used during childbirth can cross the placenta and affect the baby.

25. The average baby weighs a little over 7 pounds (3,200 grams) at birth; girls weigh slightly less than boys.

26. Low-birthweight babies (under 5½ pounds, or 2,500 grams) fall into two categories: those who were born prematurely, and those who are **small-for-dates,** meaning that they didn't grow as much as they should have during their time in the uterus. Small-for-dates babies tend to remain slightly smaller than average throughout their lives, whereas premature babies eventually catch up.

27. Prematurity is more common in teenage and disadvantaged mothers, and in the case of multiple births. Nowadays, a majority of babies weighing over 1,500 grams (3.3 pounds) can be saved. Very small premature babies are generally kept in **isolettes,** which maintain their body temperature and guard them against infection. Although such babies run a higher risk of brain damage and other problems, most turn out to be normal.

28. In **natural childbirth** the mother receives little or no medication and uses exercise and breathing techniques to deal with the pain of labor. Childbirth tends to be somewhat easier if the father is there to give encouragement and support.

29. With the **Leboyer method** ("gentle birth"), an effort is made to make birth less frightening and unpleasant for the baby.

30. Birthing centers, which provide a homelike, relaxed atmosphere and in which family and friends are welcome, have become popular in recent years.

31. Childbirth procedures differ greatly from one culture to another. Such differences probably have less impact on the newborn baby than the much greater difference between life within the uterus and life outside it.

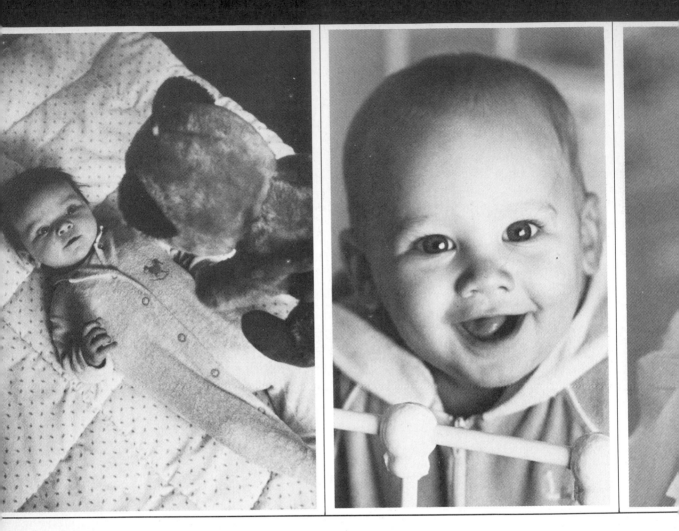

Chapter Five

THE BABY

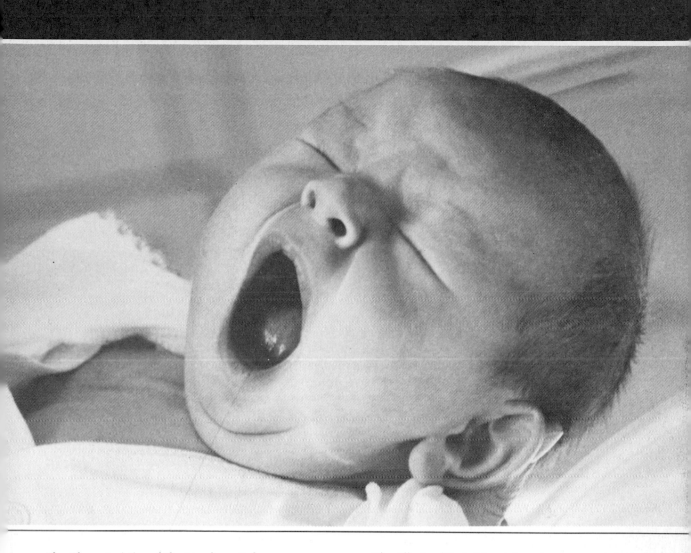

Five

The baby whose birth we witnessed at the beginning of the last chapter now lies quietly in his mother's arms. Although he's not even half an hour old, he already has a name: Michael. Michael appears to be rather unimpressed with his new environment; the vast difference between his life within the uterus and his present surroundings does not seem to have fazed him. One has the impression that he's neither frightened nor confused—just rather sleepy.

To his parents, and also perhaps to us, the newborn baby is one of the world's most interesting people. And yet, he can't tell us a thing! There are so many questions we'd like to ask him, if we could: What was it like being born? What was it like in the uterus? Are you glad to be here? When you dream, what do you dream about? Alas, we can get no answers to any of these questions. But there are many questions to ask about the newborn that *can* be answered. In fact, we now know a great deal more about the **neonate**—the newborn baby—than we did 10 or 15 years ago. Research on the neonate has been a very active and very productive field.

THE CHARACTERISTICS OF THE NEWBORN BABY

At this point, Michael bears little resemblance to the smooth, dimpled babies shown in diaper commercials. His hair is still plastered down with **vernix,** a fatty substance that protected his skin in the uterus and helped to grease his passage down the birth canal. His skin is blotchy and bruised. His eyelids are puffy. He's decidedly hairy, especially on the upper back. (This fine hair, called **lanugo,** will fall out in a few weeks.) But his color is a healthy pink now; he was somewhat blue for the first minute or two after birth, due to a temporary drop in oxygen in his blood. That blueness is perfectly normal for a newborn—it takes a little while for the lungs to clear and start working properly.

Because a quick glance *doesn't* always discriminate a healthy newborn from one that is in serious trouble, most hospitals rate the condition of babies one minute and five minutes after birth by a scoring system known as the **Apgar test** (after Virginia Apgar, its originator). The baby's heart rate, breathing, muscle tone, response to an irritating stimulus, and pinkness of skin are all quickly judged; each gets a score of 2 for good, 0 for poor or absent, and 1 for intermediate. Thus, the highest possible Apgar score is 10, lowest is 0. The lowest scores are generally found in low-birthweight babies and in those few whose umbilical cords have been pinched closed during the birth pro-

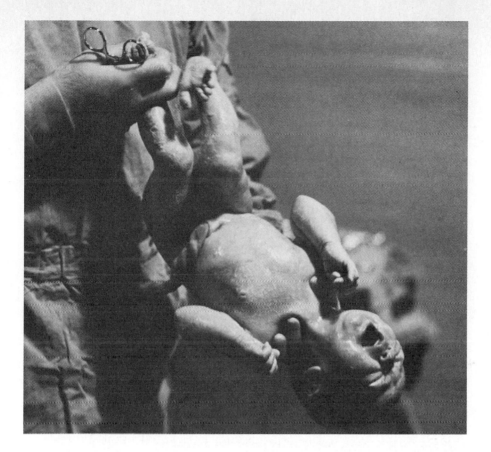

cess. A baby with a low Apgar score has a greater risk of dying, and a slightly greater risk, if he or she survives, of being handicapped in some way.

States of Sleep and Wakefulness

Having successfully navigated the crucial transition from fetus to neonate, Michael sleeps peacefully. As everyone knows, newborn babies spend much of their time sleeping.

Sleep used to be considered a do-nothing time, a time of rest and recuperation from the day's activities. That made it hard to understand why young infants need to sleep so much. Now sleep is known to consist of active periods, as well as quiet ones. In **active sleep,** also known as **REM** (for rapid-eye-movement) sleep, the eyes can be seen moving beneath the closed lids. Muscles twitch, breathing is faster and less regular than in quiet sleep. Adults who are awakened during active sleep usually say they have been dreaming.

Adults spend about a quarter of their sleep time in active sleep. The newborn is in this state about half of his total sleep time—that's about eight hours of active sleep a day, on the average (Roffwarg, Muzio, and Dement, 1966). Premature babies spend even more time in active sleep. Psychologists don't know what purpose active sleep serves, but they believe it's important to the normal functioning of the brain. If adults are deprived only of active sleep, by being awakened every time their eyelids begin to move, they tend to become irritable. When they are allowed to sleep without interruption they will make up the loss by devoting a greater percentage of sleep time to active sleep (Dement, 1974).

How Do Babies Spend Their Spare Time?   When they are not being fed, bathed, or diapered, what do young infants do? To say that they're either asleep or awake is an oversimplification: just as there is more than one kind of sleep, there is more than one kind of wakefulness. Some researchers use the word **state** to describe these various types of sleep and wakefulness. We can think of the baby as going from state to state during the course of a day. Each state is associated with a different level of responsiveness to external stimuli and to stimuli from within the body.

We've already described the two states of sleep, active sleep and quiet sleep. A third state is **drowsiness,** a state between sleep and wakefulness, in which the baby lies fairly quietly while his eyes open and close sleepily. While fully awake, the baby may be **fussy**—whimpering occasionally and moving his arms and legs at times—or **crying,** which includes vigorous movements of the face and body, as well as the conspicuous sound effects. Finally, there's the state that mothers and developmental psychologists like best of all: it's called **quiet alertness.** The baby lies quietly but fully alert, with his eyes wide open. He appears to be very attentive to visual or auditory stimuli. When researchers investigate the abilities or preferences of babies, they generally must wait until babies are in this state.

Psychologists have studied the behavior of neonates as they lie in their cribs between feedings (Berg, Adkinson, and Strock, 1973). Figure 5-1 shows how a typical infant spends his or her time. But individual babies might differ considerably from the percentages shown in this figure. An infant named

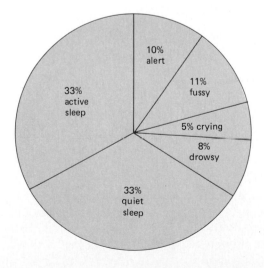

figure 5–1
How newborn babies spend their time. (Data from Berg, Adkinson, and Strock, 1973; Roffwarg, Muzio, and Dement, 1966.)

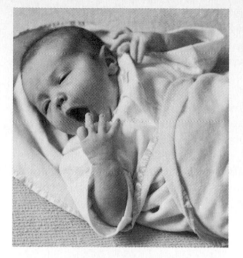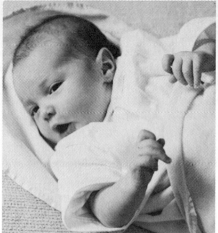

Five states of the young baby: quiet alertness (right top), fussiness (right middle), crying (left middle), drowsiness (left top), and sleeping (bottom).

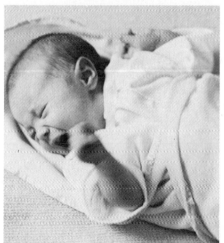

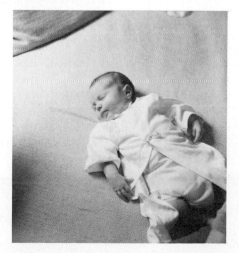

Charles, whose behavior was observed during his first week of life (Brown, 1964), spent more than a third of his time in the state of quiet alertness. Another infant, Ted, spent most of his time sleeping. Dorothy slept a fair amount, but when she was awake she was almost always crying.

Babies do differ enormously in how much they cry. Some cry hardly at all, others spend three or four hours a day at it—most commonly in the early evening. (This "colicky" crying is almost always outgrown by the age of 3 months.) Although babies also differ in how consolable or soothable they are, most will stop crying (at least temporarily) if held in an upright position against an adult's shoulder, especially if the adult is moving rhythmically—rocking in a rocking chair or walking around (Smart and Smart, 1978). Babies also cry less when placed on their stomachs than when lying on their backs (Brackbill, 1973). It seems that they're least happy in a horizontal, face-up position—yet this is the position in which American and European babies tend to spend most of their time. The practices in other cultures differ. For example, a mother of the !Kung San people of southwest Africa holds her infant sitting or standing in her lap, or in a cloth sling on her hip. Melvin Konner, an American anthropologist who studied childrearing practices among the !Kung San, reports:

> Infants are rarely permitted to lie down while awake. Mothers consider that this is bad for infants and that it retards motor development. This is the opposite of the folk belief in the Northwestern United States where vertical posture is considered bad, at least for very young infants. (Konner, 1977, p. 291)

Konner found that !Kung babies score very high on tests of motor development, and speculates that their "vertical posture" might have something to do with their rapid progress.

What Can the Newborn Do?

Immediately after birth, the new baby is able to respond to a wide variety of stimuli. Most of these responses are of the simple kind we call **reflexes.**

Reflexes of the Neonate.   A number of reflexes are essential for life outside the uterus. Human babies share these mechanisms with all baby mammals. The most important are those associated with breathing. A buildup of carbon dioxide in the blood causes breathing to deepen and quicken. In the newborn, whose breathing rhythm is still not firmly established, there may be temporary lulls in breathing and then extra breaths in order to "catch up." Obstructions of the breathing passage trigger sneezes or coughs. A period of shallow breathing leads to a yawn, another way of "catching up."

Second in importance are the reflexes associated with feeding. Michael's mother will not have much milk in her breasts for three or four days, but Michael is already capable of sucking and swallowing. A baby born very prematurely usually *can't* suck or swallow adequately. Such a baby will probably have to be fed through a tube that carries liquids directly to the stomach.

When Michael is put to his mother's breast he shows another reflex called

A touch of the nipple near his mouth or on his cheek causes him to turn his head and move his lips toward the touch, enabling him eventually to get the nipple into his mouth. (He'll do the same thing if you touch his cheek with your finger.)

Among the responses that are important for the baby's survival, we should include crying. It's the baby's signal to his parents that he's hungry or in pain, too hot or too cold. The piercing sounds of a baby's cries are *supposed* to be unpleasant: their function is to motivate the parent to turn them off, by meeting the baby's needs.

Although the baby is entirely dependent on his caregivers for relief from hunger, there are other reflexes for dealing with pain and temperature regulation. A painful stimulus to a limb causes the baby to withdraw the limb. When a doctor must take a few drops of blood from the heel of a newborn baby, the baby will try to pull the leg away. When that proves impossible, the other foot comes up and tries to push the doctor's hand away (Brazelton, 1969).

Babies react to heat and cold in the same ways that older people do. Heat causes the blood vessels in the skin to expand, so that more heat can be lost through the skin. Cold produces the opposite reflex: the blood vessels in the skin contract, so that heat is conserved inside the body. It's easy to tell when babies are cold—they turn pale, then blue. (These color changes are usually detectable even in babies who are destined to be dark-skinned, since the skin is not fully pigmented at birth.) Babies do need to be protected against chilling, because their response to cold is much less efficient than an adult's. They lack the layer of fat that helps to insulate the body of an older person. Furthermore, their small size means that even when most of their blood supply is withdrawn from the skin, it's still much closer to the surface than it is in an adult.

"Useless" Reflexes.   There are a number of reflexes present in the normal newborn that appear to serve no useful purpose at all. Most of these gradually disappear during the first three or four months of life. The **Babinski, Moro,** and **tonic neck** reflexes are all in this class. The Babinski reflex is a response to being stroked on the sole of the foot: when Michael's foot is tickled, his big toe sticks up and the other toes fan outward. The Moro reflex is a startle response to a loud noise or a sudden loss of support. The baby's arms are first flung wildly outward, then quickly brought toward the chest again. The tonic neck reflex can be seen when Michael is lying on his back with his head turned to one side, as it usually is. The arm is extended outwards on the side to which his face is pointing, and the other arm is bent up so the fist is near the back of his head. The baby's body tends to arch away from the side where his face is pointing. This characteristic position makes him look a little like a fencer with sword outstretched.

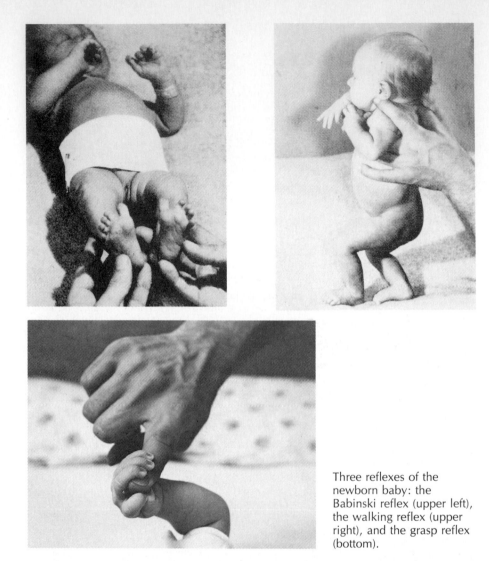

Three reflexes of the
newborn baby: the
Babinski reflex (upper left),
the walking reflex (upper
right), and the grasp reflex
(bottom).

There are other "useless" reflexes that appear to be relics, leftovers from
an earlier evolutionary stage. The **swimming** reflex is one of these: when
placed on his stomach, Michael may rhythmically extend his arms and legs.
The **grasp** reflex causes him to close his hand tightly if something is pressed
in his palm. He grasps so tightly that he can support almost his entire weight
by the grip of his two little fists. Premature babies grasp even more tightly—
they will grip an adult's index fingers firmly enough to be lifted entirely into
the air! The grasp reflex is present in baby monkeys, too. It enables them to
cling to their mothers as they are carried through the trees.

Some "useless" reflexes look forward, rather than backward, in time. The
most interesting of these is the **walking** (or **stepping**) reflex. If Michael is held
firmly in an upright position with his feet touching a solid surface, his legs

will make stepping movements, very similar to real walking—except that, of course, his diminutive legs can't possibly hold the weight of his body. This reflex disappears within a few weeks, and real walking doesn't appear until many months after that. But the walking reflex of the newborn is clearly related in some way to the walking of the toddler. A group of infants were "walked" for three minutes at a time, four times a day, during the first two months of life. Later, these children began to walk independently some five to seven weeks earlier than children who hadn't had this practice (Zelazo, Zelazo, and Kolb, 1972). Notice that during the walking practice the infants were being held upright, like the !Kung San babies—and apparently with similar results. What isn't clear is whether there are any long-term advantages in walking early. Rapid progress in one area of development is not necessarily related to progress in other areas of development, or to development at a later stage.

Some Remarkable Abilities of the Newborn.   The talents of newborns have been studied by T. G. R. Bower, a psychologist at the University of Edinburgh (Scotland) who specializes in infant development. Bower has generated considerable controversy with his claims that newborn babies have a number of

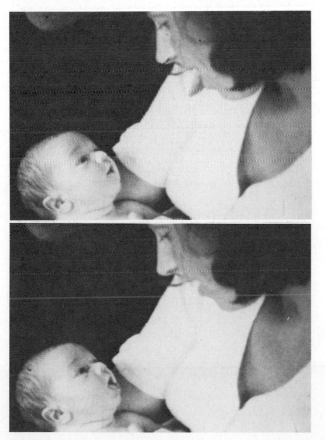

A 6-day-old baby imitates her mother's action.

previously unsuspected abilities. For example, earlier investigators had found that babies begin to reach successfully for nearby objects when they are 4 or 5 months old. Bower has reported successful reaching by babies only a week or two of age. Although these reaching movements are not very accurate, he claims that newborns can hit things and occasionally even grasp them. Bower believes that there are two reasons why this ability generally goes unrecognized. First, most newborns do not ordinarily have objects placed within their reach. Second, Bower (1977b) says that a newborn's body is shaped in such a way that he will roll from side to side unless he uses his arms to support himself. If he is to use his hands to reach for things, the baby must be supported in such a way that his body is steady. It should be noted, however, that other investigators have failed to obtain coordinated reaching movements in newborns (Ruff and Halton, 1978).

At any rate, according to Bower, these early reaching movements disappear at around 4 weeks of age. They don't reappear until three or four months later.

An even more complex type of response has been reported in newborn babies: imitation of adults' facial movements (Bower, 1976; Meltzoff and Moore, 1977). The photographs on page 147 show a baby girl only 6 days old sticking out her tongue in imitation of her mother's action. Think what an incredibly complicated kind of behavior this is: the newborn infant has presumably never seen her own tongue, yet she must somehow make the connection between her mother's tongue and her own. In addition, she must copy a movement that she can see but not feel, with one that she can feel but not see!

It isn't always easy to get very young infants to perform in this way—newborns are easily distracted by other sights or sounds. Developmental psychologist Robert McCall has some comments on getting a young baby to imitate an adult:

> First, infants do not imitate each and every action they see. To be imitated, a behavior must be something that the infant already does frequently. For example, infants are more likely to imitate adults sticking out their tongues than adults who say "bah-bah-bah"....Second, infants will imitate only in special circumstances. Adults must be close enough for the infant to see their behavior clearly; the adults' behavior must be highly distinctive (for instance, the only movement of the face should be made by the tongue); and adults must wait patiently for the baby to perform. After sticking out their tongues, adults should wait motionless, sometimes as long as fifteen or twenty seconds, before trying it again because the sight of their moving face will distract the infant from imitating. (McCall, 1979, pp. 89–91)

Like walking and reaching, imitating also disappears after a short time, not to reappear until the second half of the first year. But this early behavior is interesting, because it implies that the ability to learn through imitation is a very important, very basic human characteristic.

Why the baby appears to be so much cleverer at a week or two than at 2 or 3 months is still not clear. The early abilities seem to be of a primitive, reflexlike nature, and perhaps these abilities must go away for a while so that they can re-emerge at a more complex level.

THE PERCEPTUAL WORLD OF THE INFANT

Almost 100 years ago, the noted American psychologist William James said that newborn babies must perceive the world as a "blooming, buzzing confusion." For many decades after James, the prevailing belief was that babies start out seeing only a meaningless blur of lines and colors swimming around in their visual field, and gradually learn to interpret these stimuli as stationary or moving objects of various shapes and sizes. But we have already given you some evidence against this point of view: the photograph of the 6-day-old baby girl imitating her mother. How could she do this if she saw her mother's face only as a formless blob? Notice, too, how intently she's staring up at her mother. One gets the impression that she's extremely interested in what she sees.

What *are* newborn babies able to see, hear, smell, taste, and feel? How do their sensory capacities develop during infancy? Modern methods for studying perceptual development have revealed that babies are a lot less confused than William James thought, and a lot more capable of perceiving things. (See box.)

Vision

Puppies, kittens, and rats are born with sealed eyes that don't open till a week or two after birth. But newborn monkeys, apes, and humans are born with eyes that are ready to function immediately. Even a baby born two months prematurely can see at birth: the essential working parts of the eye are complete at seven months after conception. The body of a newborn human is only a twentieth of its adult weight; the brain is a fourth. But the human eye only doubles in volume during the course of development. Its diameter at birth is more than 70 percent of an adult's (Maurer, 1975). A baby's eyes look big because they *are* big, compared with the rest of the baby!

A normal neonate like Michael can track a slowly moving object with his eyes, right from the start, and will even turn his head to follow it. But a newborn cannot at first adjust the focus of his eyes to near or far stimuli, the way an older person can. He can see things best when they are between 7 and 15 inches (18–38 cm) away from him. Even at this optimal distance, his acuity is not as good as an older child's—things probably look fairly blurry to Michael. Nevertheless, his vision is good enough to enable him to see a

Some Methods for Finding Out about Infants' Perceptions

Systematic testing of infant visual perception was first performed by Robert Fantz in the late 1950s. Fantz's technique was simple: he put a baby in a little booth and placed two pictures on the ceiling of the booth, not far above the baby's face. Then he watched to see which one she looked at. (He could see the baby's eyes through a peephole in the top of the booth. The lighting was arranged in such a way that whatever the baby looked at was reflected on the shiny surface of her eyes.)

What Fantz found was that babies would usually look at one of the pictures significantly more often than at the other picture, regardless of whether that picture was on the right or the left. Certain kinds of pictures seemed to be preferred over other kinds, and the preferences sometimes changed as the babies got older. This indicates more than just the likes and dislikes of babies: it shows that they could tell the pictures apart. They couldn't very well consistently choose one picture over another (regardless of position) unless they could see that the pictures were different (Fantz, 1958).

So if a baby prefers to look at one picture (or one object) instead of at another, we can be pretty sure that she can see them and that she can tell them apart. But the reverse is not true: if the baby looks equally often at two pictures,

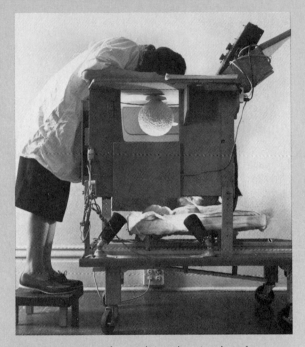

Fantz's apparatus for studying the visual preferences of babies.

that doesn't mean she *can't* see that they're different—only that she likes them equally well. Thus, Fantz's **preferential-looking** technique doesn't enable us to tell if the baby can discriminate between two very similar pictures, since

medium-size freckle on a person's face 11 inches (28 cm) away (McCall, 1979). His vision will improve rapidly: in one month there will be some ability to focus, and in two months his eyes will focus almost as well as an adult's (Aslin and Dumais, 1980). Within six months he will be able to see about as clearly as he ever will.

similar pictures are likely to be similarly attractive. However, there's another technique that does work in this situation—it makes use of a phenomenon called **habituation,** which is the simplest form of learning. First, a baby is shown one picture and given a chance to look at it. After a while, this picture no longer arouses her attention or interest—in other words she **habituates** to it. Then she's shown *two* pictures, the old one and a new one. Almost invariably, babies (like anyone else) will prefer to look at a new picture, rather than one they've seen before—that is, if they can tell the two pictures apart. So if the two pictures are looked at equally, the assumption is that the baby *can't* tell them apart. This technique allows us to test whether babies can detect rather subtle differences between stimuli. It also enables us to test the baby's *memory:* if the two-picture test isn't made until a month after one of the pictures is shown, and the baby *still* prefers the newer one, then she must have some memory of the one she saw previously (Fagan, 1972).

The habituation method can be used to test other sensory systems than vision. One experiment (Bronshtein and Petrova, 1967) was designed to find out whether babies could discriminate between sounds of different pitch. The babies were sucking on a pacifier; when a musical tone was played they showed their interest by slowing, or briefly stopping, their sucking. After several repetitions of the sound they ceased to pay attention to it. But when a different sound was played they once again stopped sucking on the pacifier, showing that they could hear the difference. Similar procedures have been used to test infant discrimination of odors, and of the shapes of objects handled (by older infants) in the dark (Engen and Lipsitt, 1965; Soroka, Corter, and Abramovitch, 1979).

There is a third method that is useful for testing an infant's **visual acuity**—her ability to see things clearly, so they don't look blurred. This technique makes use of the sideways reflex movements of the eyes that result from the visual scene passing in front of the face, as when one looks out a train window or spins around in circles. In this test a curved hood is placed over the baby's head, and a striped pattern moves sideways across the inside surface of the hood. If the stripes are extremely narrow, so narrow that they blur together in the baby's vision, no reflex eye movements will occur. If they do occur, we know that the stripes are wide enough for the baby to see them—in other words, the baby's visual system is capable of distinguishing the stripes. This method is quicker than the preferential-looking or habituation techniques, and it can be used to test the vision of babies who might not respond to pictures—for example, brain-damaged babies (Gorman, Cogen, and Gellis, 1967).

Finally, there are the older, cruder techniques that can tell us, not *what* a baby sees, hears, or feels, but only *whether* she does. When a bright light shines into their eyes, babies who are not totally blind will squeeze their eyes shut. Babies who can hear a loud noise will startle at the sound. (In the early weeks the response is the Moro reflex; later this becomes a more mature form of the startle reflex, minus the outflung arms.) And babies who can feel a pinprick or a mild electric shock inform us of this by pulling away or crying. ∎

Three-dimensional Vision. The ability to see things in three dimensions—some things closer, some farther away—is an important part of human vision. Even with one eye closed you can tell the approximate distance of the objects in an unfamiliar room: you judge by their size, and by the fact that the things that are closer to you block your view of things that are farther away. But the

A baby being tested on the visual cliff.

world seen with one eye has a flat, unconvincing appearance, like a photo instead of the real thing. The world assumes its full three-dimensional appearance only when seen with two eyes. Psychologists call this **stereoscopic vision.** It depends on the fact that the left eye's view is slightly different from the right eye's view. There are specialized neurons in the brain, called **binocular cells,** that receive inputs from both the left eye and the right eye. These cells are responsible for stereoscopic vision.

For a baby to see stereoscopically, he must be able to coordinate his two eyes, so that both point in the same direction. This he can do from birth, to some extent—though not perfectly, not as well as he will be able to in two or three months (Aslin and Dumais, 1980). But we cannot tell just from looking at his eyes whether he sees things in three dimensions. Behavioral tests are required.

The first behavioral evidence that babies have stereo vision came from a well-known experiment by Eleanor Gibson and Richard Walk, of Cornell University. It made use of a setup called a **visual cliff.** This is a sort of big table with a top made of heavy-duty glass. A slightly raised platform runs down the middle. A patterned surface can be seen directly under the glass on one side. On the other side, the patterned surface is way below the glass— this is the ''cliff'' side. In the experiment, babies from 6 to 14 months of age were put on the platform. Their mothers called them, either from the cliff side or the shallow side. Gibson and Walk found that babies were willing to crawl across the shallow side to get to their mothers, but they generally refused to go onto the cliff side. Some babies just sat and cried; some actually crawled in the wrong direction. The experimenters concluded that babies can perceive depth as soon as they can crawl (Gibson and Walk, 1960; Walk and Gibson, 1961).

It's not too surprising that babies of crawling age perceive depth. What about younger babies? In one study (Campos, Langer, and Krowitz, 1970), 2-month-old babies were simply *placed* on the visual-cliff apparatus, on their stomachs. Then the experimenters measured the babies' heart rates. Greater changes in heart rates occurred on the cliff side than on the shallow side, so apparently the babies could at least tell the difference between the two sides.

More direct proof of three-dimensional vision in young infants has been hard to come by. Currently, the best evidence suggests that stereo vision is poor or absent in babies under 3 months of age, but definitely present by 5 months (Fox, Aslin, Shea, and Dumais, 1980).

A related, but slightly different question has to do with **space perception** in infancy: Can babies perceive the locations of objects in space—especially, how far away they are? Even if they have stereo vision, they might not be able to judge distances and directions very well.

The evidence is that they can locate objects in space fairly well, at least in some situations. In two studies, infants between 1 and 11 weeks of age were seated in infant seats. A foam cube, suspended from a pulley, was moved either directly toward the baby's face or moved in a path that would carry it to one side of the baby's face. When the cube was on a "miss" path the babies just watched it calmly, but when it came directly toward them they actually cringed—pulled their heads back and brought their hands up in front of their faces. Even week-old babies, who had certainly never been struck in the face by a moving object, did this! (Bower, Broughton, and Moore, 1970; Ball and Tronick, 1971.)

What Do Babies Like to Look at?   In general, babies of all ages decidedly prefer to look at complex patterns, containing many lines or contours, rather than at plain surfaces or simple patterns. They also prefer patterns with curved lines to patterns with straight lines. For newborns, whose vision is still somewhat fuzzy, size matters too—a pattern with large squares, for example, is preferred to a pattern with small squares (Fantz, Fagan, and Miranda, 1975). Newborns also prefer close objects to distant ones. In fact, a small cube close up is preferred to a large one far away, even if they both take up exactly the same percentage of the visual field (McKenzie and Day, 1972). This, by the way, is additional evidence that young babies can perceive distances.

The contrast of the pattern also matters, especially to younger babies. Black on white (or white on black) produces the greatest contrast, so a young baby will look at a black disk on a white background longer than at a colored disk. Older babies (3 to 6 months) also show no particular attraction to color. Babies of this age will look equally long at a black disk and a colored one (Fantz, Fagan, and Miranda, 1975).

Color Vision.   It's surprising how unimportant color seems to be to babies under 6 months of age. In fact, their lack of interest in color has made it very difficult to determine whether young babies have color vision at all. We still don't know whether neonates can see colors. An experiment with 2-month-olds, however, showed that some color vision is present at this age. The experimenters (Teller, Peeples, and Sekel, 1978) illuminated all but a small area of a testing booth with white light. The small area, which was either on the right or the left side of the booth, was illuminated with colored light. Then the experimenters watched to see whether the babies' eyes would turn toward the colored area. (The intensities of the lights were varied so the babies couldn't respond simply to differences in brightness.)

The 2-month-old babies showed no signs of seeing the colored light when it was greenish-yellow or purple. But they *did* look at the colored area when it was blue, red, orange, or green—so evidently they were able to see those colors. (There's no way of knowing, of course, if blue looks the same to a baby as it looks to you. But then, there's no way of knowing if blue looks the same to *us* as it does to you!)

Even at 4 or 5 months, when given a choice of colors to look at, babies tend not to look at greenish-yellow. By this time they will look at purple, though. Whether they still can't see greenish-yellow isn't clear. Perhaps they just don't like that color. Most adults don't care much for greenish-yellow, either (Bornstein, 1975).

Where Do Babies Look? When babies look at a picture, an object, or a face, where do they look? The answer depends on the age of the baby. New-borns tend to look at the edges of things, at the contours where contrast is greatest. For example, when 1-month-old babies are shown a pattern such as a square with some spots inside it, they will look at the edge of the square instead of at the spots. Similarly, when looking at a face they tend to point their eyes at the line between the forehead and the hair, or at the line between the hair and the background (Salapatek, 1975).

The transition to looking at the features *inside* the contours occurs at about the fifth or sixth week. At that point, a parent might notice that the baby has finally begun to "look me in the eye," or to make **eye contact.** The eyes, in fact, are about all they do look at, at this stage: a 6- to 10-week-old baby will smile at a drawing of a face that contains only eyes. By 3 months the mouth must be there, too (Bower, 1977b).

The Effects of Early Visual Experience.   In our discussion of the development of the nervous system (Chapter Four), we said that useless or erroneous neural connections are eliminated in the first months of life. Neurons and neural connections seem to be kept or discarded on the basis of experience—on what proves to be useful and what doesn't. Thus, the structure of the nervous system is not entirely determined in advance—there is a certain amount of flexibility, or what psychologists call **plasticity.** This plasticity enables the brain to compensate for damage, if the damage occurs early in life, by having undamaged areas of the brain take over some of the functions of the damaged parts. It also provides a mechanism for adapting to the environment: the neural circuits that work best in one environment may be useless in another environment.

But this plasticity has its disadvantages, too. The clearest example of a disadvantage involves stereoscopic vision. Those binocular cells in the brain simply disappear—or become some other kind of cell—if they do not receive input from both eyes in the first few months of life.

Much of the data we have on this topic was gathered by two Nobel-prize-winning neurologists from Harvard Medical School, David Hubel and Thorsten Wiesel. Their subjects were not humans, but cats and monkeys. The monkey's visual system is very similar to that of humans; even a cat's is not that different.

What Hubel and Wiesel (1970; Wiesel, 1975) found was that an animal's visual system could be permanently impaired if one of its eyes was kept closed for a period of time, early in its life. If, during this period, the binocular cells in the brain receive inputs from only one eye, they cease to be binocular cells. Even when the animal is later allowed to see through its closed eye, these cells no longer respond to inputs from this eye. The animal is **stereoblind**—it lacks three-dimensional vision. In a cat, the period during which one-eyed vision can produce this effect is very brief—it must occur before the kitten is 3 months old. In a monkey, the period of risk is longer—perhaps as long as 18 months.

What about humans? According to one estimate (Julesz, 1971), 2 percent of adults are stereoblind. Stereoblindness will result if a baby is born with crossed eyes and they are not corrected by surgery in the early months of life. It may also result from anything that impairs the sight of one eye, even if the impairment is temporary. The period of risk for stereoblindness is not known in humans. More is known about the critical period for **amblyopia,** sometimes called "lazy eye." Amblyopia is the failure to use one eye for vision, even though the eye itself is perfectly normal. The "lazy" eye is, in effect, virtually blind.

In humans, the period of risk for amblyopia may be as long as 5 years (Mitchell, 1980). For example, if a child becomes cross-eyed at the age of 3 and remains that way for a year, the result is permanent amblyopia. Crossed eyes result in double vision if both eyes can see, so vision from one eye is suppressed. Amblyopia also results if a child is born with a defective eye, or if one eye is injured early in life. Even if that eye is later restored to health, it may be too late. As little as a month or two of one-eyed vision, early in infancy, may permanently impair vision in the "bad" eye. The brain simply takes back some of the space that is normally assigned to that eye and gives it to the other eye instead.

Visual experience can produce more subtle kinds of adjustments, too. A cat has some cells in its brain that send out signals only when the animal sees a vertical line. Other cells respond only to horizontal lines; still others specialize in the various in-between slants. Rear a kitten in an environment that contains only horizontal lines, and you'll find few cells that respond to verticals or diagonals (Blakemore and Cooper, 1970). Something similar may occur in humans. Most people in our society can see vertical and horizontal lines slightly more clearly than they see diagonals. Could this be because so many of the important lines in our environment are straight verticals and horizontals? Perhaps so. A group of Cree Indians reared in traditional tepees were found to see diagonal lines just as well as verticals and horizontals (Annis and Frost, 1973; Mitchell, 1980).

Hearing

A fetus has no opportunity to use its eyes—Michael had to wait until he was born before he could see anything. But his ears have already been functioning for three months or more. In the last third of her pregnancy Michael's mother noticed that her child would "jump" if a loud noise, such as a car horn, sounded nearby. Presumably, he could also hear the assorted thumps, swishes, and gurgles of her heart and digestive system. Perhaps he found those internal sounds soothing: one study (Salk, 1962) showed that newborns cry less when a recording of heartbeats is played. But other rhythmical sounds, such as lullabies, seem to work just as well (Brackbill, Adams, Crowell, and Gray, 1967). On the other hand, newborn babies cry *more* when they hear a tape of another baby crying (Simner, 1971). They also fuss more when high-pitched sounds are played. Low-pitched sounds tend to soothe them (Eisenberg, 1970). Clearly, babies are responsive to the sounds in their environment.

Even very young babies seem to be particularly attuned to the sounds of human speech. Month-old infants can detect the subtle difference between two speech sounds: after they have habituated to a recording that goes "pah-pah-pah," they will respond to a new recording that goes "bah-bah-bah," and vice versa (Eimas, 1975). Newborns appear to listen with greater interest to a tape of a woman's voice than to a tape of a man's voice (Ashmead, 1976). And babies only 2 or 3 weeks old would rather listen to their mother's voice than to the voice of a stranger (Hulsebus, 1975; Mills and Melhuish, 1974).

Sound Localization.   Some years ago, a psychologist named Michael Wertheimer, whose specialty is perception, was permitted to enter a hospital delivery room and perform a simple test on a newborn baby girl (Wertheimer, 1961). He clicked a metal "cricket" noisemaker to the baby's right, and the baby turned her eyes to the right. When he clicked it on the left, the baby looked to the left. This baby was only a few minutes old! Similar results have since been found with other newborns—not *quite* as young—and with 2½-month-olds (Mendelson and Haith, 1976; Field, DiFranco, Dodwell, and Muir, 1979).

An infant soon learns to connect his mother's voice with his mother's face and expects them to appear in the same location. One experimenter (Carpenter, 1975) devised a setup in which a stranger's voice seemed to come from the baby's mother, or the mother's voice came from the stranger's face. Babies as young as 2 weeks of age reacted by turning actively away from these confusing stimuli, in apparent dismay. In another experiment the baby saw his mother in one location and heard her voice (through a loudspeaker) coming from another location. This, too, was a distressing experience for young infants (Aronson and Rosenbloom, 1971). So apparently babies are able, quite early in life, to judge what direction a sound is coming from.

Taste and Smell

"Newborns," says Lewis Lipsitt of Brown University, "come into the world with all of their sensory systems functioning at a level that enables them to assimilate and 'appreciate' their environment" (Lipsitt, 1980, p. 96). Lipsitt and his colleagues have conducted a number of studies of infants' responses to tastes and smells.

A newborn infant sucking on a nipple doesn't suck steadily—she sucks in bursts and pauses. If each time she sucks she receives a drop of a sweet liquid (such as sugar-water), her rhythm of sucking will depend on the sweetness of the liquid. The sweeter it is, the more times she will suck per burst, with shorter and fewer pauses between bursts. But—and here's what seems odd at first—the sweeter the liquid, the *slower* she will suck within a burst. Lipsitt explains it this way:

> The slower sucking . . . suggests that the baby is savoring fluid that goes into his/her mouth. The phenomenon is not unlike that found in adults who tend to slow down their sucking and licking behavior when savoring an especially delectable substance. (1980, p. 81)

If the infant is switched from a sweet liquid to one that is *less* sweet, she will react with apparent "distaste" by sucking less—even less than a baby who hadn't first tasted the sweeter substance. For this reason, Lipsitt (1980, p. 93) warns that it is unwise to try to "prime a baby with something very sweet before putting the baby to the breast." The baby is more likely to reject the milk after a taste of something sweeter.

Babies don't care for salty-tasting fluids. If sucking produces a drop of something salty, they suck less and less. The higher the concentration of salt, the sooner they stop sucking (Crook, 1978). Bitter- or sour-tasting fluids, on the other hand, don't seem to be distinguished from plain water (Maller and Desor, 1974).

As for smells, infants (like adults) have definite likes and dislikes. Newborns will grimace in apparent disgust at the smell of rotten eggs; they tend to turn their heads away from unpleasant smells (Steiner, 1974; Bower, 1977a).

It is possible that smells mean even more to a baby than they do to us. One investigator (Russell, 1976) wondered whether breast-fed infants can recognize the scent of their mother's breasts. He had nursing women wear cotton pads inside their bras, and then used these pads to test the infants' sensitivity to smells. He found that by 6 weeks of age, babies were more likely to respond to the scent of their own mother's pads than to the scent of a pad worn by a stranger. They responded by becoming alert and by making sucking movements.

The Skin Senses

Traditionally, there are supposed to be five senses, of which the fifth is commonly called "touch." But touch itself actually consists of five senses: sensitivity to pressure, to pain, to heat, and to cold (the four **skin senses**); and **proprioception,** the sense that tells you the positions of the parts of your body, even when your eyes are closed. We'll discuss proprioception in the next section, under Visual-Motor Coordination.

Sensitivity to pressure begins very early in prenatal life: several months before it's due to be born, a fetus will move if its skin is touched. A newborn infant responds to touches on various parts of the body with the reflexes described earlier—for example, a touch on the cheek produces the rooting reflex. Babies also show that they can tell approximately *where* they are touched. An irritating stimulus on his nose or on his leg will cause the neonate to swipe in the appropriate direction with his hand or his other leg. Mild stimulation of a baby's skin—for instance, patting him on the stomach—will sometimes temporarily soothe a fussy baby. The stronger stimulation produced by **swaddling**—wrapping a baby tightly in cloth—is more effective and is used for that purpose in many societies.

Newborns seem not to be very sensitive to pain—they cry only briefly in response to medical procedures such as circumcision. Experiments with mild electric shock (how much current does it take to produce a reaction?) show that their sensitivity to pain increases rapidly in the first few days of life (Lipsitt and Levy, 1959).

MOTOR DEVELOPMENT

Among the most striking changes that occur in the first year or two of life are changes in motor abilities. The human newborn can do relatively little. Arms, legs, and body are capable at most only of reflex (or reflexlike) motions. The head, however, is relatively sophisticated: Michael can already turn his head from side to side; open, close and move his eyes; suck and swallow; open and close his mouth; and move his tongue around. Within a few weeks he will be able to hold his head up steadily and look around, when he is on his stomach or is held upright.

In general, motor development starts at the top and works its way down. Michael will gain control of his head before he can use his hands for accurate reaching. He will use his hands for reaching before he can use his legs for walking. Table 5–1 shows the average ages at which American children achieve the major motor milestones. The table also lists the age ranges within which 90 percent of children achieve these milestones.

TABLE 5–1   Motor Milestones and When They Are Achieved

Motor Behavior	Average Age in Months	Usual Range
Sits with support	2.3	1 to 5 months
Sits alone steadily	6.6	5 to 9 months
Stands up holding on to furniture	8.6	6 to 12 months
Stands alone	11.0	9 to 16 months
Walks alone	11.7	9 to 17 months
Walks downstairs alone (both feet on each step)	25.8	19 to over 30 months

From the Bayley Scales of Infant Development, 1969

figure 5–2

The development of the baby's ability to grasp objects, from 16 weeks to 1 year. (The numbers on this figure give the age of the baby in weeks.)

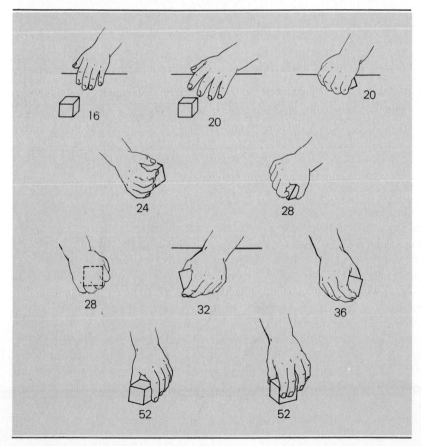

Adapted from H. M. Halverson, 1931.

Motor development also proceeds from the general to the specific, from large muscles to small ones. For example, reaching and grasping start with clumsy swipes at an object, using mostly arm muscles rather than hand muscles. Grasping at first is with four fingers against the palm, then with the thumb and palm, then with thumb and fingers. Finally, at the end of the first year, a baby can pick up very small objects with his thumb and index finger.

Experience versus Maturation

Larval frogs begin to make swimming movements with their tails even before they are hatched. These movements gradually become smoother and more vigorous. The tadpoles are able to swim as soon as they are hatched. In a famous experiment performed in the 1920s (Carmichael, 1927), a psychologist kept unhatched frogs under light anesthesia for several days. Their growth was unaffected but they couldn't move. As soon as the anesthetic wore off, however, the tadpoles were able to swim just as well as unanesthetized tadpoles that had been "practicing" swimming movements for several days. The experimenter concluded that swimming of tadpoles results from maturation, not practice. The ability to move around in their environment is "programmed" in advance in the animals' genes, and experience plays no role.

The results of another experiment performed at about the same time suggested that human babies are similar to frogs in this respect. A pair of identical twin girls were the subjects. One twin was given lessons in stair-climbing, the other wasn't. At a year of age the trained twin could crawl up a flight of stairs far more rapidly than her sister. But only two weeks later the second twin caught up and could climb the stairs as quickly as the trained twin (Gesell and Thompson, 1929).

A third study, some years later, involved Hopi Indian babies who spent most of their first year of life tightly swaddled and strapped to a cradleboard, in the traditional Hopi manner. These babies learned to walk at the same age—about 15 months—as other Hopi children who hadn't been tied down (Dennis and Dennis, 1940).

All of these studies seem to imply that motor milestones occur at a certain stage of physical maturation, and that experience doesn't much matter. These studies, however, leave some questions unanswered. Traditionally reared Hopi children are removed from their cradleboards before they are a year old. Thus, they've had at least three months to ready themselves for walking. In the stair-climbing experiment the "trained" twin was simply moved passively up the stairs in the practice session. Probably a better way to prepare for stair-climbing is to practice crawling around on the floor—and *both* twins were evidently allowed to do that.

It is true that normal children reared in a normal environment will invariably learn to sit, to stand, and to walk. But under certain extreme conditions the normal schedule of events can be interfered with. Children who were reared under very deprived conditions, in an orphanage in Lebanon, were greatly retarded in motor development. These children were kept in bare cribs, with nothing to look at and nothing to do. They received a minimum

The baby in this photograph is strapped to a cradleboard.

of adult attention. Some of these children couldn't sit alone at 1 year, or walk at 2 (Dennis, 1973).

Motor development can also be speeded up somewhat. Earlier in this chapter we described an experiment (Zelazo, Zelazo, and Kolb, 1972) in which babies under 2 months of age were given practice in using the walking reflex. Later these babies learned to walk unusually early. As it happens, this experiment has received quite a bit of criticism (Ridenour, 1978). Some psychologists have claimed that babies who walk exceptionally early are more likely to injure their legs (because their muscles aren't strong enough to protect their bones) or, if they fall, to injure their brains (because there are still "soft spots" on the head, where the skull hasn't yet grown together).

Fortunately, normal children reared in a normal environment don't need to be given special practice for motor development: they practice on their own. Esther Thelen, a developmental psychologist at the University of Missouri, has described how babies gear themselves up for motor milestones by repeating certain movements over and over again, in a rhythmic fashion. Such **stereotyped** movements, which include kicking, rocking, waving, and bouncing, take up an average of 5 percent of an infant's day. Thelen has observed that these rhythmic movements occur shortly before the appearance of a motor milestone that uses the same group of muscles:

For example, kicking movements had their greatest frequency just before the onset of locomotion [crawling and walking]. . . . Rocking on hands and knees appeared just before crawling, and rhythmical hand and arm movements appeared before complex manual skills. (Thelen, 1981, p. 239)

After the motor milestone is achieved, the stereotyped behavior goes away, its purpose served. But blind babies and babies in institutions often get stuck at the level of stereotyped behavior. For them, Thelen says, the self-stimulation resulting from these rhythmic movements is a substitute for the sensory stimulation their environments fail to provide.

Visual-Motor Coordination

Sitting, crawling, and walking are motor skills—to do them, all the baby needs is her own sturdy little body and the surface beneath it. But reaching for an interesting-looking object, or stacking one block on another block, or getting a spoon under a piece of food, or drawing a circle are **visual-motor skills:** the baby must learn to guide her movements by what she sees. Another name for this ability is **hand-eye coordination.**

Reaching for a visible object is the earliest form of hand-eye coordination. After that brief period in the first month of life in which babies (under certain conditions) may bat at things, babies do not reach again for several weeks. What are they doing in the meantime? They are watching their own hands. They are, in fact, quite fascinated by the sight of their moving hands (White, Castle, and Held, 1964).

T. G. R. Bower believes that it is precisely this fascination with the sight of their own hands that keeps 1- or 2-month-old babies from reaching for things. When a baby of this age sees something, she'll start to reach for it until she catches sight of her hand. Her attention will switch to the hand. At 1 or 2 months, says Bower (1977b), a baby can't pay attention both to an object and her hand. The hand wins.

But all this gazing at the hand will soon make accurate reaching possible. By moving her hand and watching it move, the baby is getting **visual feedback** from her actions—she's seeing the visible results of what happens when she directs this muscle or that muscle to contract. She's also developing an accurate sense of proprioception in her hands and arms—she's coming to feel her hand in the locations and positions she sees them in. Accurate proprioception *can't* be built in, the way accurate vision apparently is, because the limbs (unlike the eyes) change so drastically in size during development. So the greater accuracy of the visual system is used to "calibrate" proprioception. This can be shown even in an adult, by letting a person see his hand through special goggles that make it look a few inches to the side of its true location. The hand soon comes to feel that it's in the location in which it's seen (Harris, 1965, 1980).

Experiments with animals show what happens if a young organism doesn't get to see the parts of its body. Some kittens were raised with big circular collars around their necks that kept them from seeing their paws. When the collars were taken off, the kittens couldn't use their paws accurately, the way normal kittens can (Hein and Held, 1967; Hein, 1980). Similar results were found with monkeys. Monkeys deprived of the sight of their paws (but not deprived of other sights) couldn't reach accurately for things. After a period in which they spent a lot of time watching their paws, their reaching became normal. A monkey that was allowed to see only *one* paw could

A kitten wearing a collar that prevents it from seeing its own paws. (From Hein and Held, 1967.)

PROBLEMS IN DEVELOPMENT

Sudden Infant Death

Stephen Richard Raring was born on November 18, 1970, in Washington, D.C. He was what we called in Chapter 2 an "easy baby"—good-natured, adaptable and regular in his habits. In his routine medical checkups, his pediatrician gave him a clean bill of health.

Here's how Stephen's father describes the last day of his son's life:

On February 8, 1971, just short of 12 weeks of age, he awoke at his usual time of 7 A.M., and had his early liquid breakfast, as usual, followed by a period of conversation with his mother, a short nap, a bath, more conversation and play, and a second breakfast, became sleepy—again on schedule—and did not object to retiring for his regular 11 A.M. nap.

During the next hour his mother looked in to see that all was well—again a usual procedure. The third time she found him face down in the center of his crib—in a non-normal position and very still. (Raring, 1975, p. 42)

Stephen was dead—a victim of what used to be called "crib death" and is now called **Sudden Infant Death Syndrome,** or **SIDS.**

The next 24 hours were a nightmare for Stephen's parents. The doctor on duty at the emergency room of Georgetown University Hospital pronounced Stephen dead, "cause unknown." An autopsy was ordered. A homocide detective arrived at the Rarings' home to question them—child abuse is often suspected in cases of SIDS.

The next morning, Stephen's father had to go to the morgue to identify his son's corpse. The tiny body, with the marks of the autopsy clearly visible, lay on a gray slab. Raring (p. 43) describes these painful events in the third person. "When the father was able to speak," he says, "he identified the body of his dead son."

The hospital sent the Rarings a bill for their services, but provided them with no information about the cause of the baby's death. It was the Rarings' own pediatrician who told them that Stephen had died of SIDS. But the emergency-room doctor was correct, in a way: the precise cause of SIDS *is* unknown. There are several promising theories, but no one knows for sure.

There have always been theories of SIDS, because SIDS has undoubtedly always existed. A theory that remained popular for millennia was first recorded in the Old Testament, in one of the stories about King Solomon: "And this woman's child died in the night, because she overlaid it" (1 Kings 3:19). When babies slept in the same beds with their mothers, it was easy enough to say the mothers caused these deaths by rolling over onto their babies. When it became customary to keep the baby in a separate bed, the death was blamed on suffocation by a blanket (although even a newborn can push a blanket out of the way), or by a cat (the cat was supposed to have "sucked the life" out of the baby!).

What makes SIDS so puzzling is that ordinarily there are no signs of a struggle; parents who

reach all right with that one but not with the other one (Held and Bauer, 1967).

Normal human infants learn how to reach accurately for things by the time they are about 6 months old. This reaching is visually guided reaching. The baby sticks out her hand and then uses vision to guide it toward the object (White, Castle, and Held, 1964; Bower, 1977a).

have been nearby have heard no sounds of distress. The baby goes to sleep in the usual way and, while he's asleep, he simply stops breathing. In the United States alone, an estimated 7,000 infants die each year in this way—it's the leading killer of babies between 1 month and 12 months of age. SIDS claims about one infant out of every 500, most often when they are 2 or 3 months old (Naeye, 1980).

Because many babies who died of SIDS have symptoms resembling those caused by suffocation, attention has focused on the respiratory (breathing) system. According to one theory of SIDS, these babies have something wrong with the parts of the brain that control breathing, due to genetic factors, to unfavorable prenatal influences, or both. Many of these babies appear to have inadequate breathing reflexes. All babies stop breathing for brief periods, from time to time, but SIDS babies seem to have a weaker-than-normal impulse to begin again and to "catch up." More than half of the babies who died of SIDS show signs of having gotten slightly less oxygen than their bodies needed, probably ever since they were born (Naeye, 1980).

This theory is plausible; yet it leaves some questions unanswered. What about the babies who don't show any signs of long-term oxygen deprivation? If the breathing reflexes are at fault, why didn't the baby die in the first month of life? (Deaths due to SIDS are rare in the first three weeks.) And why does it almost always happen while the baby is asleep? One group of investigators (Harper and others, 1981) believe that the problem is not in the breathing centers of the brain, but in those that regulate the states of sleep and wakefulness. In active (or REM) sleep, breathing is irregular, but most babies apparently wake up if breathing stops for too long. A group of infants at risk for SIDS showed abnormal sleep patterns: they seemed, the investigators said, "to have difficulty in making the normal transition from sleeping to waking states" (p. 1031). Thus, the baby may be unable to wake up in time to resume breathing. There are devices currently available to monitor the breathing of infants who are believed to be at risk for SIDS. These devices sound an alarm if the baby stops breathing for any length of time.

In autopsy, certain symptoms or abnormalities are found in many SIDS babies; yet no single finding is true of all SIDS babies. It's possible, therefore, that the deaths lumped under the SIDS label may be due to more than one cause. The theory that certain viruses or bacteria are responsible may account for some SIDS deaths. About half of the babies who succumb to SIDS had mild colds at the time of their deaths. Breast-fed babies are more resistant to infections than bottle-fed ones, because their mothers' milk conveys partial immunity to many illnesses. Breast-fed babies are less likely to die of SIDS than are bottle-fed babies.

Other risk factors include having a mother who smokes or who was addicted to opiates during pregnancy. SIDS babies are more likely to have had Apgar scores below 7 at birth and to have weighed less than 5½ pounds (2500 grams). Boys are at greater risk than girls, later-borns are at greater risk than firstborns. But all of these facts are just statistics. They're of little consolation to the nonsmoking parents of a first-born girl who weighed 7½ pounds at birth, who was breast fed, and who appeared to be in perfect health at the time of her death. ■

FROM INFANCY TO TODDLERHOOD: PHYSICAL GROWTH

One of the most noteworthy characteristics of the human newborn is his small size. Michael weighs about as much as a plump roasting chicken. His length, 20 inches, is less than a third of his mother's height. Within a year he will add 10 inches to his height, 15 pounds to his weight. Then his rate of growth will slow considerably. Dramatic changes in size and shape won't occur again until adolescence.

Many people wonder whether it is possible to predict from a baby's size how tall he or she will be as an adult. For a newborn baby, the answer is *no:* size at birth correlates hardly at all with size at maturity. In fact, we can do a better job of predicting by ignoring the baby's size at birth and measuring the *parents* instead. The correlation between two parents and their grownup child is .70 (Tanner, 1978).

The growth pattern of the individual child begins to be noticeable early in the first year: babies destined to be tall adults grow faster than those destined to be short. By age 2 there is already a good indication of how tall the child will eventually become—height at that age correlates .80 with height at maturity. We can make a rough estimate of eventual adult height by multiplying the height at 2 years by 2 for a boy, by 1.9 for a girl. But that estimate may be off by as much as 2 or 3 inches, one way or the other (Tanner, 1978).

Sex Differences in Growth

Notice that a girl has achieved more than half of her adult height by age 2, despite the fact that since birth she's been slightly shorter and slightly lighter in weight than her male agemates. J. P. Tanner, a British biologist who does research on child growth, reports that girls are physically more mature than males, even four months before they are born! At birth there is a difference of four to six weeks in physical maturity.

The Brain after Birth

Almost all of the cells in our body continue to divide after birth—continue, in fact, all our lives, so that dead or damaged cells can be replaced with new ones. Neurons are an exception. For some reason neurons lose their ability to divide at about nine months after conception. The 100 billion neurons in the brain of that newborn baby are just about all he's ever going to have. And yet his brain is only a quarter of the size of an adult brain. In six months it will have almost doubled in weight; in two years it will have tripled (Tanner, 1978).

What causes this rapid increase in brain size, if not an increase in the number of neurons? Three factors are involved. First, the neurons themselves increase in size—they send out more branches, form more synapses with other neurons. Second, there's another type of cell in the brain, called the **glial** cell, whose chief function is to support and nourish the neurons. Glial cells continue to increase in number throughout childhood; by adulthood they outnumber the neurons about 10 to 1. If a neuron dies it is not replaced—instead, the gap is filled by a glial cell. (But don't worry too much about your neurons dying. It has been estimated that only 3 percent of the brain's neurons die during a normal lifetime.)

The third cause of brain growth after birth is **myelination.** During the first years of life many neurons develop a coating of a fatty substance called **mye-lin.** This insulating jacket greatly speeds the transmission of neural signals. Myelination plays an important role in the physical maturation of the brain.

Changes in Body Proportions

The newborn isn't just smaller than an adult: he's shaped differently. His body proportions are different. Compared with an older child or an adult, his limbs are very short, his head is very large. In fact, while the head makes up only an eighth of an adult's total height, it's a full quarter of the baby's length. Before birth the head is even larger, compared to the rest of the body. We might say that the head is "physically more mature" than the rest of the body, because all during prenatal life, infancy, and childhood it is closer to its adult size than any other part of the body (except the eyes). This reflects the rapid growth of the brain. At birth the brain has achieved 25 percent of its total growth, as measured by its weight. The body as a whole has achieved only 5 percent of its adult weight. At age 10 the growth of the brain will be 95 percent complete, whereas the body will be only about half grown in terms of weight (Tanner, 1978).

A big head is characteristic not only of human babies—it's characteristic of baby animals as well. In general, the young of all warm-blooded species have small limbs and bodies and relatively large heads. The head itself is proportioned differently from an adult's: the eyes are relatively large and are located lower down on the head; the other features are small and close together. As you can see in Figure 5–3 (p. 168), these characteristics are what makes a face look babyish and cute. The artists who draw cartoon animals make use of these principles. When they want an animal to look appealing, they give it a large forehead and big, low-set eyes (Gould, 1979).

Cuteness Counts. Newborn babies are totally dependent on other, older members of their species. This is true of all baby mammals—a newborn kitten, calf, rabbit, or monkey will usually die if its mother abandons it. But mammal mothers *don't* ordinarily abandon their young. A female rat will repeatedly cross an electrified grid in order to reach her squealing pups, even though the current is strong enough to keep her away from food when she is hungry, from water when she is thirsty (Warden, 1931). Even female animals that have never given birth, even (in some cases) *male* animals, will nurture young members of their species. And even the boundaries between species do not necessarily interfere with this willingness to nurture: mother cats have suckled puppies, female wolves (if the old stories are to be believed) have suckled human infants, humans of both sexes have tenderly bottle-fed the orphaned young of virtually every mammal on the face of the earth.

Konrad Lorenz, the well-known biologist, believes that this nurturing impulse is "released" or triggered by the babyish features of young animals, and that this response is innate and instinctive—in humans as well as animals. In other words, the big heads and eyes, the small, low-set features of baby mammals evoke in most of us an automatic, involuntary response of affection

figure 5–3
The location and
relative size of the facial
features are what
determine whether a
face looks babyish and
cute.

and protectiveness. The existence of such an instinctive response would
clearly have adaptive value for any species, since it would increase the
chances that the young of that species would survive (Lorenz, 1971).

Whether or not Lorenz is correct in assuming that this "maternal" reaction
is due to nature rather than nurture, there is good evidence that it does, in
fact, exist in many humans. Moreover, it exists in the male as well as in the
female. In several studies, a majority of people of both sexes judged pictures
of young humans or animals to be more attractive, appealing, and likable
than pictures of older humans and animals. Some of these studies showed
that this preference was stronger for women than for men; others found no
overall difference between the sexes (Jackson and Jackson, 1978). However,
the preference does seem to appear at an earlier age in girls than in boys.
Children under 11 prefer pictures of *adult* humans and animals. Girls switch
to a preference for baby humans and animals by about age 13, boys by about
17 (Fullard and Reiling, 1976).

Human babies are not able to move around and find food on their own a
few hours after birth, the way the young of some species can. But they can
do something that's perhaps even more remarkable: they can make the older
members of their species *want* to feed them and take care of them.

summary

1. In the past 10 or 15 years, a great deal has been learned about the characteristics and abilities of the **neonate** (the newborn baby).

2. The **Apgar test** is a quick way of assessing how healthy neonates are and how well they are adjusting to life outside the uterus.

3. Babies sleep an average of 16 hours a day; roughly 50 percent of this time is spent in quiet sleep, the other 50 percent in **active** (or **REM**) sleep. Active sleep is the phase in which dreaming occurs.

4. Babies' behavior can be described in terms of **states:** they go from state to state during the day. Six states that have been described are active sleep, quiet sleep, drowsiness, fussiness, crying, and quiet alertness. It is in the state of quiet alertness that the baby is most attentive to visual and auditory stimuli.

5. Babies differ enormously in how much they cry. During the first three months, some babies cry for three or four hours a day, most commonly in the early evening. Holding babies in an upright position, a common practice among the !Kung San people of Africa, seems to decrease their crying.

6. Babies are born with a number of reflexes. The most important of these are associated with breathing: breathing deepens and quickens, or the baby yawns, if there is too much carbon dioxide in the blood; obstructions of the breathing passages produce coughs or sneezes. Temporary lulls in breathing are normal in newborns; the baby then takes extra breaths in order to "catch up."

7. Reflexes associated with feeding include sucking, swallowing, and **rooting,** in which a touch on the cheek causes the baby's head to turn in that direction.

8. Other reflexes occur in response to pain, to heat, and to cold. Crying can be considered to be in this category, too—it is a response that has survival value for the baby, because it motivates his parents to meet his needs.

9. "Useless" reflexes found in newborn babies include the **Babinski reflex** (which occurs when the infant's foot is tickled) and the **Moro reflex** (which is a startle response to a loud noise or a sudden loss of support). In the **tonic neck reflex,** the baby lies on his back with his head turned to one side and his arm on that side outstretched. The **swimming reflex** may occur when he's placed on his stomach, and the **grasp reflex** (found also in baby monkeys) occurs when something is pressed in his palm.

10. The **walking** (or **stepping**) **reflex** can be seen in newborns when they are held upright with their feet touching a solid surface. A group of babies were "walked" in this way during their first two months; later these babies began to walk independently at an earlier age than babies who hadn't had this practice.

11. T. G. R. Bower has reported successful reaching movements in babies only a week or two old. He claims that this ability disappears at around 4 weeks and that it occurs only if the baby's body is given steady support. Other investigators have failed to obtain reaching movements in newborns.

12. Babies only 1 or 2 weeks old seem to have the ability, under certain conditions, to imitate adults' facial movements. This ability also disappears after three or four weeks.

13. The **preferential-looking technique** is one way of finding out about a baby's visual perception. If a baby looks at one picture significantly more than at another, she must be able to see that the pictures are different. However, even if there's no preference, the baby may be able to see the difference. We can find out by **habituating** the baby to one picture, then noticing if she looks more at the new picture. The **habituation technique** can also be used to test other senses.

14. **Visual acuity,** the ability to see things clearly, can be tested by moving stripes of various widths across the baby's field of view and checking for sideways reflex eye movements.

15. Babies' eyes are ready to function im-

mediately after birth. Newborns can track moving objects with their eyes, but they cannot at first adjust their focus to near or far stimuli. Things that are at a distance of 7 to 15 inches (18–38 cm) look clearest to newborns. Babies' eyes focus almost as well as an adult's by the time they are 2 months old; by 6 months they can see as clearly as they ever will.

16. **Stereoscopic vision** is the ability to see the world in three dimensions; it depends on the fact that the left eye's view is slightly different from the right eye's. **Binocular cells** in the brain, which receive inputs from the two eyes, are responsible for stereo vision.

17. The **visual cliff** experiment showed that babies of crawling age can perceive depth. Other evidence suggests that stereo vision is present in 5-month-olds, poor or absent in 3-month-olds. But even babies under 3 months of age seem to have some ability to perceive the locations of objects in space, at least in some situations.

18. Babies prefer to look at complex patterns rather than at plain surfaces; curved lines are preferred to straight ones. Newborns prefer large patterns to small ones, close objects to distant ones.

19. Young babies show surprisingly little attraction to color. Experimental results indicate that 2-month-olds can see blue, red, orange, and green. At 4 or 5 months they can also see purple. Greenish-yellow is either not perceived at this age, or is perceived but disliked.

20. Month-old babies tend to look at edges of patterns, rather than at what's inside them. By the fifth or sixth week, they start to look at the features inside the contours—their parents' eyes, for example.

21. The structure of the nervous system has a certain amount of **plasticity**—neural connections are strengthened or discarded on the basis of what occurs in the first months of life. If the binocular cells do not receive inputs from the two eyes during this time, **stereoblindness** results. The period of risk lasts around three

months in cats, 18 months in monkeys, and probably much longer in humans. An estimated 2 percent of humans are stereoblind.

22. **Amblyopia** is the failure to use one eye for vision, even if the eye itself is perfectly normal. (The problem is probably in the brain, rather than in the eye.) The period of risk for amblyopia may be as long as five years in humans—anything that impairs vision in one eye during that period may lead to amblyopia.

23. People in our society see vertical and horizontal lines slightly more clearly than diagonals. Some psychologists believe that this is because we were reared in an environment in which most of the important lines are verticals and horizontals.

24. The hearing of a newborn baby has already been functioning for three months or more. Newborns cry less when they hear low-pitched, rhythmic sounds; they cry more when they hear other babies crying. Month-old infants can hear the difference between the speech sounds "pah" and "bah"; they prefer their mother's voice to that of a stranger.

25. Even newborns seem to be able to tell what direction a sound is coming from. Quite early in life, they expect to hear their mother's voice coming from the direction where they see her face.

26. Newborn babies appear to like sweet liquids—the sweeter the better. They dislike salty liquids. They show no reaction to bitter or sour tastes.

27. Newborns perceive odors and have definite likes and dislikes. Breast-fed babies seem to be able to recognize the scent of their mothers' breasts by 6 weeks of age.

28. The sense called "touch" consists of the four **skin senses** (pressure, pain, heat, and cold), plus **proprioception,** which tells us the positions of the parts of our bodies even when our eyes are closed. Sensitivity to pressure begins very early in fetal life. Babies seem not to be very sensitive to pain until a few days after they are born.

29. Motor development tends to start at the top and work its way down: babies can control their heads first, then their hands, then their legs. It also proceeds from large muscles to small ones: babies can control their arm movements before they can control their finger movements.

30. Tadpoles' ability to swim when they are hatched is due to maturation, not to practice. There are some indications that this may also be true of motor development in humans. A baby who was given practice in stair-climbing was only two weeks ahead of her untrained twin sister in this skill; Hopi babies who spend most of their first year strapped to cradle boards learn to walk at the usual time. However, there are other interpretations of these findings.

31. Children who are reared under extremely deprived conditions may be retarded in their motor development.

32. Babies who were given early practice in using the walking reflex learned to walk earlier than usual, but some psychologists feel that stimulating walking in this way is unwise.

33. Stereotyped movements—rhythmic movements such as kicking, rocking, waving, and bouncing—tend to occur shortly before the appearance of a motor milestone that uses the same group of muscles. Handicapped children, and children in institutions, may continue to make rhythmic movements because of the self-stimulation such movements provide.

34. Stacking blocks or reaching for an interesting-looking object requires **visual-motor coordination** (or **hand-eye coordination**). Such actions are guided by means of **visual feedback**—the visible results that occur when a particular movement is made. Babies spend a lot of time looking at their hands; this will enable them to reach accurately for objects by the time they are 6 months old, and to gain an accurate sense of proprioception.

35. The **Sudden Infant Death Syndrome (SIDS)** claims an estimated 1 out of 500 babies, most often when they are 2 or 3 months old, and generally when they are asleep. According to one theory of SIDS, these babies have something wrong with the parts of the brain that control breathing; another theory locates the problem in the brain areas that control sleep and wakefulness. Babies who are at greatest risk of SIDS are male rather than female, later-borns rather than firstborns, bottle-fed rather than breast-fed, and have mothers who smoke or who were addicted to opiates during pregnancy. Low birthweight and low Apgar scores at birth also increase the risk. About half of SIDS babies had mild colds at the time they died.

36. Size at birth correlates hardly at all with size at maturity, but height at age 2 correlates .80 with adult height. At age 2 a boy is roughly half his adult height; a girl is more than half of her adult height. Girls are physically more mature than boys all through childhood—even at birth.

37. The neurons in the brain do not continue to divide after birth. Increase in brain size after birth is due to an increase in the size of the neurons, to an increase in the number of **glial cells,** and to **myelination.** Myelination speeds neural transmission and plays an important role in brain maturation.

38. The newborn's head is closer to its adult size than is the rest of his body. The brain is 25 percent of its adult size at birth, 95 percent of its adult size at age 10.

39. The big heads, big foreheads, and big, low-set eyes of baby humans and animals make them look cute and appealing, and (according to some theorists) make us want to nurture them. Whether or not this tendency is innate, it exists in many humans, both male and female. People of both sexes react favorably to pictures of human and animal babies, but girls do so at an earlier age than boys.

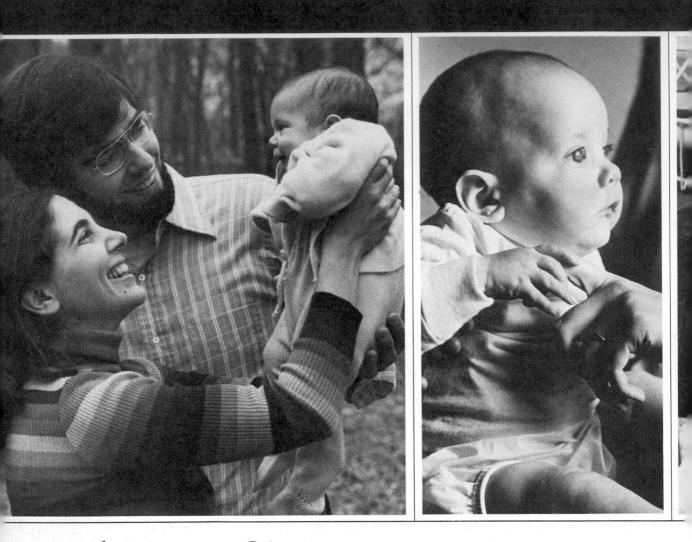

Chapter Six

THE FIRST SOCIAL RELATIONSHIPS

Six

An adult who doesn't happen to like people can get along without them. He or she can decide to become a hermit, or to live alone on an island like Alexander Selkirk, the historical person who served as the inspiration for Defoe's *Robinson Crusoe*. But living alone is hardly an option for a child, much less for an infant. Young humans don't have any choice: they *have* to associate with other people in order to survive. And the course of their lives will be very much affected by how successful these associations are.

Much of this chapter will focus on the relationships between babies and their mothers. Although in our society there are now a growing number of families in which fathers have an equal share in the responsibilities of child-rearing, these families are still only a small minority (Eiduson and Weisner, 1978). The recent increase in father involvement is a dramatic departure from a pattern that has prevailed not only in Western culture but in all known human cultures: all over the world, babies have been cared for primarily by women. This pattern has changed very little throughout human history, according to anthropologist Melvin Konner. But, he says, "it may do so in the very near future" (1977, p. 96).

In this chapter we will summarize what is known about interactions between fathers and babies. We will have considerably more to say about interactions between *mothers* and babies, simply because so much more is known about that topic.

PARENT-INFANT INTERACTIONS

The newborn baby is not a particularly sociable person. Very young infants are in a receptive state—a state of quiet alertness—only for brief periods. More often they are sleeping or crying or being fed. Pediatrician I. Berry Brazelton and his colleagues have described what happens if you prop up a week-old baby in an infant seat and ask the mother to "communicate" with her child.

> Our mothers were faced with the problem of communicating with infants who, if they were not crying or thrashing, were often hanging limply in the infant seat with closed or semiclosed eyes or, just as frequently, were "frozen" motionless in some strange and uninterpretable position—staring at nothing. While infants in the first few weeks did seem to look directly into the faces of their mothers, the communicative aspects of eye-to-eye contact sometimes were dampened when the mothers moved their heads and found the infants still staring off in the original direction. (Brazelton, Koslowski, and Main, 1974, p. 67)

The situation improves with almost breathtaking rapidity. Occasionally during the first three weeks a mother may notice a "strange little smile" appearing while the infant is drowsy or asleep (Bell, 1974, p. 10). By the end of the third week, this smile occasionally occurs in response to the sound of her voice. By the fourth or fifth week, the baby starts to focus on her face, and true eye-to-eye contact begins. By 6 or 7 weeks the baby is looking right at her and smiling, and perhaps making cooing noises as well. Social interactions have begun.

A baby's smile is a delightful event. Most parents find it irresistible—it's nearly impossible not to smile back. But eye contact may be even more important than the smile in establishing a bond between parent and child. Once eye contact is made, the parents feel that their baby is "becoming a person." Some mothers report their first feelings of love at this time (Robson, 1968).

Now parents begin to play with their babies instead of simply taking care of them.

Playful Interactions

Child psychiatrist Daniel Stern has videotaped many hundreds of hours of mothers and babies at play. He has studied three aspects of the mothers' behavior with their infants: their speech, their facial expressions, and the direction of their gaze. In all three kinds of behaviors, Stern finds, mothers act differently with babies than they would with an adult. Their speech contains exaggerated variations in pitch and loudness and is very slowed down, especially in the duration of the vowels:

Hi- swee-e-e-et-ee, Hi-i-i, Hi-i-iya, watcha lookin' at?, Hu-u-uh? O-o-o-o-o-o. Yeah, it's mommy, ye-e-a-ah. (Stern, 1974, p. 192)

Stern believes that this kind of slowed-down "baby talk" is a better match to the baby's perceptual abilities than the pace of normal, adult speech would be.

Mothers' *facial* expressions, too, are highly exaggerated:

> The often seen "mock surprise" expression of mothers is a good example. The eyebrows go way up, the eyes open very wide, the mouth opens and purses and usually emits a long "Ooooooooo," and the head comes up and forward sometimes to within inches of the baby's face. This expression may take many seconds to slowly come to a full bloom and then may be held for an unusually long time. Such an expression directed toward an adult would be experienced as quite bizarre. (p. 192)

Finally, mothers and babies gaze at each other for unusually long periods of time—sometimes for 30 seconds or more. Such long gazes seldom occur among adults, except between people who are in love or people who are about to fight.

The three kinds of behavior—looking, talking, and facial expressions—generally go together. However, there *is* one time the gaze occurs alone: mothers often look steadily at their babies during a breast- or bottle-feeding. These gazes tend to be one-way—the infant seldom looks back. Such is the potency of social stimuli for the infant that if eye contact is made and the mother smiles or speaks, the baby may stop sucking in order to return her smile.

The Baby's Behavior During Social Interactions. During play, while the mother is speaking, gazing, and changing her facial expressions, what is the infant doing? For the answer we return to the observations of Brazelton and his colleagues (Brazelton and others, 1974). These investigators have found that as early as 4 weeks of age, a baby's response to a human face is noticeably different from the response to an inanimate object. When confronted with an interesting object—say, a stuffed animal—babies sometimes stare at it fixedly for as long as two minutes at a time. Then they will suddenly turn aside to look at something else. In contrast, their response to a person tends to be more up and down in nature—a short period of increasing interaction followed by a short period of withdrawal. It seems that social interactions are so intensely stimulating for young infants that they must take frequent breaks, perhaps in order to avoid becoming overstimulated or perhaps just to rest up for the next interaction.

A typical interaction begins with the mother looking at the infant. The baby looks back at her, his face brightens and he turns his body and face in her direction. He is paying close attention to what she is doing. If he starts to smile and she smiles back, his smile is reinforced and he smiles more broadly. He waves his arms and legs. If she speaks to him and then is quiet for a moment, he may **vocalize** (make some sounds); he is less likely to vocalize if she talks without stopping. As his intensity builds up, his movements tend to become jerky and to involve more of his body. Then, gradually, he begins to relax. His smiles fade and his eyes lose their bright look. At this point he appears to withdraw his attention from his mother; he looks away.

But he is still aware of her, because if *she* now looks away, he's likely to return his gaze to her face. A brief period without eye contact seems to be what he wants. If he gets it—if the mother doesn't insist on trying to maintain his attention—he will soon be ready for another interaction, perhaps in a matter of seconds.

Whether the mother and baby enjoy these interactions, whether all goes smoothly, depends to a large extent on the mother's sensitivity to her baby's signals. If she gives him time to respond, if she allows him his "time-outs" without overwhelming him with stimulation, if she adjusts her behavior to his rhythms, then their interactions are likely to be successful. But if she ignores his signals and continues to try to get the infant's attention when he's had enough, her efforts may backfire. He may respond to her less and less. Stern describes an extreme example of an unsuccessful interaction of this kind: the case of Jenny, a 3-month-old baby girl, and her mother. Whenever Jenny looked at her mother, her mother would overwhelm her with exaggerated facial expressions, continuous speech, tickling, and so on.

> Jenny invariably broke gaze rapidly. Her mother never interpreted this temporary face and gaze aversion as a cue to lower her level of behavior, nor would she let Jenny self-control the level by gaining distance. Instead, she would swing her head around following Jenny's to reestablish the full-face position. Once the mother achieved this, she would reinitiate the same level of stimulation with a new arrangement of facial and vocal combinations. Jenny again turned away, pushing her face further into the pillow to try to break all visual contact. Again, instead of holding back, the mother continued to chase Jenny. . . . With Jenny's head now pinned in the corner, the baby's next recourse was to perform a "pass-through." She rapidly swung her face from one side to the other right past her mother's face. When her face crossed the mother's face, in the face-to-face zone, Jenny closed her eyes to avoid any mutual visual contact. (Stern, 1977, pp. 110–111)

Having an Effect on the World

One reason that things went badly for Jenny and her mother was that Jenny's behavior didn't seem to have any effect on her mother's actions. Babies—like everyone else—apparently like to feel that what they do matters, that people are responding to them. (Think how frustrating it is to try to communicate with someone who never answers your questions, never gives any signs of having noticed what you said.) Perhaps the feeling of having some effect on what's happening is particularly important for babies, since there are so few things they can actually do.

When babies find out that something they *can* do makes something else happen, they are usually delighted. For example, in one study (Field, 1977) mothers simply imitated the actions of their 3½-month-old babies—they did whatever their babies did. When these babies realized that they were "controlling" their mothers' behavior, they smiled and laughed. They smiled and laughed more when their mothers imitated them than they did when their mothers played with them in the ordinary way.

Robert McCall (1979) has described how one baby reacted when her father made his own responses **contingent** (dependent) on her vocalizations. This father sat his 8-week-old baby girl on his knee, and every time she sighed or gurgled or cooed he would immediately give her a big smile, bounce her gently on his knee, and say "bumpety-bump." Since he was reinforcing her vocalizing, just as B. F. Skinner reinforced *his* daughter for lifting her arm (see the box on Behavior Modification, Chapter 3), it's not surprising that the baby's vocalizing increased. By the third day she had turned into a real chatterbox. But the point here is that the baby *delighted* in this game, once she found out how to make her father go "bumpety-bump." In fact, within a week the baby was bursting into smiles and coos whenever she saw her father.

Crying and Helplessness.   Not all babies can make their fathers go "bumpety-bump." But all babies can cry. Crying is usually the most effective way a baby has of producing a response from the people around her. A tiny baby has been known to move a full-grown adult up an entire flight of stairs, just by the force of her cries!

When parents respond reasonably quickly and reasonably consistently to their babies' cries, the babies seem to acquire what Erikson calls **basic trust.** They come to see the world as a friendly place, a place where their needs will be met, a place where what they do matters. Not surprisingly, these babies turn into reasonably contented toddlers who cry relatively little. By the end of the first year, a group of babies whose mothers had responded to them quickly and consistently were crying significantly less than some other babies whose mothers often ignored them (Bell and Ainsworth, 1972).

Babies who are usually ignored are in danger of developing what has been called **learned helplessness.** They cease to feel that what they do makes any difference. The extreme case of this was seen in babies in old-fashioned institutions, with too few caregivers and too many babies. The babies were fed on a schedule; their cries had little or no effect on their caregivers' behavior. By the end of the first year they were crying very little, like the babies with highly responsive parents. But the institutionalized babies hadn't just stopped crying—they had stopped laughing, as well. Their faces were expressionless, they showed little interest in their surroundings, and their motor and language development was retarded (Spitz and Wolf, 1946; Provence and Lipton, 1962).

Babies whose cries are answered relatively quickly, and babies whose cries are not answered at all, end up crying the least. Therefore, the babies who cry the most are the ones whose caregivers respond sometimes, but either slowly or inconsistently. There are three possible explanations for this finding, and no sure way of deciding among them. Very likely all three are right, in the sense that each accounts for the behavior of *some* babies, *some* of the time.

The first explanation is the one we've already given you: the baby who feels ineffective, who can't rely on her caregivers to meet her needs, is relatively unhappy—though, unlike the institutionalized baby, she's not totally

Babies whose cries often go unanswered may come to feel that the world is an unfriendly place and that what they do doesn't make any difference.

without hope. Her cries signify her lack of contentment, her lack of trust in her environment.

The second is the operant conditioning explanation. Suppose that the caregiver doesn't respond to all of the baby's cries, but responds a fifth of the time, or a tenth, or a twentieth. An operant conditioning theorist would say that this baby has had **partial reinforcement** (see p. 102) for her cries. (Partial reinforcement, as we know from experiments with rats and pigeons, leads to much higher rates of responding than reinforcement for every response.) Furthermore, a caregiver is more likely to come when the baby cries very loudly or for a very long time. In other words, this baby has been reinforced for crying frequently, persistently, and loudly, so it's not surprising that she does so!

The third explanation is that the correlation works in the other direction: it's due to a difference in babies, not in parents. We know that some babies cry more than others, right from the start. Naturally, parents who have a baby who cries constantly will eventually pay less and less attention to her cries—especially if they find that they're seldom able to stop her from crying by feeding her or picking her up.

Although the third explanation is as plausible as the other two, it doesn't seem that it can be the *only* explanation. The investigators who found the correlation between crying babies and unresponsive mothers (Bell and Ainsworth, 1972) also have some evidence that the mother's behavior does have an effect: they showed that a mother who ignored her baby's cries during one three-month period had a baby who cried more in the *next* three-month period. But the reverse was true, too: if a baby cried a lot in one period, her mother ignored her more in the next. So it appears to be another one of those "vicious circles" we mentioned in Chapter 2: the baby cries, the mother ignores the crying, the baby cries more, the mother pays even less attention, and so on.

Babies Are Not All Alike

From the point of view of the baby, the best kind of parents are ones who respond quickly and appropriately to her cries and to her other efforts at communication. Parents who act in this way tend to have successful interactions with their babies (Ashton, 1978).

But it takes two to make a successful interaction. Babies are not all alike. Some babies are born experts at letting their parents know what they want, and at administering reinforcement when their parents do the right thing. (All the baby has to do is stop crying—that's a reinforcer for parents. A smile is even more reinforcing.) Most babies are, in fact, amazingly good at "training" an inexperienced parent. Some, however, are not (see Box).

Other Differences.   Besides obvious things like how much they cry and how they react to new things, there are also more subtle differences among babies. In one investigation (Horowitz, 1980), a number of newborn babies were tested by five different examiners. When they were finished testing, the examiners were asked simply to say whether they liked the baby or not. There was considerable agreement among the different examiners—some babies were generally liked, others were not. Responsive, alert babies who didn't cry too easily tended to be most popular, but other factors—such as the babies' physical appearance—probably also influenced the examiners. What's interesting is that there were some indications that mother-infant interactions were more successful with the likable babies. The likable babies were held closer and for longer periods, and were spoken to more. Their mothers seemed to find it fairly easy to feed them; the mothers of the less popular babies had more problems during feeding sessions.

There are group differences, as well as individual differences, among babies. Chinese-American babies, on the average, get upset less readily than babies of European ancestry. When they *do* cry, the Chinese-American babies tend to be easier to soothe (Freedman, 1979). Another group of babies who were observed to differ from the typical American infant were members of the Zinacanteco Indian tribe of southeast Mexico (Brazelton, 1977). These babies were less active than American babies. They cried less often and less hard, and their sleep was not as deep. In general, the states of the Zinacanteco babies were "smoothed out"—extremes were rare and the babies moved more gradually from one state to another.

The "Difficult" Baby

When interactions between babies and parents don't go well, most parents assume that it's *their* fault. But some babies are more difficult to deal with than others. These babies may be unusually poor at informing their parents of their needs, or at reinforcing their parents for taking care of them. We've already mentioned the clearest example of this: the baby who cries continuously, no matter what her anxious parents do. Most babies cry and fuss a good deal in the first three months; the average is almost eight minutes an hour (Bell and Ainsworth, 1972). But crying generally diminishes after that. If it doesn't, the "tolerance limits" of the parents may be exceeded and they may become less responsive to the baby (Bell, 1974).

It's also true that some babies are "hard to read." One report (Thoman, Becker, and Freese, cited in Jackson and Jackson, 1978) described a baby with a rather unusual characteristic: he often kept his eyes open when he was in the state of active sleep. In addition, this baby tended to change states frequently—from sleep to wakefulness and back. The problem was that the baby's mother couldn't always tell whether he was awake or asleep. Sometimes he was asleep when she thought he was awake, and her efforts to feed him or to get him to respond to her were unsuccessful. This baby's cues were so difficult to interpret that the mother never was sure what he wanted.

Another unusual case involved the first child of a young professional woman who had eagerly awaited his birth. Right from the start this baby

Babies differ in how they react to new situations.

was capable of being in only two states: either he was in a deep sleep or he was screaming at the top of his lungs. When he was screaming, nothing would comfort him except being tightly swaddled. Swaddling caused him to fall back into a deep sleep, in which he was unresponsive to all efforts to reach him. His mother felt rejected by this baby and unable to cope with the task of mothering him. A psychotherapist helped her to see that she wasn't responsible for the ba-

Cuddlers and Noncuddlers. Babies may differ in many ways, but all babies need their minimum daily requirement of hugs and cuddling, right? Wrong! Some infants not only don't seem to need cuddling—they show a positive dislike for it. They struggle and protest when their mothers (or other people)

by's problems. This woman was able to have a successful relationship with her second child, a baby who behaved in a normal way (Brazelton, 1961).

The two babies we've just described are exceptional—they are extreme examples of how the baby's characteristics can affect parent-child relationships. A less severe but much more common problem is the baby who continues to wake his weary parents during the night, month after month. Although most babies are sleeping through the night by 6 months of age, 20 to 25 percent are not (Anders, 1980). When a researcher in England (Richards, 1977) asked a group of mothers about difficulties they were having with their 14-month-old babies, sleep problems headed the list.

The researcher wondered why certain babies were still waking up during the night. Were their mothers more anxious, or less responsive? The answer, apparently, was *no*. No differences were found, between the mothers of sleep-problem babies and mothers of other babies, in attitudes toward childrearing. The mothers of the sleep-problem babies were no less responsive to their babies' cries. Whether the baby was a first-born or a later-born, a boy or a girl, made no difference.

The sleep-problem babies *did* differ from other babies in some ways, though. When tested at 8 or 9 days of age, they had been unusually irritable and quick to cry, and they were fussy babies all through infancy. The investigator concluded that the sleep-problem babies had had distinctive characteristics from the time they were born, and that "sleep problems are not the result of any particular style of parental handling" (p. 485).

It's clear that babies differ from birth in the way they respond to people and to situations.

These differences in styles of interaction reflect differences in **temperament,** which we discussed in Chapter 2. In that chapter we described the work of psychiatrists Alexander Thomas and Stella Chess. It was Thomas and Chess who classified babies as "easy," "difficult," or "slow to warm up." (Not all babies fall into these three categories, however—some show no clearcut patterns of behavior.)

The easy babies were cheerful, adaptable, and regular in their habits. In Thomas and Chess's longitudinal study of differences in temperament (1977), 40 percent of babies fell into this category.

The difficult babies were those whose biological cycles were irregular, who showed negative reactions to new people or new situations, whose reactions tended to be intense, and who were often irritable or unhappy. Only 10 percent of the babies in Thomas and Chess's sample were classified as difficult.

The final category was the slow-to-warm-up babies—15 percent of the sample. These babies, like the difficult ones, reacted negatively to anything new; however, unlike the difficult babies, their reactions tended to be mild.

According to Thomas and Chess, the quality of the relationship between parents and baby depends partly on the "goodness of fit" between the baby's characteristics and the parents' expectations and attitudes. Awareness of their baby's temperament can help parents to develop a style of interaction that is satisfying both for them and for their baby. For example, the parents of a difficult or slow-to-warm-up baby can introduce new experiences gradually. Such a baby, if given time to adjust, will eventually come to accept new people and new situations. In a supportive environment, a difficult baby is less likely to turn into a problem child. ∎

try to hold them close. Yet there is no evidence that these babies are "frustrated," or that they are any less capable than other babies of forming close ties with their parents.

These findings emerged from a longitudinal study of 37 infants, carried out in Scotland by Rudolph Schaffer and Peggy Emerson (1964). About half of the children in this study *loved* being cuddled. All through infancy they enjoyed being held, hugged, and carried. Here are some of the things the mothers of these cuddlers said about them:

"Cuddles you back."

"Loves it."

"Laps it up."

"Would be up on my lap all day if I let her."

"Snuggles into you."

"I have to rock him in my arms every night till he falls asleep."

About a quarter of the children *never* liked cuddling, even when they were tired or ill. The comments of the noncuddlers' mothers were sometimes rather wistful:

"He's just like his father—not one for a bit of love."

"Gets restless when cuddled, turns face away and begins to struggle."

"Will kick and thrash with his arms, and if you persist will begin to cry."

"You can't calm him by picking him up even when he is teething."

"Holding her up on her feet is the best way of calming her."

"Asks to be lifted, yet the moment you hold him on your lap he pushes against you till he is down again."

The remaining quarter of the babies fell in between the other two groups—they liked cuddling some of the time.

Being a cuddler or a noncuddler didn't depend on birth order: firstborns and later-borns were no different in this respect. There was also no significant relationship with the babies' sex, although there were slightly more girls in the cuddler group and slightly more boys in the noncuddler group.

The noncuddlers didn't shun their parents altogether—like other babies they went to their mothers when they were frightened. They allowed themselves to be held during feedings (at least until they were old enough to sit in a high chair). In play they didn't mind being kissed, stroked, or tickled, as long as they weren't being held. They enjoyed being bounced or swung around just as much as the cuddlers did, even though these activities *did* involve being held. What they seemed to mind was the restraint of movement that resulted from being cuddled or hugged. These babies were generally more active and restless than the cuddly babies. The noncuddlers disliked being wrapped up or having their clothes put on, and when they were tucked into bed they struggled free of the blankets. In motor development they were ahead of the cuddlers.

Schaffer and Emerson reasoned that if the noncuddlers really had a need for cuddling that was not being met, then these babies should look for other ways to satisfy that need. But there were no signs of a frustrated need. In fact, the noncuddlers were less likely than the cuddlers to become thumbsuckers. They were also less likely to become attached to a favorite blanket or stuffed animal.

What determines whether a baby is a cuddler or a noncuddler? Schaffer and Emerson didn't feel that these characteristics resulted from differences in the way their mothers treated them. There were no differences in how quickly the mother responded to the baby's cries, or in whether she was a "handler" (who sought physical contact with her child) or a "nonhandler" (who preferred to interact in other ways). The babies seemed to be cuddlers or noncuddlers right from the start. Eventually the noncuddlers' mothers stopped trying to cuddle them and learned other ways of giving comfort. These differences in maternal behavior were apparently a *result* of those babies' characteristics, not the cause of them. Schaffer and Emerson concluded that the tendency to be a cuddler or a noncuddler is inborn—that it depends on nature, not nurture. Of course, like other inborn characteristics, this tendency can be either increased or decreased by environmental influences.

The Effects of the Baby's Sex and the Parent's Sex. Among the factors that affect a baby's relationship with parents and other people, surely one of the most important is the baby's sex. "What a cute baby," strangers say. "Is it a girl or a boy?" Unless the baby is dressed in pink ruffles or blue overalls, it's not easy to tell, is it? Girls and boys seem pretty much alike at this age.

There *are* measurable differences between male and female infants, even in the first week or two of life. But these differences are small—statistical differences between the "average boy" and the "average girl." The differences between one baby boy and another, or between one baby girl and another, are likely to be far greater than the differences between the averages for the two sexes.

What, though, are these sex differences? The most reliable one is the difference in size and strength. Boys are larger at birth and remain so, on the average, during most of childhood. A boy baby tends to have a larger head and a larger face than a girl, and to have less fat and more muscle (Tanner, 1974). He is able to hold up his head at an earlier age.

The other differences between male and female infants are slight enough so that they show up in some studies and not in others. These differences may all be due to the fact that, at birth, girls are somewhat more advanced in physical development than boys. Infant girls have been found to be more sensitive to various kinds of stimuli, especially touch, cold, pain, and taste. Some studies find that boys tend to cry more than girls and are a little harder to soothe; they also tend to startle more easily.

Differences in the ways parents treat male and female infants have been found, too. A number of studies have shown that mothers are more likely to cuddle and hold close their infant sons. They are more likely to smile at or

Boy or girl? Unless the baby is wearing distinctively masculine or feminine clothing (or, of course, no clothing at all), it's hard to tell.

talk to their infant daughters—in other words, to give them stimuli from a distance. One investigator (Korner, 1974) speculated that these differences might be partly a reaction to the differences in the babies: for example, new-born boys are larger and stronger, so mothers may be less hesitant about picking them up; or mothers may hold them close as a way of controlling their startles.

Explanations like these are attempts to account for the *mother's* behavior. For many years, psychologists talked about mother-infant interactions but seldom about *father*-infant interactions. This was mainly because mothers were thought to be much more important in infant development, but it may also have been because mothers were more likely to be available at the times of day when psychologists like to do their research!

Recently, however, there have at last been some studies of fathers' behavior with their babies. It turns out that fathers, too, behave differently with girl and boy infants, but in *opposite ways* from mothers. Fathers hold and cuddle their daughters more than their sons, and they give their sons more stimuli from a distance. In general, both fathers and mothers tend to show more *affection* toward a young infant of the opposite sex, and to give more *attention* and stimulation to an infant of the same sex (Parke and Sawin, 1977). Since the mother and the father respond in different ways to the same infant, it's hard to see how these differences could be based on differences in the infant's size, tendency to startle, or whatever.

If mothers act toward sons the way fathers act toward daughters, and vice versa, does that mean that male and female infants end up even—end up getting the same amount of affection and stimulation? No, it doesn't. For one thing, fathers tend to be around a lot less of the time than mothers (Weinraub, 1978). For another thing, when they *are* around, fathers are more likely than mothers to be playing with the baby, and less likely to be feeding, diapering, or giving other kinds of care. And finally, fathers and mothers play in different ways with their babies (Lamb, 1978). Fathers' play tends to be of a physical sort—they will roughhouse with their sons, though they're gentler with their daughters. Mothers tend to play in less active ways with both boys and girls—their play is more likely to be vocal than physical, and more likely to involve conventional games such as peek-a-boo and patty-cake. So fathers and mothers are not equal and interchangeable parents. They tend to assume different roles in their interactions with the infant.

As babies turn into toddlers and then preschoolers, the differences between girls and boys become more numerous and more noticeable. We'll return often in later chapters to the important matter of sex differences.

Cultural Differences in Baby Care

When people become parents, many of their attitudes and opinions about childrearing are already formed. These attitudes may change, of course, as the parents encounter the day-to-day realities of childrearing. They may also change as the parents adjust to the particular characteristics of the individual child. But to some extent the attitudes and beliefs that people start out with *do* influence their parental behavior (Moss and Jones, 1977).

This is most obviously true when it comes to cultural differences in child-rearing styles. In industrialized societies like those of North America and Western Europe, young babies spend much of their time lying in their cribs. They are taken out from time to time for feeding or for playing, but they sleep alone—often, in fact, in a separate room.

The pattern in other societies, preindustrial societies, is quite different. In many parts of South America and Africa, and in some parts of Asia, babies are held almost constantly. There is usually some sort of cloth sling or shawl that holds the baby against the mother's body but leaves her hands free. Typically, these babies are breast-fed every time they cry, even at the slightest whimper. It's not surprising that they appear to be very contented.

But there's a catch. Typically, in these societies, little attention seems to be paid to the baby's social or intellectual development. The kind of mother-infant interactions we see in our own society are rare: there is much less eye contact, much less smiling, between mother and baby. She seldom plays with him face to face. She seldom speaks to him.

One possible reason for these cultural differences is that so many babies in the preindustrial societies will never live to become adults. Most of the deaths occur in the first two years. In these societies, the important thing is that the baby survives. All the parents' concern is focused on the infant's *physical* welfare. Concern about other aspects of development can wait until later on.

Class Differences. Even within our own culture there are differences in childrearing styles. Some of these differences are related to the socioeconomic class of the parents. One study of childrearing in the United States (Tulkin, 1977) compared a group of white, college-educated parents with a group of white, working-class parents. (*Working class,* in this case, meant that one or both parents had dropped out of high school and that the father was working at an unskilled or semiskilled job.)

The babies in the working-class homes were almost always bottle-fed, rather than breast-fed. Many of them slept in their parents' bedrooms, even when a separate room was available. They spent more time in front of a TV set than the babies of college-educated parents.

The babies of the college-educated parents slept in a separate room. The majority were breast-fed. Compared with the working-class mothers, the college-educated mothers gave their babies more things to play with and more freedom to crawl around on the floor. (These were babies of crawling age, 10 months old.) But the biggest difference between the two groups was that the college-educated mothers talked to their babies more and responded more often to the assorted coos, goos, and babbles that their babies uttered. They responded by imitating the sound the baby made, or by "answering" the baby's vocalization.

It's important to note that in many ways the two groups of mothers did *not* differ. There were no differences in the amount of time the mother spent with the baby, in the number of times the baby was picked up, kissed, tickled, or bounced, or in the way the mother responded when the baby touched her or handed her something.

ATTACHMENT

When Sarah was 3 or 4 months old, *any* kind person could care for her—rock her or diaper her or give her a bottle. In those days Sarah smiled at everyone: little old ladies in the supermarket, visiting aunts and uncles, even at her pediatrician. But now Sarah is 12 months old, and the situation has changed. Just anybody won't do. There are times—times when Sarah is tired, frightened, or in pain—when she wants her mother and only her mother. If her mother is available, Sarah will cling to her and be comforted. If her mother is not around, Sarah may cry and cry, refusing to be consoled, until her mother returns. If her mother is gone for a period of time that seems endless to a 1-year-old—a week, say—Sarah may fall into a deep depression.

A special relationship now exists between Sarah and her mother, a relationship that didn't exist 6 months ago. Psychologists call this relationship **attachment;** a nonpsychologist might simply call it love. Attachment is a bond between Sarah and her mother. This bond developed over a period of

time. It causes Sarah to want to be near her mother, especially when she is in need of security or comfort.

Attachment is a remarkably universal aspect of development. Virtually every normal child becomes attached to someone (provided, of course, that there is someone there to become attached to). Moreover, the age at which attachment occurs is virtually the same in societies all over the world. Babies generally cry (or at least look unhappy) when a person to whom they are attached leaves them alone in an unfamiliar place. This is called **separation distress.** Separation distress shows up in pretty much the same way, and at pretty much the same time, in babies raised in a variety of settings:

> . . . American cities, Latin American barrios, Israeli kibbutzim, or !Kung San bands in the Kalahari. Such crying usually emerges when babies are about eight months old, rises to a peak in the middle of the second year, and then declines in all those cultures. (Kagan, 1978, p. 72)

Fear of strangers shows a similar trend in time. As attachment to familiar people increases during the second part of the first year, *un*familiar people are no longer smiled at so readily. A 7- or 8-month-old might stare intently at a stranger, then frown or look away. By 12 months many babies will burst into tears if someone they don't know tries to pick them up. Fear of strangers is another aspect of the attachment relationship.

Unlike attachment, however, fear of strangers is not universal. Babies have positive feelings, as well as negative ones, toward strangers who act friendly. Which feeling wins out depends both on the baby and on the situation. Some babies continue to smile at strangers, even at 12 months. More commonly, the baby's reaction will depend on who the stranger is and on what he or she does. Babies are seldom afraid of other babies or of children; they are less afraid of women than of men (Brooks and Lewis, 1976). Adult strangers are likely to get a friendly response from a baby if they approach her gradually, if they offer her a familiar toy, and if her mother is nearby. They're likely to get a negative response if they try to get too close too quickly, especially if the baby is in an unfamiliar place or if her mother isn't with her.

To Whom Are Babies Attached?

Many babies—the majority, in fact—are attached not only to their mothers but to their fathers as well. Babies often become attached to both parents at around the same time, usually between 6 and 9 months. At 12 or 13 months, most babies are equally attached to both parents. Under normal conditions they show no consistent preference for one parent rather than the other. However, in stressful situations, when they are upset, year-old babies generally go to their mothers for comfort (Lamb, 1978).

It is not surprising that babies at this age turn to their mothers in times of trouble, since in almost all families the mother is the primary caregiver—the one who does most of the feeding, diapering, bathing, dressing, and so on. The father is much less likely to be involved in caregiving, especially during the first year.

The amount of caregiving does make a difference. In one study (Ross, Kagan, Zelazo, and Kotelchuck, 1975) babies' attachment to their fathers was found to correlate with the number of times per week the father changed the baby's diaper! Babies who *aren't* attached to their fathers are likely to be those whose fathers took no part in their care. When fathers of this sort were encouraged to share in the caregiving and to interact more with their babies, the babies soon became attached to them (Kotelchuck, 1975; Zelazo, Kotelchuck, Barber, and David, 1977).

It's not always the father's attitude, though, that leads the mother to do all or most of the caregiving. Some mothers are convinced that only a woman is capable of taking care of a young infant. They believe that males are incompetent in that department. There is no evidence to support this belief. On the contrary, as we mentioned before, fathers appear to be just as responsive to their newborn babies as mothers are, just as sensitive to the babies' signals, and just as capable at giving care (Lamb, 1978; Parke, 1979).

Attachment without Caregiving.   In order for a baby to form an attachment to someone, the baby has to have many opportunities to interact with that person. Caregiving is one way to make sure that those interactions occur, but it isn't the only way. Babies often become attached to people who never take

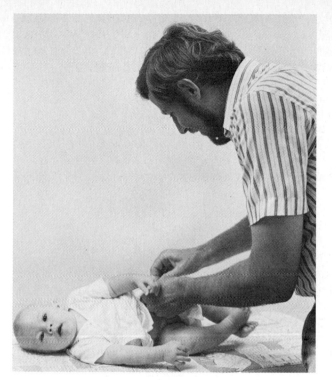

Caregiving provides an opportunity for a father to interact with his baby.

care of them at all—not only fathers, but also other people such as siblings and grandparents. Moreover, babies sometimes *fail* to become attached to people who *do* take care of them—people such as housekeepers and day-care-center workers. Babies who spend their days at a day-care center generally become attached to their mothers, not to the people who take care of them at the center. They are as attached to their mothers, in fact, as babies who stay at home all day (Ashton, 1978; Kagan, Kearsley, and Zelazo, 1978).

What seems to count most in the attachment process is not who changes the diapers or how much time (within reasonable limits) that the baby and the parent spend together. It is the *quality* of their interactions—the sensitivity of the parent's response to the baby, the emotional intensity of their interactions, the sheer delight each takes in the other's company.

Attachment in the Second Year. We've already mentioned that fathers and mothers tend to interact in different ways with their babies. When a mother picks up an infant or a toddler, it's most often for some caregiving chore. When a father picks the child up, it's more likely to be for play. In addition, fathers tend to play in more lively and unpredictable ways than mothers. Fathers are especially active and stimulating in their play with their sons. Perhaps for these reasons, almost all boys come to prefer their fathers to their mothers by the end of their second year. Two-year-old girls are more variable. Some prefer their fathers, some their mothers, and others remain equally attached to both parents (Lamb, 1978).

Why Do Babies Form Attachments?

The bond that forms between a baby and his mother was a subject of interest to Sigmund Freud. Freud believed that a baby's first attachment is to his mother's breast, the source of his greatest pleasure during the first stage (the oral stage). Later the baby enlarges his attachment to include *all* of his mother. His love for his mother is based primarily on the fact that she feeds him when he's hungry. He also associates her with other pleasant sensations that she produces in his body as she holds him and cares for him.

Other theorists (Sears, 1963; Bijou and Baer, 1965; Gewirtz, 1972) have also connected the baby's attachment to his mother with the fact that she feeds him. Some behaviorists, for example, believe that the baby comes to associate his mother with reinforcers such as food and warmth. By providing the baby with these things, she becomes a **secondary reinforcer**—a stimulus that has acquired reinforcement value of its own simply by being linked repeatedly with a real reinforcer.

Although these theories sound reasonable, they can't account for all that we now know about attachment. Babies *don't* become attached just to their mothers, and they *don't* become attached just to the person who feeds them or takes care of them. Reinforcement in the form of food does not seem to be necessary. The kind of pleasurable sensations that result from being held or stroked also do not seem to be necessary. In fact, *visual* contact between the baby and the other person seems to be more important than *physical* contact (Rheingold, 1961; Roedell and Slaby, 1977). But visual contact, too, is not essential: babies who are blind from birth do become attached to their mothers (Fraiberg, 1977). And finally, even babies whose mothers have beaten them or neglected them become attached to their mothers (Egeland and Sroufe, 1981).

But what if there *is* no mother, no permanent caregiver? Even then, given half a chance, babies will form attachments. This was poignantly illustrated many years ago, by some young Jewish children who had spent their infancy in a Nazi concentration camp. Their parents were dead. They were kept together in the concentration camp and cared for by an ever-changing series of adults, all of whom were killed before the war was over. At the end of the war these six children were sent to England, where they came to the attention of Anna Freud (Sigmund's daughter). She was amazed to discover that these 3-year-olds cared not a bit for any adult. They were attached solely and completely to one another!

> The children's positive feelings were centered exclusively in their group. It was evident that they cared greatly for each other and not at all for anybody or anything else. They had no other wish than to be together, and became upset when they were separated from each other, even for short moments. . . .
>
> On walks they were concerned for each other's safety in traffic, looked after children who lagged behind, helped each other over ditches, turned aside branches for each other to clear the passage in the woods, and carried each other's coats. In the nursery they picked up each other's toys. After they had learned to

play, they assisted each other silently in building and admired each other's productions. At mealtimes handing food to the neighbor was of greater importance than eating oneself. (Freud and Dann, 1967, pp. 497, 500)

The Ethological Approach.   Because babies seem to have such a strong predisposition to form attachments, even under the most unfavorable conditions, many developmental psychologists now believe that this is a built-in characteristic of the human species. The study of animals' and humans' built-in patterns of behavior (sometimes called *instincts*) is the concern of a field known as **ethology.** Thus, this view of attachment is called the **ethological** approach. John Bowlby, a British psychologist, was the first to propose an ethological theory of attachment.

Bowlby (1969) points out that attachment of the infant to its mother is not unique to the human species—it is found in most bird and mammal species as well. Baby ducklings, for example, follow their mother wherever she goes. Their tendency to follow is innate and instinctive, but ducklings must *learn* to recognize their mother. The way this is learned, in ducklings, is through a process called **imprinting:** ducklings will follow the first moving object they see after they hatch. Normally, this is their mother. But occasionally it turns out to be something else—for example, a large, featherless ethologist named Konrad Lorenz. Some ducklings that were imprinted on Konrad Lorenz followed him wherever he went and totally ignored full-grown female ducks. Once ducklings are imprinted on someone or something, it's virtually impossible to *un*imprint them.

Konrad Lorenz and friends.

Another feature of imprinting is that it must take place soon after the duckling is hatched, or it won't take place at all. The period of time during which the duckling can be imprinted—the **critical period**—lasts only about a day. If the duckling is not allowed to see its first moving object until after it is 24 hours old, little or no imprinting will occur (Hess, 1970).

Imprinting is a quick and simple form of attachment. The attachment process is more gradual and more flexible in the higher animals, especially in monkeys and apes. The end result is similar, though: the attached baby animal stays close to its mother. A newborn monkey at first clings to its mother only by reflex—it doesn't recognize her yet. But a month or so later, when it has begun to explore its environment, its attachment to its mother is clear. The young monkey always remains near its mother. Although it may approach other monkeys (including other adult females), at the first sign of danger it leaps towards its mother and clings tightly to her (Bowlby, 1969).

Unlike ducklings, orphaned monkeys can become reattached to other monkeys—or to other people, for that matter. A young monkey reared by a human caretaker becomes attached to that particular person and protests vehemently if its caretaker tries to leave. But a new caretaker is eventually accepted, and new attachments can be formed. There is no critical period in monkeys—no definite age after which they can no longer form or change attachments. Instead, there is what ethologists call a **sensitive period,** a time when attachments are formed most readily. After that, the monkey's capacity to form new attachments gradually declines.

The tendency for a young animal to become attached to its mother and to remain close to her is adaptive—it increases its chances of survival. A baby mammal that remains with its mother is less likely to be taken by predators, less likely to lose its only source of food. Thus, the tendency to become attached is passed on from generation to generation, preserved by the process of natural selection.

According to the ethological view, the same is true of the human baby's tendency to form attachments. That is, the predisposition has been inherited by human babies because, in the primitive environment of the early humans, it had survival value.

In line with this idea, we might point out that attachment seems to occur at just the time it's needed most—just when the young organism develops some mobility. Human babies begin to form attachments at about 6 months of age; most are attached by 9 or 10 months, the age of crawling. Attachment behavior tends to reach a peak at around 13 or 14 months—precisely the age when they begin to walk. A young rhesus monkey starts to move away from its mother at about 2 weeks of age. It takes only a week or two for these monkeys to become attached to their mothers (Harlow and Harlow, 1965; Bowlby, 1969). Ducklings can walk almost as soon as they hatch, and ducklings become imprinted almost immediately.

Security and Comfort.   In human babies, as in young monkeys, attachment behavior is a compromise. Two different desires motivate the young human or monkey: the desire to stay with its mother, and the desire to explore its environment and to play. In both human and monkey babies we can see the pull of these two opposing interests. The typical human baby of 12 or 18 months will explore and play happily within sight of his mother, now and then returning to her (or glancing at her) for reassurance. The child uses the mother as a "secure base from which to explore" (Ainsworth, 1977, p. 59).

Attachment shows up most clearly when a child is in pain, afraid, tired, or ill. Anything that worries or frightens a young child is likely to increase his or her clinginess, and that includes being punished or threatened for clinging too much! The same is true in baby ducklings. A psychologist who studied imprinting in ducks (Hess, 1970) noticed that if he accidentally stepped on the toes of a duckling that was beginning to follow him around, the duckling followed him more closely than ever. In a similar manner, human babies become attached even to caregivers who physically abuse them: the child in pain may go for comfort to the very person who caused his pain. One little boy who was badly beaten by his mother was removed from his home and placed in a children's residential center. When the nurse in the center held him, he told her, "Nobody holds me when I hurt like my mama does" (Blount, 1981, p. 5).

The Quality of Attachment

A leading figure in the ethological approach to attachment is Mary Ainsworth, of the University of Virginia. Ainsworth has been studying infant-mother attachments since the early 1950s. Her work has had significant influence on the course of child psychology in the United States.

Ainsworth's main interest has been in the *quality* of the attachment relationship. She believes that an infant is either attached to someone or not attached, and that it makes no sense to talk about the *strength* of the attachment. How attached a given baby appears to be at a particular moment depends on the situation, and on whether the baby is frightened or not, happy or not, and so on. But attachment relationships do vary along another dimension, a qualitative dimension. Ainsworth (1977) calls this dimension the **security** of the child's attachment. Virtually all children are attached by 12 or 14 months, but some are **securely attached** and some are **insecurely attached.**

To assess the security of babies' attachments, Ainsworth and her colleagues (Ainsworth, Blehar, Waters, and Wall, 1978) have developed a procedure called the "strange situation." The baby and his mother are brought into a room where they've never been before, a room with toys for the baby to play with. They remain in the room for a little while and the baby is allowed to play. Then during the course of the next 20 minutes, the mother leaves the room twice. The first time, there is another person in the room—a person whom the baby doesn't know. The second time the baby is left alone.

Many babies cry when their mothers leave, whether or not the stranger is present. Crying isn't the important thing, though. Securely attached babies may or may not cry; the same is true of insecurely attached babies. What the investigators look at is the whole pattern of the baby's behavior during the course of the session. A securely attached baby will generally be attracted to the toys and will play happily as long as his mother is there. (He's using his mother as a "secure base from which to explore.") When his mother leaves he may not cry, but he'll stop playing or play with less enthusiasm. Then, when his mother returns, he'll greet her joyously. If he wasn't greatly upset by her leaving, he may just smile or babble at her. If he was upset, he'll rush to her and cling to her, and he'll calm down quickly.

That's the typical pattern for the securely attached child. Children with insecure attachments are more variable in their behavior. Some do little playing and exploring, even when their mothers are present—they may cry or cling even before their mothers leave. But it's their reaction to their mothers' return (after the mother does leave) that is most revealing. An insecurely attached child will not greet his mother with unmixed joy. He may alternate between clinging to her and pushing her away. He may ignore her entirely. Or he may continue to cry in an angry way and refuse to be comforted (Sroufe, 1978).

About 60 to 70 percent of babies from middle-class homes are securely attached to their mothers by age 12 months (Ainsworth and others, 1978). But remember: we said that attachment is a *relationship*. The security or insecurity of a child's attachment to someone resides in the child's *relationship* with that person, and not necessarily in the child. A child may be insecurely attached to one person and securely attached to someone else (Londerville and Main, 1981).

What Determines the Quality of an Attachment?   We said earlier that what seems to count most in the attachment process is the quality of the interactions between the baby and the other person. Now we can make that statement more precise. The quality of a baby's attachment to his mother (assessed in the "strange situation" at age 12 months) is correlated with the kinds of interactions the mother and baby had when the baby was younger. A baby who is securely attached at 12 months generally had good interactions with his mother at age 2 or 3 months—and, presumably, in the following months as well. An insecurely attached baby tended to have unsuccessful interactions with his mother when he was 2 or 3 months old. During these interactions he was more likely to fuss, and less likely to smile, than the babies who would later form secure attachments. The mother of the insecurely attached baby was abrupt or unresponsive, and she didn't gear her actions to the baby's signals. Remember Jenny and her mother (p. 178)? That's the kind of interaction that shows a lack of sensitivity on the mother's part. An insensitive mother tends to end up with an insecurely attached child (Blehar, Lieberman, and Ainsworth, 1977).

This makes it sound as though unsuccessful interactions and insecure attachments are all the mother's fault: she hasn't been sensitive enough to the baby's signals. But other investigators (Osofsky, 1976; Waters, Vaughn, and Egeland, 1980) have shown that the baby's own characteristics are also important. Differences in babies that showed up in the first week of life were found to correlate with the success of infant-mother interactions, and also with the quality of later infant-mother attachments. The babies who will have poorer interactions and less secure attachments are less "with it" in the first week of life. They are less responsive to stimuli, less alert, more irritable. And it's unlikely that these characteristics are the result of their experiences, since they're only a few days old.

The conclusion, then, is just what you'd expect: the relationship between two people depends on *both* of them.

The Effects of Experiences Right after Birth. Is the relationship between a mother and her baby affected by what happens in the first few hours after the

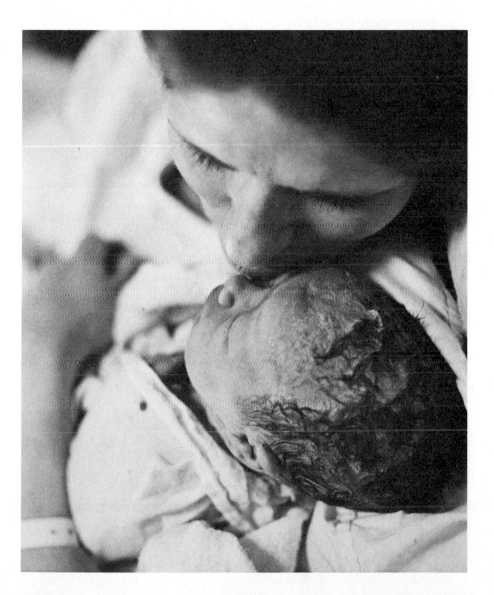

baby is born? Some investigators think so. They feel that the hours immediately after birth are extremely important. They feel that the mother needs a chance to be alone with her newborn baby right away, in order for their relationship to get off to a good start. A group of mothers were permitted some time alone with their babies in the first hour or two of the baby's life. Later, these mothers had more affectionate relationships with their infants than other mothers whose babies had been whisked off to a hospital nursery. The investigators concluded that separation in the first few hours after birth is harmful to the mother-infant relationship (Klaus and Kennell, 1978).

Most of the mothers in the report we just referred to were economically deprived: they were North or South Americans of low socioeconomic status. A study of middle-class families in the United States (Rode, Chang, Fisch, and Sroufe, 1981) yielded different results. The babies in this second study had been hospitalized for an average of 3½ weeks right after birth, due to prematurity or other health problems. They were tested a year or so later in the "strange situation." Seventy percent were found to be securely attached—about what you'd expect in a middle-class sample. Early hospitalization (and separation from their mothers) hadn't affected the attachment process.

A psychologist who looked into this question has concluded that a period of togetherness right after birth might be helpful for babies and mothers who are "at risk." It isn't necessary, though, when "one has no reason to be concerned about the mother's adequacy in caretaking" (Horowitz, 1980, p. 120). That conclusion is backed up by tens of thousands of adopted children, some of whom weren't adopted until many months after they were born. Most of them formed close ties with their adoptive parents.

The Toddler's Struggle for Autonomy

As Sarah approaches her second birthday, her need to stay in close contact with her mother begins to lessen. Her interest in play and exploration remains high. She can walk well now. Her new mobility, coupled with her increasing willingness to leave her mother's side, enables her to explore more of her environment. During toddlerhood, children are moving toward independence. (To toddle means to take short, uncertain steps. Roughly speaking, **toddlerhood** is a period that begins in the second year of life, when the child begins to walk. It ends at age 2 or 2½, when the child becomes a preschooler.)

Erikson has pointed to the struggle for **autonomy** as the big issue in the toddler's life. Autonomy means self-determination. It means "Me do it!" It means "No!"

Toddlerhood is also the time when **socialization** begins in earnest—when a child must begin to learn the attitudes, behaviors, knowledge, and skills that are necessary to get along in her society. Thus, the child's desire to do what she wants conflicts with the pressures on her to conform to the rules of the society. (This conflict, as you may recall, is a central part of Freudian theory.)

Socialization of a toddler is primarily the parents' job. When a parent tells a toddler to do something (or not to do something), will she obey her parent's command or will she resist and rebel? A study of the behavior of toddlers and their mothers (Londerville and Main, 1981) found that the average 21-month-old toddler obeys about half of her mother's commands. But toddlers who were securely attached to their mothers at 12 months obeyed more often than toddlers who were insecurely attached. The securely attached children were also more cooperative when a stranger asked them to do something. Insecurely attached toddlers were much more likely to defy their mothers and do exactly the opposite of what she asked. They were also much more likely to throw a tantrum when they were told to stop doing something.

Other studies (Sroufe, 1978; Matas, Arend, and Sroufe, 1979) have focused on the *kinds* of commands that toddlers do and don't obey. When mothers told their toddlers not to play with a certain toy, or told them to put their toys away, securely attached children were just as disobedient as insecurely attached ones. But when securely attached toddlers were given a problem they couldn't solve alone, they listened to their mothers' advice and solved the problem with their mothers' help. The insecurely attached toddlers, on the other hand, wouldn't let their mothers help them. They had tantrums or gave up.

A toddler may like to feel that she is independent and autonomous, but of course she really isn't. She still has a lot to learn, and she still needs her parents' help. The path is smoother for a toddler who can accept help when it's offered.

The Unattached Child

Toddlers who have formed attachments to their parents are often desperately unhappy if they must be separated from them. As Ainsworth (1977, p. 56) has put it, "Young children may well respond to an involuntary separation with an intensity appropriate to matters of life and death." If the separation is prolonged, the frantic unhappiness that many of these children display gives way in time to sadness and depression. Eventually, though, the wounds are healed and new attachments are formed (Burlingham and Freud, 1967; Rutter, 1974).

Far more serious are the consequences of a failure to form attachments in the first place. There is only one situation in which this is likely to happen: when a child is reared in an institution where there are many caregivers, all of the "here today, gone tomorrow" variety. If a child never has the chance to interact with one particular person over a period of time, he or she will form no attachments. Even in a "good" institution, where the care is adequate and the children are given many things to look at and play with, the long-range forecast is not cheerful. These children will probably turn out to be of near-average intellectual ability, but their social and emotional development will probably not be normal. As toddlers, they tend to follow and cling to any available adult. As preschoolers they are likely to be overly friendly with strangers and very demanding of attention. By middle childhood they are often restless and disobedient, and they tend to get along poorly both with adults and with other children. Few appear able to form lasting relationships

THE CHILD IN SOCIETY

Toilet Training

Every human society places some restraints on its members with regard to elimination—nowhere are people allowed to urinate or defecate wherever and whenever they please. Eventually, all young children are expected to conform to the toileting customs of their culture. But societies differ greatly in when and how this demand is made. Children may be trained harshly or with gentleness. They may be trained in early infancy or in late toddlerhood.

Gentle, late training is often found in preindustrial societies where the climate is warm and toddlers go naked (at least from the waist down). The practices of the Siriono, a South American Indian people, are a good example:

Almost no effort is made by the mother to train an infant in the habits of cleanliness until he can walk, and then they are instilled very gradually. Children who are able to walk, however, soon learn by imitation, and with the assistance of their parents, not to defecate near the hammock. When they are old enough to indicate their needs, the mother gradually leads them further and further away from the hammock to urinate and defecate, so that by the time they have reached the age of 3 they have learned not to pollute the house. (Holmberg, cited in Whiting and Child, 1953, pp. 75–76)

We often think of early toilet training as harsh and late training as gentle. But there is no necessary connection between these two aspects of training. The Digo of East Africa train their babies early, but the training is by no means harsh. Babies in this society are generally trained by 6 months! Here's how it's done:

Bowel and bladder training are initiated simultaneously and extremely early, at about 2 to 3 weeks of age. The mother takes a teaching role and assumes all responsibility in the initial phase of the training process. She places the infant in a special training position outside the house, at first at times when she senses that the infant needs to eliminate (after feeding, when waking from naps, etc.), with the idea that he will soon learn to let her know more independently.

At about 2 to 3 weeks of age, the mother begins by putting the infant in a position assumed to facilitate elimination. For voiding [urination], the mother sits on the ground outside, with her legs straight out in front of her. The infant is placed between the mother's legs, facing away from her, in a sitting position, supported by the mother's body. The mother then makes a "shuus" noise that the infant learns to associate with voiding. This is done many times during the day and at night. When the infant voids as the "shuus" sound is

with anyone, although many have a considerable amount of superficial charm (Rutter, 1974, 1979).

Ducklings have only a day to form an attachment; monkeys may have as much as a year. At what point does it become too late for a young human? Children taken out of an institution and adopted into a family by age 3 generally turn out all right. Children adopted after age 4 may form very close attachments to their new parents, but the damage has been done. In school they show the same social and emotional problems as the children who remade, he is rewarded for his behavior by feeding, close contact, or other pleasurable activity. Gradually, the infant is expected to become more articulate in communicating his needs or by climbing to the appropriate position. He is expected to urinate in position and on command at least by 4 to 5 months. (deVries and deVries, 1977, p. 173)

The procedure is similar for bowel training. Only the position is different:

The mother again sits on the ground or floor but with her knees bent. The infant sits facing her, supported on the lower parts of her legs, with his legs over hers and leaning slightly forward, the support of her feet providing a kind of "potty." (p. 173)

The Digo do not regard bladder and bowel training as private or unclean—rather, it is accepted in a relaxed way as a normal part of infant care, something a mother might do while she was socializing with her friends. During the first year, occasional slips that occur during the day or night are taken casually—perhaps only with an exclamation of surprise. After the baby is walking he is scolded if he eliminates in the house, but apparently that happens very rarely.

In our own culture, toilet-training practices have changed considerably over the years. The severest training occurred in the 1920s (Wolfenstein, 1967). In those days, mothers were told to begin training when the baby was a month old and to adhere to a strict schedule: the baby

This Digo baby has learned to urinate in response to his mother's signals.

should be held over a potty at certain times of day, and these times mustn't vary by as much as five minutes! That attitude gradually went out of style. Nowadays children are seldom put under any pressure to use the potty until after their second birthday, and even then the pressure tends to be of the mildest sort.

(Continued on page 202.)

main in the institution. So there seems to be a sensitive period for the formation of human attachments. An attachment to someone in infancy or toddlerhood paves the way for later close relationships (Rutter, 1979).

Relationships with Other Children

Although attachments in infancy or toddlerhood are necessary for normal development, it is possible that attachments to *parents* (or parent substitutes) are

From the child's point of view, the timing of training probably matters less than the *manner* of training—whether the trainer is impatient and critical, or gentle and understanding. But what about timing? Is it correct to assume that late training is better for the child? It *is* better in some ways: The child can understand what's expected of him, can participate in a conscious, voluntary way, and can take pride in his accomplishment.

But late training has its disadvantages, too. Urination and defecation start out as simple reflexes, triggered by the pressure of a full bladder or bowel. Like other reflexes (salivation, for example), these reflexes are subject to the laws of classical conditioning (see p. 102). This means that they can become linked with neutral stimuli, if the neutral stimuli often are present when the reflex occurs. The Digo's training technique makes use of this principle. The sounds the mother makes, and the positions in which she puts the baby, become associated with urination or defecation, and eventually these stimuli can themselves trigger the reflexes.

We don't use those techniques in our culture, but that doesn't mean that the reflexes don't get conditioned. Babies in our society have spent two years urinating and defecating with their diapers on. Perhaps they have also gotten used to doing it in a certain place or in a certain position—standing in the crib, for instance. Now we ask them to change—to do it with their pants off, in a different room, and in a different position. Even if they're perfectly willing, it may not be that easy. Our astronauts discovered how dif-ficult it is to abandon the toilet habits of a lifetime and to get the reflexes to function under totally new conditions. Here's astronaut Russell Schweickart describing what it's like to urinate in space:

> You just . . . urinate into it [a bag] through the one-way valve. There are lots of little cute problems and uncertainties. Unless you're an extremely unusual person, since the time you were about a year and a half old or so, you probably have not taken a leak laying flat on your back. And if you think that's easy, let me tell you, you've got some built-in psychological or survival programs, or something which you've got to overcome. So that's a tricky little problem. (Schweickart and Warshall, 1980)

What about other psychological effects of toilet training practices? Freud believed that a child trained too early or too harshly might in later life become an "anal personality"—stingy, stubborn, and overly finicky. But researchers have not been able to find a connection between toilet training and later personality (Gleitman, 1981). There might be a connection with bedwetting in later childhood, though. A study done in England in the 1950s (Douglas and Blomfield, 1967) showed that early-trained babies were less likely to become bedwetters than later-trained ones. However, this may just have been a result of social-class differences. Bedwetting was more common in the lower socioeconomic classes, and (at that time in England) so was late training. ■

not essential. As the study of the concentration-camp children showed, a close and lasting relationship with other children may at least partially fill the gap.

This conclusion seems to hold for monkeys, too. Monkeys that are reared in isolation (with or without terrycloth "surrogate mothers"—see p. 40) become very abnormal adults. They are incapable of getting along with other monkeys, extremely fearful, and even self-destructive (many of them bite themselves). But motherless monkeys reared in groups—four of the same age

These four monkeys were raised together in one cage, without their mothers.

caged together—develop normally. As infants the group-reared monkeys spend most of their time clinging to one another, just as they would ordinarily cling to their mothers. A friend in need is a friend indeed.

The companionship of other young monkeys can even to some extent reverse the effects of a long period of isolation. A monkey that is kept in isolation for its first six months and then placed in a cage with other monkeys is terrified—it cringes in fear when another monkey approaches. But there's a way of "rehabilitating" the isolated monkey: a much younger monkey is used as a "therapist." A baby monkey isn't as aggressive as older monkeys are, and it seems to be less frightening to the isolated one. Also it keeps trying to cling to the older monkey. Eventually the isolated monkey warms to its younger companion, and soon the two are playing together like normal monkeys (Harlow and Harlow, 1962; Suomi and Harlow, 1972).

The Beginnings of Friendships. Children begin to be interested in other children very early in life. Attachments to older siblings are often among babies' first attachments, even though the older siblings may be scarcely out of toddlerhood themselves.

To study how relationships with agemates develop, researchers (Eckerman, Whatley, and Kutz, 1975) put babies or toddlers of various ages into a room with another child of the same age and watched to see what would happen. (There were toys in the room, too, and the babies' mothers were present.) The study showed that as early as 10 months of age, babies' responses to another baby were mostly friendly and positive—they looked at the other baby and smiled and vocalized. This was different from their response to a new toy—a toy was touched and manipulated. So babies aren't attracted to other babies because they look like interesting *things*. Even to a 10-month-old, a baby is a person.

The older babies in this study (16 to 24 months) didn't just look and smile at each other: sometimes two toddlers actually played together. For example, one child might hand the other a toy, or both children might play side by side with the same kind of toy. Sometimes they even imitated each other's actions. (Imitation is a firmly established ability by the end of the first year.) Of course, not all of the things the toddlers did were friendly. They were about as likely to take a toy *away* from the other child as to give him one, and sometimes that led to a struggle.

One more finding emerged from the study we just described—an important finding, though not a surprising one. The older the two babies in the room were, the more attention they paid to each other and the less attention they paid to their mothers. As a more recent study showed (Pastor, 1981), this is particularly true of toddlers who have formed secure attachments. By the end of the second year, the securely attached child can loosen her ties to her parents, knowing that they'll always be there when she needs them. She can move a little away from them, into a world that contains people her own age—people who will soon be her friends.

summary

1. Newborn babies are not, at first, very sociable, but by the time they are 6 or 7 weeks old they have begun making eye contact and smiling at people.

2. Mothers act differently with babies than they do with adults—their speech and facial expressions are slowed down and exaggerated. Mothers and infants gaze at each other for longer than is usual in social interactions.

3. As early as 4 weeks, babies' responses to a human face are different from their responses to an object. Their responses to a person tend to consist of brief periods of interaction; in between, they seem to want brief periods without eye contact. If the mother tries to get the infant's attention during these "time-outs," their interactions may be unsuccessful.

4. Babies apparently enjoy having an effect on someone—controlling the other person's actions. When the other person makes his or her behavior **contingent** upon what the baby does, the baby is delighted.

5. Crying is another way that babies can control the behavior of adults. Babies whose parents respond quickly and consistently to their cries end up crying very little, perhaps because they have developed what Erikson calls **basic trust.** Babies who are completely ignored also end up crying little—they apparently cease to feel that what they do makes a difference **(learned helplessness).**

6. Babies whose parents respond slowly or inconsistently to their cries end up crying the most. One possible explanation for this is that they are discontented, though not totally without hope. Another is that they've received partial reinforcement for crying. A third possibility is that the correlation works the other way—when the baby cries a lot, the parent eventually pays less and less attention. There is some evidence to support the third explanation, but this is clearly not the *only* explanation.

7. Some babies are better than others at communicating their needs to their parents and at reinforcing their parents for meeting their needs. "Difficult" babies include those who cry a lot, those whose cues are hard to interpret, and those who frequently wake at night. Many of these problems appear to be present from birth. How "easy" or "difficult" a baby is will also be affected by built-in differences in temperament. The babies that Thomas and Chess classified as "difficult" or as "slow to warm up" showed negative reactions to anything new. Parents who understand their baby's temperament are in a better position to keep minor problems from becoming major ones.

8. Responsive, alert babies who don't cry too easily tend to have the most successful interactions with adults.

9. There are group differences, as well as individual differences, among babies. For example, Chinese-American babies tend to cry less readily and be easier to soothe than European-American babies; Zinacanteco babies show "smoothed-out" states.

10. Another way in which babies differ is in how much they like to be cuddled. Noncuddlers go to their parents when frightened and enjoy being bounced or tickled, but they seem to dislike the restraint of movement that is involved in hugging. There are indications that the tendency to be a cuddler or a noncuddler is present from birth.

11. Sex differences are negligible in infancy; nonetheless, parents treat male and female infants differently. Mothers tend to cuddle their infant sons and to give their daughters stimuli from a distance. Fathers to tend to act in the opposite way. Both parents seem to give more affection to a baby of the opposite sex, more attention and stimulation to one of the same sex.

12. Fathers tend to play in a physical manner, especially with their sons. Mothers' play is more likely to be vocal than physical, and more likely to involve conventional games.

13. Babies in industrialized societies tend to spend much of their time lying alone in their cribs. In contrast, babies in many preindustrial societies are held almost constantly; however, they are played with and spoken to less. Where infant death rates are high, parents' concern seems to focus on their babies' physical welfare, rather than on their social or intellectual development.

14. In our own society, there are social-class differences in childrearing styles. As compared with babies in working-class homes, the babies of college-educated parents are given more freedom and more playthings, are more likely to be breast-fed, and watch less TV. They are also spoken to more, and more of their vocalizations are responded to. No class differences have been found in the amount of attention or affection given.

15. Virtually every normal child develops an **attachment** to someone (provided there is someone to become attached to). Babies show **separation distress** when a person to whom they are attached leaves them alone in an unfamiliar place; this behavior emerges at about 8 months of age in babies all over the world. Fear of strangers appears at about the same time; many babies will cry if a stranger tries to get too close too quickly. Babies are less afraid of children than of adults, less afraid of women than of men.

16. By 12 or 13 months, most babies are attached to both parents, but when they are under stress they are more likely to turn to their mothers. If a father does little or no caregiving, his baby is less likely to become attached to him; however, babies often do become attached to people who don't take care of them (e.g., siblings), or fail to become attached to people who do take care of them (e.g., day-care center

workers). What seems to matter is the *quality* of the baby's interactions with the other person.

17. Mothers are more likely to pick up a baby for a caregiving chore; fathers are more likely to pick up a baby for play. By the age of 2, most boys seem to prefer their fathers to their mothers; girls are more variable in this respect.

18. Some theories attribute attachment to the pleasures (or reinforcers) parents provide to babies. But reinforcement doesn't seem to be necessary for attachments to form—in fact, visual contact may be more important than physical contact (but blind babies become attached, too). Even abused children typically become attached to the parents who have beaten them.

19. Anna Freud reported that some children who had been reared in a concentration camp, cared for by an ever-changing series of adults, had become deeply attached to one another.

20. According to the **ethological** view, the tendency to become attached is a built-in characteristic of the human species, inherited because it had survival value for early humans.

21. Attachment is found in other warm-blooded species, too. A duckling learns to follow its mother by a process known as **imprinting,** which can occur only within a **critical period** lasting about a day. For monkeys, attachment takes longer to occur; there is no critical period, but rather, a **sensitive period** when attachments are formed most readily.

22. A baby of 12 or 18 months has two opposing desires: to remain near his mother, and to explore and play. If his mother is nearby, he can use her as "a secure base from which to explore." He is likely to cling most to his mother when he is frightened, tired, ill, or in pain; thus, punishing a child (even punishing him for clinging!) is likely to increase his clinginess.

23. Mary Ainsworth distinguishes between **secure attachments** and **insecure attachments;** the difference shows up most clearly in babies' reactions to the "strange situation." A securely attached baby tends to greet his mother joyously, whereas an insecurely attached one may ignore his mother or act as though he's angry at her. Babies can be securely attached to one person, insecurely attached to another.

24. Successful mother-infant interactions in early infancy are correlated with secure attachments later on. The baby's characteristics, as well as the mother's, affect the success of early mother-infant interactions.

25. Under some circumstances, separation of infant and mother immediately after birth may be harmful to their relationship. However, contact immediately after birth does not invariably appear to be essential.

26. **Toddlerhood** starts when the child begins to walk and ends at age 2 or 2½. Toddlers have more mobility than infants and are more willing to leave their mother's side. According to Erikson, the struggle for **autonomy** is the major issue in the toddler's life.

27. The average toddler obeys about half of her mother's commands; securely attached toddlers are more likely to obey than insecurely attached ones. Insecurely attached toddlers tend to be unwilling to let their mothers help them, even when they need help.

28. Societies differ greatly in toilet-training customs. In many preindustrial societies, toilet-training is gentle and accomplished at a relatively late age; however, the Digo people of Africa train babies gently but very early. The manner of training—gentle or harsh—probably matters more than the timing. Late training has some advantages, but it has a disadvantage, too: the reflexes may already have become conditioned to certain places or positions. Research has not supported Freud's belief that too early or too harsh toilet training can lead to personality problems later on.

29. When children are separated from the people to whom they are attached, they are likely to be desperately unhappy at first, then sad and depressed. Eventually they are able to form new attachments. The consequences of a failure to form attachments at all are far more serious. Children who have no opportunity to form attachments before the age of 4 may later have social and emotional problems and may be unable to form deep and lasting relationships with anyone. The first four years seem to be a sensitive period for the formation of human attachments.

30. Attachment to peers may, to some extent, take the place of attachment to parents. Monkeys raised in isolation become very abnormal adults, but motherless monkeys raised in groups develop normally. The companionship of a baby monkey may even reverse the effects of isolation in an older monkey.

31. Babies as young as 10 months of age are attracted to other babies; their responses to other babies are not the same as their responses to objects. Older toddlers pay more attention to one another, and less attention to their mothers, than younger toddlers. By the end of his second year, the securely attached child can move a little away from his parents and begin to form friendships with other children.

Chapter Seven

THE BEGINNINGS OF INTELLIGENCE AND LANGUAGE

<u>S</u>even

Stephanie was born four days ago. She's just come home from the hospital and lies in her crib, awake. As neonates go, she's a rather attractive one, with a full crop of dark hair and big, alert-looking eyes.

Someday Stephanie may become a mathematician, or a concert pianist, or a Supreme Court justice. But right now, frankly, she doesn't appear to be awfully bright. When we ask her to add 1 and 1, she merely purses her lips. When we ask her to hum "Mary Had a Little Lamb," she turns her head away. When we ask her to give us her opinion on the Equal Rights Amendment, she closes her eyes. She can't read, she can't count, she can't even speak English! Stephanie has a long way to go.

But before Stephanie learns to read or count or even to speak, she has some much more basic things to find out. She must learn about herself—which parts of what she experiences are "me" and which parts are "the world out there." She must learn about her own body—the shape of its contours, and how to make its various parts move where she wants them to. She must learn that people and objects exist "out there," and that they continue to exist even when she isn't looking at them. She must learn some simple laws of cause and effect (if you let go of a rattle it will fall down) and some simple rules about solids and liquids (you can stick your hand into water, but not into the wall). She must learn about relationships like *under* and *on top of,* *behind* and *inside.*

Stephanie may seem dumb, but in fact she is one of the most efficient learning machines on the face of the earth. A baby chimpanzee is way ahead of her at this point, but in less than two years she will be doing things that no chimpanzee has ever learned to do. She will be doing things that no computer has ever been programmed to do. How will it come about—this remarkable transformation from the ignorant creature she is now to the clever person she is destined to become? We are talking now about **cognitive development**—the growth of intelligence, reasoning, knowledge, and understanding.

COGNITIVE DEVELOPMENT IN INFANCY

The outstanding leader in the field of cognitive development has been Jean Piaget, whom we've already introduced to you in Chapter 3. Piaget's influence on this field has been so overwhelming that only Sigmund Freud can be said to have had a greater impact on developmental psychology. We will start out, therefore, by giving you Piaget's view on cognitive development in infancy.

The Piagetian Approach: the Six Stages of Sensorimotor Development

As we mentioned in Chapter 3, Piaget believes that cognitive development proceeds in stages. Each child must go through the same stages in the same order. However, the rate of progress may vary considerably from child to child, and transitions from one stage to another are usually gradual rather than clear and distinct.

What causes the child to progress from stage to stage? According to Piaget, cognitive development depends both on **maturation**—the gradual unfolding of a genetic plan—and on the child's interactions with the environment. Maturation provides the child with the necessary biological equipment. Children put that equipment to good use in their active exploration of the environment (Phillips, 1975).

Above all, human beings are *adaptable*. Adaptability means that an organism can adjust to the demands of the environment and *re*adjust if the environment changes. Thus, **adaptation** depends both on the challenges provided by the environment and on the organism itself—what it's capable of doing, what it's capable of understanding. In the chameleon, adaptation may result only in a change of skin color. In the young human, adaptation leads to cognitive development.

Adaptation, according to Piaget, occurs in two different ways. The first he calls **assimilation.** Assimilation means applying something you already know (or already can do) to something new. You've learned to wash walls; now you can also wash windows. You've said hello to Gramma and Grampa; now you can say hello to Aunt Jane and Uncle Jack.

The other kind of adaptation is called **accommodation.** In accommodation you don't do (or think) the same thing—you modify your **scheme** (Piaget's term; see p. 95) in order to suit some new situation. You do this because the old scheme wouldn't work.

Here's an example of the two kinds of adaptation. Young Alex, age 14 months, sits on the floor putting small objects into his pail. (He's using his putting-things-into-the-pail scheme.) We hand him several objects he's never seen before: a sea shell, a spool of thread, a pocket watch, a small plastic box. He **assimilates** them all into his putting-things-into-the-pail scheme—in other words, he puts them all into the pail. Now we hand him a cardboard tube from a roll of paper towels. He tries to put it in the pail, but he's holding it crosswise and it's too long to fit in that way. So he **accommodates:** he turns the tube sideways so it can go into the pail vertically.

When he's older, Alex's *ideas,* as well as his actions, will undergo assimilation and accommodation. Alex may believe, for example, that all dogs are friendly and playful. Then he meets a dog that backs off and runs away when Alex approaches. Alex can assimilate this experience to his previous belief

("The dog did that because he was trying to get me to play with him"), or he can accommodate and modify his idea ("Not all dogs are friendly").

Using assimilation and accommodation, children constantly widen their ability to cope with a variety of situations—increasingly complex situations. We will see how this happens during the first major period of development, which Piaget calls the **sensorimotor period.** The sensorimotor period itself is divided into six separate stages (see Table 7–1), the six stages of cognitive development in infancy. Bear in mind that the ages given for these stages are all very approximate.

Stage 1: The First Month of Life. The first stage involves the use of inborn reflexes such as sucking and rooting. Even with schemes this simple, there is adaptation: Stephanie nurses clumsily at first, but quickly becomes more skillful at finding the nipple and taking it into her mouth.

Another built-in scheme that is used during the first month is looking at things. Newborn babies gaze at large, brightly illuminated objects, and they can track slowly moving objects with their eye movements. Their ability to focus on visual stimuli improves considerably during the first month, and so does their tracking ability.

Thus, the first stage of life, in Piaget's view, involves the use—and consequently the improvement through adaptation—of abilities the baby is born with.

Stage 2: 1 to 4 Months. The second stage marks the entrance of what Piaget (1952) calls "the first acquired adaptations." Thumb-sucking is a good ex-

TABLE 7–1   The Six Stages of Piaget's Sensorimotor Period

Stage	Approximate Age	Description
1	Birth to 1 month	The use and adaptation of built-in reflexes.
2	1 to 4 months	The first acquired adaptations. Simple circular reactions.
3	4 to 9 months	More complicated circular reactions. Procedures to make interesting events happen again.
4	9 to 12 months	Applying known procedures to new situations.
5	12 to 18 months	The discovery of new procedures through active experimentation.
6	18 to 24 months	The invention of new procedures through mental representations. Insight and planning.

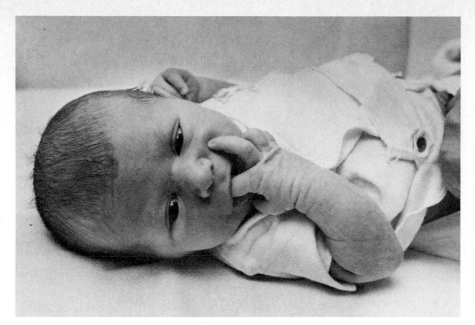

According to Piaget, babies aren't born with a desire to suck their fingers—they learn to do it by means of a circular reaction.

ample. As Piaget points out, babies haven't inherited an instinct to suck their fingers: they discover by accident that it feels good, so they do it again. But it takes most babies a while to coordinate their head movements with their hand movements.

Piaget describes how his son Laurent learned to suck his thumb during the second month of life. At first, Laurent's hands flailed around wildly, but one day his left hand happened to land on his face, and the rooting reflex enabled him to get his thumb into his mouth. Until it escaped again, Laurent sucked his thumb, as Piaget puts it, "with greed and passion" (1952, p. 51).

A day later, Laurent's hands no longer seemed to be moving randomly— they were approaching his mouth more often. On the following day, Piaget noted, "There is no longer any doubt that coordination exists. The mouth may be seen opening and the hand directing itself toward it simultaneously" (p. 52). A month and a half later, Laurent routinely used his thumb to comfort himself when he was hungry or tired: "When Laurent cries his thumb goes to the rescue" (p. 54).

What does this show? Laurent sucked his thumb at first only because his random hand movements chanced to bring it near his mouth. But once he had discovered the joys of thumb-sucking, Laurent began to move his hand toward his mouth on purpose, and he soon got to the point where he could do it without a struggle. Piaget calls this a **circular reaction:** "The child does something at random, and when he gets an interesting result, he repeats the action indefinitely. In this way, he learns to suck his thumb, to seize objects, to make noises by knocking hard things together, and so on" (Piaget, 1927/1977, p. 202).

A similar development occurs with vision. By 1 month, 9 days,

> Having learned to direct his glance, Laurent explores his universe little by lit-
> tle. . . . He systematically explores the hood of his bassinet which I shook
> slightly. He begins by the edge, then little by little looks backward at the lowest
> part of the roof. . . . His examination of people is just as marked. . . . When
> one leans over him, as when dressing him, he explores the face section by section:
> hair, eyes, nose, mouth, everything is food for his visual curiosity. (1952, pp. 68–
> 69)

Two schemes—looking and moving the hands—come together during the
second stage: the baby begins to enjoy looking at his hands. As with sucking,
the hand movements are at first not under voluntary control—the baby looks
at his hands when they happen to be in front of his face. When they move
out of his field of view he seems to have no idea where they've gone, and in
fact "seems very much surprised to see them reappear" (p. 96). But by the
end of the second stage, babies have more control over their hand movements. Now, when they look at their hands, the hands cooperate and remain
in the visual field.

Stage 3: 4 to 9 Months.   A new kind of circular reaction appears in the third
stage: Piaget (1952) calls it "procedures to make interesting sights last." Now
the baby is interested not only in what he can do with his own body, but also
in the effect he can produce on his environment.

For example, Piaget hung a rattle from the hood of Laurent's bassinet and
attached a string to it. The other end of the string was tied to Laurent's right
hand. When Laurent chanced to move his arm, the rattle moved and made a
noise. At first this startled him, but soon he began to wave his arms around
in order to produce this interesting result. Three days later, Laurent had
learned to move only his right arm to make the rattle shake. When Piaget
switched the string to Laurent's left arm, the baby quickly adapted to the
change, and moved his left arm instead of his right. Laurent clearly enjoyed
this game. He smiled and even laughed when he succeeded in shaking the
rattle.

Piaget credits the stage-3 baby with understanding that his action (in this
case, his arm movements) was what produced the interesting result (the rattle
shaking). That kind of understanding can't occur until stage 3 because, Piaget
believes, the baby must first have experienced some of the simpler circular
reactions, the ones that involve just his own body. As Piaget puts it,

> After reproducing the interesting results discovered by chance on his own body,
> the child tries sooner or later to conserve also those which he obtains when his
> action bears on the external environment. (1952, p. 154)

Here it seems that Piaget underestimates the baby. Much younger babies—
babies in the second stage and perhaps even in the first—can apparently tell
when something they've done has had an interesting effect on the environ-

ment. Apparently it is only their lack of motor skills that ordinarily keeps them from doing this. If you give them a way of having an effect on the environment that uses a skill they already possess, they will show this stage-3 ability much earlier than Piaget would have predicted.

This conclusion follows from an experiment done by psychologist John S. Watson (not to be confused with the early behaviorist John *B.* Watson). Watson (1972) set up an apparatus that made a mobile rotate whenever a baby moved his head in a certain way. (Babies gain control over their head movements well before they can control their hand movements.)

What Watson found was that 2-month-old babies quickly learned to make their mobiles turn. The number of head movements they made increased from session to session. Furthermore, the babies *loved* being in Watson's experiment: when they got the mobile turning they would smile at it and coo. Watson tried a similar setup with an 8-month-old baby who was so severely retarded that she seldom moved and had never smiled at anyone. This baby, too, was soon making the mobile turn and—more impressive—was smiling and cooing at it!

To Watson as to Piaget, the smiles and coos are a sign that babies are thrilled to discover that they have the power to make something happen. That's why they delight in the kind of "contingency game" we described in Chapter 6, a game in which the parent reacts in a distinctive way whenever the baby makes a particular response. Remember the little girl who so enjoyed making her father go "bumpety-bump"? That baby was only 8 weeks old.

Stage 4: 9 to 12 Months.   Even babies 2 or 3 months old seem to be able to understand that what they just did made something else happen. They don't understand *why* it happened, though, or *how.* They see that there's a connection between their action and some environmental reaction, but the connection is a "magical" one. Piaget's daughter Jacqueline, in stage 3, learned to move a doll hanging from her bassinet by pulling a string that was attached to it (Piaget, 1952). Then when her father held up his pocket watch out of her reach, she tried to make *it* move by pulling the doll's string!

Now in stage 4, we see the beginning of "intelligent" behavior. When Jacqueline was 9 months old, Piaget took her toy duck and tangled it in the strings leading to two other toys suspended above her crib. Jacqueline wanted the duck, but it was too high for her to reach.

> She grasps both strings, one in each hand, and pulls. She looks at the duck who shakes when she shakes. Then she grasps both strings in one hand and pulls, then grasps them in the other hand a little higher up and pulls harder until the duck falls. (1952, p. 215)

As Piaget points out, Jacqueline is not simply repeating an action that worked in the past. It's true that she is using methods that she learned in the past, but she is applying them to a new situation. Her "act of intelligence," he says, consists of finding the appropriate method to achieve her goal. Now she appreciates cause-and-effect relationships in a new way: for the first time she's beginning to pay attention to the *why* and the *how*.

This dawning intelligence is also shown in the way stage-4 babies act when you give them something they've never seen before. When Piaget gave Jacqueline a new object, she examined it carefully. Then she tried out all her old schemes on it: she shook it, tapped it, rubbed it against the side of her crib, put it in her mouth, and so on. She seemed to be trying to understand this new thing by systematically exploring all of its possibilities.

Finally, stage-4 babies show that they are able to anticipate the future. Jacqueline would begin to cry whenever her mother put on her hat, because she knew it meant that her mother was about to go out.

Stage 5: 12 to 18 Months. In the previous stage, babies began to explore objects in a systematic way, using schemes they already knew. Now, in stage 5, toddlers can work out *new* schemes to suit new situations. Piaget (1952) calls their method for doing this, "discoveries of new means through active experimentation." A stage-5 child may perform a series of experiments just to see what will happen.

Piaget gives many examples of the kinds of "experiments" his own children performed. Laurent, for instance, spent a lot of time discovering that objects of all shapes and sizes would fall down when he let them go. He

Stage-4 babies explore the possibilities of new objects by trying out their old schemes on them.

varied the position of his hand or arm and they still fell down. Piaget says that at the beginning of stage 5,

> The child has not yet perceived the role of gravity. In other words, when he lets go of an object, it is without knowing what is going to happen; and, when he tries to send it to the ground, he believes himself to be obliged to push it down, without confining himself simply to letting it go. (1952, p. 270)

Through his experiments, the child eventually realizes that objects inevitably fall to the ground unless something is holding them up.

Jacqueline, with similar concentration, spent many hours investigating the properties of water. She filled containers of all sorts with water, studied it as she poured it out, let the water run along her arm, squeezed it from a sponge, and so on. Jacqueline studied the behavior of water in much the same manner, and with the same seriousness of purpose, that Piaget studied the behavior of Jacqueline!

The stage-5 child approaches problems in a flexible, sometimes even inventive way. In many cases this approach is successful. Jacqueline tried over and over again to put the chain from her father's watch into a small matchbox. She put one end of the chain into the box, but when she released it in order to grab the other end the first part slid out. She did this 14 times in a row! Then she tried a different method: she held the chain by the middle and got both ends into the box before she let go. That worked better, but sometimes the middle part fell outside of the box and then the chain slipped out again. Finally, she had a new idea: she rolled the chain into a ball and put it all into the box at once (Piaget, 1952).

Stage 6: 18 to 24 Months. Jacqueline, in stage 5, solved the problem of the chain and the matchbox by trying things out until she found something that worked. But Lucienne, when just entering stage 6, solved a similar problem—not by trial and error—but by a flash of insight. Piaget had given her a matchbox with his watch chain already inside it. She wanted to get it out, but the matchbox was partly closed and the opening was too narrow to permit the chain to come out. Here's what Lucienne did (this is a very famous passage):

> She looks at the slit with great attention; then, several times in succession, she opens and shuts her mouth, at first slightly, then wider and wider! . . . Lucienne, by opening her mouth thus expresses, . . . her desire to enlarge the opening of the box.

Then,

> Lucienne unhesitatingly puts her finger in the slit and, instead of trying as before to reach the chain, she pulls so as to enlarge the opening. She succeeds and grasps the chain. (1952, p. 338)

Stage-5 babies love to do "experiments" with water.

Piaget explains that Lucienne, at this point, still couldn't think out the situation in words or in clear visual images. So she used mouth-opening as a symbol, as a means of representing to herself what she wanted to do.

What's particularly interesting about Lucienne's behavior is that it marks a transition between stage 5 and stage 6 abilities. In stage 5, children actually have to try out solutions to problems. Later in stage 6, they can *think* out the possibilities—do them mentally. This is a real breakthrough. It enables children to plan ahead, to envision the consequences of their actions without actually having to experience them. Here's Jacqueline at age 1 year, 8 months:

> Jacqueline . . . arrives at a closed door—with a blade of grass in each hand. She stretches out her right hand toward the knob but sees that she cannot turn it without letting go of the grass. She puts the grass on the floor, opens the door, picks up the grass again and enters. But when she wants to leave the room things become complicated. She puts the grass on the floor and grasps the doorknob. But then she perceives that in pulling the door toward her she will simultaneously chase away the grass. . . . She therefore picks it up in order to put it outside the door's zone of movement. (1952, p. 339)

Thus, we have reached the stage where the child can work things out in her head, using mental **representations,** as Piaget calls them. Representations are something like ideas and something like memories—they can be mental images of things seen, of things heard, or even of actions performed. They can also be words or sentences, but they don't have to be. The child has mental representations before she has words. Jacqueline, early in stage 6, imitated a little boy she had seen having a tantrum the day before. At that age she couldn't possibly have described the scene in words. Her **deferred imitation** (see p. 96) was based on her mental representation of the event.

The Concept of Object Permanence

The stage-6 child understands that she lives in a three-dimensional space which also contains a number of other people and objects. She understands that these people and objects have a permanent existence, even when she doesn't see them or feel them. How does this understanding develop?

Stages 1 and 2.   By the end of stage 1, according to Piaget, the baby is able to recognize certain sights and sounds: the sight of the nipple from which she gets her milk, the sight of her mother's face, the sound of her mother's voice. But, says Piaget, this kind of simple recognition does *not* mean "that in the first weeks of life the universe is really cut up into objects, that is, into things conceived as permanent, substantial, external to the self, and firm in existence" (1954, p. 5). There are simply "pictures" that come and go, and some of the pictures start to look familiar after a while. The disappearance of one of these pictures causes no particular concern. If the baby sees her mother's face she may stare at it for a time, but if it disappears she simply stops looking and does something else (Ginsburg and Opper, 1969).

In stage 2, there are already signs of progress. The baby now shows some kind of simple expectation that things looked at or touched can be looked at or touched again. For instance, Laurent grasped the edge of his blanket, let it go, and grasped it again. Lucienne looked at her father, looked away, and then looked back again—clearly expecting to see him in the same place. But this kind of behavior is very limited. It consists only of continuing to do something that was done a few seconds before. If the blanket and the father *aren't* there when the baby looks for them again, they're quickly forgotten (Piaget, 1954).

Stage 3.   The first hints of object permanence appear in this stage: "The child no longer seeks the object only where he has recently seen it but hunts for it in a new place" (1954, p. 18). That means that when Laurent sees his father drop a toy, he'll look for it on the floor—but only if he has seen the toy fall.

What happens when you cover up an object that he's been looking at? The reaction at this stage is interesting. Laurent was screaming for his bottle (which Piaget was holding), but when Piaget hid it behind his back, the baby stopped crying. Similarly, when Piaget showed Laurent a small bell,

> Laurent's arm is outstretched and about to grasp the little bell at the moment I make it disappear behind my hand (which is open and at a distance of 15 cm. from him); he immediately withdraws his arm, as though the little bell no longer existed. I then shake my hand, always revealing the back of it and gripping the little bell in my palm. Laurent watches attentively, greatly surprised to rediscover the sound of

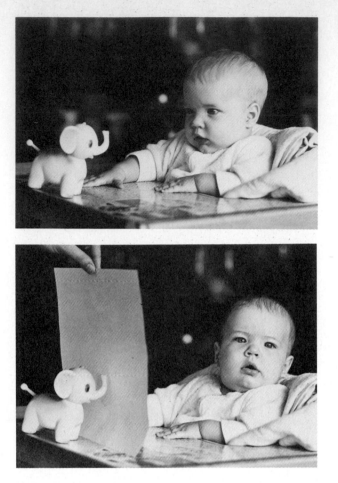

For the stage-3 baby, when an object is "out of sight" it is also "out of mind."

the little bell, but he does not try to grasp it. I turn my hand over and he sees the little bell; he then stretches out his hand toward it. I hide the little bell again by changing the position of my hand; Laurent withdraws his hand. (pp. 39–40)

Piaget says that as long as any little piece of the bell was visible, Laurent would try to grab it. But when it was totally covered it was still—at this stage—totally gone.

What about people? As we mentioned in the last chapter, most babies start to become attached to people somewhere between 6 and 8 months of age (the second half of Piaget's stage 3). One of the signs of attachment is separation distress, also known as **separation anxiety.** Here's what one Piagetian psychologist has to say about separation anxiety:

Psychiatrists have coined the term "separation anxiety" to refer to the distress that is occasioned by the absence of the mother. But how can the child be distressed about being separated from her if she does not exist when she is not present? The answer is, he can't, and in point of fact, separation anxiety does not occur in Stages

1 or 2. Its development is correlated, as one might suspect, with that of object permanence; until then, it is literally a case of "out of sight, out of mind." (Phillips, 1975, p. 33)

So the emergence of separation distress, at around 7 or 8 months, implies that the baby now realizes that his mother is a "permanent object"—that even if she isn't here, she is *somewhere*. As it turns out, he evidently comes to that realization a little before he draws the same conclusion about inanimate objects. Piaget (1954) describes how Jacqueline, at 8½ months, uncovered her father when he was hiding behind a blanket. She was still stumped, though, when he hid one of her toys in the same way.

Later studies have supported Piaget's finding that "person permanence" comes a little before object permanence. In one investigation (Bell, 1970) a number of babies were tested several times between the ages of 8½ and 13½ months. Each baby was given two kinds of tasks: to find a hidden toy, and to find Mommy (who hid behind a screen or a couch). The results at both ages showed that the babies' concept of person permanence was ahead of their concept of object permanence. Moreover, the babies who did well on one kind of test tended to do well on the other, too.

One more noteworthy finding came out of this study. The babies who did best on both kinds of tasks were the ones who had formed secure attachments to their mothers (see Chapter 6). As we've said, securely attached children tend to have mothers who respond quickly and appropriately to their signals. So these findings fit together nicely: a baby who learns that his mother will generally appear when he really needs her will naturally begin to believe that she exists all the time, not just when he can see her. Once he has had this realization about a person, he can apply it to inanimate objects as well. Thus, a secure attachment not only fosters healthy social and emotional development—it also aids in cognitive development.

Stage 4. Removing a cover to find a totally hidden object or person is stage-4 behavior. (In Piaget's view, the baby enters stage 4 with regard to people before he enters stage 4 with regard to objects.) Babies in this stage have some understanding of the permanence of objects—enough so that they will search for a vanished toy. But there's a strange limitation to their understanding. Here's Laurent at 9½ months:

Laurent is placed on a sofa between a coverlet A on the right and a wool garment B on the left. I place my watch under A; he gently raises the coverlet, perceives part of the object, uncovers it, and grasps it. The same thing happens a second and a third time . . . I then place the watch under B; Laurent watches this maneuver attentively, but at the moment the watch has disappeared under garment B, he turns back toward coverlet A and searches for the object under that screen. I again place the watch under B; he again searches for it under A. (Piaget, 1954, p. 53)

Laurent searched in a place where he had previously found the watch, even though he saw his father put it in a different place. It's hard to believe that a clever baby like Laurent would make such a stupid mistake! But Laurent is not an exception. Jacqueline and Lucienne behaved in a similar way at that stage, and so do other babies—babies whose last names are Thompson or Romero or Wong, and not Piaget.

Piaget's explanation for this behavior is that the baby's concept of the object is still not complete at stage 4. He does not yet have an understanding of the object as a unitary thing that is independent of its surroundings. Take the case of Piaget's nephew Gérard. Gérard was playing with a ball. It rolled under an armchair and he got it out. Then the ball rolled under the sofa. Gérard tried to get it out from under the sofa but was unable to. So he crossed the room and again searched for the ball under the armchair! Piaget says that, to Gérard at this age, the ball was not an object in itself but part of a larger context. It's perfectly possible for the child to have *two* contexts that include the ball: "ball-under-the-armchair" and "ball-under-the-sofa." When Gérard failed to find the "ball-under-the-sofa," he went in search of the "ball-under-the-armchair" (Piaget, 1954).

Stages 3 and 4: Other Views.   To the stage-3 child, a toy is apparently gone and forgotten the moment you cover it up with a blanket. The stage-4 child sees you cover the toy with a blanket and looks for it under the rug, where you previously hid it. These reactions have been observed many times, in many babies, by many different psychologists (Gratch, 1975). However, not all of these psychologists agree with Piaget's interpretations.

Jerome Kagan of Harvard University interprets the baby's reactions in a straightforward way: as simple forgetting. An adult looks up a phone number and then forgets it, unless he dials it within 20 seconds or so. The baby forgets even faster—in as little as a second—that her father has a bell hidden behind his hand. Kagan (1978) says that the baby's memory improves dramatically at about 8 months (the end of stage 3). He attributes this improvement simply to the physical maturation of the brain.

Another interpretation comes from T. G. R. Bower (whose research we discussed in Chapter 5). Bower (1975) thinks that the baby's problem is not that she lacks the concept of permanent objects, but that she lacks concepts such as *under, inside, behind,* and even *on top of.* The stage-3 baby starts to reach for a toy, but stops when the toy is covered by a barrier. In Piaget's view, this is because the toy is no longer there, to the baby, if she can't see it. But Bower disagrees. He describes an experiment in which babies were shown a toy and then, when they started to reach for it, the lights were turned out. The babies continued to reach for the toy, even though they couldn't see it. So the fact that the baby can't see the toy isn't the important thing: what matters is whether or not it's covered up by another object. According to Bower, this is because the baby can't understand the concepts *under* and *behind*—she can't understand that two things can be in the same place and still be separate things. To a young baby, when one object is on top of another, both objects lose their previous identities. A 5-month-old, says Bower,

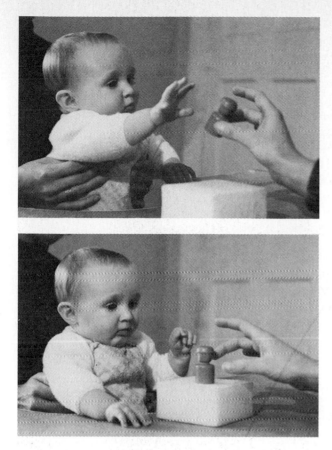

According to Bower, this 5-month-old baby is bewildered when a toy is put down on a foam block because she lacks the concept "on top of."

will reach for a dangling toy, but if you put the toy down on *top* of something, she'll stop and look puzzled.

Bower believes that the concepts of *on top of* and *behind* are generally understood by the time the baby is in Piaget's stage 4. *Inside of* still presents some problems, though. If you show the baby a toy and then cover it with a cup, she will lift the cup in order to get the toy. If you then, while the baby is watching, put the toy under a different cup, the baby looks again under the first cup. Piaget says that this is because the baby doesn't yet have a concept of the toy as an independent object that can be moved from place to place. But Bower has tried the same test using *transparent* cups, so the toy is clearly visible the whole time—and the baby still makes the same error! Bower concludes that what the baby lacks is not an object concept but an understanding of how one object can be *inside* another. Notice, though, that this theory doesn't explain why the baby looks again under cup A when she's seen you put the toy under cup B. It explains only why she has difficulty with this task.

Perhaps Bower and Piaget are *both* right. Perhaps the baby has difficulty because of the *inside* relationship, and she looks again under cup A because she lacks the concept, "a-toy-that-can-be-under-either-cup-A-or-cup-B."

Stage 5. By stage 5, the toddler knows that things can be moved from place to place (see Table 7–2). She searches for an object in the place where she saw it hidden, and not necessarily where she previously found it.

> Jacqueline watches me hide my watch under cushion *A* on her left, then under cushion *B* on her right; in the latter case she immediately searches in the right place. If I bury the object deep she searches for a long time, then gives up, but does not return to *A*. (Piaget, 1954, p. 67)

There's still a catch, though. The child can take account of movements of

TABLE 7–2   Piaget's View of the Development of Object Permanence

Stage	Approximate Age	Description
1	Birth to 1 month	No signs of object permanence.
2	1 to 4 months	No particular reaction if objects vanish, but there seems to be some expectation that an object looked at or touched can be looked at or touched again.
3	4 to 9 months	Still "out of sight, out of mind" for hidden objects, but if an object is seen to fall it may be searched for on the floor.
4	9 to 12 months	The child now searches for a hidden object, but if it is hidden in a new place the child may continue to search for it in the place where it was previously found.
5	12 to 18 months	The child searches for hidden objects in new as well as old locations, but only if the movements of the object are visible.
6	18 to 24 months	Invisible movements of objects can now be followed in the imagination, by means of mental representations. Object permanence is complete.

the object only if she sees them happen. She still can't allow for what Piaget calls "invisible displacements."

> Jacqueline is sitting on a green rug and playing with a potato. . . . putting it into an empty box and taking it out again. For several days she has been enthusiastic about this game.
>
> I then take the potato and put it in the box while Jacqueline watches. Then I place the box under the rug and turn it upside down thus leaving the object hidden by the rug without letting the child see my maneuver, and I bring out the empty box. I say to Jacqueline, who has not stopped looking at the rug and who has realized that I was doing something under it: "Give papa the potato." She searches for the object in the box, looks at me, again looks at the box minutely, looks at the rug, etc., but it does not occur to her to raise the rug in order to find the potato underneath. (p. 68)

Stage 6. In stage 6 the child becomes capable of forming mental representations, and that makes all the difference. At 19½ months, Piaget reports,

> Jacqueline watches me when I put a coin in my hand, then put my hand under a coverlet. I withdraw my hand closed, Jacqueline opens it, [finds it empty,] then searches under the coverlet until she finds the object. I take back the coin at once, put it in my hand, and then slip my closed hand under a cushion situated at the other side (on her left and no longer on her right); Jacqueline immediately searches for the object under the [correct] cushion. (p. 79)

Piaget then complicated the situation by putting his closed hand first under a cushion and then under a coverlet. Jacqueline still reacted appropriately: she searched under the cushion, then under the coverlet.

The stage-6 child is able to follow all the movements of the coin, even when she can't see them happen, because now she can imagine them.

VARIATIONS IN INTELLIGENCE: INFANCY AND LATER

One thing is very clear about babies' development: some babies progress more rapidly than others. This was true even in Piaget's own family—at any given age, Lucienne and Laurent were ahead of Jacqueline.

Two questions are often asked about these differences in rate of development. First, is an advanced baby likely to turn into an intelligent child, a slow baby into a dull one? Second, do environmental factors that affect infant development—either favorably or unfavorably—result in a difference in later intelligence?

The first question is easily answered: not necessarily. In general, rate of development in the first year of life does not correlate with later IQ. There's

The Origins of Self-Awareness

Jean Piaget and Sigmund Freud have very different views on infant development, but they agree on one point: both theorists believe that the newborn baby has no concept of self, no concept of the distinction between "me" and "not me." The baby at first doesn't realize that the sounds he hears are his own cries, that the moving thing passing in front of his eyes is his own hand. Piaget puts it very well:

> When a baby discovers his own body—his fingers, feet, arms—he looks at them no differently than he regards other objects, without any idea that he himself is the one responsible for moving the particular objects that he is admiring. . . . To begin with a baby has no sense of self at all. (1927/1977, p. 200)

The concept of self develops gradually during infancy. Many aspects of the baby's experience are responsible for this development. He discovers that he can control the movements of his hands and feet, but that he can't make the wall move, nor the table, nor the family dog. He discovers that his hands and feet and mouth and chest are always there, while other things—such as Mommy and Daddy—come and go. (This, according to Freud, is how the baby learns to distinguish himself from his mother.) He learns

that certain sensations derive from the "me" parts of the world and not from the other parts—biting down hard on his toe feels dramatically different from biting down hard on a teething ring!

By the second year of life, most babies in our society have access to another way of finding out about themselves: mirrors. Babies' reactions to their own mirror images change as they get older (Rheingold, cited in Lewis and Brooks, 1975). A 4-month-old baby seems to regard his mirror image as an entertaining playmate—as another baby who is playing an exciting contingency game called "I do everything that you do." Naturally, he smiles enthusiastically at this appealing companion. (He'll smile less vigorously at a motion picture of a baby, since the movie doesn't act contingently.)

In the second half of the first year, babies begin to make deliberate, repetitive movements in front of a mirror, apparently in an effort to explore the mirror's possibilities. (See Jacqueline's stage-4 behavior with a new object, pp. 216.) They also look *behind* the mirror. Later in the second year there may be a time when the child avoids looking at himself in the mirror (Amsterdam, cited in Lewis and Brooks, 1975). This seems to be the beginning of that kind of em-

only one case in which the rate of infant development gives us any hints about the child's future: a baby who progresses abnormally slowly during infancy may turn out to be retarded, because of brain injury or a genetic mishap such as Down's syndrome. On the other hand, very rapid progress during infancy tells us nothing about later intelligence. In fact, children who will have unusually high IQs at age 4 years are not unusually advanced at age 8 months—at least not in any way we can measure. At 8 months these

When will this baby realize that the interesting little boy in the mirror is "me"?

barrassment commonly called "self-consciousness."

Can we tell when the baby first recognizes that the image in the mirror is "me"? There is a clever technique that psychologists have used to answer this question: a red mark is put on the baby's nose without his knowing it—his mother puts it on while pretending to wipe his face. Then the baby is shown his face in a mirror.

What will he do when he notices the red mark? If he just stares, or if he touches the mirror, we haven't found out anything. But if he touches his *own* nose when he sees his mirror image, he must realize that the red-nosed baby in the mirror is himself.

This experiment was tried on 96 babies (Lewis and Brooks, 1975). The results are given in Table 7-3. You can see that self-recognition

future geniuses are completely indistinguishable from their agemates (Willerman and Fiedler, 1974).

In the second year of life, some hints of the child's eventual intelligence begin to emerge. The correlation between measures of infant development and IQ in late childhood, which is close to zero in the first year of life, increases to around .50 by the end of the second year (McCall, Eichorn, and Hogarty, 1977).

TABLE 7–3   Self-Recognition of Mirror Image in Babies of Different Ages

Age	Number Tested	Percent of Babies Who Touched Their Noses
9 and 12 months	32	0
15 and 18 months	32	25%
21 and 24 months	32	75%

From Lewis and Brooks, 1975, p. 124.

increases as the baby grows older: no babies under a year touched their reddened noses, but 75 percent of the babies over 1½ did so.

An experiment of this sort (Gallup, 1970) has also been tried on rhesus monkeys and chimpanzees. (Chimpanzees are apes. Apes are considered to be higher on the evolutionary scale than monkeys.) The monkeys and chimpanzees were given a general anesthetic, and red dye was painted on one ear while they were unconscious. Then each animal was put in front of the mirror. The chimpanzees immediately reached for the offending ear; the monkeys didn't. So we can say that, in this respect, a year-old baby is still at the level of a monkey, whereas a 21-month-old has reached the more advanced level of the chimpanzee!

By 21 months, many toddlers can also recognize photographs of themselves, and can even discriminate such photos from photos of other babies of the same sex and age. A 21-month-old named Erika was shown a photo of herself, and her mother asked, "Who is that?" "Erika," she replied. When she was shown a photo of a different 21-month-old girl, her response was, "No, not Erika." Erika also recognized a photo of her mother ("Mommy," she said) and labeled a photo of another woman "lady." Not all the children in this study (Lewis and Brooks, 1975) did as well as Erika. Only 7 out of 25 toddlers correctly identified photos of themselves—six gave their own names and one said, "Me." But these toddlers did just about as well in identifying themselves as they did in identifying their mothers. That's rather remarkable, since babies presumably spend much more time looking at their mothers than they do looking at themselves.

That finding, however, fits in well with Piaget's view of the stage-6 child. Piaget believes that the development of the child's self-image progresses hand-in-hand with his development of the concepts of object and person permanence. Once representation is possible, Piaget says, the child can visualize his own body as "an object among other objects," localized in space and existing through time (1954, p. 86).

Infant Development and Later Intelligence

In recent years there's been quite a lot of emphasis on enriching the baby's environment. Parents have been made to feel that if they don't provide the proper toys, the proper stimulation in infancy, all is lost. But is it true, as some have claimed, that the first two years are the most important in the development of intelligence?

It's not easy to answer this question. Parents who provide a good environment at age 1 are also likely to provide a good environment at age 2, at age

3, and at age 5. Thus, if the child ends up with a high IQ at age 7, how can we tell that the first two years mattered? Maybe it was just the next five!

Adoption studies are of some help here. Children adopted into middle-class homes in early infancy end up with higher IQs than children born into a deprived environment and adopted later on. Clearly, then, infancy does matter—on the average, children who had an enriched environment in infancy do better than ones who had a deprived environment in infancy, even if their environments in later years were about the same (Rutter, 1979). But we still don't know whether infancy matters *more* than the later years. To find out, we'd have to show that two years of deprivation at the beginning of life has a worse effect than two years of deprivation later on. For obvious reasons, such an experiment has never been done.

Intelligence and Extreme Early Deprivation. Another way of assessing the importance of early experiences is to look at children who've had extremely poor environments in the first couple of years. Can they ever recover from the effects of severe early deprivation?

Jerome Kagan, the Harvard developmental psychologist whom we mentioned earlier in this chapter, believes that the answer is *yes*. He describes what infancy is like in an Indian village called San Marcos, in western Guatemala. In this society,

> Infants typically spend their first year confined to a small, dark hut. They are not played with, rarely spoken to, poorly nourished, . . . and their health [is] poor. (Kagan, 1978, p. 70)

As we would expect, this kind of environment has an unfavorable effect on cognitive development:

> When compared to American babies of the same age, the Guatemalan infants are retarded. Some of the major developmental milestones, such as the ability to recall past events, the belief that objects continue to exist when they are out of sight (object permanence), symbolic play, and language appear from two to 12 months later than they do in American infants. . . . American children begin to speak their first words about the middle of the second year; San Marcos children do not begin to speak until the middle or end of their third year. (pp. 70–71)

If an American toddler were that far behind at age 3, it would be cause for serious concern. But the retardation of these San Marcos children is only temporary. Their lives grow more stimulating after the first year or so, when "they are allowed to wander outside the hut and encounter the rich variety of the world" (p. 71). By adolescence, these children have nearly caught up with their American counterparts and are performing at normal levels on tests of memory and reasoning.

In our own culture, cases of children who have been the victims of appalling neglect occasionally come to light. In 1967, for instance, a pair of twins was discovered in a small town in Europe. These boys, who were 7 years old at the time they were rescued, had spent their preceding years in a small, unheated closet. They had been kept in almost total isolation by their father and stepmother; at times they were brutally beaten. When the twins were discovered, they could barely walk and had less language than the average 2-year-old. After weeks of hospitalization they were tested by psychologists. According to the test results, the twins were in the moderate-to-severe range of mental retardation.

After 7 years of such cruel and complete deprivation, could these boys possibly recover? To everyone's surprise, they did. They were adopted by a normal family and were eventually enrolled in a school for normal children. They were several grades behind their agemates at first, but by the age of 14 they were only one grade behind, and their tested IQs were around 100—exactly average (Koluchová, 1972, 1976).

PROBLEMS IN DEVELOPMENT

Does Early Malnutrition Have a Permanent Effect on Intelligence?

It seems to be possible to overcome the effects of intellectual deprivation in infancy, if the later environment is good. But what about the effects of *nutritional* deprivation? Poor nutrition has been assumed to have its worst effects on intelligence when it occurs very early—before birth or in the first year or two after. The reason has to do with the physical development of the brain: as we've seen, the most important stages of brain growth take place before the age of 18 months.

There are still many parts of the world where babies and young children do not get enough to eat. Many of these children die from starvation or disease. What happens, though, to the ones who survive?

Myron Winick, the director of the Institute of Human Nutrition at Columbia Medical School, has been studying these children since the early 1960s. In 1968 he concluded that children who are severely undernourished in infancy are left permanently handicapped. Even if their diet improves later on, their brains remain smaller than

normal and have fewer cells. Winick (1968) had little hope that these children could ever attain normal levels of intelligence.

In 1980 Winick changed his mind. New data indicated that the lowered IQs found in undernourished children from Africa, Central America, and South America were not due to starvation alone. The cause seemed to be malnutrition *plus* an impoverished environment. Children who had been just as undernourished in infancy but who had been raised in good environments had normal IQs. For example, a study was made of a group of undernourished Korean babies who were adopted into middle-class American homes. Several years later, these children were performing at average American levels, both in school and on IQ tests. Other data came from children who were malnourished as infants because of medical problems involving their digestive systems. These children, too, turned out to have normal intelligence (Winick, 1980).

What about children who are undernourished *before* birth, as a result of starvation of their

It is important, however, to distinguish between intellectual deprivation and emotional deprivation. As we saw in the previous chapter, failure to form any attachments early in life may be very difficult or even impossible to repair. The twins we just described had each other during those early years in the closet. Otherwise, they might not have been able to recover at all.

ACQUIRING LANGUAGE

In the first year or so, the baby's development is marked by important motor milestones: she learns to turn over, to sit, to crawl, to walk; and she learns to use her hands and fingers to perform increasingly skilled movements. But

mothers during pregnancy? Again, death rates are higher but the survivors will have normal intelligence if they are raised in an adequate environment. At the end of World War II there was a severe famine in some parts of the Netherlands. The children born in these areas during and soon after the famine are now adults. IQ tests have detected no differences between these people and people born in areas where there was no famine (Stein, Susser, Saenger, and Marolla, 1975).

A good environment can prevent early starvation from affecting intelligence. Malnutrition has physical effects, though, that are permanent. People who were undernourished in infancy or early childhood are likely to be short of stature. Their heads are smaller than average; the missing brain cells are never replaced.

How, then, can they achieve normal intelligence? A British pediatrician named John Lorber has reported some almost incredible facts about brain size and intelligence. Lorber has done research on a group of people born with a disorder called *hydrocephalus* ("water on the brain"). There is always fluid in the brain, but in a baby with hydrocephalus the fluid gradually builds up to an excessive level. The brain begins to swell; the head becomes misshapen. Hydrocephalus can be treated with brain surgery—a shunt is inserted that carries away the excess fluid. But in some cases the operation is not successful, and in others the buildup of fluid is gradual

enough that it is not noticed and no treatment is given.

With the aid of modern computerized brain-scanning devices, Lorber has studied more than a hundred people who grew up with their brains severely distorted from the pressure of excess fluid. Because the fluid takes up so much room, there is much less space for brain cells. Nevertheless, Lorber found that most of these people were normal, intellectually and physically. Several had IQs of 130 or more (well above average). Lorber described one young man whose brain was so filled with fluid that the cerebral cortex—the "thinking" part of the brain—occupied only one-twentieth of its usual space. Yet this young man had a university degree in mathematics and had graduated with highest honors!

Lorber concluded that we can manage very well with a brain that is "substantially reduced in size, as long as the loss occurs before birth or early in infancy, thus giving the brain a chance to adjust. It appears that the brain has greater plasticity than was previously thought possible" (1981, p. 126).

Lorber speaks of "plasticity." Piaget refers to "adaptation." What it boils down to is that the human is flexible—the most versatile organism on the face of the earth. The human baby is fully capable of profiting from a good environment in the first year or two of life. But if things go badly during infancy, all is not lost. ∎

in the second year of life the striking milestones are in the realm of cognitive development: the baby makes impressive gains in knowledge and understanding, and speech begins. The acquisition of language, in particular, is one of the most fascinating aspects of human development.

Learning to Talk

Remember Stephanie, the 4-day-old baby we met at the start of this chapter? She can communicate with the people around her in only one way: by crying when she's unhappy, and by not crying when she's not unhappy. It's a simple system, but it works.

Soon, however, Stephanie will want to communicate more complicated ideas and make a wider range of sounds. In two or three months she will have discovered the sound of her voice and will play with it, producing a variety of cooing sounds—a typical stage-2 circular reaction. She'll also make cooing sounds during face-to-face interactions with her mother or father, particularly if they talk to her and then pause, allowing her to take her turn in the conversation.

By the second half of her first year, Stephanie will be able to produce a large number of different sounds—perhaps, as some have claimed, all the sounds that occur in all the languages of the world! This is the period of babbling: ba-ba-ba-ba, ma-ma-ma-ma, assorted goos, and various juicy

sounds. It's also clear by this time that the baby can modify the sounds she makes in response to the sounds she hears. If Stephanie is saying "goo-goo" and her mother says "da-da," Stephanie may switch over to "da-da." She'll practice her sounds when she's alone in her crib, sometimes for long periods of time.

By her first birthday, Stephanie (if she's an average baby) will probably have a word or two: "ma-ma" or "da-da," or perhaps "hi!" A few babies seem to be starting to talk even earlier, at 8 or 9 months, but these early words may be misleading—they may disappear as mysteriously as they appeared. Most babies wait until two or three months after their first birthday to begin talking in earnest. Perhaps they are concentrating on learning to walk and can't turn their full attention to language until after that milestone has been reached.

In the meantime, many babies engage in what seems to be a pretend kind of speech—they'll come out with what sounds like long, complicated sentences, complete with expression, except that the "words" are totally unintelligible. This kind of pseudospeech is called **expressive jargon.** Some babies continue to produce it for months, even after they've learned to say real words.

Once the baby can produce 10 understandable words, true speech has begun. This occurs, on the average, at 15 months; the age range in one study (Nelson, 1973) was from 13 to 19 months. At about 18 months the average baby starts to acquire new words very rapidly: she'll have 50 words at 20 months (range: 14 to 24 months). At 2 years she'll know close to 200 words (range: 23 to 436 words).

The baby's ability to understand the speech of the older people around her—her **receptive language**—at every age is greater than her ability to express herself in speech—her **productive language.** (This continues to be true all through life. Most people can understand words that they themselves have never used.) Thus, by the end of the first year most babies can understand words such as "no" and "bye-bye." In the second year they can understand sentences that are far more complex than those they can produce.

The One-Word Stage. Joshua, 18 months old, sits by his mother's side. They're "reading" a picture book together: Joshua's mother points at a picture of, say, a house and says "house." Joshua tries—more or less successfully—to imitate her. In some cases he can say the word as soon as his mother points to the picture—he knows dog ("doh"), baby ("ba-ba"), and car ("cah"), for example. Joshua's productive vocabulary now contains about 20 words. Not much, actually, when you consider that he said his first word ("da-da") more than 6 months ago. In the time since then he's acquired only three or four words a month.

But his rate of learning new words is about to increase dramatically. He'll pick up around 15 words a month between 18 and 20 months, and more than 30 a month between 20 months and 2 years. What's the reason for this sudden acceleration?

John McShane, a psycholinguist who teaches at a university in Scotland, has an intriguing explanation. According to his theory, the toddler learns words by imitation and learns by imitation when to use them. But at first the child has no idea that the word he is speaking is the *name* of the object he is pointing at—that it is a symbol, a representation, of the object itself. According to McShane, this realization comes to him suddenly, as a flash of insight, after he's learned a certain number of words. "The child first learns the words and later learns that these words are names. The key element in learning that words are names is an insight by the child" (1980, p. 49). If McShane is right, this flash of insight comes at about 18 months—just before the dramatic increase in vocabulary. Once the child has gotten the idea that things have names, he wants to know the name for everything.

McShane's proposal—that the child doesn't really understand what words are until he has a sudden insight about language in the middle of the second year—fits in very well with Piagetian theory. In Piaget's view, insight is a mental process that isn't possible until stage 6 of the sensorimotor period. Stage 6 begins at approximately 18 months.

Are there any other indications—other than the sudden acceleration in learning new words—that this insight actually occurs? Unfortunately, toddlers can't tell us if and when it happens, and later (when their language ability is up to the task) they'll have forgotten. But what if a child were introduced to language at a later age, when she's old enough to retain a memory of her experiences? That happened in the case of Helen Keller, and Keller's memories provide striking support for McShane's theory.

Helen Keller lost her sight and hearing in infancy, and was without language until she was almost 7 years old. At that point Anne Sullivan became her teacher and began to teach her a new language. The words in this language were tapped into her hand, letter by letter, by her teacher's fingers. Here's Keller's description of how her lessons began:

> The morning after my teacher came she led me into her room and gave me a doll. . . . When I had played with it a little while, Miss Sullivan slowly spelled into my hand the word "d-o-l-l." I was at once interested in this finger play and tried to imitate it. When I finally succeeded in making the letters correctly I was flushed with childish pleasure and pride. Running downstairs to my mother I held up my hand and made the letters for doll. I did not know that I was spelling a word or even that words existed; I was simply making my fingers go in monkey-like imitation. In the days that followed I learned to spell in this uncomprehending way a great many words, among them *pin, hat, cup,* and a few verbs like *sit, stand,* and *walk.* But my teacher had been with me several weeks before I understood that everything has a name. (Keller, 1905, p. 22)

Years later, Keller still remembered the excitement of the moment that she came to that realization:

> We walked down the path to the well-house, attracted by the fragrance of the honeysuckle with which it was covered. Some one was drawing water and my teacher placed my hand under the spout. As the cool stream gushed over one hand she spelled into the other the word *water,* first slowly, then rapidly. I stood still,

my whole attention fixed upon the motions of her fingers. Suddenly . . . the mystery of language was revealed to me. I knew then that "w-a-t-e-r" meant the wonderful cool something that was flowing over my hand. That living word awakened my soul, gave it light, hope, joy, set it free! . . . I left the well-house eager to learn. Everything had a name, and each name gave birth to a new thought . . . I learned a great many new words that day. (pp. 23–24)

There's one more thing to note about the one-word stage: the toddler's use of a word may not correspond exactly to the way adults use a word. Commonly, children tend to overgeneralize: call all four-legged mammals *dog,* anything round a *ball,* or *moon.* One toddler—the son of two psycholinguists—pointed to a bowl of salad and said "Nunu," the name of the family dog. His parents (de Villiers and de Villiers, 1979) were puzzled until they noticed that the shiny black olive on the top of the salad resembled their dog's shiny black nose!

To the toddler who can still say only one word at a time, a single word may have to take the place of a whole sentence. A child who says, "Cat!" may mean many things by that utterance: "There's a cat!" "I want the cat!" "Get that cat away from me!" and so on. Often it's possible to tell what is meant from the context and from the child's gestures and facial expressions.

Two- and Three-Word Phrases.   The average child begins to put words together at about 20 months—approximately the same age that the milestone of 50 words is achieved. At first there may be a brief pause between the words: "Car . . . go," "See . . . dog." Other phrases are produced more rapidly, as ready-made packages: "Thank you," "Go away," "What's that?" Or, the phrase may be only partly ready-made. In phrases like "Tie it," "Push it," and "Get it," the word *it* serves as a so-called **pivot word**—the child just has to insert a verb in front of it to form a phrase (Braine, 1963). Pivot words can also occur at the beginning of phrases. *Allgone* is used as a pivot word in phrases such as "Allgone milk," "Allgone cookie," and "Allgone doggie."

Once children have gotten the idea that words can be combined into phrases, it would seem that they should be able to combine any number of words. But that is not the case. The length of their utterances is still very restricted. Try saying, "A boy is walking down the street," to a toddler at the two- to three-word stage, and ask her to repeat it. She'll say "Boy street," or "Boy walk," or "Downa street." Table 7–4 shows some actual attempts by toddlers to imitate adults' sentences. Notice what gets repeated and what's left out. There's usually a noun such as *dog* or *shoe,* and there might be a verb such as *go* or *drink.* But verb endings such as *-ing* are dropped, and so are unimportant words such as *the* and *is.* What's left has been described as **telegraphic** speech (or **telegraphese**), because it sounds like the language used in telegrams: "Come home quick. Father ill. Bring money."

The phrases children construct on their own are very much like the ones they use when they imitate an adult—short and to the point. Almost always, the words appear in the proper order, the order they would have in a complete sentence. They say "My chair" or "Billy chair," not "Chair my" or

TABLE 7–4   Toddlers' Imitations of Adults' Sentences

What the Adult Said	What the Child Said
Fraser will be unhappy.	Fraser unhappy.
He's going out.	He go out.
It's not the same dog as Pepper.	Dog Pepper.
I'll make a cup for her to drink.	Cup drink.
Is it broken?	Is broken?
No, you can't write on Mr. Cromer's shoe.	Write Cromer shoe.

From Brown and Bellugi, 1964; Ervin, 1964.

"Chair Billy." They say "Hit Mommy" to mean they hit Mommy, and "Mommy hit" to mean Mommy hit them.

The characteristics of toddler speech that we have described here appear to be universal—toddlers all over the world speak in basically the same way, and the subject matter of their speech is similar, too. Table 7–5 shows some samples of the speech of toddlers from a variety of countries (Slobin, 1971).

Toddlers all over the world also tend to make the same kinds of errors in pronunciation. Difficult sounds like *th, l,* and *r* are often dropped, and easier sounds like *d, y,* and *w* may be substituted. *That* becomes *dat, lady* becomes *wady* or *yady, run* becomes *wun.* Combinations of two consonants are particularly difficult, and one consonant is usually omitted, as in *poon* for *spoon.* It's also easier for a toddler to say the same consonant twice than to switch to a different one in the middle of a word, so *doggie* may become *doddie* or *goggie.* It's clear that the problem is in pronunciation, not in hearing. A child who pronounces *mouse* and *mouth* in exactly the same way will have no trouble responding appropriately to the instructions "Point to the mouse" and "Point to the mouth" (de Villiers and de Villiers, 1979).

How Older People Speak to Toddlers

Here's a typical dialogue between a 2-year-old and his mother:

      Adam: See truck, Mommy. See truck.
    Mother: Did you see the truck?
      Adam: No I see truck.
    Mother: No, you didn't see it? There goes one.
      Adam: There go one.
    Mother: Yes, there goes one.
      Adam: See a truck. See truck, Mommy. See truck. Truck. Put truck, Mommy.
    Mother: Put the truck where?
      Adam: Put truck window.
    Mother: I think that one's too large to go in the window.
            (Brown and Bellugi, 1964, p. 135)

Notice that the mother speaks in a characteristic way—different from the way she would speak to another adult. It's not only mothers who do this. Researchers have found that other adults, and even children as young as 4, modify their speech appropriately when they are talking to a toddler. Adults speaking to toddlers use short, clear, simple sentences, and they say the words clearly and with greater than usual stress and expression. They pause between sentences. Many of their sentences are repetitions of all or part of their previous sentence, or they may correct or expand on the child's previous sentence. Many more questions are used than in speech directed at another adult.

The *content* of the adult's speech also differs when he or she is talking to a toddler. Their conversation is generally focused on the here and now, rather than on the past or the future. It concerns concrete objects, animals, or people, rather than abstract ideas. The objects and animals tend to be named at an intermediate level of specificity: *flower*, not *plant* or *chrysanthemum; dog*, not *animal* or *Shetland sheepdog* (Brown and Bellugi, 1964; de Villiers and de Villiers, 1979).

Finally, adults have a tendency to avoid using words that toddlers find hard to say, and to substitute words better suited to the toddler's pronunciation ability. Thus, *Mommy* and *Daddy* replace *Mother* and *Father; Nana* may be used instead of *Grandmother*. This special language—which has been called **motherese**—also includes words like *choo-choo, boo-boo, wee-wee, tick-tock,* and *bow-wow*. (See Box.)

When an adult speaks to a toddler, she uses many repetitions and questions, and she avoids using words that toddlers find hard to say.

Learning to Take Turns in Conversation

It makes sense that a parent would speak to a toddler in the manner we've described. The parent's speech presumably has two functions—communication and language teaching. Both of these functions are better served if the parent's speech is simple enough that the child can easily understand it.

What's surprising, though, is that parents speak in the same manner even to very young babies—babies who are nowhere near being able to understand speech, much less produce it. Mothers speaking to 3-month-old babies use the same kinds of simple sentences and just as many repetitions and questions as mothers speaking to toddlers. Why do they do this?

Catherine Snow, a psycholinguist at the University of Amsterdam, has a plausible answer. She believes that the mother's goal, right from the beginning, is to teach the child to be a partner in a conversational game that involves taking turns.

The process starts in early infancy. Here's a "conversation" Snow recorded between Ann, a 3-month-old baby girl, and her mother:

Ann: (smiles)
Mother: Oh what a nice little smile! Yes, isn't that nice? There. There's a nice little smile.
Ann: (burps)
Mother: What a nice wind as well! Yes, that's better, isn't it? Yes. Yes.
Ann: (vocalizes)
Mother: Yes! There's a nice noise. (Snow, 1977, p. 12)

Despite Ann's inadequacies as a partner in the conversation, Ann's mother attempts to keep the dialogue going. She indicates to the baby that it's *Ann's* turn now, by asking a question or by pausing. Then, almost anything Ann does is interpreted as a conversational response—a turn. Ann can coo, smile, burp, cough, or look attentively at something, and her mother will accept that response as an attempt to communicate.

But what if Ann does nothing at all? Then her mother will take Ann's part, too—she'll fill in

Individual Differences in Language Development

One of the ways that psycholinguists measure the development of children's speech is with an index called **mean length of utterance (MLU)**. An utterance is a phrase or a sentence said all in one piece. The length of an utterance is calculated by counting the number of words it contains and adding the number of grammatical suffixes such as the verb endings *-ing* and *-ed* and the plural or possessive*–s*. (Thus, in "See the dog," the length of the utterance is 3; in "See the dogs," or "Seeing the dog," it is 4. In "I'm seeing the dog," it is 6, since *I'm* counts as 2.) So the MLU is the average length of a child's recorded utterances at a given age.

Figure 7–1 shows the relationship between MLU and age in three children

the gap in order to keep the conversation going:

> Mother: Oh you are a funny little one, aren't you, hmm? Aren't you a funny little one? Yes. (p. 13)

Gradually, as the baby gets older, the mother gets more particular about what she will accept as a response in the conversation. At 7 months, Ann plays imitation games with her mother, and her mother clearly expects her to play by the rules:

> Mother: Ghhhhh ghhhhh ghhhhh ghhhhh. Grrrrr grrrrr grrrrr grrrrr.
> Ann: [whines]
> Mother: Oh, you don't feel like it, do you?
> Ann: Aaaaa aaaaa aaaaa.
> Mother: No, I wasn't making that noise. I wasn't going aaaaa aaaaa.
> Ann: Aaaaaa aaaaa.
> Mother: Yes, that's right. (p. 16)

At 12 months, the mother often interprets Ann's babbles as attempts at words:

> Ann: Abaabaa.
> Mother: Baba. Yes, that's you, what you are. (p. 17)

Finally, by 18 months, Ann is using words in true conversations with her mother:

> Ann: Hot.
> Mother: Hot, hot.
> Ann: Tea.
> Mother: No, it's not tea, it's coffee.
> Ann: Coffee. (p. 18)

At this stage, any clearly spoken word from Ann will evoke a response from her mother. Her mother will even interrupt a conversation with another adult in order to respond to Ann!

It seems that the language known as "motherese" is designed not just to teach sentence structure, nor just to communicate information at a level the child can understand. Part of its purpose is to teach the child what Snow calls "the conversational mode" of interaction with another person. Snow concludes,

> Recognition of the skill and insistence with which mothers introduce the conversational mode into their interactions with their children may help to explain how children acquire turn-taking skills, both in conversation and in other types of interaction. (pp. 21–22) ∎

studied by a group of Harvard psycholinguists. There are two things to note about this graph. First, MLU increases fairly steadily with age. This increase reflects the children's growing vocabularies and their ability to say more words at a time, and also their greater use of grammatical forms as they get older. Second, notice how rapidly Eve's MLU increases, relative to Adam's and Sarah's. Eve reaches a MLU of 4 at about 26 months; Adam and Sarah reach that point at 3½ years—more than a year later. Such large individual differences in speed of language acquisition are not rare. Most children don't use 10-word sentences until they are 3 or 4 years old; yet one young girl we know said things like "Wish we could get a cute little puppy like that," before the age of 24 months. Albert Einstein, on the other hand, is said to have been speechless until he was nearly 3!

It's possible to make some generalizations about differences in the rate of

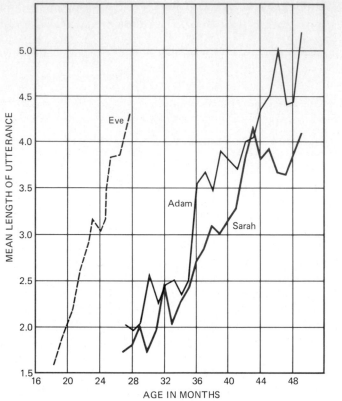

figure 7–1
Children speak in longer and longer utterances as they get older. This graph shows how MLU increased with age for Eve, Adam, and Sarah. (Brown, 1973, p. 57)

language development. First, on the average girls tend to progress slightly more rapidly than boys. Second, there is a correlation between how early a little girl begins to speak and how well she will do on IQ tests later on. For little boys, the correlation between language development and later IQ doesn't become significant until they're 21 months old (McCall, Eichorn, and Hogarty, 1977).

Third, both heredity and environment play a role in the rate of language development. One study (Hardy-Brown, Plomin, and DeFries, 1981) has separated these two factors by examining early language development in adopted children. (Receptive language, as well as productive language, was tested in these children.) There was a significant correlation between the children's language ability and the general cognitive ability of their biological mothers. The children's language ability also correlated significantly with the way their *adoptive* mothers reacted to their vocalizations. Adoptive mothers who responded to most of their children's vocalizations in some way—even just by imitating the sounds that the child produced—had children who were more advanced in language development.

Different Styles of Language Learning.   Language development, as it's usually described in textbooks, proceeds in an orderly fashion: the toddler begins by saying one-word utterances ("Mama," "Dada," "cookie," "kitty"), goes

on to two-word utterances ("See kitty," "Car go"), and so on. That description *does* fit the majority of children. But there's a sizable minority who come to language in a different way. "Some children," says psycholinguist Katherine Nelson, "are aiming at sentence targets rather than single-word targets right from the beginning" (1981, p. 176).

Nelson found that toddlers vary widely in their approach to learning to speak. Some specialize at first in learning words, especially nouns. Others use many ready-made phrases and relatively few nouns—instead they use all-purpose pronouns such as *it* (as in "Don't do it" and "I don't want it," two phrases used by a 16-month-old girl). Other children fall somewhere in between these two extremes.

The phrases said by a 16- or 18-month-old phrase-user are said all at once, without pauses. The words tend to be pronounced very poorly, so a person who's unfamiliar with the child (or unaware of the context) may not understand the phrase at all. However, the intonation of the phrase, the expression in the child's voice, is very clear. These children may not have learned all the words of the language, but, as Nelson puts it, they already know the "tune."

At a given age, the phrase-users and the noun-users have equal MLUs, though the phrase-users have a smaller vocabulary. Some of these children will actually fill in a phrase with meaningless sounds when their vocabulary fails them. For instance, one phrase-user said "Uh-uh down," presumably to mean "Put me down," or "I want to go down." A noun-user would have been perfectly content just to say "Down."

Nelson believes that the difference in language style between the two groups of children reflects their different ideas about the function of language. The noun-users assign it a cognitive, information-transmitting function. The phrase-users seem to employ language mainly for social purposes—to attract an adult's attention, or to keep an interaction going. Noun-users tend to be firstborn children; phrase-users are more often later-borns.

Perhaps these two groups of children differ in temperament—perhaps phrase-users are simply more sociable. But Nelson (1981) thinks that the difference is based more on their experiences with language, with the way that language is used in their presence. She feels that a mother who uses language to transmit information and who teaches by asking questions is likely to have a noun-using child. On the other hand, a mother who doesn't pay a lot of attention to what her child says, and who uses language mostly to tell the child what to do, is more likely to have a phrase-using child.

Theories of Language Learning

In 1957, B. F. Skinner published a book called *Verbal Behavior,* in which he interpreted language as a set of responses controlled and shaped by reinforcement. It all starts when the baby says "ma-ma," and Mother comes running with smiles, caresses, and perhaps even good things to eat. Later, Mother gets fussier about pronunciation—wants "Mommy" rather than "ma-ma,"

perhaps. She also selectively reinforces longer and more grammatical utterances. In some cases the child is reinforced by getting what he wants, as when he says "Put me down," or "Milk, please." In other cases the reinforcer is simply the approval of his audience, as when he makes statements such as "Teddy bear is brown," or "I have two shoes." And sometimes the reinforcer can be his own knowledge that he has produced the kind of acceptable English sentence that *would* be approved of, if anyone had happened to hear it.

Skinner views language as just another kind of behavior. He believes that it's subject to the same laws, controlled by the same sorts of consequences, as all human and animal behavior. The way he works out the details of this theory is complex and ingenious. Many of the psycholinguists who have attacked Skinner have never really attempted to understand all the intricacies of his theory.

Nevertheless, some of the attacks have been successful. Psycholinguists soon came up with a finding that went against the predictions of Skinner's theory. Skinner claimed that children's utterances become more grammatical as they grow older because parents selectively reinforce grammatical utterances and fail to reinforce ungrammatical ones. But studies show that parents don't actually do that with toddlers. They approve or disapprove of their children's statements on the basis of their truth, their accuracy—not on the basis of grammatical correctness. For instance, one little girl said "Mama isn't boy, he a girl," and her mother said approvingly, "That's right." But when another child made the perfectly grammatical statement, "Walt Disney comes on Tuesday," his mother replied, "No, he does not" (Brown and Hanlon, 1970, p. 49). One would think that children would grow up speaking ungrammatically but truthfully, since parents reinforce truth and don't bother much about grammar. But as one group of researchers put it, "the usual product of such a training schedule is an adult whose speech is highly grammatical but not notably truthful" (Brown, Cazden, and Bellugi-Klima, 1969, pp. 57–58).

Even parents who *are* concerned about grammar or pronunciation have found it very hard to influence their children's utterances. Here's one mother's unsuccessful attempt to speed up her child's acquisition of grammar:

    Child: Nobody don't like me.
  Mother: No, say "Nobody likes me."
    Child: Nobody don't like me.
  Mother: No, say "Nobody likes me."
    Child: Nobody don't like me.

        [They continue like this for a while.]

  Mother: No, now listen carefully: "Nobody likes me."
    Child: Oh! Nobody don't *likes* me. (McNeill, 1966, p. 69)

Correction of pronunciation yields similarly unencouraging results. This is the child whose parents are both psycholinguists:

Father: Say *tur.*
Nicholas: *Tur.*
　　Father: Say *till.*
Nicholas: *Till.*
　　Father: Say *turtle.*
Nicholas: *Kurka.* (de Villiers and de Villiers, 1979, pp. 109–110)

Is Language Innate?　The same four-legged animal would be called *un chien* in France, *un perro* in Mexico, *ein Hund* in Austria, and a *dog* in the United States. That makes it seem ridiculous to ask whether language is innate. But a noted linguist, Noam Chomsky, has proposed that a knowledge of certain universal aspects of language is built into the human brain. In Chomsky's view, the child knows without having to learn it that the same underlying idea can be expressed in superficially different ways (such as "The boy carried the box" and "The box was carried by the boy"). The child knows that her job is to figure out the underlying idea—what Chomsky (1968) calls the "deep structure." The child is also furnished with the innate knowledge that learning language doesn't just consist of memorizing a bunch of words—one must also discover the rules for putting the words together. According to Chomsky, the child has an inborn tendency to look for regularities in the utterances she hears, and to make guesses about the rules that govern these regularities.

Part of this theory has not held up very well. There is no good evidence that children know anything about the "deep structure" of language. But the second part of the theory—that children have an inborn tendency to figure out the rules of language—has fared better. In fact, many psycholinguists agree with it (Aitchison, 1977).

It seems clear that *something* about language is innate. Babies appear to be "tuned in" to speech right from the start. They can detect subtle differences in speech sounds, such as the difference between "pah" and "bah" (see p. 156). At a very early age they prefer to listen to speech, or to songs sung by a human voice, rather than to instrumental music (Butterfield and Siperstein, 1974).

The development of language follows a fairly fixed, universal pattern. The baby progresses from crying to cooing to babbling. (Even deaf babies begin to babble at the usual age. They eventually stop babbling, though, if they can't hear the sound of their own voice.) The first words generally appear early in the second year of life. Later, the child's utterances become longer and more complicated. She does not need lessons in learning to speak—in fact, formal training is usually of little use. She does not need to be particularly intelligent—only the most severely retarded or brain-damaged children are totally without language. All in all, the normal course of language acquisition is much like the normal course of learning to walk. At a given level of maturation the behavior appears. It can be speeded up or slowed down a little, but not very much.

If a child must reach a certain level of maturation before she can learn to

TABLE 7–5 Children's Two-Word Sentences in Five Different Languages

		Language		
English	**German**	**Russian**	**Finnish**	**Samoan**
there book that car see doggie	buch da [book there] gukuk wauwau [see doggie]	Tosya tam [Tosya there]	tuossa Rina [there Rina] vettä sünä [water there]	Keith lea [Keith there]
more milk give candy want gum	mehr milch [more milk] bitte apfel [please apple]	yeshchë moloko [more milk] day chasy [give watch]	anna Rina [give Rina]	mai pepe [give doll] fia moo [want sleep]
no wet no wash not hungry allgone milk	nicht blasen [not blow] kaffee nein [coffee no]	vody net [water no] gus' tyu-tyu [goose gone]	ei susi [not wolf] enää pipi [anymore sore]	le ái [not eat] uma mea [allgone thing]
Bambi go mail come hit ball block fall baby highchair	puppe kommt [doll comes] tiktak hängt [clock hangs] sofa sitzen [sofa sit] messer schneiden [cut knife]	mama prua [mama walk] papa bay-bay [papa sleep] nashla yaichko [found egg] baba kresio [grandma armchair]	Seppo putoo [Seppo fall] talli 'bm-bm' [garage 'car']	pa'u pepe [fall doll] tapale 'oe [hit you] tu'u lalo [put down]
my shoe mama dress	mein ball [my ball] mamas hut [mama's hat]	mami chashka [mama's cup] pup moya [navel my]	täti auto [aunt car]	lole a'u [candy my] polo 'oe [ball your]
pretty dress big boat	milch heiss [milk hot] armer wauwau [poor dog]	mama khoroshaya [mama good] papa bol'shoy [papa big]	rikki auto [broken car] torni iso [tower big]	fa'ali'i pepe [headstrong baby]
where ball	wo ball [where ball]	gde papa [where papa]	missä pallo [where ball]	fea Punafu [where Punafu]

From Slobin, 1971.

speak, what happens if she *passes* that level without having learned it? Can she be *too* mature to learn a language? Certain kinds of birds learn to sing the characteristic song of their species through hearing it sung by adult birds. But there's a *critical period* (see p. 194) for that kind of learning: if the bird reaches sexual maturity without having heard its song, it will never learn it.

In humans, there's some evidence of a critical period for language learning that ends at adolescence. A person who learns a second language after early adolescence will never speak it like a native. A retarded child who hasn't acquired a first language by early adolescence will never acquire it (Lenneberg, 1964).

But humans' ability to acquire language doesn't cease abruptly—it just gradually declines. A tragic illustration of this is provided by the case of Genie. In 1970, a 13½-year-old girl in shocking condition came to the attention of California authorities. Genie could not speak, nor stand erect, nor control bowel or bladder, nor eat solid foods. She weighed only 59 pounds (27 kg). It turned out that Genie had been confined in a small room since infancy, harnessed by day to a potty chair and by night to her crib. No one ever spoke to her. Her mentally ill father used to bark or snarl at her like a dog; he beat her whenever she made a sound. (He was charged with child abuse, but on the day he was to appear in court he shot himself.) Genie's mother was partially blind, and terrified of her husband.

Genie was hospitalized for several months and then went to live with a foster family. She learned to say many words, and eventually she began to combine them into two- and three-word phrases. But her language development was extremely slow, and her speech never became normal. She never learned to use pronouns like *I* and *you,* or to ask questions. She never got beyond the stage of "telegraphic speech" (Curtiss, 1977; Pines, 1981).

Even so, her progress surprised psychologists. No one thought that a child that old could still acquire a first language. The only comparable case before Genie was that of Victor, the "wild boy of Aveyron." Victor was captured by hunters in a forest in France in 1799. A young French doctor named Jean Itard tried to teach him to speak, starting when Victor was about 12 years old. But Victor never learned to say more than a few simple words. It's possible, though, that Victor was retarded—perhaps that's why he was abandoned in the first place (Lane, 1976).

Putting all the evidence together, many psychologists, psycholinguists, and biologists have concluded that the ability to learn language is a built-in human trait—a species-specific characteristic (Lenneberg, 1964).

Can Chimpanzees Learn a Language?   Is the human species *alone* in its language-learning ability? Obviously, parrots don't really learn language—they just learn to imitate a sequence of sounds, without any understanding of what they mean. But dogs can learn to follow dozens of different spoken commands. And chimpanzees are much more intelligent than dogs—why don't they learn to speak?

One reason is that their mouths and vocal cords don't seem to be designed for it. However, their hands are quite nimble, and a pair of psychologists at the University of Nevada (Gardner and Gardner, 1971) had the clever idea of teaching a chimp American Sign Language (ASL), the gestural language used by many deaf people in the United States. Washoe was a year old when she started to learn ASL. Within three years she had learned the signs for 130 words, including *fruit, toothbrush, gimme,* and *tickle.* She also was using combinations of signs, such as *"gimme tickle"* and *"more fruit."* There was one problem, though. It wasn't clear whether Washoe was combining signs

Nim makes the sign for *cat*.

in a specific *order,* the way children do at the two-word stage. Was Washoe as likely to say *"tickle gimme"* as *"gimme tickle"*?

To answer that question, a psychologist at Columbia University (Terrace, 1979) taught ASL to a chimp named Nim. Nim learned his first sign-language word *(drink)* when he was only 4 months old. He learned his 125th sign *(peach)* 3½ years later, just before the experiment ended. Nim was also able to combine signs—he produced combinations of two, three, four, and even more signs.

In some ways, Nim's use of language was much like that of a human child's. He was clearly capable of naming things. Nim used signs like *dog, cat, bird, apple, red,* and *play* at appropriate times—for instance, he would see a picture of a cat and sign *cat.* But the chimp's "phrases" were not like those of a normal child's. Some of Nim's two-, three-, and four-word phrases are shown in Table 7–6. The two-word combinations seem pretty reasonable, but the three- and four-word ones don't seem at all like what a child would say. They seem more like random strings of words. There are many repetitions. Nim's longest "utterance" was 16 words long. It went, *"Give orange me give eat orange me eat orange give me eat orange give me you"* (Terrace, 1979, p. 210).

Most of Nim's utterances were much shorter than 16 words. His MLU reached 1½ words at 26 months—not too different from Adam's and Sarah's

TABLE 7–6   Sign-Language Phrases Used by Nim, a Chimpanzee

Two-Word Phrases	Three-Word Phrases	Four-Word Phrases
play me	play me Nim	play me Nim play
me Nim	eat me Nim	me Nim eat me
eat Nim	eat Nim eat	Nim eat Nim eat
Nim eat	banana Nim eat	banana me eat banana
drink Nim	banana eat Nim	banana eat me Nim
tickle me	tickle me Nim	eat drink eat drink
more tickle	tickle me tickle	tickle me Nim play
sorry hug	hug me Nim	banana me Nim me

From Terrace, 1979, pp. 212–213.

at that age (see Figure 7–1). But Nim's *remained* at about 1½ words from then on, until the experiment ended 20 months later. Nim's utterances did not get longer and more complex as he got older, the way children's utterances do.

So the answer about chimpanzee language is yes, chimpanzees can learn to use words. But they don't seem to be able to use *sentences*—at least not in the way people use them. It seems unlikely that an ape could ever figure out the rules of grammar, the rules that young children use when they combine words to form phrases.

Figuring Out the Rules.   For that matter, it seems unlikely that *children* could ever figure out the rules of grammar from the incredible variety of sounds they hear. Can you say how you know that "I have hurt myself" is a grammatical English sentence, and "He has hurt myself" isn't? Can you say what the rule is for deciding which is correct, "Where is Mommy?" or "Where Mommy is?"

But children don't have to *know* the rules, you may be thinking. They just have to imitate what they hear other people say.

It turns out, though, that that's not exactly the case. They *don't* learn only by imitation. For one thing, children seem not to be able to acquire a language from passively listening to radio or TV shows (de Villiers and de Villiers, 1979). For another, young children routinely come out with utterances that they've never heard anyone else say, such as "Two feets," "Daddy goed 'way," "Dat's mines," and even "I have a clo" (instead of "some clothes").

What's interesting about these examples is that all of them are incorrect applications of general rules. What's more interesting is that a child might say *feet, went,* and *mine* before she's 2 years old, and then a few months later switch to *feets, goed,* and *mines*. At some point she notices that most past tenses end in -*ed* and most plurals and possessives end in -*s*, and she tries to apply this rule consistently. Still later she'll learn the exceptions to the rule.

Learning the rules of grammar is really something that preschoolers do, and we'll discuss it in more detail in Chapter 10. Right now we just want to point out that young children *do* seem to be willing and able to notice patterns in the speech they hear, and to make guesses about the rules that underlie the patterns. Sometimes their guesses are right, sometimes they're wrong. The wrong rules eventually get replaced with better ones. It's rather like an experimental science. The main difference is that the children aren't consciously aware of what they're doing, and couldn't actually tell you the theories they're testing at the moment. But the comparison between the toddler and the scientist is a valid one. Remember Laurent, doing experiments on the behavior of falling objects, and Jacqueline, studying the properties of water?

Human babies are born knowing nothing. But they come equipped with the most valuable equipment in the world: a thirst for knowledge and understanding, and the ability to acquire them.

summary

1. **Cognitive development** is the growth of intelligence, understanding, reasoning, and knowledge. Piaget believes that cognitive development progresses in stages (each child must go through the same stages in the same order, though the rate of progress may vary), and that both maturation and the child's interactions with the environment play a role in this progress.

2. **Adaptation** depends on the challenges provided by the environment and on what the child is capable of doing and understanding. Piaget distinguishes two kinds of adaptation that occur in children: **assimilation,** which involves applying previously acquired abilities or ideas to new situations, and **accommodation,** which involves modifying previously acquired abilities or ideas to suit new situations.

3. Piaget calls the first major period of development (roughly the first two years) the **sensorimotor period.** This period is divided into six stages.

4. Stage 1 (the first month of life) involves the use, and the improvement through adaptation, of inborn **schemes** such as rooting, sucking, and looking at things.

5. Stage 2 (1–4 months) marks the entrance of the first acquired abilities, such as thumbsucking and visual exploration. Piaget believes

that these schemes are acquired by means of **circular reactions:** the baby does something by accident, and if the results are pleasant or interesting he does it again. During stage 2, babies also begin to enjoy looking at their hands; by the end of this stage they have gained some control over the movements of their hands and arms.

6. In stage 3 (4–9 months) the baby becomes interested in the effects he can produce on his environment—e.g., causing a rattle to make a noise. Piaget believes that before stage 3, babies cannot understand the connection between their actions and the results of their actions; however, other evidence suggests that it is only their lack of motor skills that ordinarily prevents younger babies from making this connection. In one experiment, 2-month-old babies quickly learned to move their heads to make a mobile turn; they appeared to enjoy doing this very much.

7. For stage-3 babies, the connection between their actions and the results of their actions is a "magical" one—they don't understand cause-and-effect relationships. That understanding begins to develop in stage 4 (9–12 months)—now babies search for an appropriate method to achieve a particular goal. Previously acquired schemes are applied to new objects as

a means of systematically exploring their possibilities. There is also some ability to anticipate the future.

8. In stage 5 (12–18 months), babies begin to use active experimentation in order to develop new schemes to suit new situations. Stage-5 babies may perform series of experiments just to see what will happen; they approach problems in a flexible, sometimes even inventive way.

9. In stage 6 (18–24 months), problems may be solved, not only by trial and error, but also by insight. Children in this stage can think out possibilities, and plan ahead, by means of mental **representations.** At this point, representations generally consist of visual, auditory, or motor images. Such representations also make **deferred imitation** possible.

10. During the sensorimotor period, the concept of **object permanence** is acquired. The stage-1 baby can recognize familiar sights, but she has no conception of the permanent existence of things outside of herself. By stage 2, the baby begins to show some expectation that things seen or touched can be seen or touched again.

11. The first real signs of object permanence appear in stage 3: now the baby begins to look for things, not only in the place where they were last seen, but also in a new place (e.g., on the floor, for an object that is seen to fall). However, when an object is completely hidden, babies will immediately act as though they've forgotten about it. "Person permanence" occurs a little before object permanence—many babies will search for a completely hidden parent (a stage-4 action) while they're still in stage 3 with regard to objects. Securely attached babies tend to develop "person permanence" and object permanence at an earlier age than insecurely attached ones.

12. Stage-4 babies will search for a completely hidden object, but they are likely to search in the place where they previously found it, even if they see it being put somewhere else.

Piaget thinks that this is because babies still don't have a concept of independent objects that can be moved from place to place; another view is that they lack concepts such as *under* and *behind.*

13. In stage 5, toddlers will search for an object in the place where they saw it hidden, but they cannot yet use mental representations to take account of movements they didn't actually see. This ability appears in stage 6.

14. Piaget and Freud agree that the newborn baby has no concept of self and cannot distinguish between "me" and "not me." The concept of self develops gradually during infancy, due at first to the infant's increasing ability to gain control of the movements of his body (and not of the movements of other things) and to his experiences with the sensations he feels in his body.

15. Babies at first seem to regard their mirror images as amusing companions. Later they begin to explore the mirror's possibilities; they may also go through a stage in which they avoid looking at themselves in the mirror. The understanding that the image in the mirror is "me" generally arises between 18 and 24 months; chimpanzees (but not monkeys) also show this awareness. Piaget believes that a stage-6 child can conceive of his own body as a permanent object, existing in space and through time.

16. Rate of development in the first year of life cannot be used to predict later IQ. A significant correlation between early development and later IQ first appears in the second year; it is around .50 by age 2.

17. Environment in the first years of life clearly affects later intellectual ability, but we don't know whether experiences in the early years matter more, less, or the same as later experiences. Even severe early deprivation may be overcome, if the later environment is favorable.

18. Children who have suffered starvation or malnutrition in the early years of life will be smaller, both in body and in brain, than well-nourished children. However, if they are reared in good environments, their intelligence is likely to be normal. The brain is apparently able to adjust to a loss of size and of brain cells, provided that this loss occurs early in development.

19. A baby discovers the sound of her voice in early infancy, and enjoys playing with it and using it in interactions with other people. In the second half of the first year, the baby can produce a wide variety of sounds; this is the period of babbling. Most babies can say a word or two at 12 months, but true talking generally doesn't appear for another two months or more. In the meanwhile, some babies use **expressive jargon,** which sounds like speech but is unintelligible.

20. The average baby can produce 10 words at 15 months, 50 words at 20 months, and close to 200 words at age 2. At every age, **receptive language** is ahead of **productive language.**

21. The productive vocabulary begins to increase dramatically at around 18 months. According to one theory, this increase comes at the point when the child has the insight that words are representations of objects.

22. Toddlers at the one-word stage often overgeneralize—e.g., by calling any four-legged animal a *dog.* They may also use a single word in place of an entire sentence.

23. The average child begins to combine words at around 20 months. At first there may be pauses between words, or the child may use ready-made phrases (e.g., "What's that?") or **pivot words** (e.g., *it,* in "push it" and "get it"). A toddler at the two-word stage cannot repeat a longer sentence; if she attempts to do so, she will probably leave out verb endings and unimportant words. The words in such **telegraphic speech** generally occur in the proper order. Toddlers all over the world speak in much the same way.

24. Toddlers have trouble with pronunciation, though they can hear the differences that they can't pronounce. They tend to drop difficult sounds and substitute easier ones.

25. Adults and older children speak in a characteristic way to toddlers: they use short, clear, simple sentences, with greater than usual stress and expression, more pauses, more repetition, and more questions than they would use with an adult. Their speech generally relates to concrete objects, which they tend to name at an intermediate level of specificity. There is also a tendency to avoid using words that toddlers find hard to say.

26. Mothers apparently try, right from the beginning, to teach their babies to take turns in conversation. At first, almost anything the baby does is interpreted as a conversational response; later the rules get stricter.

27. One way that psycholinguists measure the development of children's speech is in terms of **mean length of utterance (MLU).** MLU increases fairly steadily with age, but there are large individual differences. For girls, the speed of language development correlates with later IQ; for boys, the correlation does not become significant until the age of 21 months.

28. Although the majority of children start with one-word utterances and go on to longer utterances, a sizable minority aim at sentences right from the start. These children tend to use ready-made phrases and relatively few nouns; they seem to employ language more for social purposes than to convey information.

29. Skinner believes that children's use of language improves with time because parents selectively reinforce grammatical utterances and don't reinforce ungrammatical ones. But parents seem to approve or disapprove of toddlers' statements on the basis of their truth, not their grammatical correctness; and parents who do attempt to correct grammar or pronunciation often get nowhere.

30. Chomsky believes that children are born with a knowledge of certain universal aspects of language: that understanding a statement consists of discovering its "deep structure" (underlying idea), and that words are put together according to rules that they must figure out. There is no good evidence that children know anything about the "deep structure" of language, but many psycholinguists agree that children have an inborn tendency to figure out the rules of language.

31. Babies appear to be "tuned in" to speech right from the start. All but the most severely retarded or brain-damaged learn to speak without any special training. There is some evidence for a critical period for language learning that ends at adolescence. However, the ability to learn a language probably doesn't end abruptly—it gradually declines.

32. Chimpanzees have been taught to communicate in sign language; one chimp learned to make 125 signs and could combine them into phrases. However, these phrases appeared to be strings of words arranged in random order, unlike children's phrases. Chimps seem to be unable to do what children do—figure out the rules for combining words into grammatical sentences.

33. Children do not learn a language simply by imitating what they have heard. Some of their early speech errors are incorrect applications of general rules—evidence that they have noticed patterns in the speech they hear and have made guesses about the rules that underlie these patterns.

Chapter Eight

THE PRESCHOOL CHILD: PHYSICAL, MOTOR, AND PERCEPTUAL DEVELOPMENT

Eight

The 2½-year-old child no longer toddles—he or she walks and even runs steadily. Toddlerhood is over, and what is called the **preschool period** has begun. Of course, not all children attend a preschool during this period. The term **preschooler** means only that the child is too young to enter elementary school.

Many changes—in size, shape, motor skills, intellectual abilities, and so on—will come about before the 2½-year-old will be ready to enter first grade. But many important changes have already taken place.

You've Come a Long Way, Baby!

At 2½, Neil is a sturdy-looking little boy, with short, chubby arms and legs and a rounded body. He has lost that fragile, helpless look that he had for the first few months of his life, and the roly-poly look that succeeded it. Preschool children are attractive people—many adults find this the most appealing age of all. Neil still has the big head and eyes, the small features set low in his face, that made him so irresistible in infancy. His skin is still soft and smooth. But in infancy he was virtually bald—now he has a full head of shiny curls. In infancy he was toothless—now he has a complete set of 20 baby teeth, white and even. In infancy his head was set squarely on his shoulders—now a short but slender neck holds his head erect.

In behavior as well as appearance, Neil has come a long way since infancy. He has been talking for barely a year, but he can already communicate a wide range of ideas and information to anyone he happens to meet. A year and a half ago Neil could only crawl; now he can run and jump, walk up and down the stairs, and even climb a short ladder (putting both feet on each rung). He's recently begun to use the potty and now he wears diapers only at night. He can eat with a fork or spoon and drink from a cup he holds himself. He's not too good at putting on his shoes or clothes (buttons and shoelaces are still beyond him), but he's quite capable of taking them off. He can build a tower of blocks, knock it down with enthusiasm, and build it up again. He can even sing "Row, row, row your boat"—well, it sounds *something* like "Row, row, row your boat"!

Physical Growth

At 2½, Neil is exactly 3 feet tall (91 cm), which is just a shade above the mean for boys his age. If we were to try to predict his eventual adult height

The preschooler can do a great many things that are beyond the capabilities of the toddler.

at this point, our best guess would be 5'10" (177 cm), or 1.94 times his present height (Tanner, 1978). But the correlation between height in early childhood and height in adulthood is not perfect—it is only .80 to .85. Thus our estimate has about a 5 percent chance of being off by more than 3 inches (7½ cm).

Neil's growth depends on many things. He will end up shorter if he is undernourished or if his health is poor. His body must produce the right hormones for growth. He should get at least a minimal amount of exercise: children who are confined to bed do not grow as much as active children (Teeple, 1978).

Neil weighs 32 pounds (14½ kg)—again, slightly above the mean for 2½-year-old boys. Note that Neil is now more than 50 percent of his adult height but only about 20 percent of his adult weight. Furthermore, the different parts of his body have not all grown at the same rate. Neil's brain growth is more than 75 percent complete; by the time he's 5 it will be 90 percent complete (Tanner, 1978). His bulging abdomen attests to the fact that his internal organs are closer to their adult size than is the rest of his torso. His legs have the most growing to do, because preschoolers are proportionately short-legged, relative to adults.

Growth during the preschool period is considerably slower than growth during infancy. Neil grew 16 inches (41 cm) in the first 2½ years of his life; he'll grow only 7 inches (18 cm) from 2½ to 5 years. Considered in proportion to body size, the difference in growth rate is even greater: an 80 percent increase in the first 2½ years, a 19 percent increase in the second 2½ years. A similar trend exists in weight gain: Neil gained 24 pounds (11 kg) in infancy and toddlerhood; he'll gain only 10 pounds (4½ kg) in his preschool years. (In percentages, that's a 300 percent gain for the first period, versus 31 percent for the preschool period.)

Despite the fact that growth during the preschool period is not rapid, changes in proportions and in overall appearance do occur. By the time he is ready to begin elementary school, Neil will look less like a baby and more like an adult. His limbs will be longer relative to his body. His body will have grown more than his head, so he will be less top-heavy in appearance. Due to the growth of his torso and the development of his abdominal muscles, Neil's stomach will gradually stop protruding and will be fairly flat by the end of the preschool period.

Preschool boys are slightly taller and heavier than girls of the same age. The differences are small—they amount to less than an inch, and no more than a pound, between the heights and weights of the average boy and the average girl. Despite their slight advantage in weight, boys have less fat on their bodies than girls do—boys lose their baby fat more quickly. Girls, however, are ahead in other ways: they will lose their baby teeth, and get in their permanent teeth, at an earlier age than boys. They will also complete their growth and become sexually mature adults at an earlier age.

The Importance of Nutrition

The baby gained weight very rapidly; the preschooler does not. This rapid decline in weight gain goes along with a noticeable change in appetite. Neil's mother has observed that he's not nearly as hungry as he was as a baby; in fact, many mothers of preschoolers describe their children as "picky eaters." The decrease in appetite follows naturally from the decrease in growth rate— a child who *did* continue to eat as hungrily as he did in infancy would quickly become obese.

Because of their children's "picky" appetites, some mothers try to tempt them to eat by offering sweets or snack foods. The danger here is that such "junk foods" provide only the empty calories of refined carbohydrates, without the needed nutrients. Thus, children may enjoy the food they are eating and may feel full when they are done, but they may not be getting vital nutrients. Indeed, it has been estimated (Schaefer and Johnson, 1969) that about 30 percent of American children have a deficiency of Vitamin A, and that an even larger percentage have anemia (too few red blood cells, due to an inadequate intake of iron in the diet). Vitamin C deficiency is also common.

Despite these facts, and despite the amount of "junk food" in the modern diet, unfavorable effects of diet on growth are not very evident in our society. American preschoolers are larger today than children of the same age were 30 or 40 years ago, when fewer processed foods were eaten. Differences in size among children in this country are related more to racial background

than to diet: the average black child is a little taller than the average white child; the average Asian-American is a little shorter (Meredith, 1978).

Growth, Nutrition, and Intellectual Ability. What we just said about diet and growth applies to most children in countries such as the United States and Canada, where the standard of living is relatively high. Even in those countries, however, there are some children who don't get enough to eat over long periods of time, and there are parts of the world where sizable proportions of the children are chronically undernourished.

Chronically undernourished children are, of course, shorter and thinner than their well-fed agemates. In addition, undernourished children tend to score lower on IQ tests and on tests of motor development. A study of 2-year-olds in rural Guatemala (Lasky and others, 1981) found a significant correlation between the children's heights and their test scores. The taller children were presumably the ones who were better-nourished and healthier; these children were more advanced in their intellectual and motor development than their smaller agemates. These findings were interpreted as showing that good nutrition has a direct influence on intellectual development, as well as on physical and motor development.

A later study (Politt, Mueller, and Leibel, 1982) suggests that the relationship between nutrition and intelligence is a little more complicated than that. A group of preschoolers in Cambridge, Massachusetts, were weighed and measured and were given IQ tests. All of these children were well-nourished; yet, the correlation between their physical growth and their IQ scores was about as high as in the Guatemalan children. The investigators concluded that these correlations reflected differences in rate of physical maturation. Those children who were physically more mature than their agemates tended, on the average, to score a little higher on IQ tests. (It's possible that the other children will eventually catch up.) In places like rural Guatemala, where many children are undernourished, the rate of physical maturation will depend to a large degree on nutrition. But in places where almost all children are well-nourished, the rate of maturation will depend primarily on genetic factors.

We do not know the precise reason why speedier physical maturation should give a child an intellectual advantage, but it is not surprising. A body that matures more rapidly implies a brain that matures more rapidly, too. And, as we will see in Chapter 10, a child who does well on an IQ test is one whose intellectual ability is developing at a faster rate than average.

Other Aspects of Physical Growth

Besides the changes in size and shape we mentioned earlier, other physical changes take place during the preschool period. For instance, breathing becomes slower and deeper, heart rate decreases, blood pressure goes up. The child's general physical health is likely to improve, as well. Many younger preschool children, especially those who go to nursery school or to a day-care center, get one cold after another. Ear infections are also common at this age. By the end of the preschool period, children tend to get sick less often. When they do run a fever, the fever is likely not to be as high (Lowrey, 1978).

Compared with the toddler, the preschooler is a sturdy individual. He no longer requires special foods—he can leave the high chair and take his place at the family dining table. He doesn't need to snack as often as he did in toddlerhood; he doesn't need as much sleep. He can go for increasingly longer periods without access to a toilet. All of these changes make it possible for him to participate more fully in the society of which he is a member. The experiences that come from this participation contribute to his cognitive and social development.

MOTOR DEVELOPMENT

Neil spends his waking hours in almost constant activity—in his mother's words, "He's never still for a moment." Preschool children don't have to be told, "Practice your running and jumping, your jungle-gym climbing, your

tricycle-riding, and your puzzle-putting-together skills.'' They apparently have ample motivation to do these things on their own.

When not asleep or watching TV, the typical preschooler is almost continuously on the go. The physical changes we described in the last section, plus increased muscular strength and the development of the motor areas of the brain, enable the preschooler to engage in vigorous, sustained physical activity. The games that preschoolers like to play are action games—games like Follow the Leader, or Hide and Seek. It is during this period that children begin to engage in physical competition with each other—to race each other across the yard, or to see who can build the highest tower of blocks. Such activities not only aid in the further development of motor skills, but also give children new opportunities for learning to get along with their peers.

Motor Development as Increased Control

By the time he is 3 years old, Neil will be able to climb stairs without putting both feet on the same step, jump down from the bottom step, walk on tiptoe, and ride a tricycle. His manual skills will have improved, too: he will be able to pour milk from a pitcher, unbutton buttons, put on his shoes, and draw a circle or a straight line.

At age 4, Neil will be able to hop on one foot, catch a large ball, and dress himself. He will be able to draw designs (and perhaps even letters) and will be able to cut on a line with a pair of scissors. By age 5, Neil will be able to run smoothly, skip, fasten the buttons on his shirt, and maybe even tie a bow in his shoelaces.

As these examples suggest, motor development involves motor control. Significant advances in motor control occur during the preschool period. These advances depend both on physical maturation of brain and body systems, and on the increasing skill that comes through practice. They involve both the large muscles, such as those that are used in running, jumping, and climbing; and the small muscles, such as those that are used in drawing, cutting with scissors, and tying a bow.

One way to appreciate the development of motor skills during the preschool years is to focus on the word *voluntary*. In many ways the infant and toddler were still using inborn reflexes to guide their actions. But now, in the preschool years, the child begins to use his body to do what he *wants* to do, what he *chooses* to do. And this new goal—to get his body to do what he wishes it to do—becomes a motivation to exercise a variety of physical and motor skills.

The development of good motor control is an important task of the preschool years. Once achieved, this control will serve as the foundation for more advanced motor skills that are acquired in later childhood and adulthood.

Motor Patterns and Motor Skills

Motor development can be divided into two broad categories: **motor patterns** and **motor skills.** A motor pattern is the basic sequence of movements involved in performing some action. Motor skills, on the other hand, involve accuracy and precision. A child who has acquired a motor pattern has not necessarily acquired the ability to perform it skillfully.

Walking and Running.   For example, the toddler can walk, but his gait is awkward—he walks with his feet wide apart and he falls down easily. As toddlerhood ends and the preschool years begin, walking becomes a skilled activity. The stride lengthens, speed increases, balance is more stable. The child becomes able to walk for longer periods of time without resting.

The changes that take place in running patterns are more noticeable than those involved in walking, but they are similar in nature. Figure 8–1 shows the difference in running style between an 18-month-old toddler and a 3-year-old preschooler.

Throwing a Ball.   In many cases, the development of a motor skill involves the gradual integration of already existing movements—what start out as sep arate pieces of behavior are eventually combined into a smooth, continuous pattern. In other cases, new movements are acquired. Learning to throw a ball skillfully is an example of an activity that involves acquiring new movements as well as integrating existing ones.

At 2 or 3 years of age, the child merely swings his arm while holding his trunk steady. There is no rotation of the trunk and the feet are fixed. Next, horizontal movements of the arm and body begin to occur, producing some

rotation of the body. Although the child is now rotating his trunk to compensate for the greater power of his arm movement, his feet still remain fixed in one place.

Toward the end of the preschool years, the child will begin to take a forward step with his right leg (or, if he throws with his left hand, his left leg). Next, he increases the movement of his hip, getting greater power and accuracy. Finally, in the ideal throwing pattern, his weight is moved forward from his right to his left foot, while at the same time the trunk rotates to the left. This mature, highly skilled throwing procedure typically does not appear full-blown until about the time the child enters first grade (Malina, 1982).

Manipulation Skills. The preschool period is also the time when children develop important skills at **manipulation** (literally, acting on something with the hands). Most 4- or 5-year-olds delight in making things with scissors and paper, glue and popsicle sticks, and all sorts of small materials. Their increasing manual dexterity is applied to more practical activities, too—for example, combing their own hair or helping with family chores. All of these things are done rather awkwardly at first, but children's manual skills gradually improve as they approach the time they will enter elementary school. Such skills are essential if they are to deal successfully with the many paper-and-pencil activities of kindergarten and first grade.

Variability in Motor Development

Individual differences in motor development are striking—some children are decidedly better coordinated, stronger, or more athletic than others. These individual differences tend to persist throughout the life span. What makes for such differences? Genetic factors unquestionably play an important role—there is evidence that identical twins are more alike than fraternal twins in

The preschooler period is an important time for the development of manipulation skills.

their expression of motor skills during the preschool years. What's inherited may be a certain physique (some individuals may have larger muscles than others), a talent for coordinated movements, or even a tendency to be more active than most children and thus to devote more time to practicing motor skills.

Nutrition, which we have already mentioned, is also important. It appears that children who have been undernourished for long periods of time are likely to be retarded in their motor development. It may take them many years to catch up with their better-nourished agemates, or (if the undernutrition went on too long or was too severe) they may never catch up.

We should mention in passing that there are difficulties involved in the assessment of a particular preschooler's motor development. For one thing, day-to-day variations in performance are much greater in preschoolers than in older children, due to changes in motivation and in willingness to cooperate, and to other factors. For another thing, no test of motor abilities has been accepted as the established standard, the way the Apgar test has been accepted as the standard for assessing the physical condition of the neonate. Work in the area of motor development has generally focused on establishing norms—that is, on determining the average ages at which various motor skills are acquired. But children who are ahead in one motor skill are not necessarily ahead in others.

Sex Differences. In infancy, there are no consistent differences between boys and girls in motor development: the average girl sits up, crawls, and walks at virtually the same age as the average boy. By the preschool period, however, some differences have emerged. Boys, on the average, have more muscle and less fat on their bodies than girls do. Partly for this reason, they can run faster, jump farther, climb higher, and throw a ball harder. Girls, on the other hand, are ahead in other aspects of motor development, particularly in manipulation skills such as using scissors and fastening buttons. They're also a little ahead in large-muscle activities that require coordination, rather than strength—for instance, skipping, hopping, and balancing on one foot (Cratty, 1979).

None of these differences is particularly surprising, since many factors combine to produce them. Boys are physically more muscular than girls; girls are physically more mature. In addition, boys spend far more time than girls do in large-muscle activities such as running, jumping, and climbing; girls spend more time in activities that involve manipulation and precise coordination. A study of preschoolers in a California nursery school (Harper and Sanders, 1978) showed that the boys spent considerably more of their time in vigorous outdoor play, whereas the girls spent relatively more time indoors. Perhaps these children were yielding to social pressures to do "boy things" and "girl things," but these investigators thought not. They summed up their findings this way:

> In summary, we found little evidence that the behavior of the nursery school staff, the expressed concerns or the overt practices of the children's parents, or the nature of the available apparatus could account for the observed sex differences in behavior. (Harper and Sanders, 1978, p. 48)

The investigators concluded that the different styles of play reflected, at least in part, biological differences. They point out that in other mammalian species the males explore over a wider territory, and engage in more vigorous forms of activity, than the females.

DEVELOPMENT OF THE BRAIN

Growth of the head and brain occurs early in the life of the human—brain growth, in fact, is most rapid in the period just preceding birth. By age 2, brain growth has slowed considerably. It has not ended, however—the neurons in the brain will continue to increase in size and to form new connections with other neurons, and there will be a small increase in the number of glial cells. The process of myelination (see p. 166) also contributes to brain growth. Myelination is not complete until adolescence, or perhaps even later (Tanner, 1978).

The Two Sides of the Brain

In appearance, the human brain is symmetrical—its two wrinkled hemispheres are almost perfect mirror images of each other. But although they look alike, the two hemispheres are not, in fact, identical. It has been known for over a century that the part of the brain that enables us to speak, to understand language, and to read and write is generally located on the left hemisphere. The left side of the brain is also in charge of the right hand and foot—each side of the body is controlled by the brain hemisphere on the opposite side.

Because the left hemisphere controls both verbal ability and the right hand—the dominant hand, in most people—it used to be called the "dominant" side of the brain. But more recent evidence shows that *both* sides of the brain are important—the two hemispheres simply serve somewhat different functions. The left hemisphere is the verbal one, the one that specializes in reasoning and numerical skills. The right, on the other hand, specializes in nonverbal things: for example, spatial ability, perception of patterns and melodies, and the expression and recognition of emotions (Geschwind, 1979).

The Left Hemisphere and Language Acquisition. One way psychologists and neurologists have found out about these hemispheric differences is by seeing the results when one hemisphere or the other is injured (generally by a stroke or in an accident). An adult who suffers an injury to the left side of the brain might lose the ability to speak or to understand what someone is saying. But what happens when damage to the left hemisphere occurs in infancy or childhood? The answer is that damage in infancy seldom causes any language problems, although there may be other difficulties (in motor skills, for instance). Damage a little later on—after the child has learned to

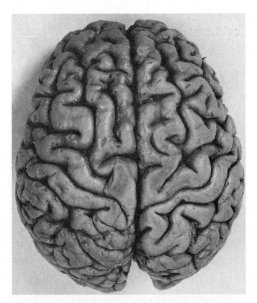

The human brain.

talk—may produce temporary loss of language, but recovery is usually complete. The effects of the injury become more serious with age. Once the child has reached adolescence, injury to the speech area in the left hemisphere is likely to produce permanent language disability (Lenneberg, 1964).

When the left hemisphere is damaged in early life, it appears that the right hemisphere may take over the job of handling language. But does that mean that the two hemispheres start out equal? Some psychologists and neurologists have assumed that **lateralization** of the brain—the tendency for the two sides to serve different functions—happens gradually during development, and that there are really no important differences between the hemispheres at first. But there's evidence that the two hemispheres *aren't* the same, even in very young babies. It's possible to measure the electrical activity inside the brain with sensors placed on the scalp. One study (Molfese, Freeman, and Palermo, 1975) showed that brain activity is greater in a baby's *left* hemisphere when the baby is hearing speech, and greater in the *right* when the baby is hearing music. Thus, it seems that the two hemispheres have different specialties right from the start. In spite of this, the young human brain is amazingly flexible. The ability of a young child to acquire (or reacquire) speech after left-hemisphere damage shows that parts of the brain not originally destined for language functions can take over those functions if necessary.

Right- and Left-Handedness. Given that the two hemispheres of the brain are used somewhat differently right from the start, it comes as no surprise to find that the two sides of the *body* also tend to be used differently. It was noticed many years ago that newborn babies usually hold their heads turned to the right, rather than to the left or straight ahead. Moreover, this tendency is related to handedness—the few babies who did keep their heads turned to the left later turned out to be left-handed (Gesell and Ames, 1947). Although young infants generally show no preference for reaching with one hand rather than the other, most are able to hold a rattle for a longer time in the right hand than in the left (Caplan and Kinsbourne, 1976).

By the preschool period, many children have settled down to using one hand to hold a spoon or a crayon, or to throw a ball. Although they're by no means as consistent in their preference as older children or adults, the *direction* of their preference is just as clear: the overwhelming majority favor the right hand (Coren, Porac, and Duncan, 1981).

Right-handedness is not just a cultural convention. In every known human society most of the people are right-handed. This has been true ever since the dawn of our species (Corballis and Beale, 1976).

These observations suggest that handedness is an innate characteristic of the human species. In fact, the tendency to be right- or left-handed does run in families: the probability that a child will be right-handed is about 92 percent if both parents are right-handed, 80 percent if one parent is left-handed, and close to 50 percent if both parents are left-handed (Rife, 1940; Longstreth, 1980). Overall in our population, something like a tenth of people are lefties. The proportion is a little higher in males than in females; it's also a little higher in twins (Corballis and Beale, 1976).

Do left-handed children differ from right-handed children? One way they *don't* differ is in intelligence. In a study involving over 7,000 children, no IQ differences were found between lefties and righties (Robert and Engle, as reported in Hicks and Kinsbourne, 1977). Nevertheless, there is evidence that the lefty's brain is organized a little differently from the righty's. Earlier we said that the brain area involved in producing and understanding language is "generally" located on the left hemisphere. The exceptions are lefties. Virtually all right-handed people have their language areas on the left (the hemisphere that controls their dominant hand). But among lefties, the situation is rather complicated. Slightly over half have language areas on the left (the side associated with the *non*dominant hand), about a third have language areas on the right, and the remainder use both hemispheres for language (Kinsbourne and Hiscock, 1977).

How do we account for lefties? One hypothesis that tries to explain the presence of these nonconformists in an overwhelmingly right-handed world is that lefties were "meant" to be right-handed but were brain-damaged before or during birth (by lack of oxygen, for example). If the damage involved the motor areas on the left side, the right hand might be affected. Thus, the child would tend to favor the left hand. If the damage also involved the language area on the left, the child would develop a language area on the right. What supports this hypothesis is the higher proportion of males and twins among lefties—both groups are known to be at higher risk for brain damage than female and single-born children.

Brain damage *does* seem to be involved in some small percentage of left-handedness. But the great majority of lefties have brains that work just as well as righties' brains, as shown by the equal IQs of the two groups. In fact, in some ways the lefty's brain is *better:* a left-handed person who suffers a stroke, and who loses the power of speech because of damage to the speech area, is more likely to regain the use of language than a right-handed person (Geschwind, 1979). That would hardly be the case if lefties were left-handed because they had *already* lost the use of some part of their brains!

Another hypothesis is that left-handed people (particularly those with language areas on the right) were simply "made backwards," like the proverbial "mirror-image twin." This, of course, would account for the higher proportion of lefties among twins. The trouble with this theory is that the internal organs of these supposedly mirror-image people are not backwards at all—the heart and the appendix, for instance, are in their normal locations. Truly "backwards" people are extremely rare, among twins as well as in the singly born (Corballis and Beale, 1976).

The theory of left-handedness that currently seems most reasonable is the one that answers the question, What is inherited? What is inherited seems to be either a strong tendency towards lateralization—carried by a dominant gene—or the *lack* of a genetic tendency towards lateralization, which is recessive. A child who inherits a strong tendency towards lateralization will inevitably be right-handed and will use the left hemisphere for language (unless brain damage intervenes). A child who inherits little or no tendency towards lateralization may be either right- or left-handed, and may use either the right or left hemisphere for language. The outcome seems to be determined more or less at random, which is why only about half of children with two left-handed parents are lefties, and why only about half of lefties use the left hemisphere for language. Consistent with this theory is the fact that lefties are known to be less one-sided than righties: they're better at using their nondominant hand, and they're better at switching brain hemispheres if one side gets injured (Annett, 1974; Corballis and Beale, 1976).

What are the implications of all this? If left-handed children are not really *born* left-handed, doesn't that mean it's all right to switch them—to force them to write with their right hand? No, it doesn't. For one thing, even if left-handedness is determined by random factors, these factors may have their effects during very early prenatal life, so the child may, indeed, be born a lefty. Second, some psychologists believe that a child who has been forced to switch handedness has a higher risk of becoming a stutterer or having problems with reading.

Finally, parents and teachers have many more important things to hassle a child about. Why add one more requirement to the list of things we already expect from our children? True, being left-handed in a right-handed world is a little inconvenient. But it doesn't seem to have held back Leonardo da Vinci, or Harry Truman, or Babe Ruth, or Charlie Chaplin, or Paul McCartney.

Regardless of whether the child is right-handed or left-handed, there are certain practical advantages in having a dominant hand. That hand now gets twice as much practice in carrying out skilled tasks as it would if both hands were used equally. More precisely, the two hands can each become adept at their own specialties: the nondominant hand will be used to hold objects, the dominant hand to manipulate them. (See Box.)

PERCEPTUAL DEVELOPMENT

Well before the preschool period, the normal child's sensory systems are functioning fully and efficiently. After 1 year of age there are, at most, only minor gains in the acuity of vision and hearing. The typical toddler sees the world clearly, in full color, and stereoscopically—in three dimensions (see p. 152). This doesn't mean that sensory and perceptual development have ceased entirely. It does mean, though, that the changes still to come are not dramatic ones. Among the most important of these changes are improvements in the accuracy of what are called **visual constancies.**

The Visual Constancies

When you move toward an object, its image on the back of your eye grows larger and larger the closer you get, yet you perceive the object as constant in size. You perceive a piece of paper lying on your desk as rectangular, even though—from the angle you're seeing it—it's trapezoidal in shape. You might

PROBLEMS IN DEVELOPMENT

Left-Right Confusions

Another advantage of handedness is that it gives the child a convenient way of telling left from right. By age 4 or 5, many children can tell you which is their right hand and which is their left. The majority can make that judgment by age 6. Frequently, a 5- or 6-year-old will make writing motions with the right hand before answering that question. People who do not have one hand clearly dominant over the other (that is, ambidextrous people) tend to have difficulty even in adulthood with making quick decisions about left and right.

Children learn to discriminate the left and right sides of their own bodies before they can make that judgment about objects and other people. The judgment about other people—the understanding that when someone is facing you their right hand is at your left—is a particularly difficult one, even for school-age children.

Before children can learn to read they must be able to make *visual* left-right distinctions: for example, they must be able to distinguish between *d* and *b*, between *p* and *q*. Preschoolers tend to have a great deal of difficulty in making such distinctions. There's been some confusion over the nature of this difficulty.

In a classic experiment performed back in the 1930s, young children were given a sheet of paper with a sample letter on the left side and some other letters in the box in the middle. They were asked to mark all the letters in the box that were exactly like the sample letter. The children had little difficulty distinguishing letters such as *b* and *p*, which differ only in up-down orientation. Yet many 5-year-olds confused *b* and *d*. When the sample letter was *b*, they marked all the *d*'s as well as the *b*'s.

Do *b* and *d* actually look the same to these children? To answer this question, the experimenter pointed to a *d* that a child had marked, and to the sample *b*, and asked, "Is this the same as that?"

> Some children replied in the affirmative to all. One or two said "yes," then added: "This faces this way and that faces that way." These observations were made on only one or two isolated cases but seemed to indicate that the child noticed the difference in orientation of the letters but did not consider that this fact made them different. (Davidson, 1935, p. 464)

It is not so surprising, when you think about it, that a child might consider two things that differ only in left-right orientation to be equivalent. A baby learns early on that Mommy is Mommy, whether he sees her left profile or her right profile. A chair is the same chair, whether its seat is facing right or left. When we walk around an object its left-right orientation changes, but it is still the same object.

wish to attribute such mundane observations to your knowledge that things really stay the same size and shape, despite the angle or distance you view them from. But knowing that something is true and perceiving it that way are two different things. (The illusion shown in Figure 8–8 is a good example: knowing that the two lines are the same length doesn't make them *look* the same.) In fact, most psychologists who study perception believe that the visual system *automatically* takes into account distance and angle, to produce

Preschoolers *can* learn to distinguish visual stimuli that differ only in left-right orientation, but it's not easy for them. In one study, 4-year-olds were shown two stick figures, one pointing left and one pointing right. Each of these figures was given a different name: one was called "Jack," the other, "Jill." The children's task was to learn to call each figure by its correct name. Most of the children were unable to do this. Then the experimenter gave the children a much easier task: simply push a button on the left if the figure was pointing to the left, a button on the right if the figure was pointing to the right. They learned to do this without any difficulty, proving that they could see the difference between the two figures. Afterwards the experimenter again asked them to try to learn the figures' names. Now their performance on this task was greatly improved. What's interesting is the way that many of the children used the button-pressing response in learning to apply the names:

> In one case, a child who had to be told twice to discontinue the button pressing started lifting the appropriate shoulder for each stimulus before applying labels. Other children would look at the appropriate button before supplying the name of the figure. (Jeffrey, 1958, p. 274)

A later study confirmed these findings and showed that even a *single* type of motor response could help the child to make a left-right discrimination—provided that the response itself was, as the experimenters put it, "asymmetrical." The children in this study had to learn to distinguish two circles: one was red on the left half, green on the right; the other was green on the left, red on the right. One circle was called "good," the other, "bad." Some children were told to touch a spot on the right side of the circle whenever they looked at a circle. (The experimenters indicated the spot to be touched before the circle was shown.) Other children touched a spot in the *center* of the circles. The first group quickly learned to discriminate the two circles; the members of the second group learned only with great difficulty or not at all (Clarke and Whitehurst, 1974).

Apparently, it's easier for most children to make left-right distinctions by means of asymmetrical motor responses than by means of visual memories. This is not invariably the case, however. We know of one little boy who learned to tell left from right by summoning up a visual image of his kindergarten classroom while saying to himself, "The flag is on the right."

If we're to help children cope with confusing stimuli such as *b* and *d*, we must be clear about the source of their confusion. There's no reason to believe that the two stimuli actually *look* identical to them. Preschoolers have trouble with such distinctions because at first they don't realize that the difference is important. Once they've realized that, their difficulty lies in remembering which is which, which orientation goes with which label. Giving them an asymmetrical motor response to tie to the stimuli helps them to keep the stimuli straight, to remind them that this is Jack, not Jill. ∎

a certain perception of size and shape. It's not easy for a person to cancel out these automatic adjustments and see the world as a camera would. Artists must learn to do it as part of their training—it doesn't come naturally.

The perceptual mechanisms we have been talking about are called *constancies* because they result in a constant perception despite changes in the actual stimuli reaching your eyes. We have described **size constancy** and **shape constancy.** (There is also **position constancy,** which keeps an object looking stationary despite movements of your eyes, head, or body; and **brightness constancy,** which keeps a black object in bright sunshine looking black even though it's reflecting far more light to your eyes than a white object in dim illumination.) Ordinarily, we are aware of constancies only when they break down, which they do under certain circumstances. For example, size constancy works best at small and medium distances. At great distances, when one is looking at cars or people from an airplane or a tall building, size constancy breaks down, and the cars and people appear toylike in size. Figure 8–2 shows another way—simpler though less impressive—of achieving a breakdown of size constancy.

In the past, most psychologists assumed that babies start out without constancies and acquire them through experience. The assumption was that babies learn gradually that, for instance, distant objects may look smaller but they're really just as big as closer objects. They were presumed to learn this in late infancy and early childhood, by moving around in their environment, approaching and touching things. But recent evidence does not support this view. Two Australian psychologists (Day and McKenzie, 1973, 1981) have shown that size constancy is present in babies as young as 4 months of age—much too young to have learned anything through exploration of their environment. The same investigators have also found that shape constancy is present in early infancy. Since these mechanisms can be detected at such an early age, they are in all probability innate—nature provides them, not nurture. (It's also possible, though unlikely, that they are somehow learned in the first few weeks of life.)

Although the constancy mechanisms appear to be built in, they are not very accurate at first. A baby may not have to learn that a distant object takes up less of her visual field than a closer object, but what she probably does have to learn is *how much less*. Young children do not have very accurate size constancy. Their constancy improves with age (Rosinski, 1977). Undoubtedly, information obtained from moving around in the environment is a major source—perhaps even the *only* source—of this improvement. That is why the preschool period, a period of lively and active exploration of the

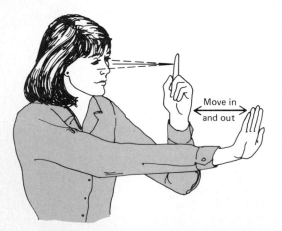

Move in and out

figure 8–2

A breakdown of size constancy. Hold your right hand out in front of you, at arm's length, and move it toward your face and away again, several times. Notice that your hand does not appear to change in size. Then try this: hold up the index finger of your left hand about 8 inches (20 cm) in front of your face, and look at it. Keep your eyes fixed on your finger while you again move your other hand back and forth. This time you probably *will* see your right hand appear to get bigger as it approaches your face, and smaller when it's at arm's length. Focusing on your finger has diverted some of your attention from your moving right hand and produced a partial loss of size constancy. (Coren, Porac, and Ward, 1979, p. 337.)

environment, is an important time for the development of accurate size, shape, and distance perception.

Picture Perception

Another aspect of perception that we take for granted is picture perception. When we see a picture of something—even if it is in black and white (and therefore very different in coloring from the original)—we see it as a replica of the original. We are not fazed by the distortions involved when a three-dimensional scene is reduced to two dimensions. Even an outline-drawing of an object—different in so many ways from the object itself—is generally recognized without difficulty. Is our ability to interpret pictures innate, or have we learned it in infancy or early childhood?

To answer that question, two experimental psychologists (Hochberg and Brooks, 1962) raised their son from infancy without showing him any pictures (photos or drawings) or letting him watch TV. Although he must have seen *some* pictures during infancy, purely by accident, no one ever pointed to a picture and told him what it was. Normally, in our society, parents do quite a lot of picture-naming with their older infants and toddlers.

When the child was 19 months old and had a sizable vocabulary, his parents finally showed him some pictures (see Figure 8–3). The child had no difficulty naming the pictured objects, whether they were photographs or drawings. Although this experiment involved only a single child, the results are clear-cut: recognizing pictures of things does not depend on experience with pictures.

Pictorial Depth. But there is more to seeing pictures than simply knowing what objects they represent. Pictures are two-dimensional, but usually they

figure 8–3
A 19-month-old boy who had never been shown any pictures was able to name all the things in these photos and drawings. (Adapted from Hochberg and Brooks, 1962, p. 626)

depict three-dimensional objects or scenes. Although actual depth is absent, there are many ways that a picture can give the viewer an impression of depth—for example, by shadings and shadows, by the relative sizes and positions of pictured objects, and by the way lines converge toward the horizon. Are young children responsive to pictorial depth cues of this sort?

For preschool children in the United States, the answer is yes. Experiments have shown that 2- and 3-year-olds respond appropriately to depth cues such as shading and the convergence of lines in the distance. But experience does appear to play a role in this kind of perception, as shown by the fact that sensitivity to such cues improves with age. Young babies (under 6 months) don't seem to respond to the kinds of depth cues that pictures contain (Yonas, 1979).

There are other indications that picture perception depends on nurture, as well as nature. If you look at the picture in Figure 8–4 you probably see a man about to spear a gazelle, with an elephant in the distance. But when this picture was shown to people from remote areas in Africa, they tended to see it as a man about to spear a very small elephant. To interpret the picture correctly requires some experience with the way distance is depicted in Western culture (Hudson, 1960).

Illusions.   Look at Figure 8–5. The two children shown here are actually the same size—measure them if you doubt it! This illusion depends on two factors: a perception of depth caused by the convergence of lines, and the effects of size constancy. Size constancy normally makes distant things look as large as near things. Here, since the children are already the same size, it makes the one that appears to be farther away look larger.

A simpler illusion, based on the same principles, is shown in Figure 8–6. This is called the *Ponzo illusion*. The Ponzo illusion depends on the use of converging lines to produce an impression of depth. Since sensitivity to this depth cue increases as a child gets older, it is not surprising that the effectiveness of the Ponzo illusion also increases with age (Coren and Girgus, 1978).

figure 8–4
People from remote areas in Africa, who were unfamiliar with the way distance is depicted in Western art, saw this picture as a man about to spear a very small elephant. (Adapted from Hudson, 1960, p. 186)

figure 8–5
A size-distance illusion. Although the two children are actually the same size, the one that looks farther away appears to be larger. (Rosinski, 1977, p. 64)

figure 8–6
The Ponzo illusion. The two horizontal lines are actually of equal length.

Another illusion that seems to increase with age is called *illusory contours*. Figure 8–7 shows three drawings that produce this effect: most viewers see a triangle in 8–7a, a rectangle in 8–7b, and a circle in 8–7c. These figures are often seen as slightly brighter than the rest of the paper and a little bit in front of it. The contours of the figures appear to be fairly clear and sharp. Yet the figures exist only in the eye of the beholder—they're not actually there on the paper.

Children between the ages of 3 and 6 were recently tested with the stimuli shown in Figure 8–7. For example, a child would be shown one of these stimuli and asked, "Do you see any of these shapes in this picture?" She could respond by pointing to one of three shapes—a triangle, a rectangle, or a circle—cut out of white cardboard, or by naming the shape. Slightly more than half of the 3-year-olds saw the illusory contours. The proportion of children who got the illusion increased with age—by 6 it was nearly 100 percent (Abravanel, 1982).

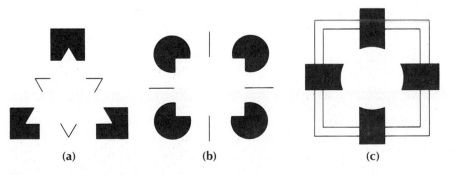

(a)   (b)   (c)

figure 8–7
Illusory contours. (Abravanel, 1982, p. 282)

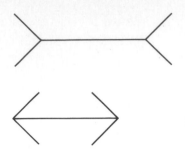

figure 8–8
The Mueller-Lyer illusion. The two horizontal lines are actually of equal length.

Although most illusions become more powerful with age, there are exceptions. The best known illusion of all, the *Mueller-Lyer illusion* (Figure 8–8), is one of these exceptions. For reasons that are still unclear, this illusion decreases as children get older.

How Children Look at Pictures.   We've discussed some of the ways that the picture perception of a preschool child differs from that of an adult. The differences we've mentioned, however, are relatively minor. Visual perception doesn't change that much after the preschool years. Still, we know that a preschool child doesn't always see a picture in the same way that an adult would. One reason for this is obvious: preschoolers simply don't know as much about the world—they lack the extensive store of memories and experiences that adults bring to any situation. But there's another factor involved. Preschoolers see a picture differently from adults partly because they *look* at it differently.

With sensitive cameras that take photographs of a person's eyes, psychologists can tell exactly what part of a picture the person is looking at. When someone is looking at a picture, she **fixates** (or focuses) her eyes on one location, then moves them to another location. These eye movements occur about four times a second. During the movement itself the eyes are essentially "turned off." It's during the brief periods of fixation (between eye movements) that seeing takes place (Sperling, 1963).

Both children and adults look at pictures in the manner we just described. The differences have to do with the kinds of eye movements they make and what parts of the picture they fixate. Adults scan systematically. They use long, leaping eye movements to sweep around the picture as a whole, and short eye movements when they are concentrating on particular details of the picture. Young children, on the other hand, tend to get stuck on certain conspicuous details. Their eye movements are much shorter and their fixations tend to be restricted to small areas of the picture, generally near the middle. The edges are often ignored. Thus, children tend to miss a lot—they don't get all the information that a picture has to offer (Davidoff, 1975).

Children don't need a lot of experience in order to know how to see things. They need much more experience in learning how to *look* at things.

The Drawings of Preschool Children

With a purple felt-tip pen clutched firmly in her fist, 2½-year-old Elaine makes a series of curvy lines on a piece of paper and punctuates them with several emphatic dots. She appears to be quite satisfied with her creation in purple and white. "I wanna 'nother paper," she announces firmly.

In the months to follow, Elaine will continue to cover pieces of paper with various samples of abstract art. She'll experiment with scribbles-in-the-middle versus scribbles-in-the-corner. She'll also discover certain geometric forms: the straight line, the cross, the rectangle, and the circle. The circle seems to be particularly fascinating to her. She covers whole sheets of paper with roundish forms. Understand that we're using the term *circles* loosely here—not one of these forms is perfectly round, and many of them are not even completely closed. The preschool child is plagued by what one psychologist (Goodnow, 1977, p. 89) has termed "budget problems": "The difficulty is one of 'making ends meet.'"

Somewhere around her third birthday, Elaine will begin to combine forms—circles within circles, crosses within circles, squares filled with dots. Sometimes she'll look at something she's drawn and claim, "It's a fish," or "a car," or "a baby." But her identifications are very much after the fact. She didn't plan on making a fish or a car—it just looked that way to her when she was done.

The time will soon come when Elaine will put pen to paper with a definite idea in mind, and produce a recognizable facsimile of whatever she's thinking of. That crucial moment will probably occur between her third birthday and her fourth. Her first real drawing is quite likely to be a person—the so-called **tadpole person** of the preschool period (Gardner, 1980).

The tadpole person of a preschooler's drawings has no body—only a big head with some sticks for legs (see Figure 8–9a). The head usually has eyes; it may also have a nose, mouth, and possibly hair. If there are arms they will emerge horizontally from the head, roughly where the ears would be. If there are ears, there probably won't be arms. The preschooler's motto about such things seems to be "When in doubt, leave it out."

The armless drawings often produced by preschoolers do not represent a lack of understanding of human anatomy or a perceptual problem. In most cases the children who produce these drawings have previously drawn people *with* arms. Some psychologists believe that the arms are left off because the child feels that the drawing looks better without them (Kellogg, 1969). Others have noted that the arms, when they are included, are usually put on last—more or less as "extras." In many cases the child simply doesn't bother to go back and add them (Goodnow, 1977).

The tadpole person usually appears during the year that the child is 3, so some 3-year-olds are still producing "scribbles" while others are drawing families of tadpole people. By 4, most children are beyond the scribble stage and some have begun to produce a more complete person, with a body as well as a head (Figure 8–9b). In one study (Taylor and Bacharach, 1981) 99 preschoolers, ranging in age from 3 to 5, were asked to draw a person. Figure 8–10 shows the proportions at each age who drew tadpole people, complete people, or scribbles.

In the same study, the children were also given three cardboard figures (shown in Figure 8–11) and asked to pick the one that looked "most like a real man." The results were interesting. The children who had drawn tadpole

figure 8–9a

Tadpole people. These bodyless people are typical of the drawings of 3- and 4-year-olds. (Top row: Goodnow, 1977, p. 54, Second row: Taylor and Bacharach, 1981, p. 374)

figure 8–9b

Complete people. Most 5-year-olds draw people with bodies. (Taylor and Bacharach, 1981, p. 374)

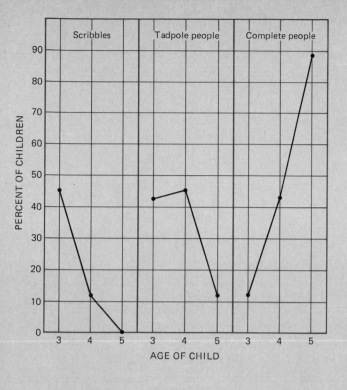

figure 8–10
What preschool children drew when they were asked to draw a person. The three graphs show the percentages of children of different ages who drew scribbles (left), tadpole people (center), and complete people (right).

figure 8–11
The three cardboard figures used in the study described in the text (Taylor and Bacharach, 1981, p. 375). The children who drew tadpole people said that the figure on the right looked "most like a real man."

people tended to say that the tadpole figure (the one on the right) was most like a person. But this doesn't represent any kind of cognitive or perceptual immaturity, because *younger* children—children who were still drawing scribbles—generally picked the complete person, and so did the older children who were already drawing complete people. The experimenters concluded

that there's an interaction between children's concepts about things and the way they draw those things. Not only do the concepts influence the drawings—the drawings also influence the concepts.

Two other characteristics of preschoolers' drawings should be noted here. The first is *economy*. Jacqueline Goodnow, an Australian

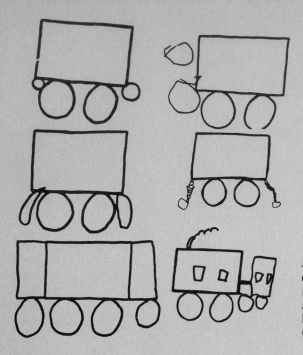

figure 8–12
Children were shown a rectangle with two circles under it and asked to put two more wheels on the "train." Here are some of the ways the children solve the problem of how to add two wheels without overlapping them. (Goodnow, 1977, p. 45)

psychologist who studies children's art, puts it this way:

> Children are thrifty in their use of units. They will use one graphic unit (a particular kind of circle, a particular sun shape, a particular type of human figure) over and over. The same line often doubles as an arm or a leg; the same human figure stands for every member of the family. . . . The repetition of units helps create a sense of charming simplicity or unity. . . . When children do make a change, they are usually conservative. Typically, a change in meaning will be carried, especially among younger children, by varying only one unit (sometimes only by varying the name given to the drawing). (1977, p. 141)

The second characteristic is that children like to put only one thing in a given space—they are very reluctant to overlap things. Thus, in drawings of people, the arms stick straight out, seldom crossing each other or another part of the body. Hair tends to remain well on top of the head, where there's less danger it will intrude on the space given to the arms or ears. If there's a hat it may even float above the head, so it won't

intersect with the border of the head or the hair. Goodnow studied this dislike of overlapping by having preschoolers finish a drawing of a train by giving it two more wheels. The train already had two wheels, and they took up all the space underneath the train. Only one child out of almost 100 overlapped the second pair of wheels on top of the first. Figure 8–12 shows some of the ingenious solutions the other children used to avoid overlapping.

Preschoolers are vivid people who see the world with fresh eyes. Their drawings are often delightful, sometimes even beautiful. In the opinion of one expert on children's art:

> A summit of artistry is achieved at the end of the preschool period. . . . Drawings by youngsters of this age are characteristically colorful, balanced, rhythmic, and expressive, conveying something of the range and the vitality associated with artistic mastery. . . . And the often striking products reinforce a general notion of the child at this age as a young artist—an individual participating in a meaningful way in processes of creation, elaboration, and self-expression. (Gardner, 1980, p. 11) ∎

summary

1. At age 2½, toddlerhood is over and the **preschool period** has begun. The preschooler is noticeably more advanced than the toddler in physical and motor development, in the ability to communicate, and so on.

2. It's possible to predict adult height from the height of the preschooler, but such predictions are not precise. Adult height will depend on many factors, including nutrition, health, hormones, and exercise.

3. The different parts of the body grow at different rates. A 2½-year-old boy is more than 50 percent of his adult height but only about 20 percent of his adult weight. His brain growth is more than 75 percent complete.

4. Growth during the preschool period is considerably slower than growth in the first 2½ years. Preschool boys are slightly taller and heavier than preschool girls; they have less fat (and more muscle) than girls do. In other ways, girls are physically more mature.

5. Because preschool children are not growing rapidly, they may become "picky" eaters. "Junk food" may tempt them, but it does not provide needed nutrients. Despite the popularity of "junk food," preschoolers in the United States are taller today than their agemates of earlier generations.

6. Chronically undernourished children are shorter and thinner than their well-fed agemates; they are also less advanced in their intellectual and motor development. In places where all children are reasonably well-nourished, those children who are ahead in physical development (most likely because of genetic factors) also tend to be ahead in intellectual development.

7. Children's general health improves during the preschool period.

8. Many physical changes make the preschooler better able than the toddler to participate in the society of which he is a member, and hence to learn from the experiences that such participation provides. Physical maturation also enables the preschooler to engage in vigorous, sustained activity.

9. Significant advances in motor control occur during the preschool period. These advances involve both large-muscle and small-muscle activities; they will serve as the foundation for the later acquisition of more advanced motor skills. The preschooler has achieved voluntary control over his body; the goal of getting his body to do what he wishes it to do becomes a motivation for exercising motor skills.

10. A child may acquire a **motor pattern** without having acquired much skill. For example, walking and running are acquired in infancy and toddlerhood, but are not performed skillfully until the preschool period. The acquisition of a **motor skill** may involve only the integration of separate movements into a smooth, continuous pattern, or it may involve acquiring new movements. For example, throwing a ball skillfully involves acquiring new movements.

11. **Manipulation skills** undergo important advances during the preschool period. These skills will be essential when the child enters kindergarten and first grade.

12. Individual differences in motor development are noticeable in the preschool period; they tend to persist throughout life. Genetic factors apparently play an important role in such differences; so does nutrition. Assessing the motor development of individual preschoolers is difficult because of day-to-day variability and because no standardized method for testing such development has been established.

13. The average preschool boy can run faster, jump farther, climb higher, and throw a ball harder than the average preschool girl. Girls are ahead in manipulation skills and in skills that require coordination rather than strength. Such differences are due to a combination of factors, including the tendency of preschool boys to engage in more active, vigorous play than preschool girls.

14. Brain growth has slowed considerably by age 2, but the neurons continue to increase in size. Myelination, which continues through adolescence, also contributes to brain growth.

15. The two hemispheres of the brain look

alike but serve different functions. The left side of the brain, which controls the right hand and foot, is generally used for language, for reasoning, and for numerical skills. The right side specializes in nonverbal skills such as spatial ability, perception of patterns and melodies, and the expression and recognition of emotion.

16. An adolescent or adult who receives an injury to the left side of the brain might lose the ability to use or to understand language. Damage in infancy seldom causes language problems; damage in later childhood may produce temporary difficulties. When damage to the left side occurs early in life, the right side can apparently take over language functions.

17. Some researchers have assumed that **brain lateralization**—the tendency for the two hemispheres to serve different functions—occurs gradually during development. But there is evidence that the two hemispheres serve different functions even in very young babies.

18. Infants show no strong tendency to use one hand rather than the other, but by the preschool period most children favor the right hand. The tendency to right-handedness is apparently a built-in characteristic of the human species.

19. The chances of being left-handed are higher in children whose parents are left-handed; it's also higher in boys and in twins. Some left-handed people have language centers on the left side of the brain, some on the right side, and some on both sides. Lefties are as intelligent as righties; most of them do not appear to be brain-damaged or to have been "made backwards." According to a plausible theory of left-handedness, left-handed people have failed to inherit a tendency toward lateralization. Nevertheless, it's probably unwise to try to force a lefty to become right-handed.

20. There are practical advantages in having a dominant hand: that hand now gets twice as much practice in manipulation skills, and it gives the child a way of telling her left from her right. Most children can make that distinction by age 6.

21. Making visual left-right distinctions (such as *d* versus *b*) is difficult for preschoolers. Their difficulty, however, does not appear to be perceptual: at first they seem not to realize that the distinction is important, and then they have trouble remembering which is which. Giving them an asymmetrical motor response is one way of helping them to remember.

22. Most preschoolers see and hear quite well. One form of perceptual development that goes on during the preschool period involves the **visual constancies**—for instance, **size constancy**, which keeps distant objects from appearing smaller than close ones. This mechanism is automatic, not based on knowledge; it is probably built in. What develops through experience is the *accuracy* of the constancies.

23. The ability to recognize a picture of something does not need to be learned. However, experience does seem to play a role in certain aspects of picture perception, especially in sensitivity to pictured depth cues such as shading, convergence of lines toward the horizon, and relative size.

24. Since sensitivity to pictured depth cues increases as children get older, so does their tendency to be fooled by illusions that are based on such cues. Response to another illusion, called *illusory contours,* also increases during the preschool period. However, the response to some illusions decreases with age.

25. One reason that children don't always see pictures the way adults do is that they don't *look* at them in the same way. Adults scan a picture systematically, whereas young children do not.

26. The first recognizable drawing that children produce on purpose usually occurs at age 3. It is likely to be a **tadpole person**—a head with legs attached. The tadpole person generally has eyes; it may also have a nose, mouth, arms, and possibly hair. Such drawings do not signify

perceptual or cognitive immaturity, since even the younger child apparently knows what people look like. However, evidence suggests that children's concepts are influenced by their drawings.

27. Two other characteristics of preschoolers' art are (1) a tendency to use the same graphic unit over and over, to represent many different things; and (2) a tendency not to let the parts of a drawing overlap.

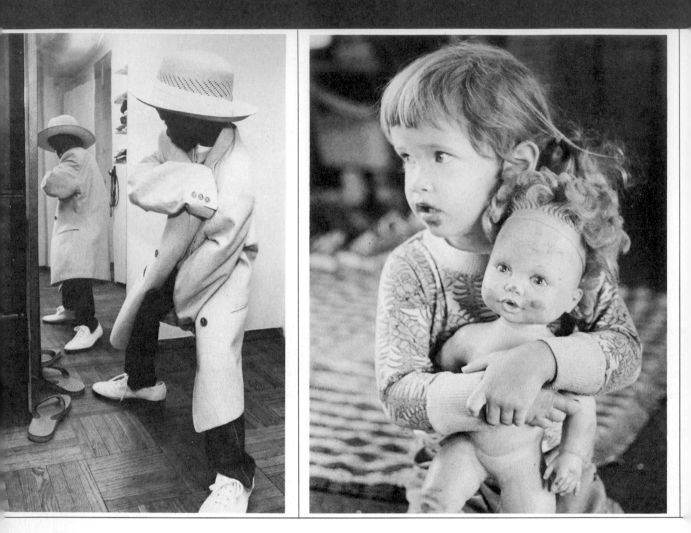

Chapter Nine

PERSONALITY AND SOCIAL DEVELOPMENT IN THE PRESCHOOL PERIOD

Nine

Thirty-month-old Julia finds herself alone in the kitchen while her mother is on the telephone. A bowl of eggs is on the table. An urge is experienced by Julia to make scrambled eggs.

Julia reaches for the eggs, but hesitates as she realizes that her mother wouldn't approve. There's a brief period of indecision that is resolved in this way:

When Julia's mother returns to the kitchen, she finds her daughter cheerfully plopping eggs on the linoleum and scolding herself sharply for each plop, "NoNoNo. Mustn't dood it. NoNoNo. *Mustn't* dood it!" (Fraiberg, 1959, p. 135)

The story of Julia and the eggs illustrates two important points about preschoolers. First, even though you can't always rely on their doing the right thing, they at least have some knowledge of what things they should and shouldn't do. Julia, age 2½, made scrambled eggs *despite* the fact that she knew she shouldn't. We can consider this progress of a sort. At 1½, Julia might have done the same thing, but in complete innocence. At that age she would have been genuinely surprised when her mother failed to share her enthusiasm about the results. Now she knows better. She appears ashamed and embarrassed when her mother returns and catches her egg-handed.

The second point that this story illustrates is the preschooler's growing independence from her mother. When Julia was 1½ her mother might not have left her alone in the kitchen, or if she did Julia might have toddled out after her. Toddlers and their mothers, while at home and awake, spend almost all of their time in the same room with each other. Preschoolers spend less time in close proximity to their mothers. This was shown by a recent longitudinal study of nonworking mothers and their young children (Clarke-Stewart and Hevey, 1981).

The same study revealed other important changes in the period from 12 months to 2½ years. When mothers and children *are* in the same room, they look at each other less often as the child gets older. They speak to each other less often when the child is 2½ than when she is 2—conversation between mother and child reaches a peak at 2 years and then declines. Physical contact between mother and child also tends to decline as the child gets older. In this case, the findings depend on whether the child is securely attached or insecurely attached to her mother (see Chapter 6). Children who were judged insecurely attached at 12 months seem to have problems at age 2½, too. At 2½ years, many of these children are still physically clinging to their mothers. It is the securely attached children who are able to move away on their own.

These observations translate very nicely into the descriptive terms used by psychoanalytic theorist Erik Erikson. As we explained in Chapter 6, the securely attached child is generally one whose mother was sensitive and responsive to her needs during infancy. Her secure attachment reflects what Erikson calls *basic trust*—she believes that the world will not let her down. Now, in the early preschool years, this child has moved on to develop a sense of *autonomy*—a sense of confidence and pride in her ability to do things on her own.

For the rest of the preschool period, the child will be in Erikson's third stage, which corresponds to Freud's phallic (or Oedipal) stage. One of the important milestones of this stage, according to Freud and Erikson, is the development of a superego, a conscience.

"GOOD" AND "BAD" BEHAVIOR

In order to become a useful member of society, it's not enough for a child to learn what kinds of behavior are approved of and what kinds aren't. He or she must also develop the ability to *act* according to these rules, even if no adults are around. Psychologists agree that much of this kind of development takes place during the preschool period. There is less agreement on *how* it takes place.

The Psychoanalytic View

Selma Fraiberg, the child psychologist who described the incident with Julia and the eggs, goes on to present a psychoanalytic view of the development of a preschooler's conscience:

> Even when the child of this age [2½] acquires some control over his urges and his impulses we can't properly use the word conscience. At this age children are capable of guilt feelings over misbehavior, but the guilt feelings do not emerge until the act is discovered. It's when the mother comes into the kitchen and finds scrambled eggs on the linoleum that Julia feels ashamed at her lapse. An older child, one who possesses a conscience, will be troubled with self-reproaches and feelings of shame for his naughtiness, even if he is not discovered. The older child, then, has taken the voice of criticism, the voice of authority into his ego where it functions as the voice of conscience. But our two year olds and our three year olds experience guilt feelings only when they feel or anticipate disapproval from the outside. In doing this they have taken the first steps toward the goal of conscience, but there is a long way ahead before the policeman outside becomes the policeman inside. (Fraiberg, 1959, p. 138)

How does the policeman outside become the policeman inside? In Freud's view, the emergence of the conscience (or superego) is closely connected with the Oedipal conflict. When a little boy gives up his hopes of possessing his mother, out of fear of his father's wrath, he ends up **identifying** with his father. This means that he starts wanting to be like his father and that he takes on many of his father's characteristics—including his father's standards of right and wrong. By doing this, according to the theory, the boy feels safer from his father's wrath and thus from the danger of castration.

For girls the situation is different. They're clearly in no danger of castration, so they have less to fear. Consequently they have less motivation to identify with their mothers than boys have to identify with their fathers. In fact, Freud (along with most of the males of his time) believed that women have weaker consciences than men!

Attempts to verify Freud's view of the superego have not been successful. If anything, young girls seem to have *stronger* consciences than young boys, at least in terms of resistance to temptation. Another prediction derived from Freudian theory is that a boy with a stern, threatening father should develop a stronger conscience than a boy with a mild, loving father. Again, if anything, the reverse is the case (Shaffer, 1979).

The Effects of Punishment

Another view is that children learn to behave according to the rules of their family and their culture simply because "good" behavior has been reinforced and "bad" behavior has been punished. For the preschooler, the issue is mainly one of avoiding "bad" behavior—of resisting temptations such as the temptation to make scrambled eggs on the kitchen floor. Thus the question here is: does punishment really make the preschooler better able to resist temptation?

The answer is that it depends. It depends on the age of the child, the type of punishment, and the quality of the child's relationship with the person doing the punishing. It depends on when the punishment is given, how severe it is, and whether an explanation is given in addition to the punishment. It is undoubtedly influenced by many other things as well—the temperament of the child, the kind of behavior that is being punished, and so on.

In a study done in the 1960s, a group of 4-year-olds were tested in a situation in which there was a strong temptation to cheat. The children were shown a bean-bag game and told that they would win a prize if they could hit the target a certain number of times. Then each child was left alone in the room to play the game. The children didn't know that the experimenters were carefully monitoring the game and could tell if anyone broke the rules—for example, by standing too close to the target or by hitting it with their hand instead of with a beanbag.

The experimenters found that many of the preschoolers were unable to resist the temptation to cheat. They also found that the ability to resist this temptation was related to certain methods of childrearing. The children who resisted temptation were more likely to come from homes where misbehavior was punished by spankings or scoldings. The children who broke the rules were more likely to come from homes where misbehavior was dealt with by psychological methods—reasoning, temporary withdrawal of the parent's love, and so on (Burton, Maccoby, and Allinsmith, 1961).

Other research suggests that reasoning *does* help, especially with somewhat older children. Some kindergarten boys were told "That's bad" when they started to play with a certain toy; other boys were told the same thing but were also given an explanation for why they shouldn't play with it. The boys who had heard the explanation were less likely to touch the toy when they were left alone with it than those given no explanation. The explanation was even more effective with third-grade boys (Cheyne and Walters, 1969). Given what we know about cognitive development, it makes sense that reasoning with a child becomes more successful as the child grows older.

Timing of punishment has been tested in a number of experiments similar to the one we just described: children are punished for playing with a particular toy and then left alone in a room with that toy. The punishment usually consists of the experimenter saying something like "No!" or "That's bad!"; or a loud buzzer might go off. A hidden observer watches to see what the child does.

These experiments have shown that a punishment given as soon as a child reaches for a toy is more effective than a punishment given a few seconds later. In other words, a child who receives immediate punishment is less likely to touch the forbidden toy a second time than a child who receives late punishment. The intensity of the punishment matters too: an extremely loud buzzer is more effective than a moderately loud one. In fact, the extremely loud buzzer is so effective in this situation that it hardly matters whether the punishment is given early or late (Parke, 1970).

Children receive most of their punishments from their parents. The effects of a punishment given by a parent will depend on the parent's personality and on the quality of his or her relationship with the child (which, as we've seen, depends partly on the *child's* personality). Mothers who generally have a warm and affectionate relationship with their children seem to find spanking a fairly effective punishment. Mothers whose relationship with their children is cold and rejecting report that spanking doesn't do much good (Sears, Maccoby, and Levin, 1957).

A sizable majority of American parents admit that they occasionally spank or slap their children. As we will shortly see, the short-term effectiveness or ineffectiveness of this kind of punishment isn't the only issue. Even if it works, physical punishment can have some unfortunate side effects. We will describe them in the section on aggression.

The Social Learning Approach

Freudian theorists believe in an underlying conscience that tells a child what to do (or not to do) in a variety of situations. Social learning theorists do not. According to the social learning view, a child learns bit by bit about individual kinds of behaviors—that it's all right to do this and this and this, but it's *not* all right to do that and that and that. Unlike the strict behaviorist view, however, the social learning view doesn't require the child to be punished

Patterns of Parenting

Developmental psychologist Diana Baumrind, of the University of California at Berkeley, has been studying the effects of various methods of discipline since 1960. She has examined the behavior of children from preschool age through adolescence, at home and in the laboratory. She has investigated parents' childrearing styles by interviewing them and by observing how they interacted with their children in real-life situations.

On the basis of her work with preschoolers, Baumrind (1967, 1975) distinguished three major patterns of childrearing. Not all families fall into one of these three categories, but most do.

The first childrearing style is called **Authoritarian**—old-fashioned strictness. Authoritarian parents follow the "traditional" viewpoint: obedience is viewed as a virtue, and conflicts between child and parent are met with punishment and force. The child is expected to do what the parent says without argument, and that includes helping with household chores. The children of Authoritarian parents are not given much freedom or independence.

Baumrind calls the second childrearing style **Authoritative.** Authoritative parents, like Authoritarian ones, believe in firm enforcement of family rules; but there's a difference: Authoritative parents give their children the reasons behind their decisions and permit verbal give-and-take. They listen to their children's objections and take them into consideration, but the final decision belongs to the parents. On the other hand, their children are not hemmed in by restrictions and they are encouraged—even pushed—to be independent.

The third type of parenting style is called **Permissive.** Permissive parents behave in a kind, accepting way toward their children and demand very little. Their children are given as much freedom as possible (short of endangering their health or safety). These parents see their role as helping or serving their children, rather than the opposite.

What Baumrind discovered about these three major patterns of childrearing was rather surprising. She found few differences between the children of Authoritarian parents and the children of Permissive parents. Both groups of children were less motivated to achieve and less independent than the children of Authoritative parents. Both groups tended to be discontent, distrustful, self-centered, and (in the case of boys) hostile. Authoritative parents, in contrast, produced the most successful children. These children were responsible, assertive, self-reliant, and friendly.

One interesting finding that emerged from these studies is that parental warmth—defined as expressions of tenderness and compassion—had no significant relationship to the measured aspects of the children's behavior. In fact, unconditional love or acceptance (given most commonly by Permissive parents) did not produce its expected results. Children who were given unconditional acceptance—who were shown love no matter what they did—were *not* especially independent, cooperative, friendly, or assertive. According to Baumrind, these traits were more likely to follow from "parental practices that were stimulating and to some extent tension-producing" (1975, p. 16). Baumrind goes on to state,

The exalted value placed upon unconditional love has, in my view, deterred many parents from fulfilling important parental functions. Since unconditional acceptance of a child's misbehavior is a psychological impossibility over the long haul for any parent, the attempt to achieve this illusory goal results in disguised efforts to shape the child's actions through withdrawal of love when the child disappoints the parent. Thus the effects on children of attempts at unconditional love are that the child

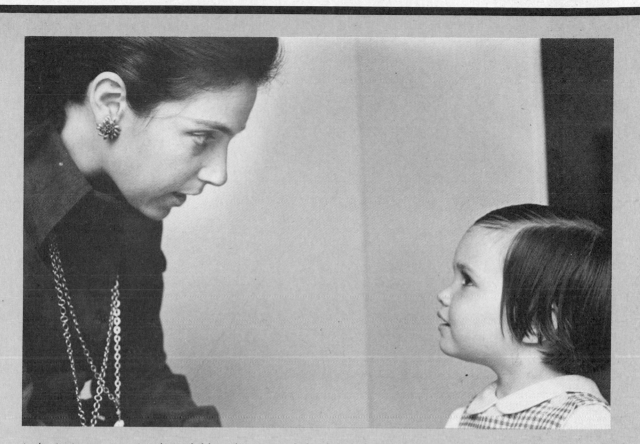

Authoritative parents give their children the reasons behind their decisions and permit verbal give-and-take.

becomes overly dependent upon parental love and unduly concerned about distinguishing between subtle signs of approval and disapproval. (p.20)

Baumrind comes out strongly in favor of firm but reasonable parental control, enforced by punishment when necessary. She believes that parents should listen to the child's point of view, but they shouldn't feel they have to accept it. Reasons should be given for rules and restrictions; when rules or restrictions are not needed they shouldn't be used. Finally, instead of unconditional love, Baumrind proposes something that she considers more important—she calls it *unconditional commitment:*

By this is meant that the parent continues to take care of the child because it is his or her child, and not because of the child's merits. Since the parent is human, the quality of his or her feeling for the child will depend on the child's merits. This abiding parental interest is expressed not by gratifying the child's whims, nor in being gentle and kind when the child is being obnoxious, nor in making few demands upon the child, nor in approval of his actions, nor even in approving of what he is as a person. Unconditional commitment means that the child's interests are perceived as among the parent's most important interests, and that (no matter what the child does) the parent does not desert the child, physically or emotionally. (1975, p. 21)

One objection can be made to Baumrind's theories. She seems to take it for granted that the children's characteristics she observed *resulted* from the childrearing patterns she identified. But there is another possibility, one we've mentioned a number of times. Perhaps the characteristics of the child *determine*—to some extent, at least—the parents' methods of childrearing.

for every unacceptable act, or reinforced for every acceptable one. A lot of learning can be accomplished through observation—through seeing how other people behave and the consequences that their behavior leads to. (We discussed this in Chapter 3.)

It's clear to anyone who has spent time with children that they do many things that they've never been reinforced for. Often, they are simply imitating the behavior of other people—of models. A little boy, for instance, might watch his father shaving or painting the house or yelling at the dog, and later the child might perform some of these same actions himself. But little boys don't imitate just their fathers; nor do little girls imitate only their mothers. Young children of both sexes learn from parents of both sexes. Children also imitate other children, people they see in stores or on the street, people they see on television, and even—on occasion—developmental psychologists. They imitate words as well as actions. They imitate gestures, facial expressions, and subtle intonations of voice. They imitate behaviors we'd like them to acquire, and also behaviors we *don't* want them to acquire.

Acquiring Prosocial Behavior.   Among the kinds of behaviors we want our children to acquire are those called **prosocial,** which include sharing, cooperation, helpfulness, and the like.

Developmental psychologists have carried out a number of studies in an effort to find out when and why children cooperate with one another. In one such study (Madsen, 1971), children were tested in pairs. Their task was to guide a marble into a cup by means of strings attached to a "marble holder." This goal could only be accomplished if the two children cooperated, because if they both pulled at once the marble holder came apart and the marble rolled away (see Figure 9–1). The experimenter found that successful cooperation was quite common among 4- and 5-year-olds. But, strangely enough, older children (age 7 to 10) generally failed to cooperate and hardly ever got the marble into the cup. The reason seems to be that children in our society become more and more competitive as they grow up—so much so that they would rather lose altogether than permit another person to win! Children raised in villages in Mexico, or on kibbutzim (collective farms) in Israel, have been found to be less competitive and more cooperative than American children (Madsen, 1971; Shapira and Madsen, 1974).

Competitiveness, of course, is not necessarily bad: it goes along with a desire to excel that is likely to be of some benefit both to the individual and to the society as a whole. But competitiveness should not override cooperation to such an extent that children cannot cooperate to achieve a mutual goal. How can we encourage children to be more cooperative?

One possible way is to reward them for cooperating. When both members of a pair of preschool children received a reward whenever they succeeded in a task, they soon learned to cooperate in order to succeed. But when only the winning member of each pair received the reward, there was much less cooperation. The children could still have succeeded if they simply took turns collecting the reward, but few of them hit on this strategy (Nelson and Madsen, 1969).

figure 9–1
The apparatus shown here is used for the experiment on cooperation and competition (Madsen, 1971). If the children failed to cooperate, the marble holder would come apart and neither would win.

A better way to foster cooperation in children is to provide them with good models for the desired behavior. A group of children were shown a movie in which a girl and a boy are both eager to use the only available swing on a playground. Instead of fighting over the swing, one of the children suggests that they take turns using it and that the other child should go first. All ends happily. Although this film lasted only 30 seconds, the children who saw it did significantly better, when tested in a cooperation task, than children who hadn't seen it (Liebert, Sprafkin, and Poulos, 1975). The film subsequently became a public service announcement on national television.

Modeling is also a very effective way of teaching other kinds of prosocial behaviors. A number of experiments have shown that children who see an adult give something to charity are more willing to share some of their own possessions.

Children commonly imitate the behavior of the people who take care of them. Mothers who are helpful and sympathetic toward their children (and toward other people in the presence of their children) tend to have helpful and sympathetic children (Zahn-Waxler, Radke-Yarrow, and King, 1979).

It is quite clean that preschool children are influenced by the behavior of models.

Even part-time caregivers make an impression. In one study, a group of children were cared for by an adult who treated them in a helpful and considerate way. The period of care was only 30 minutes a day for two weeks. A second group of children spent the same amount of time with an adult who ignored or criticized them. In a test, the children with the kind caregiver were found to be more helpful and sympathetic to other people than the children with the unkind caregiver (Yarrow, Scott, and Waxler, 1973).

A noteworthy finding of studies like these is that "preaching" isn't as effective as "practicing"—that is, modeling—the desired behavior. If there's a discrepancy between what we do and what we say, children do as we *do*, not as we say.

Delay of Gratification and Self-Control.   Which would you rather have, a single jellybean right now or a whole bag of them tomorrow? A dollar today or ten dollars next year? Most adults would choose to wait and receive the larger reward—they accept what psychologists call **delay of gratification.** This is one of the things we want children to acquire—the ability to withstand the temptation of immediate gratification for greater benefits in the long run. How can we help them to acquire this ability?

A number of experiments on this question, involving children of various ages, have been carried out by social learning theorist Walter Mischel and his colleagues. These experiments have shown that children are very much influenced by the choices they see other people make. A child who hears an older person say, "No, I don't want that piece of candy—I'll wait till tomorrow and get a whole bag of candy," becomes more likely to make that decision himself when faced with a similar choice. It has also been shown that older children are more willing than younger ones to accept a delay (Mischel, 1974; Mischel and Metzner, 1962).

Other factors also affect a child's ability to resist the immediate temptation. In one study (Mischel and Ebbesen, 1970), preschoolers 3 to 5 years old were asked which they liked better, pretzels or cookies. Then they were told that they could have the treat they preferred—cookies, for example—if they could wait alone in a room for 15 minutes. If they *couldn't* wait that long they could call the experimenter back, but then they would receive only the *non*preferred food—pretzels, in our example. The outcome of this test depended heavily on whether the children stayed in a room without any food, or whether one or both of these foods were left where the children could see them. The children who were able to see the foods were able to wait only about 5 minutes, on the average. But the children left without any food waited an average of 11 minutes—in fact, more than 75 percent of them held out for the entire 15 minutes. Apparently, seeing the food made it much harder for the children to withstand the immediate temptation. The experimenters also discovered how some of the children were able to wait *despite* the fact that food was present: many of these children avoided looking at the food by covering their eyes or resting their heads on their arms!

These children hit on this strategy on their own. But it's also possible to *give* children strategies to help them resist temptation. In a later study (Mischel and Patterson, 1976), preschool children were asked to work on a boring task. To do this they had to ignore the distraction of an appealing "Clown Box." The children who were most successful at doing this were the ones who were given concrete advice about how to handle the situation: "When Mr. Clown Box says to look at him, say to yourself, 'I'm just not going to look at Mr. Clown Box!' "

Thus, it's not always necessary for children to see others model the desired behavior—in some situations verbal instructions are quite effective. Teaching children to instruct *themselves* seems to be particularly effective (Toner and Smith, 1977; Miller, Weinstein, and Karniol, 1976). Preschoolers can be helped to wait longer for gratification by the simple procedure of telling them to say to themselves, "It is good if I wait."

Aggression

- Douglas hits Seth, who has just taken his crayon.
- Elena shouts "You dummy!" at her father, who has just stopped her from going outside.
- Mark crumples up the pieces of a cardboard puzzle he was unable to put together.

- Margaret takes hold of her baby brother's foot and squeezes it until he begins to whimper.

These actions are examples of **aggression.** Aggression may be physical or verbal; it may be directed against people, animals, or things. Its aim is to hurt, damage, or destroy. Usually, aggression is accompanied by other outward or inward signs of anger, such as reddening of the face or increases in breathing and pulse rate. It is also possible—as in Margaret's case—for anger to be present in a more subtle form.

A theory proposed in the 1930s by a group of psychologists at Yale (Dollard, Doob, Miller, Mowrer, and Sears, 1939) linked aggression to frustration. This theory, which was popular for a time, stated that all aggression is caused by frustration and that frustration invariably leads to aggression. "Frustration" was defined as anything that interferes with goal-directed behavior. For example, Elena's goal was to go outside; being stopped by her father produced frustration. Her anger was directed at the source of the frustration—her father. If she had previously been punished for insulting her father, the aggression might be **displaced:** she might tear up her father's newspaper, or break one of her own toys, or even kick the cat.

Since it is clear that frustration does frequently lead to aggression, what was wrong with the frustration-aggression theory? Only that it attributed *all* aggression to frustration, and it predicted that *all* frustration would lead to aggression. That is clearly not the case. As we will see, there are other sources of aggressive behavior. And children's responses to frustration differ, depending on the individual child and on the particular situation. In a classic study that tested responses to frustration (Barker, Dembo, and Lewin, 1943), preschool children were given attractive toys and then the toys were taken away and locked behind a wire screen. Some children did react aggressively—they attacked other children, the experimenters, or the wire screen. But others reacted passively, putting their thumbs in their mouths and sitting quietly. Others cried or attempted to leave the room. And some children simply forgot about the toys and turned their attention elsewhere.

Of course, it's possible to claim that the children who did not react aggressively were just storing up their aggression and that it would come out later, perhaps in a different form. But there is no evidence that a person can "let out" or "store up" aggression as though it were water in a tank. If anything, "letting out" aggression—for instance, by encouraging children to use aggressive language—makes it *more* likely that they will hit or push another child (Slaby, 1975).

Learning to be Aggressive. It's clear that children's aggressive behavior is affected not only by the events of the moment but by their past experiences. A number of experimental studies have shown that children's tendency to behave aggressively can be increased by rewarding aggression with gifts or nods of approval. This is true even when the aggression that is rewarded is harmless "make-believe." Some of the children in one study were given marbles when they punched a life-sized doll made of inflated plastic. Later, the experimenters observed them while they played group games. The children who had received the marbles were significantly more aggressive with other children than the ones who had not been rewarded for punching the doll. These experimenters (Walters and Brown, 1963, 1964) also found that rewarding children only when they punched the doll very hard made them still more aggressive with other children.

Experiments like these have some very important implications. Some parents buy their sons punching bags or boxing gloves, in the hope that hitting a punching bag might serve as a harmless outlet for some of their child's aggressive energies. But the evidence suggests that the opposite outcome is more probable—the child will become more aggressive, not less.

A child's aggression tends to be directed most often against other children, rather than adults. The response of these other children has a very powerful effect. If a child launches an attack on another child and the second child fights back, the aggressor is less likely to tackle that particular victim in the future (Patterson, Littman, and Bricker, 1967). On the other hand, if the victim reacts by crying or withdrawing, the aggressor feels that the attack has "succeeded" and is likely to attack that child (or other children) again. For this reason, the neighborhood bully is usually a strong, muscular child whose aggressive attacks on other children are generally successful. Later, such children are more likely to become teenage delinquents than those without a history of successful aggressive acts (Glueck and Glueck, 1950).

Aggressiveness is definitely increased by seeing someone else—particularly an adult—perform an aggressive act. In Chapter 3 we mentioned an experiment (Bandura, Ross, and Ross, 1963) in which children were shown a movie of an adult attacking a large "Bobo" doll (the kind that bounces back when it is knocked down). They were far more likely to punch or kick the doll than children who had not seen that film. Some psychologists pointed out that the fact that the children behaved aggressively to a doll doesn't mean they would do the same to a person. This objection was met by a later experiment (Hanratty, Liebert, Morris, and Fernandez, 1969), involving 4- and 5-year-old boys. Half of the children in this study saw a movie in which an adult was shown hitting and insulting a person dressed as a clown. Later, the children were put in a room with an adult dressed in the same clown costume. Some of the children who had seen the movie behaved quite aggressively toward the clown—one even hit the clown's arm hard enough to leave a bruise. None of the children who hadn't seen the movie behaved in this way.

Watching aggressive and violent TV shows has been shown to have similar effects. In one major, long-term study reported recently (Singer and Singer, 1981), there were highly significant correlations between how much TV children watched at home and how aggressive they were with their nursery school classmates. In particular, watching action and adventure shows tended to increase aggressiveness, whereas watching *Sesame Street* and *Mr. Rogers* did not. It is worth noting that the 3- and 4-year-olds involved in this study spent an average of 23 hours a week watching television. One child watched 72 hours a week!

How to Deal with Aggression. When a child behaves aggressively, parents and teachers generally feel that punishment is called for. But does punishment stop aggression? In the case of physical punishment, the answer is clear: spanking a child is more likely to *increase* aggressiveness than to decrease it. There are two reasons for this. The first is that a parent who is dishing out physical punishment is, at the same time, providing a very clear model of aggressive behavior. A parent administering a spanking is saying, in effect, "The best way to get people to do what you want is by hurting them."

The second reason that physical punishment is not a good way to curb aggression is that it tends to produce the very behavior it is designed to stop. Most people realize that hitting a child for crying doesn't work because crying is the child's natural reaction to being hurt—the child will cry more, not less. Similarly, hitting a child for hitting doesn't work because aggression is a natural response to pain. If two white rats are put into a cage and then given painful electric shocks, they will attack each other. A monkey whose tail is pinched will bite the experimenter or anything else that happens to be handy.

Of course, it is possible to suppress aggressive behavior (or any behavior) if the punishment is severe enough. But such severe punishment may depress behavior in general and produce a fearful, passive child. A more likely result is that the aggression will be temporarily inhibited in the presence of the punishing adult but will increase when the adult isn't around. It's been found that children who are highly aggressive in school and at play tend to come from homes in which physical punishment is used (Eron, Walder, Huesmann, and Lefkowitz, 1974; Patterson, 1976, 1979). Severe, punishing parents also produce a larger proportion of the teenagers who are arrested for aggressive acts (Bandura and Walters, 1959).

How, then, *should* aggression be handled? Although physical punishment creates more problems than it solves, milder forms of punishment may be effective—for example, isolating a child for a short period. Isolation is probably a particularly sensible punishment, in fact, because there are indications that the attention paid to a child who speaks or acts aggressively may serve as a reinforcer for such behavior. However, we can't simply *ignore* aggressive behavior. What we can do, though, is to reinforce other kinds of behavior—behavior that is incompatible with aggression. When the teachers in a nursery school began to reinforce their pupils for sharing and for playing cooperatively, physical and verbal aggression decreased (Brown and Elliot, 1965).

Undoubtedly, the best way to deal with aggression is through prevention, rather than cure. Since aggression frequently results from frustration, one way to prevent it is to avoid putting children into situations where frustration is extreme or prolonged. Better still, we can try to provide them with models who behave responsibly and thoughtfully, rather than ones who behave aggressively or impulsively.

GIRLS AND BOYS: ALIKE OR DIFFERENT?

We have just been talking about aggression. There's one more thing to say on that subject: studies almost invariably show that boys, on the average, are more aggressive than girls (Maccoby and Jacklin, 1974, 1980; Whiting and Edwards, 1973). This is true both of verbal aggression and physical aggression. It is true not only in our own society but in virtually every society that has been studied. (When there is an exception it is due to the fact that, in a few studies, girls and boys were found to be equally aggressive—not that girls were found to be more aggressive than boys.)

Sex Differences

The difference in aggressiveness between boys and girls is an example of a **sex difference.** When a given study turns up a sex difference, it means that on some measurement the girls' scores and the boys' scores differed significantly. As you may recall from Chapter 1, a significant difference is one that *could* have occurred by chance (by coincidence, if you prefer that term), but it's a difference that is highly unlikely to have occurred this way. However, a difference doesn't have to be large in order to be significant—just reasonably consistent. And, in fact, although significant sex differences are frequently found, they are seldom large.

For instance, girls are a little ahead of boys in verbal ability. (The difference is slight in early childhood; it becomes somewhat greater in late childhood and adolescence.) Two developmental psychologists put together the data from many different studies on children's verbal ability—scores from more than 67,000 children in all. The sex difference was significant, all right, but it was small: it accounted for only 1 percent of the variation among the children. As those psychologists put it, "If all we know about a child is the child's sex, we know next to nothing about the child's verbal ability" (Plomin and Foch, 1981, p. 383).

Two other well-substantiated sex differences involve mathematical ability and visual-spatial ability. (*Visual-spatial ability* refers to such skills as the ability to visualize how a figure would look if it were turned upside down. It is used in map-reading, putting together puzzles, and so on.) Males tend to be better in both mathematical and visual-spatial ability, but again the differences are negligible in early childhood. They become greater in adolescence and adulthood (Maccoby and Jacklin, 1974).

On the other hand, the difference in aggressiveness is not negligible. There is a related difference, again sizable, in rough-and-tumble play: as a recent study showed, preschool boys play this way far more often than preschool girls (DiPietro, 1981). Preschool boys are also more likely than preschool girls to take risks—to come close to potentially dangerous animals, to climb onto narrow ledges, and so on (Ginsburg and Miller, 1982).

Bear in mind that even a sizable sex difference doesn't mean that *every* boy is different from *every* girl. In the study of rough-and-tumble play, for instance, the difference was great enough so that 20 percent of the boys had higher scores than *any* of the girls. But what would happen if we take this 20 percent of the boys, put them in a separate room (let's hope it's a room with tough walls and sturdy furniture) and observe the remaining children? We'd see some boys who were moderately high in rough-and-tumble play, and some girls who were equally high; we'd see some boys who were moderately low in rough-and-tumble play, and some girls who were equally low. The 80 percent of the boys who *didn't* score high in rough-and-tumble play are not very different from the girls in that respect (Jacklin, 1981).

The fact remains, though, that there are real differences between boys and girls in general aggressiveness. These differences show up quite early—as early as 2 or 2½ (Maccoby and Jacklin, 1974, 1980). What is the source of this difference?

Why Do Boys Fight More Than Girls?   One possibility—the possibility that comes quickly to most people's minds nowadays—is that little boys are encouraged to be aggressive and little girls are *dis*couraged. As it happens, there's not much evidence to support that theory. There's better evidence *against* it, in fact. When nursery school teachers are observed in their classrooms, it turns out that they are more likely to let *girls* get away with aggressive acts—they're more likely to scold or punish a boy for being aggressive (Serbin, O'Leary, Kent, and Tonick, 1973; Hyde and Schuck, cited in Maccoby and Jacklin, 1980). Mothers, too, seem to be more aware of boys' aggression—and more on the alert to discourage it—than they are with girls. In a study of how mothers act towards opposite-sex twins, this observation was made: "Although Ruby, aged 2, repeatedly pulled her baby brother's hair, mother twice wrongly suspected Ruben [the male twin] of hitting the baby" (Goshen-Gottstein, 1981, p. 1260).

Eleanor Maccoby and Carol Jacklin, of Stanford University, have done a considerable amount of research on sex differences. In their opinion, neither reinforcements and punishments nor imitation of aggressive models can account for the sex difference in aggressiveness. It's true that there are more male than female models for aggression: TV offers many examples. But Maccoby and Jacklin don't believe that male models influence preschool boys more than preschool girls. Older children do tend to imitate models of the same sex, but this tendency is weak or absent in the preschool period. In fact, young boys and girls are *both* more likely to imitate aggression displayed by a male model than by a female model. This, of course, would not lead to the sex difference in aggression seen in preschool children (Maccoby and Jacklin, 1974, 1980).

Then what *is* it due to? Maccoby and Jacklin feel that this sex difference is basically biological in origin. It shows up not only in humans, but in most other mammals as well. It is quite clear in chimpanzees: male chimps, young and old, are more aggressive than female chimps. The young males also engage in more rough-and-tumble play than the young females.

The source of this male aggressiveness appears to be hormonal. The male sex glands—the testes—produce male hormones (androgens), both before birth and afterwards. Male animals that have had their testes removed are known to be more docile after the operation: a steer is easier to handle than a bull, a gelding is gentler than a stallion. The aggressiveness can quickly be restored by the artificial administration of androgens. Hormone treatments can also make *female* animals behave as aggressively as males. Female monkeys that are exposed to male hormones during their prenatal development behave more like male monkeys than like normal females (Young, Goy, and Phoenix, 1964).

The fact that some human societies are much more aggressive than others shows that social learning does play an important role in human aggressiveness. But the sex difference in aggressiveness within a society seems to be at least partly biological. Maccoby and Jacklin conclude that boys are innately more *prepared* (see Box, p. 109) to learn aggressiveness than girls are.

Sex Similarities. Maccoby and Jacklin (1974) reviewed a large number of studies that looked for other kinds of sex differences. Surprisingly, not many of the characteristics that have been measured have shown consistent differences between girls and boys. Girls and boys appear to be similar in more ways than they are different.

There is no good evidence, for example, that girls are more sociable than boys. In childhood they do not appear to be more dependent than boys are, and they're not less willing to remain alone.

Nor do girls seem to be more suggestible than boys. Girls and boys are equally likely to imitate other people, and equally susceptible to persuasion.

Intellectually, few differences are found (only the ones we've already mentioned in verbal, mathematical, and visual-spatial ability). Boys are not more "analytic" than girls, or better at reasoning. Girls are not better at simple rote learning.

Finally, the research that Maccoby and Jacklin reviewed did not indicate a sex difference in self-esteem. Boys and girls from preschool to high school appear to be equally satisfied with themselves.

Gender Identity

Despite the many similarities between the sexes, by the preschool years one can usually tell at a glance—and not just by clothes or hairstyle—whether a child is male or female. Let a group of children into a roomful of toys and many of the girls will head straight for the dolls. Many of the boys will go for the tricycles and toy trucks. The girls tend (even this early) to spend more of their time with other girls than with boys; the boys show a similar preference for members of their own sex. Ask a little boy what he wants to be when he grows up and he might say, "a fireman," or "an airplane pilot." A little girl might reply, "a mommy." Children at this age have already absorbed a great deal of our society's sexual stereotypes. This is true even of children raised in "liberated" homes. One 4-year-old girl insisted that only boys could become doctors—girls have to be nurses (Maccoby and Jacklin, 1974). Yet this child's own mother was a physician!

The social influences that produce **sex typing,** or **sex-role development,** may be subtle, but they're persistent. They begin at birth, from the moment the announcement is made, "It's a girl!" or "It's a boy!" The baby is given a girl's name or a boy's, and is referred to as "her" or "him." Children are generally kept in clothing and hairstyles that clearly indicate their sex, so all the people a child meets know at once whether they're dealing with a girl or a boy. Their attitude toward the child is inevitably influenced by that knowledge. This was shown by an experiment (Condry and Condry, 1976) in which adults watched a movie of a 9-month-old baby who was identified either as Dana, a girl, or David, a boy. Their comments were different, depending on whether they thought the baby was male or female. For example, they tended to interpret a certain facial expression as fear if they thought they were seeing a girl, but as anger if they thought they were seeing a boy.

There are biological differences between girls and boys, based on the male and female hormones that affected their prenatal development. A male brain isn't identical to a female brain. But these biological differences are slight, compared to the steady barrage of environmental pressures that tell a child, "You're a girl—act like a girl," or "You're a boy—act like a boy." Nothing illustrates this point more forcefully than the story of identical twins—genetically equal—of whom one was reared as a boy, the other as a girl (see Box).

Gender identity is firmly
established in most children
by age 3.

Sex-Role Development

Sex-role development doesn't end at age 3, when most children can tell you
with assurance, "I'm a girl," or "I'm a boy." Although most young preschoolers can tell girls from boys and men from women, they are often unclear on
the nature of the difference. They might believe that the distinction is based
on clothing or hairstyle, and that a girl can become a boy simply by having
a haircut. They may also be unaware that little girls become women and little
boys turn into men—that boys can't become mommies, even if they want to.
The understanding that sex is based on differences in genitals and is (almost
invariably) permanent is called **sex constancy.**

The development of sex constancy, around the end of the preschool period, is an important milestone. It marks the end of the period when children
pay equal (or nearly equal) attention to models of both sexes. The understanding of the permanence of sex goes along with a greatly increased tendency to imitate models of one's own sex (Kohlberg, 1966; Slaby and Frey,
1975). One consequence of this is a closer identification with the parent of
the same sex—an identification that Freud attributed to the resolution of the
Oedipal conflict.

The Case of the Opposite-Sex Identical Twins

The parents were a young couple of rural background, with only a grade-school education. Their children were identical twins, grown from a single fertilized egg. They were both born normal boys. But at the age of 7 months, one twin suffered a tragic accident in which his entire penis was destroyed.

Doctors explained to the parents that there was no satisfactory way of replacing a penis. They recommended raising the child as a girl, and said that reconstructive surgery could produce the outward appearance of female genitals (though, of course, there would be no ovaries or uterus). With hormone treatments, the child would develop breasts and all the other feminine characteristics that appear during puberty.

For several months the parents agonized over the decision. Finally, when the child was 17 months old, they decided to follow the doctors' advice. The child was given a girl's name. Surgery was performed a short time later. The little boy became a little girl.

The child was treated at the Johns Hopkins Hospital. Two psychologists there, John Money and Anke Ehrhardt, counseled the parents on how to handle a situation for which their own experiences had given them little preparation. Money and Ehrhardt continued to see them from time to time, up until the children were 7 years old. Their published report quotes the comments the mother made to them on the progress of her new daughter.

For a first step, the mother said, "I started dressing her not in dresses but, you know, in little pink slacks and frilly blouses . . . and letting her hair grow." By the preschool period, her daughter preferred dresses to slacks, and took pride in her long hair. "She just loves to have her hair set; she could sit under the drier all day long to have her hair set" (Money and Ehrhardt, 1972, pp. 119–120).

At 4½, the mother reported, the girl liked to be neat and clean, whereas her brother preferred being dirty. "She seems to be daintier. Maybe it's because I encourage it . . . I've never seen a little girl so neat and tidy as she can be when she wants to be" (p. 119).

Clearly, though, the parent of the same sex isn't the only model children follow. As Maccoby and Jacklin (1974) pointed out, much of children's **sex-typed behavior** (behavior that is more typical of their own sex than of the opposite sex) is *not* based on parents' behavior. Young boys play with cars and trucks, though they may see their mothers driving the family car more often than their fathers. They tend to play in all-male groups, though their fathers do not shun the company of women. Similarly, young girls are unlikely to have seen their mothers playing jacks or hopscotch.

Identification with the parent of the same sex is a relatively minor factor in sex-typed behavior. Children do not always turn out to be just like the same-sex parent—in fact, their personality characteristics are just as likely to resemble those of the opposite-sex parent (Shaffer, 1979). Children who are reared

It was also during the preschool period that the parents' "double standard," for what behavior is acceptable in a boy and not in a girl, became evident. "In the summer time, one time I caught him—he went out and he took a leak in my flower garden in the front yard, you know. He was quite happy with himself. And I just didn't say anything. I just couldn't. I started laughing and I told daddy about it." She was asked whether the girl ever did anything like that. She replied, "I've never had a problem with her. She did once when she was little, she took off her panties and threw them over the fence. And she didn't have no panties on. But I just, I gave her a little swat on the rear, and I told her that nice little girls didn't do that, and she should keep her pants on. . . . And she didn't take them off after that" (p. 120).

"One thing that amazes me," said this woman about her daughter, "is that she is so feminine." Nevertheless, there seemed to be certain aspects of her personality that Money and Ehrhardt describe as "tomboyish":

> The girl had many tomboyish traits, such as abundant physical energy, a high level of activity, stubbornness, and being often the dominant one in a girls' group. Her mother had tried to modify her tomboyishness: ". . . of course, I've tried to teach her not to be rough . . . she doesn't seem to be as rough as him . . . of course, I discouraged that. I teach her more to be polite and quiet." (p. 122)

Many little girls who were *born* little girls are tomboyish, too. Nonetheless, they think of themselves as girls—their **gender identity** (or **sex identity** is firmly female. Money and Ehrhardt believe that the identical twin reared as a girl was able to develop a secure gender identity as a female because her parents treated her consistently as a girl, and because the change of sex was made before 18 months. It's not a good idea to try to change a child's sex much later than 18 months, because his or her gender identity has begun to develop. In most children it is firmly established by age 3.

On rare occasion, usually for unknown reasons, a child will fail to establish a gender identity in accord with social pressures and biological sex. The writer Jan Morris, born James Morris, was such a case. Morris describes vividly what it's like to feel that one has been assigned the wrong gender:

> I was three or perhaps four years old when I realized that I had been born into the wrong body, and should really be a girl. I remember the moment well, and it is the earliest memory of my life. (Morris, 1974, p. 3)

Many years later, after marrying and fathering five children, James Morris underwent hormone treatments and surgery and became Jan Morris. ∎

by a single parent of the opposite sex may have some problems in sex-role development, but almost all are able to acquire the appropriate gender identity and behavior.

There are so many different ways that a society imposes its sex-role standards that it is virtually impossible for a child to avoid them. Models are everywhere—they consist not only of parents but of other adults and other children. They are seen in real life, on TV, and in books. Even a slight tendency for 3- or 4-year-olds to imitate same-sex models would make a difference in the long run. So would any tendency, even a slight one, for parents and other adults to encourage certain kinds of behaviors in one sex and not the other. And many parents show a *strong* tendency to encourage sex-typed behavior, as we saw in the case of the opposite-sex identical twins. Fathers are more likely than mothers to feel strongly about this sort of thing, particularly with their sons. Lower-class parents tend to be more concerned about it than upper-middle-class parents (Shaffer, 1979).

Androgenous People.   Many societies—in Arab countries and in Africa, for example—prescribe much more rigid roles for males and females than our own society does. Furthermore, in our own society there is now a very clear trend against distinctions based on sex. Increasingly, men and women have similar careers, similar household chores, and play similar roles in childrearing. Increasingly, little boys and little girls are treated the same. Girls are encouraged to strive for achievement and independence. Boys are less likely to be shamed for expressing love and tenderness, or fear, or pain.

The evidence suggests that this trend is a healthy one. It has been found that men who are not exclusively masculine and women who are not exclusively feminine have some psychological advantages over those who follow the sexual stereotypes more closely. People who have some characteristics of both sexes—**androgenous** people—tend to be more flexible, more competent, and to have greater self-esteem (Bem, 1974; Spence and Helmreich, 1978). We will return to the topic of androgeny in the last chapter of the book.

Children today are growing up in a society where male role models and female role models are not nearly as different as they once were. Girls and boys are under much less pressure to acquire sex-typed behavior, and the pressure will probably continue to lessen. The children reared under these conditions will probably make even fewer distinctions based on sex when they rear their own children.

Nevertheless, we do not expect sex differences ever to vanish entirely. The sex differences we see in children today are probably not entirely a function of their environment; they are a product of the *interaction* between their own built-in characteristics and the environment. As we have pointed out many times, parents act differently to different children partly in response to the differences in the children themselves. Some of these differences may well be correlated with sex.

In a study of childrearing in modern Israel, it was found that most of the parents provided dolls for both sons and daughters of toddler and preschool age. These parents were perfectly happy to have their sons play with dolls. Some of the boys *did,* in fact, play with dolls, but usually not in the same way the girls did:

> [The boys] used dolls differently than the girls, treading on them or beating them like hammers against pieces of furniture. (Goshen-Gottstein, 1981, p. 1261)

PLAY AND IMAGINATION

The scene is a day-care center for preschool children aged 2½ to 5. Aileen and Darrell sit at the clay table side by side. Aileen is using her index finger to poke holes in a roundish lump of clay; Darrell is rolling out "snakes." Heather sits by herself at another table, stringing brightly colored wooden beads on a long shoelace. In the "kitchen" corner, Michelle and Verna are pretending to make dinner for Jeannie and Manuel. Jeannie, the "baby," is indicating her impatience by waving her arms and whining. David is watching them with interest, but making no attempt to join in their game. Eric and Casey, meanwhile, are galloping loudly through the large room, pretending to ride horses—or perhaps to *be* horses.

With minor variations, scenes like this one can be found all over the world and all through history. We call such activities *play,* and we distinguish them from what we consider the important business of life, which we call *work.* But anyone who has observed the energy and intensity that young children devote to their play probably realizes that it, too, is important business to a child.

Types of Play

One way of classifying children's play is according to how much interaction with other children is involved. Five categories of play can be distinguished in this way (Parten, 1932). Examples of these types of play can be found in the day-care center we just described.

Categories of Interactive Play.   The first type is called **solitary play.** Heather provides the example. A frequent activity of infants and very young toddlers, solitary play involves no interaction at all with other children.

Onlooker behavior (shown by David) is the second. The onlooker simply watches other children play, perhaps asking a question or making a comment occasionally. This is often the first stage of a young preschooler's interaction with other children. In a week or so, David will be participating in the game instead of just looking on.

Aileen and Darrell exemplify **parallel play.** Children often play side by side at the same activity, but without taking much notice of each other. Again, this is common in the early part of the preschool period.

Associative play is shown by Eric and Casey. In the slightly older preschooler, play becomes interactive to a certain extent. Two or more children will take part in the same activity, all doing basically the same thing. There is still no attempt to organize the activity or to take turns.

Michelle, Verna, Jeannie, and Manuel are engaged in **cooperative play.** This type of play doesn't usually appear until age 3. It involves organized activity in which the individual children cooperate to achieve some sort of group goal—for instance, by taking different roles in a game of make-believe.

As children mature they become more able and more eager to participate in the social forms of play, but solitary play does not ever disappear. Most children are capable of playing alone if a companion is not available. Onlooker behavior, too, persists—even into adulthood, as shown by the amount of time people spend watching sports events or dramatic presentations.

Preschoolers enjoy "dressing up" for sociodramatic play.

The Piagetian View. Piaget (1962) was very interested in children's play because of its connection with cognitive development. In Piagetian theory, the earliest kind of play is called **sensorimotor play.** This involves moving the body and, usually, manipulating things: a baby bats at a toy hung above her crib; Heather strings wooden beads on a shoelace.

At around 12 months a new form of play appears: **pretend play.** In its earliest form it is very simple—a toddler may pretend to go to sleep, or to drink out of an empty cup. But once the child has entered the last stage of the sensorimotor period, at about 18 months, a new type of pretend play is possible. Children at this point have become capable of representational thought (see pages 218–219), and that means they can use things in symbolic ways. Now a child may pretend to drink from a seashell or from a round block; a stick may be used to represent a sword or even a baby.

Representational thought also permits deferred imitation. A child can pretend to cook a meal or to drive a car, using memories of what was seen and heard in the past. Deferred imitation is particularly important in **sociodramatic play,** a kind of pretend play that usually appears around age 3. Sociodramatic play involves *group* imagination and symbolism—"playing house" is a good example.

Pretend play—especially sociodramatic play—reaches a peak around age 5 and then declines. What takes its place is play that involves games with rules (Fein, 1981).

The Functions of Play

An adult considers play to be, almost by definition, unproductive. But for a child the time spent in play is extremely productive. When a kitten plays by pouncing on a leaf and shaking it, it's plain that she is rehearsing movements that later will be used on real prey. In humans, too, play enables young organisms to practice many of the skills they will need as they grow older. These include social and cognitive skills, as well as motor ones.

In play, children are able to experiment with the environment in ways that generally do not have serious consequences. It is trial and error with no penalty for error. That kind of experimentation can tell the child something about the nature of things—Darrell's rolling of clay balls into "snakes" can be seen in this light. Or it may tell the child something about the nature of social interactions, about what is permitted and what is not. The rules for social behavior are more lenient in a play situation. Preschool boys sometimes play quite roughly with each other, but it's accepted as fun rather than as aggression if the participants are smiling or laughing. (In the same way, older children and adults say "I'm only kidding," and get away with insults that would otherwise not be tolerated.)

Fantasy

Play also permits children to act out in fantasy what they cannot achieve in reality. A child may pretend to be an astronaut, a doctor, a king, or a queen. Many psychologists and educators believe that this kind of fantasy has a wish-fulfillment function. Although in reality young children are weak and powerless, in fantasy they can be Wonder Woman or Superman.

The Psychoanalytic Interpretation.   In the classical Freudian view, fantasy serves as an outlet for repressed feelings, for wishes that are contrary to society's rules. The idea is that fantasy provides a **catharsis** of these drives: by acting out the wish in fantasy form, the child is partially relieved of the desire to act it out in reality. For example, a little boy playing with dolls might cause the boy doll to crush and "kill" the father doll. According to the theory, the fantasy action drains the boy of some of his desire to act aggressively toward his real-life father. Play therapy, based on this theory and applied by Anna Freud and others, is still much used by psychotherapists who work with disturbed children.

On the other hand, experimental tests have failed to provide any support for the notion of catharsis. Earlier we noted that encouraging a child to hit a doll or to speak aggressively produces an *increase* in general aggressiveness, not a decrease. Aggressive fantasies seem to be no different from aggressive words or actions in that respect. For example, one experimenter (Feshbach, 1956) found that after playing imaginative games involving soldiers or pirates, children were more aggressive than before. In another study (Biblow, 1973), children were divided into two groups: those who did a lot of fantasizing and those who did little. It was found that the high-fantasy children did react to frustration with less aggression than the low-fantasy children. However, the reduction of aggressiveness didn't depend at all on what these children's fantasies were about. It seemed that the children who were good at fantasizing used that ability to put themselves in a better mood—to make themselves happier or less angry—and that was why they were less aggressive. The investigator concluded that his results went against the catharsis theory of fantasy.

Fears. Children's fantasy games often concern matters that worry them: burglers or kidnappers, fire, sickness and death. Playing out their fears in fantasy form seems to give children a way of dealing with them, of making them less scary. A child who is soon to be hospitalized—say, for minor surgery—will often play imaginative games involving doctors, operations, even death. These fantasies may also continue for a while *after* the hospital experience, until the child feels comfortable with the thoughts and memories of the hospitalization.

At other times, fantasy seems to have the opposite effect—contributing to fears, instead of taming them. The fears of the infant and toddler usually concern actual stimuli: loud noises, the dark, being dropped, strangers. But by the age of 3, many of a child's fears are of imagined dangers. A 5-year-old is afraid, not so much of the dark itself, but of the imaginary monsters with which he populates it.

All children seem to have frightening fantasies of this sort—even those whose parents have tried hard to keep them away from scary movies, TV shows, and comic books. Such fears have often been interpreted as having symbolic meaning. For instance, the witch, in fantasies and fairy tales, is thought to represent the angry, punishing aspect of the child's mother (Bettelheim, 1976). Imaginary lions and tigers are attributed to a child's worries about being dependent and powerless, or to his fears about his ability to handle his own aggressive feelings.

The parent or caregiver is less concerned about what these fantasy fears represent than about how to handle them. The truth is that no one method for dealing with such fears has proven generally successful. Eventually—no matter how they're handled—most children simply outgrow them. Of course it *is* possible to make things worse, but nowadays few adults would be so unfeeling as to make fun of a child's fears, or to force a child who is afraid of the dark to sleep without a night-light.

It is a little discouraging to think that one can't do much to help a young child deal with the monsters that inhabit his or her imagination. It might help, however, to realize that such fears may actually be of *benefit* to the child in the long run. In laboratory experiments with white rats (Levine, 1960), some baby rats were taken out of their cages and subjected to stressful experiences—experiences that were somewhat frightening or painful. These rats developed normally and as adults were able to cope well with stress. But the *other* rats—the ones that had remained peacefully in their cages—grew up to be much more fearful and excitable. They even turned out to be a little smaller than the stressed rats.

Something similar may occur with human children. Just the minor physical and emotional stress involved in being innoculated against smallpox or other diseases produces a small but significant difference in growth. Innoculated children grow slightly taller than ones who haven't been innoculated, and the difference can't be attributed to differences in general health or to genetic differences (Whiting, Landauer, and Jones, 1968).

It is well known that stress or fear produces all sorts of temporary changes in the body—hormonal changes, changes in the nervous system. Perhaps the body needs those occasional jolts in order to function at its highest level of efficiency (Levine, 1971).

Imaginary Playmates. A nicer kind of fantasy is the one that involves an imaginary companion. No scientific description of this invisible friend could possibly match A. A. Milne's (1927) ode to "Binker":

Binker—what I call him—is a secret of my own,
And Binker is the reason why I never feel alone.
Playing in the nursery, sitting on the stair,
Whatever I am busy at, Binker will be there . . . .

Binker's always talking 'cos I'm teaching him to speak:
He sometimes likes to do it in a funny sort of squeak,
And he sometimes likes to do it in a hoodling sort of roar. . .
And I have to do it for him 'cos his throat is rather sore. . . . .

Binker's brave as lions when we're running in the park;
Binker's brave as tigers when we're lying in the dark;
Binker's brave as elephants. He never, never cries . . .
Except (like other people) when the soap gets in his eyes. . . .

Binker isn't greedy, but he does like things to eat,
So I have to say to people when they're giving me a sweet,
"Oh, Binker wants a chocolate, so could you give me two?"
And then I eat it for him, 'cos his teeth are rather new. . . .

Well, I'm very fond of Daddy, but he hasn't time to play,
and I'm very fond of Mummy, but she sometimes goes away,
and I'm often cross with Nanny when she wants to brush my hair . . .
But Binker's always Binker, and is certain to be there.

It is quite normal for a preschool child to invent an imaginary playmate; these persistent and sometimes annoying characters are quite common, especially among firstborn and only children. It has been estimated that from

15 to 30 percent of children engage in this kind of fantasy for at least some portion of their preschool years. The fantasy fades as the child grows older, and the friend makes fewer and fewer appearances. Many people of college age can still remember having an invisible playmate. Such people tend, on the average, to be higher in creativity than their classmates (Schaeffer, 1969).

Although imaginary playmates are particularly common among children who do not have siblings, this doesn't mean that these children are shy or maladjusted. On the contrary: a child who has an imaginary companion is likely to be better than average in adjusting to nursery school and in cooperating with other children and adults (Singer and Singer, 1981). The playmate may be imaginary, but the benefits to the child are real.

Lying. If a child breaks something and blames it on her little brother, we consider that a lie; but what if she blames it on her imaginary playmate—is that fantasy or fib? For a young preschooler, the distinction is often a hazy one: although a story may be an obvious attempt to avoid punishment, the child may actually believe it. Many of the "tall tales" that children tell at this age fall into the same category. A story about owning a pile of diamonds, or seeing an elephant in the backyard, may be partly motivated by a desire for attention or importance. At the same time, the preschooler may be at least partly convinced that these stories are true. Punishing such behavior could have the undesirable effect of making the child feel guilty about being imaginative.

On the other hand, adults should not encourage tale-telling by pretending that they believe the child's stories when they are obviously untrue. A child must learn to distinguish between fantasy and reality. Most are able to do so by the time they are ready for first grade: studies show that tale-telling reaches a peak between the ages of 4 and 5, and then declines rapidly (Macfarlane, Allen, and Honzick, 1954).

Friendship

The fact that a child without playmates will sometimes invent an imaginary one shows how important the companionship of other children is to the preschool child. A sociologist who spent several months observing 3- and 4-year-olds at a nursery school (Corsaro, 1981) reported that these children seldom played by themselves for very long. They spent most of their time interacting with other children. However, these interactions tended to be brief—most of them lasted less than 10 minutes. Often, they ended abruptly. Two children would be playing together and one might simply walk off, without even saying goodbye. Usually, a child who was left alone would sooner or later wander over to a place where two or three other chidren were playing, and try to gain entry into the group. Only about half of these attempts were successful. Equally often, the children who were already playing together resisted the entry of a newcomer.

As these observations suggest, friendships in the preschool years are highly unstable. Whomever a child is playing with at the moment is "my friend,"

whoever is being excluded is "not my friend." In the nursery school we just described, two 3-year-olds named Denny and Leah were playing together, pretending to be lions. Glen, age 3½, who had played with Denny earlier in the day, approached them.

Denny to Glen:	Grr-Grr. We don't like you.
Leah to Glen:	Grr-Grr.
Glen to Denny:	You were my friend a minute ago.
Denny to Glen:	Yeah.
Glen to Denny:	Well, if you keep going "grr" you can't be my friend anymore.
Denny to Glen:	Well, then I'm not your friend.
Leah to Glen:	Yeah. Grr-Grr. (Corsaro, 1981, p. 219)

PROBLEMS IN DEVELOPMENT

Autism

Most preschoolers are rather sociable people— if not with strange adults, at least with other children and with members of their own families. But there is one kind of child whose most striking characteristic is an almost complete withdrawal from human interaction. The technical name for this disorder is **infantile autism.** Here's a mother's description of her autistic daughter:

> She is at the beach, two years old now. . . . A bronzed, gold baby of unusual beauty, she walks along the sand. Many people are looking at her because she is so pretty, but she is looking at no one. On she walks, into family groups, by picnic baskets, sand castles, and buckets. She grazes human beings by a quarter of an inch. You would think she did not see them. But she does see them, because no matter how close she comes, her eyes fixed, it seems, on some point beyond them or to one side, she never touches them. On she goes. . . . When I can hardly see her, I begin to run. She might have walked straight ahead, delicately swerving to avoid an occasional collision, without a backward look, forever, so little did she need of human contact. (Park, 1967, p. 5)

As the term *infantile* autism suggests, this disorder appears very early in development, usually in infancy or toddlerhood. However, it is seldom diagnosed before the preschool years. In most cases, the parents can then recall that there were signs of trouble much earlier. Babies who will later be diagnosed as autistic often fail to make eye contact with their parents in infancy (or, for that matter, later on). They tend not to lift up their arms in anticipation of being picked up, as normal babies do. Most telling of all, they fail to develop attachments. As toddlers they don't run to their parents when they're hurt or frightened. If an autistic child does develop an attachment, it's likely to be to an object, rather than to a person. One autistic child spent hours every day looking at a water heater. He even loved to look at *pictures* of water heaters (Rimland, 1964).

Another symptom of autism is an intense desire for sameness in the environment. Typically, autistic children become upset if there's any change in the furnishings of their house. Some insist that the objects in a room remain in certain exact positions, and will fly into a rage if

Despite the instability of preschool friendships, some children are consistently more popular than others. Studies (Charlesworth and Hartup, 1967; Masters and Furman, 1981) have shown that popular children give other children more "social reinforcements." (Social reinforcements are actions like praising or smiling at another child, showing affection, giving or accepting a gift, complying with a request, or simply paying attention to the other child.) The children who gave many social reinforcements also *received* many of them. And, as you would expect, the children who dispensed a lot of social punishment (teasing, blaming, hitting, insulting, grabbing toys away, or ignoring another child) were unpopular with their peers.

These studies also showed a strong tendency for preschool children to give

even a single item is slightly shifted (Kanner, 1951).

Almost all autistic children have speech and language problems. About half do develop some speech, but they tend to use it in unusual ways. An autistic child may simply echo samples of speech that he's heard—TV commercials, for instance. A question such as "Do you want some milk?" may be answered with "Do you want some milk?" (meaning "yes"). Normal children generally learn to refer to themselves as *I* or *me* by the age of 2½. An autistic child may go on calling himself *you* for many years (Rimland, 1964; Rutter, 1978).

The long-term outlook for these children is pretty grim. Of one group of 96 autistic children who were followed through to adulthood, only 11 were able to become fully self-sufficient (Kanner, 1973). Various treatments have been used, ranging from psychotherapy to behavior modification. Some successes have been reported, but they tend to be modest and short-term, or to involve the less serious cases.

Fortunately, autism is an extremely rare disorder. According to a recent estimate (Hanson and Gottesman, 1976), only one child in 10,000 is autistic. Boys are affected three or four times as often as girls.

What causes autism? It has been blamed on parental unresponsiveness, but there's no evidence that the parents' behavior is at fault. Studies of the parents of autistic children have failed to find anything unusual about them—they are not less friendly or more neurotic than other parents (Rutter and Bartak, 1971). Furthermore, it's very rare for a family to have more than one autistic child. Siblings of the affected child are likely to be normal. And finally, the early onset of infantile autism makes an environmental explanation improbable.

At present, the best guess about the cause of autism is that it's due to some physical abnormality of the brain. A sizable proportion of autistic children are also mentally retarded. They remain mentally retarded even if they recover from autism. More than a quarter of autistic children eventually develop epileptic seizures (Rutter and Bartak, 1971). Perhaps autism is due to some unusual kind of brain damage, suffered during prenatal development or birth (Hanson and Gottesman, 1976). A genetic factor may also be involved, so that certain babies are more vulnerable than others to this kind of damage (Folstein and Rutter, 1978).

What makes autism interesting is that it makes us appreciate how many aspects of normal development we take for granted. One child walks silently through the crowded beach, never seeing another person except as an obstacle in her path. The hundreds of other children on the beach are digging holes in the sand and running back and forth. They're looking at each other, talking to each other, and playing with each other. ∎

and receive reinforcements from members of their own sex, rather than the opposite sex. When asked which of their nursery schoolmates they liked, girls named girls and boys named boys almost 80 percent of the time (Masters and Furman, 1981). That's not too surprising, but it *is* a little surprising to find the same tendency appearing in the home, between siblings. Two young siblings—one a preschooler, one a toddler—give each other more social reinforcements if they're the same sex. They show more hostility to each other if they're opposite sexes (Dunn and Kendrick, 1981).

Toward the end of the preschool period, children begin to form lasting friendships. They tend to choose as their friends children they perceive to be similar to themselves—children of the same sex, the same race, and roughly the same age. There is even a tendency for young children to pick friends who are similar to themselves in physical attractiveness: pretty children tend to like other pretty children, homely ones choose homely friends (Langlois and Downs, 1979).

summary

1. As compared with toddlers, preschoolers spend less time in close proximity to their mothers. When a preschooler is in the same room as her mother, there's less interaction between them than there was in infancy and toddlerhood.

2. At age 2½, children have some knowledge of what kinds of behavior are approved of and what kinds aren't. The tendency to *act* according to these standards develops with time; much of this development occurs during the preschool period.

3. According to the psychoanalytic view, the superego—or conscience—develops when the Oedipal conflict is resolved and children **identify** with the same-sex parent. Two predictions follow from that view: (1) that boys should have stronger superegos than girls; and (2) that boys with stern, threatening fathers should have stronger superegos than boys with mild, loving ones. Neither prediction has been upheld.

4. Behaviorists believe that children learn to act according to society's rules as a result of the reinforcements and punishments they've received for particular actions.

5. Whether punishment is an effective means of eliminating undesirable behavior depends on many factors. Preschoolers who are scolded or spanked seem better able to resist temptations than those whose parents use reasoning or withdrawal of love; however, for older children, reasoning is more effective. Immediate punishment works better than delayed punishment; a very loud buzzer works better than a softer one. Mothers who have warm, affectionate relationships with their children find spanking to be a fairly effective punishment; cold, rejecting mothers say that spanking doesn't do much good.

6. Baumrind distinguishes three major styles of childrearing: (1) **Authoritarian** parents expect their children to do what they're told without argument. (2) **Authoritative** parents believe in firm enforcement of rules but give reasons for the rules and listen to their children's objections; their children are encouraged to be independent. (3) **Permissive** parents behave in a kind, accepting way toward their children and demand very little. No important differences were found between the children of Authoritarian parents and those of Permissive parents. The children of Authoritative parents were found to be the most responsible, assertive, self-reliant, and friendly. Baumrind believes that parents should give their children unconditional commitment, rather than unconditional love.

7. Social learning theorists agree with behaviorists in believing that children learn bit by bit about the acceptability of various kinds of behaviors, but they do not believe that all of this learning depends on reinforcements and punishments received—much of it is learned through observing other people's behavior and the consequences that follow from their behavior.

8. Children imitate, often in surprising detail, the behavior of other people. Their models are not only their parents, but also other children and other adults.

9. **Prosocial behavior** includes sharing, cooperating, and helping. Evidence suggests that children in our society tend to become less cooperative and more competitive as they grow older. The most effective way to foster cooperativeness is to provide them with models who behave cooperatively. Children with kind and helpful caregivers are likely to be relatively kind and helpful themselves.

10. Children's ability to tolerate **delay of gratification** is influenced by the behavior of models. It is also influenced by other factors, such as whether or not the immediate temptation is visible. Children may themselves devise strategies to help them resist the immediate temptation, or we can instruct them in the use of such strategies.

11. Aggression may be physical or verbal; its aim is to hurt, damage, or destroy. According to one theory, aggression results from frustration. Frustration frequently does lead to aggression, but not invariably; and not all aggression results from frustration.

12. There is no evidence that children can "store up" or "let out" their aggressions. Encouraging them to use aggressive language only increases the chances that they will be physi-

cally aggressive. Similarly, rewarding children for punching a doll makes them more aggressive with other children, not less. Their likelihood of attacking other children also depends on the reactions of the victims—when the victims cry or withdraw, further attacks are more apt to occur. Exposure to aggressive models (such as those on TV) is another factor that increases children's aggressiveness.

13. Because a parent administering a spanking is providing a very clear model of aggressive behavior, physical punishment is not an effective solution for aggressiveness. Another reason spanking is not effective is that aggression is a natural response to pain. Highly aggressive children tend to come from homes in which physical punishment is used.

14. Probably the most effective ways of dealing with children's aggressiveness are (1) using isolation as a punishment; (2) reinforcing behavior that is incompatible with aggression; and (3) providing them with models who behave responsibly and thoughtfully, rather than ones who behave aggressively or impulsively.

15. Most sex differences detectable in early childhood are minor, but there are sizable differences between boys and girls in aggressiveness, in rough-and-tumble play, and in risk-taking behavior. According to one theory, boys are more aggressive than girls because their aggressiveness is more likely to be encouraged or tolerated; the evidence does not support this theory. It's true that there are more male than female models for aggression, but preschoolers don't imitate only models of the same sex. Evidence from animal studies suggests that the sex difference in aggressiveness is at least partly biological in origin—a product of the male hormones.

16. Girls and boys are similar in more ways than they are different. There is no consistent evidence that girls are more sociable, more dependent, more susceptible to persuasion, lower in reasoning ability, or lower in self-esteem than boys.

17. By the preschool period, children have already absorbed a great deal of our society's sexual stereotypes. The biological differences between girls and boys are slight, compared to the steady barrage of environmental pressures that tell a child, "You're a girl—act like a girl," or "You're a boy—act like a boy." The effectiveness of such pressures is shown by the case of the identical twin boys, one of whom was reared as a girl and developed a female **gender identity.** Gender identity is generally firmly established by age 3.

18. **Sex constancy**—the understanding that a person's sex is permanent and is determined by the reproductive organs—is achieved around the end of the preschool period. It is accompanied by a greatly increased tendency to imitate models of the same sex.

19. Identification with the same-sex parent seems to be a relatively minor factor in **sex-typed behavior** (behavior that is considered typical of a given sex). Many parents, especially fathers, do show a strong tendency to encourage sex-typed behavior; however, there is a growing trend against making distinctions based on sex. Evidence suggests that **androgenous** people have some psychological advantages over those who fit the sexual stereotypes more closely.

20. Five types of play, varying in the type of social interactions they involve, are **solitary play, onlooker behavior, parallel play, associative play,** and **cooperative play.** Cooperative play doesn't usually appear until age 3.

21. The Piagetian categories of preschool play are **sensorimotor play, pretend play,** and **sociodramatic play.** Pretend play appears at around 12 months of age. Sociodramatic play appears around age 3 and reaches a peak around age 5; it involves group imagination.

22. Play is extremely important for a child. It enables children to practice many of the skills they will need later on, and to experiment with the environment in ways that do not have serious consequences. It also permits children to act out in fantasy what they cannot achieve in reality.

23. In the Freudian view, fantasy serves as an outlet for expressing feelings or wishes that are contrary to society's rules, and thus provides a **catharsis** of such drives. There is no experimental support for this view.

24. All preschool children seem to have fantasies that frighten them. Playing out their fears in fantasy form may give children a way of dealing with them; on the other hand, fantasies often seem to contribute to their fears, rather than decreasing them. There appears to be little we can do to help children deal with their fantasy fears; however, such fears may provide some biological benefits in the long run.

25. From 15 to 30 percent of children invent imaginary playmates; they are most common among firstborn and only children. The fantasy seems to produce some benefits: children with imaginary playmates are better than average at getting along with other children and with adults. The fantasy fades naturally as the child grows older.

26. The distinction between a fantasy and a lie may be difficult to make with a preschool child. A story may serve the function of a lie, but the child who tells it may actually believe it. Tale-telling reaches a peak around age 4 or 5 and then declines.

27. Friendships in the preschool years are highly unstable—a friend is whomever a child happens to be playing with at the moment. Two or three children playing together will resist the entry of another child about half the time.

28. Preschool children who give other children many "social reinforcements" tend to be popular with their peers. Even at this age, children give more social reinforcements to members of their own sex than to members of the opposite sex. Children tend to choose friends who are similar to themselves in sex, race, age, and even in physical attractiveness.

29. *Autism* is characterized by an almost

complete withdrawal from human interaction. It generally appears early in development but is seldom diagnosed before the preschool period. Autistic infants fail to make eye contact with their parents and fail to become attached to them. Most have an intense desire for sameness in the environment; almost all have language difficulties. There is no evidence that parental unresponsiveness is at fault—some physical abnormality of the brain is a more likely explanation.

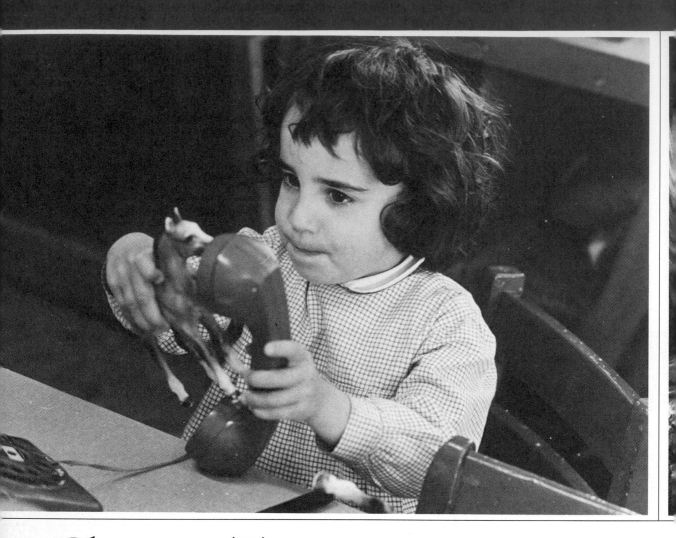

Chapter Ten

PRESCHOOLERS THINK AND COMMUNICATE

Ten

We went to see Uncle Walter and he was sitting on the sofa. And he gave me some chocolate lollipops. They were in a red box. And he pulled me in the wagon.

Nomi, age 3, is talking about things that happened a couple of days earlier. She is describing people and events that are not, at the moment, part of her environment—they are present only in her thoughts and memories. Nomi can think about future events, too, as when she asks her mother, "We go to the beach today?" She can also make and carry out simple plans, as when she drags out her box of blocks to make a "house" for her stuffed animals. All of these abilities depend on mental representations.

REPRESENTATIONAL THOUGHT

What, exactly, are mental representations? Cognitive psychologist Jerome Bruner distinguishes three kinds: **enactive** representations, **iconic** representations, and **symbolic** representations. "Their appearance in the life of the child," says Bruner, "is in that order, each depending upon the previous one for its development, yet all of them remaining more or less intact throughout life" (1973, pp. 327–328).

Here's Bruner's description of the first kind of representation:

> By enactive representation I mean a mode of representing past events through appropriate motor response. We cannot, for example, give an adequate description of familiar sidewalks or floors over which we habitually walk, nor do we have much of an image of what they are like. Yet we get about them without tripping or even looking much. Such segments of our environment—bicycle riding, tying knots, aspects of driving—get represented in our muscles, so to speak. (p. 328)

Enactive representations are present in infancy. Later, during the second year of life, iconic representations become possible. These are mental images—often visual (Nomi might have been picturing to herself that red box of candy, for example), but not necessarily so. One can have an iconic representation of a song, of an odor, or even of the way something feels. Bruner believes that iconic representations are responsible for the development of object permanence (see Chapter 7). It's when the toddler can form a mental image of an object, even when it's not physically present, that she comes to believe in its continued existence.

The last kind of representation, the symbolic kind, appears early in the preschool period but (according to Bruner) doesn't become dominant until about the age of 8. It is closely associated with the acquisition of language. A word is a symbol; it is linked to the thing it represents solely by arbitrary convention. We call the white liquid we get from cows *milk,* but we could just as easily have learned to call it *la leche,* or *le lait,* or *Milch.* For that matter, we could just as easily call it *mud,* or *Joe.* Whatever we call it, having a word for it helps us to ask for some when we're thirsty, to remember to buy some when we're at the store, and to respond appropriately when someone asks us for a glass of it. Symbols are representations that have been freed from the fetters of sensory and motor images. They can be combined in an infinite number of ways. And the resulting combinations are readily stored as memories. Perhaps some people remember how to tie a square knot by means of enactive representations. We do it by thinking to ourselves the words, "Right over left, left over right."

Thinking in words is not, of course, the only kind of symbolic thought. There are other kinds of symbols. Some are arbitrary and conventional, such as numbers, mathematical signs, and religious symbols. There are also personal, relevant symbols: a piece of lace or the smell of cookies being baked can symbolize "Grandma," for instance. But for Bruner, symbolic thought essentially means thinking in words.

Other psychologists do not give language the central role in cognitive development that Bruner gives it. To Bruner, language is what makes thinking and reasoning possible. To Piaget, on the other hand, language is an indication of the child's increasing cognitive capacities, not a cause of them. The child must develop a concept before he or she can put it into words.

Who is correct in regard to the importance of language, Piaget or Bruner? There is evidence on both sides. Bruner's position is supported by the fact that deaf children who cannot speak and are not taught sign language tend to be quite delayed in their cognitive development. For example, their understanding of conservation (that the amount of a liquid doesn't change when it's poured into a container of a different shape, or that the amount of clay doesn't change when it's rolled into a snake or flattened like a pancake) lags a year or two behind that of hearing children (Piaget and Inhelder, 1969). Yet deaf children *do,* eventually, come to an understanding of conservation. Language helps considerably, but it doesn't seem to be essential.

There's one more thing to note about the relationship between language and thought. Older children and adults can think by means of words and sentences that are "heard" in the mind but not spoken out loud. It's not clear whether young children can do this. When they think in words, they seem to have to say the words out loud. At any rate, they *do* carry on a lot of thinking out loud, to themselves, in what is called **private speech** (Goodman, 1981). As children grow older, this speech becomes more and more internal (Vygotsky, 1962).

CHARACTERISTICS OF PREOPERATIONAL THINKING

In Piagetian terms, preschoolers are in the **preoperational period.** Despite its acknowledgement of the impressive achievement of representational thought, Piagetian theory puts more emphasis on what preoperational children *can't* do than on what they *can*. We discussed some of these inabilities in Chapter 3: according to Piaget, preoperational children can't **decenter**—they can't consider more than one aspect of a situation at a time. Their thought is **egocentric**—they can't see something from another person's point of view. It isn't that preoperational children simply think less well or less clearly than older children and adults, or that they simply possess less information about the world. Piaget believes that their thought processes are *qualitatively* different from those of older people. That assertion deserves careful consid-

Is Preschool Thought Always Egocentric?

Let us start with Piaget's assertion that the thought of the preoperational child is egocentric. As you probably remember from Chapter 3, that term (as it is used here) isn't meant to imply selfishness or conceit. Piaget puts it this way:

> One of the first results of childish egocentrism is that everything is judged from the individual's own point of view. The child experiences the greatest difficulty in entering into anyone else's point of view. Consequently, his judgment is always absolute, so to speak, and never relative, for a relative judgment involves the simultaneous awareness of at least two personal points of view. (1928, pp. 215-216)

As evidence of this inability to take another's point of view, Piaget cites the results of his well-known "three mountains" experiment (Piaget and Inhelder, 1956). In this experiment, children were shown a three-dimensional scene made out of pasteboard. The scene was of three mountains, differing in size and in color. The display also included a small doll, which was facing the mountains. The children were asked to show (by means of cardboard cutouts of the mountains) what the mountains would look like from the *doll's* point of view, which was different from their own. Children were unable to do this before the age of 7 or 8—the age, according to Piaget, that marks the beginning of the next stage, the period of concrete operations. The younger, preoperational children depicted their *own* view of the mountains, instead of the doll's. Later experimenters made the task a little easier by supplying pictures of the various views of the scene, but preschool children are generally unable to indicate the doll's point of view.

This seems like undeniable evidence of egocentric thought: apparently, the child imagines that everyone sees things in the same way that *he* sees them. But it isn't as clear-cut as that. The three-mountain situation is a very difficult task for a preschool child. As recent studies have shown, even indicating his *own* point of view is difficult for a preschooler. If several blocks are put down in front of a 3- or 4-year-old and he is asked to pick the picture that shows his own view of them, he tends to pick one that shows *all* the blocks—even if some of them are not visible from his position because other blocks are in the way (Liben and Belknap, 1981). So the preschooler makes errors in this kind of task, but they're not necessarily egocentric errors.

A number of other observations about preschoolers have been attributed to their alleged egocentricity. In most cases, alternative explanations are possible. For example, Piaget asked a preschool boy, "How many brothers have you got?" The child said, "One, Paul." "And has Paul got a brother?" Piaget asked. "No," said the child. He doesn't realize that if Paul is his brother, he must be Paul's. Piaget states that this is due to his "thinking solely from his own point of view" (1928, p. 217). But consider: if Piaget had asked a little *girl* if she had any brothers and she had said, "One, Peter," then the correct answer to the second question *would* be "No" (Peter has no brothers). Or suppose Piaget had asked the little boy a different question, "How many uncles have you got?" and had been told, "One, Uncle Fred." If the child then said that Uncle Fred has no uncles, he could be either right or wrong! The fact of the matter is that *kinship terms*—in our English or in Piaget's French— are quite complicated. A few are reciprocal (if she's your cousin, you're hers); most are not (if he's your father, you're not his). It takes considerable experience to get clear on all these relationships. Paul's brother may be ignorant, but that doesn't mean he must be egocentric.

Adult: Can I see you?
Child: No.

One final example: if you ask a 2½- or 3-year-old to cover his eyes with his hands and then ask him, "Can I see you?" he is likely to answer "No." But, as shown in a study by three Stanford psychologists (Flavell, Shipstead, and Croft, 1980) it's not simply because he thinks *you* can't see if *he* has his eyes covered. He will answer correctly if you ask him whether you can see his arm, or some other object in the room. What these experimenters concluded was that children are taught by adults to regard the location of "you" and "me" as the eye area of the face. When an adult says to a child, "Look at me when I'm talking to you!" she doesn't mean "Look at my arm," or "Look at my left hip." She means "Look at my face—at my eyes." So if your eyes are covered, the child can't see "you," and vice versa!

The Evidence Against Egocentricity.   There is evidence that preschoolers *can* take another's point of view, if the situation is simple enough. In one experiment (Hobson, 1980) preschoolers were asked to position dolls in a game of hide-and-seek. Their task was to place one doll in a position (behind some barriers) where it couldn't be seen by two other dolls. Even 3-year-olds were able to place the doll correctly—despite the fact that their own perspective (looking down at the scene from above) was quite different.

Evidence from many other studies indicates that preschoolers are not invariably egocentric. Children as young as 2½ show another person a picture by turning it away from themselves, toward the other person (Lempers, Flavell, and Flavell, 1977). And when preschoolers talk to other people, they can appropriately modify their speech according to the needs of their listener. They speak louder when the other person is farther away (Johnson and others,

1981). They talk in short, simple sentences when they're speaking to a toddler, and with longer, more complicated utterances to older people (Shatz and Gelman, 1973; Sachs and Devin, 1976).

It's true that preschool children have more difficulty than older children in adopting someone else's viewpoint. But in the absence of *additional* difficulties, they are capable of doing it.

Can Preschoolers Decenter?

This question isn't really very different from the one about egocentricity: instead of asking, Can the preschooler consider more than one point of view? we are now asking, Can the preschooler consider more than one aspect of a situation? In this case, much of the data involve the problem of **conservation.** We described Piaget's famous experiment on the conservation of liquid volume in Chapter 3. When liquid is poured from a normal-shaped glass into a tall, skinny beaker, the preschooler says that the quantity has increased, because she centers on the height of the liquid and ignores the other dimensions. Note, however, that even adults find it difficult to estimate liquid volume (a difficulty that beverage manufacturers often take advantage of!). The reason it's hard is that volume increases with the liquid's height in a one-to-one fashion: double the height and you've doubled the volume. But, in a cylindrical container, liquid volume increases with the *square* of the radius. Thus, it takes only a small change in the diameter of the glass to produce a large change in the height of the liquid. That change in height is very impressive to a preschooler—the sensory evidence overrides any other ideas she might have on the subject. But if you prevent her from seeing the change of height in the containers, by keeping the second container covered up, she is quite likely to say (correctly) that the amount of liquid has remained the same—"It's the same water. You only poured it" (Bruner, 1973, p. 336).

Conservation of Number.   Another problem that preschoolers fail—again, apparently, because of their tendency to be swayed by appearances—involves the conservation of number. Take seven or eight pennies and the same number of jellybeans and put them in two rows of equal length, one jellybean under each penny. Preschoolers will tell you with assurance that there are the same number of jellybeans and pennies. But if you then spread out the jellybeans so that the row of candies is longer than the row of coins, they will claim that there now are more jellybeans than pennies. According to Piaget (1965), they have again centered on one aspect of the situation—length of row—and ignored the other—the distances between the objects.

Rochel Gelman, of the University of Pennsylvania, has done a series of studies on preschoolers' understanding of the concept of number. She feels that preschoolers *do* possess such a concept, but that it only extends to numbers they feel comfortable with—numbers no bigger than 4 or 5. In some of her experiments she shows preschoolers a small set of objects (two, three, or four) and then makes one object "magically" disappear or an extra one appear. The children are quick to notice the change in number.

Preschoolers can handle problems involving numbers only if the numbers are ones they feel comfortable with—numbers no bigger than 4 or 5.

They not only recognize the resulting change; they tell us what must have happened, i.e. that somehow an item was either removed or added. On the other hand, when the experimenter surreptitiously lengthens or shortens a row or changes the color or identity of items in a row, the children notice the changes but say that they are irrelevant to number. (Gelman, 1978, p. 301)

This is just what Piaget claims that preschoolers can't do. Indeed, they *can't,* if you make the situation too difficult by giving them numbers that are beyond their grasp.

Class-Inclusion Problems. There is another type of problem that preschool children have trouble with. It has to do with classification—with what things are included in what classes (hence, the term **class inclusion**). The question that is typically asked is of the form, "Are there more black horses or more horses in this barnyard?" or, "Are there more square blocks or more blocks?" Here the difficulty does not involve numbers, because even if the numbers are quite small the preschooler gives the wrong answer: "More black horses" (when there are five horses—three black, two white), or "More square blocks" (when there are four blocks—three square, one round). According to Piaget, this is another instance of preoperational children's inability to decenter: they can't conceive of something belonging simultaneously to the class *black horses* and to the larger class *horses* (Inhelder and Piaget, 1964).

That young children can't handle questions of this type has been reconfirmed time and again, and investigated in many studies. It has been shown

Metacognition: Learning How To Learn

One thinks of the mind of the preschooler as fresh and open, all ready to soak up knowledge like a sponge. It's a little surprising, therefore, to find that preschoolers actually learn most things *less* readily than older children. Let's say, for instance, that you give them a short list of objects to memorize, by showing them pictures of the objects. Preschoolers will remember fewer of them than older children (Flavell, Friedrichs, and Hoyt, 1970). In fact, for just about any learning task you can think of, preschoolers do less well than school-age children.

There's nothing the matter with preschoolers' minds. They have the most wonderful cognitive apparatus in the world, sitting inside their heads. Their only trouble is that they haven't learned all the tricks of using it. It's as though they had an elaborate new computer up there, that hasn't been fully programmed yet. It can do all the basic things, but it still can't handle the fancy stuff. It will be able to do a lot more, once the necessary programs are written and running.

"Learning how to operate the memory" is how some psychologists describe one of the skills that preschoolers are in the process of acquiring. It's not exactly a cognitive skill: it's a *metacognitive* skill.

The study of **metacognition** is a new field within developmental psychology. A leading researcher in this field is John Flavell, of Stanford University. Flavell and his associates were the ones who did the study we just mentioned, which showed that preschoolers are not as good as older children at memorizing a list of items. But that wasn't the most noteworthy part of the results. A more interesting finding was that the

that even if you make the question less tricky by asking, "Which are there more of, the black horses or *all* the horses?" preschoolers still tend to give the wrong answer. They do a little better, but not much. It's also been shown (Grieve and Garton, 1981) that the problem isn't simply the black horses' dual membership in two classes (*black horses* and *horses*), because preschoolers also give the wrong answer when you ask them to compare the black horses with the *cows*.

What the problem seems to involve is the children's interpretation of the question they've been asked. As some psychologists in Australia pointed out, the question they answer isn't always the same as the one you've asked (Grieve and Garton, 1981). When you ask them to compare "black horses" and "horses," they do something different: they compare the black horses with the *white* horses. And when you ask them to compare the black horses and cows they generally compare the black horses with the *black* cows. They interpret the question as being "symmetrical"—as involving two classes of the same level, rather than one subordinate class and one superordinate class.

But isn't this the natural thing to do? Isn't this what people *usually* do? The younger children *thought* they had memorized the list, when in fact they hadn't. As Flavell puts it,

> Preschool and elementary school children were asked to study a set of items until they were sure they could recall them perfectly. . . . The older subjects studied for a while, said they were ready, and usually were, that is, they showed perfect recall. The younger children studied for a while, said they were ready, and usually were not. . . . [They] incorrectly thought they had memorized and could recall the items. Results such as these have suggested that young children are quite limited in their knowledge and cognition about cognitive phenomena, or in their *metacognition,* and do relatively little monitoring of their own memory, comprehension, and other cognitive enterprises. (1979, p. 906)

What does "learning how to learn" actually involve? You probably are aware that if you want to learn something, the first thing you have to do is pay close attention to it. Then, if it's something that can be understood or not understood, it helps if you can manage to understand it. If it's something like a name or a list of words,

it's a good idea to *rehearse* it—to say it over and over to yourself. It's also helpful to organize what you are trying to learn. For example, if you're trying to learn a list of object names, it's easier if you can categorize them—put all the names of tools together, all the kinds of fruit, all the kinds of furniture. Then, when you want to recall them, you can think of the things that are in each category. Finally, if you want to find out whether you've succeeded in learning something, you can test yourself on it.

In general, preschoolers have little or no understanding of the principles we just summarized, and this seems to be the main reason why their learning is relatively inefficient. They gradually acquire this kind of knowledge, and the ability to apply it, as they grow older.

Metacognition is not just learning how to learn. It's also thinking about thinking. It's paying attention to whether you're paying attention. Any aspect of cognitive activity can become the focus of metacognitive activity. But learning how to learn, how to remember, is especially important. We may eventually come to the conclusion that this kind of cognitive development is even more important, in the long run, than the kinds of things Piaget was interested in. ∎

kind of question we normally ask is, "Are there more cars or more trucks? More pens or more pencils?" How often do we ask, "Are there more cars or more vehicles? More pens or more writing implements?" In fact, questions of the second type are not always answered correctly by adolescents—or even by college students! (Brainerd, 1978)

Perhaps there's a moral here. Crudely stated, it goes, Ask a stupid question, get a stupid answer.

The Preoperational Child: Conclusions

Obviously, the cognitive abilities of preschool children are more advanced than those of younger children and less advanced than those of older children. But are they *qualitatively* different from those of infants and toddlers? From older children and adults?

To the first question, we believe the answer is yes. Representational thought—especially symbolic thought—makes preschoolers' mental abilities a clear step above those of infants and toddlers. It's not like the difference between crawling and walking—it's more like the difference between crawling and flying.

On the other hand, the case for a qualitative change between preschool thinking and later thinking is much less clear. Yes, older children and adults can perform most cognitive tasks better than preschoolers, but part of this difference is due simply to their greater knowledge and experience.

What *is* clear is that the cognitive advances still to come are not going to be as dramatic or impressive as those that have already occurred. Cognitive development from here on in will be a more gradual and continuous process.

INTELLIGENCE

It's pretty clear by the beginning of the preschool period that children's cognitive abilities vary considerably from one individual to another. Some children come much earlier than others to the understanding of principles such as conservation of liquid volume. Some are speaking in long, complicated sentences when others are using only a few words. Some can put together a puzzle in record time or figure out how to unlatch a cabinet, while others are stumped. Of course, these different abilities don't necessarily go together—one child may be verbally advanced but no good at puzzles; for another, the reverse may be true.

IQ Tests

Although intelligence testing doesn't usually begin until the school years, it is possible to give an IQ test to a preschooler. Moreover, the results of such tests correlate reasonably well with IQ tests given to the same children when they're older. This is in contrast to what happens when you test infants and toddlers. Tests given much before the age of 2 have essentially no predictive value—their correlation with tests given in middle or late childhood is approximately zero.

Why is this? One reason is that infants and toddlers are notoriously difficult to test. They are highly distractible, and their performance will depend heavily on irrelevant factors such as their mood at the time (fussy or cheerful) and their reaction to the test-giver (friendly or shy).

A more important reason is that infant and toddler tests simply can't include many of the kinds of things that are measured in tests given to older children. Preschoolers and school-age children can be tested on memory, reasoning ability, and verbal ability (for example, vocabulary). In contrast, infant tests primarily involve assessment of perceptual and motor functioning: Does the baby look at a toy? Can she reach for it or pass it from hand to hand? Toddler tests might involve building a tower of three blocks, or imitating some simple action demonstrated by the test-giver.

What Do They Measure? This brings us to an important issue—one that we didn't really go into in our brief discussion of IQ in Chapter 2. What are intelligence tests supposed to measure? And how well do they measure it?

Psychologists have tried for a long time to say exactly what characteristics an "intelligent" person has and an "unintelligent" person lacks. There is a fairly long list of characteristics that are usually mentioned. The list includes the ability to learn things quickly and forget them slowly, to reason correctly with words and with numbers, to understand spoken or written words and sentences, to see relationships and differences between things, to think up insightful solutions to problems, and so on.

IQ tests are designed to measure all of these abilities and more. When we speak of a child's "IQ" we are referring to how well he or she does on an IQ test. When we speak of "intelligence" we are speaking of the quality (or qualities) that IQ tests are supposed to measure. But if the children being tested are tired, ill, frightened, or uncooperative, or if the language of the test is not their native language, then their test performance might be a very poor measure of their actual intelligence. A test might also be a poor measure of intelligence just by being a poor test. A good test is one that succeeds in measuring what it is supposed to measure. Such a test is said to have **validity.**

How They Began.   The idea of testing children's intelligence started in France, around 1900. The Paris school system wanted a way of identifying those children who would have problems in school and would need extra help. They asked a psychologist named Alfred Binet to help with this task. Binet and his co-worker Théophile Simon devised the first successful IQ test. It was successful because it produced results that agreed pretty well with teachers' opinions of their students' intelligence. It also did a fairly good job of predicting how well the students would do in school. These two criteria are still used in judging the validity of an IQ test. The IQ tests used today correlate about .60 with grades in elementary school (Jensen, 1981). They don't correlate perfectly, because grades depend on many other factors in addition to intelligence.

The Binet-Simon test was based on the concept of **mental age.** Binet decided that an intelligent child of 5 might be the intellectual equal of an average child of 6. That meant that the bright 5-year-old could answer as many questions or solve as many problems as the average 6-year-old. Then this 5-year-old would have the mental age of 6. Binet and Simon spent a lot of time finding test items (questions or problems) that most 6-year-olds could answer but most 5-year-olds couldn't, items that most 7-year-olds could answer but most 6-year-olds couldn't, and so on. A child who could answer all of the test items for 5-year-olds, most of the items for 6-year-olds, and few of the items for 7-year-olds would have a mental age of 6.

Later psychologists found a convenient way to express the relationship between mental age and chronological (actual) age. They divided the mental age by the chronological age to get what they called the **intelligence quotient,** or IQ for short. A 5-year-old with a mental age of 6 would have an intelligence quotient of 6 ÷ 5, or 1.20. For convenience the decimal point was dropped, so the child's IQ was expressed as 120. A 5-year-old with a mental age of 5 (or any child whose mental age and chronological age were the same) would have an IQ of 100. A 5-year-old with a mental age of 4½, and a 10-year-old with a mental age of 9, would have IQs of 90.

The problem with this way of expressing intelligence was that it was difficult to apply it to older teenagers and adults. A brilliant 5-year-old might have a mental age of 7 (IQ = 140), but it's meaningless to say that a brilliant 25-year-old has a mental age of 35. So nowadays IQ tests are scored a little differently. IQ is defined entirely in terms of how well a person does compared to others of the same age. A person who scores exactly at the mean will have an IQ of 100. The other IQ scores are distributed in such a way that IQs close to 100 are very common and IQs much higher or lower than 100 are relatively rare. About 50 percent of people have IQs between 90 and 110, but only 0.4 percent—fewer than 1 in 200—have IQs of 140 or more.

Remember that an IQ score tells us only one thing: how well a child did on a particular IQ test, compared to others of the same age who also took that test. A child with an IQ score of 140 has performed in the upper 0.4 percent and a child with an IQ score of 70 has performed in the lowest 3 percent, but it would be misleading (and incorrect) to say that the first child is "twice as smart" as the second.

IQ Tests for English-Speaking Children.   The Binet-Simon IQ test was, of course, written in the French language. An English translation of that IQ test attracted the attention of Lewis Terman, an American psychologist at Stanford University. He and his colleagues at Stanford revised the test so that it would be more suitable for American children. The new test, called the **Stanford-Binet,** first appeared in 1916. It has been necessary to update the test several times since then; the latest revision appeared in 1972. The Stanford-Binet is designed to be administered individually; it can be used with children from age 2 on up. It consists of a wide variety of test items, with some items used mostly for younger children, some for older ones. A young child might be shown a picture of a common object and asked to say what it is, or to copy a square. An older child might be asked to define a vocabulary word, or to discover what is missing in a picture of a familiar object.

Another popular IQ test is the Wechsler, which is also meant to be administered individually. There are three versions of the Wechsler: one for adults, one for school-age children (the Wechsler Intelligence Scale for Children, or **WISC**), and one for younger children aged 4 to 6 (the Wechsler Preschool and Primary Scale of Intelligence, or **WPPSI**). The Wechsler tests consist of several different subtests, which are designed to measure two different kinds of ability. The verbal subtests measure language ability and general knowledge. The performance subtests are for nonverbal abilities such as assembling puzzles or copying patterns with colored blocks. A child who takes the WISC or the WPPSI receives a verbal IQ score, a performance IQ score, and a full-scale score that is a combination of the other two.

We said a little while ago that a child who is verbally advanced, for instance, is not necessarily good in nonverbal things such as putting together puzzles. That's true—there's no *necessary* connection. The fact is, though, that a child who is way ahead verbally is likely to be above average in puzzle

IQ tests for preschool children must be administered individually. The results of such tests correlate fairly well with IQ tests given in later childhood and adulthood.

assembly. To put it another way, there is a correlation between the scores on one subtest and scores on others. These correlations aren't always very high, but they're almost invariably positive.

There are two different ways of interpreting these correlations; as yet, there is no agreement as to which is more accurate. The first way is to assume that intelligence is made up of a number of separate abilities, and that whatever genetic and environmental factors cause a child to be high in one ability are likely to cause him to be high in others as well. The second is to assume that all the different kinds of tests are different ways of getting at one underlying characteristic, which has been called g (for the *general factor* in intelligence). None of the tests measures it perfectly, but all of them measure it to some extent. To the extent that they measure it, the scores will be correlated. In other words, a child who is high in g will tend to do better at all kinds of intelligence tests than a child who is low in g.

Stability of IQ. A question that people often ask about IQ scores is: How stable are they? Does a 3-year-old with a measured IQ of 110 become a 10-year-old with an IQ of 110 and eventually an adult with an IQ of 110? One way of answering this question is to say that IQ scores obtained in middle to late childhood correlate quite well (about .75) with adult IQ. Scores obtained in the preschool period correlate less well with adult scores (about .50).

The reasonably good correlations between IQ scores in childhood and adulthood don't mean that IQ can't change, though. In some children IQ scores change quite a lot. In one long-term study (McCall, Appelbaum, and Hogarty, 1973) a group of children were tested many times over the course of 14½ years. Each child was given a total of 17 IQ tests, starting at age 2½ and ending at age 17. About half the children stayed pretty much the same, but the other half varied considerably. Some IQs went steadily up, some went up for a while and then down, and so on. In one out of three children, the differences between the lowest and the highest of the 17 scores was 30 points or more. One child's IQ went up 74 points! This study shows how unwise it is to pigeonhole a child on the basis of a single IQ score.

What could be the cause of such major changes in IQ scores? Part of the variation must have resulted from developmental changes in individual children. Some children, no doubt, are "late bloomers"; for others, the opposite may be true. In some cases, there may have been a drastic change in the child's environment—due, perhaps, to an improvement in family finances, or to parental divorce or unemployment.

But for a sizable portion of these children, the changes in IQ scores were probably due, not to actual changes in intelligence, but to **error of measurement.** Even when a test is measuring the right thing, it may not measure it perfectly. All sorts of things can interfere: the test-giver may drop the testing materials, or be in a grumpy mood, or make a mistake in presenting an item or in scoring it. The child being tested may have a bad cold, or may have missed lunch, or may not feel like cooperating that day (or, for that matter, that *year*). And luck comes into it too—perhaps a vocabulary word happens to be one that the child just encountered (and learned) yesterday; or perhaps it's a word he won't encounter till tomorrow. Perhaps he guesses, and he's right—or wrong.

All of these random factors (and many others) affect what is called a test's **reliability.** Theoretically, one way of checking on a test's reliability is to give the same test twice to the same child, a week or two apart, and see how similar the two scores are. In fact, though, this isn't ordinarily done because the child will remember the test items and also his responses to them. So reliability is usually assessed in one of two ways. Some tests have two alternate forms, containing different items that have been chosen to be equivalent in difficulty. The correlation between children's scores on the two forms is one way of measuring reliability. The second, more common way is to correlate the scores on half of the items on a single test (all the odd-numbered items, say) with scores on the other half (the even-numbered ones). This method takes into account only the kinds of unreliability that would make a child do better on some items than others—for instance, lucky guesses and lucky recent encounters with test items. It leaves out things such as whether the test-giver and the child being tested are feeling grumpy or cheerful, healthy or ill. (continued on page 335)

Can Preschool Enrichment Programs Boost IQ?

Preschoolers growing up in economically disadvantaged homes, whose parents are employed in unskilled jobs, or are unemployed, or are absent, tend to score lower on IQ tests than children from middle-class homes. The average IQ score for the disadvantaged preschooler might be 10 to 20 points below the middle-class average.

The IQ scores of the disadvantaged youngsters have about the same predictive power as the scores of the middle-class children. That is, there is a moderate correlation between these scores and later school performance. The disadvantaged group contains a disproportionate share of those children who will do poorly in elementary school—who will be held back, who will be placed in special classes for slow learners, who will fail (in the long run) to graduate from high school.

Starting in the mid-60s, there have been attempts to improve the outlook for these children by improving their environments. Efforts have been made to give children growing up in slums and ghettos some of the advantages their homes seem to lack and that middle-class children take for granted. One such effort is Operation Head Start, which began in the 60s and is still going on. There have been several similar programs, all with the goal of providing deprived preschoolers with intellectual stimulation and verbal skills in a group setting, under the supervision of trained educators. In addition, some of these programs have provided health services for the children and counseling for their mothers.

The initial studies of the effects of such programs were extremely encouraging. Preschoolers' IQ scores often shot up by 10 points or more within their first year in the programs. But the long-term results were disappointing. When the children graduated from the enrichment programs their IQ scores gradually declined. After two or three years in public school, the children who had been through the enrichment programs were scoring no higher on IQ tests than other children from similar homes (Bronfenbrenner, 1974).

Some educators have concluded from such results that enrichment programs are pointless—that these children are genetically inferior and hence cannot be helped (Jensen, 1969). But there are several arguments against that conclusion. For one thing, the programs undoubtedly brought benefits in improved health care to the children involved. In all probability, there were also beneficial effects on their social and emotional development (Zigler, 1973).

For another thing, we know from studies of adopted children that the environment *does* affect cognitive development and scores on IQ tests (see Chapter 2). Children reared in middle-class adoptive homes tend to have considerably higher IQs than their biological parents. Then why did the Head Start program (and other similar programs) fail to produce any long-term gains in intellectual development?

To answer that question, let us contrast the Head Start type of program with the kind of program that *did* succeed in producing long-term intellectual gains. Head Start children attend what is basically a middle-class nursery school, provided with educational toys and a kindly teacher who leads them in group activities. They spend a few hours a day in this setting, five days a week. They spend their remaining hours in a family—in many cases, a one-parent family—that has been affected only in minor ways by the child's enrollment in the enrichment program. If anything, the child's mother may feel that her child's enrollment in the program has relieved her of the responsibility of providing intellectual stimulation for him.

The programs that have worked have two

characteristics (Bronfenbrenner, 1974). First of all, intellectual stimulation was given on a one-to-one basis: one child and one adult. Second, the program was begun at an earlier point in the child's life, generally by the age of 2, and hence was able to continue for a longer period of time (at least two years).

The most radical of these programs was called the Milwaukee Project (Heber, 1978; Heber and others, 1972). It involved a group of black infants born to mothers with IQs below 75, living in a Milwaukee ghetto. From the age of 3 months, these children spent their entire day (8:45 a.m. to 4 p.m.) at a learning center, in an intensive, cognitively structured program. Each child had his or her own teacher, a person from the same neighborhood who had been given special training for the job. At 12 to 15 months the children were combined into small groups of two to four, and the program continued until they entered first grade. Simultaneously, the children's mothers were given instruction in homemaking and childrearing skills, and were kept informed about their children's progress. Only 20 children were involved in this program, and one hesitates to rely too much on such small numbers. Nevertheless, the results were remarkable. At age 15 these children's IQ scores averaged 105. A control group of children from comparable homes averaged about 80.

Is such an intensive program necessary? It may not be. In another successful program, children and their mothers were visited in their homes only twice a week by people called "toy demonstrators." The purpose of these visits was to show the children's mothers how to use language to increase their children's cognitive skills, and to teach them some cognitive games that they could play with their children. These children showed intellectual gains that persisted at least through third grade (Levenstein, 1970; Madden, Levenstein, and Levenstein, 1976).

Thus, a twice-a-week program can succeed where five-day-a-week programs have failed. The important difference may be the close involvement of the child's mother—or a mother

Children in a Head Start classroom.

substitute—in the program. It seems that the intellectual stimulation must be provided on a one-to-one, or nearly one-to-one, basis. It also appears that the person providing it should feel that he or she has the power to affect the child's cognitive development, and should have some knowledge about how to do so. And finally, it may be the case that the best teacher for a child is someone who cares very much about that particular child.

With this second method of checking reliability, the reliability of individually given IQ tests is generally found to be between .85 and .95; it's lower for preschoolers than for older children. A reliability in the neighborhood of .90 means that a child who receives an IQ score of 105 might have a "true" IQ (what we'd get if we measured him again and again and averaged all the scores) of anywhere from 100 to 110. In fact, there's a one-in-three chance of his obtained score being even more than 5 points off the "true" score (Anastasi, 1976).

In light of all this, a 30-point spread between the highest and lowest of 17 IQ scores, collected over 14½ years, doesn't sound like so much. And when you also take into account the fact that the first IQ test was given at age 2½, it seems even less surprising. Preschoolers may not be as difficult to test as infants and toddlers, but testing them does require their cooperation—and their cooperation isn't always forthcoming. Some are stubborn or negative, some are uninterested, and some are simply more inclined to chat with the test-giver than to answer questions or draw squares (Harris, 1982).

LANGUAGE DEVELOPMENT

Among the achievements of the preschool period, surely the most impressive is in the realm of language development. The average 2-year-old has a vocabulary of 200 or 300 words; he or she is likely to be talking mostly in 2- and 3-word sentences: "See Teddy." "Car go home."

Six-year-olds, in contrast, speak in much longer, much more complex sentences and phrases. They show a sophisticated grasp of the grammar of their language—of verb forms, possessives, definite and indefinite articles, and so on. They have a productive vocabulary of some 2,500 words. Their receptive vocabulary—the words they can understand, at least to some extent—may be as high as 14,000 words (Carey, 1978). That's nine new words for every day they've been alive! One book about language development informs the reader, "Our story will end at school age because by the age of six the child's language is in many respects like an adult's" (de Villiers and de Villiers, 1979, p. 4). The authors of this book ask, "How does the child learn language so well in so short a time?" (p. 2). That question reminds us of the old joke in which a tourist in New York asks a native, "How do you get to Carnegie Hall?" The answer, of course, is "Practice! Practice!" Preschoolers do just that. Parents and nursery school teachers will freely admit, with a mixture of pride and irritation, that these children "never shut up."

It takes a lot of talking and a lot of listening to learn a language. It's not only *words* that must be learned. Think of all the rules involved in speaking the English language! Think of all the *exceptions* to the rules!

Learning the Rules of a Language

To appreciate the kinds of problems that face young learners of the English language, and the ways they deal with these problems, consider the following dialogue. The speakers are a developmental psycholinguist named Peter de Villiers and a 2½-year-old named Katie. They've been playing with some pieces of Play-Doh, and their conversation concerns the ownership of some disputed pieces.

> Katie: Don't crush mines up!
> [de Villiers]: What was yours? What was it? Had you made it into something?
> Katie: Dis is mines.

Katie has probably never heard anyone refer to anything as *"mines."* But she has heard words like *yours, ours, theirs,* and *hers,* and from these examples she has apparently generalized a rule: that possessive pronouns should end in *s.*

> Katie: Dat's yours.
> [de Villiers]: That's mine. Ok. I'll keep that. Is that as well? I have lots of pieces now, don't I?
> Katie: Dis is mine.

Now Katie has noticed that de Villiers says *mine,* not *mines,* and she follows suit. She seems to have decided that her previous rule is incorrect, so she comes up with a new one:

> [de Villiers]: Did you steal some more? You stole some more! Keep stealing all mine, don't you?
> Katie: I keep stealing all your. (de Villiers and de Villiers, 1979, p. 111)

Not all children are as quick to change their minds about a rule as Katie is. Here is perhaps a more typical example:

> [Child]:   My teacher holded the baby rabbits and we patted them.
> [Adult]:   Did you say the teacher held the baby rabbits?
> [Child]:   Yes.
> [Adult]:   What did you say she did?
> [Child]:   She holded the baby rabbits and we patted them.
> [Adult]:   Did you say she held them tightly?
> [Child]:   No, she holded them loosely. (Gleason, 1967)

It is possible that this child, at an earlier age, used the word *held.* It is probable that Katie, at an earlier age, used the word *mine.* In English the exceptions to the rules often involve the most common words, and some of these are learned in the early phases of language acquisition. But then, at a later point in time, a child who previously used *mine, held, went,* or *feet,* begins to use *mines, holded, goed,* or *feets* (we've mentioned this before in Chapter 7). To the casual observer, it appears that the child is progressing backwards. That is far from the truth, however. On the contrary: she has apparently worked out some of the general rules of the English language—a remarkable achievement, when you think about it. A child who says *holded,* for example, seems to be following a rule that goes, To form the past tense of a verb, add *ed*. Yet she's not consciously aware that she's following a rule, and it's hard to believe that she possesses the concept of a verb. What's more, she's somehow managed to come up with this generalization despite the sizable proportion of common English verbs that don't follow the rule (such as *bring–brought, ring–rang, eat–ate, break–broke, get–got,* and so on).

At a later time—usually before they enter first grade—most children are correctly using the common irregular verbs (such as *held*), plurals (*feet*), and possessives (*mine*). At this point they have learned both the rules *and* the exceptions. We know that they do use rules (and haven't just memorized each verb form, plural, and possessive individually) because they can apply them to words they have never seen before. This was demonstrated in a classic experiment carried out in the 1950s. The experimenter (Berko, 1958) made up nonsense words such as *wug* and *zib,* and used pictures to teach children these words—"This is a wug," or "This is a man who knows how to zib." If a child saw the picture of the wug, for instance, she would then be shown a second picture containing two of the birdlike creatures (see Figure 10–1), and the experimenter would say, "Now there are two of them. There are two _____." If the child said "wugs," it had to be because she knew the rule for forming plurals, since it's unlikely that she'd ever heard the word *wugs* before. In answering questions of this sort, children between the ages of 4 and 7 proved that they know how to form plurals (*wugs*), present progressives (*zibbing*), and past tenses (*zibbed*).

Acquiring Grammatical Morphemes. Roger Brown is a Harvard psycholinguist whose work includes a careful study of the language development of three children—Adam, Eve, and Sarah (see p. 239). Over a period of almost two years, Brown and his co-workers visited these children in their homes every week or two and made tape recordings of everything the children said. The recordings were later transcribed into written form and analyzed (Brown, 1973).

This is a wug.

Now there is another one.
There are two of them.
There are two _____ .

figure 10–1
The fact that 4- to 7-year-olds can give the correct response (wugs) shows that they know the rule for forming plural nouns (Berko, 1958).

What Brown was interested in was how children go from saying sentences like "Kick truck," and 'Daddy chair," to sentences like "I kicked the truck," and "Daddy is sitting in his chair." He paid particular attention to the acquisition of words such as *in, on, is, are,* and *the,* and of suffixes such as *-ing, -ed,* and *-s.* Linguists call these **grammatical morphemes.** (A **morpheme** is defined as the smallest unit of meaning. Prefixes and suffixes are morphemes, and so are words. A word with a suffix counts as two morphemes.)

Brown found that there was a fairly orderly sequence of appearance of grammatical morphemes. The order wasn't exactly the same for the three children studied, but the differences were minor.

The first grammatical morphemes acquired by Adam, Eve, and Sarah were the *-ing* ending on verbs (which was used at first without the auxiliary verbs *is* or *are,* as in "Mommy sitting"), the prepositions *in* and *on,* and the plural *-s.* Next came the possessive *-'s,* the articles *a* and *the,* some irregular past tenses such as *went* and *ate,* and some forms of *to be,* used not as auxiliaries but as verbs in themselves (as in "Here I am," and "What is it?"). The regular past-tense ending *-ed* appeared after the children had started to use the irregular forms such as *went.*

Another group of morphemes appeared relatively late: they were the *-s* that goes on the third person singular of English verbs ("He run*s*") and the forms of *to be* used as an auxiliary ("Mommy *is* sitting," "The dogs *were* running") and as a contractible verb ("I*'m* here," "They*'re* nice"). These forms didn't appear until the children's MLU (mean length of utterance—see p. 238) had exceeded 4. To give you some idea of the variability of the rate of language acquisition, this milestone was reached at age 3½ for Adam, at age 4 for Sarah, and at age 2 years 3 months for Eve.

Why do these grammatical morphemes appear in this particular order? Brown and his colleagues thought it might depend on the frequency with which these morphemes are used in adult speech—perhaps the earliest morphemes to be acquired would be the ones children hear their parents use most frequently. This proved not to be the case, however. In fact, there was no relationship between the parents' frequency of using a grammatical morpheme and the children's acquisition of that morpheme.

Brown concluded that the order of appearance of grammatical morphemes is determined chiefly by the difficulty or complexity of the rules governing their use. The forms of the verb *to be* are more complex than morphemes like *-ing* and *on* because the child must take into account both time (as in *is* versus *was*) and person (*is* versus *am* or *are*).

If this is the case, then order of acquisition might differ in other languages, because other languages make some distinctions that English doesn't, or fail to make some distinctions that English does. For example, the concepts conveyed by *in* and *on* in English are conveyed quite differently in Serbo-Croatian, a language spoken in Yugoslavia. These concepts require a preposition *plus* a special ending on the noun it accompanies, and the ending differs according to the way the noun is used in the sentence. As might be expected, children learning Serbo-Croatian take longer to use these morphemes correctly (de Villiers and de Villiers, 1979).

Negatives. Children begin to express negative ideas as soon as they begin to combine words—"No bath!" they might say, or "No wet!" (pointing to their diapers). At this stage, negative statements are constructed simply by adding *no* or *not* in front of (or occasionally after) a word or phrase. "All-gone," used as one word, or "bye-bye," as in "bye-bye bird," may also be used to express the nonexistence or disappearance of something.

A little later, *no* and *not* or *can't* and *won't* are used within the sentence, as in "He no bite you," and "I can't catch you." But full and correct use of negatives takes a long time to achieve. A 3- or 4-year-old might say "I didn't did it," and even a school-age child might say "I didn't see nothing," or "Don't let someone touch this" (de Villiers and de Villiers, 1979; Clark and Clark, 1977).

Questions. The first questions, like the first negatives, appear quite early. They are recognizable as questions only by the rising intonation of the child's voice: "See baby?" "Daddy come home?" At about the same time, some *wh*-words (such as *who, what, where* and *why*) begin to be used: "What's dat?" "Where milk go?"

Even after children have acquired most of the important grammatical morphemes, they may still be having trouble with the word order in questions. Young preschoolers often use constructions such as "Why kitty can't stand up?" or "What he can ride in?" There is also the problem of putting both the verb and the auxiliary into the proper tense: in "Did I caught it?" the child has put both verbs into the past tense—reasonable, but (as it happens) incorrect (Clark and Clark, 1977).

The complexities of learning the English language are well illustrated by so-called **tag questions.** In "Chuck plays tennis, doesn't he?" and "You can't do it, can you?" the tag questions are "doesn't he?" and "can you?". To produce such questions, the speaker must perform three separate operations on the first part of the sentence: (1) if the subject is a noun, turn it into a pronoun; (2) turn a negative construction into a positive one or vice versa; and (3) invert the word order to form a question. Adults who learn English as a second language may find tag questions so difficult that they don't even attempt them—they simply use the all-purpose "Right?" or "True?" But, by the time they enter first grade, most English-speaking children understand the basic principles of tag questions and are able to produce them correctly in at least some contexts. Complete mastery of the tag question takes several more years, however (Dennis, Sugar, and Whitaker, 1982).

Words and Meanings

Young children do not always use words in the same way as adults do. We mentioned in Chapter 7 that toddlers may **overextend** a word (apply it to more things than an adult would), or **underextend** it (*not* apply it to things an adult would). Overextensions seem to be most common in toddlerhood. For example, one toddler used the word *moon* for anything round; another called any toy that he played with in the bath a *turtle* (de Villiers and de Villiers,

1979). Toddlers haven't had time to acquire a very large vocabulary, and they're faced with a world filled with a tremendous variety of objects, so such overextensions are quite reasonable. Overextensions decline in frequency as the child learns more and more words, and as parents correct the child's usage: "No, that's not a turtle, that's a *fish*." By the late preschool period, overextensions tend to consist of the same kinds of mistakes that adults sometimes make—calling a chimpanzee "a monkey," for instance, or a spider "a bug."

Although most preschoolers have sizable vocabularies and are, to say the least, reasonably talkative people, it is not easy to find out whether their concepts of words exactly match those of adults. Jeremy Anglin, a psycholinguist who teaches at a Canadian university, tried to find out what preschoolers know about words by the straightforward technique of interviewing them. He told them they were playing a "word game," and asked them questions about words such as *car, food,* and *dog.* As you will see from these sample interviews, his method was not an unqualified success. The first interview is with Peter, age 2 years, 8 months.

Interviewer:	Can you tell me what a car is, Peter?
Peter:	Okay. A car is a truck and a truck is a car (*laughs*).
Interviewer:	What does a car look like?
Peter:	A truck.
Interviewer:	A truck? What does a car do?
	(*Peter crawls on hands and knees away from table, demonstrating what a car does.*)
Interviewer:	Peter, Peter, come on back. . . . Can you tell us what a car does?
Peter:	Voom, voom. (*He demonstrates by acting like a car again.*)
Interviewer:	It vooms. What else does it do?
Peter:	Yeah.
Interviewer:	What else does it do?
Peter:	It goes and they run.
Interviewer:	Oh, that's very good, Peter. What does it look like?
Peter:	Voom, voom, voom (*demonstrating again*).
Interviewer:	Peter, what does a car look like?
Peter:	Voom, voom, voom. (*He acts like a car.*)
Interviewer:	Peter, OK, why don't you drive back here.
Peter:	No. (Anglin, 1977, p. 193)

The second interview is with a slightly older child—Danny, age 3 years, 4 months.

Interviewer:	The first word we're going to talk about is *dog.* Do you know what a dog is?
Danny:	No.
Interviewer:	Tell me, I bet you do. What's a dog?
Danny:	I don't know.
Interviewer:	Don't know?
Danny:	No, I don't know what, what, what a dog is.
Interviewer:	Do you know what it looks like?

Danny:	Mm. Mm. Brown.
Interviewer:	Brown?
Danny:	Yeah.
Interviewer:	Uh huh.
Danny:	And white.
Interviewer:	And white?
Danny:	Yeah.
Interviewer:	OK, can you tell me a little story about a dog?
Danny:	Yeah.
Interviewer:	OK, will you?
Danny:	(silence)
Interviewer:	When was the last time you saw a dog?
Danny:	I saw it at a playground.
Interviewer:	Uh huh, and what was it like?
Danny:	Brown and white.
Interviewer:	Um hum.
Danny:	And at the playground.
Interviewer:	And what was it doing?
Danny:	It was going away, and we named him Dutch. (p. 195)

Just in case you think girls can do much better at this "game," here's Sharon, age 4 years, 7 months.

Interviewer:	Tell me, what's a dog?
Sharon:	I don't know, it has soggy ears that go, that hang down.
Interviewer:	Mm hm, and?
Sharon:	Um, it chases cats.
Interviewer:	Mm hm.
Sharon:	Guess what?
Interviewer:	What?
Sharon:	My cat got bit by a dog.
Interviewer:	Really.
Sharon:	Yeah.
Interviewer:	Where did the dog bite him?
Sharon:	On both sides.
Interviewer:	Really.
Sharon:	He got bit on both sides.
Interviewer:	Aaa, that's too bad.
Sharon:	And his dog is the animal doctor.
Interviewer:	Uh huh. OK, do you know what kind of dogs there are?
Sharon:	Yeah, um, there are plain doggies, and let's see, there are, um, there are igloos doggies, and let's see, there are scouts doggies, um, there are, there are minuteman doggies.
Interviewer:	Minuteman doggies? What kinds of doggies do minutemen have?
Sharon:	They have ones that um that's, that can get, that go, that is that stay, they um, that go in, that get in the house, that that man, minuteman doggies are ones, minuteman has, has a doggie in the house.
Interviewer:	Uh huh. (p. 205)

Older preschoolers are better able to answer questions of this type than younger ones. Five-year-olds were able to tell Anglin that a dog is a kind of animal, and that food is "something what I eat." When asked to name some kinds of foods, one 5½-year-old girl was happy to do so:

> There's cinnamon crackers. There is meat. Yuck. Spinach. Yuck. There is noodles. There is chocolate bars. There is turkey. There is chicken. There is rice. There's Chinese food. There is eggplant. Yuck.   (p. 216)

The Names of Things.   Fortunately, Anglin used other techniques besides interviewing to find out more about preschoolers' understanding of words. His most successful method was to show preschoolers pictures, or groups of pictures, and ask questions like "What is this?" "What are they all?" "Is this a dog?" "Is this an animal?"

The results showed that underextensions were twice as common as overextensions, in the preschool period. For example, when shown a picture of a tree and asked, "Is this a plant?" most children said no—"That's a tree, not a plant" (Anglin, 1977, p. 113). Similarly, few children were willing to apply the word *animal* to a caterpillar or a praying mantis, and none would apply it to a picture of a woman.

But this is not too surprising, is it? Although most adults know that people are animals, few parents would be likely to point to a person (or to a picture of a person) and tell their child, "This is an animal." On the contrary, the parent is more likely to contrast the two groups: "Let's put the people here, the animals there." Children have no way of figuring out that people, caterpillars, and praying mantises are all "animals," unless someone happens to tell them that. Many acquire this knowledge for the first time when they learn to play the game "Twenty Questions."

As Anglin found, mothers do not always use the same words when they're naming things for their children as when they're naming them for adults. When asked to identify some pictures for their 2-year-olds, mothers used the word *dog* for a picture of a collie; they used the word *collie* when they were talking to another adult. Similarly, they labeled pictures *shoe, money,* and *bird* for their children; to an adult they called these pictures *sandal, dime,* and *pigeon.* And when a group of preschoolers were shown these same pictures, they used the same words that the mothers had used with the 2-year-olds: *dog, shoe, money, bird*—not *collie, sandal, dime,* or *pigeon.*

Note that it's not invariably the more general term (or the shorter one) that parents teach their children. For instance, mothers gave their 2-year-olds the words *pineapple, typewriter,* and *butterfly,* rather than *fruit, machine,* and *insect.*

What determines the kind of label that parents use and that children learn? Several psycholinguists have come to the same conclusion: the words children acquire are those that can be applied to things that have similar characteristics and that are used or responded to in similar ways (Anglin, 1977; Brown, 1958; Rosch and Mervis, 1978). A butterfly is admired, a cockroach is not. To call them both *insects* would be throwing away a lot of useful information. On the other hand, a collie and a chihuahua are both called *dogs,* even if they don't look very much alike, because one can behave in similar ways to both of them: they can both be patted, they may (or may not) come when you call them, they may (or may not) bite.

Recent work points to another factor that affects parental naming practices and the labels children use: whether a thing is a typical member of its general class, or an atypical member. If the thing is *not* a typical member of its class, and if a more specific name is readily available, parents use (and children learn) the more specific name. For example, one researcher noticed that mothers used the word *bird* when showing their preschoolers pictures of robins or bluejays; they used the word *turkey*—*not* the word *bird*—for a picture of a turkey. At another time these preschoolers were shown a picture of a turkey and asked (by the researcher) "Is this a bird?" Seventy percent said no (White, 1982).

The important point here is that preschoolers' use of names or labels does not necessarily tell us anything about their cognitive development or their understanding of subordinate and superordinate categories. What it mainly seems to reflect is the way adults label things when they're talking to children.

Environment and Language

We have mentioned several times in the course of this book that people talk differently to very young children than to older children or adults. To do this is so natural, so compelling, that even young children themselves "talk down" to still younger children. When we're speaking to a 2- or 3-year-old, we don't use long, complicated sentences and we don't talk about philosophy, politics, or plane geometry. Even the words we use are different from those we'd use with an adult.

The way a mother speaks to her child will be influenced by the child's level of verbal development.

Some Difficulties that Preschoolers Have with Language

To investigate children's understanding of the structure of English sentences, a psycholinguist (C. Chomsky, 1969) showed some children a doll with a blindfold over its eyes and asked them, "Is the doll easy to see or hard to see?" Most 5-year-olds, and many 6- and 7-year-olds, answered "hard to see." The psycholinguist concluded that preschoolers can't correctly interpret sentences of this type—sentences in which the noun at the beginning of the sentence (in this case, *doll*) does not serve its usual role as the performer of the specified action *(see)*. To understand "Is this doll easy to see?" one must convert it to the idea, "Is it easy (for me) to see this doll?"

A later experiment (Perry and Shwedel, 1979) suggested another possible source for the children's misunderstanding. The experimenters made a simple modification of the original situation: they showed the children *two* dolls—one with a blindfold over its eyes and one with a sheet of paper covering everything *but* its eyes. Then they asked the same question, referring to the blindfolded doll: "Is this doll easy to see or hard to see?" This time all the children 5½ or older answered correctly; so did about half of

the 4½- and 5-years-olds. The investigators concluded that older preschoolers *can* understand sentences of this type if they're not thrown off by the context. The blindfolded doll was a misleading clue that caused the children in the other experiment to interpret the question incorrectly. We have noted before that preschoolers are easily swayed by what they see.

Nevertheless, it is true that preschoolers have trouble with sentences in which the actor and the acted-upon are not in their usual order. This means that passive sentences—*the cow is kicked by the horse, the truck is bumped by the car*—are often misunderstood, especially by younger preschoolers. Three- and 4-year-olds tend to assume that the first thing mentioned *(cow, truck)* is the thing that did the acting *(kicked, bumped)*. In a similar way, a 3-year-old who responds appropriately to "After you clean your teeth, brush your hair," is likely to do these chores in the wrong order if told, "Clean your teeth after you brush your hair" (de Villiers and de Villiers, 1979).

Another source of confusion for young preschoolers concerns the words *same* and *different*. What happens if you show a young pre-

In a study of mothers' and children's conversations, one investigator (Moerk, 1975) examined the way that mothers' speech is adjusted to their children's level of verbal development. The mothers' speech was closely related to the children's MLUs—as a child's MLU increased, so did the length and complexity of his mother's utterances to him. The mother's utterances were somewhat longer and more complex than the child's, but still within his capacity to understand. By remaining always a little ahead of her child, the mother stimulated the child to make continual progress.

How important is this kind of stimulation? From the fact that a child cannot

schooler an object—say, a blue toothbrush—and ask her to give you something that's "different in some way"? Her possible choices are a blue toothbrush, a red toothbrush, and a white eggcup. Surprisingly enough, she is likely to give you the other blue toothbrush (Donaldson and Wales, 1970). She will also give you the blue toothbrush if you ask for something that's "the same in some way"!

Does this mean that preschoolers don't know the difference between *same* and *different*? An experiment by Princeton professor Sam Glucksberg and his colleagues shows that preschoolers *do* know. When they are given a red bead and asked for one of the "same color," they hand the experimenter a red bead; when asked for one of a "different color," they select a blue one. Then why do they err when asked for something that's "different in some way" from a blue toothbrush? Glucksberg and his associates believe that it's because preschoolers interpret a request for a "different" object to mean a request for *another* object:

> When someone holds up an object, for example, a pencil, and says, "Give me one that is different in some way," one may very well interpret that utterance as a request for another writing implement and not a request for a watermelon, a chair, or any other "different" object in the universe. (Glucksberg, Hay, and Danks, 1976, p. 738)

Finally, it is often said that preschoolers' speech is egocentric. Piaget noted that "conversation" between young children often consists of two monologues—neither child appears to pay much attention to what the other child says. What's worse, preschoolers who *are* trying to communicate are likely to assume that the listener possesses the same knowledge that *they* do. For instance, a preschooler trying to describe something to another child said it looked like "Mommy's hat," a description that conveyed little or no information to the second child (Glucksberg, Krauss, and Weisberg, 1966). Similarly, a 3-year-old might ask her father, "What's the man doing?" blithely assuming that her father will know *which* man she is talking about.

It's true that preschoolers' communications are egocentric in these ways. But the difference between preschoolers and adults is merely one of degree: it's not that preschoolers are egocentric and adults aren't, it's just that preschoolers are more so. Adults, too, sometimes have problems in communication. Some psycholinguists reported the following phone conversation between two adults, *A* and *B*.

A: Come here for dinner.
B: OK. . . . It'll just take me 10 minutes to walk to the parking structure, then I'll leave.
A: Oh, you have the car? I thought you were walking.
B: Yes, I have the car.
A: It's 2222 Regent Street.
B: *What's* 2222 Regent Street?
A: C's house. That's where I am.
B: Oh! I thought you were home. (Gumperz and Tannen, 1979, p. 309) ∎

become a competent language-user solely by sitting in front of a television set all day (see p. 247), it appears that verbal interactions with other people are essential. But one of the remarkable things about human language is the way it develops in virtually every child—in all but the most severely retarded or brain damaged—under an incredibly wide range of conditions. In the 2-year period between 12 months and 3 years, just about every child has acquired some sort of language. A totally deaf child who hears no spoken language, even if given no training in sign language, will develop some simple gestural language of his own in order to communicate with the people around him. As one husband-wife team of psycholinguists have put it,

> Normal human children all acquire their native tongue at a high level of proficiency by the age of four or five years. The learning is much the same for Greek and Chinese as it is for English or Hungarian; as true for dull children as for wiser ones; as true for children of kind and talkative mothers as for children of nasty or taciturn ones; and as true for children from intellectually primitive backgrounds as for those from more sophisticated ones. In sum, we find for language learning a uniform and early success with a complex task, despite differences in the learners, their motivations, their environments, and the languages they have to learn. . . .

> It seems that, for all its complexity, language is an irrepressible human activity. (Gleitman and Gleitman, 1981, p. 383)

There is, of course, a catch. Within an incredibly wide range, the environment has no effect on whether or not a child will develop language. But the environment will inevitably have an effect on what kind of language the child acquires and on how well he acquires it. A child cannot learn words he never hears. He *will* learn words he does hear, even if those words are ones his parents would prefer he *didn't* learn. He will learn from his playmates and acquaintances as well as from his parents: if his friends are native speakers of English he will learn to speak English without an accent, even if his parents cannot.

How important *is* the verbal environment provided by the parents? That question is surprisingly hard to answer. A classic study (Hess and Shipman, 1965) found that the quality of mothers' communications to their children (how informative, how encouraging, and so on) correlated highly with their children's verbal competence. But the problem in interpreting the results of this study—and those of many similar, later studies—is a familiar one: How much were the mother's communications affecting the child, and how much were the child's characteristics affecting the mother's communications? How much of the child's verbal competence reflected his verbal environment, and how much reflected genetic factors, inherited from a mother whose communications partly reflected her own genetic characteristics?

There is some evidence that differences in verbal environment affect children's verbal ability, but it's weak evidence. Firstborn children tend, on the average, to be slightly more verbal than later-borns, and parents talk more to firstborns than to later-borns (Jacobs and Moss, 1976). Similarly, single-born children tend to be more verbal than twins, and parents tend to talk more to single-borns than to twins (Conway and Lytton, 1975; Lytton, Conway, and Sauvé, 1977). The reason this is weak evidence is that many other aspects of the environment are presumed to differ for firstborns versus later-borns, and for single-borns versus twins. It's clear, however, that genetic factors can't be responsible for the small differences in verbal ability that were observed.

In conclusion, it is probable that the speed and quality of children's verbal development depends to some extent on their verbal environment—on their verbal interactions, or lack of verbal interactions, with the people around them. But as yet we know very little about the magnitude of such effects, or the way in which they operate.

summary

1. Preschoolers can think about the past and the future and can make plans. These abilities depend on mental representations.

2. Bruner distinguishes three kinds of mental representations: (1) **enactive representations,** based on motor responses; (2) **iconic representations,** based on mental images of things seen, heard, or otherwise sensed; and (3) **symbolic representations,** which are generally, in Bruner's view, words. Bruner believes that language is what makes thinking and reasoning possible; Piaget believes that language is an indication of cognitive advances, rather than a cause of them. Evidence suggests that language does help in the development of reasoning ability, but it doesn't seem to be essential.

3. Children tend to "think out loud," in what is called **private speech.** As they get older, this speech becomes more and more internal.

4. Piaget believes that thought in the **preoperational period** is qualitatively different from thought in older children and adults. He calls preschoolers' thought **egocentric,** by which he means that they can see a situation only from their own point of view. For example, preschoolers are unable to depict the doll's point of view in the three-mountains experiment; they tend to answer incorrectly when asked questions such as "Does Paul have a brother?" (asked of a boy who has a brother named Paul), or "Can I see you?" (asked of a child whose eyes are covered). There are alternative explanations for all these findings, based on preschoolers' difficulties with complex situations and on their lack of general knowledge. Newer evidence shows that preschoolers *can* adopt another point of view, if the situation is simple enough.

5. Another characteristic of preschoolers' thought, according to Piaget, is that they are unable to **decenter**—to consider more than one aspect of a situation at once. His famous experiment on the conservation of liquid volume is used to support that view. Preschoolers do seem to be very easily impressed by sensory evidence, but in the absence of misleading sensory evidence they are likely to respond correctly.

6. Preschoolers tend to reply incorrectly in Piaget's experiment on the conservation of number—they say that a spread-out row of jellybeans contains more candy than a closely spaced row. However, if the situation is simplified by using only small numbers of objects (no more than four or five), they can usually respond correctly.

7. Preschoolers generally respond incorrectly to **class-inclusion problems** of the form, "Are there more black horses or more horses in this barnyard?" Piaget attributes their difficulty to their inability to conceive of something as belonging simultaneously to two classes, but other investigators believe that the children simply misinterpret the question to mean, "Are there more black horses or more *white* horses?" This is a reasonable misinterpretation—even adults sometimes make it.

8. Preschoolers' thought is qualitatively different from the thought of younger children, because preschoolers are capable of thought based on symbolic representations. The case for a qualitative change between preschool thinking and later thinking is much less clear.

9. Preschoolers learn most things less readily than older children. This is due, at least in part, to the fact that they haven't yet learned how to learn. Learning how to learn comes under the heading of **metacognition**—knowledge and understanding about cognitive processes. The acquisition of such knowledge and understanding is undoubtedly an important aspect of cognitive development.

10. Individual differences in cognitive abilities are quite noticeable by the preschool period. IQ tests can be given to preschoolers; their IQ scores correlate reasonably well with IQ scores obtained in later childhood or adulthood. In contrast, IQ scores obtained much before the age of 2 have little or no predictive value. This is partly because infants and toddlers are very difficult to test, and partly because there's no way to measure in younger children most of the abilities that are measured in tests given to older children.

11. A child's IQ score tells us how well that child did on an IQ test; ''intelligence'' refers to the qualities that IQ tests are designed to measure. These qualities include the ability to learn quickly and forget slowly, to reason correctly with words and with numbers, to understand spoken and written words and sentences, to see relationships and differences between things, to think up insightful solutions to problems, and so on. Performance on an IQ test is not invariably a good measure of a child's intelligence. A test that measures what it's supposed to measure is said to have **validity.**

12. Binet and Simon devised the first successful IQ test. Their test was based on the concept of **mental age:** a bright 5-year-old might have a mental age of 6. IQ, or **intelligence quotient,** originally meant mental age divided by chronological age (with the decimal point dropped). Nowadays, IQ is defined entirely in terms of how well a child does compared with other children of the same age. Children who score at the mean have IQs of 100; 50 percent have IQs between 90 and 110; fewer than one in 200 have IQs of 140 or more.

13. The two IQ tests most often used with children are the Stanford-Binet and the Wechsler; both are administered individually. The Wechsler has one version for preschoolers and another version for school-age children; each of these tests contains verbal subtests (which yield a verbal IQ score) and nonverbal subtests (which yield a performance IQ score).

14. There is usually a significant correlation between children's scores on various IQ sub-tests—a child who does well on some kinds of test items tends to do well on others, too. There are two possible explanations for this finding: (1) that intelligence is made of separate abilities, but that whatever factors cause a child to be high in one ability cause him to be high in others as well; or (2) that the different tests are different ways to get at one underlying characteristic, which has been called g.

15. Childhood IQ scores correlate reasonably well with adult IQ scores, but that doesn't mean IQ can't change—some children show dramatic changes in IQ scores. Such changes may reflect actual increases or decreases in the rate of cognitive development; they may also result from **error of measurement.** Tests vary in their **reliability**—a reliable test is one that (theoretically, at least) would yield similar scores if the child took it twice within a period of a week or two. If the test is reliable, a child's obtained IQ score is likely to be fairly close to his ''true'' IQ.

16. Preschool enrichment programs such as Operation Head Start have produced sizable IQ gains in children, but these IQ gains are generally only temporary. Other programs, though, have produced lasting gains. These programs share two characteristics: (1) they start in infancy or toddlerhood; and (2) intellectual stimulation is given on a one-to-one (or nearly one-to-one) basis. It also appears that the person providing the stimulation should feel that he or she has the power to affect the child's cognitive development, should have some knowledge of how to do so, and, ideally, should care about the child.

17. The average 2-year-old has a vocabulary of 200 or 300 words and speaks mostly in two- or three-word sentences. In contrast, 6-year-olds have a productive vocabulary of around 2,500 words and a receptive vocabulary that may be as high as 14,000 words; they speak in complex sentences and show a fairly sophisticated grasp of the grammar of their language.

18. A child who uses words such as *mine, held, went,* and *feet* may later say *mines, holded, goed,* and *feets.* Although this appears to be backwards progress, it shows that the child has worked out some of the general rules of the English language—a remarkable achievement, especially considering how many exceptions there are. Evidence from the "wug" experiment shows that children between the ages of 4 and 7 know how to form plurals, present progressives, and past tenses.

19. Prepositions such as *in* and *on,* and suffixes such as *-ing* and *-ed,* are **grammatical morphemes.** Children's acquisition of the various grammatical morphemes follows a fairly orderly sequence, which seems to depend on the complexity of the rules governing the use of these morphemes, rather than on their frequency in adult speech. Thus, children who speak other languages don't necessarily acquire morphemes in the same order as English-speaking children.

20. Children at first express negative ideas by putting *no* or *not* in front of a word or phrase. Later, negative words appear within the sentence. Full and correct use of negatives takes a long time to achieve—even school-age children sometimes make errors.

21. The first questions may be recognizable as such only by the child's intonation; some *wh-* words begin to be used at about the same time. Young preschoolers are likely to have trouble with the word order in questions and with putting the verb and the auxiliary into the proper tenses. **Tag questions** are particularly difficult; nevertheless, most children understand the basic principles of tag questions by the time they enter first grade.

22. It's not always easy to tell what children mean when they use a particular word. Interviewing them on that topic produces results that may be amusing but are often not very informative.

23. In toddlerhood, **overextensions** of words are common; these decline in frequency as the child gets older. In the preschool period, **underextensions** are twice as common as overextensions; children of this age are unwilling to call a tree *a plant,* or a person *an animal.* But preschoolers' use of words does not necessarily tell us anything about their cognitive development—it may simply reflect the way adults label things when they're talking to young children. Mothers do not always use the same words when they're naming things for preschoolers as when they're talking to adults: with preschoolers they tend to use words that can be applied to a class of things that are used or responded to in similar ways, and to use that term only for typical members of the class.

24. Mothers adjust the level of their speech to their children's level of verbal development, but their utterances are longer and more complex than the child's.

25. Language develops in virtually every child—all but the most severely retarded or brain-damaged—under an incredibly wide range of environmental conditions. The speed and quality of children's verbal development almost certainly depends, at least to some extent, on their verbal environments. At present, however, we know very little about the magnitude of such effects or the way in which they operate.

26. Young children have difficulty with sentences such as "Clean your teeth after you brush your hair," "Give me the one that's different in some way," and "Is the doll easy to see or hard to see?" These difficulties arise from a variety of sources, not all of which are linguistic in nature.

27. As Piaget noted, preschoolers' speech is often egocentric—for example, they may assume that the listener possesses the same knowledge that they do. But making that assumption is not unique to preschoolers—even adults do it occasionally.

Chapter Eleven

THE SCHOOL-AGE CHILD: PHYSICAL AND MENTAL DEVELOPMENT

Eleven

We call the years from 6 to 12 the years of **middle childhood.** We could just as well call them the *elementary school years,* because the years from 6 to 12 correspond fairly closely to the school grades first through sixth in the U.S.

Although these are important years in a child's life, they are relatively calm ones. Behind us is the period of rapid physical growth of infancy and toddlerhood; the period of rapid physical growth of early adolescence is still to come. The dramatic improvements in motor abilities and in language use and understanding are also in the past. But some very crucial changes occur during middle childhood. There is a striking increase in intellectual competence—in the child's ability to make use of that superb piece of biological engineering, the human brain. There is a similar increase in the fund of knowledge that the brain holds. And there is a noteworthy change in the child's relationships with others. When children enter middle childhood, they are dependent on their parents and on other adults—not just for food and shelter, but also for emotional support and companionship. By the end of middle childhood, adults have become much less central in their lives. Their social and emotional needs are filled to a large extent (though, in most cases, not entirely) by their friends and agemates—their **peer group.**

Children enter middle childhood looking and acting much more similar to one another than they do when they leave it. Differences in size, shape, facial features, intellectual ability, talents and inclinations, and so on, are not as evident in the early school years as in the later ones. It is really in middle childhood, more than at any time since birth, that the child becomes a unique individual.

PHYSICAL CHANGES AND PERCEPTUAL-MOTOR SKILLS

Adam is 9 years old; he's in the fourth grade. He is 49 inches (125 cm) tall and weighs 50 pounds (23 kg)—well below the means for his age in both height and weight. There's a child in his class—a girl, as it happens—who's almost 8 inches (20 cm) taller than he. There's also a child—his best friend, Charlie—who's a little shorter than Adam. Charlie will be short all his life; both of his parents are small people. But Adam is destined to become an average-sized man: he is simply maturing at a slightly slower rate than most of the other boys in his class. A physician could determine this by taking an X-ray of Adam's bones: Adam's "bone age" is only 7½, and his height is average for a boy with a bone age of 7½. In adolescence, most of his male classmates will start to look and sound like young men while Adam will still look like a boy; at that point he will appear even shorter (compared to his agemates) than he does now. But his classmates will also *stop* growing before Adam does, and he will eventually catch up with many of them in height (and, of course, in other ways as well). Right now, though, his slower growth means that he can't run as fast or throw a ball as far as most of the boys in his class. That's one of the reasons that Charlie is his best friend—Adam doesn't feel at such a disadvantage when he's with Charlie.

Although in physical attributes Adam is young for his age, he does not look like a preschooler. He is taller and leaner—less fat, more muscle. His proportions are more like those of an adult: his legs are longer, relative to his body, than those of a younger child. His face and head have also changed. The brain and skull do most of their growing in the first few years after conception; later, the lower part of the face fills out. The top-heavy look that made Adam look so appealing as a baby (see p. 167) has greatly diminished. The pads of fat that used to round out his cheeks have also decreased; as a result, his nose now looks more prominent. This is not to imply that Adam is unattractive—on the contrary, he is a nice-looking boy. But he no longer looks appealing in a babyish way. The final blow to his baby cuteness came when his first set of front teeth fell out. The permanent teeth that replaced them seem much too big for his face. His smile, which had formerly revealed an even row of perfect baby teeth, now shows a pair of large incisors with serrated edges, slightly askew. (A few years from now, Adam's teeth will no

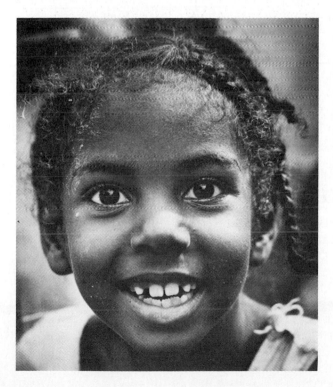

The loss of the front baby teeth, and their replacement by the much larger permanent teeth, makes a noticeable change in the child's appearance. This girl's charming smile reveals two new permanent teeth on top and four on the bottom.

longer look too big for his face, and their sawtooth edges will have worn off. Whether they will straighten up is another matter; Adam may need braces when he is older.)

School-age children always seem to be losing teeth. The first two (the bottom front teeth) usually fall out around age 6; the last of the 20 baby teeth (the canines, or "eye teeth") fall out around age 12. Middle childhood is the period that keeps the Tooth Fairy busy!

In the past, middle childhood was also the period that kept the doctor busy. So many diseases used to be prevalent at this age: measles, mumps, chicken pox, rubella, polio, rheumatic fever, scarlet fever, diptheria, whooping cough, and chronic ear and mastoid infections. Many of these diseases were potentially life-threatening—even measles, which occasionally leads to a dangerous brain infection called *encephalitis*. But all of these diseases except chicken pox are now either preventable (through innoculations) or treatable. Childhood is a healthier time today than it was when your parents were growing up; it is far healthier than it was in your grandparents' time. At present, the most frequent threat to a child's life is from accidents, particularly car accidents. The most frequent threat to a child's health is the common cold.

Size, Strength, and Athletic Ability

Growth in middle childhood is relatively slow: less than 2½ inches (6.3 cm) and 8 pounds (3.6 kg) a year. In contrast, growth during the first year of life averages 10 inches (25 cm) and 14 pounds (6.4 kg). During the growth spurt of early adolescence, a boy might add as much as 5 or 6 inches (12 to 15 cm) to his height in a year.

Because the gain in weight consists more of muscle than of fat, strength increases considerably during middle childhood. The average 10-year-old boy can throw a ball twice as far as the average 7-year-old (Keogh, 1973). Muscle development is also partly responsible for the disappearance of the bulging stomach that characterized the preschooler. The other reason for the school-age child's flatter contour is the fact that his larger trunk provides more room for the internal organs.

Sex Differences. Sex differences in height and weight at age 6 are negligible. The average 6-year-old boy is slightly taller and heavier than the average 6-year-old girl. But by the end of middle childhood, that will have changed. Girls begin their adolescent growth spurt a full two years earlier, on the average, than boys. Thus, by age 11 or 12, the average girl is taller and heavier than the average boy—an awkward situation in some ways, but a temporary one.

We said in Chapter 5 that baby girls are physically more mature than baby boys. This difference, which amounted to about five weeks at birth, becomes greater all through childhood. The average 12-year-old girl is two years closer to physical maturity than the average 12-year-old boy. And yet, despite this seeming advantage, girls persistently lag behind boys in most measures of physical ability and physical strength. Take running speed, for example. Between 6 and 11 years of age, running speed increases by approximately 1 foot (30 cm) per second; but all through this period, boys run about ⅓ foot per second faster than girls. After age 11 the difference becomes even greater, because boys' performance continues to improve, whereas girls' levels off or even declines.

Similar results are found with throwing distance. Boys throw 5 feet (1½ m) farther than girls at age 5, and 30 feet (9 m) farther at age 11. Boys also jump higher and farther than girls, kick a ball farther, and are better at catching (Herkowitz, 1978).

What are the reasons for these differences in athletic ability? One obvious one is amount of practice: boys in our culture spend more time throwing and catching balls, running and jumping, than girls do. From the preschool period on, boys spend more time in active outdoor play than girls (Harper and Sanders, 1978). The one athletic skill in which girls tend to beat boys is hopping,

School-age girls are better at hopping than school-age boys. The probable reason is that girls tend to practice this activity more than boys do.

and hopping is an activity that girls are likely to practice more than boys. School-age girls can hop a given distance slightly faster than school-age boys (Herkowitz, 1978).

Another obvious source of the difference in athletic ability is the physical difference between the sexes. At every age, boys' bodies have a higher proportion of muscle and a lower proportion of fat than girls'; the difference increases as they get older. Other differences also increase with age: boys have longer legs, slimmer hips, and wider shoulders. Boys' hearts are larger; their circulatory systems are more efficient (Tanner, 1978).

It may seem that these are reasons enough to account for the observed differences in athletic ability. But there is a third possible source of these differences: in mixed-sex situations, girls seem to be unwilling to compete with boys. A recent study (Weisfeld, Weisfeld, and Callaghan, 1982) involved 12-year-old girls and boys who were playing dodge ball, a game that involves (among other things) competition for the possession of the ball. Since these children had played the game only in school, girls and boys had had equal experience with it; however, the boys had probably had more practice with ball games in general.

The investigators divided the children into four groups: high-skill and low-skill girls, and high-skill and low-skill boys. They reported that although the boys were in general better at the game than the girls, the high-skill girls were noticeably better at it than the low-skill boys—that is, they were better at it when they were playing against other girls. But in mixed-sex games the boys always won—even when low-skill boys played against high-skill girls, and even though the girls were taller and heavier than the boys. These results were found in two very different cultural groups: a group of middle-class black children in Chicago, and a group of Hopi Indian children from a reservation in Arizona. (Hopi Indian culture tends to give equal importance to males and females.)

Why did these highly skilled girls lose? Analysis of movie films of the games made the answer clear: most of the girls were much less competitive when they were playing with boys than when they were playing against other girls. The girls stood in an alert, ready-to-go posture when they were playing against other girls. Playing against boys, the Hopi girls tended to stand with their legs crossed, their arms folded. The black girls stopped paying attention to the game when boys were present—they talked to each other, teased the other players, or ate potato chips. Yet neither group of girls were aware of these striking changes in their behavior. In fact, as the investigators discovered in a second study, the girls' explanation for why the boys always won was that the boys "cheated." But the boys *hadn't* cheated (Weisfeld, Weisfeld, and Callaghan, 1982).

We should mention that similar results have been found in other age groups (especially adolescents) and in a variety of situations. Many—though not all—females seem to be unwilling to compete against males. They compete more vigorously against other females. And, in general, they are unaware of this tendency.

Catching a ball requires the rapid and accurate coordination of the body's movements with information gained through vision.

Perceptual-Motor Abilities

Running, jumping, and hopping are motor skills that involve only the body itself and the ground beneath it. But many of the skills that we expect children to acquire involve more than that. Catching a ball, for instance, is a complex perceptual-motor task. The ball catcher must first be able to perceive, through the sense of vision, the movements of the thrower and the motion of the ball in flight. This information is then used to predict where the ball will end up and exactly when it will get there. This prediction, in turn, must be used to direct the movements of the catcher's body and hands, so they are in the right position at the right time. And all these complicated calculations must be made in the proverbial twinkling of an eye. No wonder that young children have trouble with catching, unless the ball is pretty much thrown into their waiting hands! If the ball goes too high or too low, too far to the right or left, a 6-year-old is likely to miss it. It's not that she doesn't see where the ball is or how fast it's moving—her visual perception is fine. But

PROBLEMS IN DEVELOPMENT

Bed-Wetting

Some children, for a variety of reasons, never get very good at catching balls, or riding two-wheelers, or roller-skating. Such children generally manage to get through childhood with their self-respect intact. After all, they can tell themselves, catching balls isn't *that* important. Lots of grownups never catch balls at all.

Children who wet their beds at night are less fortunate. Nearly every morning brings them renewed proof of their inability to do something that most 4-year-olds can do. They *know* a dry bed is important: people who wet beds can't sleep over at friends' houses or have friends sleep over at theirs, they can't go to sleep-away camp, and they *certainly* can't get married!

Who wets the bed? Bed-wetting is more than twice as common among boys as among girls. The percentage of children who cannot retain their urine at night declines with age: it is around 15 percent at age 6 and around 3 percent at age 14 (Azrin and Thienes, 1978).

The cause of bed-wetting, or **enuresis**, has always been a subject of controversy. Emotional factors such as stress and anxiety have been blamed. So have physical factors, such as too small a bladder. Behaviorists feel that the child's reinforcement history is at fault. Geneticists can point to the part that heredity plays: about 50 percent of bed-wetters have close relatives who were also bed-wetters. Some authorities claim that bed-wetting is due to the simple fact that the child sleeps too soundly. There *is* some evidence that bed-wetters sleep more deeply than other children (Baller, 1975), but this is not necessarily an explanation. The question still remains, *Why* do these children sleep more deeply than other children?

Even the role of toilet training practices is unclear. Some studies find a connection between bed-wetting and early, strict toilet training (Bindelglas, Dee, and Enos, 1968). Others find *fewer* bed-wetters among children whose mothers began toilet training them before they were 6 months old (Douglas and Blomfield, 1967).

The role of emotional factors is of particular concern to child psychologists. Some regard bed-wetting as a symptom of emotional disturbance. The fact that bed-wetters tend to have other behavioral problems (Rutter, Yule, and Graham, 1973) seems to provide support for this view. But psychologists generally see these children only after they have been wetting the bed for several years. A child who wets the bed lives in constant fear that his friends at school will find out about his problem. His parents, no matter how patient they are, must occasionally reveal their feelings about the child's bed-wetting—about the extra work it causes them, about the persistent smell it produces. Bed-wetting, then, may be a *cause* of the child's other problems, rather than a result of them. In line with this view, it has been observed that curing

she can't predict the ball's destination and arrival time quickly or accurately enough, and she can't get into the right position fast enough (Kay, 1970).

There is a sizable increase in all these skills during middle childhood. An experiment done by a research team in Canada tested children's ability to anticipate when a moving stimulus will reach its destination, and to respond with speed and accuracy (Bard, Fleury, Carrière, and Bellec, 1981). The children in this study ranged in age from 6 to 11. The "moving" stimulus cona child of bed-wetting generally produces an improvement in other aspects of the child's life as well. As one psychologist puts it,

> The important fact is that with the correction of the bed-wetting habit, most, if not all, of the symptoms of emotional disturbance tend, in a high majority of cases, to disappear. (Baller, 1975, pp. 9–10)

How, then, can bed-wetting be cured? The single method that has proven to be by far the most successful is the use of the **bell-and-pad device** (Mowrer and Mowrer, 1938). This device, which consists of a pair of copper screens separated by an absorbent pad, is put in the child's bed before he goes to sleep. If he urinates during the night the urine instantly soaks into the absorbent pad and closes an electrical circuit, activating a loud alarm that awakens him. The idea is based on classical conditioning (see Chapter 3): an association is made between urinating and waking up. Eventually, it is hoped, the child will wake up *before* he starts to urinate, rather than afterwards.

The fact is that it works. A summary of studies using the bell-and-pad method shows that 75 percent of the children stopped bed-wetting during the course of treatment. Unfortunately, a good many of these children—about 40 percent of the ones who had stopped wetting—have a relapse within 6 months (Doleys, 1977). However, if the bell-and-pad device is used again, those children become dry more quickly the second time, and further relapses are far less common.

For a "cured" bed-wetter, a relapse after a period of dryness can be shattering. Thus, efforts have been made to prevent relapses. One method that's been used with some success is called **overlearning.** It's based on the idea that the strength of the conditioning depends on how many times the child experiences the connection between urinating and hearing the alarm go off. If he becomes dry at night after setting off the alarm only a few times, then there are only a few occasions for the conditioning to occur. So in overlearning, the child, after he has had a certain number of dry nights, is asked to drink a quantity of fluid before he goes to bed. If this procedure causes him to wet the bed again, then he experiences more occasions on which urination sets off the alarm. Better still, he may not start to wet again but instead wake up and go to the bathroom, thereby strengthening that habit. Use of the overlearning procedure has produced significant decreases in the number of relapses (Young and Morgan, 1972).

Another technique that has been used to prevent relapses is called **retention control training** (Kimmel and Kimmel, 1970; Fielding, 1980). The child is asked to postpone urinating during the daytime, first by a few minutes and then by longer and longer periods. The idea is to increase the capacity of the bladder and to strengthen the muscle that is used in holding back urination.

Very good results have been found when all three methods—bell-and-pad, overlearning, and retention control training—have been used at once. A study that employed all three techniques led to dry beds for 81 percent of the children who participated. A year later, only a quarter of these children had had relapses (Houts, Liebert, and Padawer, 1983). ∎

---

sisted of a stationary row of lights. The lights flashed on and off in sequence, producing an illusion of movement—*apparent movement,* psychologists call it. The children's task was to anticipate when this "moving light" would reach a target at the end of the row of lights. In one test they responded simply by pushing a button. In a second test the response was more complex and involved more of the body: they had to throw a ball so that it would hit the target at the same time as the light.

The results showed that skill at both tasks improved steadily with age. In the button-pressing task, 6-year-olds were off in their timing by twice as much, on the average, as 11-year-olds. In the throwing task, too, the older children were far more accurate in their timing than the younger ones. Throwing accuracy also improved steadily with age. And finally, the boys did better than the girls in every respect.

THE TRANSITION TO OPERATIONAL THOUGHT

Between the ages of 5 and 7 some important advances occur in cognitive development. It is no coincidence that these advances take place at just around the age when children begin their formal education: over the generations, educators have found that this is a good age to begin schooling. Progress that has already occurred makes the 6-year-old ready for school; what he or she learns in school leads to further progress. In countries where not all children go to school, the schooled children are found to be more advanced in cognitive development than the unschooled ones (Greenfield, 1966). It's not that the schooled children are simply more verbal or better at arithmetic. They're also ahead in acquiring concepts such as the conservation of liquid volume.

The Period of Concrete Operations

In the Piagetian view, the preoperational period gives way to the period of concrete operations somewhere around the age of 7. The transition is gradual, rather than sudden. With regard to the concept of conservation, for instance, the child does not wake up one morning thinking, "Aha, now I see it! How could I have been so foolish!"

Instead, the changeover is less dramatic. A child who at 5 says with assurance that the tall skinny glass holds more juice than the short fat one, at 6 or 7 is no longer so sure. She looks back and forth from one glass to the other, perhaps noticing first the difference in height, then the difference in diameter. By age 8 this child has become certain again: "They're just the same. All you did was pour the juice from one glass to the other."

It's also the case that different kinds of conservation appear at different ages. Piaget and his colleague Bärbel Inhelder showed children two balls of clay, identical in size. Then they changed the shape of one of the balls— rolled it into a sausage, or flattened it into a pancake. By age 8, most children realized that the amount of clay in the two pieces is still the same, "because it's the same stuff," or "because nothing has been taken away or added" (Piaget and Inhelder, 1977, p. 355). But it isn't until they're 9 or 10 that children realize that the two pieces of clay still *weigh* the same. Still later comes the understanding that the *volume* remains the same, too—that the pieces of clay will still displace the same amount of liquid when they're dropped into half-filled glasses of water.

The ability to decenter—to consider more than one aspect of a situation at once—is not something that children either have or don't have. We have seen (Chapter 10) that preschoolers have difficulty decentering: they can do it only if the situation is a very simple and familiar one. With increasing maturity the child becomes better at decentering. The school-age child can decenter with increasingly greater ease and in a growing variety of contexts. She can notice, for instance, that although the level of liquid in one glass is higher, the other glass is wider.

A similar improvement occurs in children's ability to consider things that occur over a period of time. Preschool children tend to focus primarily on the present, rather than on what happened in the past or what might happen in the future. As they get older, though, they become better able to take the past and the future into account (Flavell, 1977). The preschooler sees the juice in the two glasses and compares them directly. The school-age child notes that "all you did is pour it," a reference to the past. She may also anticipate the future: "If you pour it back into the other glass it will be the same again."

With their ability to decenter and to consider changes that occur over time, school-age children are not as likely as younger children to be misled by appearances. They understand that things are not always what they seem to be at first glance. Their judgments are based not just on what they *perceive,* but also on what they *know* (Flavell, 1977). Most school-age children understand the difference, for example, between "looks bigger" and "really is bigger." Most preschoolers do not.

Can We Speed Up Cognitive Development?   In 1967, Jean Piaget gave some lectures in the United States. In one of these lectures, he raised what has become known as "the American question":

> If we accept the fact that there are stages of development, another question arises which I call "the American question," and I am asked it every time I come here. If there are stages that children reach at given norms of age, can we accelerate the stages? Do we have to go through each one of these stages, or can't we speed it up a bit? (Quoted in Elkind, 1973, p. 172)

Many studies have been carried out to answer this question. The results have been quite variable. Consider, for example, the many attempts that have been made to teach the principles of conservation to children who have not yet acquired them on their own. Some of these attempts have been unsuccessful: few or none of the "trained" children have shown new understanding of the concept of conservation. Other attempts have been partially successful: children have learned to conserve certain qualities such as number, but the training hasn't **generalized**—they show no advances in related things, such as conserving liquid volume. Also, the results of the training often seem to be temporary. A few weeks later the children have gone back to saying the same things they said before the training.

Still other attempts, however, have been notably successful. A good example is a study by Dorothy Field, of the University of California at Berkeley. The children in Field's study were only 3- and 4-year-olds. They were trained on two types of conservation tasks: number (the number of candies stays the same, whether they're strung out in a long line or all bunched together), and length (if two sticks are the same length when they're right next to each other, they're *still* the same length when one is moved ahead of the other). During training the children heard explanations of conservation a total of 60 times over three different sessions. Three kinds of explanation were given. The first was **identity,** which stresses that these are the same candies or the same sticks we started out with: ''No matter where you put them, the number of candies is just the same.'' The second explanation was **reversibility,** which points out that what we did to these objects can be *un*done, and then they will be the same as before: ''Look: we just have to put the sticks back together again to see that they're [still] the same length.'' The third explanation was **compensation,** which draws the child's attention to the fact that a change in one aspect of the stimulus is balanced by a change in another: ''Yes, this stick does go farther in this direction, but look here: at the other end the other stick is going farther, so they balance each other'' (Field, 1981, p. 328).

After training, these children were tested not only on length and number conservation, but on other conservation tasks as well—weight and liquid volume, for example. The results were remarkable. Of the 39 children who were at least 4 years old at the time of testing, only six gave no conservation responses after training. Sixteen showed understanding of conservation of length, number, or both. Seventeen gave conservation responses not only for the qualities they had been trained on, but for other qualities as well—liquid volume, for instance. And the majority of these children *still* gave conservation responses when they were tested again five months later!

Age does make a difference, though. The training was much less successful with 3-year-olds. Fewer of them learned to conserve number and length, and hardly any of them generalized their training to other qualities. Five months later, most of them had forgotten what little they had learned. Clearly, there's a limit to how much acceleration is possible.

We've been talking about speeding up children's transition into the period of concrete operations. It's also possible to speed up their transition *out* of this period, into the period of formal operations. Formal operational thought, according to Piaget, is necessary for dealing with tasks such as the pendulum problem (see p. 98). In one study (Siegler, Liebert, and Liebert, 1973), a group of 10- and 11-year-olds were asked to find out what determines the length of time it takes for a pendulum to complete its swing. Fewer than 10 percent of these children succeeded. A second group of 10- and 11-year-olds were given the same problem, but first they went through an instructional procedure that trained them in the use of scientific methods. About 70 percent of these children solved the pendulum problem.

Piaget himself admits that acceleration is possible, just as he had previously acknowledged that the speed of children's cognitive development will be affected by their intelligence and also by their social and cultural environments. It's the *order* of the stages that Piaget believes is universal, and the fact that stages can't be skipped entirely (Piaget and Inhelder, 1969).

Whether or not it's a good idea to speed up cognitive development is another question—one that is still unanswered. Many American psychologists seem to feel that "the sooner the better." But Piaget is skeptical. He points out that human babies take nine months or more to develop the first four stages of object permanence, whereas kittens do it in three months.

> Is this an advantage or isn't it? We can certainly see our answer in one sense. The kitten is not going to go much further. The child has taken longer, but he is capable of going further so it seems to me that the nine months were not for nothing. . . . It is probably possible to accelerate, but maximal acceleration is not desirable. There seems to be an optimal time. What this optimal time is will surely depend upon each individual and on the subject matter. We still need a great deal of research to know what the optimal time would be. (Quoted in Elkind, 1973, p. 172)

Advances in Knowledge and Understanding

Along with the transition to operational thought comes a better understanding of various aspects of the world. Like the concept of conservation, such understanding doesn't occur overnight. Piaget and his colleagues interviewed children of all ages to find out their viewpoints on a number of questions and to determine how these viewpoints changed as the children matured.

Many 5- and 6-year-olds, Piaget found, believe that anything that moves (such as a river or a bicycle), or anything that does something (such as a stove that cooks dinner or a gun that shoots) is alive. This belief is called **animism,** and it's very common in the preschool period. The belief wanes gradually, rather than all at once: 8- or 9-year-olds might still claim that things like fires and rivers are alive. By the end of middle childhood, though, most children will state that only plants and animals are alive (Piaget, 1929).

Another belief that is popular in the preschool years and is gradually outgrown is the belief that certain things are "real." (Piaget calls this kind of thinking "realism," but that's a rather misleading term for it.) Young children often think, for instance, that something's name is as much a part of it as its shape or color. As one developmental psychologist put it,

> The child at this point is like the old gentleman who, when asked why noodles are called noodles, replied that "they are white like noodles, soft like noodles and taste like noodles so we call them noodles." (Elkind, 1973, p. 169)

A similar kind of reality is attributed to dreams. Many preschoolers think that a dream is actually there in the room so that anyone can see it. By age 7 or 8 most children realize that another person can't see their dreams, but they still localize the dream as being "in the room." It isn't until they're 9 or 10 that they localize dreams "in the head" (Piaget, 1929).

"Where Do Babies Come From?"

At the age of 3 years, 3 months, Piaget's daughter Jacqueline asked her father "her first question about birth." Referring to her sister Lucienne, she asked, "Daddy, where did you find the little baby in a cradle?" "My reply," says Piaget (1962, p. 246), "was simply that mummy and daddy had given her a little sister." (Remember that this happened back in 1928.)

Two years later Jacqueline still didn't know where babies come from, and her parents gave her a pair of guinea pigs "to help her discover the true solution." "Where do little guinea pigs come from?" she asked her father. Piaget continued to beat around the bush. "What do you think?" he asked. "From a factory," the child replied (p. 247).

Modern parents are unlikely to be as close-mouthed on the subject as parents were in the 1920s. Nevertheless, notions such as Jacqueline's, that babies are made in factories, are still to be found in preschoolers today. Piaget calls this kind of thinking **artificialism.** Preoperational explanations of natural phenomena often contain artificialisms. For example, many preschoolers think that lakes and rivers were dug out by hand and supplied with water from hoses or watering cans, and perhaps even that the sun and the moon are products of human construction.

A recent cross-sectional study examined present-day children's ideas about the origins of babies. Two psychologists from Australia, Ronald and Juliette Goldman (1982), interviewed 838 children from Australia, England, Sweden, and North America (the United States and Canada), to determine their views on this question. The children ranged in age from 5 to 15. The Goldmans found that, despite the fact that modern parents are considerably more informative than Piaget and his contemporaries, an understanding about conception and birth develops slowly. Moreover, it develops in much the way that Pi-

aget would have predicted, starting with preoperational explanations in the preschool period and progressing to more sophisticated explanations later on.

To be specific, the 5- to 7-year-olds in the Goldmans' sample said things like this in answer to the question, "How are babies made?":

A 5-year-old North American girl: I don't know, I never saw. Jesus makes them in a factory.

A 7-year-old Australian boy: The father does it. He buys the seed from the seed shop and puts it into the mummy.

A 7-year-old English boy: By eating good food. She swallows it and it grows into a baby, if it's good food. (Goldman and Goldman, 1982, p. 494)

In the 9- to 11-year-old period, the explanations have grown a little more complicated. Most of the children have by now figured out that both a mother and a father are essential, but they're not sure exactly *why* they're essential. A third party, the doctor, is also thought to be very important.

An 11-year-old North American boy: The baby just grows from the food mother eats. Father warms her tummy in bed and it grows.

A 9-year-old North American boy: When the lady likes a man they get an egg in their stomach, and then it goes into a baby. He has to be by her side to help her.

A 9-year-old English girl: The doctor gives an injection and that starts it to grow. . . . it's a kind of tube that grows and grows until it becomes a baby. (p. 494)

In middle childhood, many children think that a miniature baby is present in the egg or,

Although modern parents give their children plenty of information about reproduction and birth, it takes most children several years to reach a full understanding of these facts.

alternatively, in the sperm (see the medieval notion of *preformationism*, p. 83):

> *A 7-year-old English boy:* Sperm hits the egg and sets it off. The baby's in the egg.

> *An 11-year-old English girl:* By an egg of the man. It turns into a baby inside the mother's stomach. (p. 495)

Although nowadays most children hear the basic facts at least by middle childhood, they seldom understand them completely at this stage. It's generally not until they've progressed to the period of formal operations (at around age 12) that they get the idea of two things—an egg and a sperm—uniting to form one thing, the beginning of a baby.

> *A 13-year-old English girl:* When the man and woman have sex, the sperm from his penis goes into the vagina and fertilizes the egg. It goes inside and joins it. It forms a cell which then goes into two, then four, then eight, and so on and forms a baby. (p. 495)

It would be a mistake to presume that chil-dren's understanding of sex and babies depends solely on their level of cognitive development—that simply giving them the information doesn't work until they're ready for it. It *is* possible to advance a child's understanding if the information is given in a suitable form. The Goldmans found that, in middle childhood, the Swedish children were about 2 years ahead of the English-speaking children in their understanding of reproduction. Swedish children receive sex education in public school, starting at age 8. Their society tends to be frank and open on the subject of sex. (Only 5 percent of Swedish parents refused to give the Goldmans permission to interview their children. The refusal rate averaged 20 percent in the other countries.)

Piaget wouldn't have been surprised to hear that education can hasten understanding. His daughter Jacqueline didn't figure out until she was 5½ that baby guinea pigs came out of the mother's "tummy." But Lucienne, Piaget's second daughter, achieved this level of sophistication a full two years earlier. It wasn't because her father had become any more communicative, though. It was because Jacqueline told her. ■

DEVELOPMENT OF THE HIGHER MENTAL PROCESSES

As children grow older they become more skilled in most cognitive tasks. One reason for this is their growing facility with language. Words and symbols play an increasingly greater role in their mental processes. In the terms of cognitive psychologist Jerome Bruner, school-age children have entered the *symbolic* mode of representational thought. Bruner (1964, 1966) believes that the transition between the iconic mode and the symbolic mode (see p. 320) occurs around age 7.

To illustrate this transition, Bruner and Kenney (1966) devised a special test. They placed a set of nine plastic glasses in a three-by-three arrangement, as shown in Figure 11–1. Each glass differed from the others in shape—one was short and narrow, one was tall and narrow, one was medium-tall and wide, and so on. The glasses were arranged on a board in such a way that in one direction they varied in height (from tall to short) and in the other direction they varied in width.

A child was shown this display and asked to study it. Then the glasses were scrambled and the child was asked to reproduce the original display—to set them up in the way they had been at first. Next, the glasses were scrambled again and a new task was given. The glass that had formerly been in the lower left corner of the board (the shortest and thinnest glass) was put in the lower *right* corner, and the child was asked to set up the other glasses around that glass in the same arrangement as before. This time, though, the display would have to be **transposed**—either rotated around or converted into its mirror image.

The experimenters tested children from 3 to 7 years of age. As Figure 11–2 shows, 3-year-olds couldn't do either task, and 4-year-olds weren't much better. But the interesting results were for the 5- and 6-year-olds. Over 60 percent of them were able to reproduce the original display, but few of them were able to transpose it. Bruner feels that these children performed the reproduction task by means of the iconic mode—in other words, with visual imagery. They had a visual image of the original arrangement and they used that image to reproduce it. But they weren't able to transpose the arrangement, because the glass in the lower right hand corner of the board didn't

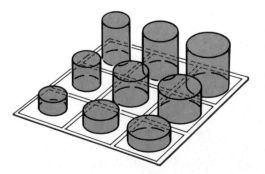

figure 11-1

The display used in the experiment described in the text (Bruner and Kenney, 1966). Children were asked either to reproduce this arrangement or to transpose it—to reproduce it in a rotated or mirror-image orientation.

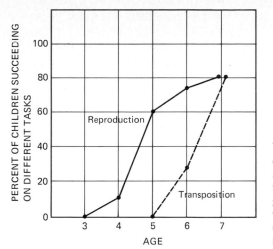

figure 11-2

The results of the transposition experiment. Three-year-olds were able neither to reproduce nor to transpose the arrangement of glasses shown in Figure 11-1; 7-year-olds could do both. Five- and 6-year-olds could reproduce it but not transpose it.

correspond to their visual image—they hadn't ever seen the glasses in the transposed arrangement.

Most of the 7-year-olds, on the other hand, were able to do both tasks. According to Bruner, these children solved the problem by means of the symbolic mode—thinking in words. When they were shown the display they described the arrangement to themselves in verbal terms such as, "It gets fatter going one way and taller going the other." Then they could use that rule to set up the transposed arrangement.

Verbal Mediation

The experiment we've just described suggests that some tasks are easier if you can "talk to yourself" about them. In particular, many kinds of learning are facilitated by the ability to verbalize. As Harold Stevenson, a specialist in children's learning, puts it,

> When the child's experiences can be summarized or coded by means of words, learning can occur with greater rapidity, effectiveness, and generality. Words enable the child to form rules. They become a dominant factor in thinking. Concepts gain firmness and durability when they can be put in the form of words. Before the child can use words to govern his behavior, he must act in order to know. Later [around the age of 6 or 7], he may use words to short-circuit action; behavior may be guided by the application of rules, concepts, or other components of the inner world of thought. (1972, p. 57)

Stevenson describes the following experiment. A number of geometric figures are drawn, each on a separate card. There's a small circle, a large circle, and a middle-sized circle; a small square, a large square, and a middle-sized square; and so on. One set of cards—let's say the squares—is placed in front of a child. He is told, "See these cards? One of these is a lucky card. If you point to the lucky card you will win a penny." The child points to a card and is told whether or not that was the "lucky" one. Then the three cards are rearranged (so that the correct card can't be chosen simply on the basis of position), and a new trial begins. Eventually the child learns that the middle-sized square is always the "lucky" one. Then these cards are put away and three new figures—triangles, perhaps—are introduced. Again the child is reinforced only for responding to the middle-sized figure.

This kind of problem—psychologists call it a **discrimination task**—is learned very slowly by 3-year-olds. But a 6-year-old learns it very rapidly. By the time the third or fourth set of figures is produced, he is choosing correctly on the first try. As he gathers up his pile of pennies, we ask him how he knew which card to pick. "Well," he replies, "it was always the middle-sized picture" (Stevenson, 1972, p. 56).

In all probability, says Stevenson, the child was saying the same thing to himself—"It's always the middle-sized picture"—during the experiment, once he was choosing correctly. The words served as what we call **verbal mediators**—they directed his responses. A verbal mediator comes between a stimulus and a response: the stimulus sets off the verbal mediator and the verbal mediator controls the response.

An experiment that demonstrated the importance of verbal mediators was performed back in the 50s (Spiker, Gerjuoy, and Shepard, 1956). The subjects were children between the ages of 3 and 6. Their task was to learn to pick the middle-sized square from a set of three. But squares of a number of different sizes were used, and the correct choice depended on the sizes of all three squares—a given square might be middle-sized on one trial but be the largest or smallest on another trial. Thus, to solve this problem the children needed to have a concept of "middle-sizedness."

The experimenters found that some of the children solved the problem fairly easily. These were the children who, in a test before the experiment began, were able to use the term "middle-sized" (or "medium-sized") appropriately and who knew what it meant. But the children whose vocabularies *lacked* that term, and who didn't seem to understand what it meant when the experimenter used it, failed to solve the problem in the allotted time. They tended to be the younger children in the group.

The Discrimination-Shift Problem. Another way of finding out about verbal mediators is the **discrimination-shift** problem, which has been studied extensively by Tracy and Howard Kendler of the University of California at Santa Barbara (Kendler and Kendler, 1962; Kendler, 1963, 1974). The task involves a discrimination between stimuli that vary in two ways—for example, shape and color. On some trials the subject is given a choice between, let's say, a large black square and a small white one. The large black one is the "lucky" one. On other trials in the same session, the choice is between a large *white* square and a small *black* one. This time the large white one is the one to pick. Thus, size is the relevant dimension—whether the square is black or white makes no difference. Children can learn this discrimination fairly readily. So, for that matter, can rats.

But now the situation grows tricky: the experimenter changes the rules.

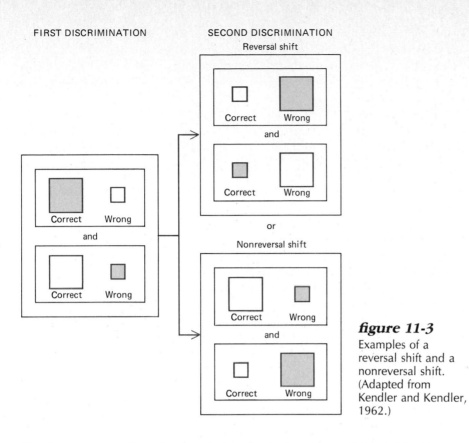

Reversal shift

Correct   Wrong

and

Correct   Wrong

Correct   Wrong

and

Correct   Wrong

or

Nonreversal shift

Correct   Wrong

and

Correct   Wrong

figure 11-3
Examples of a reversal shift and a nonreversal shift. (Adapted from Kendler and Kendler, 1962.)

The large square abruptly stops being the lucky one, and the subject is now reinforced only for choosing the small square, regardless of its color. This is called a **reversal shift**—the rule is the exact opposite of what it was before. Alternatively, the rule might change and *not* be the opposite of what it was before—this is called a **nonreversal shift.** In a nonreversal shift, the subject will now be reinforced on the basis of color instead of size: for example, the large white square and the small white square will be correct choices, and the black squares will be incorrect (see Figure 11–3).

Which is easier to learn, a reversal shift or a nonreversal shift? For a rat, the answer is a nonreversal shift. With a nonreversal shift, one of the previously correct stimuli—the large white one, in this case—will still be correct. Only one of the previously correct stimuli, the large black square, will now be incorrect. The rat has less trouble learning this new rule than learning that *both* of the previously correct stimuli are now wrong.

College students, on the other hand, find the reversal shift easier. Presumably this is because college students use verbal mediators. In the first part of the experiment the subjects could tell themselves, "Pick the big one." It seems to be easier to change that verbal rule to "Pick the small one" (or "*Don't* pick the big one") than to make an entirely new rule ("Pick the white one").

What about children? The answer is that it depends on the age of the child

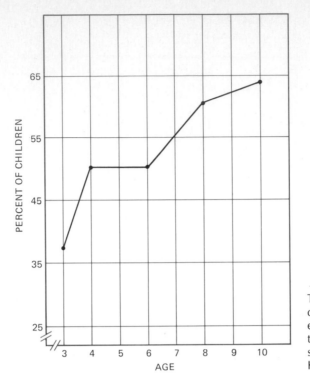

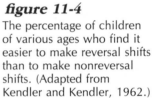

figure 11-4
The percentage of children of various ages who find it easier to make reversal shifts than to make nonreversal shifts. (Adapted from Kendler and Kendler, 1962.)

(see Figure 11–4). The majority of 3-year-olds, like rats, find it easier to make nonreversal shifts. The majority of 8- to 10-year-olds, like college students, find reversal shifts easier. Children in the 4- to 6-year-old range—"middle-sized children," we might call them—are in a transitional stage. About half of them give evidence of using verbal mediators—that is, they find reversal shifts easier (Kendler and Kendler, 1962; Kendler, Kendler, and Learnard, 1962).

We should mention that a large number of additional experiments have been done on the discrimination-shift problem in the past 20 years, and not all of them support the verbal mediation interpretation. Clearly, the ability to verbalize isn't the *only* difference between older and younger children. Nor is verbal mediation the *only* thing going on between the stimulus and the response. A crucial factor is what aspects of the stimuli the child pays attention to. Verbalization may serve simply as a reminder to direct attention in a particular way (Stevenson, 1972).

Production Deficiency. In the case of the middle-sized square, the younger children failed to solve the problem because their vocabularies lacked a term for "intermediate in size." But in the case of the discrimination-shift problem, that explanation won't work. Even 3-year-olds know the words "big," "small," "black," and "white." It seems that just *knowing* the terms isn't enough—what matters is whether the child *uses* them in this context. The evidence suggests that most school-age children do use verbal mediators when using them would be helpful. Most preschoolers, on the other hand, don't. Preschoolers' tendency not to use verbal mediators has been labeled **production deficiency,** which simply means that they are deficient in producing verbal mediators.

Because children usually move their lips when they talk to themselves, it's possible to investigate verbal mediation in a more direct way. A classic study that did this involved 5- and 8-year-olds who were given a memory task (Flavell, Beach, and Chinsky, 1966). Each child was shown a set of seven pictures of common objects. An experimenter pointed to three or four of the pictures, one at a time. Then the pictures were removed and a new set of the same pictures were put down in a different order. The child's job was to point to the pictures that the experimenter had pointed to, in the same order.

In the interval between when the experimenter pointed at the pictures and when the response was made, what would these children do? The experimenters watched the children's lips carefully during that interval, to see whether they were repeating to themselves the names of the objects they had to remember. It turned out that most of the 8-year-olds did use this technique, which psychologists call **rehearsal.** Of the 5-year-olds, though, only 10 percent used rehearsal to help them remember the pictures.

Production deficiency is not just a function of age. Among school-age children of a given age, some will spontaneously use verbal mediation and rehearsal, whereas others will not. A second study (Keeney, Cannizzo, and Flavell, 1967), using the same memory task as the one we just described, provides a closer look at this difference. The experimenters tested a group of 7-year-olds and found that some (about a quarter of the group) used rehearsal on virtually every trial. These children were labeled "producers." A smaller number of children virtually never rehearsed the names of the pictures. This group was called the "nonproducers." Not surprisingly, the producers did significantly better at the memory task than the nonproducers.

Then the experimenters tried to turn nonproducers into producers. The children were instructed in the use of rehearsal. They were told to whisper the names of the pictures out loud to themselves, over and over, after the experimenter pointed at them. The children did as they were told. This time the former nonproducers did as well on the task as the producers had.

Then a third set of trials was given. The ex-nonproducers were told that they no longer had to whisper the names of the pictures to themselves, but they could do so if they wanted to. And they promptly went back to being nonproducers, and their scores promptly went down again!

These results shouldn't be interpreted as showing that it's impossible to train children to use verbal mediators. (It undoubtedly *is* possible, in fact—it just takes a lot more training than the children had in the experiment we just described.) What the results do show is that, first of all, there are large individual differences in the tendency to use verbal mediators spontaneously. Second, verbal mediation works—even among children who *don't* use it spontaneously.

Metacognition

Using rehearsal to keep from forgetting something is pretty much automatic to an adult. For instance, if you look up an unfamiliar phone number and then have to go into another room to use the phone, you will probably repeat the number to yourself several times on your way to make your call. If your rehearsal is interrupted—say, if someone asks you a question—you will probably forget the number and have to go back and look it up again.

Rehearsing a telephone number is a metacognitive technique (see the box on metacognition, p. 326). So is rehearsing the names of pictured objects that an experimenter just pointed to, in order to remember them. And the knowledge that repeating something to yourself is a good way to keep from forgetting it is metacognitive knowledge.

There is a steady and sizable increase in metacognitive knowledge, and in the use of metacognitive techniques or **strategies,** all through childhood. Of particular interest is the increase in the use of strategies having to do with learning and memory. We have seen that preschoolers are less likely to use rehearsal than school-age children. It's also the case that young school-age children are less likely than older school-age children or adolescents to use **categorization** to help them remember things. (Bjorklund and Hock, 1982;

Rehearsing a phone number to keep from forgetting it is a metacognitive technique. School-age children are more likely to use such techniques than are preschoolers.

Moely, Olson, Halwes, and Flavell, 1969). Categorization means organizing what you're trying to learn by grouping similar things with each other.

Another memory strategy is called **elaboration.** Elaboration is most useful in what is called **paired-associate learning,** where the task is to remember that two things go together—"Atlanta" and "Georgia," for instance, or "le lait" and "milk." When paired-associate learning is studied in the laboratory, the subjects' job is usually to link together in memory a number of pairs of arbitrarily selected words—"cow" and "table," for example. There are two different ways that elaboration can be used to link these words together. The first is verbal elaboration: a sentence such as "The cow is on the table" is thought up. The second is elaboration using imagery: the subject forms a visual image of a cow standing on a table. Both of these methods are found to improve memory, and both of these methods are much more likely to be used spontaneously by older children than by younger ones (Pressley, 1982).

That the use of the imagery method increases with age is a little unexpected. Jerome Bruner's theory, which we discussed earlier in this chapter, appeared to suggest that visual imagery is *replaced* by verbalization. It seems, though, that verbalization *supplements* imagery, rather than replacing it. The child who can use verbal mediators has access to *two* modes of thought, not just one.

Increases in Metacognitive Understanding.   It's not only learning and memory that can be the subject of metacognitive knowledge. For instance, children's understanding of the various factors that enable them to pay attention to a task comes under this heading. Such knowledge, too, increases with age: older school-age children are more likely than younger ones to realize that paying attention to something is easier to do if you're highly motivated, and harder to do if there are distracting sights or noises (Miller and Weiss, 1982).

Children's ability to judge how accurately they are performing a cognitive task is another kind of metacognitive understanding that increases with age. For example, some children were shown a beaker containing about 30 beans and asked to "count" them—without taking the beans out of the beaker. Five-year-olds gave an answer and then confidently asserted that they were sure their judgments were correct. Seven- and 9-year-olds recognized that their judgments were unlikely to be exactly right (Saxe and Sicilian, 1981).

Knowing whether you're successfully communicating an idea to another person, or whether you're understanding what another person is saying to you, also falls into the realm of metacognition. The fact that the speech of young children sometimes conveys very little to their listeners has often been noted; so has the fact that the children themselves are usually unaware of their failure to communicate (Piaget, 1926; Glucksberg and Krauss, 1967). The ability to transmit ideas in an understandable way gradually improves with age. Piaget believes that this is because older children can decenter— thus, they can take on the point of view of the listener.

Newer work suggests that there is more to it than that. Young children are not only poor at knowing when *they've* failed to communicate; they're also poor at knowing when someone has failed to communicate with *them*. John Flavell, whom we previously mentioned in connection with metacognition (see p. 326) has studied what he calls "children's ability to monitor and regulate their own understanding of messages" (Flavell, Speer, Green, and August, 1981, pp. 3–4).

Flavell and his associates carried out an experiment with kindergarten children (5- and 6-year-olds) and second-graders (7- and 8-year-olds). The children's task was to build a "house" out of different-colored blocks, according to some instructions they heard on a cassette recorder. The instructions on the cassette were recorded by a 12-year-old girl named Kiersten. The children were told that they were supposed to build a house "exactly like Kiersten's." They could replay the instructions, or parts of the instructions, as often as they wished.

Kiersten's instructions were purposely unclear. For example, the instructions started out, "Put the blue block on top of the blue tape. Then, put the next block on top of it" (p. 12). Which *is* the next block? There was no way of knowing. But the younger children in this study didn't seem to realize that the instructions were faulty:

> The child puts the blue block on the blue tape while listening to the first sentence of the instructions. When he hears the second sentence he looks puzzled, picks up both the yellow and the red blocks, hesitates, and says, "What's the next block?" (the experimenter says "hmmm"). "Blue block? I guess the red one." The child puts the red block on the blue block. [The experimenter asks, "Do you think the building you made looks exactly like Kiersten's?"] "Yah. Exactly like Kiersten's." ["Why?] "Because she said to put the blue block, block on the blue tape and a block on the next tape, the next block."

The experimenter then asked the child if he thought Kiersten did a good job or a bad job of telling how to build the house.

> "Good." ["Why?"] "Because she tol—she told us in such a good way—in a good way." (p. 49)

Another kindergartener said that Kiersten had done a good job with the instructions "cuz it keeps on looking pretty" (p. 50).

The second-graders were much less likely to overlook the problem. They were quicker to notice the ambiguities in the instructions, and more of them gave some sign (verbal or otherwise) that they were aware of a difficulty. They were also more likely than the younger children to realize that their house might *not* be "exactly like Kiersten's," and less likely to think that she did a good job with the instructions. In the investigators' words, the second-graders "appear to monitor their own comprehension better than the kindergarteners do" (p. 51).

Their ability to "monitor their own comprehension" will undoubtedly continue to grow throughout the school years. The power to recognize when you do understand something and when you don't is an important cognitive tool.

Memory

We have seen the way that children's tendency to use metacognitive memory strategies increases with age. Older children, as compared with younger ones, are more likely to rehearse, to categorize, and to use elaboration. They're also more likely to remember things. But is their use of metacognitive strategies the sole reason for this improvement in memory? The answer is no: memory improves during childhood, and not all of this improvement is due to metacognitive actions or knowledge.

Short-Term Memory. Psychologists distinguish between **short-term** (or *immediate,* or *working*) memory and **long-term** (or *permanent*) **memory.** That telephone number that you will forget if someone interrupts your rehearsal—it's in short-term memory. Short-term memory has a very limited storage capacity. An adult can generally hold six or seven items in short-term memory—the seven numbers of a phone number, say. Interestingly enough, however, although the capacity is severely limited, the nature of the "item" is not. Adults can remember a list of six or seven letters of the alphabet, whether they're read out loud or appear briefly on a screen. They can remember a similar number of *words,* even though each word is composed of several letters. If the words form a meaningful sentence, more than seven are likely to be remembered—the sentence provides a structure for remembering the words, just as the words provide a structure for remembering the letters.

The number of individual items that can be held in short-term memory is called the **memory span.** Memory span increases during childhood, even under circumstances that allow no metacognitive "tricks." It is about three items at age 3, four or five items at age 6, and five or six items at ages 8 to 12 (Case, Kurland, and Goldberg, 1982; Linton, 1980).

Why does memory span increase? There are probably several reasons, but a major one seems to be a gradual improvement in the speed and efficiency of **information processing.** Information processing is a term that has been used to describe some of the very complex things that go on inside the brain when a person sees or hears a stimulus. The sensation produced by the stimulus can last only for a second or so after the stimulus is gone. Then it will ordinarily be lost forever unless it is "processed" and "stored." What this means is that when we see or hear a word, for example, we are unlikely to remember it unless we have first identified it—recognized it for the particular word it is. This identification process is sometimes called **encoding.** It is the encoded version of the word that is stored in short-term memory. And both the encoding and the storing seem to be done with greater and greater efficiency as children grow older. This is to be expected, since older children have had more practice in information processing than younger ones. But there may also be physical reasons for the improvement: myelination (see p. 166) is still going on during middle childhood, and myelination speeds neural functioning. There may also be other, more subtle changes taking place in the brain (Case, Kurland, and Goldberg, 1982; Wilkinson, 1981).

Long-Term Memory.   Things stored in short-term memory are lost almost at once unless they are rehearsed. If we want to retain something for the long run, it must be put into long-term memory. Everything that is stored in long-term memory has first been in short-term memory. The reverse, however, is not true. That telephone number, for instance, will probably never enter long-term storage if it's an unimportant number—one that is used only on a single occasion. Most people have to make a special effort to commit a number to long-term storage.

On the other hand, our long-term memory undoubtedly contains more things than we can get at, at any given time. Information-processing theorists speak of memory storage and memory **retrieval.** A memory that is stored is not necessarily one that can readily be retrieved. We feel irritation when we have trouble retrieving a memory that we know we possess—a person's name, for instance. "It's right on the tip of my tongue," we say.

Though we might not be able to think of that name ourselves, we will instantly recognize it if someone else says it. Psychologists distinguish between two kinds of memory tests, **recall** and **recognition.** In recall, the subjects have to retrieve the actual memory, say by remembering a word or a number. Recognition is an easier test—the subjects only have to decide whether a given word or number is or isn't the correct one. It's much harder to answer the question, "Where was the first battle of the Civil War fought?" than to say true or false to the statement, "The first battle of the Civil War was fought at Fort Sumter."

Recognition is a simple sort of memory. It is present even in very young babies, as shown by the procedures described in Chapter 5 (see p. 151). In fact, for a time it was thought that recognition memory doesn't change at all during development—that all the change was in recall memory. Since recall memory is the sort that is aided by the metacognitive strategies of categorization and elaboration, it seemed possible that metacognitive advances might account for *all* the improvement in long-term memory during childhood.

That no longer appears to be the case. Recent work has made it clear that recognition memory, too, improves during childhood. In one experiment (Sophian and Stigler, 1981), the children's task was to say which of two very similar drawings of faces had previously been shown to them. There was no improvement during the preschool years, but first graders did considerably better than older preschoolers (and not nearly as well as college students).

The Growth of Selective Attention.   There's a connection between memory and attention: we are most likely to remember those things we pay attention to. The ability to focus attention on a specific thing—**selective attention**—is yet another cognitive skill that grows during the school years.

Selective attention is often measured by means of a memory task. Let's say that a child is shown a set of pictures of various animals. In the background of each picture are some miscellaneous objects. The child is told that her job is to remember the animals. But later she is also questioned about the objects in the background. What she can remember about the animals is evidence of

Selective attention—the ability to focus attention on one specific thing and to ignore other things—improves during middle childhood.

central learning; what she can remember about the background objects is evidence of **incidental learning.**

As we would expect, central learning improves throughout the elementary and high school years. In contrast, incidental learning changes little between grades 2 and 5. Between grades 5 and 8 it actually *decreases*—less incidental material is learned. The reason is the older child's greater ability to focus attention selectively (Miller and Weiss, 1981).

At the beginning of Chapter 7 we described Stephanie, age 4 days, as "one of the most efficient learning machines on the face of the earth." High among the features that make that machine so remarkable is its ability to improve as it goes along, by the process of learning how to learn. Thanks to this ability, Stephanie will be an even more efficient learning machine at age 12 years than she was at age 4 days.

summary

1. **Middle childhood** (ages 6 to 12 years) is an important period in the child's life. Though physical growth is relatively slow, there are striking changes in intellectual competence and in relationships with others. Individual differences (in appearance, intellectual abilities, talents and inclinations, and so on) show up clearly during this period.

2. School-age children differ from one another in the rate of physical maturation. A small child may be destined to become a small adult, or may instead be maturing at a slower rate.

3. School-age children are taller, leaner, and more muscular than preschoolers. The proportions of face and body are closer to those of adults. Middle childhood is the period when children lose their baby teeth and get in their permanent teeth.

4. Most of the diseases that formerly threatened the lives of school-age children are now preventable or curable. Accidents—especially car accidents—now pose the greatest threat to the school-age child.

5. Although girls are physically more mature than boys, boys surpass them in most measures of physical ability and strength. One reason for this is that boys practice their physical skills more than girls do. There are also physical differences: for example, boys have more muscle and less fat than girls. A third factor is that many girls seem to be unwilling to compete with boys in sports (and in other situations, too).

6. Catching a ball is an example of a **perceptual-motor skill.** Such skills increase markedly during middle childhood. The younger child has no trouble perceiving the locations or movements of objects, but she is less able than the older child to predict such movements quickly and accurately, and less able to produce quick and accurate movements of her own body.

7. The percentage of children who are bedwetters declines with age; it is twice as high among boys as among girls. The cause of bedwetting is unclear, though heredity appears to play some role. Emotional problems may be the result, rather than the cause, of bedwetting. A device that rings an alarm when the child begins to urinate has proven to be the single most successful cure for bedwetting; **retention control training** also seems to be helpful.

8. According to Piaget, the preoperational period gives way to the **period of concrete operations** around the age of 7. The ability to decenter gradually increases, as does the ability to consider the past and the future. Similarly, the concept of conservation is not acquired all at once—different types of conservation appear at different ages. School-age children are not as

likely as preschoolers to be misled by appearances.

9. With special training, children as young as 4 can acquire conservation concepts; school-age children can be taught to use some of the concepts of formal operational thought. Piaget himself admits that it's possible to accelerate cognitive development. Whether doing so is a good idea is still not clear.

10. Preschoolers are likely to believe (1) that anything that moves or does something is alive (this belief is called **animism**), (2) that their dreams are "real" and are visible to other people, (3) that something's name is as much a part of it as its shape or color, and (4) that lakes and rivers, and the sun and moon, are the products of human construction (a belief called **artificialism**). All these beliefs gradually disappear during middle childhood.

11. The understanding of where babies come from develops slowly: preoperational children may say that babies are made in factories; older children know that a mother and a father are essential, but they're not sure why. Although it's possible to accelerate the understanding of reproduction, American children seldom have a complete understanding of the facts until they reach the period of formal operations.

12. According to Bruner, the transition from the iconic to the symbolic mode of representational thought occurs around age 7. Because they are able to think in words, 7-year-olds can put a display of glasses in a transposed arrangement, even though they've never seen this arrangement. Five- and 6-year-olds can reproduce the original arrangement, but they can't transpose it.

13. Many kinds of learning are facilitated by the ability to verbalize. Words serve as **verbal mediators:** a stimulus sets off the verbal mediator, which then directs the response. For example, only those children who could use the term "middle-sized" were able to solve a **discrimination task** in which the middle-sized figure was always the correct one.

14. In the **discrimination-shift** problem, a subject must choose between stimuli that vary on two dimensions—for example, size and color—of which only one dimension determines the correct stimulus. Then the rules are changed so that the correct stimulus is either the opposite one of the same dimension (a **reversal shift**), or is now determined by the other dimension (a **nonreversal shift**). Children under 7 find nonreversal shifts easier. Older children find reversal shifts easier; this is assumed to be because they use verbal mediators.

15. Preschoolers and some school-age children seem to have a **production deficiency**—that is, they tend not to use verbal mediators, even when they know the words that would help them solve a problem or perform a memory task. If given suitable instructions, school-age nonproducers can use verbal mediators to improve their performance on such tasks, despite the fact that they do not use them spontaneously.

16. An example of metacognition is the knowledge that **rehearsal**—repeating something over and over to yourself—is a good way to keep from forgetting it. This type of knowledge, and the use of metacognitive **strategies** such as rehearsal, **categorization,** and **elaboration,** show steady and sizable increases during childhood. Children's increasing use of elaboration involving visual images suggests that verbalizing supplements imagery, rather than replacing it.

17. Other metacognitive knowledge that increases with age includes children's understanding of the factors that enable them to pay attention, the ability to judge how accurately they are performing a cognitive task, and knowing how well they are communicating to another person. Their knowledge of how well another person is communicating to *them* also develops gradually—unlike older children, kindergarteners may not realize that their failure to understand what someone is telling them may be due to faulty communication on the other person's part.

18. **Short-term** and **long-term memory** both improve during childhood; not all of this improvement is due to metacognitive advances. The **memory span** (the number of items that can be held in short-term memory) increases gradually from about three items at age 3 to six or seven items in adulthood. This increase seems to be due, at least in part, to an improvement in the speed and efficiency of **information processing.** Both practice and physical maturation are probably responsible for this improvement.

19. To remember something for a long time, the sensation produced by the stimulus must first be **encoded,** then stored in short-term memory, then put into long-term memory. Not all items stored in long-term memory can readily be retrieved—**recall** tests of memory depend on memory **retrieval. Recognition** tests are easier—the task is simply to decide whether a given stimulus is or isn't the correct or familiar one. Recognition memory, too, improves with age.

20. **Selective attention,** the ability to focus attention on what matters, also improves during the school years. As a result of this increased ability to focus attention selectively, **incidental learning** actually decreases between grades five and eight, while **central learning** improves steadily throughout childhood.

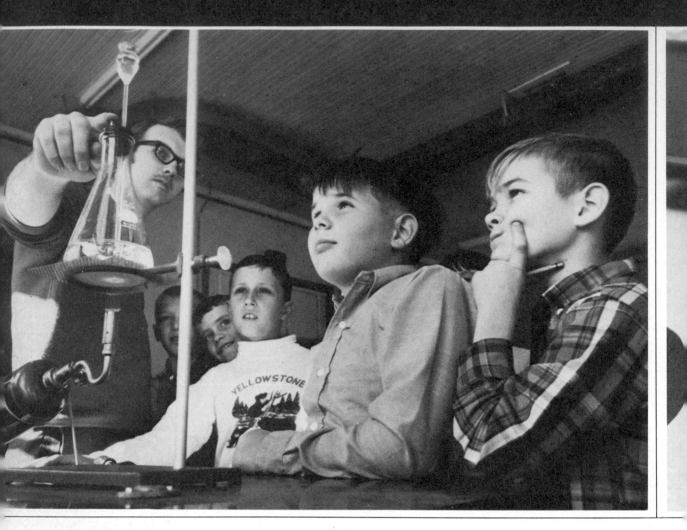

Chapter Twelve

LEARNING IN SCHOOL

Twelve

It's a sunny morning early in September, in a small town or a big city somewhere in North America. Children are waking up early, with a touch of butterflies in the stomach. This is the big day: the day school starts! For weeks they have been anticipating this day—some with eagerness, some with dread, most with a complicated mixture of the two. They've been told by older children that first grade (or whatever grade they're going into) is "really hard." Perhaps they've also been told that the teacher is "mean" or "dumb" or "weird."

The children dress and comb their hair with greater care than usual. They assemble pencils, pens, rulers, and notebooks. There are tears and smiles, skimpy breakfasts, and extra trips to the bathroom. All too soon it's time to go. The younger children permit their mothers or fathers to walk with them; some children (and some parents) are reluctant to let go at the door to the classroom. The older children refuse to be accompanied. They say goodbye to their parents with exaggerated casualness.

For the parents, too, there may be a touch of butterflies in the stomach. They know—better than their children—how much hinges on what happens in that school building. They know how much depends on whether their child does well or poorly in school.

The first day of school produces a complex mixture of emotions, both in children and in their parents.

Going to school is the job, the career, of middle childhood. It is likely to be a challenging job, perhaps even an anxiety-producing one. It's a job at which one can succeed brilliantly or fail miserably, in which one is judged and possibly found wanting. For those children who do poorly at it, their school years may be by far the most difficult period of their entire lives. Their preschool years, the "play years," were likely to be fairly carefree. As adults they can usually find a niche in society.

For those who succeed in school, there are long-term benefits that become cumulative over the years. A child who does well in first grade, especially one who learns to read rapidly and easily, will have a head start in second grade. By early adolescence, the good student is likely to be on a different "track" from the poor student—a track consisting of advanced or accelerated courses, a track leading directly to college. The child who does well in her school subjects will probably end up in a very different kind of career, and lead a very different kind of adult life, than the child who does poorly. We don't mean to imply that all of these later differences result directly from school performance: in many cases they are simply *correlated* with school performance. This is because there are many factors—the child's intelligence and personality, the parents' socioeconomic level—that affect both school performance *and* adult status.

On the other hand, there have always been some individuals who thrive in school, but who wither once they're out of it—or vice-versa. A study of the life histories of eminent people showed that the majority of them had hated school (Goertzel and Goertzel, 1962).

INTELLIGENCE AND ACHIEVEMENT

The study of eminent people suggests that not all of the qualities that lead to outstanding success in adult life are equally well suited to the school environment. It is nonetheless true that many of the qualities required for success in school are also extremely useful outside of school. Such qualities include the ability to concentrate on a task in the face of difficulties or distractions, the motivation to achieve, and, of course, intelligence. All three of these qualities—especially, it is assumed, intelligence—are also likely to influence performance on an IQ test. Thus, it is not surprising that measured IQ correlates highly with academic achievement. Here's what one psychologist has to say about the implications of the IQ score:

> No other single fact that one can determine about a child is considered more informative about his probable educational attainments, eventual occupational level, and socioeconomic status than is the child's IQ. This is especially true of his average IQ, based on several testings over three or four years after he has entered school. Neither the parents' IQ, nor their education, nor their occupational level, nor their social status, nor their income, nor all of these combined is as predictive of the child's educational and occupational future as is his own IQ. This is not to

PROBLEMS IN DEVELOPMENT

The Mentally Retarded Child

Mental retardation refers to intellectual abilities that are below normal. Generally, a score below 70 on an IQ test is taken as a sign of mental retardation. By this criterion 6 million Americans, or 3 percent of the population, are retarded.

Most retarded children are *not* in institutions. Almost 90 percent of retarded children are in the *mildly retarded* category (see Table 12–1), with IQs in the range of 55 to 69. Only 1 percent of children in this category are ever institutionalized. Johnny is a typical example of a mildly retarded child:

> Johnny was a 6½-year-old blond, blue-eyed youngster who was spending his second year in the kindergarten of a school in a predominantly middle-class neighborhood. He was the fifth of eight children of a rather pleasant, quiet mother. . . . His father, a cloth man in a textile mill, provided the family living by loading finished bolts of material from weaving machines onto carts to be taken elsewhere in the mill. . . . Three of Johnny's four older brothers and sisters were in the slowest group in their schoolrooms. . . .
>
> Johnny's parents, their children, and the maternal grandmother lived in a four-room house situated on the edge of town. . . . Johnny shared a bed with three older brothers; three sisters were in another bed. The house was untidy and run-down. Meals were cooked somewhat erratically, and the children often ate their meals cold while walking about the house. . . .
>
> Johnny was not able to master the reading-readiness materials of the kindergarten. He had difficulty in wielding a pencil, folding paper, coloring within lines, and differentiating one symbol from another. He usually had a pleasant smile and often seemed to be listening carefully to what the teacher told him, but half the time he was unable to repeat her instructions. . . . Johnny liked the other children, but they paid him little attention and usually left him out of their play at recess. . . .
>
> His mother reported that Johnny was a very good child who played outdoors much of the day and seldom cried. . . . She was somewhat surprised by the teacher's interest in Johnny's "special" problem, since he seemed so much like her other children and had never given her any trouble. (Robinson and Robinson, 1976, pp. 167–168)

According to an IQ test given to him by the school psychologist, Johnny's mental age was 4 years, 9 months. His IQ score was 67.

say that the IQ is a very good predictor of these things, but it is a better predictor than any others we know of. (Jensen, 1981, pp. 10–11)

Not all psychologists consider the IQ to be so important. Furthermore, as the author we just quoted goes on to state,

> It is important to realize that for any given IQ there is a considerable range of behavioral capabilities. But that range is much narrower for the most intellectually demanding activities. The IQ predicts academic performance better than it predicts anything else. Except at the lowest levels, IQ is not a very good clue to performance on many of the ordinary tasks of life, or to overall social adjustment. (p. 12)

Educators call children like Johnny the **educable mentally retarded** (often abbreviated as *EMR*). Most children in this category can learn to read and write and to do simple arithmetic, but it takes them much longer than usual to acquire these skills. Even with special help, a child in this category is not likely to progress beyond a fifth- or sixth-grade educational level.

For most of the children in the mildly retarded group, no specific cause can be found for their retardation. Their brains have not been injured, they do not have a disease. Human intelligence varies over a wide range, and some children simply fall at the low end of the range. The majority, like Johnny, come from the lowest socioeconomic levels.

For these mildly retarded children, typically, neither genetic nor environmental factors have been favorable. Genetically, they may have inherited a limited intellectual potential—yet in an enriched, stimulating environment, these children might have ended up with IQs in the normal range. Unfortunately, their parents are seldom able to provide them with that kind of

TABLE 12–1   The Mentally Retarded

Level of Retardation	IQ Range	Percent of Retarded Children	Description
Mild	55–69	89%	Educable mentally retarded (EMR). Few are institutionalized. Most learn to read and write. As adults, most are capable of holding unskilled jobs.
Moderate	40–54	6%	Most learn to talk but not to read and write. Capable of performing routine jobs under supervision.
Severe	25–39	3½%	Need constant supervison at home or in an institution. Many learn to walk and to speak simple phrases. Require considerable training to learn self-help behavior such as feeding and toileting.
Profound	Below 25	1½%	Many are bedridden. Life expectancy is short. Some eventually learn some self help behavior. May walk, may say a few words.

Knopf, 1979; Ross, 1980.

What this means is that two children with equal IQ scores can differ greatly in social skills and in many other ways. They can also differ in academic achievement, though they're likely to differ less in academic achievement than in other ways. The correlation between IQ scores and school performance is not perfect—it is around .60. Intelligence, as we have said before, is not the only characteristic that affects school performance; nor is an IQ test a perfect measure of intelligence. But when IQ score and school performance differ considerably, it is likely to be in a high-IQ child who does quite poorly in school. The low-IQ child who does very well is rare indeed. Although high intelligence does not guarantee high achievement in school, low intelligence generally makes it impossible to attain. (See Box.)

environment. They are likely to receive a minimum of adult attention. They may also be nutritionally deprived and have uncorrected health problems.

This kind of mental retardation, in which both heredity and environment play a role, is called **familial retardation.** A child like Johnny has a hard time in school, but Johnny will probably grow up to become a functioning member of society. He is likely to have an unskilled job like his father's. He may marry; if he does, his wife will probably be of low intelligence too. The chances are good that some of his children will also be mentally retarded.

The other type of mental retardation is found in children from all socioeconomic levels. It is called **biologically caused** (or *organic*) **retardation.** Some cases are due to brain damage, resulting from head injuries, brain infections (encephalitis), or oxygen deprivation before or during birth. Other cases are due to genetic abnormalities. Down's syndrome (see p. 54) is responsible for 10 to 15 percent of institutionalized retarded children. A number of metabolic disorders also produce retardation. Most are due to missing or defective enzymes and are carried by recessive genes.

Children with biologically caused retardation generally have IQs below 55. These children are often institutionalized. In their appearance and behavior, they are likely to differ from normal children. Most have multiple problems. Their motor coordination is usually poor, and vision or hearing may also be affected.

Retarded children tend to pass through the same developmental sequences as normal children (for example, sitting up, then standing, then walking), though at a much slower rate. A 10-year-old with a mental age of 5 is similar to a normal 5-year-old in some ways, but not in all. The retarded 10-year-old has, after all, lived for five more years. And those years have been filled with failure, not success (Ross, 1980).

How can we be sure that a child is mentally retarded? A low score on an IQ test is the usual criterion, but it is a risky one. Children may do poorly on a single IQ test—or even on a number of IQ tests—for many reasons. Shy or fearful children, children with visual or hearing problems, children with language disabilities or whose native language differs from that of the tester, children with motor disabilities (cerebral palsy, for example), and even children who prefer to work slowly or children who are easily discouraged—all are penalized (Harris, 1982). For this reason it is unwise to base a decision about a child's future on IQ tests alone, and unreasonable to base a decision on a *single* IQ test.

The dangers of incorrectly labeling a child "mentally retarded" are obvious and frightening. But it can also be tragic when we continually expect more from a child than he or she is able to accomplish. ■

IQ Differences

IQ has undoubtedly been investigated more thoroughly than any other psychological characteristic. Thousands of studies have been performed to answer questions about the relationship between IQ and other factors. Hundreds of correlations have been found between IQ and other measurements or classifications. Here, for example, are some of the things that IQ has been found to correlate with:

- Teachers' opinions about children's intelligence—children who teachers think are intelligent tend to do well on IQ tests.

- Parents' socioeconomic class and educational attainment—the children of college-educated, middle-class parents tend to test higher than the children of less educated, lower-class parents.

- Height and weight—children with high IQs tend to be slightly taller and heavier than those with low IQs.

- Activity level—very active children tend to have lower IQs (Halverson and Waldrop, 1976).

- Birth order—firstborn children tend to have slightly higher IQs than second-borns, second-borns slightly higher than third-borns, and so on (see p. 54).

- Family size—the more siblings a child has, the lower his or her IQ is likely to be.

Racial and Ethnic Groups.   It has also been found that people of different racial and ethnic groups perform somewhat differently on IQ tests. Some groups tend to do slightly better, others do slightly less well. Some do better on verbal test items, others on nonverbal items. Although there are many examples of group differences in IQ scores, the one that worries people most is the black-white difference. On the average, black children and adults score about 15 points lower than white children and adults. Controlling for socioeconomic class (by taking into account average socioeconomic level) reduces the difference to 11 or 12 IQ points. Just for comparison, the average IQ difference between two siblings in the same family is about 12 points.

The racial difference in performance on IQ tests is often blamed on the IQ tests themselves. It has been claimed that IQ tests are "culturally biased," biased against black culture and in favor of white culture. But serious efforts to construct "culture-free" tests have not eliminated the racial difference in IQ. Completely nonverbal tests such as Raven's Progressive Matrices (Fig 12–1) show about the same black-white IQ difference as the Stanford-Binet (Jensen, 1974). In the early 1970s a group of black people sued the state of California because standard IQ tests were putting too many black children into classes for the educable retarded. But banning the use of IQ tests had little effect. Before the ban, 27 percent of the children in these classes were black; three years after the ban, 25 percent were black (Lambert and Meyers, 1977).

Although "culture bias" of IQ tests doesn't seem to be the cause of racial differences in performance, that doesn't mean that the differences are genetic. In fact, there's a fair amount of evidence that the differences are mostly cultural or environmental. The evidence comes from three different studies.

The first (Eyferth, 1961) concerns the biological children of U.S. servicemen, born during and after World War II to unwed German mothers. Some of the fathers of these children were white, others were black. When the children's IQs were tested, no difference was found between the all-white children and the children who were racially mixed.

The second study (Willerman, Naylor, and Myrianthopoulos, 1974) also has to do with racially mixed children. The comparison was between one

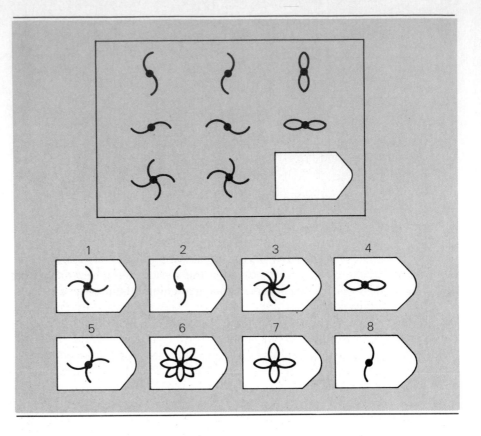

figure 12–1

A problem similar to those in Raven's Progressive Matrices test. (Liebert and Wicks-Nelson, 1974.)

group of children who had black mothers and white fathers, and another group who had white mothers and black fathers. The results were surprising. Although by the customary social standards all of these children were black, the ones with white mothers had a mean IQ score of 102. The ones with black mothers had a mean IQ score of 93. Thus, the race of the child wasn't the important factor—the difference seemed to depend on whether the child was reared by a white mother or a black one.

The third study (Scarr and Weinberg, 1976) supports this conclusion. It concerns a group of black children who were adopted by white families. Adoption agencies always prefer to place a child with adoptive parents of the same race, but sometimes that isn't possible. When the alternative is to let the child grow up without any permanent home at all, many agencies will permit a white family to adopt a black child. Psychologists tested a group of black children who had been adopted by upper-middle-class white families in Minnesota. The average IQ of these black children was 106. The ones who had been adopted in infancy had an average IQ of 110, well above the national average for white children.

Undoubtedly, there would tend to be many differences in the childrearing styles of white mothers and black mothers. Perhaps we should not be surprised that the white childrearing style produces children who perform well on tests devised by white psychologists.

Sex Differences on IQ Tests.   People often ask, "Which are smarter, boys or girls?" The answer is that it depends on what you mean by "smart." IQ tests have many different items, designed to tap many different aspects of intelligence. The average girl does better on some kinds of items, especially items having to do with words and language. The average boy does better on other kinds of items, especially those having to do with spatial and mathematical skills. IQ tests are designed in such a way that these kinds of items are fairly evenly balanced. The result is that the average girl has about the same overall IQ score as the average boy.

It's very important to keep in mind that the differences between one girl and another girl are likely to be greater than those between the "average girl" and the "average boy." Similarly, the differences between one white child and another white child are likely to be greater than those between the "average white" and the "average black." For this reason, the group differences found by researchers are often of little practical value. Teenage girls perform less well in math, on the average, than teenage boys. But if we wanted to have separate math classes for good math students and poor ones, it would make no sense to divide students up by sex. We'd have to test them individually. We might find, then, that the proportion of boys was slightly higher in the more advanced class. But there would be many girls who were better mathematicians than the "average boy."

As psychologists or statisticians, we sometimes find it useful to think about statistical differences between groups of children. But as parents, as teachers, as people who care for and about children, we deal only with individuals.

The Intellectually Gifted Child.   The child with the exceptionally high IQ is often depicted in popular literature in an unfavorable light. People tend to think of such a child as smaller and weaker than average, wearing glasses, and socially inept. Only in one respect does the evidence support this stereotype: the bright child *is* more likely to be nearsighted, and hence to need glasses (Jensen, 1981).

The best-known study of gifted children is a large, longitudinal one begun in California in the 1920s. Psychologist Lewis Terman and his associates selected a group of almost 1,500 schoolchildren on the basis of their very high IQs. The IQs in this group ranged from 140 to 200; the mean was around 150. The children were repeatedly examined over the course of their lives.

In middle childhood these children measured roughly an inch (2.5 cm) taller than their agemates. They were superior in physical development and in health and were judged better than average in social skills and psychological adjustment. On achievement tests they ranked far ahead of their agemates—not just in one or two areas, but in a wide variety of school subjects.

The record of high achievement and good adjustment continued into adulthood. Close to 90 percent attended college. Many of the men became doctors, lawyers, college professors, and writers. (This was not generally true of

The intellectually gifted child is likely to be ahead of her agemates in other ways, too.

the women, however—they tended to become housewives. Remember, though, that these women were born in the 1910s.) As a group, these people exhibited far lower than average rates of alcoholism, insanity, ill health, criminality, and divorce (Terman, 1954a).

Later studies by other investigators led to the same conclusions: gifted children *don't* tend to be maladjusted weaklings. Where, then, did this stereotype come from? The fact that many of these children wear glasses has no doubt contributed to the popular image. That they are pictured as small and weak is probably due to the fact that many have skipped a grade or two, and thus are younger than their classmates. But why are they thought of as maladjusted?

This idea may have had its origins in newspaper and magazine articles about some of the exceptions to the rule—those occasional ''child prodigies'' who do turn out to be misfits. The most widely publicized of these cases was that of William Sidis.

William Sidis was born in 1898, the son of Russian immigrants, both psychiatrists. William was ''trained'' according to his parents' theories; most of his early education took place at home. William was able to read English before he was 3; by 5 he was also reading French, Russian, and German. By age 10 he had mastered algebra, geometry, trigonometry, and calculus.

In 1909, at the age of 11, William Sidis entered Harvard. Before he reached his twelfth birthday he had given a lecture on higher mathematics to the Harvard Mathematical Club. Newspapers of the time were full of the exploits of the "boy prodigy."

The same newspapers gleefully recorded his decline. Although William Sidis did graduate from Harvard (at the age of 16), his adult life was a failure. He became an eccentric recluse, supporting himself with low-paid clerical jobs and devoting most of his energies to his hobby, collecting bus and trolley transfers. At his death, at the age of 46, he was alone, unemployed, and impoverished.

Sidis was never forgotten by the press during his lifetime. Reporters continued to hound him all through his adult life. No matter how hard he tried—he even sued one magazine for invasion of privacy—he couldn't escape the notoriety of his extraordinary past. The boy wonder had become a subject of ridicule. People would read these articles and shake their heads. "Early ripe, early rot," they would say (Montour, 1977).

But Sidis was not a typical case. More often than not, child prodigies grow up to lead successful and productive lives. A good example is Norbert Wiener, who, as a 15-year-old *graduate student* at Harvard, attended William Sidis's lecture at the Mathematical Club. Wiener eventually became a well-known professor at M.I.T. and the founder of a field called cybernetics. His early history was as astounding as that of William Sidis.

If the Sidis case attracted more publicity than the success stories of other grown-up prodigies, it may have been simply because it made a better story. But there may also have been an element of sour grapes involved. Reading about the accomplishments of prodigies like William Sidis often makes people feel inferior by comparison. Perhaps they find consolation in the idea that children like Sidis are destined for failure.

One more thing to note on this topic: those exceptional child geniuses—the real prodigies—for some reason are usually boys. Perhaps parents aren't as quick to encourage extraordinary talent, or to publicize it, when it appears in a girl. On the other hand, there may be some biological reason for the shortage of female prodigies. Mental retardation is also more common in males than in females. Although *average* intelligence is equal for the two sexes, perhaps males tend to vary more widely—to reach the extremes more often. That possibility has been raised before (Maccoby and Jacklin, 1974). The question is still not settled.

OTHER FACTORS AFFECTING ACHIEVEMENT

What are the factors other than intelligence that affect achievement? Why did William Sidis end up a failure whereas Norbert Wiener became a success? Kathleen Montour, of Johns Hopkins University, attributes Sidis's later problems to the way he was reared. She feels that his mother and father exploited William, and that they weren't capable of giving him ordinary parental love.

Boris and Sarah Sidis, it seems, could not provide William with even the most basic emotional security a child needs to grow up normally, let alone the special care that a child prodigy requires to face the rebuffs he is certain to encounter from the world. (Montour, 1977, p. 273.)

By the time he was in his 20s, William was totally estranged from his parents—he didn't even attend his father's funeral. According to Montour, "William Sidis deliberately ruined his own life to thwart his father's efforts at making him the perfect man" (p. 274).

Terman's study of gifted children gives further indication of the importance of the home and the family. When the children in that study had become middle-aged adults, Terman and his associates examined the lives and histories of 800 of the male subjects. The men were divided into three groups: the highest achievers (in terms of occupational success and productivity), the lowest achievers, and those in between.

Comparing just the highest and lowest achievers, Terman (1954b) found many differences in their childhood homes and families. The highest achievers were far more likely to have had parents who were college graduates; their homes had contained twice as many books as the homes of the lowest achievers. Divorce occurred only half as often among the parents of the highest achievers as among the parents of the lowest achievers.

There were also differences in the children themselves. In childhood, the highest achievers were rated considerably above the lowest achievers in desire to excel, persistence, self-confidence, sensitivity to approval and disapproval, and popularity. By the high school years, the lowest achievers had begun to slump academically: only 14 percent graduated from high school with honors, as opposed to 52 percent of the highest achievers. Interestingly enough, the highest achievers were most likely to have skipped grades: at college graduation they averaged 15 months younger than the lowest achievers.

This last finding suggests that skipping grades is not as likely to be harmful in the long run as some educators believe. Nowadays many school systems are reluctant to allow gifted children to move ahead of their agemates. Instead, these children are frequently put into what are called *enrichment programs*. In many cases, what this means is that the gifted children are expected to do all the schoolwork that the other children in their grade are assigned, *plus* additional work on a higher level. If the "reward" for being more intelligent is that one is given more work to do, surely these children are bright enough to realize that being intelligent doesn't pay!

Differences in Personality and in Cognitive Style

The study of the highest and lowest achievers indicates that certain nonintellectual characteristics measured in childhood correlate with achievement in adult life. Not surprisingly, such characteristics also tend to correlate with

figure 12–2
A sample problem from the Matching Familiar Figures Test (Kagan, Rosman, Day, Albert, and Phillips, 1964). The children's task is to find the picture that exactly matches the one at the top. Impulsive children respond quickly but make many errors; reflective children respond more slowly and more accurately.

achievement in school. In this section we will discuss three characteristics that have been studied extensively.

Impulsive and Reflective Children. Figure 12–2 shows a sample problem from the Matching Familiar Figures Test, devised by Harvard psychologist Jerome Kagan and his associates (Kagan and others, 1964). The task in this test is to find the picture that exactly matches the one on the top.

When this test is given to school-age children, it is found that some of them respond quickly, without checking carefully to see if their answer is correct. As a result, they tend to make many errors. These children are said to be **impulsive**.

The **reflective** children, on the other hand, respond much more slowly.

Because they tend to examine each picture carefully, they make fewer errors than the impulsive children.

Kagan believes that reflectiveness or impulsiveness are, to some extent, enduring characteristics of a child's cognitive style. Although all children tend to become more reflective as they grow older, the classifications are fairly stable—a child who is rated as impulsive at age 7 (relative to other 7-year-olds) is also likely to be rated as impulsive at age 12 (relative to other 12-year-olds). The same is true for a child who is rated reflective (Kagan, 1965).

Although impulsive and reflective children don't differ consistently in IQ, they do differ in many other ways. Reflective children tend to do better in school—they make better grades and are better readers. Impulsive children tend to make more errors in reading—they are more likely to jump to conclusions and identify a word incorrectly on the basis of one or two letters. When given a list of words to memorize, both groups forget approximately the same number of words, but the impulsive children are more likely to name words that *weren't* on the original list (Kagan, 1965). When younger school-age children are given Piagetian conservation problems, the reflective ones are more likely to have the concept of conservation. The impulsive ones are more likely to respond on a preoperational level (Cohen, Schleser, and Meyers, 1981).

Differences show up in other kinds of situations, too. Impulsive children are more likely to do things that involve a risk, such as walking on a narrow plank or joining a group of children they don't know well. Reflective children tend to be more cautious, more anxious not to make mistakes. However, they're more likely than impulsive children to choose difficult problems to work on, and less likely to give up easily (Kagan, 1965).

What is the basis of these differences in cognitive style? Kagan has proposed that reflective children are motivated by an anxiety to do well on intellectual tasks, coupled with a belief that they *can* do well if they try. Impulsive children, on the other hand, have less confidence in their intellectual abilities. They are motivated by a desire to escape from the situation (Kagan and Kogan, 1970). It seems likely that such attitudes would persist or even get stronger, in a vicious-circle sort of effect: reflectivity *does* tend to lead to greater success in intellectual tasks, so it is not surprising that reflective children should have greater confidence in their abilities. Similarly, impulsiveness *does* more often lead to failure, so it is not surprising that impulsive children should have less self-confidence.

Can impulsive children be trained to slow down and become more careful and analytic in their thinking? To some extent, yes. But when reflective and impulsive children were both given such training, *both* groups became more reflective. Thus, after the training the children who were reflective to begin with remained more reflective than the ones who were impulsive to begin with (Cohen, Schleser, and Meyers, 1981).

Achievement Motivation.   The concept of **achievement motivation** (or the **need for achievement,** sometimes abbreviated as *n Ach*) came into prominence in the 1950s. Its leading proponent was David McClelland, a social psychologist then at Wesleyan University. McClelland viewed achievement motivation as something that parents teach (or fail to teach) their children; the parents, of course, are not necessarily aware that they are doing this. Their own attitudes toward achievement are a function of their culture, their ethnic group, and their socioeconomic class (McClelland, Atkinson, Clark, and Lowell, 1953).

McClelland believed that an entire society can be characterized in terms of the strength of its achievement motivation, at a given point in its history. He reasoned that one way of assessing the strength of a society's achievement motivation was to look at the storybooks given to beginning readers in that society. The stories of an achieving society should contain more themes having to do with competing, succeeding, working toward a goal, and so on. McClelland and his associates rated each of 23 countries on the amount of achievement motivation shown in its storybooks used in the 1920s. The results were quite interesting. A country's achievement motivation, judged in this way, correlated significantly with the economic growth of that country over the next 20 years (McClelland, 1961).

Consistent differences in achievement motivation have also been found between members of different socioeconomic classes and of different ethnic groups. To show such differences, achievement motivation is measured in individuals in much the same way that McClelland measured it in societies: people are shown pictures and asked to make up stories about them, and then the stories are rated for the number of achievement themes they contain. When this method is used, middle-class children tend to score higher in achievement motivation than lower-class children. When socioeconomic class is held constant, Protestant and Jewish children tend to score higher than Catholic children; white, English-speaking children score higher than black children or those from Spanish-speaking families (Shaffer, 1979). Recently it has been noted that Asian-American children are likely to show evidence of unusually high achievement motivation (McGrath, 1983).

Most psychologists agree with McClelland in believing that the need to achieve is something that children acquire as a consequence of their parents' behavior toward them. The classic study was done in the 50s. This study (Winterbottom, 1958) linked achievement motivation with **independence training**—parental pressure to be self-reliant. It was found that the mothers of highly motivated boys expected various signs of independence at an earlier age than the other mothers. They were also more likely to reward independence and achievement by hugging or kissing their sons.

A later study examined school-age boys with high or low achievement motivation, but who were comparable in IQ and social class. Each boy was tested in his own home—given a series of problems to solve—in the presence of his parents. The parents were permitted to talk to their sons during the experiment, to offer help or advice. It was really the parents' behavior, more than the sons', that interested the experimenters.

Clear differences showed up between the parents of the highly motivated boys and the parents of the less motivated ones. The parents of the highly motivated boys became more involved in their sons' performance and seemed to take more pleasure in their sons' achievements. In the words of the experimenters,

> They set up standards of excellence for the boy even when none is given, or if a standard is given will expect him to do "better than average." As he progresses they tend to react to his performance with warmth and approval, or, in the case of the mothers especially, with disapproval if he performs poorly. (Rosen and D'Andrade, 1959/1975, p. 448)

The fathers of the highly motivated boys tended to give their sons a fair amount of autonomy—they were willing to stand back and let their sons perform on their own. Dominating or rejecting fathers were more likely to be found in the low-motivation group. According to the experimenters (p. 449), "The dominating father may crush his son (and in so doing destroys the boy's achievement motive)." Dominating mothers didn't seem to have this effect on their sons.

The parents of the highly motivated boys in this study *expected* their sons to do well. The important role played by parental expectancies was confirmed by a study done recently (Parsons, Adler, and Kaczala, 1982). This study examined beliefs and attitudes towards achievement in mathematics, in girls and boys in grades five through eleven. Both the children and their parents were questioned in detail. The investigators concluded that the primary way that parents influence their children's achievement attitudes was as "conveyors of expectancies regarding their children's abilities" (p. 320). In fact, how well the parents thought their children would do had more of an influence than how well the children actually *had* done, in the past! That finding, by the way, shows that achievement attitudes aren't simply a side effect of innate differences in ability. In other words, children don't develop the desire to succeed, or even the belief that they *can* succeed, merely as a consequence of having been born with greater than average ability.

We've discussed the causes of high or low achievement motivation; what about the effects? Do children with high motivation do better in school than children with low motivation? The answer, oddly enough, is: not always. Some studies do find a significant relationship, others do not (Crandall, 1967). There seem to be two main reasons for these inconsistent results. One is that the motivation to achieve is not necessarily focused on academic work. Children can direct their motivation toward achievement in sports, in music or art, or even toward attaining social successes. Second, the usual method for measuring achievement motivation—by looking for achievement themes in the stories children are asked to tell—seems not to be very accurate or reliable (Beck, 1978). For unknown reasons, it tends to be a better measure for boys than for girls (which may be why some investigators have avoided using girls as subjects).

Locus of Control. What's the point of striving for success if you feel that nothing you do is going to make any difference? There's no point at all. That's

The motivation to achieve is not necessarily focused on reading, writing, and arithmetic.

why, in recent years, psychologists have been less interested in achievement motivation and more interested in a factor called **locus of control.**

Some children believe that they are responsible for their own successes and failures, and that if they do well at something, it's because they've worked hard or have ability. These children are said to have an **internal locus of control;** they're called **internalizers.** Other children feel that they have little control over events—they attribute their successes and failures to luck or to the attitudes and actions of other people. These children are **externalizers**—they have an **external locus of control.** (Of course, many children fall between these two extremes.)

Locus of control has been assessed in school-age children by means of a test devised by Virginia Crandall and her associates (Crandall, Katkovsky, and Crandall, 1965). Some sample items from this test, called the Intellectual Achievement Responsibility Questionnaire, are shown in Table 12–2.

Locus of control, as measured by this test, correlates significantly with achievement motivation: children high in achievement motivation tend to be internalizers. Moreover, internalizers tend to come from the same social classes and ethnic groups that produce high achievement motivation. But, perhaps because the locus-of-control test is a more direct and accurate measure than the story-telling method of judging achievement motivation, locus of control is a better predictor. It usually predicts school achievement more

TABLE 12-2 Sample Items from the Intellectual Achievement Responsibility Questionnaire

1. If a teacher passes you to the next grade, would it probably be
   a. because she liked you, or
   b. because of the work you did?
2. When you do well on a test at school, is it more likely to be
   a. because you studied for it, or
   b. because the test was especially easy?
3. When you read a story and can't remember much of it, is it usually
   a. because the story wasn't well written, or
   b. because you weren't interested in the story?
4. Suppose your parents say you are doing well in school. Is this likely to happen
   a. because your school work is good, or
   b. because they are in a good mood?

Note: Children with an internal locus of control are likely to choose answers 1b, 2a, 3b, and 4a.
Courtesy of Virgina C. Crandall.

accurately than does measured achievement motivation. Internalizers are better students than externalizers (Crandall, Katkovsky and Preston, 1962; Coleman and others, 1966).

Since locus of control seems to be closely related to achievement motivation, it is not surprising that it has been linked to similar sorts of parental behaviors and attitudes. For example, parents who warmly praise achievement are likely to foster their children's belief in an internal locus of control (Katkovsky, Crandall, and Good, 1967). The granting or encouragement of independence seems to be particularly important. Children who are allowed at an early age to do independent things (such as sleep over at a friend's house) tend to become internalizers; children who are granted these privileges relatively late tend to become externalizers (Crandall, 1973; Wichern and Nowicki, 1976). It makes sense that having the opportunity to do things on your own should make you feel more in charge of your own destiny.

Perhaps some of this discussion has sounded vaguely familiar. Remember those babies (p. 215) who smiled and cooed when they discovered that their head movements could make a mobile turn? Remember the baby girl (p. 179) who was so delighted when she was able to make her father go "bumpety-bump"? And remember, on the other hand, those babies (p. 179) whose cries were often ignored and who cried more as a result? Even in infancy, a child is happier (and, presumably, better off) if she feels she has some control over her world. The unfortunate ones are those babies, those children, who feel they are powerless to have any effect on what goes on around them. It is reasonable to assume that eventually they just give up trying—a reaction that has been named **learned helplessness** (Seligman, 1975).

As far as we know, there is as yet no published evidence along these lines—no studies that have shown a connection between methods of baby care (for example, how quickly do the parents respond to the baby's cries?) and the child's locus of control later on. To show such a relationship would be very difficult, in fact. Longitudinal studies are arduous and time-consuming. And because so many factors intervene between the infant experiences and the later results, the relationship might not be detectable. Certainly we don't believe that internalizers and externalizers are formed, once and for all, in the first year of life. Later experiences will unquestionably have a strong influence. But if a child is given the impression, right from the start, that he or she has the power to make things happen, then that child will almost certainly have an advantage over one who *isn't* given that impression.

The School's Influence on Achievement

When children fail, often it is not they who are blamed, or even their parents. Often, the schools are held responsible. How much influence *can* schools and teachers have on children's achievement?

According to a recent article by British psychologist Michael Rutter, they exert quite a bit of influence. Rutter reviews the evidence for "school effects," gathered both in the United States and in England. His conclusion is that there are "successful schools" and "unsuccessful schools," judging by the students' performance on standardized achievement tests and by other criteria such as absence rates.

One factor that helps make successful schools successful is what Rutter calls the "academic balance" of its students: "the proportion of intellectually able and less able children." In his words,

> A child of any level of ability is likely to make better progress if taught in a school with a relatively high concentration of pupils with good cognitive performance. In other words, there is some kind of group effect; the school performance as a whole is influenced by the composition of the student body. (1983, p. 19)

Only the *intellectual* composition of the student body was found to be important. Whether there's a racial mixture or an ethnic mixture makes little difference. Rutter notes that studies done in the United States have shown that putting black children into predominantly white schools, or white children into predominantly black ones, has had no consistent effects on the academic achievement of either group.

Although an academic balance is helpful, it's not essential. There are successful schools with low proportions of bright students; there are also *un*successful schools with more than their share of them. Rutter cites studies in which schools are "matched" on the basis of the IQs of the students, measured when they first enter school. Despite this restriction, a successful school can produce notably better results than its less successful "match." Rutter mentions an extreme example: children who measured in the lowest 25 percent in verbal ability, and who attended the most successful school, did about as well on standardized achievement tests as children in the *top* 25 percent in verbal ability at the least successful school.

What accounts for such sizable differences in achievement? Rutter lists a number of factors that make a difference, and also a number of other factors that don't seem to matter much. Some of the factors that one would expect to make a big difference turn out not to. Among these *un*important factors are the amount of money per pupil allocated to a school, the number of books in the school library, the size and luxuriousness of the school building and of the schoolrooms, and the proportion of teachers with advanced degrees. In England, where some schools are co-ed and others are segregated by sex, that factor had no consistent effect on school achievement. Even the size of the classes—the number of children per teacher—mattered much less than one would expect. It was only in the first few years of schooling, for the teaching of beginning reading and math, that a small class size provided a real advantage.

What things *did* matter? They tended to be subtle things, things that are hard to measure: the attitude of the teachers and administrators, the overall atmosphere or spirit of the school. The successful schools, through the behavior and attitude of its staff, fostered a sense of purpose, a love of learning. In the successful schools, teachers took their jobs seriously: they arrived on time, assigned and graded homework papers, and spent a larger proportion of their time in actual teaching than the teachers in the less successful schools. The successful schools—even if they were old and crowded—were kept clean and orderly. Discipline was good, but there was not an excessive emphasis on punishment. Students who did well were publicly praised for their achievements, and all the students were given opportunities to take on responsibilities and to participate in school activities.

The Role of the Teacher.   Clearly no school can be successful unless the teachers within that school are successful, too. Rutter's review discusses teacher effects as well as school effects—we've already mentioned some of the things that teachers can do to further their students' progress.

There seem to be three main ways in which teachers influence their student's achievement. The first has been called "classroom management." Rutter lists some of the factors that are involved in successful classroom management:

> . . . a high proportion of lesson time spent on the subject matter of the lesson (as distinct from setting up equipment, handing out papers, dealing with disciplinary problems, etc.); a high proportion of teacher time interacting with the class as a whole, rather than with individuals; minimum disciplinary interventions; lessons beginning and ending on time; clear and unambiguous feedback to pupils on both

Children tend to learn more in school if their teacher practices good classroom management, if she models desirable behavior, and if she has high expectancies for her students.

their performance and what was expected of them; and ample use of praise for good performance. (1983, p. 21)

Why is it beneficial to have teachers spending a good proportion of their time in actual teaching? It's not simply the fact that more teaching leads to more learning. It's also that interruptions for any purpose—whether it's to distribute materials or to enforce discipline—tend to interfere with the class's concentration on the subject matter. The attention and interest of the students are likely to be lost. In addition, when the interruptions do involve discipline and reprimands, they're likely to have a negative effect on the classroom atmosphere.

The second way the teacher can influence his or her students is as a role model: to some extent at least, students do imitate their teachers' behavior. In schools where teachers are frequently late, attendance is likely to be poorer. Schools where the teachers don't bother about the maintenance of school property are likely to have higher rates of vandalism. And schools in which teachers break rules by slapping or shoving their students are likely to have higher rates of student misbehavior (Rutter, 1983).

Teachers can serve as role models in more subtle ways, as well. In one study of teacher effects (Yando and Kagan, 1968), 20 first-grade teachers were classified as either impulsive or reflective. By the end of the school year, first graders who had been in the classes of the impulsive teachers had become more impulsive. Those who had been in the classes of the reflective teachers had become more reflective.

The third way that teachers influence their students is by their expectancies and attitudes toward the students. We have seen that parents who expect their children to do well tend to have children with a strong desire to achieve. The same appears to be true of teachers with high expectancies: teachers who expect their students to do well tend to have students with good motivation—students who *do,* in fact, do well.

There is a possible catch here. As Rutter puts it,

> Of course, it might be thought that the observed association between high teacher expectations and high pupil achievement simply means that teachers are good judges of children's abilities. However, the findings make clear that this cannot be the whole explanation. (1983, p. 21)

What are these findings? The first important study of the effects of teacher expectancies is a well-known one. It was reported in 1968 by Robert Rosenthal and Lenore Jacobson. These investigators told some teachers in grades one through six that certain children in their classes were likely to be "spurters"—that these children might show sudden, rapid growth in intellectual ability. Actually, the names of the "spurters" were simply chosen at random. But at the end of the school year, these children (especially those in first and second grade) showed significantly larger gains in IQ scores than the other children in the same classes. Rosenthal and Jacobson felt that the IQ increase was due to the fact that the teachers *expected* these particular children to show increases in intelligence. This effect is often called a **self-fulfilling prophecy**—a prediction that comes true because of its having been predicted (Rosenthal and Jacobson, 1968).

Since 1968, a number of studies have investigated the effects of teacher expectancies. Not all of these studies have supported Rosenthal and Jacobson's conclusions, and their study has been severely criticized for having various weaknesses. But the teacher expectancy effect has been found often enough so that most psychologists believe in its existence.

For example, consider the effect on a child of having an older sibling who did either well or poorly in school. Let's say that this child has the same first-grade teacher as his or her older sibling. Will the child's teacher expect this child to do well if the older sibling did well, and poorly if the sibling did poorly? And will these expectancies have an effect on the younger sibling? The answer to both questions appears to be yes. Children with older siblings who were good students tended to do better in first grade if they had the same teacher as their older sibling. That is, they did better than children with equally bright older siblings but who had a *different* first-grade teacher. Similarly, children with older siblings who did poorly also tended to do poorly if they had the same first-grade teacher as their sibling. They did less poorly if they had a different teacher (Seaver, 1973). This study shows that teacher expectancies can work in both directions: good expectancies are likely to lead to better student achievement, low expectancies tend to depress achievement (Shaffer, 1979).

Think about what this means. Surely there are many teachers who expect white children to do better than black children. Surely there are many teachers who expect upper- and middle-class children to do better than lower-class ones. Surely there are many teachers who expect clean, good-looking children to do better than dirty or homely or overweight ones. The implications are saddening. It's another vicious circle: the less a child's teachers expect from him, the worse he does. And the worse he does, the less they expect from him. Of course, the circle works the other way too: high expectancies lead to better performance, and that in turn leads to higher expectancies. (See Box.)

Open Classrooms versus Formal Teaching. From time to time in the United States and in other English-speaking countries, there are movements in favor of "progressive education" or "open classrooms." These movements are based on a viewpoint very similar to Jean-Jacques Rousseau's (see Chapter 3)—that children merely have to be provided with the proper materials and left alone, and they will educate themselves. The idea is that children are endowed by nature with the motivation to learn and explore, and that traditional schooling stifles that motivation.

The pendulum in educational styles tends to swing back and forth, from the progressive view to the traditional, conservative one and then back again. In the past few years the pendulum has been swinging toward the traditional. The motto of this movement is "Back to Basics."

Some of the impetus for the "Back to Basics" movement came from a book written by a British investigator, Neville Bennett. Bennett (1976) made an extensive survey of 37 third- and fourth-grade classrooms in schools in northern England. The teachers of these classrooms were chosen as examples of

In the open (or informal) classroom, the students are permitted to choose their own activities and to move freely around the classroom.

An Apple for Miss A

The time was the 1940s. The setting was an old, fortresslike school located in a poor section of a large city in northeastern North America. It was a distinctly urban setting, surrounded by busy streets and factories.

> Across the street from the [school's] front entrance, the buildings of a brothel, thinly disguised as residences, blocked the view of a junkyard. Crowded tenement houses were interspersed with an automobile repair shop, a dry-cleaning plant, and an armature-wiring factory. The asphalt schoolyard was enclosed by a chain-link fence and the ground-floor windows were protected with vertical iron bars. (Pedersen, Faucher, and Eaton, 1978, p. 2)

Of the 400 to 500 children attending this elementary school at a given time within this period, about a third were black. The rest were mostly white Protestants. Only a minority of any of these children would ever graduate from high school, much less go to college. Fights and behavior problems were common. Unruly children were strapped—a school policy. There were about 500 strappings a year.

In the early 1950s a graduate of this school— one of the relatively small proportion who "made good"—returned to the school as a teacher. His name was Eigil Pedersen. Pedersen remained at the school for a number of years. During this time he began to look into the school records of the children who had been students there in the 1940s. Eventually he and his associates located a number of these ex-students—now adults, of course—and interviewed them. The results of this research were reported a number of years later in the *Harvard Educational Review* (Pedersen, Faucher, and Eaton, 1978).

Pedersen began his research in an attempt to find out why so few graduates of the school ever finished high school. But somewhere along the way that original purpose was abandoned. He came across something that startled him so much that he ended up just studying that phenomenon. That phenomenon was the effects on her students of one particular first-grade teacher, whom Pedersen calls "Miss A."

The school still had the records of all its former students—their marks in each grade, teachers' comments, and so on. Pedersen noticed that Miss A's students got higher grades in first grade than the students of the other first-grade teachers, although the school always made an effort to give each teacher a fairly equal selection of children. But perhaps Miss A was an "easy marker."

In this school, each time a class was promoted it was split up into equivalent groups so that each of the teachers in the next grade received an even share of the good students and the poorer ones. Thus, Miss A's former pupils had several different second-grade teachers. Nevertheless, these children got significantly better marks in second grade than children who hadn't had Miss A. The same was true in third

three different styles of teaching: formal, informal, and mixed. Formal teaching meant that the teacher told the children what to do and when to do it; their seats were assigned, and they were expected to stay in them and not

grade, in fourth, and in fifth. The difference was still detectable in seventh grade! The differences weren't small, either. In second grade, 64 percent of Miss A's ex-pupils got overall marks of "excellent" or "very good plus." Only 28 percent of the former students of other first-grade teachers did that well.

The most remarkable result emerged when Pedersen and his colleagues interviewed some graduates of the school and rated them on their adult socioeconomic status. There was a significant and sizable difference, with Miss A's former students being rated higher than those of other teachers. (The ratings were based on such factors as number of years of schooling completed, occupational level, and quality of housing.) Thus, Miss A's students not only did better in first grade than the students of other teachers— they *kept on* doing better.

Clearly, Miss A had quite an impact on her pupils. During the interviews, people were asked to recall their first-grade teachers of 25 year earlier.

> Many of the subjects could not remember the names of their teachers, and sometimes their memories were actually wrong, as we discovered when comparing their recollections with information on the permanent record cards. Despite the general difficulty of remembering every teacher, not a single subject who had been in Miss A's class failed to recall that fact correctly. Of those who had *not* been Miss A's pupils in first grade, 31 percent had no recollection of who their teacher had been, fewer than half identified their first-grade teacher correctly, and four subjects incorrectly named Miss A as their teacher. Memory seems to have been influenced by wishful thinking! (p. 19)

Apparently, Miss A was as fond of her students as they were of her. A reporter from a popular magazine interviewed some of her ex-pupils. They told him that Miss A could still remember them by name even 20 years after they graduated from her class. Every one of her students learned to read, regardless of background or abilities—she devoted many of her after-school hours to the children who were having trouble. If children forgot their lunches, she'd share her own lunch with them. She never lost her temper with her students: she kept control of the class by the power of her personality and the obvious affection she had for them.

Most of all, Miss A believed in her students. Pedersen's report sums it up this way:

> If children are lucky enough to have a first-grade teacher who has high expectations for their achievement, they will be more likely to develop positive academic self-concepts and to be more successful in school. (p. 22)

Out of school, too. It's a clear case of the *nonvicious* circle. Miss A expected her students to do well, and they *did* do well. What they learned in first grade, plus their heightened self-esteem and achievement motivation, gave them an advantage in second grade. This led their second-grade teacher to expect good things from them, too. And so it went.

There are just two more things to say about Eigil Pedersen and Miss A. Pedersen never got to talk to Miss A himself. By the time he had discovered her remarkable effect on her students' lives, she was dying of a terminal disease. And Pedersen himself, despite the fact that he was one of the more successful graduates of that school, was not one of the "lucky" ones. Pedersen's first-grade teacher had been Miss B. ∎

talk out of turn. Homework was given and tests were administered and graded.

With informal teaching, the children were allowed to decide where to sit and what to work on. They were permitted to talk to one another. The different school subjects were not kept separate and distinct—they were integrated in various ways. Homework, tests, and grades were not given.

Mixed teaching combined some aspects of formal teaching with some aspects of informal. The exact nature of the mix differed for different teachers.

Bennett's comparison of these three teaching styles was in terms of "pupil progress"—how much the children actually learned between September and June, as measured by achievement tests. He found that children simply didn't learn as much in the informal classes. In math and in English grammar and punctuation, children in formal classrooms learned considerably more than those in mixed or informal ones. In reading, children made more progress in formal and mixed classrooms than in informal ones.

When Bennett looked for a reason for these results he quickly found one: "Pupils in formal classrooms more frequently engage in work activity" (p. 113). In informal classrooms, where the teacher did not direct the children's activities, the children wasted more time—they talked to one another more, moved around the room more, fidgeted more. This was particularly true of the boys with high scholastic ability: "These pupils display a very low level of actual work activity, preferring to talk about it or simply to gossip socially" (p. 113). Bennett reports that the high-ability boys learned much less in informal classes than in formal ones—the difference in achievement was greater for this type of student than for any other.

Bennett did find one informal teacher whose students made above-average progress. It turned out that the students in her classroom spent as much time working on basic subjects as the children in the formal classes.

What about other aspects of development—social and emotional, for example? What about creativity? Don't children in open or informal classes do better in these respects than children with strict teachers? Bennett didn't find much support for this view. With regard to creativity, the stories written by children from informal classrooms were judged no more imaginative than the stories from formal classrooms. (The only difference was that the stories from the informal classrooms contained more errors in punctuation.) There were no major differences in the children's self-esteem, nor in sociability, even though the children in the informal classrooms talked to one another more. It's true that the informal students did enjoy school more—they had more positive attitudes toward school and schoolwork—but there was a catch. Some children, especially the nervous or insecure ones, became more anxious in the unstructured environment of the open classroom. Such children did better in the more predictable environment of the formal classroom.

Although not all studies comparing formal and informal teaching have led to the same conclusions, Bennett's study is an important one. It involved about 1,200 children. An even larger American study (Stallings, 1975), involving more than 6,000 children, led to similar conclusions: traditional teaching methods produced greater achievement in reading and math. Progressive, informal teaching resulted in better attitudes toward school and schoolwork.

If other studies have sometimes gotten different results, it suggests that the method of teaching may not be as important as the teacher herself (or himself). In Bennett's study there was that one informal teacher whose students spent as much time on schoolwork as those in the formal classrooms. This teacher did not use strict methods of control—she simply encouraged her students to be "work-minded." Their chief incentive was not grades but, as she put it, "They know I will be pleased if they do well" (Bennett, 1976, p. 98). Talented, dedicated teachers such as this woman and Miss A (see the Close-Up Box) seem to bring out the best in their pupils, regardless of the particular teaching method they use.

Intrinsic versus Extrinsic Motivation.   With a few exceptions, when teachers don't tell children what to do and see that they do it, the children seem to end up doing less schoolwork. Does this mean that Rousseau and his present-day followers are all wrong—that children won't learn anything if they're left to their own devices? Of course it doesn't mean that. But children are motivated to do and to learn many different things, and all of these things are competing for their time and attention. If we leave children to their own devices, they will certainly not sit around doing nothing. The trouble is, they probably won't spend their time learning their multiplication tables, either.

This brings us to the question of motivation. Let's say we see 10-year-old Cynthia reading a book about life in colonial America. We ask her why she's reading it. Looking somewhat annoyed at the interruption, she says, "Because it's interesting." A month later we see 10-year-old Jeff reading the same book and we ask him the same question. Looking somewhat annoyed at the interruption, he says, "Because I'm having a social studies test tomorrow, and I have to read this book so I'll get a good grade on the test."

If this child is reading her book because she likes to read or because she finds the book interesting, then her motivation is intrinsic.

Clearly, both of these children are motivated to read the book. But the first child has an **intrinsic motivation:** she's reading it because she *wants* to. The second child has an **extrinsic motivation**—he wants to make a good grade on the test. So reading the book can either be an end in itself (intrinsic motivation) or a means to an end (extrinsic motivation). In the case of extrinsic motivation, the incentive can be of many different sorts—we do things because we fear the consequences of not doing them, or because we want to gain praise, approval, gold stars, money, or other rewards.

The effects of such rewards on children are not always easy to predict. Assuming that Jeff had no prior interest in colonial America, he probably wouldn't even have considered reading that book without the extrinsic motivation provided by the test. Where no intrinsic motivation exists, an extrinsic one *can* produce results. But what about the cases where there already is an intrinsic interest? Let's say we got to Cynthia before she started reading the book and offered to pay her a dollar for reading the first four chapters. Naturally, she'll read the first four chapters and get her dollar. But will she then go on to finish the book? The evidence (from studies involving subjects from preschool age through college) suggests that she might not. The evidence suggests that she will be less likely to read the rest of the book than if we *hadn't* paid her to read the first part (Deci, 1971; Lepper, Greene, and Nisbett, 1973; Dollinger and Thelen, 1978). Interestingly enough, if we let her read the first four chapters and then *surprise* her by paying her a dollar for having done so, her intrinsic motivation probably won't diminish. The effect seems to depend, not on the reward itself, but on knowing about it in advance. If Cynthia knows she will get a reward for reading those chapters, perhaps she'll feel that she's only reading them because of the reward. Then, when no reward is offered for reading the remaining chapters, she may see no point in continuing (Lepper and others, 1973).

Fortunately, the effect we've just described seems to be fairly well confined to cases when tangible rewards such as money or candy are given. Praise and approval seem not to have a depressing effect on intrinsic motivation; nor do symbolic rewards such as gold stars. Since school grades fall into the category of symbolic rewards, they probably don't have much of an influence on intrinsic motivation.

Grades seem to have one unfortunate effect, though: they appear to make children less willing to take on challenges. In one study (Harter, 1978), 11-year-olds were asked to solve anagrams (sets of letters that can be unscrambled to make a word). The anagrams varied in difficulty, from easy three-letter ones to hard six-letter ones. The children were allowed to choose the level of difficulty of the anagrams they would do. One group of children were told that this was a game. A second group were told that they would be graded on their performance. The investigator found that the "grades" children chose easier problems to work on than the "game" children. The "grades" children also seemed to get less pleasure from solving the anagrams—they were less likely to smile when they had found the solution. And their comments indicated that being graded made them feel more anxious about their performance. The investigator felt that being graded in school might have similar effects—it might cause children to derive less enjoyment from their work, and make them less willing to attempt anything they weren't certain they could do well.

Does this mean that schools shouldn't use grades—that we should get rid of them? Not necessarily. The studies of open classrooms suggest that children do not have much intrinsic motivation to learn their math facts and the rules of English grammar. If we want children to learn these things—and most educators agree that we *do*—then the extrinsic motivation provided by grades may be better than no motivation at all. On the other hand, the de-emphasis on testing and grades found in open classrooms may be the reason why these students have more positive attitudes toward school and schoolwork.

LEARNING TO READ

Of all the things a child acquires in school, the ability to read is unquestionably the most important. Reading is the skill that most later learning is based upon. A great deal hinges on whether a child reads well or poorly or not at all.

In Chapter 10 we pointed out that virtually every child—all but the most severely retarded or brain-damaged—develops some sort of language. To communicate in words (or, in the totally deaf, in gestures) seems to be an ability that is built into the human species. Such is not the case with reading. Reading is a cultural invention, not a biological legacy. Speech develops in almost all children between the ages of 1 and 3; if it hasn't been acquired by adolescence, it probably never will be. Reading, on the other hand, is much more uncertain and variable in its appearance. It is seldom acquired before the age of 2½, but there is no upper age limit. Some people learn to read in adulthood. Some never do. Estimates of the proportion of adults in our society who, for all practical purposes, are illiterate range as high as 10 percent.

The Teaching of Reading

Given the variability of this ability, it isn't surprising that so much attention has focused on the issue of how to teach children to read. And given the importance of reading, it isn't surprising that this subject has generated some strong feelings. In 1955 a book by Rudolf Flesch, called *Why Johnny Can't Read*, became a nationwide best seller. Flesch argued in his book that the reason some children didn't learn how to read (he called them the "remedial reading cases") was that they were taught by the wrong method. His prose was vivid, inflammatory, and often sarcastic. Here's a sample:

> And how do the educators explain all the thousands and thousands of remedial reading cases? This is what really got me mad. To them, failure in reading is *never* caused by poor teaching. Lord no, perish the thought. Reading failure is due to poor eyesight, or a nervous stomach, or poor posture, or heredity, or a broken home, or undernourishment, or a wicked stepmother, or an Oedipus complex, or sibling rivalry, or God knows what. The teacher or the school are never at fault.

As to the textbook or the method taught to the teacher at her teachers' college—well, that idea has never yet entered the mind of anyone in the world of education. (Flesch, 1955, p. 18)

The method of teaching reading that Flesch objected to is called the **whole-word method**, or the *sight* method, or *look-and-say*. With this method, children are taught to recognize words as wholes, by their overall shape, rather than sounding them out letter by letter. Flesch thought that this was a ridiculous procedure. He believed in teaching children **phonics**—the correspondences between letters and speech sounds. He felt that they should be taught that way right from the beginning. And he felt that if they *weren't* taught that way, they were quite likely never to learn to read at all.

In that last belief at least, Flesch was overly pessimistic. The fact is that the great majority of children *do* learn to read, regardless of the method used to teach them. American children *are* able to recognize by sight a great many words—just as Chinese children learning the traditional Chinese characters have done for centuries. But American children have an advantage in that their written language is phonetic. Once they have learned to recognize a certain number of English words, some children are able to figure out for themselves the correspondences between letters and sounds. Proof that they have done this is their ability to read words they've never seen before—something that a child who simply recognizes words by their overall shape cannot do.

Perhaps you feel that figuring out the "code" of English phonics is an impossible task—that English spelling is too irregular. But, although English spelling and pronunciation are full of exceptions, they are exceptions to the *rules*. That there *are* rules is clear. People are quite able to offer pronunciations for nonwords like "snurb" and "flape"; moreover, there is usually good agreement on the pronunciation of such nonwords. As for the exceptions, they exist in spoken language, too—remember (from Chapter 10) "mines," "holded," "goed," and "feets"? Toddlers make such errors, showing that they have learned the rules despite the irregularities of spoken English. They soon learn the exceptions to the rules, as well. Both in written and in spoken English, the exceptions tend to involve the most commonly used words, which means that children get plenty of practice in learning them.

Why Can't Johnny Read?

We said that *some* children can work out the phonic code on their own, even if no one teaches it to them. Not all children do this. Children with higher than average intelligence, and children who are strongly motivated to learn to read, are more likely to do it than children who lack these assets. The brighter, well-motivated ones tend to become good readers regardless of the teaching method used. But what about the others? Is Flesch right in believing that many children can't learn to read with the whole-word method and that they *would* have learned with the phonic method?

The ability to read is undoubtedly the most important skill that children learn in school.

Why Johnny Can't Read started a tremendous controversy. Although educators tended not to take the book seriously, the questions it raised couldn't easily be stilled. Though the questions weren't answered, many publishers of school textbooks began hedging their bets by slipping some phonics into their early readers.

Then, in 1967, a book appeared that educators *had* to take seriously. It was a scholarly book, written by a faculty member at the Harvard Graduate School of Education. The book's title was *Learning to Read: The Great Debate*. The author, Jeanne Chall, started off by admitting that the "great debate" began with the publication of *Why Johnny Can't Read*. She ended up by coming to the same general conclusions that Flesch did—in a quieter, more moderate way, of course, and with heavy use of footnotes. Chall reviewed the research on the teaching of reading, much of it done after Flesch's book came out. She concluded that children who are taught phonics right from the start—taught to *decode* written words, as she put it—are better off. They're more likely to become good readers, less likely to become Flesch's "remedial reading cases," than children taught by the whole-word method.

Since Chall's book came out, the whole-word method in its purest form has virtually disappeared. Most reading teachers teach at least some phonics, although it's still common to try to sneak it in little by little, or to introduce it only after a number of words have been learned by sight. Perhaps as a result of the increase in the teaching of phonics, reading achievement has increased. Between 1971 and 1980, scores on a standardized reading test taken by 9-year-olds went up by 4 percent. Black and disadvantaged 9-year-olds showed even greater gains during that period—the improvement for black children was an impressive 10 percent (Micklos, 1982).

What Does It Take to Learn How to Read? Although the gap has narrowed a little, children from disadvantaged homes still do not read as well, on the average, as middle-class children. What is the source of the difficulty for the disadvantaged children? Research points to a previously unsuspected problem. Here's how one report describes it:

> In order to be able to make use of the relations between letters and sounds in learning to read, a child must, of course, be able to recognize the sounds when they occur in spoken words. But large numbers of the low-income first graders with whom we have worked had great trouble "hearing" the sounds in words when we tried to have them do so. . . . Middle-class children, on the other hand, frequently seem to find sound recognition to be a very easy task even well before the start of school. In one middle-class preschool we visited, in fact, the *four-year-olds* were already quite competent not only at recognizing a word's starting sounds but also at producing that sound for almost any word that we could give them! (Wallach and Wallach, 1976, pp. 46-47)

The problem the "low-income" children are having isn't really a hearing problem. They can easily hear the difference between *bat* and *cat,* for instance. The problem comes in knowing that these two words differ only in their first sounds.

There is much evidence that children who will have trouble learning to read are unable to divide up spoken words into their separate sounds. They're unable to tell that *bat* consists of a *b* sound followed closely by an *a* sound and then a *t* sound. They hear the word as a unit; they can't break it up into its component parts.

In one experiment, children were given the task of deciding how many sounds there were in some short words—three, for example, in the word *bat.* They were asked to indicate the number of sounds in each word by tapping a stick on the table. Before they had that test, they were given some training on a number of sample words, with the experimenter demonstrating the correct response for each one.

The test was given to 4-, 5-, and 6-year-olds. None of the 4-year-olds could do it, only 17 percent of the 5-year-olds, and 70 percent of the 6-year-olds. The 6-year-olds were first graders. When they became second graders, they were given a test of reading achievement. Of the children who scored in the bottom third of the class, half had failed the tapping test. Of those in the highest third of the class in reading achievement, not one had failed the tapping test (Liberman and others, 1977).

The same sort of problem shows up in many other ways. Children who are having, or will have, difficulty in learning to read are likely to be unable to say that *boy* and *button* begin with the same sound, or to give you a word that rhymes with *cat.* They are unable to speak in Pig Latin, which involves separating the first sound of a word from the rest of it. They have trouble responding to requests like "Say a little piece of *gate,*" or "Say *man.* Now say it again without the *m*" (Rozin and Gleitman, 1977; Liberman and others, 1977; Stanovich, 1982).

It's not clear why some children lack these abilities when they enter first grade. It *is* clear that if they lack them, they're going to have a hard time learning to read. Fortunately, it seems to be possible to teach children to "hear" the sounds in words. A training program designed to do this has shown promising results (Wallach and Wallach, 1976).

Good Readers versus Poor Ones.   Although some children have trouble dividing up spoken words into separate sounds, they seem *not* to have trouble dividing up written words into letters. Nor do they have much trouble learning to tell the letters apart. A considerable body of research done in the 1970s and 80s has led to a surprising conclusion: reading difficulties are seldom caused by a problem in visual perception, or even by a problem in visual information processing. The problem lies elsewhere.

Some psychologists (Rozin, Poritsky, and Sotsky, 1971) did an experiment with a group of second graders who had been unable to learn to read. They taught these children to read Chinese characters. The traditional Chinese characters are abstract symbols of the words they represent—they stand for ideas and generally not for sounds. The nonreaders were taught 30 Chinese characters—for example, the characters for *mother, good,* and *car* (see Figure 12–3). With only three to six hours of instruction, the children could read and understand simple stories written in these Chinese characters. And yet the hundreds of hours of instruction in first grade had failed to teach them to read English! It was clear that their problem was not in discriminating or remembering the 26 English letters—they had readily learned to distinguish and remember 30 Chinese characters.

If children with reading problems are able to recognize nonphonetic word symbols, it seems as though they'd be better off learning to read English with a whole-word approach. Why teach them phonics if phonics are where they're having trouble? Because, for one thing, if they don't know how to decode written English words—to analyze them phonically—they will never be able to read a word they haven't seen before, even if it's a word they frequently use in speech. And second, because there seems to be a rather

figure 12–3
Three sentences written in Chinese characters, successfully read by American children who couldn't read English. (Rozin, Poritsky, and Sotsky, 1971.) The top sentence, read from left to right, means "Father buys [a] black car." The middle one means "Older brother says Mother uses [the] white book." The last one says "Good older brother [would] not give [the] man [a] red car."

PROBLEMS IN DEVELOPMENT

Learning Disabilities

The term **learning disability** is used quite often nowadays. In general, it's applied whenever a child's achievement in school is considerably below—a grade or two below—what you'd predict from his IQ. We say *his* IQ on purpose. Among the learning disabled, boys outnumber girls by three or four to one (Farnham-Diggory, 1978).

A big difference between IQ and school achievement can be due to any number of causes. When it's a case of emotional or motivational problems, "learning disabled" is probably a misleading term. It's also misleading when applied to children who have serious visual, hearing, or motor disabilities, or who haven't been able to go to school for some reason. That still leaves a large number of children in the learning disabled category: 2 to 3 percent of American children is the usual estimate (Tucker, Stevens, and Ysseldyke, 1983). Most of these children fall into two categories: those with a reading disability, or **dyslexia**, and those who are hyperactive.

Children with dyslexia—especially when they're fairly bright children—have long interested psychologists. Because their problems resemble those of adults with certain kinds of brain injuries, their disability has been blamed on something wrong with their brains. One frequently mentioned possibility is that it results from abnormalities of brain lateralization—from a lack of clear-cut dominance of the left side of the brain (see Chapter 8). It's been said that reading problems are associated with left-handedness or with mixed dominance—when a

right-handed child is left-eyed or left-footed, for example. There is some weak support for this belief: dyslexic children are slightly more likely to be left-handed, to have mixed dominance, or to have less lateralized brains. But the differences are so slight that if you look at a large number of unselected children, you'll probably find no correlation between reading ability and various measures of lateralization (Hynd, Obrzut, and Obrzut, 1981; Watson and Engle, 1982).

Dyslexia has traditionally been attributed to problems in visual perception or in visual information processing. Children with this condition were said to "see things backwards"—to confuse *b* and *d*, for instance, or *was* and *saw*. Given the way the visual system is constructed, it's hard to imagine how such errors in seeing could occur. It makes more sense to blame errors of this kind on *memory* problems (see the Box on Left-Right Confusions, p. 268). But even that explanation may not be necessary. Recent evidence shows that, though dyslexic children do make many reversal errors, they make many other kinds of errors, too. The proportion of errors that are reversal errors is not higher in dislexics than in good readers (Stanovich, 1982).

Although the visual theory of reading disabilities has been rejected by researchers, the theory is not dying an easy death. It persists in the minds of many teachers and learning specialists. As one recent journal article complains,

> The visual perceptual deficit hypothesis assumes that problems in learning, and particularly in

severe limit on how many words can be remembered purely by sight. The average high school student in our society can read approximately 50,000 written English words. An adult Chinese *scholar,* on the other hand, can iden-

learning to read, can be attributed primarily to inaccurate perception of letters and words. . . . Though the visual perceptual deficit hypothesis has been severely criticized for the past two decades, it is still accepted by reading and learning disability practitioners. . . . Considering the criticism of the perceptual deficit hypothesis, it seems somewhat surprising that many practitioners still adhere to it, particularly in light of the dismal record perceptual training has in promoting reading or readiness skills. (Allington, 1982, p. 351)

Perhaps the reason for the persistence of this belief is the fact that the real problem is something a great deal more complicated. It's also a great deal harder to know what to do about it. And we're no closer than we were before to knowing the precise cause of the problem—where in the brain it resides and what it consists of. That it *is* somewhere in the brain is pretty clear. It's probably not an injury, though, but rather some difference in the way the brain developed. There's a hereditary factor involved. The siblings of dyslexic children, even when they are not dyslexic themselves, score behind their agemates in reading and spelling. One or both of their parents are also likely to have had learning difficulties when they were in school (Farnham-Diggory, 1978).

Hereditary factors are also known to be involved in **hyperactivity** (Willerman, 1973). Hyperactive children are the children who can't sit still, who are always getting into trouble. Here, for example, is how one 7-year-old boy feels about his own hyperactivity:

I am very tired of everything always being wrong and having to go for tests and my mom and dad look awful worried and soon I might have to go to another school. And what I would like a lot would be if I could just sit still and be the way the other kids are and not have all these things happen. And most of all I wish I did not break that mirror at Teddy Work's birthday party. (Ross and Ross, quoted in Farnham-Diggory, 1978, p. 80)

In school, hyperactive children are described by their teachers as inattentive, fidgety, and unpredictable. They speak out or leave their seats without permission. They are more impulsive and less reflective than other children. Most serious, from the point of view of the educator, is their inability to focus their attention on something and *keep* it focused. They are highly distractible (Brown, 1982). It is this problem, above all, that interferes with their learning.

Hyperactivity has been successfully treated with drugs, most often with methylphenidate (trade name: Ritalin). The drug helps them to calm down, to sit still, and to focus their attention. But there is concern about the long-term effects of drug therapy. There have been reports, for example, of interference with growth and of elevated blood pressure. Moreover, drug therapy does not work with every hyperactive child. For these reasons, behavior modification techniques (see Box, p. 104) have been used to treat hyperactivity. When parents and teachers gave praise and rewards for desirable behavior, the symptoms of hyperactivity declined (O'Leary, Pelham, Rosenbaum, and Price, 1976).

In the past, parents were told that their hyperactive children would eventually "outgrow it." This is no longer believed to be true: hyperactive children tend to become hyperactive adults (Farnham-Diggory, 1978). Fortunately, hyperactivity does not present such a problem in adulthood. In our society we ask children to spend their days sitting in a classroom and to pay attention to the teacher. Once they're adults, they are free to apply themselves to whatever they do best. ∎

tify only about 4,000 characters. Chinese characters are more distinctive than written English words; furthermore, many of them have some pictorial value that reminds the reader of their meaning. It's harder to recognize English words purely by sight. As a matter of fact, adult nonreaders in our society—the so-called functional illiterates—generally can recognize a certain number of common words by sight. They acquire a reading vocabulary of a few hundred words, but do not progress beyond that point. Their progress in reading stops at about the fourth-grade level (Rozin and Gleitman, 1977).

Interestingly enough, children who are born totally deaf and who are without a spoken language also have great difficulty progressing beyond the fourth-grade level in reading. Deaf children very seldom become good readers (Quinn, 1981).

Then *is* it some kind of a hearing problem that distinguishes good readers from poor ones? Not exactly. It seems to be more of a *speaking* problem. Not in speaking out loud, though—it's more of a problem with *internal* speech, speech that is thought rather than spoken. Nonreaders seem to have trouble with the kind of unspoken words that, in a different context, we've labeled *verbal mediators* (Chapter 11). In fact, they appear to have what's been called a *production deficiency,* a deficiency in producing verbal mediators (see p. 371). Although deaf children probably do use verbal mediators, they're likely to be sign-language verbal mediators rather than spoken words, spoken (or heard) inside the head. And it seems to be precisely the spoken (or heard) aspect of internal speech that matters.

Here's a typical experiment. It involved two groups of second graders, one group consisting of good readers, the other of poor ones. The two groups were matched in IQ—they differed only in reading ability. The children's task was simple. Strings of five letters, all consonants, were projected on a screen for three seconds. All the children had to do was to write down the five letters, which did not form a word. (The children could all write letters.) Sometimes they wrote down the letters as soon as as they saw them. Sometimes they had to wait 15 seconds before writing the letters.

As we know from Chapter 11, these letters have to be stored in short-term memory. To keep them there until they're written down, it's necessary to encode them (see p. 375), which in this case simply means saying "H" to yourself when you see an H. Then, to hang onto them for 15 seconds, they have to be rehearsed.

Two different sets of letters were used in this experiment. In one set the five letters might be, for example, H, R, K, L, and S. In the other set the five letters might be B, G, P, C, and T—all letters with rhyming names. If you have to say to yourself, "B, G, P, C, T," over and over, it's easy to get mixed up. It's harder to mix up "H, R, K, L, S."

The experimenters found that the good readers did significantly better than the poor ones when they wrote down the letters right away. The good readers also did much better than the poor ones when there was a delay—but only when the letters were nonconfusable. With the confusable letters, they were no better than the poor readers. For the poor readers, it made hardly any difference whether the letters were confusable or not. The experimenters concluded that good readers and poor ones differ in the extent to which they are able to use internal speech to keep things in short-term memory (Liberman and others, 1977).

A later experiment (Katz, Shankweiler, and Liberman, 1981) contributed some additional information but led to the same conclusion. The subjects were again second graders, good readers and poor ones. The stimuli were again of two sorts. One kind of stimuli were "nonsense drawings" or "doodles"—random squiggles chosen precisely because they couldn't easily be given names but had to be remembered visually. The other stimuli were pictures of familiar things that are easy to name—for instance, a fish and a tree. Both the good readers and the poor ones found it quite difficult to remember the unnamable doodles and to put five cards containing these pictures into the order in which they had been shown. On this task the good readers and the poor ones did not differ significantly. But with the namable stimuli, the good readers were much better than the poor ones. Apparently, the good readers were better able to say to themselves, "kite, horse, fish, sheep, tree."

Finally, a recent experiment used letters for stimuli and involved slightly older children. We won't go into the details, but the conclusions were basically the same. There was a further finding, though: the investigators concluded that the poor readers, just like the good ones, scanned the letters from left to right. (Some theories of reading difficulties are based on the idea that poor readers don't look at the letters in the right order—that they sometimes scan backwards, for instance. But this doesn't seem to be the case.) Moreover, the good readers and the poor ones both used—or attempted to use—the same strategy, that of encoding and rehearsing the letters from left to right. The difference, say the investigators, is only in the "speed and efficiency of carrying out the strategy" (Manis and Morrison, 1982, p. 84). That means that we can't turn poor readers into good ones simply by telling them, "Hey, why don't you name the letters and say the names over and over again inside your head."

Whatever the reason for the poor readers' inefficient use of internal speech, it's a serious problem. Even if they can decode the words in a sentence, if they can't hold the words in short-term memory, they'll have forgotten the beginning of the sentence before they get to the end of it.

summary

1. Going to school is the career of middle childhood; the child who does well at it will probably end up leading a very different kind of adult life than the child who does poorly. Some of the qualities required for success in school are the ability to concentrate on something despite difficulties or distractions, the motivation to achieve, and intelligence. Since all of these qualities influence performance on an IQ test, it is not surprising that IQ scores correlate highly with academic achievement. When the two differ considerably, it's likely to be in the case of the high-IQ child who does poorly in school.

2. An IQ score below 70 is generally taken as a sign of mental retardation (though that is a risky criterion, since a child may do poorly on an IQ test for many reasons). The great majority of retarded children fall into the category of the **educable mentally retarded** (EMR): few are ever institutionalized; most learn to read and write; in adulthood they can hold unskilled jobs. Their retardation is generally of the **familial** type, caused by a combination of genetic and environmental factors. The other type of retardation

is **biologically caused**—it results from a physical abnormality or injury of the brain. Such retardation is likely to be more severe in nature; many of the children in this group require constant supervision.

3. IQ is correlated with many other variables, including socioeconomic class, height and weight, activity level, birth order, and family size.

4. There are many examples of racial and ethnic-group differences on IQ tests, but the one that seems to worry people most is the black-white difference. Evidence from studies of black and mixed-race children reared by white mothers suggests that differences in childrearing styles play an important role in the difference in IQ scores.

5. The average girl does slightly better than the average boy on verbal items on IQ tests; she does slightly worse on spatial and mathematical items. Since IQ tests are designed in such a way that these kinds of items are fairly evenly balanced, there are no overall sex differences in IQ scores.

6. Gifted children, contrary to the common stereotype, tend to be taller than their agemates and superior to them in health, physical development, psychological adjustment, and social skills. They also tend to be high achievers, both in childhood and in adulthood. Although some "child prodigies" turn out to be misfits, they are the exceptions, not the rule.

7. Many factors influence the likelihood of a gifted child becoming a highly successful adult. These include characteristics of the home and the family, and various aspects of the child's own personality.

8. **Impulsive** children respond quickly on the Matching Familiar Figures Test, but they're likely to make many errors; **reflective** children respond more slowly and accurately. Reflectiveness or impulsiveness is, to some extent, a stable characteristic of a child's cognitive style, although all children tend to become more reflective as they get older.

9. Reflective children generally do better in school and on Piagetian conservation problems than impulsive children. According to one theory, reflective children are motivated by anxiety to do well on intellectual tasks plus a belief that they *can* do well if they try, whereas impulsive children have less confidence in their intellectual abilities and are motivated by a desire to escape the situation. Training can help all children to be more reflective, but it doesn't eliminate the differences between reflective and impulsive children.

10. **Achievement motivation,** according to one view, is something that parents teach their children. The parents' own attitudes toward achievement are influenced by their culture, their ethnic group, and their socioeconomic class. There is evidence that **independence training**—parental pressure to be self-reliant—leads to higher achievement motivation. Highly motivated children also tend to have parents who take pleasure in their children's achievements, who grant a fair amount of autonomy, and who have high expectations that their children will succeed. Measured achievement motivation is not necessarily a good predictor of success in school.

11. A better predictor of school achievement is **locus of control.** Children who believe in an **internal** locus of control feel that their successes or failures depend on their own efforts and abilities; such children tend to do well in school. Children who believe in an **external** locus of control attribute their successes and failures to luck or to the actions and attitudes of other people; they feel they have little control over events. Locus of control, like achievement motivation, is correlated with social class and ethnic group; it has been linked to similar sorts of parental behavior, such as encouraging independence. It seems to be important to give babies and children the feeling that they have some control over what goes on around them.

12. There are "successful schools" and "unsuccessful schools," judged by students' achievement scores, absence rates, and so on. Among the factors that appear to influence a school's success are its proportions of intellectually able and less able students, the attitude of

its teachers and administrators, and its overall atmosphere and spirit. The factors that seem not to matter are racial and ethnic mixture, whether a school is co-ed or all one sex, the size and luxuriousness of the building, the number of books in the library, and the proportion of teachers with advanced degrees.

13. Teachers can further their students' progress in three ways: (1) through good "classroom management," which includes such things as spending a high proportion of time on subject matter and a low proportion on discipline, beginning lessons on time, and praising students for good work; (2) as role models; and (3) by their expectancies and attitudes toward the students. What a teacher expects from a student may become a **self-fulfilling prophecy**—a prediction that tends to come true because of its having been predicted. Even a single outstanding teacher with high expectancies can produce a sizable improvement in the future achievements of her students.

14. An extensive study, done in England, compared pupil progress in formal (traditional) and informal ("open") classrooms. The children in formal classrooms made the most progress in math, in English grammar and punctuation, and in reading, mainly because the children in the informal classrooms spent less time at their schoolwork. There were no major differences in the students' creativity, self-esteem, or sociability, but the informal students did tend to have more positive attitudes toward school.

15. A child with an **intrinsic motivation** to do something is doing it because she wants to; a child with an **extrinsic motivation** is doing it as a means to an end. When intrinsic motivation does not exist, an extrinsic motivation (such as the offer of a reward) can produce results; but when intrinsic motivation *does* exist, the offer of a reward can diminish it under certain circumstances. Symbolic rewards such as school grades probably don't have much influence on intrinsic motivation, although they do seem to make children less willing to take on challenges.

16. Reading is unquestionably the most important skill a child acquires in school. Unlike language, the ability to read is not built into the human species: some people never learn to read.

17. Much controversy has surrounded the teaching of reading—particularly the issue of teaching **phonics** versus teaching by the **whole-word method.** Although the great majority of children learn to read regardless of the teaching method, there is evidence that children who are taught phonics right from the start are more likely to become good readers. The whole-word method is seldom used now in its purest form; perhaps as a result, reading scores have been going up.

18. Children who are unable to divide up spoken words into their separate sounds are likely to have trouble learning to read.

19. Reading difficulties are seldom caused by an inability to discriminate the letters of the alphabet. Poor readers seem to have a problem with internal speech, speech that is thought rather than spoken.

20. The term **learning disability** is used when school achievement is considerably below what you'd expect from a child's IQ. An estimated 2 to 3 percent of American children are considered learning disabled; the majority are boys. Most of these children either have a reading disability (**dyslexia**) or are **hyperactive**.

21. Dyslexia has traditionally been attributed to problems in visual perception or in visual information processing; such children were said to "see things backwards." Although this theory persists in the minds of many teachers and learning specialists, the evidence indicates that it is erroneous. Dyslexia probably does involve some kind of minor brain abnormality (in which heredity seems to play a role), but it does not appear to be due to a simple lack of brain lateralization.

22. Hereditary factors are also involved in **hyperactivity.** Hyperactive children have trouble learning in school because they are highly distractible—they are unable to focus their attention on something and keep it focused. Both drug therapy and behavior modification have been used successfully to treat hyperactivity.

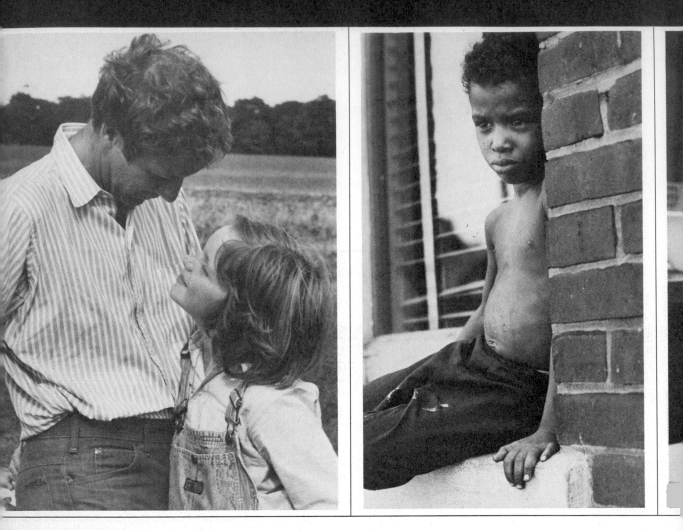

Chapter Thirteen

GETTING ALONG WITH ONESELF AND WITH OTHERS

Thirteen

Until quite recently in human history, the 8- or 10-year-old child was given many of the duties and responsibilities of an adult. Even today, in some parts of the world, 8-year-old girls are entrusted with the care of young infants, while 8-year-old boys work side by side with their fathers to provide the family with food. The fact that school-age children can successfully take on such responsibilities shows how far they have come—how much they have absorbed of the knowledge, the skills, the beliefs, and the attitudes of their society. It shows, in other words, how far along they have come in the process of **socialization.**

In our own society, in the twentieth century, we do not make, or even allow, school-age children to perform the work of adults. Like the lilies of the field, they toil not, neither do they spin (Matthew 6:28).

But don't be misled. Although we don't send 8- or 10-year-olds into the mills or the mines, we do expect a lot from them. As we pointed out in the previous chapter, we expect them to sit in a schoolroom for five or six hours a day, printing letters and numbers on sheets of paper, answering questions,

Less than a century ago, it was not unusual for school-age children to have to put in a full day's work in a factory. This photo, taken in a cotton mill in Georgia, is from the early 1900s.

deciphering printed text. We also expect them to know how to behave in a wide variety of situations—in the classroom, in the cafeteria, in the playground, in the library, on the street, in the supermarket, at the dentist's office, at a birthday party. We expect them to know the numerous and intricate rules of how to act with different people—with neighbors, grandparents, Dad's boss, other children, strangers. A 4-year-old can get away with remarks like "Mrs. Jones, how come you're so fat?" or "Mr. Smith, my daddy isn't really sick—he just didn't want to come to work today." An 8- or 10-year-old cannot. We expect school-age children to be sophisticated members of our highly complex society.

How well children live up to these expectations varies, of course. Some are more successful at it than others. A given child is likely to be more successful at one time than at another. One of the things we will discuss in this chapter is what we know about the reasons behind such variations.

SOCIALIZATION IN MIDDLE CHILDHOOD

Perhaps the most important part of what comes under the heading of socialization has to do with morality—with what our society considers is "right" and "wrong." School-age children are expected to know that lying, stealing, and harming others are "wrong," and that honesty and kindness are "right." We may not expect perfection as far as behavior is concerned, but we do expect children at least to feel guilty if they break one of these rules of morality.

The Psychoanalytic View

According to Freud, these feelings of guilt are the product of the superego, which is assumed to be fully developed by middle childhood. The superego, as you may recall from Chapter 3, is said to result from the resolution of the Oedipal conflict (or, in girls, the Electra conflict), at around age 6. Once children have become reconciled to the fact that they cannot possess the parent of the opposite sex, they identify with the parent of the same sex. With this process of identification, Freud says, the child takes on the moral beliefs and attitudes of the same-sex parent. At the same time, the sexual motive declines in power, to remain submerged until puberty arrives and reawakens it. Thus, the Freudian view of middle childhood is that not much is happening—it's the calm between storms. The turmoil of adolescence has not yet begun. The turmoil of the Oedipal period, with its strong desires and fears, is over. The important aspects of moral development have already occurred.

Erikson's View. But important things *are* going on. According to Erikson (1963, p. 260), middle childhood is "socially a most decisive stage." School-age children, in Erikson's view, have accepted the fact that their future lies, not within the family, but in the larger world outside the home. They therefore take on the task of learning the skills that will equip them for that future. They learn to apply themselves to work, rather than play. Getting along with people outside their immediate family becomes crucial.

The danger in this stage, according to Erikson, is that the child may feel himself to be less able than his peers to carry out the work society assigns him, or less able to win their respect and friendship. Consequently, he may develop a sense of inferiority that interferes with his ability to apply himself to his work. Inferiority versus industry is the central issue of Erikson's fourth stage. Thus, personality development and school achievement (discussed in the previous chapter) are closely related.

Social Learning

Erikson's view, unlike Freud's, recognizes that the parents aren't the only ones involved in the child's adaptation to society. By middle childhood, a variety of socializing forces have started to exert an influence. Aside from parents, many other people—siblings, other children, teachers, other adults—make their influence felt.

Reinforcement and Punishment.   These other people can serve, for example, as givers of reinforcement and punishment. The reinforcements and punishments can be as concrete as a piece of candy or a spanking, or as abstract as a nod or a frown. They can be given—in fact, often are given—without conscious intention to produce a particular effect. A study of families with "problem" children (Snyder, 1977) showed that these families were unintentionally reinforcing their children's displeasing behavior (with smiles or favorable comments, for example) and punishing good behavior (with frowns, criticism, and so on) to a greater extent than families with well-behaved children.

In other cases, an adult may act with the conscious intention to produce an effect, but the effect turns out to be the opposite of what was desired. A study done within a school setting (Madsen and others, 1968) showed that when first-grade teachers said "Sit down, John," and, "Sit down, Susan," whenever children left their seats, the children left their seats more often in the long run. (They'd sit down when the teacher told them to, but they'd soon pop up again.) It was only when the teachers started ignoring children who got up and praising children who remained seated that their behavior improved. Apparently, gaining the attention of the teacher was rewarding to these children. Being given attention, either from adults or from other children, often functions as a powerful reinforcer.

Learning by Observing the Behavior of Others.   Parents, teachers, and other adults exert a socializing effect in another important way: by serving as models. The influence can be a subtle one, as shown by the study of the impulsive and reflective first-grade teachers (see p. 401). And again, neither the

A girl with an older brother is likely to be more active and daring than a girl who doesn't have an older brother.

adults nor the children are likely to be consciously aware of what's going on.

Other children serve as models, too. In fact, by the middle of the elementary school years, the influence of other children is probably stronger in many ways than that of parents and teachers. Siblings, as well as unrelated children, serve as models. For example, it has been found that a child who has an older brother is more likely to be physically active and daring than one without an older brother. Somewhat surprisingly, this is true for girls as well as for boys—school-age girls with older brothers tend to be more active and adventurous than girls with older sisters or girls with no older siblings (Longstreth, Longstreth, Ramirez, and Fernandez, 1978).

Television. Children's behavior may also be influenced by characters they see on TV or in movies, or whom they read about in books and magazines. It's true that such characters cannot provide rewards and punishments; they may also seem to us to be quite unconvincing and unrealistic. But, particularly in the case of TV, these lacks are more than made up for by the vividness of the portrayals and by children's long and frequent exposures to them. Television is a potent socializing force. Unfortunately, because of the amount of violence it depicts, its overall influence is more likely to be negative than beneficial (see pp. 19, 296). Socialization can mean the acquisition of undesirable behaviors, as well as desirable ones.

Inductive versus Power-Assertive Discipline. In addition to learning from models and learning by means of rewards and punishments, school-age children are capable of another kind of learning, based on cognitive processes—on understanding and reasoning. Unlike the other two methods of influencing children's behavior, this one is likely to be used quite consciously by parents and other adults. It is called **inductive discipline,** and it consists of explaining to the child the reasons and justifications for behaving in a particular way (or *not* behaving in a particular way). This method is often contrasted with **power-assertive discipline,** which consists of enforcing standards of behavior with threats and punishment (Hoffman, 1977). For example, a parent using the inductive method might tell a child, "You shouldn't have taken Tommy's truck away from him. Look how sad he is! How would *you* feel if a bigger kid took *your* toys away from you?" A parent using a power-assertive technique, on the other hand, might say, "Give that truck back to Tommy and get in the house immediately! No more playing for you today!"

School-age children are far less egocentric in their thought than are preschoolers; they find it considerably easier to imagine, and sympathize with, the feelings of other people. They find it considerably easier to consider future consequences of current actions. Their reasoning ability is far better than the preschooler's. For all these reasons, inductive discipline is a successful method when used with school-age children, although it is usually not very successful when used with preschoolers (Brody and Shaffer, 1982; Johnson and McGillicuddy-Delisi, 1983).

With school-age children, when parents rely more on inductive techniques than on power-assertive techniques, a number of studies have shown that the children tend to be advanced in their moral development. They tend to **internalize** the parents' moral standards—to take them on as their own, to believe in them. If they deviate from these standards, they are likely to feel guilty. They may confess their wrongdoing and accept the blame for it.

Children whose parents rely primarily on power-assertive techniques, on the other hand, seem to be primarily motivated by a desire to avoid punishment. They have a tendency to break rules if they think they can get away with it. In terms of Kohlberg's theory (see the box on Moral Development, pp. 98–99), both their behavior and their reasoning are at a lower level of moral development than the children given inductive discipline (Hoffman, 1975a, 1977; Brody and Shaffer, 1983; Olejnik, 1980).

Theoretically, it all sounds quite clear-cut. The actual situation is really a lot more complicated, though. The problem is that, as we have pointed out often in this book, parent-child interactions are a two-way affair. We know that children's behavior does influence the way their parents act toward them. Could it be that parents tend to use power-assertive discipline chiefly with children who have proven to be unresponsive to reasoning?

There's some evidence that this is the case. Psychologists at the University of Virginia (Keller and Bell, 1979) trained three 9-year-olds to pretend to be either responsive or unresponsive to adults' instructions. The adults were college students. One adult and one child were left alone in a room, and the adult's job was to try to get the child to perform certain tasks, some of which involved benefiting other people. If the child was told in advance by the experimenters to be responsive, she looked often at the adult's face, smiled readily, and answered promptly when spoken to. If she was told to be unresponsive, she looked and smiled infrequently at the adult and answered very slowly or not at all. What the study showed was that when the children were responsive, the adults who interacted with them tended to behave in an inductive fashion. When the children were acting unresponsive, the adults who interacted with them tended to use power assertion.

It is probably the case, then, that both effects are going on: the parents' method of discipline is affecting the children's behavior, and the children's behavior is affecting the parents' method of discipline. It should also be noted that few parents use one method of discipline exclusively: it's generally a combination of the two. Many parents will start out by giving the reasons for why they don't want their child to do something, and then, if the child does it anyway, they will resort to punishment. Thus, children probably realize that the threat of punishment is present, even though unstated, when their parents reason with them (Kuczynski, 1983).

Sex-Role Development

By the time they enter school, boys are quite clear that they are male and destined to remain so, and girls are equally clear that they are female and will continue to be so. They have also absorbed a good many of our society's stereotypes of the sexes: they believe that males are strong, aggressive, and independent, and that females are emotional, gentle, and somewhat foolish (Williams, Bennett, and Best, 1975).

Such stereotypes have been shown to be well-established in children's thinking by the time they are second graders. After that point there seems to be no increase in belief in the sex stereotypes. In fact, one study of girls' sex-role attitudes showed that 11-year-old girls were *less* stereotyped in their thinking than 7-year-olds (Meyer, 1980).

Whether the same would be true of boys is doubtful. Boys are under much more social pressure to be "masculine" than girls are to be "feminine." Perhaps because they were subjected to these pressures while they were growing up, fathers seem to be much more stereotyped in their sex-role attitudes than mothers. In general, fathers are much more concerned than mothers that their sons be tough and active and that their daughters be sweet and "ladylike." In accordance with these concerns, fathers act differently with their sons than with their daughters. For instance, in one study of third graders (Tauber, 1979), a psychologist observed the behavior of child-parent pairs in a playroom provided with an assortment of toys. In this situation, there was no difference between girls and boys in their tendency to engage in active, physical play. Nor did mothers differ in their behavior, according to whether the child was male or female. But fathers did differ. When a boy engaged in active, physical play, his father tended to be supportive and to talk to him a lot. But when a girl played that way, her father tended to withdraw from her.

School-age children generally segregate themselves into all-girl and all-boy groups.

Relationships between the Sexes. At no time in their lives are girls and boys further apart than in middle childhood. In the preschool period, girls and boys sometimes play together, although mixed-sex friendships are less common than same-sex friendships even then. In adolescence, of course, the sexes get back together again. But school-age children segregate themselves rigidly by sex. A psychologist who spent some time observing preadolescents in an urban middle school (Schofield, 1981) reported that virtually no sixth graders or seventh graders sat at lunch with a member of the opposite sex. At one point in a science class, the teacher, forming groups of three for doing an experiment, told a sixth grader named Juan to join "Diane's group" of two girls. Juan refused. The teacher became angry when he was unable to make Juan give in and ended by sending him out of the room. Juan accepted this punishment as preferable to joining the girls' group. Perhaps, more than his teacher's anger, Juan feared the taunts of the other children: "Juan and Diane, sitting in a tree, K-I-S-S-I-N-G!"

However, as Figure 13–1 indicates, not all preadolescent boys are so reluctant to admit they are interested—even *romantically* interested—in girls. The rigid sex segregation masks a great interest, by both boys and girls, in the opposite sex. It is not all that uncommon nowadays for a sixth-grade boy, or even a *fifth*-grade boy, to claim to have a girlfriend.

Girl Friend X

figure 13–1
A drawing by a 10-year-old boy of himself and his girlfriend. (Smart and Smart, 1978, p. 200)

RELATIONSHIPS WITH OTHER CHILDREN

Interacting with other children plays a central role in the growing-up process. In Piaget's view, it is one of the factors responsible for the decline in egocentric thought. School-age children are likely to spend a good deal of time with other children who are on the same level of development. The necessity for cooperation, and the conflicts that arise when two egocentric children interact with each other, lead to an increased ability to take the other person's point of view.

What makes interactions between children particularly important is that they involve people of roughly equal status. An adult cannot interact on an equal basis with a young child. It is in equal-status interactions that children learn to take on different roles—for instance, leader on one day, follower on the next. They also learn that laws and rules, such as those that govern children's games, are made by mutual agreement and can be changed by mutual agreement (Piaget, 1965).

Relationships with other children serve many functions. A close friend or an older sibling can sometimes provide the kind of caring that, for one reason

THE CHILD IN SOCIETY

Desegregation in America

Children tend to choose friends whom they perceive as similar to themselves. This is true in nursery school (see pp. 313–314), but it is even more the case in elementary school. In a school where there are white children and black children of both sexes, friendships tend to be formed between children of the same sex and the same race. Of these two factors, sex is considerably more important than race in determining relationships between preadolescents. In the incident in which Juan was asked to join a group of two girls, both Juan and the girls were black. Had Juan been asked to join a group of two white boys, he probably would have obeyed. In the cafeteria of Juan's school, it is unusual for black students to sit next to white ones. But it is virtually unheard of for a girl to sit next to a boy.

Juan's school is located in a large city in the northeastern United States. Its sixth and seventh grades are roughly 50 percent black, 50 percent white. The administration and faculty are biracial. Both the blacks and the whites on the staff are openly committed to furthering good relationships between the black students and the white ones.

As yet, this goal is unmet. Black children and white ones eye each other with wary mistrust.

Both races perceive the black children as being aggressive and tough and the whites as soft, unable to defend themselves. This is true for girls as well as for boys.

Donna (black): The white girls are scared of the black girls.
Interviewer: Why do you think that is?
Donna: They (black girls) just like to bully.
Interviewer: Do they bully other black girls?
Donna: Those who let them. Most of the time white girls can't defend themselves as well as a black girl can. (Schofield, 1981, p. 76)

One of the problems at this school is that the whites, who are mostly from middle- and upper-middle-class homes, do much better academically than the blacks, who are mostly from lower-class homes. Not surprisingly, this produces a lot of resentment among the black students. They think of the white children as "conceited," as "goody goody two-shoes" (p. 77). Sometimes a higher-achieving white student will offer to help a lower-achieving black student in a school subject.

or another, a child's parents may be unable to give. Other children can also act as corrective influences in another direction. For instance, a child who has been overindulged by her parents and made to feel that she should have everything her little heart desires will quickly be brought down to earth by the no-nonsense attitude of her peers (Rubin, 1980; Sullivan, 1953).

Children's social behavior is influenced in a variety of ways by the actions and attitudes of other children. One study asked children what a child should

Black students often see such offers of help as yet another indication of white feelings of superiority and conceit. White students who do not perceive themselves as conceited feel mystified and angry when what seems to them to be friendly and helpful overtures are rejected. (p. 79)

There is a good deal of social pressure on the black students in this school to avoid friendships with whites. If a black child, especially a girl, is nice to white children, her actions are likely to be interpreted by her fellow blacks as disloyalty to her race. They may treat her badly. Similarly, when a black student shows any signs of doing well academically, he or she may be pressured by other blacks not to work so hard. Doing well in school is seen as another kind of disloyalty.

For black students . . . succeeding academically often means leaving their friends behind and joining predominantly white groups within their classes. (p. 78)

All in all, the attempt to foster good white-black relationships through desegregation seems to have failed at this school. Why is this the case? There are two reasons. One is that most of these children came from elementary schools that were overwhelmingly white or overwhelmingly black. It wasn't until sixth grade that they were thrown together. Clearly, it was too late.

Second, and perhaps more important, was the difference in social class. The superior aca-demic performance of the whites, and the greater tendency of the blacks to be aggressive and to break rules, was attributed by both blacks and whites to racial factors. In reality, socioeconomic factors were undoubtedly more responsible for these differences. But social-class distinctions are not as obvious, not as easy to make, as racial distinctions. Thus, the racial stereotypes held by both races were strengthened, rather than weakened, by the situation at the school.

Better results follow from desegregation that involves children from the same socioeconomic class. Girls and boys, 8 to 12 years of age, attended a summer camp that was roughly half black, half white. All these children were from economically deprived homes, so all were of the lower socioeconomic classes. After living together for as little as a week, both black and white children had significantly more favorable attitudes towards each other (Clore, Bray, Itkin, and Murphy, 1978).

Another study, done in the Midwest, involved black and white children who had attended desegregated schools from kindergarten onward. Most studies of race relationships in children have involved asking the subjects to "name your best friend" or "your three best friends"; such studies invariably show that most children choose their friends from within their own racial group. This study, however, asked children how much they liked to work or play with each of their classmates. These children gave rather high ratings to classmates of the other race—far

do in 10 different social situations, if friends and parents gave contradictory advice. The tendency to choose the friends' advice rather than the parents' advice increased steadily between the ages of 8 and 12, but even the 8-year-olds chose the friends' advice a little more often than the parents' advice (Utech and Hoving, 1969).

It has been observed that children who behave disruptively in school tend to be reinforced for their behavior by gaining the attention of their classmates.

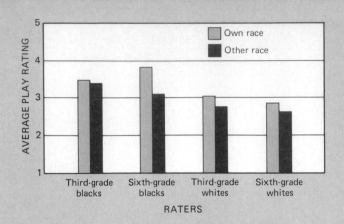

figure 13–2

Average play ratings given by third-grade and sixth-grade children to classmates of the same race and of another race. The ratings were given in answer to the question, "How much do you like to play with this person at school?" A rating of 5 meant "like to a lot" and a rating of 1 meant "don't like to." (Singleton and Asher, 1979)

higher than they gave to classmates of the opposite sex! Although they did rate members of their own race a little higher than those of the other race, the differences were relatively small (see Figure 13–2). Moreover, the white children showed no tendency to increasingly prefer the members of their own race as they went from third grade to sixth. The black children did show such a tendency, but again it was relatively slight (Singleton and Asher, 1979).

A final source of encouragement comes from a study in which children in first, third, and fifth grade were asked to give rewards to other children. They were instructed to decide how many "reward chips," supposedly redeemable for prizes, these other children should get. The rewards were to be given on the basis of the other children's ability to build a high tower out of blocks. The subjects were shown photos of the other children and photos of the towers they had supposedly built. Some subjects were white, some black; the children shown in the photos were also white or black.

Since the children were made to believe that the chips were rewards for good tower-building, they naturally gave more chips to the child who they believed had built the taller tower. And, in fact, the race of the pictured child made no difference at all. When one photo showed a black child and the other a white child, both black and white subjects gave out chips according to the height of the pictured towers. In other words, these children—from a rural area in northeast Georgia—were able to ignore race, when race was irrelevant to the matter at hand. They were able to concentrate on what *was* relevant—the other children's skill at performing a task (Graziano, Musser, Rosen, and Shaffer, 1982). ■

When the children in a sixth-grade classroom were trained to ignore disruptive acts and to give approval for desirable acts, the behavior of the disruptive child improved considerably (Solomon and Wahler, 1977).

Getting to Know Oneself

An essential function served by peer-group relationships is that it provides children with the opportunity for self-knowledge. Without standards of comparison, how can they know if they are tall or short, clever or dull? How can they tell what things they are good at and what things they are not? It is

Relationships with other children serve many functions in a child's development.

mainly by comparing themselves with their peers that children are able to develop a realistic self-concept.

By the time a child is in third or fourth grade, it is possible to predict with fairly good accuracy some of the characteristics of the future adult. School-age children's IQ scores, for example, correlate highly with IQ measures made 10 or 20 years later. An exceptionally tall child is unlikely to become a shorter-than-average adult; a well-coordinated one is unlikely to turn into a "klutz"; a social butterfly will probably never end up as a recluse. Although sizable changes are still possible, they are not probable. We can look at an 8- or 9-year-old and get at least a glimpse of the person he or she is destined to become. It is this relative permanence of the school-age child's character-istics that makes self-knowledge possible. The development of a self-image is a slow and gradual process.

The Development of Self-Knowledge.   Self-knowledge begins in infancy (see the box, on Origins of Self-Awareness, pp. 226–228), as the child comes to recognize that this baby in the mirror, this baby in the photograph, is *me*. According to a recent review of studies of self-knowledge, the toddler or the young preschooler conceives of himself in terms of physical characteristics and physical possessions: "I am different from Johnny because I have blonde hair, different from that tree because I am smaller, different from my sister because I have a bike" (Damon and Hart, 1982, pp. 849–852). Older pre-schoolers think of themselves in terms of activities: "I play baseball"; "I walk to school" (p. 853). Children of this age would rather be described in terms of activities and abilities than in terms of appearance: "Johnny can brush his teeth'' is preferred to "Johnny has a nice face'' (Keller, Ford, and Meacham, 1978).

At around 7 or 8 years of age, children begin to describe themselves relative to others. Activities are still important, but now it's not simply a question of what a child does, but of how well he or she does it compared with others: "I can ride a bike better than my brother" (Secord and Peevers, 1974). This is the age when they start to judge how well they did something—their performance on a test, for example—by comparing it to how well other children did (Damon and Hart, 1982).

Susan Harter, of the University of Denver, has constructed a test to assess children's self-concepts. It's designed to provide information about children's notions of their own competence or ability to succeed. Three different sorts of competence are included: cognitive ("doing well at schoolwork, being smart, feeling good about one's classroom performance"), social ("having a lot of friends, being easy to like, and being an important member of one's class"), and physical ("doing well at sports, learning new outdoor games readily, and preferring to play sports rather than merely watch others play"). There's also a fourth part of the test, aimed at measuring "general self-worth." This refers to "being sure of oneself, being happy with the way one is, feeling good about the way one acts, and thinking that one is a good person" (Harter, 1982, p. 88). A sample item from the test is shown in Table 13–1.

Harter and her colleagues have tried out this test on a number of children in grades three through six in schools across the country. They found that school-age children are able to rate themselves in these four different ways, and that their answers are consistent and reliable. (Reliability was judged by retesting nine months later—see p. 332.) Moreover, the children were reasonably accurate in their self-assessments. Their scores on the cognitive part of the test correlated significantly with their teachers' assessments of their abilities and with their achievement test scores. (The correlations were generally in the range of .40 to .50.) Scores on the social part correlated highly (around .60) with popularity ratings by classmates. Scores on the physical part correlated highly (also around .60) with ratings by gym teachers.

Last and most important, the correlation between perceived competence in these three areas, and actual competence (as measured by teachers' ratings, academic achievement tests, and popularity ratings) becomes steadily

TABLE 13–1 A Sample Question from Harter's Test of Children's Concepts of Their Own Competence

Really true for me	Sort of true for me			Really true for me	Sort of true for me
☐	☐	Some kids often forget what they learn	but Other kids can remember things easily	☐	☐

From Harter, 1982, p.89.

stronger from third grade to sixth. It appears that during the elementary school years, children develop a self-image that corresponds ever more closely to reality (Harter, 1982).

Friendship

It goes without saying that interactions with other children are important in their own right. Having friends, being with friends, playing with friends— these are among the chief joys of childhood.

Children play together in every society and have done so throughout human history. Similar behavior is seen in apes and monkeys. Young rhesus monkeys, for example, spend more time with other young monkeys than with their mothers by the time they are 4 months old. If a young monkey is raised in a cage with its mother but without peers to play with, its later social behavior will be abnormal. It will avoid other monkeys, or attack them out of fear. Monkeys are sociable animals by nature, but they must have the opportunity to develop patterns of social interaction while they're still young. Interaction with the mother is not enough (Suomi and Harlow, 1975).

Theories of Friendship. Harvard psychologist Robert Selman has proposed that children's friendships proceed in four stages (see Table 13–2). The first stage can be seen in the preschool period:

> A close friend is someone who lives nearby and with whom the self happens to be playing with at the moment. Friendship is more accurately playmateship. (Selman, 1981, p. 250)

Preschool friendships, then, tend to depend on the needs and feelings of the moment, on the physical presence of the other child, and on the toys or facilities that are available (see p. 310).

The second stage is characteristic of the early school years. Selman calls it "one-way assistance":

> Friendship conceptions are one-way in the sense that a friend is seen as important because he or she performs specific activities that the self wants accomplished. (p. 250)

In other words, the child's attitude towards a friend, in the first part of middle childhood, is "What can you do for me?"

In the latter half of middle childhood, starting at around age 9, children become able to view friendship as a two-way relationship. This advance is made possible by their increased ability to take the other person's perspective—to see things from another's point of view. There's a new concern with cooperation, a new awareness of the reciprocal nature of friendship: "If you do that for me, I'll do this for you." But relationships are still only "fair-weather friendships":

> Arguments are seen as severing the relationship. . . . No underlying continuity is

seen to exist that can maintain the relation during the period of conflict or adjustment. (p. 251)

"I wouldn't worry," said Selman in an interview with a newspaper reporter, "if a 7-year-old has a friend who is here today and gone tomorrow. That's the nature of child friendships" (Siegel, 1982, p. 49).

In late childhood or early adolescence, if all goes well, the fourth stage emerges. Selman calls it "intimate and mutually shared relationships":

TABLE 13–2 Selman's Stages of Friendship

Stage	Approximate Time Period	Description
Playmateship	Preschool period	A friend is someone who lives nearby and whom one happens to be playing with at the moment.
One-way assistance	Early school years	A friend is important because he or she does specific things that the child wants done. A close friend is someone who is known better than other people, where "known" means being aware of the other person's likes and dislikes.
Fair-weather cooperation	Later school years	There is a new awareness of the reciprocal nature of friendship and a new willingness to adjust to the likes and dislikes of the other person. But there is no long-term continuity—arguments are seen as a cause for breaking off the relationship.
Intimate and mutually shared relationships	Late childhood or early adolescence	There is a closer bond between friends and a new awareness of the continuity of the relationship. Friendship is not seen merely as a way to avoid being bored or lonely, but as a basic means of developing intimacy and mutual support. Friends share intimate problems. Conflicts do not necessarily bring an end to the relationship.

Based on Selman, 1981.

The importance of friendship does not rest only upon the fact that the self is bored or lonely; . . . friendships are seen as a basic means of developing mutual intimacy and mutual support; friends share personal problems. The occurrence of conflicts between friends does not mean the suspension of the relationship. (Selman, 1981, p. 250)

Having a "Chum."   Although Selman does not emphasize this point, it's assumed that in the last two stages children begin to care about their friends in an unselfish way—their friends' feelings begin to matter to them. Back in the 1950s, psychiatrist Harry Stack Sullivan proposed a simpler theory of school-age friendships: a self-centered stage, from age 4 or 5 to age 8, followed by a period of what he called **chumship,** from 8 to 11. Chumship, in Sullivan's view, was based on intimacy and on an unselfish kind of mutual concern:

If you will look very closely at one of your children when he finally finds a chum . . . you will discover something very different in the relationship—namely, that your child begins to develop a new sensitivity to what matters to another person. And this is not in the sense of "what should I do to get what I want," but instead "what should I do to contribute to the happiness or to support the prestige and feeling of worthwhileness of my chum." (Sullivan, 1953, p. 245)

Sullivan, like Piaget, believed that associating with other children helps to free a child from egocentric thought. In Sullivan's view, having a chum causes the child to learn to see things from another's point of view and, consequently, to care more about the other person's feelings.

Two developmental psychologists at the University of North Carolina recently revived Sullivan's theory and put it to the test. They studied fifth graders and sixth graders who had a close, mutual friendship with one of their classmates—meaning, say, that Claire names Heather as her best friend and Heather names Claire, and that they do things together such as tell each other secrets and sleep over at each other's houses. Just as Sullivan would have predicted, such children were more likely than other children to act in helpful and unselfish ways, and better at taking another person's viewpoint. These children scored higher in a test in which they were asked to imagine the feelings and motivations of characters in a tape-recorded story. On the playground or in the lunchroom, they were more likely to offer assistance to a child who was hurt and more likely to share their lunch with someone who didn't have one. Incidentally, only 87 out of 230 fifth and sixth graders in the school had the kind of close mutual friendship that met the researchers' definition.

As the researchers themselves pointed out, the direction of causality in this study isn't clear. Does friendship make children less selfish (as Sullivan thought), or does being less selfish make a child more likely to develop a close friendship? The answer, say the researchers, must wait "until the appropriate data have been gathered" (McGuire and Weisz, 1982, p. 1483).

School-age girls tend to form close, one-to-one friendships. They tend to reveal more of themselves to their friends than boys do.

Girls' Friendships and Boys' Friendships. Sullivan talked about how a child will change when "he" finally finds a chum. Actually, the kind of close, mutual friendship Sullivan described is more characteristic of girls than of boys. It has been noted in a number of cultures—not just our own—that boys are more likely to play in groups than girls, and that girls are more likely to form pairs. Closeness and the sharing of personal concerns are more apt to occur in a one-to-one relationship, and girls' friendships are likely to be more intimate than boys'. Girls tend to reveal more of themselves to their friends (Rubin, 1980; Dweck, 1981).

Zick Rubin, a professor at Brandeis University who specializes in the study of children's friendships, points out another difference between girls' friendships and boys':

Along with their greater concern with intimacy, girls have been found to be more exclusive than boys, in the sense that they are less likely to expand their two-person friendships to include a third person. Girls appear to have a more acute appreciation than boys of the fragility of intimate relationships and of the ways in which one friendship may sometimes threaten another. Eleven-year-old Sarah reports: "Joan's now trying to hang around the older kids so as to be admitted into their gang so she has no time to be with Liz who therefore tries to be friends with

School-age boys tend to play in groups, rather than to form pairs. There is less jealousy and fewer attempts to exclude outsiders, but there is more competitiveness.

Christine which doesn't please Sally." Boys . . . are typically less sensitive to such dilemmas of intimacy. And because of girls' greater concern with intimacy, jealousy seems more likely to arise in girls' than in boys' groups. (Rubin, 1980, p. 108)

The greater tendency of girls to have chums, in Sullivan's sense of the word, has its drawbacks—more jealousy, more attempts to exclude third parties, more hurt feelings. But the boys' style of friendship has some disadvantages, too: boys are more likely to compete with their friends and less likely to share with them. In one study (Berndt, 1981), kindergarteners, second graders, and fourth graders were tested in pairs. The pairs were always of the same sex and grade, but some pairs were close friends, whereas others were just acquaintances. Both children had to color a color-by-number design; they were told that the one who colored the most areas would get 10 cents and the other child would get a nickel. The catch was that there was only one crayon of each color, so the children had to share.

The results were informative. When a girl asked the other girl if she could use a particular crayon, her partner usually handed it to her. It made no difference whether or not they were friends. But boys were less likely to hand over the crayon, and they were significantly *less* likely to give it to a friend than to an acquaintance! Apparently, the boys were more relaxed with a friend than with an acquaintance, so they felt more free to do what they wanted to do. And what they wanted to do was to *win*.

That girls seem more inclined to share goes along with Sullivan's theory that unselfishness results from chumship. There's other evidence, too, that girls perform more **prosocial** acts (sharing, helping, and so on) than boys do. For example, a study of children in fourth through sixth grades (Payne, 1980) involved five situations in which the children had an opportunity to help, share, or cooperate with others. Girls behaved more prosocially than boys in four of the five situations; in the fifth there was no difference.

These results suggest that Sullivan was right—that chumship, found more often in girls, leads to unselfishness. (The opposite hypothesis—that because girls are less self-centered they are more likely to have a close friend—seems a lot less plausible.) But there is another logical possibility. The study we just mentioned also showed that older children behaved more prosocially than younger ones. Since girls are developmentally more mature than boys all through middle childhood, the difference in prosocial behavior may be due to their greater maturity.

Popular and Unpopular Children. We have mentioned studies in which children are asked to name their best friends, or three children they especially like, or to say how much they like working or playing with the various members of their class. In other studies, children have also been asked to name three children they *don't* like (as well as naming their friends), or to go through a list of the names (or pictures) of their classmates and rate each on a scale of 1 to 5 according to how well they like them. All of these methods produce what are called **sociometric measures** of children's popularity with their peers—that is, measures of their **sociometric status.** (The data from such studies are considered highly confidential—the names and scores of individual children are never made public.)

Sociometric measures consistently show that children vary considerably in how well they are liked by their peers. Moreover, these variations tend to persist over time—a child who is well-liked in third grade will probably be well-liked in fourth grade, too. It is equally true that an unpopular third grader is likely to become an unpopular fourth grader. The question, then, is obvious: How do children with low sociometric status—unpopular children—differ from their more popular classmates? In recent years there have been a number of attempts to answer this question.

It has been found that unpopular children do less well, on the average, on measures of academic achievement (Green, Forehand, Beck, and Vosk, 1980). They are likely to be less attractive, physically, than the popular children. They are more likely to be firstborn or only children and less likely to be later-borns (Shaffer, 1979).

It also seems that a child who is different in any way from his or her classmates bears a greater risk of having popularity problems. We mentioned earlier that children tend to name as their friends other children of the same race. Thus, the one or two white children in a mostly black class, or the one or two black ones in a mostly white class, may have a rough time of it. But much less obvious differences matter, too—even a child's first name. Children who have odd or unusual first names have been found to be less popular with their peers than children with common names (McDavid and Harari, 1966).

In one study, children in third and fifth grades were asked to suggest ways to help another child who is in trouble—for example, a child who is being teased by his classmates. The popular children tended to make standard kinds

A child who's different in any way from his classmates is less likely to be popular.

of suggestions—suggestions that many of their classmates made, as well. The unpopular children were more likely to come up with unusual suggestions—suggestions no one else made. The experimenters felt that these unpopular children "lack knowledge of peer norms or values" (Ladd and Oden, 1979, p. 408).

Another study showed that unpopular children differed from popular ones in their knowledge of how to make friends. The children were asked to pretend that the experimenter was a new child at school with whom they wanted to make friends. Popular children were more likely than unpopular ones to make suggestions such as "Wanna come over to my house sometime?" or to offer information such as "My favorite sport is basketball" (Gottman, Gonso, and Rasmussen, 1975, p. 712). On the other hand, the popular children did no better than the unpopular ones in tests of imagining another person's point of view. This result might seem at first glance to conflict with what we said a little while ago: that children with chums were better at imagining other people's feelings and motivations. But having a close friend isn't the same as having high sociometric status. Popularity as defined by sociometric measures depends on being liked by many children, not by just one. In the study of chumship, sociometric status was *not* correlated with the ability to imagine other people's feelings or to behave in unselfish ways (McGuire and Weisz, 1982).

In fact, when it comes to *behavior,* it's rather hard to find consistent differences between popular and unpopular children. In Chapter 9 we mentioned that popular children gave more "social reinforcements" to their classmates than unpopular ones did. ("Social reinforcements" were defined as praising or smiling at another child, showing affection, complying with a request, and so on.) But that was in nursery school. In elementary school, the situation is more complicated. One study did find that popular third and fourth graders were giving out more social reinforcements than unpopular ones (Gottman, Gonso, and Rasmussen, 1975). Other studies have failed to find any differences at all in the social behavior of popular and unpopular children (Oden and Asher, 1977; Hymel and Asher, 1977).

Failure to find a difference, however, doesn't mean that there *are* no differences. The differences may be subtle and difficult to observe, or they may show up only in certain situations that don't occur very often in a classroom or on the playground. What happens, for instance, if an adult instructs a child to join two other children who are playing a game in another room? This was the situation used in one recent study. The behavior of the three children was videotaped by a hidden camera and later analyzed.

What the experimenters found was that the popular and the unpopular children had different ways of trying to gain entry into the game—different **entry strategies,** as the experimenters called them. Unpopular children generally tried to gain the attention of the other children by asking questions, by disagreeing with what one of them said, by saying something about themselves, or by stating their feelings or opinions. Here's an example of an unpopular child's unsuccessful bid for entry. Janet and Vera have been playing together for 10 minutes (they're now choosing playing pieces again), and Terry is the third girl who's trying to join their game.

Janet:	Okay, I want this one again.
Terry:	This is fun, ain't it?
Janet (to Vera):	Do you want this one again?
Vera:	I want this one.
Terry:	This is a nice room, ain't it?
Janet (to Vera):	You can have this one. Here.
Terry:	This is a nice table, ain't it? (Putallaz and Gottman, 1981, p. 141)

In contrast, the popular children tried to blend into the ongoing activities, rather than draw attention to themselves. Here's an example of a popular child's successful bid for entry. Sam and Craig are the pair who have been playing together and Matt is the newcomer.

Sam:	Animals.
Craig:	What'd you get . . . B?
Matt:	What'd you go and pick?
Sam:	Take another turn.
Matt:	Bear.

Sam: Gorilla. Thank you, Matt.
Matt: Let's see . . .
Sam: Move ahead . . .
Matt: Your turn.
Craig: Animals. Bear.
Matt: Hey. Mix these up.
Craig: I know. Okay, hold it. Yeah, do that. I got move ahead 3. Ooh.
        How lucky can you get. 1, 2, 3. Your turn, Matt. (pp. 141–142)

Not surprisingly, the popular children were much more likely than the unpopular ones to be accepted into the game. Unpopular children were not so much rejected outright as simply ignored.

Different Types of Unpopular Children.   We have so far spoken as though unpopular children are all the same—a single, distinctive type of child. That is not the case. There are several different personality patterns that characterize children who have been labeled "unpopular." The composition of the "unpopular" group in a given study depends on the particular sociometric measure that is used. That's one reason why results in this field have been so inconsistent.

The most common method of determining sociometric status is to ask the children in the class to name their best friends or to name some children they especially like. (Sometimes they have to name a certain number, sometimes they can name as many as they wish.) The problem is that this measure doesn't always agree with other measures.

For instance, one study (Hymel and Asher, 1977) involved 205 third, fourth, and fifth graders. Of this group, 23 were not named by a single child as being "especially liked." But the children were also asked to rate each of their classmates on a scale of 1 to 5 according to how much they like to play with that child. (Smiling and frowning faces helped them to remember that 1 means "don't like to" and 5 means "like to a lot.") When this was done, it was found that 11 of the 23 children whom no one had named as "especially liked" nonetheless received fairly high play ratings—an average of 3 or above. Clearly, these 11 children were acceptable to many of their peers—they simply weren't considered as a best friend by anyone in the classes that were tested. (Perhaps they had best friends in other grades or going to other schools.) Moreover, of the 46 children who received play ratings that averaged *below* 3, 22 of them *were* named as "especially liked" by one child in the class, and 12 were named by two or more children. It appears that there is little relationship between being generally popular with one's classmates and having a good friend. There are "unpopular" children with close friends, and there are probably "popular" children without them.

In the study we just described, only 12 of the 205 children got no "especially like" nominations and received low play ratings, too. Even this small group (about 5 percent of the total) may not consist of a single type of unpopular child. Some studies, as we mentioned earlier, also ask children to name classmates they "don't like very much." When children are asked to make both kinds of nomination—to name children they especially like and children

Training Children in the Art of Being Likable

It has been found in the past that children who are unpopular with their peers bear a greater risk of a number of problems later in life. The problems include delinquency, dropping out of school, bad-conduct discharges from the military, and mental health difficulties. The unpopular children who run these risks are probably the disliked ones, rather than the ignored ones. Children who simply have low rates of interaction with their peers—children who are alone a lot—are probably *not* at greater risk than their more sociable classmates. There is little relationship between how much children interact with other children and how well they are liked (Asher, Markell, and Hymel, 1981; Asher and Hymel, 1981).

For this reason, simply getting children to interact with their peers—for example, by reinforcing them for doing so—is not a solution to the problems of the disliked child. It's not the quantity of their interactions that's at fault, it's the quality.

Several attempts have been made to improve the quality of children's interactions with their peers. The most successful of these attempts have involved direct one-to-one coaching of unpopular children, in order to teach them the social skills they seem to lack. One study involved third and fourth graders who received very low ratings from their classmates on two questions: "How much do you like to play with this person at school?" and "How much do you like to work with this person at school?" (Oden and Asher, 1977, p. 497).

The unpopular children who were selected for the training participated in six sessions over the course of a month. Each child was paired with a moderately popular classmate, and the two children were taken to a separate room where they played games together. Before each of these sessions except the first, one of the experimenters—the "coach"—took the unpopular child into a private room and asked whether he or she enjoyed playing the game last time. Then the coaching began:

> The coach then said, "I have some ideas I'd like to talk to you about what makes it fun to play a game with another person."

> The child was then instructed for 5–7 minutes on the following concepts: participation (e.g., getting started, paying attention); cooperation (e.g., taking turns, sharing materials); communication (e.g., talking with the other person, listening); and . . . being friendly, fun, and nice (e.g., looking at the other person, giving a smile, offering help or encouragement). (Oden and Asher, 1977, p. 499)

Here's an example of part of a typical coaching session:

> Coach: Okay, I have some ideas about what makes a game fun to play with another person. There are a couple of things that are important to do. You should *cooperate* with the other person. Do you know what cooperation is? Can you tell me in your own words?

they don't like—there is often very little relationship between *those* measures, too. In other words, the fact that some children receive a lot of positive nominations (meaning that they are often named as especially liked) doesn't prevent them from receiving some negative ones. And a child who receives *no*

Child: Ahh . . . sharing.

Coach: Yes, sharing. Okay, let's say you and I are playing the game you played last time. What was it again?

Child: Drawing a picture.

Coach: Okay, tell me then, what would be an example of sharing when playing the picture-drawing game?

Child: I'd let you use some pens too.

Coach: Right. You would share the pens with me. That's an example of cooperation. Now let's say you and I are doing the picture-drawing game, can you also give me an example of what would *not* be cooperating?

Child: Taking all the pens.

Coach: Would taking all the pens make the game fun to play?

Child: No!

Coach: So you wouldn't take all the pens. Instead, you'd *cooperate* by *sharing* them with me. Can you think of some more examples of cooperation? [The coach waited for a response.] Okay, how about taking turns . . . (p. 500)

After the training session, the other child was brought in and the two children played together. Then, afterwards, the other child was sent back to the classroom, and the coach asked the unpopular child, "Did you get a chance to try out some of the ideas we talked about?" and "Did you think that [the other child] liked playing the game?" (p. 500). The coach went on to review the concepts that were discussed in the training session.

A few days after the last training session, all the children in these classrooms again made work ratings and play ratings of their classmates. The play ratings of the children who were coached—the ratings of them by their classmates—were significantly higher than they had been a few weeks earlier. (The work ratings were unchanged. But then, the coaching had involved *playing*, not working.) There was no change in the work or play ratings of a control group of equally unpopular children who had received no coaching but who had played games with more popular peers.

A year later, the play ratings were made again. The coached children were now in different classrooms; many of their current classmates had not been in their class the previous year. The play ratings that the coached children received from their classmates were even higher than they had been right after the coaching sessions. In fact, they were now only slightly below the mean for the class. It would seem that the coaching sessions gave these children a shove in the right direction, and once they were started, they continued to move ahead on their own.

Aside from the particular social skills taught in the training sessions, it's possible that these children learned something even more important: that their behavior can influence how another person feels about them. During one of the later training sessions, one of the coached children suddenly came to this realization. "You mean, what I do affects whether kids like me or not?" she exclaimed (quoted in Asher and Renshaw, 1981, p. 289).

It probably seems obvious to you that what you do affects how others feel about you. But what if you were a child who believed in an external locus of control (pp. 396–398)? Mightn't you feel that what you did made no difference—that if people didn't like you it was simply because you weren't any good? There *are* children like this. And probably the most valuable gift we can give them is the feeling that they have some control over other people's reactions to them (Dweck, 1981). ∎

positive nominations doesn't necessarily receive negative ones. In fact, some children receive very few nominations of either sort. These children are said to be *neglected* by their peers. The ones who receive few or no positive nominations and who do receive negative nominations are said to be *rejected* by their peers. Neglected children tend to be the shy, quiet ones nobody notices. Rejected children, in contrast, are noticed but disliked (Asher, Markell, and Hymel, 1981).

ALTRUISM, SELF-CONTROL, AND MORALITY

Earlier in this chapter we mentioned Piaget's theory that cooperation and conflicts with agemates are important factors in the decline of egocentric thought. As we said in Chapter 3, "egocentric thought" does not refer to selfishness. It means the inability to see things from another person's perspective or point of view. The decline in egocentricity involves, among other things, an increased ability to imagine another person's thoughts, feelings, and motivations. This is often called **role-taking ability.** Role-taking ability is closely linked to **empathy.** Role-taking involves being aware of another person's feelings; empathy means actually sharing in them. When we get pleasure from someone else's happiness, or when we wince when someone's finger gets pinched in the door, we're empathizing.

Many developmental psychologists believe that there is a connection between empathy and prosocial behavior. Prosocial behavior generally means doing something beneficial to others. When the beneficial act is done without an apparent selfish motive, the act is called *altruistic*.

Helping and Sharing with Others

Altruism is the opposite of selfishness—it's doing something for someone else despite cost, inconvenience, or even danger to oneself. (The classic example of altruism is the person who risks his or her life to rescue another person.) Altruism has been observed in other species: porpoises will help a sick or injured porpoise by lifting it to the surface so it can breathe. Altruism has also been observed in very young human beings:

> Michael, aged 15 months, and his friend Paul were fighting over a toy and Paul started to cry. Michael appeared disturbed and let go, but Paul still cried. Michael paused, then brought his teddy bear to Paul but to no avail. Michael paused again, and then finally succeeded in stopping Paul's crying by fetching Paul's security blanket from an adjoining room. (Hoffman, 1975b, p. 612)

Empathy and Role-Taking Ability. Even newborn babies tend to start crying when they hear another baby cry. That suggests to some psychologists that "empathic distress"—the tendency to become distressed by the sight or sound of someone else's misery—may be an innate, involuntary response in human beings. Such a response would provide a motivation for altruistic acts: by helping to relieve the other person's misery, one's own distress is relieved as well. Cases when people do *not* help other people who are in trouble make headlines, but psychologists have found that most adults will immediately rush to someone's aid when it's clear that it's needed and there's no one else around to share the responsibility (Hoffman, 1975b).

Empathy depends on role-taking ability—because if we don't know what another person is experiencing, how can we share it? Since babies and young children are not very good at role-taking, they are able to empathize only when the other person's distress is particularly obvious. Altruism appears in toddlers, but it is rare and undependable. In general, as children grow older, their role-taking ability and their tendency to behave in altruistic ways both increase. This finding supports the theory that role-taking ability, empathy, and altruism are closely related to one another (Hoffman, 1975b; Shaffer, 1979).

One of the clearest demonstrations of the link between role-taking ability and altruism was reported recently (Hudson, Forman, and Brion-Meisels, 1982). The investigators gave a battery of tests to second-grade children to assess their role-taking ability. The tests involved answering various kinds of questions about the intentions, thoughts, or feelings of people shown in videotaped enactments. On the basis of their responses to these questions, the children were classified as high role-takers, low role-takers, or average. Only the high and low role-takers served in the second part of this study. The effects of IQ differences were controlled by selecting a group of high role-takers and a group of low ones that did not differ significantly in IQ.

In the second part of the study, each second grader who participated was given the task of teaching two kindergarteners to make paper caterpillars,

As children grow older, they show an increasing awareness of other people's feelings and an increasing tendency to behave in altruistic ways.

using scissors, glue, and crayons. There were clear and consistent differences between the ways that the high and low role-takers carried out this task. The high role-takers answered the younger children's questions and helped them when they were having trouble, even if the younger children didn't ask for help. The low role-takers often failed to answer questions or else gave inadequate answers, and they were much less likely to offer assistance. The high role-takers were also more likely than the low ones to offer encouraging words such as "It doesn't have to be perfect. Mine isn't perfect."

Other Factors that Influence Helping and Sharing.   Besides age and role-taking ability, several other factors have been found to influence whether or not children will help or share with other people. Two we've already mentioned are the child's sex and whether the child has a chum. Many studies show no differences between girls and boys in altruistic or prosocial behavior, but when differences are found, it's usually the girls who are more helpful.

Whether or not a child will come to the aid of someone who needs help will depend partly on the situation. Seventh-grade girls were taken individually to a private room where they were asked to fill out a questionnaire and were then left alone. The experimenter told some of the children that when they were done, they could play with some games in the next room. Others were told not to bother the girl in the next room. A minute or two after the experimenter left, the children heard tape-recorded sounds coming from the next room: a crash (as of a chair overturning) and sounds of a girl crying. Of the children who had been told that they could go into the next room, more than 90 percent went to see if they could help. Of the ones who were told not to go into the other room, only 45 percent made an effort to help (Staub, 1974).

Exposure to models who behave altruistically is quite effective, even if the exposure is brief. In a typical experiment, fourth and fifth graders played a game in which they won gift certificates redeemable at a local toy store. Some of the children saw an adult donate some of his gift certificates to a charity—he put them in a box labeled "Orphans Fund," which showed a picture of some children in ragged clothes. Later, when they were alone, almost half of these children put some of their gift certificates into the box. In contrast, of the children who hadn't seen the generous adult model, none made a donation (Rosenhan and White, 1967).

The adult models to whom children are exposed continuously are, of course, their parents. One interesting study involved families with two daughters, the older around 10, the younger around 8. The two girls were observed at home with their mother, and the three were asked various questions and given some games and problems to work on together. The investigators took particular note of whether, when either child expressed a need or asked for help, the mother responded to her child's request. They found that when the mother was responsive to her children's needs, the two children were more helpful and less critical toward each other (Bryant and Crockenberg, 1980).

One of the findings in this study that is difficult to explain is the lack of correlation between various kinds of prosocial behaviors. Girls who tended to comfort their sisters when their sisters were distressed were no more likely to *help* their sisters than girls who offered no comfort—comforting and helping were uncorrelated in this study. Other studies, too, have found a lack of correlation among such prosocial behaviors as helping, sharing, and donating to charity. (Some studies do show a correlation between these behaviors, though.) Prosocial behavior is influenced by many environmental factors, and these factors do not necessarily all work together in a unified way.

Even temporary factors such as whether the child is in a good or bad mood can have an effect on prosocial behavior. Three psychologists from Stanford University gave 7- and 8-year-olds 25 pennies each for participating in a "hearing test." Then they told each child that he or she could share some of the money with other children who weren't going to have a chance to participate. But before the children were given the opportunity to donate, an experimenter attempted to put them in a happy mood or a sad one. Some of the children were asked to tell the experimenter about something that makes them feel happy and were then instructed to think about that for a while. Other children were asked to think about something that makes them feel sad. There was also a control group of children who were not asked to think about anything but who remained with the experimenter for the same period of time. The children were then left alone in the room to make their donation or not make it, as they wished.

The results are shown in Figure 13–3. The children who were presumably put in a good mood by thinking about happy things donated significantly more than the controls. The children who thought about sad things donated significantly less (Moore, Underwood, and Rosenhan, 1973).

A recent study (Barnett, Howard, Melton, and Dino, 1982) elaborated on

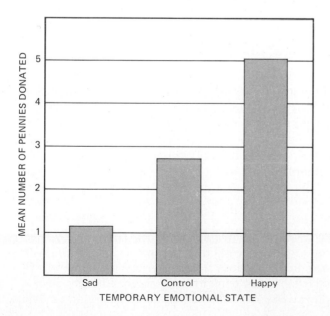

figure 13–3

Mean number of pennies donated by children after they were asked to think happy thoughts (right), and sad thoughts (left), or who were not asked to think about anything (center). (Based on data from Moore, Underwood, and Rosenhan, 1973.)

these findings in a clever way. Some sixth-grade children were asked to discuss sad incidents that had happened to them. A second group of children were asked to discuss sad incidents that had happened to *other* children. Then each child was given the opportunity to staple together some booklets for "sick children in a hospital." The results turned out to depend on whether the child was high or low in empathy. Children who had previously been classified (on the basis of ratings by teachers and peers) as having low empathy didn't help the "sick children" very much, whether they had been thinking sad thoughts about themselves or about other children. The high-empathizers didn't help very much either, when the sad thoughts had been about themselves. But the high-empathizers who thought sad thoughts about other children stapled significantly more booklets than the children in any of the other three groups. Apparently, when high empathizers feel sorry for other people, their desire to help others increases.

Self-Control

Temporary emotional states have also been shown to affect children's ability to resist temptation. In an experiment by a Canadian psychologist, 7- and 8-year-olds were taken individually into an experimental room. In the room was a table with two toys on it. One was a toy car, the other was a battery-operated mobile consisting of three toy helicopters that revolved and flashed lights when a button was pushed. The children were told that they could play with the car but that they should not touch or play with the mobile. (While the experimenter was telling them this, he casually pushed the button to demonstrate how the mobile worked.) Then some of the children were asked to think of happy and pleasurable things. Others were asked to think of things that made them sad. Children in the control group assembled a simple jigsaw puzzle.

The experimenter then said that he had to be gone for a little while. Before he left he reminded the child not to play with the helicopter mobile. The child was left alone in the room for 10 minutes while a hidden observer watched through a one-way mirror to see if the child touched the mobile.

The children who had thought about happy things resisted the temptation to touch the mobile for a long time—approximately six minutes, on the average. The children who had thought about sad things waited only half as long—an average of three minutes. The children in the control group were intermediate—they waited an average of about four minutes. It seems that children have more self-control when they are happy than when they are sad (Fry, 1975).

Delay of Gratification.   Self-control is also involved in the ability to delay gratification—the ability to wait a few minutes or a few days for a greater reward instead of going for a smaller reward right away (see Chapter 9). With this kind of self-control, too, thinking happy thoughts seems to help. Some 7- and 8-year-olds were asked to tell an experimenter about "things you like most of all." Afterwards they were put in a situation in which waiting a little longer would win them a bigger prize. These children waited longer than the children in the control group, who were asked to tell an experimenter the names of their classmates (Yates, Lippett, and Yates, 1981).

Another experiment explored the effect of self-image on the ability to delay gratification. The subjects in this experiment were kindergarten, first-grade, and second-grade girls. These children were tested individually by an undergraduate research assistant, whom they met for the first time when they participated in the experiment. The research assistant chatted with them for a few minutes and then said to some of the children, "I hear that you are very patient because you can wait for nice things when you can't get them right away." The other children were given an irrelevant compliment: "I hear that you have some very nice friends here at school." The children who were told that they were patient were able to wait considerably longer than the children who were told that they had nice friends (Toner, Moore, and Emmons, 1980, p. 619).

Giving In to Temptation

There are many temptations out there in the world—temptations to lie, to steal, to cheat. What determines whether a given child, in a given situation, will yield to these temptations?

The answer is that it depends more on the situation than on the child. Under some conditions—when the stakes are high, when the chances of

What determines whether a given child, in a given situation, will yield to temptation?

being caught are low, and when "everyone is doing it"—most children will cheat. Under other circumstances they might behave quite differently.

The Role of Models.   The tendency of children to behave prosocially is increased if they are exposed to models who behave prosocially. Similarly, seeing someone else cheat increases children's tendency to cheat, especially if these models go unpunished for their behavior.

For example, in one experiment children 8 to 12 years old were asked to perform a boring task while a cartoon film was being shown. To do the task, they had to resist the temptation to look at the cartoon. Before they started, some of the children saw an adult model yield to temptation and watch the film. Others saw the model resist the temptation and stick conscientiously to the task. A control group didn't see the adult model.

The children who had seen the adult yield to temptation were more likely than the others to yield to temptation themselves—to quit working in order to watch the cartoon. There were no differences between the other two groups, however; the children who had watched the conscientious model were no better at resisting temptation than the children who had seen no model at all (Rosenkoetter, 1973).

The knowledge that other people also yield to temptation has another effect: it makes children feel less guilty when they themselves do something they've been told not to do. Third and fourth graders in one experiment were told to sort blocks and not to turn around to watch a cartoon show on a TV set behind them. Virtually all of the children gave in to temptation and peeked at the TV set occasionally. Afterwards, an experimenter told some of the children, "Well, it's not surprising, because all of the other children that have come to the room to help us have peeked too; everyone did it." Others were told, "Well, it's surprising that you peeked because none of the other children who have come to the room to help us has peeked; you're the only one." The children in the first group—the ones who were told that "everyone did it"—showed much less remorse than the children who thought they were "the only one" (Perry and others, 1980, p. 547).

Individual Differences.   Although the tendency to yield to temptation depends more on the circumstances than on the individual, there are differences among children. Some children *are* more honest than others in a variety of situations. These differences are small, though, compared to the effects of the situation (Burton, 1976).

In contrast, sizable and consistent differences are found when moral development is judged by the way children answer questions about morality (see Box, pp. 98–99). Piaget told children a story about a boy who broke several cups accidentally and another boy who broke one cup while trying to steal some jam; then he asked the children, "Which boy is naughtier?" Kohlberg told stories that contain a moral dilemma (for instance, which is worse—stealing or letting someone die?) and recorded children's comments. Both techniques yield measures of the maturity of children's moral judgments. Moral development measured in this way has been found to correlate

PROBLEMS IN DEVELOPMENT

Antisocial Behavior

Antisocial behavior falls into two general classes. One we can label "dishonesty"—it includes lying, cheating, and stealing. The other class is aggressiveness—harming other people. As we have seen, dishonesty is not very predictable from IQ, role-taking ability, or sex. That is not true of aggressiveness. Aggressive children tend to be poor role-takers, to have lower than average IQs, and to be male. They are also more likely than nonaggressive children to be from the lower socioeconomic classes and to have parents who frequently resort to physical punishment.

Aggressive children are low in empathy (Feshbach and Feshbach, 1969). This is not surprising, since empathy involves a tendency to share in other people's feelings—to become distressed when other people are hurt or upset. A child who experienced such "empathic distress" would have a motivation to avoid hurting others.

Highly aggressive children not only seem to lack this motivation—they actually appear to find other people's distress rewarding. As we mentioned in Chapter 9, preschoolers who attack another child are likely to attack that child again if the victim cries or runs away (Patterson, Littman, and Bricker, 1967).

In an experiment with boys in fifth, sixth, and seventh grades, the subjects were made to think they were punishing another boy (for making mistakes in arithmetic problems) by sounding loud noises in his earphones. They could control the loudness of the sound by deciding which of 10 buttons to press. The other boy, who was supposedly in a separate room, would then let the subject know how much he had minded the noise by lighting up a signal on a so-called "pain indicator." The "pain indicator" had five lights, each bearing a label. The labels ranged from "Did not hurt my ears at all," for the first light, to "Hurt my ears so much that my whole head hurts," for the fifth. (The lights were, in reality, controlled by the experimenter.) The experimenter told the subject how to operate the equipment and then left the room.

The subjects had previously been classified, on the basis of ratings by peers, as "high aggressive" and "low aggressive." These two groups behaved quite differently in the experiment. The low-aggressive boys tended to send soft noises, even when the "pain indicator" told them that the other boy was not much bothered by the sounds. But the high-aggressive boys scaled their button-pushing to the feedback they were supposedly receiving from the other boy. When the "pain indicator" said that the other boy wasn't being hurt very much, the high-aggressive boys would escalate their punishment—push buttons with higher numbers and hold them down longer. Hurting the other boy apparently became their goal, and they seemed to be frustrated if they were unable to make the other boy say he was hurt.

> When the aggressive child is denied the satisfaction of knowing he has successfully injured his victim, he may in fact become extraordinarily hostile. That this may be the case was dramatically illustrated by the behavior of the high-aggressive boys in the low-pain-cues condition. Over the course of the test for aggression, as their victims continued to deny the experience of pain, many of these boys tried to evoke a pain response by simultaneously depressing noise buttons 8, 9, and 10 in an obvious attempt to maximize the noise level. (Perry and Perry, 1974, pp. 60-61)

The depressing fact about such children is that children who show high levels of antisocial behavior are quite likely to become antisocial adolescents and antisocial adults. Chronic delinquency is much more common in young men

How can we stop
aggressive children from
turning into aggressive
adolescents?

who showed early signs of unusually high aggressiveness, or who repeatedly stole things or told deliberate untruths (Loeber, 1982).

The fact that aggressive children tend to remain aggressive does not necessarily imply that their aggressiveness is an innate characteristic. Once a child starts off in that direction, many environmental factors tend to lead him further along that path. The attention he gets and his ability to dominate others serve as reinforcers. The punishments his parents mete out may increase his hostility and provide him with role models. And the companions and recreational activities he chooses may compound the problem. Boys who say that they would rather play football than act in a play, or that they'd rather play army than go swimming, are likely to be more aggressive a year later than boys who have the opposite preferences. Even boys who aren't very aggressive to begin with become more aggressive if they choose to spend their time in rough and highly competitive activities (Bullock and Merrill, 1980).

Several times in this book we have mentioned the impact of television. One more point needs to be made on that topic, though. Some people believe that televised violence doesn't make children more aggressive because the perpetrators of the violence usually end up getting punished for their crimes. It's true that children who saw an aggressive model getting punished for his behavior were less likely to imitate him than children who saw him rewarded. But seeing the model punished did *not* lead to less aggressiveness than seeing no model at all: the children in the punished-model condition were not any less aggressive than the children in the control group (Bandura, Ross, and Ross, 1963). Furthermore, on television it is likely that many minutes, and several commercials, will intervene between the crime and the punishment. Under these conditions the punishment seems to have little or no effect on children's tendency to imitate aggressive models (Collins, 1973).

What can we do to stop the vicious circle of antisocial behavior leading to more antisocial behavior? There are several things. We can make an attempt to see that desirable behavior is reinforced and undesirable behavior is not. We can advise parents to avoid severe punishments without going too far in the direction of permissiveness—moderate punishments for undesirable behavior seem to work best (Lefkowitz, Eron, Walder, and Huesmann, 1977). We should do our best to provide children with models who behave the way we want children to behave. And perhaps we can even help them to find a chum.

highly with role-taking ability, with general cognitive development, and with IQ (Krebs and Gilmore, 1982). Brighter children are better at role-taking and better at giving the kinds of answers Piaget and Kohlberg considered to be on a higher level.

But are they more honest? There is no clear and consistent tendency for children who give "better" answers to Piaget's or Kohlberg's questions to be "better" in real-life situations (Lickona, 1976). As for intelligence, there is some evidence that high-IQ children are less likely to cheat on tests at school, but that may be because they are less worried about doing well. In nonacademic situations, there seems to be no correlation between IQ and the tendency to cheat (Burton, 1976).

Finally, there's the question of sex differences. In middle childhood, girls are ahead of boys in many ways, physically and socially. Probably for that reason, they tend to be a little more advanced in the level of their moral judgments (Krebs and Gilmore, 1982). Also, since they tend to be more obedient than boys, they are sometimes found to do better in experiments on resistance to temptation—they're a little less likely to touch something that an experimenter has told them not to touch. But in real life—in resisting temptations to cheat or to lie—there seem to be no overall differences between girls and boys (Burton, 1976).

1. Although in our society we do not allow school-age children to take on the work and responsibilities of adults, we do expect a lot from them. They are expected, for example, to know the numerous and intricate rules of how to act with different people and in different situations. We also expect them to know "right" from "wrong." Although the behavior of school-age children might not adhere perfectly to these standards, they are expected at least to feel guilty if they do something our society considers "wrong."

2. According to Freud, not much is happening in middle childhood—the important aspects of personality development have already occurred. But Erikson regards this period as a socially decisive stage, because school-age children have accepted the fact that their future lies in the world outside their home. In his view, **industry versus inferiority** is the central issue of this stage.

3. Parents and many other people act as socializing forces on school-age children. One way people influence the behavior of children is by the reinforcements and punishments they dispense. In many cases, these reinforcements and punishments are given without conscious intention to produce a particular effect; in some cases their effect may even be the opposite of what was intended.

4. Children's behavior is also influenced by the behavior of models. The models may be parents, teachers, or other adults; they may also be other children, such as siblings. Characters seen on TV or in movies, or read about in books or magazines, may serve as models, too.

5. Two forms of parental discipline are **inductive discipline,** which consists of explaining to the child the reasons and justifications for various rules of behavior, and **power-assertive discipline,** which consists of enforcing rules with threats and punishments. Inductive discipline is a successful method when used with school-age children; it is not particularly successful with preschoolers, because they are at a lower level of cognitive development. With inductive discipline, school-age children tend to **internalize** their parents' moral standards and to feel guilty if they deviate from them. An adult's choice of a given form of discipline will be influenced by the child's behavior.

6. By the time they enter school, children have established a firm gender identity and have absorbed many of our society's sexual stereotypes. Boys are under more pressure than girls to act according to these stereotypes; fathers are more concerned than mothers about their children's sex-role behavior.

7. School-age children generally segregate themselves rigidly by sex. But this rigid sex segregation masks a great interest, by both boys and girls, in the opposite sex.

8. School-age children also tend to segregate themselves by race. Relationships between children of different races seem to be more successful when there are no differences in socioeconomic class and when the children attend racially mixed schools from kindergarten onward.

9. Children's relationships with other children serve many functions. According to Piaget, interactions with peers lead to an increased ability to take another person's point of view.

10. Relationships with other children can compensate, to some extent, for parental indifference or overindulgence. Children's social behavior is influenced in a number of ways by the actions and attitudes of other children.

11. The relative permanence of school-age children's characteristics makes it possible for them to develop a realistic self-concept. They do this, to a large extent, by comparing themselves with their peers.

12. Children play together in every society and have done so throughout human history; similar behavior is seen in apes and monkeys. A young monkey must have an opportunity to interact with other young monkeys, or its later social behavior will be abnormal.

13. According to Selman, children's friendships progress through four stages: (1) in the preschool period, a friend is someone whom the child happens to be playing with at the moment; (2) in the early school years, a friend is important because he or she does specific things that the child wants done; (3) in the later school years, children begin to view friendship as a two-way relationship, but arguments are seen as a cause for breaking off the relationship; (4) in late childhood or early adolescence, intimate and mutually shared relationships may be formed.

14. The theory of **chumship** states that having a close, mutual friendship makes a child more concerned about other people's feelings. Recent research showed that children with close friends tend to act in helpful and unselfish ways with other children, but it is not clear whether such behavior is an effect of the friendship or a cause of it.

15. Girls are more likely to have close, intimate, and exclusive friendships; boys are more likely to play in groups.

16. In their relationships with other children, girls tend to perform more **prosocial** acts (sharing, helping, and so on) than boys do; boys are more likely to compete with their friends and less likely to share with them. Two possible explanations for this difference are that it's due to girls' greater tendency to have a ''chum'' or to their greater maturity.

17. **Sociometric measures** show that children vary in how well they are liked by their peers; these variations tend to persist over time. Unpopular children are likely to do less well academically and to be less physically attractive than popular children; they are more likely to be firstborn or only children. Children who differ in any way from their peers are more likely to be unpopular.

18. Behavioral differences between popular and unpopular school-age children are not easy to find. One study showed a difference in **entry strategies** between these two groups. Unpopular children tried to gain the attention of other children; popular children tried to blend into the ongoing activities.

19. Some unpopular children (generally the shy, quiet ones) are neglected by their peers. Others are rejected—disliked but not ignored.

20. It seems to be possible to coach children in the art of being likable. One study showed that individual coaching sessions can produce long-term improvements in popularity.

21. Role-taking ability—the ability to imagine another person's thoughts, feelings, and motivations—increases as children get older. **Empathy,** which means actually sharing in someone else's feelings, depends on role-taking ability. Some psychologists feel that "empathic distress" may be an innate, involuntary response in human beings.

22. Altruism is doing something that's beneficial for others, without an apparent selfish motive. Children who are high in role-taking ability are more likely to behave in altruistic ways.

23. Whether or not a child will come to the aid of someone who needs help depends partly on the situation. A child's tendency to help or share is also influenced by exposure to models who behave altruistically, and by whether the child is feeling happy or sad.

24. Temporary emotional states can also influence children's ability to resist temptation and to delay gratification.

25. Children who see someone else yield to temptation are more likely to yield to temptation themselves. In addition, the knowledge that others also yield to temptation makes children feel less guilty about doing so.

26. Although the tendency to yield to temptation seems to depend more on the circumstances than on the individual, there are small differences among children in how honest they are. There are much greater differences in their answers to questions about morality. Moral development measured in this way correlates with role-taking ability and with IQ; it is a little more advanced in girls than in boys. No consistent sex differences have been found in moral behavior in real-life situations.

27. Antisocial behavior includes dishonesty and aggressiveness. Highly aggressive children are not only low in empathy—they actually appear to find other people's distress rewarding. Children who show high levels of antisocial behavior tend to become antisocial adolescents and antisocial adults, partly because the attention such behavior receives, and the ability to dominate others, act as reinforcers. The best methods for decreasing antisocial behavior are (1) to reinforce desirable behavior; (2) to give moderate, not severe, punishments for undesirable behavior; and (3) to provide children with models who behave in desirable ways, rather than models who behave aggressively.

<u>C</u>hapter <u>F</u>ourteen

CHILDHOOD'S END

Physical Development
The Growth Spurt of Early Adolescence
Attaining Puberty
Social and Behavioral Consequences
   The Role of Cultural Differences
   Individual Differences
   Effects of Maturing Early and Late

PROBLEMS IN DEVELOPMENT—EATING DISORDERS
   IN ADOLESCENT GIRLS
Cognitive Development
Appearance and Application of Formal Operations
   Characteristics of Formal Thought
Adolescent Egocentrism
   The Imaginary Audience and the Personal Fable

Fourteen

Adolescence is the transitional period from the dependency of childhood to the independence and responsibility of being an adult. At this point in their lives, young people struggle with two fundamental problems: to redefine their relationships with parents and other adults, and to establish themselves as individuals. As a result, this is a time of both dependence and independence. The adolescent is likely to act in a childlike manner at one moment and with considerable maturity at the next. There may even be open conflict between these two roles.

Developmental psychologists of every theoretical orientation acknowledge the importance of adolescence as a turning point in development. During this period many aspects of the individual's personal identity are formed. There are important decisions to make—decisions about love and work that will affect the person throughout his or her lifetime.

Adolescence can be divided into three subperiods. **Early adolescence** includes the period of initial physical change, usually marked by a sizable growth spurt. This begins while the individual is still looking, acting, and thinking like a child. **Mid-adolescence,** which begins after the noticeable changes in physical appearance have already occurred, is characterized by intense revolt mixed with extreme conformity, and a movement toward the opposite sex. There is an interest in love and sex, which may be kept quite separate by the adolescent. Mid-adolescence is also characterized by large and often unpredictable mood swings. **Late adolescence** comes at a time when physical maturity is essentially complete. It brings concerns about education, occupation, and courtship and marriage, as the young person begins to come to grips with his or her future as an adult (Lidz, 1976).

In this chapter we will consider development through the span of early and mid-adolescence. Late adolescence and entry into full adulthood will be discussed in the final chapter of the book.

PHYSICAL DEVELOPMENT

Physical growth during middle childhood was relatively calm. In sharp contrast, adolescence begins with a burst of rapid physical growth followed by an equally dramatic succession of changes in the body that lead to sexual maturity. These changes are triggered in large measure by the secretion of increased quantities of sex hormones, specifically estrogen in the female and androgen in the male.

The Growth Spurt of Early Adolescence

The first sign of childhood's end is a dramatic spurt of growth. Height may increase by as much as 4 or 5 inches (10–13 cm) in a year; weight may increase by 20 pounds (9 kg). The growth spurt and subsequent milestones in physical development come about two years earlier in girls than in boys (see Figure 14–1).

As a result of girls' earlier growth, the average 12-year-old girl is slightly taller and heavier than the average boy of the same age (See Figure 14–2). This situation has reversed itself by age 14, when the boy's later growth spurt has begun to propel him toward his adult size (Tanner, 1978).

The dramatic increase in height and weight is accompanied by the growth of most organs and bodily systems: besides the bones themselves, the muscles, heart, lungs, digestive system, and reproductive system all show marked growth during this spurt. The brain, however, does not, since it has already attained about 95 percent of its adult size in middle childhood. One system— the immunological system—actually decreases in size during adolescence. (The immunological system guards the body against attacks by viruses or bacteria. The tonsils and adenoids are part of this system.)

Glandular changes also occur, producing effects throughout the body. For example, glands near the surface of the skin begin to secrete increased amounts of sweat and oil. These secretions are responsible for a sharpening of body odor and for the acne that plagues so many adolescents.

Changes in body proportions around the start of adolescence bring about other changes in physical appearance. These changes may make the young adolescent temporarily unattractive. For example, the arms and legs become relatively long. The nose or lower jaw may become noticeably large, compared with the rest of the face. Physical growth during early adolescence is uneven, and it is this fact that accounts for the ungainly appearance of many

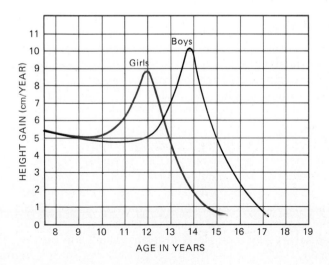

figure 14–1

Height gain of boys and girls between the ages of 8 and 17, showing that the male growth spurt occurs about two years later than the female growth spurt. (Adapted from Tanner, 1970)

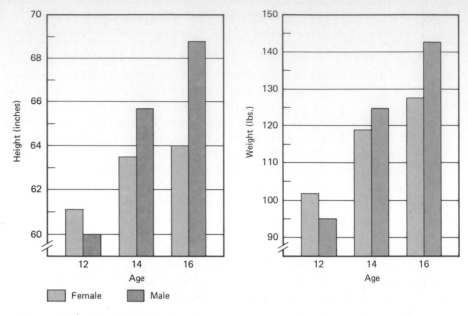

figure 14–2
Mean height and weight of boys and girls age 12, 14, and 16, showing the result of the difference between the sexes in age of onset of the growth spurt. At age 12, when the average girl has begun her growth spurt and the average boy has not, girls are actually taller and heavier than boys. By 14 the boy has caught up and passed his female agemates on these measures, and by 16 he is way ahead in physical size. (Data from Vital and Health Statistics, 1973)

young adolescents. In particular, the hands, feet, and legs actually do grow more quickly than the rest of the body during this period (Katchadourian, 1977).

Attaining Puberty

Entry into adolescence is a transitional period that becomes complete with **puberty**, or the attainment of sexual maturity. Puberty is reached when the adolescent is theoretically capable of parenting offspring, which corresponds roughly with the time when the girl experiences **menarche,** her first menstruation, and when the boy begins to produce live sperm. For girls in the United States, the average age at menarche is between 12½ and 13 years. Boys begin to discharge semen with live sperm at about 14½ years, on the average.

As puberty approaches, there are also changes in the external sex organs. At the same time, a variety of secondary sex characteristics appear, such as deepening of the voice in boys and breast development in girls: These are called **secondary sex characteristics** because they distinguish males from females biologially but are not directly related to reproduction. (**Primary sex characteristics** are the reproductive organs themselves—the penis and testes in males, the ovaries, uterus, and vagina in females.)

The path to attaining puberty follows a distinctive pattern (see Table 14–1).

TABLE 14–1   The Sequence of Physical Development in Adolescence

Girls	Boys
Initial enlargement of the breasts occurs (breast bud stage).	Growth of the testes and scrotum begins.
Straight, lightly pigmented pubic hair appears.	Straight, lightly pigmented pubic hair appears.
Maximum growth rate is attained.	Growth of the penis begins.
Pubic hair becomes adult in type but covers a smaller area than in adult.	Early changes in the voice occur.
Breast enlargement continues; the nipple and the area around it now project above the level of the breast.	First ejaculation of semen occurs.
Menarche occurs.	Pubic hair becomes adult in type but covers a smaller area than in adult.
Underarm hair appears; the sweat glands under the arms increase in size.	Maximum growth rate is attained.
Breasts and pubic hair reach adult stage.	Underarm hair appears; the sweat glands under the arms increase in size.
	The voice deepens noticeably.
	Growth of mustache and beard hair begins. Pubic hair reaches adult stage.

Sources: The Committee on Adolescence, Group for the Advancement of Psychiatry, 1968; Tanner, 1978.

In boys it begins with an increase in the size of the testes, followed by the appearance of some pubic hair and then an increase in the size of the penis. Underarm hair begins to appear next; shoulders broaden. The growth of beard and body hair is generally not complete until late adolescence.

In girls the budding breasts and the appearance of pubic hair are the first signs of approaching puberty, followed by changes in body proportions—the hips and thighs widen, the waist becomes relatively narrower. Girls begin to menstruate, on the average, about three years after the beginning of the growth spurt. Menarche generally does not occur until a girl's body weight is over 100 pounds (45 kg); those girls who reach that weight early will menstruate at an earlier age than girls who put on weight more slowly (Frisch and Revelle, 1970). Menarche does not necessarily mean that a girl is capable of becoming pregnant. For the first year or so after their first period, most girls are considerably less fertile—less likely to conceive a child—than they will be later on.

Social and Behavioral Consequences

The bodily changes we have been discussing lead to a variety of other changes, both physical and psychological. Some of these changes are nicely summarized by Mollie and Russell Smart, a team of developmental psychologists.

> New motor coordinations are both possible and necessary. Food intake has to adjust to growth demands. A fast developing body calls for frequent changes in body image, as well as continual re-evaluation of one's own body and self in relation to others'. Newly acquired sexual powers have to be understood and integrated into living. In reworking and elaborating his sense of identity, the young person has to deal with all these aspects of his bodily development. (Smart and Smart, 1978, p. 34)

The Role of Cultural Differences.   In emphasizing physical changes, we do not mean to imply that the problems of adolescence are merely the products of physical maturation and biological development. Many of the difficulties we associate with adolescence may arise from the cultural practices of technologically and economically complex societies. In such societies education tends to be prolonged, and young people often remain dependent on their parents throughout their teens and even into their 20s. The problems that arise under these circumstances may be quite different from those that occur in societies in which, for example, girls are expected to marry in their early teens and boys are expected to do a man's job.

Individual Differences.   Although on the average girls enter adolescence about two years earlier than boys, there is considerable variation among individuals. Some normal girls in the United States have not reached menarche by their sixteenth birthday, while a few on the other extreme begin to menstruate at the age of 10. This variability in rate of maturation occurs in boys, too. The photo on the next page shows three boys of the same age who differ considerably in physical maturity.

Of the considerable individual differences in rate of maturation, most are within the normal range. At some point, however, an individual no longer seems to be part of the typical range but, instead, is distinctive among his or her agemates. If development is unusually early, we speak of **precocious puberty.** Unusually late development is referred to as **delayed puberty.**

Effects of Maturing Early or Late.   Because there are such noticeable individual differences in rate of maturing, psychologists have wondered whether these differences affect social and psychological development during adolescence. The answer appears to be that they do, to a certain extent. For example, an adolescent boy's physical maturity is closely correlated with the degree to which he behaves in a "power-assertive" way. It has been shown

These boys are all 13 years old.

that the further along an adolescent boy is in the sequence of pubertal changes, the more likely he is to interrupt others in family discussions and the less obliged he feels to explain himself. This pattern not only characterizes older boys as opposed to younger ones—it is also true of physically mature boys as opposed to less mature ones of the same age (Steinberg and Hill, 1978).

Other evidence suggests that boys who develop early have the advantage over boys who develop late. Superior physical strength and a more mature appearance make it easier for the physically advanced boy to win the admiration of his agemates. Indeed, early maturers are more likely than other boys to be elected class officers in school, to have their names in the school newspapers, and to excel at sports (Eichorn, 1963; Carron and Bailey, 1974).

For girls, on the other hand, there are no clear-cut advantages (or disadvantages) in maturing early. Some early-maturing girls are embarrassed by the fact that their bodies are more womanly in shape than those of their female agemates; they may also be troubled by being taller than most of their agemates of either sex. Others take their greater physical maturity to be an asset, just as early-maturing boys do. In one study it was found that whether an adolescent girl matured early or late did not influence her prestige among her peers (Harper and Collins, 1972).

Eating Disorders in Adolescent Girls

Anorexia. At the age of 15, Tammy won a local beauty contest in the small suburban town in which she lives. No one was surprised that she won, because Tammy was outstandingly good-looking. She had a shapely figure, big green eyes, and long, blond hair. People thought she looked like a model or a movie star.

Now, three years later, Tammy's appearance has undergone a startling change.

> Anyone meeting Tammy today for the first time would not believe that she had ever once been capable of winning a beauty contest. She would not be mistaken for an actress or a model, although she could easily pass for a concentration camp victim.
>
> In the past year, Tammy's weight has dropped from one hundred eighteen to eighty-four pounds. She gives the appearance of a skeleton; her arms and legs seem to dangle from her body like wooden sticks. . . .
>
> Much of Tammy's full blonde hair has either fallen out or broken off. Whatever strands are left appear brittle and dry and hang from her head in stringy tufts. Perhaps the most dramatic difference in Tammy's appearance, however, is in her face. There's little flesh around her cheeks or chin, and her eyes seem to stare hauntingly out of her head from deeply recessed sockets. (Landau, 1983, p. 2)

Tammy is suffering from **anorexia nervosa,** a disorder that strikes an estimated 1 in 200 girls between the ages of 12 and 18 years. Ten to 20 percent of its victims will die. Many of those who survive will experience life-long health problems.

The **anorectic** simply stops eating, except perhaps for a tiny amount of food to which she restricts herself. One anorectic reduced her food intake to two small cookies a day, which she cut up into little pieces to make them last longer. Then, deciding she was still eating too much, she cut her diet in half—to one cookie a day!

Anorexia frequently begins when a teenage girl decides she's "too fat" (many anorectics were somewhat pudgy in childhood). She goes on a diet in order to lose a few pounds. But instead of resuming a normal food intake when that goal has been met, she continues or even increases her efforts to lose weight, often adding a heavy load of exercise to her regime. Many anorectics refuse treatment and give irrational justifications for their behavior.

It's clear that an anorectic tends to define her self-worth in bodily terms. But her perception of her own body does not correspond to reality—she may see herself as "fat" even when she is dying of starvation.

> Even when forced to look at themselves in a mirror wearing only a bikini, emaciated anorectics will often claim that they look disgustingly fat. One skeletonlike young woman who had lost almost sixty pounds in a year protested bitterly that her stomach still stuck out and that her thighs looked too fat and flabby. (Landau, 1983, p. 8)

COGNITIVE DEVELOPMENT

According to Piagetian theory, adolescence marks the entry into the highest stage of cognitive development, the **period of formal operations.** Unlike children, adolescents often display the ability to solve problems in a systematic

The psychiatric view of anorexia is that the anorectic outwardly seems to be an "ideal teen-ager"—obedient and hard-working—while she is actually immature and dependent, suffering from low self-esteem and chronic self-doubt. The parents of anorectic girls are described by some researchers as people who hide family problems under a false front of harmony. Such parents tend to see their anorectic child as a "good girl," and she sees herself that way, too. Typically, she has worked hard in fulfilling the expectations others have had for her.

> Unaware and unable to express what she wants, lacking identity, the anorectic changes to suit others' high expectations of her while remaining isolated, self-absorbed, anxious, and unhappy. (Cauwels, 1983, p. 40)

Anorexia halts the development of the breasts and causes menstruation to cease. Thus, the disorder is sometimes viewed as a way of escaping from the demands of sexual maturity.

We should mention that not all anorectics are female, nor does the disorder always have its onset in adolescence. Also, some researchers believe there may be an underlying physical cause for anorexia—for example, a metabolic or neurological imbalance—which could be triggered by psychological or environmental factors.

Bulimia. There is an Eating Disorders Clinic at the University of California at Los Angeles. Originally, this clinic was designed to help anorectics. To everyone's surprise, the students who came for treatment were five times as likely to be suffering from **bulimia** as from anorexia. As a result, the clinic had to change its emphasis.

Bulimia is similar to anorexia in many ways. Both disorders are most likely to appear in adolescent girls, and both are marked by a preoccupation with food and body weight. With bulimics, however, the preoccupation with food turns them toward it, rather than away from it. The bulimic pattern is to *gorge and purge:* the bulimic stuffs herself with incredible quantities of food, and then rids herself of all that has been so ravenously consumed by means of laxatives or self-induced vomiting. Bulimics can sometimes consume 50,000 calories of high-calorie food at a time; they may make themselves vomit as many as 20 times a day. The constant vomiting produces side effects—for example, the salivary glands in the mouth may swell, giving the face a puffy look. More serious is the possible disruption of the body's delicate balance of fluids and of essential chemicals such as sodium, potassium, and calcium. Such an imbalance may lead to muscle spasms, kidney problems, or even heart failure (Landau, 1983).

Nonetheless, bulimics seem better off than anorectics in a number of ways. Except for their binges, they can often maintain a reasonable diet, so their body weight typically remains normal. They tend to be more sociable than anorectics, more likely to achieve independence and occupational success as adults, and considerably more responsive to treatment. Unlike anorectics, who are usually described as having been exceptionally well-behaved children, bulimic girls were more likely to have been seen as troublesome children.

The underlying causes of bulimia and anorexia are still being debated, with consideration being given to both psychological and physical causes. ∎

way, by thinking up several alternative solutions. They may then test these alternatives in a rational, orderly fashion, according to a rough-and-ready version of the scientific method. Adolescents are beginning to distinguish between what is real and what is possible. They can now start to use imagination not merely for fantasy and play, but also to solve problems mentally, by means of symbolic manipulation. These new cognitive abilities aid adolescents in dealing with and understanding their physical development. As we shall see, the same abilities also play a central role in many aspects of personality and social development.

Appearance and Application of Formal Operations

In a famous experimental procedure devised by Piaget, children and adolescents of various ages are presented with a bucket of water and with pieces of plastic, wood, rock, metal, cork, and so on. The subjects are asked to pick up each object, say whether it will float or sink when placed in the bucket of water, and then check to see if they're right. The objects vary in size and in weight, but these characteristics don't immediately lead to accurate predictions as to which objects will float and which will sink: for example, a large block of cork which weighs several ounces will float, while a thumbtack weighing a fraction of an ounce will sink.

What determines whether an object will sink or float is its weight per cubic inch (or cubic centimeter)—if its weight per unit of volume is less than that of water, it will float. Children below the age of 11 or 12 are generally unable to discover this principle and to put it into words. Many 16-year-olds, though, can succeed at this task. The law of sinking and floating objects is an abstract or formal idea, and such ideas usually cannot be understood until adolescence.

Characteristics of Formal Thought. Since Piaget's classic experiments, many researchers have delved into the nature of adolescent thought. Their goal has been to specify the characteristics that distinguish this form of reasoning and problem-solving from other more "primitive" forms.

One important characteristic of formal thought, hinted at by the experiment on floating and sinking objects, is that it involves seeking explanations rather than mere descriptions of what has been observed. Thus, adolescents who are asked why something has happened will consider how this event is related to other events with which they are familiar. Younger children, on the other hand, are more likely just to describe the event in greater detail.

Another important characteristic of formal thought is that it involves the ability to remove oneself from the immediate context of a problem in order to get additional perspective. In fact, the development of perspective and the ability to consider long-term as well as short-term consequences are considered by many psychologists to be among the most significant aspects of cognitive development. From childhood through adolescence, young people show a gradual and steady increase in the degree to which they consider the future (short-term and long-term) in dealing with problems (LeBlanc, 1969).

One of the most socially significant characteristics of formal thought is that it leads to the metacognitive ability to "think about thinking"—that is, the ability to reflect about the thought process itself. One study examined children's and adolescents' ability to think about such statements as, "I wonder what he is thinking of me." "I wonder what he thinks I am thinking about him." "I wonder what he thinks I think he is thinking about me." The ability to reflect on such notions increases dramatically in adolescence (Miller, Kessel, and Flavell, 1970).

In sum, then, formal thought is characterized by a relative freedom from the immediate constraints of a problem—that is, flexibility. There is a tendency to identify and consider all solutions systematically, and to experiment with them in the mind and in reality. There is also a tendency to seek broad and complete explanations for what has been observed or experienced.

It is important to note that the capacity for formal operational thinking *begins* in adolescence. The capacity appears to take six or seven years to develop fully, and is only partially attained in many individuals. It is a form of thinking used much more readily with problems of an intellectual nature than with problems of a social nature. The ability to *apply* formal thought develops unevenly. It is rare to see it applied in its purest form to a person's social or personal life. Moreover, as one investigator (Lovell, 1971) has pointed out, whether a person uses formal thought in a particular situation depends on a number of factors. These factors include the exact nature of the situation and the person's familiarity with, and attitude toward, the subject matter.

Formal thought is not equally likely to be displayed by all adolescents. Those who test higher on measures of verbal and nonverbal intelligence appear to acquire formal operations earlier and more strongly than others (Cloutier and Goldschmid, 1976). The development of formal thought also depends on appropriate environmental and educational experiences designed to foster this kind of thinking. Experimental studies show that even preadolescents can be taught to use formal operations under ideal conditions. For example, in one study, children 10 and 13 years old were given instructions and examples for using formal thought to solve a problem according to the scientific method. This training procedure was found to be highly effective (Siegler and Liebert, 1975).

The tendency to think in abstract rather than concrete terms is by no means limited to matters of a scientific or academic nature. Two developmental psychologists examined the self-perceptions of children and adolescents, ages 9 to 18 years, and found substantial changes in the way these young people described themselves. The descriptions ranged from very concrete to highly abstract. Here is what one 9-year-old said of himself:

> My name is Bruce C. I have brown eyes. I have brown hair. I have brown eyebrows. . . . I am almost the smartest boy in the class. . . . I love fresh air. I *love* school. (Montemayer and Eisen, 1978, p. 92)

Contrast the above statement with one made by a 17-year-old girl in the twelfth grade:

> I am a human being. I am a girl. I am an individual. I don't know who I am. . . . I am an indecisive person. I am an ambitious person. I am a very curious person. I am a confused person. . . . I am a pseudoliberal. I am an atheist. I am not a classifiable person. (p. 94)

Adolescent Egocentrism

With the adolescent's new ability to think in abstract terms comes an over-confidence in the value of intellectual solutions to problems, which Piaget calls "the egocentricity of formal operations." Now that she has a reasonably consistent set of beliefs, the adolescent is startled to find that others do not share her opinions on all matters. She may react by becoming self-righteous or intolerant of opposing opinions. This adolescent form of egocentrism gradually diminishes as the individual passes toward late adolescence and adulthood. Eventually, most people come to appreciate the importance and legitimacy of different points of view.

The Imaginary Audience and the Personal Fable. Developmental psychologist David Elkind has applied Piaget's notion of adolescent egocentrism to teenagers' apparent preoccupation with themselves. According to Elkind (1967), young adolescents feel that they are playing to an *imaginary audience*. They also believe in what he calls their *personal fable*.

The **imaginary audience** refers to the feeling that one is constantly being observed by others. This feeling plays a role in determining certain behaviors and emotions—for example, the self-consciousness, loudness, and faddish dress that frequently characterize adolescence.

The **personal fable** involves a belief in the uniqueness of one's feelings and in one's immortality. Thus, as Elkind points out, we can see lengthy diaries depicting with great drama the special experiences and frustrations of young people, which they presumably regard to be of universal importance. Elkind also suggests that certain specific adolescent problems can be attributed partly to the imaginary audience and the personal fable:

> The imaginary audience . . . seems often to play a role in middle-class delinquency. . . . As a case in point, one young man took $1,000 from a golf tournament purse, hid the money, and then promptly revealed himself. It turned out that much of the motivation for this act was derived from the anticipated response of "the audience" to the guttiness of his action. In a similar vein, many young girls become pregnant because, in part at least, their personal fable convinces them that pregnancy will happen to others but never to them. (Elkind, 1967, pp. 1031–1032)

The Dawn of Ideology

With the development of formal operational thought comes the ability to build and understand abstract theories and ideas. In turn, this cognitive capacity paves the way for the development of commitment to ideals and ideologies, which typically appear for the first time in adolescence (Adelson, 1975). During adolescence young people often begin to refer to universal moral principles as a possible basis for making decisions about how one should act. Paralleling this development is an increasing tendency to think of laws as based on fairness rather than mere practicality (Adelson and O'Neill, 1966).

Most important, when a young adolescent does make an ideological com-

The confirmation ceremonies that many religious groups hold for adolescents are a recognition of the strong commitment to ideals that often develops at this age.

mitment, it tends to be very strong and very rigid. It should not be surprising that many social and cultural institutions adapt themselves to the idealistic strivings of this age group. Thus, it is typical for religions to provide confirmation ceremonies during adolescence. Most socially sanctioned youth groups (such as the Boy Scouts and the Girl Scouts) are built around ideals that are intensely felt and intensely expressed. Today in the Soviet Union, there is the Komosomol (the Communist Youth organization), whose members zealously uphold the ideology of communism.

Not all ideological commitment is social activism, of course. For example, a minority of adolescents express an intense commitment to self-denial or self-discipline, so that these practices also reach ideological intensity.

The Psychoanalytic View of Adolescent Idealism. Psychoanalysts believe that the superego, the part of the mind concerned with moral values, must be reorganized during adolescence. It must accommodate both the new demands of a personal ideology and also the sexual requirements of adulthood. Thus, ideological commitments during adolescence serve as channels to redirect sexual and aggressive impulses.

PARENTS, PEERS, AND THE STRUGGLE FOR INDEPENDENCE

Adolescence is a milestone on the path to the relative independence of adulthood. Through middle childhood, parents and family hold sway as models

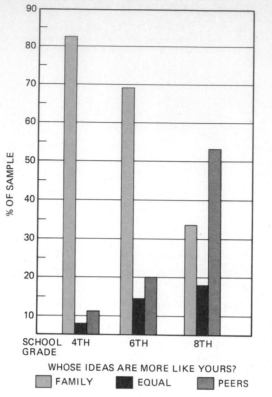

figure 14–3
The answers of fourth, sixth, and eighth graders to the question, "Whose ideas are more like yours: family or friends?" (Data from Bowerman and Kinch, 1969)

and reference groups for the young person. Then, as adolescence begins and independence from parents is desired, identification shifts to a peer group of friends who are similarly seeking their own identity. This group forms the adolescent's subculture. It is common for teenagers to learn a special slang vocabulary (or **argot**) peculiar to their generation. This vocabulary serves to distinguish them from adults and strengthens their identity with one another.

A well-known study (Bowerman and Kinch, 1969) obtained information about the value orientations of almost 700 students in a middle-class school, in the fourth through eighth grades. One question the students were asked was, "Whose ideas are more like yours: family or friends?" The results are shown in Figure 14–3.

Conflict and Revolt

In most Western cultures, conflict with parents is an inherent part of adolescence. Most psychologists believe that this conflict ultimately serves a useful purpose for both the child and the parent. Disenchantment with parental values and attitudes is a common way for young people to begin to express their independence. For the older generation, having to defend their views might be seen as a stimulating and thought-provoking experience.

Many young adolescents openly revolt against parental demands and restrictions, refusing to comply with a variety of family expectations. The phenomenon is certainly not a new one—it dates at least as far back as ancient Greece:

> Socrates described youth as disrespectful of their elders and as tyrants—not servants—of their households. "They are also mannerless," said Socrates, "and fail to rise when their elders enter the room. They chatter before company, gobble up dainties at the table, cross their legs, and tyrannize over their teachers." (Rogers, 1977, p. 6)

At the same time, teenagers typically conform quite closely to the expectations and demands of their own peer group. Thus, the young adolescent does not in fact gain true independence (which will not come until later in development), but instead breaks away from parents and moves dramatically toward peers as a first step in a larger process. A number of studies have demonstrated that youngsters are more likely to conform to group pressures in early adolescence than at either earlier or later ages (Costanzo and Shaw, 1966; Iscoe, Williams, and Harvey, 1963).

Subcultures of Early and Mid-Adolescence. Earlier, we briefly mentioned adolescent subcultures. An adolescent subculture is a group of teenagers of roughly the same age, who share knowledge, values, and experiences. The subculture may take various forms, from a formal club or gang to a loosely organized social group. One study (Cohen, 1979) found three general types of subcultures among high school youth, each corresponding to values that have their counterparts in the larger society. The **academic subculture** is associated with high interest in studies, aspirations for college, spending time at home, and relatively little interest in dating. The **delinquent subculture** is associated with frequent dating, an interest in drinking and smoking, spending time away from home, and rejection of studies and college. Status is determined partly by cars and clothes. The **fun subculture** is associated with an emphasis on being popular as a friend or a date, athletic ability, and participation in school activities. These subcultures do not necessarily correspond to particular socioeconomic classes or ethnic groups. Adolescents from every background can be found in each of the three types of subcultures.

What Is Juvenile Delinquency? **Juvenile delinquency** refers to violations of the law by youths under 16 or 18 years of age. Some acts are illegal *only* for juveniles, so juvenile delinquents should not simply be thought of as adult criminals who are underage. For example, adolescents (but not adults) may be put in prison for running away from home. The interstate agreement on runaway juveniles is so strict that it has been compared to the fugitive slave laws of the 19th century. Teenage girls may be imprisoned for being promiscuous, although teenage boys are seldom punished for similar behavior. There is now a move afoot, backed by some psychologists, to rethink the legal status of such adolescents (Melton, 1983).

Nonetheless, it is also true that some real crimes *are* associated with adolescence. For example, although persons under 18 make up only 29 percent of the United States population, they are responsible for more than half of the arrests for vandalism, burglary, and motor vehicle theft. In four cases out of five, the youthful offender is male.

Two-thirds of all crimes by those under 18 years are committed by white youths. However, black youths are more likely to be involved in crimes in which they confront their victims, including robbery, rape, and murder. White youths are more likely to commit burglary, vandalism, and car theft.

Slightly more than half (56 percent) of the juveniles who are arrested are released at the police department without court action (Hindelang, Gottfredson, and Flanagan, 1981). Of the remainder, most are referred to juvenile court (see Figure 14–4).

The causes of juvenile delinquency are many and complex. Some young people may become delinquent because of psychiatric problems. This group includes the so-called "unsocialized psychopaths"—adolescents who are aggressive and defiant toward authority, and who seem to feel no guilt when they harm someone. Other troubled adolescents are judged to be neurotically disturbed—timid, shy, and anxious.

Delinquents tend to have had a history of poor physical health as children, and to have been impulsive and restless (Glueck and Glueck, 1974). But many delinquents are also products of their family or neighborhood environments, or of their membership in the kind of delinquent subculture we mentioned earlier.

Who becomes a member of a delinquent gang? Here's one psychologist's description of the major differences between gang members and nonmembers:

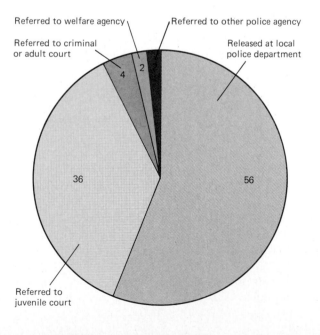

Referred to welfare agency
Referred to criminal or adult court
Referred to other police agency
Released at local police department
4
2
36
56
Referred to juvenile court

figure 14–4
What happens to juveniles taken into police custody in the United States. (Adapted from U.S. Department of Justice, 1979)

More than half of all arrests for vandalism, burglary, and car theft involve adolescents under 18.

Gang members were more violent than non-affiliated youth, and they felt significantly less guilty than non-gang-members about antisocial acts. They also had poorer relationships with their mothers and engaged more often in physical assault against their fathers. On the other hand, they did not differ from non-members with regard to such factors as backgrounds of intact or broken homes, criminal histories of their parents, the level of their intelligence, or the highest school grade completed. In fact, gang-members and non-gang-members were similar in personality traits, sociological characteristics, and family structure. Hence, gang affiliation may be highly dependent on situational factors, often an ineffectual parent-son relationship or the presence of a gang in the neighborhood. (Rogers, 1979, p. 398)

Historically, males have been more likely than females to be delinquent. Delinquency is also more common among the disadvantaged than among middle-class youth. These two gaps are closing, however. Females and middle-class youths are showing definite increases in delinquency (Kratcoski and Kratcoski, 1975).

Recent critics (Hindelang, Hirschi, and Weis, 1981) have noted that delinquency data are inevitably biased in three important ways. First, not all crime is reported. There are a variety of "reporting biases." For example, crimes committed by upper-middle-class youth are less likely to be reported than those committed by youth from disadvantaged families. Second, the methods used for processing and reporting crime data vary from state to state. Individual studies of juvenile offenders also differ—for example, the juveniles may be asked different questions, or the questions may be worded in different ways. Finally, most of what has been written about the families and social lives of juvenile delinquents comes from their own self-reports. These reports are almost certainly biased and distorted in many ways, both consciously and unconsciously.

Adolescents' friendships with others of the same sex do not seem to be harmed by the growth of opposite-sex friendships.

Friendships in Adolescence

Subcultures is a word used by sociologists; it is not in the vocabulary of most adolescents. To adolescents, the important people are their friends.

Friendship in early adolescence resembles friendship in middle childhood (see Chapter 13) in more ways than it differs from it. Friendships in the second half of middle childhood tended to last longer than those in earlier childhood, but adolescence brings no further increase in that tendency. The differences between girls' friendships and boys' friendships also continue in adolescence: it is still the case that girls are more likely to have one or a few close friends and to exclude outsiders, while boys are likely to be members of a larger, less exclusive group.

Another characteristic of friendships that persists into adolescence (and, in fact, throughout the life-span) is the tendency to choose friends who are similar to oneself. If two adolescents are good friends, they are likely to have many attitudes and preferences in common. They will probably have similar attitudes toward school and similar academic ambitions; they will probably be fairly equal in academic achievement, too. They are also likely to share similar tastes in music, clothing, and recreational activities, and to have similar views on drinking, smoking, and drug use. Not all of these similarities are due to the way young people select their friends. There is evidence that the attitudes and preferences of friends become more alike, over the course of their friendship, because of the influence the friends have on each other (Berndt, 1982).

One way that friendships in adolescence do differ from friendships at a younger age is in closeness and intimacy. Between seventh grade and eleventh grade, there is a steady increase in how strongly young people agree with statements such as "I feel free to talk with [my friend] about almost anything" and "I know how [my friend] feels about things without his (her) telling me" (Sharabany, Gershoni, and Hofman, 1981). This increase in reported closeness occurs both in boys' friendships with boys and in girls' friendships with girls. In fact, somewhat surprisingly, boys' and girls' replies to the two questions we just quoted did not differ significantly, although other measures (in this study and in others) do show girls' friendships to be generally more intimate than those of boys. It's also interesting to note that the rise of close friendships between young people of the opposite sex does not seem to interfere with same-sex friendships. Opposite-sex friendships show a sharp rise in reported intimacy, starting in seventh grade for girls and in ninth grade for boys. The reported intimacy of same-sex friendships continues to increase despite the development of close opposite-sex friendships.

Although there is a lack of long-term, longitudinal data on this topic, most developmental psychologists believe that close friendships are very beneficial for young adolescents. One recent review summarizes the views of other researchers this way:

> Intimate conversations with friends can contribute to adolescents' self-esteem . . . by showing adolescents that another person respects their ideas and wants their advice. In addition, intimate adolescent friendships can contribute to the development of the social skills and the sense of security that are necessary for intimate relationships later in life. Finally, intimate conversations with friends may reduce adolescents' fears and anxieties about the physical and emotional changes that occur during early adolescence and, therefore, improve their actual adjustment. (Berndt, 1982, p. 1450)

Very few adolescents have just a single close friend. Most are members of groups, either informal "cliques" or more formal gangs or clubs. These peer groups provide support for the adolescent, but often at the expense of being petty, intolerant, or even cruel. Erik Erikson (1963) explains that such behavior serves to help the group members protect themselves against what he calls **identity confusion.** By rejecting others who are different from themselves in race, religion, social class, abilities, or appearance (including dress), adolescents are able to derive a sense of identity from the particular group to which they belong. Erikson suggests that parents should try to understand the motivations behind this kind of intolerance, even if they don't necessarily approve of it.

Adolescent Drug Use

In a society in which adults use a wide array of legal and illegal drugs for nonmedical, "recreational" purposes, it is no surprise that adolescents also use drugs in this way. Indeed, the fact that drug use is a prerogative of adults in our society is undoubtedly one of the major reasons that the practice is taken up by adolescents. Although adolescent drug use is associated with a variety of other difficulties that adolescents may have, alcohol and drugs are typically not so much the cause of other problems as they are a result. However, excessive use of alcohol and drugs may make existing problems worse.

It is important to note that in many ways the available data on adolescent drug use are unsatisfactory or inadequate. In some surveys, adolescents are simply asked about their use. A variety of distortions can result, caused by their unwillingness to admit to the use of drugs, a tendency to play down the amount and type of use, or even a tendency to exaggerate drug use. Furthermore, many studies are done in hospitals or clinics and thus may involve a selected group of adolescents who are not really typical of the population as a whole. Finally, there is continuing debate about when use becomes abuse. The precise effects of the "recreational" use of alcohol and marijuana are still matters of public and scientific uncertainty. Nonetheless, a certain number of facts are relatively well established.

There is some evidence to support the view that adolescent drug use proceeds in stages (Kandel, 1980). According to this view, drug use progresses in a fixed sequence: nonuse, use of legal drugs such as tobacco and alcohol, use of marijuana, and use of other illegal drugs. However, fewer adolescents are involved at each stage than at the previous stage. In other words, many more students stop with beer than go on to marijuana; many more stop at marijuana than go on to heroin or amphetamines.

A recent study of ninth and tenth graders (Brook, Whiteman, and Gordon, 1983) attempted to identify the factors associated with slow or rapid progression along this sequence. Lower stages of drug use were found among those who were not rebellious and who had affectionate relationships with their mothers or friends. Typically, the parents of these adolescents were not very far along on the path to drugs themselves. In contrast, adolescents at more advanced stages of drug use tended to have parents who were drug users and to associate with friends who were also drug users. Adolescents who had experienced rejection by their peers also tended to be further along in drug use.

Anxiety is a major correlate of drug abuse in early and middle adolescence. So is the desire to escape, alone or with others, into an inner world. Finally, several factors can combine to produce drug use. Thus, unconventional adolescents whose mothers showed them little warmth or affection tended to be among the most advanced in the sequence of drug use.

Adolescent drug use can be divided into five categories, depending on the substance used. These are inhalants, tobacco, alcohol, psychoactive drugs, and narcotics.

Inhalants. Inhalants that produce a "high" are among the few intoxicating substances readily available over the counter to individuals of any age. The fumes of certain glues, spray paints, and solvents, when sniffed, have immediate physiological and psychological effects, producing a degree of light-headedness and disorientation. A recent national survey on drug abuse found that many 12- and 13-year-olds begin their drug experiences with inhalants of this type (Comer, 1982).

Tobacco.   The good news is that the percentage of teenagers who smoke has finally begun to decline. It was 20 to 25 percent through most of the 1970s. A recent report (Barton, Chassin, Presson, and Sherman, 1982) puts the figure at 16 percent for 15- and 16-year-olds, and there are indications that the rate is continuing to drop.

One of the probable reasons for this decline is that there seems to have been a change in the way adolescents and preadolescents view teenagers who smoke. Smokers are seen by present-day sixth and tenth graders as less wise, less healthy, and less likely to do well in school than nonsmokers. And instead of appearing sophisticated and mature, the teenager who smokes is seen as someone who "tries to act big" (Barton and others, 1982).

As with other drugs, having parents and friends who use tobacco considerably increases the likelihood of its use. Adolescents who smoke cigarettes tend to believe—quite wrongly—that it will be easy to give them up later. Only 1 percent of high school seniors thought they would be smoking five years later (Atwater, 1983).

Alcohol.   A review of the literature on teenage alcohol use gives an enlightening portrait of how alcohol use develops (Jessor and Jessor, 1980). Most adolescents have their first drink in their own homes, with their own families sanctioning the action. Indeed, in some families a teenager is offered his or her first drink as a sort of milestone to mark the time when adolescent experimentation with adult behaviors is first permitted.

Not all adolescents drink, of course. Whether they do so depends heavily on the region from which they come—another subcultural influence. Teenagers who drink may make up as much as 80 percent or as little as 30 percent of the adolescent population, depending on the drinking patterns of adults in their community. On an individual level, one of the best predictors of how much an adolescent will drink is how much his or her parents drink—teenagers who are high users of alcohol tend to have parents who are also high users. In fact, knowing the drinking habits of a teenager's parents is the single best predictor of how much the teenager will drink.

Peers also play an important part in adolescent alcohol use. Adolescents who abstain from alcohol in the tenth grade but who begin to drink by the eleventh or twelfth grade are typically those who have moved into a drinking subculture.

Most religions deal with alcohol in some way, either by using it ceremonially or by banning it, so it should not be surprising that religious differences are also important. It appears that Jews and Catholics are somewhat more likely than Protestants to drink during adolescence, but those Protestants who do drink are more likely than Jews or Catholics to become problem drinkers.

The interpretation usually put on these findings is that Jews and Catholics have home experiences that include the moderate and controlled use of alcohol, and thus learn both to use and to restrain their use of alcohol.

Problem Drinking.   Despite variations among families, communities, and religious groups, the majority of adolescents have established a pattern of light to moderate drinking by the time they graduate from high school. However, only one adolescent in 20 is a problem drinker—one who engages in heavy drinking that interferes with normal activities.

What type of adolescent becomes a problem drinker? Most teenage alcoholics are male. They tend to be impulsive and aggressive—angry outbursts are rather common among these young men. They are also likely to be unstable and unpredictable in their dealings with others. They often have low expectations of attaining their personal goals; many of them seem depressed. Alcohol is an escapist solution for these young people because it stimulates thoughts of success and dominance, and provides a temporary feeling of power (McClelland, 1971).

Psychoactive Drugs.   Marijuana, LSD, amphetamines, and cocaine are all considered **psychoactive drugs**—drugs that have some effect on one's psychological state or processes. Among adolescents, such drugs are more likely to be used by males than by females. In sharp contrast to narcotic users, the users of psychoactive drugs tend to come from middle- and upper-class families with professional or managerial-level parents.

Marijuana is the most used of all illegal drugs, and most of its frequent

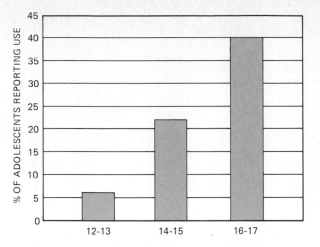

figure 14–5

Percentages of adolescents reporting ever having used marijuana, as a function of age. (Abelson and Atkinson, 1975)

users are adolescents and young adults. Figure 14–5 shows the results of one large survey done in the 1970s: the percentages of 12- to 17-year-olds who reported ever using marijuana.

Currently, about two-thirds of all high school seniors report having tried marijuana. Half say they have used it within the last year; 10 percent report daily use (Atwater, 1983). Occasional marijuana users are not very different from nonusers. Interestingly, although marijuana smoking is statistically associated with lower academic achievement in high school, academic differences between users and nonusers are not found at the college and professional school levels.

Narcotics. Most adolescent narcotic addicts come from broken homes and are members of minority groups. It has been speculated that a major cause of narcotics use among adolescents is an environment that they feel has rejected them. As one group of investigators pointed out, the early years of many adolescent addicts have been marred by mentally disturbed parents, by rejecting parents, or by the absence of one or both parents (Braucht and others, 1973). Racial discrimination also appears to play a role in narcotics addiction, which is perhaps why it is more prevalent among minority groups. Addicts in the United States tend not only to come from minority groups but also to be in their families' first generation of native-born Americans—in other words, to be the American-born children of immigrants to this country. For this reason, it has been suggested that narcotics use is partly due to a cultural clash between young people and their parents—another possible source of the feeling that their parents have rejected them.

In terms of personality variables, young narcotic addicts tend to have a low tolerance for frustration, to deal with their problems by not thinking about them, and to withdraw into fantasies. Introversion, shyness, insecurity, depression, and hypersensitivity also appear to have some association with narcotics use in adolescence.

SEX AND SEXUALITY

Sexuality is the sum of our sexual identity, sexual values and standards, and sexual behavior. We have seen that by the preschool period each child has developed a gender identity, including a set of expectations about what behaviors are appropriate for males and females. With the onset of adolescence, however, the sexual identity of childhood is suddenly complicated by powerful chemical and physical changes in the body that promote sexual and romantic interests. Two major undertakings of adolescence are to learn to deal with these interests and to adjust to social sex roles. Accomplishing these goals presents complex and subtle problems for both females and males throughout the life span.

Awakening of Sexual Interests

Sexual interests awaken in most adolescents at about the time of puberty, according to nature's usual clockwork. The experience, however, is quite different for boys and girls.

Between the ages of 14 and 16, most boys begin to have nocturnal emissions (the release of semen during sleep). These might be accompanied by vivid sexual dreams, which may contain elements of homosexuality or incest. There may also be unexpected erections and unbidden fantasies.

The situation for the girl is quite different. As one report puts it, "The sexual desire in males is centered clearly in the genitals, a factor which pushes them in an almost irresistible fashion. Although the physiological maturity of the girls is clearly evidenced by menarche, there is no corresponding immediate increase in sexual desire" (Turner and Helms, 1979, p. 264). On the basis of these differences, the writers conclude that adolescent males' interest in females is *erotic* (or sexual), whereas females' interest in males is *romantic*.

In fact, early adolescence is the time when many girls first begin to experience romantic love. Boys, on the other hand, are not usually swept up in a romantic interlude until later adolescence. Romance is embedded in Western culture: young people are *supposed* to fall in love; they are *supposed* to experience the complex set of emotions that goes along with that state. The culture, through movies, television, and novels, leads the young adolescent to interpret certain experiences as being "madly in love." Moreover, the feeling of being in love is considered by many to be a necessary and sufficient condition for sexual activity during adolescence.

Parties and Dating. The first expressions of romantic and sexual interests typically occur at parties or other gatherings of young adolescents, where they can experiment with kissing, hugging, and light petting on a relatively "safe" basis. These gatherings, of course, serve other purposes besides that of sexual experimentation. Parties and get-togethers in early adolescence provide an opportunity for social learning about a wide range of new roles, people, and relationships.

By mid-adolescence, most young people have started to have at least occasional individual dates, though about a quarter of adolescents do not date at all. A summary of data relating to the question of dating shows that girls begin dating at an earlier age than boys, and that marriage-oriented young people date more during mid-adolescence than career-oriented ones. Who is a desirable date? Sophistication and physical attractiveness, highly valued in the peer culture of early and middle adolescence, seem to be more important during the early period of dating than do traditional virtues. Thus, according to this report,

> An adolescent who is dishonest but attractive and sophisticated tends to date more than one who is honest and dependable but unattractive physically. In fact, many students would rather not date at all than date someone who is socially unsophisticated or physically unattractive, indicating that adolescents react more to social norms than they do to individual value systems. (Rogers, 1977, p. 206)

Sexual Behavior

Adolescent sexuality proceeds in a stepwise fashion, from kissing, to breast fondling and manual contact with the genitals of the partner, and then, often, to sexual intercourse. Adolescents do not seem to stay sexual beginners for very long. The majority either move on to a new partner or else have intercourse with their original partner. The most sexually experienced adolescents tend to report that magazines, movies, and television have influenced their sexual values and standards (Smart and Smart, 1978).

The motivations that adolescents give for having sexual intercourse are quite varied. Some apparently pair up into meaningful and enduring sexual relationships, others merely try sex out, and still others seem to use their sexual experiences to fulfill what are primarily nonsexual needs (Sorenson, 1973).

Since the late 1960s, teenage girls are increasingly more likely to have sexual intercourse before marriage, and to do so at an earlier age. It is still the case, however, that young adolescents experience many problems with their budding sexuality. Many find it difficult to deal with the prospect of heavy petting and sexual intercourse. Sex education as offered in the public schools has had little impact on the sexual attitudes or sexual behavior of youth. Nonetheless, sex is a topic that most teenagers would like to be able to discuss more openly.

Teenagers who have not had sexual intercourse tend to be among the most conventional in other aspects of their lives as well—they are less likely to use alcohol or drugs, for example. Late sexual activity is also more common among adolescents who are deeply involved in religion, or who lack self-confidence regarding their personal attractiveness and their social ability in mixed-sex situations (Jessor, Costa, Jessor, and Donovan, 1983). Among those who do begin to have sexual intercourse in adolescence, early sexual activity is associated with low academic achievement and with low levels of parental support or discipline.

In our culture, "falling in love" is an expected part of adolescent experiences.

There are clear similarities between adolescents who have early sex and those who are early drug users: both groups have low goals for academic and career achievement, both groups are more accepting than other adolescents of peers who behave in rebellious or unconventional ways, and both groups have a high need to establish their independence.

The Psychoanalytic View of Adolescent Sexuality. Psychoanalysts, starting with Anna Freud, have had a great deal to say about adolescents. They believe that adolescence brings with it a resurgence of Oedipal feelings. According to this view, a teenage boy may begin to idolize his mother and to believe that she is more appreciative of him or that she responds to him in a more appropriate manner than his father. A girl may have similar fantasies about her closeness to her father. For example, one adolescent girl hoped to cure her father of his alcoholism by being more understanding of him than her mother and by showing a greater interest in his work and hobbies. She began to center her life around him, so that she could take care of him after her mother divorced him (Lidz, 1976).

Parents are themselves intricately involved in their children's emerging sexuality. This may provoke jealousy in the same-sex parent and feelings of discomfort in the opposite-sex one. Moreover, the underlying dynamics can be troubling and confusing to all concerned. For example, a father may be inclined to draw away from his daughter as she matures into a young woman, precisely because he *is* unconsciously attracted to her. The daughter, meanwhile, may feel rejected by her father's withdrawal, because she does not understand its motivations. This, in turn, may cause the girl to become uneasy about her relationships with members of the opposite sex. In addition, daughters and mothers may vie for the father's attention, or the mother may be openly flirtatious with her daughter's boyfriends. Fathers, for their part, may idolize their daughters as women and then set impossibly high standards for them (or for their daughters' boyfriends).

Masturbation. Whereas boys today are about as likely to report masturbating as they were in the late 1940s, the self-reported incidence for girls has doubled (Hass, 1979). More than half of all adolescent girls and about three-quarters of adolescent boys report masturbating; the incidence for both sexes tends to increase slightly throughout the teen years. Somewhat surprisingly, the reported incidence of masturbation is lower among virgins than among nonvirgins.

Masturbation tends to be a middle-class activity. Middle-class adolescents and adults are less likely to voice strong disapproval of masturbation than those from the lower classes, who may consider masturbation to be a perversion and believe that early premarital intercourse is preferable.

Adolescents' motivations for masturbating focus on the fact that it "feels good" and provides a readily available outlet for sexual impulses. On the other hand, adolescents often report feeling guilty after masturbation. Here is a sample of comments made by 15- to 17-year-olds.

15-year-old boy: "After I masturbate I feel dirty."

15-year-old girl: "Most of the time I feel a state of euphoria, but at times if I'm trying to 'kick the habit,' I feel disgusted with myself."

15-year-old girl: "I usually regret it and can't imagine why just 30 seconds ago I was so involved with the great feeling."

17-year-old boy: "I feel satisfied but not fulfilled."

16-year-old boy: "I feel guilty and frustrated that I don't have a girlfriend instead of abusing myself."

16-year-old boy: "I feel relaxed, like all the tension has been released. All my worries go away for a while."

16-year-old girl: "I feel fine. Less horny and less tense."

16-year-old boy: "I feel satisfied. I thoroughly enjoy it." (Hass, 1979, pp. 98–101)

Homosexuality. Many children have fleeting sexual play with members of the same sex, often motivated by curiosity. Typically, such play is not a sign that the child will be homosexual. By adolescence, though, sexual contact with one's own sex is taken more seriously. Young adolescent boys tend to be highly disapproving of homosexuality. (According to psychoanalytic theory, this is by way of denial of their own homosexual impulses.) Adolescent girls seem to be somewhat more accepting than boys of homosexuality. In a study of 15- to 18-year-olds across the country, 2 percent of the girls and 3 percent of the boys said that they would be open to homosexual experiences, but 18 percent of the girls and only 11 percent of the boys said "maybe" to the same question (Hass, 1979).

Venereal Disease among Adolescents. Of the roughly 12 million cases of sexually transmitted venereal disease per year in the United States, three out of four occur among people 15 to 24 years old. The reasons for this high level of venereal disease include ignorance of the risk or of the means of controlling it (such as the use of condoms), and a personal fable that includes the belief, "It won't happen to me" (Katchadourian, 1977).

Teenage Pregnancy

The birth rate for unmarried mothers under 18 increased by 64 percent between 1966 and 1975 (Ventura, 1977), and the upward trend appears to be extending into the 1980s (see Figure 14–6). As a result, the birth rate for teenagers in the United States is among the highest in the Western world. In concrete terms, this means we have reached a point of having almost 1 mil-

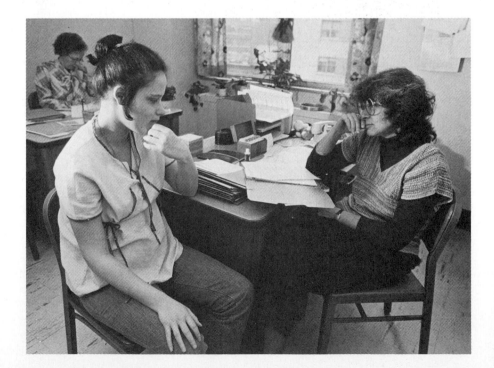

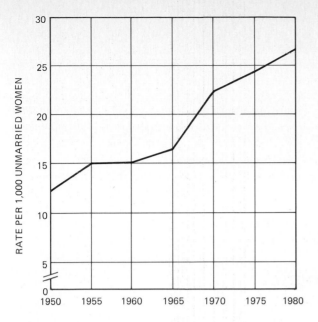

figure 14–6
Births to unmarried women
15 to 19 years old, 1950–
1980. (Data from
Hindelang, Gottfredson,
and Flanagan, 1981)

lion unwanted teen pregnancies per year. Another way to express the problem is to compare teenage girls with older women. Although teenage girls make up only 18 percent of the population of sexually active, fertile women, they account for 46 percent of all births to unmarried women. (Only 10 percent of teenage pregnancies are conceived in marriage, whereas the majority of women who become pregnant in their 20s and 30s are married.)

Why the big increase in teen pregnancy? One reason is that middle-class society in general has become much more permissive about sex. Paralleling this change, the percentage of sexually active 16-year-old white teenagers nearly doubled between 1970 and 1980. Black teenagers, who were 2½ times as likely as whites to be sexually active in 1970, also became more sexually active during this period, but the amount of change was not so dramatic (Zelnik and Cantnor, 1980).

If the increase in sexual activity is a reflection of the new sexuality in our larger society, the failure to use contraceptives appears to result from immature thinking and from ignorance of the facts. Young girls are surprisingly naive about pregnancy. Sexual activity need not lead inevitably to pregnancy, but teenagers are considerably more likely than adults to engage in sexual intercourse without using contraceptives. Research shows that about 80 percent of sexually active adolescents do not attempt to use any sort of birth control. This may be due partly to the difficulty of obtaining contraceptives, or to religious convictions. However, the fact that stands out most clearly is that most sexually active young people are ignorant of the facts of reproduction; they are also unrealistic in thinking about their own chances of becoming pregnant or of "getting someone pregnant." For example, 70 percent of the sexually active teenage girls in one study incorrectly claimed that they *couldn't* get pregnant. Among the reasons they gave were that they were too

PROBLEMS IN DEVELOPMENT

Adolescent Suicide

During the 1970s there was a sharp increase in the rate of adolescent suicide. Between 1968 and 1977 the suicide rate increased for many age groups, but for people aged 15 to 24 years the rate almost doubled (from 7.1 per 100,000 persons to 13.6 per 100,000). By 1977, suicide was second only to accidents as a cause of death in this age group. Some researchers suspect that the suicide rate may actually be underestimated, since some self-inflicted deaths are probably reported as accidents (*Monthly Vital Statistics Report,* 1979; Seiden, 1969).

There are clear sex and race differences in adolescent suicide. Girls are more likely to *attempt* suicide, but boys are considerably more likely to succeed in taking their own lives. In addition, the methods used by the sexes are different. A boy is more likely to attempt suicide with a gun, whereas girls typically choose pills or poison (Petzel and Cline, 1978). The youthful suicide rate, adjusted for overall population differences, is also higher for whites than blacks; this is true for both sexes.

Why do adolescents kill themselves? Freud saw suicide as one way a young person might respond to the death of a loved one, if the relationship between the two involved elements of hate and anger as well as love. When the loved one died, this hate and anger would be directed inward, and could lead to suicide. In fact, the death of a family member or close friend does increase the risk of suicide for young people (Tishler, McKenry, and Morgan, 1981).

Other factors, too, are associated with adolescent suicide. These include long-term isolation from others, repeated failure experiences, feelings of unworthiness and an absence of self-respect, and a sense of desperation.

Sociological explanations of suicide have also been advanced, mainly by the famous sociologist Émile Durkheim. Durkheim classified suicides as either *altruistic* (sacrificing themselves to benefit others), *anomic* (having experienced rapid life changes that led to disorientation), or *egoistic* (alienated from society and its members).

One theory of suicide is directed specifically at adolescents. In this theory, suicide is seen as a process that begins with the child's long-term problems. The turmoil of adolescence intensifies these difficulties, and the adolescent becomes increasingly isolated and unable to cope with them. A sudden loss of any remaining social relationship, combined with a philosophy that justifies suicide, may culminate in a suicide attempt (Petzel and Cline, 1978).

While depression is often considered a necessary precursor of suicide, some adolescents at-

young, or that they didn't have sex often enough to get pregnant (Shah, Zelnik, and Kanter, 1975). Another study showed that most young teenagers remained ignorant of how and when pregnancy can occur, despite having taken sex-education courses. For example, only one girl in three knew when in the menstrual cycle a girl can become pregnant. Most sex-education courses shy away from providing specific, practical, clear, and useful information on birth control (Zelnik, 1979).

In one study of pregnant girls between the ages of 12 and 15, it was found that 86 percent were not using *any* form of contraception prior to becoming

tempt suicide as a way of manipulating their environment to achieve a goal otherwise not available to them. For example, a teenager wishing to escape a distressed family situation might attempt suicide as a means of getting out of the home (and perhaps to a hospital). Unfortunately, although these young people do not actually intend to kill themselves, they pose a serious danger to themselves because they can misjudge the effects of their actions (Glaser, 1981).

In one recent study (McKenry and Morgan, 1981), adolescents themselves were asked about the events that led to their suicide attempts. The most common reasons cited were problems with parents (52 percent), difficulties with members of the opposite sex (30 percent), difficulties at school (30 percent), problems with siblings (16 percent), and trouble with peers (15 percent). (These figures add to more than 100 because some adolescents gave more than one reason.) It is not clear whether these findings can be taken at face value—whether teenagers really know why they tried to kill themselves, and whether they'd reveal the reason if they did.

Other studies have shown that adolescent suicide or attempted suicide is more likely when one or more of these factors are present: (1) previous suicide attempts, (2) a family history of suicide, (3) the death of a friend or relative, (4) pregnancy, and (5) early marriage. Early marriage is associated with an increased adolescent suicide risk, despite the fact that in older age groups married people have *lower* suicide rates than single people (Tishler and others, 1981).

Adolescent suicide not only destroys its victims but frequently devastates the surviving family members as well. The grief and confusion of parents whose teenage child has committed suicide is compounded by the shame and disgrace attached to the act. The parents may be unable to discuss their feelings with anyone, even each other. In these situations the parents may deny that the death was a suicide, or express hostility toward professionals (such as physicians or coroners) involved in its aftermath.

Although much research needs to be done in the field of suicide prevention for all age groups, two strategies for parents have been suggested to help decrease teenage suicide risk. First, all suicidal behaviors should be taken seriously, and should not be regarded as idle threats or gestures. Second, guns, dangerous drugs, and common household poisons should be kept out of sight and relatively unavailable, because adolescent suicide is often an impulsive act that can be triggered by having the means readily at hand.

Young people who try to kill themselves tend to have the same basic concerns that all young people have—concerns about their ability to succeed in life, about their relationships with parents and with peers, about their physical appearance, about drugs, alcohol, and sex, and so on. These are the typical concerns of early adolescence; we have discussed them in this chapter. Older adolescents direct more of their attention toward choosing a career and finding a mate, the issues to which we will turn in the next chapter. ■

pregnant (Salguero, 1980). What must be emphasized is that the vast majority of these girls do not wish to become pregnant. Rather, they are either completely ignorant about contraception, or they have no way of obtaining contraceptive devices or pills. Understandably, young teenagers worry about confidentiality in seeking and obtaining contraceptives. Adolescents do not discuss birth control very much—not even with friends, much less parents. Thus, laws against providing contraceptive aids to minors without the knowledge and consent of their parents are likely to deter them from using such aids.

Consistent with Elkind's views, which we discussed earlier in this chapter, adolescents display egocentric thought regarding their own chances of pregnancy (Rogel and Zuehike, 1982). There is evidence of belief in a personal fable (for example, the girl who thinks, "I am a unique and special person; therefore I won't get pregnant") and in the imaginary audience (for example, the boy who sees himself as a daredevil in life's play, and who thus sees using contraceptives as "being chicken").

Abortion.   The results of the huge increase in unwanted pregnancy in this age group are also cause for concern. Fewer young mothers today than ever before are having their babies and then giving them up for adoption. In 1979, pregnant girls under 15 were the only group more likely to have an abortion than to let the pregnancy continue and girls between 15 and 19 were the next most likely to choose this alternative (Hindelang, Gottfredson, and Flanagan, 1981).

Teenage Motherhood.   Of the teenage girls who don't have abortions, the overwhelming majority (about 90 percent) keep their babies, rather than give them up for adoption. As a result, there are now about three-quarters of a million children under the age of 4 years in the United States who are being brought up by young, unmarried mothers.

What happens when an unmarried teenager does decide to keep her baby, bringing it up with the help of parents and friends, or by herself? Although some unwed teenage mothers are quite successful, many will have physical and psychological problems with their babies that relate to their own youth and lack of experience. These problems begin even before the baby is born. Financial considerations and sheer ignorance keep many pregnant girls from getting proper prenatal care; poor nutrition is common. As a consequence of these factors and of their physical immaturity, young teenagers are considerably more likely than other age groups to experience problems in pregnancy and delivery. Low-birthweight babies (see Box, p. 131) are more common in this group.

The problems continue after the baby comes home from the hospital. Unmarried teenage mothers are likely to drop out of school. If they marry, they are more likely than others to have unsuccessful marriages. It has been found that many teenage mothers do not play with or talk to their babies enough. These young women do not appreciate the infant's need to interact with others, and often describe their babies as "doing nothing" or as "being naughty," when what the baby is in fact doing is seeking needed stimulation (Salguero, 1980). Unmarried teenage mothers are also more likely to engage in child abuse. These are all additional reasons why teen pregnancy is considered an extremely pressing national problem today (Sacker and Neuhoff, 1982).

summary

1.   Adolescence is a transitional period from the dependency of childhood to the independence and responsibility of adulthood. Many important aspects of an individual's identity are formed during this period, and many important decisions must be made.

2. Adolescence can be divided into three subperiods: (1) early adolescence, which begins while the individual is still looking and acting like a child and is usually marked by a sizable growth spurt; (2) mid-adolescence, which begins after the most noticeable changes in physical appearance have already occurred and is characterized by revolt mixed with conformity, a movement toward the opposite sex, and unpredictable mood swings; and (3) late adolescence, which brings concerns about education, occupation, and marriage.

3. The growth spurt of early adolescence, which consists of a dramatic increase in height and weight, comes two years earlier in girls than in boys. As a result, the average 12-year-old girl is taller and heavier than the average boy of the same age. By age 14, the average boy is once again taller than the average girl.

4. The spurt in height is accompanied by the growth of most organs and bodily systems, and by changes in glands and in body proportions.

5. **Puberty** is the attainment of sexual maturity. In girls, **menarche** (the first menstrual period) occurs between 12½ and 13, on the average. Boys begin to discharge semen containing live sperm at an average age of 14½.

6. The approach of puberty is accompanied by the appearance of various **secondary sex characteristics,** such as breast development in girls and deepening of the voice in boys. Changes also occur in the sex organs themselves (the **primary sex characteristics**).

7. Adolescents vary widely in the speed with which they reach physical maturity. Early-maturing boys are more apt than late-maturing ones to assert themselves at home and to be socially and athletically successful. For girls, there are no clear advantages or disadvantages to maturing early.

8. **Anorexia** affects about one in 200 girls between the ages of 12 and 18. Girls with this disorder restrict themselves to tiny amounts of food; they may refuse treatment, give irrational justifications for their behavior, and see themselves as fat even when they are dying of starvation.

9. **Bulimia** is another eating disorder that is most common in teenage girls. Bulimics gorge themselves with food and then use laxatives or self-induced vomiting to rid themselves of it. Unlike anorectics, their body weight tends to remain normal; they are more likely to achieve independence and more responsive to treatment. The exact causes of bulimia and anorexia are still being debated.

10. According to Piaget, adolescence marks the entrance to the **period of formal operations.** Formal thought is characterized by a tendency to identify and consider all solutions systematically, and to experiment with them in the mind and in reality. There is also a tendency to seek explanations of what has been observed.

11. Formal thought is more likely to be applied to problems of an intellectual nature than to personal or social problems. Individuals who test high in IQ, and those who have had appropriate environmental and educational experiences, are more likely to display formal thought.

12. Adolescents are often egocentric, in the sense that they tend to be overconfident about the value of intellectual solutions to problems, and intolerant of others who do not share their opinions.

13. According to Elkind, adolescents feel that they are playing to an **imaginary audience.** They also tend to believe in a **personal fable,** which involves feelings of uniqueness and immortality.

14. Cognitive advances in adolescence pave the way for the development of commitments to ideals and ideologies. Such commitments tend to be strongly felt and strongly expressed.

15. Conflict with parents is typical in adolescence; many teenagers openly refuse to comply with family expectations. Instead, they conform quite closely to the demands and expectations of their peer group. Conformity to peer group pressure is higher in early adolescence than in any other stage of life.

16. Teenagers may belong to an **academic subculture,** a **delinquent subculture,** or a **fun**

subculture. Adolescents from every background can be found in each of these three subcultures.

17. **Juvenile delinquency** occurs more frequently among boys than among girls, and among the disadvantaged than among middle-class youth. Other factors that have been associated with delinquency are psychiatric problems, a history of poor physical health, impulsiveness and restlessness, and membership in delinquent gangs.

18. If two adolescents are good friends, they are likely to have many attitudes and preferences in common. These similarities are due partly to the way adolescents select their friends, and partly to the influence that friends have on each other.

19. Between seventh grade and eleventh grade there is a steady increase in the closeness and intimacy of adolescents' friendships with others of the same sex. This is true for both boys and girls, although girls' friendships are generally found to be closer and more intimate than boys'. The increased closeness of same-sex friendships occurs despite the development of opposite-sex friendships.

20. Psychologists believe that adolescents' friendships contribute to their self-esteem and to the development of social skills, and serve to reduce anxiety about the changes that occur during this period.

21. Most adolescents are members of "cliques," clubs, or gangs. Erikson believes that belonging to such groups serves to protect adolescents against what he calls **identity confusion.**

22. There is some evidence that the use of drugs during adolescence proceeds in stages: nonuse, use of legal drugs such as tobacco and alcohol, use of marijuana, and use of other illegal drugs. Each stage involves fewer adolescents than the previous stage. Some of the factors associated with rapid advancement through these stages are the use of drugs by parents and friends, rejection by peers, poor relationships with parents, rebelliousness, and anxiety.

23. The percentage of teenagers who smoke tobacco has begun to decline. This decline may be due in part to the fact that present-day teen-agers tend to have a rather unfavorable view of agemates who smoke.

24. Whether or not an adolescent drinks alcoholic beverages will depend to a large extent on the drinking habits of his or her parents and peers.

25. One adolescent in 20 is a problem drinker. Most teenage alcoholics are male; they tend to be impulsive and aggressive.

26. Marijuana is the most used of all illegal drugs; about two-thirds of all high school seniors report having tried it. High school students who are regular users of marijuana tend to be less conventional and more rebellious than non-users, and to be lower in academic achievement. Academic differences between users and nonusers have not been found at the college level.

27. Adolescents who are narcotic addicts tend to be members of minority groups and to have had a disturbed family background. It has been speculated that a major cause of narcotics use by teenagers is an environment they feel has rejected them.

28. Two of the important undertakings of adolescence are to deal with newly awakened sexual and romantic interests, and to adjust to social sex roles.

29. Early adolescence is the time when many girls first begin to experience romantic love. For boys, this experience does not usually occur until later adolescence. Teenage girls' interest in boys seems to be primarily romantic, whereas boys' interest in girls seems to be primarily erotic (or sexual).

30. The first expressions of romantic and sexual interests often occur at parties or other gatherings of young adolescents. By mid-adolescence, most young people have started to date; girls begin dating at an earlier age than boys. During the early period of dating, sophistication and physical attractiveness seem to be valued most highly when it comes to choosing a date.

31. Adolescents do not tend to stay sexual beginners for very long—most move on to a new partner or have intercourse with their original partner. Early sexual activity is associated with low academic achievement and low levels of parental support or discipline. Late sexual activity is more likely to be found in adolescents who are conventional, religious, or lacking in self-confidence.

32. According to the psychoanalytic view, adolescence brings a resurgence of Oedipal feelings—boys may begin to feel close to their mothers, girls to their fathers. Such feelings may greatly complicate family relationships.

33. More than half of all adolescent girls and about three-fourths of boys report masturbating; some feel guilty about doing so, whereas others focus on the fact that it "feels good" and provides an outlet for sexual impulses.

34. Despite our society's permissiveness about sex, most sexually active teenagers are still ignorant of the facts of reproduction. As a result, pregnancy rates in teenage girls are con-

tinuing to rise. Many of these pregnancies are ended by abortion. Of those that are not, about 90 percent of unmarried teenage mothers keep their babies. The physical and psychological immaturity of these young mothers, and their ignorance about child development, make this situation risky for both mother and child.

35. The rate of suicide in adolescents almost doubled during the 70s. Girls make more suicide attempts, but boys succeed more often. An adolescent may commit suicide as a reaction to the death of a loved one, or as a result of long-term isolation, repeated failure experiences, feelings of unworthiness, or a sense of desperation. Adolescents may also attempt suicide as a way of escaping from a distressed family situation. Suicide threats or attempts should be taken seriously, and guns, poisons, and dangerous drugs should be kept out of sight.

Chapter Fifteen

BECOMING AN ADULT

Fifteen

The status of a 13- or 14-year-old is neither here nor there: he or she has one foot in childhood, the other in adolescence. An 18- or 19-year-old, on the other hand, is clearly no longer a child. Physical development is virtually complete, except for a subtle further deepening of a young man's voice and the appearance of a slight indentation in his hairline. That little indentation can be considered nature's marker that complete physical maturity has been reached in the male (Lidz, 1976).

Similarly, the most pronounced changes in the area of cognitive development have taken place, although small but observable changes can still be seen into the early twenties. Language development, too, is mostly complete by early adolescence, but again, research has shown that certain subtle developments continue to take place. For example, the ability to understand unusual language constructions continues to develop at least through the later teenage years. This was shown in a study (Kramer, Koff, and Luria, 1972) in which subjects between 8 and 19 years of age were presented with sentences such as "Ask Bob which book to read." The meaning of this statement is that you should ask Bob which book *you* should read, but the children and younger adolescents tended to misinterpret it as meaning "Bob, which book do you want to read?" These observations remind us that development is a continuing process throughout the life-span.

MILESTONES OF LATE ADOLESCENCE

Physical and cognitive changes may be small, but there are dramatic changes in social development during the final years of adolescence. By high school graduation (or, for others, when they drop out of high school), most adolescents are confronted by a whole new set of demands as they prepare for entrance into adulthood. Three closely related issues face the older adolescent during the final phase of transition to adult status: identity formation, selecting a mate, and choosing and preparing oneself for an occupation.

Because the decisions that are made during this period may have life-long effects, late adolescence is seen as a time of unique importance both by young people and by their parents. Parents are typically worried that a single rash action during adolescence will mar the adolescent's chances for a successful future life. Adolescents themselves are keenly aware that the career or marriage decisions they make today will follow them through much of the rest of their lives, and that changing directions later on will be much more difficult than making desirable choices at the outset.

As was the case earlier, underlying cognitive development assists the young person in dealing with the problems and tasks that still lie ahead. Thus,

> As the adolescent differentiates the thoughts of others from his own, he also becomes able to regard his own thinking more objectively. As thought grows more mobile and flexible, he can stand off and look at himself as a person. He can consider himself as a physical specimen, as a person-among-persons, as an intellectual being, or as a friend in any of the numerous roles he plays . . . son, friend, sweetheart, student, and so on. (Smart and Smart, 1978, p. 69)

IDENTITY FORMATION

In Erik Erikson's theory of psychosocial development, the major crisis of adolescence is **identity versus role confusion.** At first, every adolescent faces some confusion as the innocence of childhood gradually fades and dependence on parents and peer groups lessens. To attain a sense of identity is to know what kind of person one wishes to be as an adult, and to act and plan accordingly (Keniston, 1975). Equally important, the adolescent must now recognize and accept opposing forces in his own personality, and must learn more effective forms of self-control.

Themes in Identity Development

Identity formation is not—and should not be—sudden or abrupt. During adolescence the young person is encouraged to experiment with a variety of roles, attitudes, and interests. Indeed, it would be a mistake to limit one's options too soon.

Research suggests that a firm sense of identity is usually not achieved until late adolescence. The critical period for identity formation is seen as being between the ages of 18 and 21 (Meilman, 1979; Munro and Adams, 1977).

Growth in Overall Self-Esteem. **Self-esteem** refers to a person's overall regard for himself or herself. It can be assessed by asking people to indicate (on a 5-point scale: disagree, mostly disagree, neither, mostly agree, agree) their opinion of statements such as:

> I take a positive attitude toward myself.
>
> I feel I am a person of worth, on an equal plane with others.
>
> I am able to do things as well as most other people.
>
> On the whole, I am satisfied with myself.

Using this method, a recent study involving thousands of young people showed a steady increase in self-esteem during adolescence (O'Malley and Bachman, 1983). The change is not due to age itself, but rather to three factors that are related to age: an increase in physical size; an increased access to adult roles, responsibilities, and privileges; and a shift away from school as the central activity in one's life.

Involvement in Ideology. Political involvement is a favorite way to try out ways of expressing one's identity. For this reason, political causes in every generation have relied on young people at the threshold of adulthood. Thus, youth is a natural time for political activism, though the specific form of ac-

TABLE 15–1 How Youth in Every Generation Becomes Involved in the Decisive Political Events of the Period

Time period	Decisive political events	Youth movements
1900–1929	Economic growth and cultural liberalism Industrialization. U.S. develops favorable balance of trade and becomes world industrial power World War I Isolationism Prohibition Women's Suffrage "Roaring Twenties"	Youth culture challenges Victorian social and sexual mores
1930–1940	The Great Depression Poverty Election of FDR—"New Deal" Government economic programs Growth of national socialism in Germany	Youth join antiwar movement Sign Oxford Pledge Campus strikes
1941–1949	World War II Truman administration Atomic bomb Returning GIs Global reconstruction, U.N.	Little youth movement activity
1950–1959	The Cold War—Eisenhower Years Growth of "military-industrial complex"	"The silent generation"

From Braungart, 1975.

tivism that occurs in a given generation depends upon the decisive political events of that period (see Table 15–1).

Trying on various commitments and identities is done in a variety of ways. Many adolescents become concerned with philosophical issues. Often there is identification with one or more older individuals, frequently involving a type of hero worship. Settling on a vocation is particularly important in this process, and the decision is a difficult one for many young people. Even falling in love can be a means of arriving at a definition of one's identity, by seeing oneself reflected and gradually clarified through another (Erikson, 1963).

Typically, a commitment to certain ideas or political beliefs gives way to personal concerns. Young adolescents are idealistic and optimistic, presumably because they are not yet fully aware of the problems and complications

Time period	Decisive political events	Youth movements
	Dulles foreign policy	
	Recession	
	McCarthyism	
	1954 Supreme Court desegregation decision	
	House Un-American Activities Committee	
1960–1968	Kennedy-Johnson Years	New Left
	"New Frontier"	New Right
	Civil rights demonstrations	Civil rights and Black Power
	Peace Corps, poverty programs	Protest demonstrations, strikes, violence
	Vietnam escalation	
	Assassinations of Kennedy brothers and Martin Luther King	
	"Great Society" programs	
	Ghetto riots and campus disruption	
1969–1973	Nixon-Agnew Years	Women's rights
	Emphasis on "law and order"	Ecology movement
	Vietnam war ends, fighting in Southeast Asia continues	
	Inflation, job squeeze	
	Growth of multinational corporations	
	Watergate	

Involvement in political issues is a traditional way for young people to express their developing sense of identity.

involved in existing social and political systems. As they gain political realism, in the sense of being able to understand what can and cannot be easily changed, they also realize that they must come to grips with what Freud called the two greatest human needs and concerns: love and work (Adelson, 1975).

Identity Status

At any particular point in time, each adolescent has what developmental psychologist James Marcia calls an **identity status.** A person's identity status depends on the way he or she is dealing with the problems of forming a distinctive adult identity. Marcia (1966, 1976) interviewed many adolescents and talked with them about their career plans, their political convictions, and their general philosophy of life. On the basis of this research, he defined four levels of identity status, which he labeled *foreclosure, diffusion, moratorium,* and *achievement.*

Foreclosure is a status in which the identity crisis has not yet been faced squarely. Young people who have this status remain close to their parents and display a high need for social approval. They show little autonomy. On the other hand, this status produces little anxiety, which is perhaps its benefit.

Diffusion is also a status of avoidance. It is characterized by a lack of intimate relationships and a lack of commitment—a general withdrawal from life. This is a kind of drifting (sometimes called *ego diffusion*) in which the individual is not willing to make conscious decisions about the future and may instead drop out, often turning to drugs or mystical experiences rather than getting on with the business of living. *(continued on p. 502)*

CLOSE-UP

Creating Rites of Passage

In many nonindustrialized societies there is a formal **rite of passage** into the full set of privileges and responsibilities of adulthood. For example, among Australian aboriginals an adolescent male passes from childhood into adulthood by taking his *walkabout,* a six-month-long individual endurance test in the wilderness. At the end of this ordeal, if he survives, he is accepted back into his tribe with celebration. He is now considered a full-fledged adult (Gibbons, 1974).

Adolescents in industrialized societies are not provided with such a clear opportunity to demonstrate that they merit acceptance into adulthood. Rather than a sharp line marking the occasion, there is a good deal of confusing blur. For example, a degree of adult status is achieved by reaching voting age, by earning a college degree, by joining the military service, by marrying, or even by reaching the age when it's legal to drink (this age ranges from 18 to 21 in the United States). Contrast these variable and uncertain criteria with the rigor and "proof-of-manhood" quality of the aboriginal's walkabout, and we see that cultural factors can turn the formation of one's identity as an adult into a slow and uncertain process. A young person in North America may wait until his or her middle 20s or even beyond to be recognized as a full-fledged adult. Those who remain at home or who continue their education (for example, four years of college plus graduate or professional school) invariably prolong the period in which their status is ambiguous—neither child nor adult.

Maurice Gibbons, a professor of education at a Canadian university, feels we can provide a valuable service to youth by requiring "rite-of-passage" demonstrations and experiences that fit in with our own culture. He observes that the only tests we give adolescents are given in school, and in taking them the adolescents are expected to think and write, not to act. Gibbons goes on to observe:

> The young North American is faced with written examinations that test skills very far removed from the actual experiences he will have in real life. . . . He is under direction in a protected environment to the end; he does not go out into the world to demonstrate that he is prepared to survive in, and contribute to, our society. His preparation is primarily for the mastery of content and skills in the disciplines and has little to do with reaching maturity, achieving adulthood, or developing fully as a person. (1974, pp. 596-597)

Gibbons believes that the main challenge for young people in any society is to learn to make decisions on their own, and that we deal poorly with this challenge in today's educational and economic system. Although North American adolescents have neither the need nor the training for Australian-style walkabouts, Gibbons feels we need something of that sort—a formalized opportunity for adolescents to display their skills as a way of marking passage from childhood to adulthood. He suggests five basic challenges that we *could* present to adolescents. These are:

- *Adventure* (such as parachute drops, rock-climbing expeditions, and the like);
- *Creativity* (such as producing one's own poems, pictures, tooled leather purses, and so on);
- *Service* (such as political or social volunteer work on an intensive basis);
- *Practical skill* (such as cultivating the ability to make a stock-market trend analysis, or to take dictation, or to make one's own camera);
- *Logical inquiry* (such as learning what is involved in navigating in space, or providing a careful, scientific analysis of what is known about faith-healing). ∎

Those in the **moratorium** status are experiencing an ongoing identity crisis. There is a moratorium (a period in which no action is taken) on making important personal decisions. Young people with this status relate to their parents with guilt and ambivalence and have frequent conflicts with authority. They experience a considerable amount of anxiety.

Finally, there are those who have reached **achievement** status. They have been through the identity crisis of adolescence and have made their commitments; as a result, they are now achievement oriented, socially adapted in their dealings with others, and enjoy high levels of intimacy in some of their personal relationships.

As young people mature, there is generally a progression toward moratorium and then achievement status (Meilman, 1979). However, achieving identity in adolescence is not always a steady process—an identity crisis that is apparently resolved may sometimes reappear (Bourne, 1978).

An adolescent's identity status is related to the parenting style with which he or she was reared (Adams and Jones, 1983). Adolescents who have achieved identity or who are in moratorium status tend to have parents who allow them a fair amount of self-determination and who stress independence; these parents also provide much praise and encouragement. Adolescents who have foreclosure or diffusion status, on the other hand, tend to feel that their parents are simply not emotionally involved with them.

SEX, ROMANCE, AND SELECTING A MATE

Sex and romance play an important role in the life of the older adolescent. Most contacts with the opposite sex proceed from casual acquaintanceship or meeting in groups to dating or "going out with" someone. There also appears to be a newly emerging goal for men: intellectual companionship with women. As little as one or two generations ago, men would have sought their intellectual companionship largely, if not entirely, from other men.

Dating provides companionship and the opportunity to acquire experience with members of the opposite sex. There is also, of course, a sexual component. Nonetheless, dating is an activity that is oriented to the present, rather than the future. In this respect it differs from *courtship,* a series of similar activities that has marriage or at least a permanent relationship as its goal.

The New Sexuality

The rules and ideals governing male-female relationships have changed dramatically over the past 20 years. Spurred by the women's movement, by changes in the economy, and by other factors, a "new sexuality" has emerged that involves considerably more than sex (Otto, 1971). The ideal relationship is currently felt to have all the following characteristics: open

For the older adolescent, romantic relationships provide companionship and an opportunity to gain experience with the opposite sex.

communication, a willingness to reexamine gender-linked roles, an emphasis on both realism and spiritualism, a rejection of puritanical and Victorian anti-sexuality, and a strong emphasis on empathy, love, concern, intimacy, responsibility, authenticity, and mutual fulfillment. In a study of Harvard college men (Vreeland, 1972), it was found that the most important reason for dating was finding a friend who is female. The essential characteristic required by these men for a date was her ability to carry on a good conversation. This fit in well with the primary dating activity, which was "sitting around a room and talking."

Along with the emphasis on mutual fulfillment and empathy has come a definite change in the perceived acceptability of sexual intercourse before marriage. Most adolescents today believe that a person's sexual behavior is his or her own business and, if kept reasonably private, not the business of the community at all. Adolescents, particularly adolescent girls, increasingly believe that they have a right to various forms of birth control without parental approval or any "hassle" (Rogers, 1977). Nevertheless, some things remain unchanged. The great majority of adolescents still hold to the traditional ideal of a marriage in which the partners are faithful to each other (Edwards and Steinnett, 1974).

Premarital Sex

Acceptance of intimate sexual behavior between unmarried people has increased substantially over the past two decades. According to one source (Juhasz, 1976), 40 percent of college women and 60 percent of college men will have had intercourse by the end of their senior year in college. The overall likelihood of having lost one's virginity increases sharply with age. For example, while 14 percent of all 15-year-old girls have had intercourse at least once, fully 46 percent of all 19-year-old women have done so. This same general pattern is also true for boys. Within these broad trends, however, there are wide variations based on individual psychological characteristics and on educational, socioeconomic, and ethnic background.

Overall, the prevailing standard seems to be that the level of the relationship between the two people determines whether or not they will have sexual intercourse. Having had a sex-education course in high school is not very important in determining premarital sexual behavior among college students; nor is their parents' viewpoint on sexual matters (Spanier, 1975).

A generation or two ago, most girls who engaged in premarital sex did so only on the assumption that their boyfriends intended to marry them. That standard no longer prevails. Still, we should not characterize the adolescent or college student as being overly involved with sex. In fact, the frequency of intercourse tends to be quite low throughout the adolescent years.

Compared with immediately preceding generations, the behavior of college students today shows a clear easing of the "double standard," which demanded virginity for girls but not for boys. There have even been some hints of a reversal of earlier trends. While females are now *more* sexually experienced at any given age than a generation ago, males today tend to be *less* experienced than their fathers were. But women have a lot of catching up to do, and men as a group remain more likely than women to have premarital sexual intercourse during the college years, in a ratio of approximately to 3 to 2. And other gender differences remain. For example, young women tend to have had only one sexual partner, whereas young men tend to have had several.

Living Together

In 1962, a Cornell University graduate student was suspended indefinitely for living with a woman in his own apartment off campus. By 1972, however, cohabitation ("living together") was commonplace at this famous Ivy League college. This dramatic change in the attitude of colleges and universities toward cohabitation among students has produced a striking change in the nature of college life. Although there are fewer studies of noncollege adolescents, it appears that they too are cohabitating much more frequently than in the past (L. Smart, 1978).

Living-together relationships of undergraduate college students often follow a pattern. Typically, the girl moves into the boy's room in the dormitory (if he is a freshman) or into his apartment (if he is an upperclassman). His apartment is probably shared with other individuals, but the couple almost invariably live in a room of their own not shared by other people. In most cases, the girl also keeps a nominal residence of her own, either in the dormitory or in another apartment. One purpose of this second residence is to keep parents from knowing that a living-together relationship exists. The second residence may also be used for other purposes, such as getting messages or mail, changing clothes, or studying. Although some relationships are formed quite intentionally, other couples seem to drift into them, spending a night and then a weekend and then three or four days together as the relationship becomes more secure (Macklin, 1972).

The living-together relationships of college students are quite intimate in a number of ways. The typical couple are together about 17 hours a day on weekdays (5:00 p.m. to 8:00 a.m. plus lunch) and even longer on weekends. However, not all of this time is spent *alone* together—much of the time is shared with mutual friends. Generally, the couple eat two meals a day with each other. They cooperate on housekeeping chores. Food and entertainment expenses are typically shared, but it is quite rare to have a total pooling of financial resources.

In the great majority of cases, the basis of the relationship is a strong bond of affection, with neither member of the pair dating anyone else. This is consistent with the general trend among nonmarried adults today to engage in "serial monogamy": rather than cultivating several major romantic or sexual relationships at once, couples confine their sexual behavior to one another as long as the relationship lasts.

Parents often interpret living-together relationships among older adolescents as "trial marriages." The evidence suggests that this interpretation is quite wrong. As one investigator found, most undergraduate couples do not consider themselves married in any sense of the word. "When asked, 'Did you consider the possibility of getting married instead?' a frequent response was 'Heavens no!' " (Macklin, 1972, p. 467).

It appears that living together has become an ordinary part of life for young persons on the college campus, and is now accepted as one element in the courtship process and in sexual and sex-role development. The relationships are spawned in part by the impersonal atmosphere of many college and university campuses, and by the desire to try out an intimate relationship without making a deep or permanent commitment. Here's how the investigator we just mentioned sums it up:

> Given peer group support, ample opportunity, a human need to love and be loved, and a disposition to question the traditional way, it seems only natural that couples should wish to live together if they enjoy being together. One might almost better ask: why do students choose *not* to live together? (Macklin, 1972, p. 446)

In fact, about a third of all students will live with someone during college, if spending the night with the other person four nights a week is used as the criterion. On the average, living-together arrangements in college last about 4½ months.

What Are the Relationships Like and How Well Do They Work? About half of the students who live together do not find it a successful experience (Juhasz, 1976). Guilt, feelings of being overly involved, and sexual difficulties (such as lack of orgasm) are problems frequently reported by those who have lived with someone in college. The major psychological problems reported in relationships that prove unsatisfactory are overinvolvement and difficulty with holding on to one's own identity. (Although we mentioned earlier that falling in love can be a means of arriving at a definition of one's identity, a love affair can also have the opposite effect.) Some young people feel trapped in their relationships—they feel they should break up but are afraid or unable to do so. Jealousy is also fairly common. Another problem is disapproval, or fear of disapproval, by parents. More than two-thirds of college student couples who are living together try to conceal the relationship from their parents.

Equally interesting are those who did find living together a successful experience. These tend to be individuals who value emotional security, mutual affection, and loyalty more than sexual activity, and who find that they can obtain these valued qualities in their living-together relationship.

Early Marriage

There has been a drop in teenage marriage in recent years, perhaps because of a lessening of sexual taboos. One consequence of this development is an increase in the number of unwed teenage mothers—especially, unwed mothers who keep their infants (a matter we touched on in the last chapter).

What happens, though, to those who do marry in adolescence? Although some of these marriages are successful, the risk of an unsuccessful marriage is considerably greater for those who marry early than for those who marry in their middle 20s or later. Dissatisfaction typically begins within a few years after the marriage, sometimes within a few months. This dissatisfaction may take the form of sexual frustration, of unhappiness about losing one's same-sex friends, or of feeling "left out" by one's spouse (deLissovoy, 1973).

The phrase **lost-adolescence syndrome** has been used to refer to marital dissatisfaction among those who married young (Jurich and Jurich, 1975). Later on, these people come to regret that they married without gaining a wider range of personal experience with the opposite sex. Here's how one psychologist describes the lost-adolescence syndrome:

> Persons suffering from this syndrome define themselves as having "romantically" loved only one person—their spouse. Usually, they were married early, but in some cases the couple remained in a monogamous, intimate long-term relationship until they could marry, sometimes throughout all of high school and college. In the early years [of these marriages] persons with the lost adolescence syndrome usually have happy marriages with little stress. This peaceful period sometimes lasts until the first child is a year or two old. Shortly after the childbearing period begins, however, one or sometimes both spouses begin to feel trapped, and to view the single adolescent life as the ideal existence that they missed out on. The dissatisfaction grows, and the unhappy partner seeks a way out. Not infrequently the result

is a divorce, followed by loneliness and a rapid subsequent remarriage, with another cycle of the lost adolescence syndrome following. (L. Smart, 1978, p. 138)

OCCUPATIONAL CHOICE

"What do you want to be when you grow up?" This question is asked of every child, sometimes even before he or she has entered school. But it is not until late adolescence that the question of occupational choice becomes a serious and immediate one for most youngsters.

Cognitive Development and the Concept of Occupation

One can think of the development of occupational understanding as falling into three broad periods. The **fantasy period** extends until about age 11 or so; it is fantasy because the child perceives no limits on what he or she can potentially do. Then, with the appearance of formal operational thought, children enter the **tentative period.** They come to realize that jobs require specific training and abilities, and that education is costly. Finally, during the **realistic period** the individual chooses a career after considering job requirements, opportunity for training, and his or her own talents, abilities, and personal values. This mature realism about one's occupation is seen as a process that then remains active throughout one's lifetime, sometimes leading to mid-life career changes (Ginzberg, 1972).

Factors Involved in Occupational Choice

Many factors are intricately woven into occupational choice.

Parents and Children.   Traditionally, children "inherited" the occupations of their parents, generation after generation. Plainly, that is much less true today, although many young people—from musicians to plumbers to physicians—do continue in the occupations of their parents. It is still generally true that children usually have occupations at the same socioeconomic level as their parents. Financial resources, early modeling by parents, and subcultural influences all play a role in maintaining these occupational levels.

Education.   Education plays an extremely important role in determining the occupations one can and cannot pursue. In turn, education depends upon family background and circumstances, as well as one's aptitudes, abilities, and interests.

Aspiration Level and Achievement Motivation.   Level of aspiration and degree of achievement motivation have major influences on the occupational selections of young men and women. Young people with high levels of

PROBLEMS IN DEVELOPMENT

High School Dropouts

At the turn of the century, the expected minimum education for an American youngster was eight grades of public school. These eight years of schooling were expected to provide basic skills in reading, writing, and arithmetic, and a rudimentary familiarity with history, science, and literature. The expected standard gradually changed as the century advanced. State after state passed laws requiring attendance in school to a particular age—usually 16. Youngsters who failed to attend school until this age were considered truants, who were to be returned to school and punished for their absence.

Today the general expectation is that all normal youngsters will complete high school. Those who do not are considered dropouts. The overall high school dropout rate, from 1980 census figures, is just under 30 percent. Dropping out of high school is seen as undesirable by most educators and social commentators, and is associated with crime and unemployment among youth (Biddle and others, 1981). Fortu-

nately, there are fewer high school dropouts now than there were in the 1960s or 70s (Herron and Johnston, 1975). One reason for this decrease, however, may be a drop in the overall level of achievement required to earn a high school diploma, an issue to which we shall return later.

Although high school dropouts come from every social background and geographic area, a disproportionate number come from big-city schools and are members of ethnic and racial minorities. The dropout rate in New York City and Chicago, for example, is about 50 percent; it is only 6 percent in Kansas City, Missouri. Averaged across the United States, the dropout rate is about twice as high for blacks as for whites. Teenagers from broken homes, or from financially disadvantaged ones, are also considerably more likely than others to drop out.

Reasons for dropping out vary. Boredom is a reason that is commonly given by boys; girls often drop out because they have become preg-

achievement motivation are far more likely than others to aim for prestigious careers that require graduate or professional school training. Such achievement-oriented individuals tend to come from homes in which the parents made appropriate demands at appropriate times, warmly rewarded success, and established standards of excellence. At the same time, these parents gave their children opportunities to work out their problems in their own way (Veroff, 1965).

Socioeconomic background makes a difference, too. Youngsters from the lower classes tend to have less achievement motivation than those from the middle and upper classes (Haller, Otto, Meier, and Ohlendorf, 1974). Family size also seems to matter considerably, so that the lowest average levels of aspiration are found in large lower-class families.

Regardless of achievement motivation and level of aspiration, the best-laid career plans can sometimes lead to a dead end as a result of the fickle and changing job market. The past few decades have seen drastic variations in the need for people in various occupations, from assembly-line workers to

nant (see Chapter 14). Also, many young people drop out of high school simply to go to work. The consequences of dropping out are harder to pinpoint. Although more dropouts than non-dropouts are involved in crime and delinquency, the causal relationship between these factors is unclear. Personal, economic, or family problems may cause an adolescent to drop out *and* to become delinquent (Biddle and others, 1981).

In the past few years, dropout prevention has been receiving a great deal of attention and has provoked a good deal of controversy (Mauer, 1982). One reason for interest in this topic is that state funding of local schools is often linked to school attendance and dropout rates, which have come to be seen as yardsticks for evaluating school systems and administrators. The most successful way to increase retention rate of students during the high school years is to provide various forms of alternative education. Thus, many schools now allow youngsters to earn their diplomas by taking mostly vocational and recreational courses. Some schools offer alternative education in the evenings, so that those who might otherwise drop out for economic reasons are able to work while they continue their schooling. Counseling is frequently offered for those who propose to drop out.

Alternative education programs have their critics—the goal of a high school diploma for all has been attacked on several fronts. For one thing, it seems pointless to force teenagers to remain behind a school desk if they neither want nor need the traditional academic subjects of high school. Literacy, if that is the goal, should be assured at the elementary school level. According to one observer:

> Taxpayers today are supporting some students in high school only so that they can receive the stamp of approval signified by the diploma. This situation was graphically illustrated by a . . . student who said he was only staying in school to take auto mechanics. "I already know how to be a mechanic," he said. "My uncle, who is one, taught me. But they don't hire mechanics off the street. I have got to take the course so the school will recommend me, because, if the school says I am good, they'll know I am." High school, in other words, doesn't *help* such a young person get a job; it delays his doing so. It has become, in the words of David K. Cohen, a professor at the Harvard Graduate School of Education, "A sort of state-supported social service center for adolescents at loose ends." (Yaffe, 1982, p. 472) ■

engineers, teachers, and lawyers. As a result of these fluctuations, young people sometimes find themselves unable to get a job in the profession they have trained for.

Sex Roles and Occupational Choice: The Young Woman's Dilemma

Traditional sex roles dictated different occupations for men and women. That tradition has weakened to some extent, but it has not entirely vanished. The result is an ambiguity of sex roles that lends a new dimension of uncertainty to the occupational choices of young women. Compared to one or two generations ago, there has been a marked weakening of sexual stereotypes. More and more jobs are perceived as appropriate for both sexes. Temperament, personality, and physical variables other than gender are increasingly taken into account in the occupational selections of young women. Many teenage girls believe that they should plan on having an occupation outside the home, and that their nonworking mothers led nonproductive and even empty lives. On the other hand, the range of occupational roles that women can fill while still succeeding as wives and mothers is not entirely clear; those who try to be all things to all people face real difficulties.

Fear of Success.   Matina Horner, a psychologist who went on to become president of Radcliffe College, believes that many young women suffer from what she calls **fear of success.** She uses this term to refer to a young woman's concern that academic, business, or professional success may lead to negative social or personal consequences. In her doctoral dissertation and in later publications, Horner stated her belief: women fear that the consequence of success will be social rejection (Horner, 1969, 1972).

Horner tested her claim by presenting male and female college students with the first paragraph of one or two brief stories, identical except for the sex of the person described. The students' task was to complete the stories. Here's an example of the kind of lead paragraph she used:

> After first-term finals, *John* finds *himself* at the top of *his* medical school class.

Or:

> After first-term finals, *Anne* finds *herself* at the top of *her* medical school class.

Generally, both men and women responded by indicating John's understandable delight at his success, but Anne is seen—especially by young women—as having a problem or facing a conflict because of her high grades. Horner offers this "typical female story":

> Anne has a boyfriend Carl in the same class and they are quite serious. Anne met Carl at college and they started dating around their soph years in undergraduate school. Anne is rather upset and so is Carl. She wants him to be higher scholastically than she is. Anne will deliberately lower her academic standing the next term, while she does all she subtly can to help Carl. His grades come up and Anne soon drops out of med-school. They marry and he goes on in school while she raises their family. (1972, p. 227)

Equally impressive are stories within Horner's second largest category for females—namely, responses that employ frank denial of the content of the opening paragraph. Here are two such stories:

> Anne is a code name for a non-existent person created by a group of med students. They take turns taking exams and writing papers for Anne.

> Anne is really happy she's on top, though Tom is higher than she—though that's as it should be. . . . Anne doesn't mind Tom winning. Anne is talking to her

counselor. Counselor says she will make a fine nurse. She will continue her med school courses. She will study very hard and find she can and will become a good nurse. (1972, p. 226)

Subsequent research indicates that fear of success may be developed by early adolescence and may thus influence girls' career choices even before they reach high school. One researcher examined the stories of ninth grade girls in home economics classes and found that more than half of them appeared to have fear of academic and occupational success because of possible negative social consequences (Harvey, 1975).

The Myth of Male Superiority

Although men might have a sex-role advantage, their situation is by no means ideal. In a study of the attitudes of college men (Komarovsky, 1973) it was found that about a third of them were troubled by the possibility that they might date a woman who was their intellectual superior. Such men doubtless communicate their concerns in some way to their girlfriends. Often the young woman's response is to "play dumb." Here is one young man's experience:

> Once I was seeing a philosophy major, and we got along quite well. We shared a similar outlook on life, and while we had some divergent opinions, I seemed better able to document my position. One day, by chance, I heard her discussing with another girl an aspect of Kant that just the night before she described to me as obscure and confusing. But now she was explaining it to a girl so clearly and matter-of-factly that I felt sort of hurt and foolish. Perhaps it was immature of me to react this way. (Rogers, 1977, p. 265)

Another study of college men (Komarovsky, 1977) included a penetrating interview with each subject, revealing that superficially these men expressed very "liberal" attitudes, but that a much more traditional viewpoint emerged when the men were questioned more closely. The men believed, for example, that wives should definitely be able to pursue a career if they wished to, but only if (1) the home was run smoothly, (2) the children did not suffer, and (3) the wife's work did not interfere with her husband's career. Plainly, this is a rather tall order. Similarly, although the men said they were quite willing to share household chores, on closer questioning they admitted there were a few exceptions: "not the laundry," "not the cleaning," and "not the diapers." High achievement striving received moderate disapproval if it occurred in a man, but strong disapproval if it was found in a woman. For example, one young man was asked how he felt about another male student who was trying to get into a good medical school and who went to see a professor about a C in chemistry. The young man said he would be "disapproving but understanding." The same young man was then asked what he would think of the same behavior on the part of a female student, and he said he would find it "positively obnoxious." It is understandable that young women may respond by playing down their own intellectual abilities and career ambitions, to avoid being shunned by men.

Finally, the majority of the men expected to marry and have children, and felt quite strongly that their wives should be home during the children's infancy and preschool years. It also appeared that most women are still willing to accept the traditional view that the male will have the superior career while the female is primarily responsible for the children and the home. Thus, many women expected to prepare themselves for an occupation, work at it for a while, and then temporarily withdraw from work for a period of childrearing. The wife's career would therefore be secondary to the husband's, and she would be primarily, though not entirely, responsible for domestic matters. On the other hand, her right to work and to have an occupation would be acknowledged to some degree.

Although more women may be working or contemplating work as part of their lives, most working women still have jobs that are traditionally female. A study done in the United States in the mid-70s showed that 97 percent of registered nurses, 92 percent of dieticians, 85 percent of elementary school teachers, and 70 percent of health technicians were women. How fast is all this changing, and in which direction? It is extremely difficult to say. In a 1975 survey of adolescents and young adults, fully half of the females said they would choose to be an "average housewife" over a variety of other possible occupations ("Youth's Attitudes," 1975). Certainly, however, the same proportion might not hold in 1985. The instability of social values greatly increases the stresses that today's adolescents must feel as they pass through what is in any case a difficult and trying time in their lives.

Androgyny. An important concept for understanding and dealing with sex-role differences is **androgyny** which we mentioned previously in Chapter 9. Androgyny (*androgynous* is the adjective) means the state or quality of having both masculine and feminine characteristics. The word comes from the Greek roots *andros,* meaning "man," and *gynē*, "woman."

Androgyny has spurred a great deal of interest among psychologists, psychiatrists, and sociologists over the past two decades (Kaplan and Sedney, 1980). There is currently a growing feeling that males and females need to express some of the behaviors and feelings traditionally associated not only with their own sex, but with the opposite sex as well. Previously it was thought that masculinity and feminity are opposites—that more masculinity implies less feminity. The newer view is that a person can become more masculine *and* more feminine—in other words, that these characteristics represent independent dimensions, both of which play a significant role in the functioning of a healthy human being. What do these independent dimensions consist of? Research suggests that the traits traditionally valued in the female are warmth and expressiveness. In the male, the traditionally valued trait has been called *competency,* which means the ability to do things well and which has the implication of power or dominance. Figure 15–1 illustrates the idea that these are independent dimensions rather than two poles of the same dimension.

A man can have traits that are traditionally viewed as "feminine" *without* becoming less "masculine."

TRADITIONAL VIEW

ANDROGYNOUS VIEW

Warm-expressive

Competent ——————— Warm-expressive

Competent ——————— Incompetent

Cold-inexpressive

figure 15–1

The traditional and androgynous views of the relationship between *competency* and *warmth-expressiveness*. According to the traditional view these two characteristics are the opposite ends of the same dimension, whereas according to the androgynous view they are two entirely different dimensions (and thus a person can be highly warm and expressive *and* highly competent).

From Generation to Generation

Any given generation of adolescents is made up of individuals of about the same age who have experienced the same politically and socially significant events at about the same time in their lives. According to one theorist, "From these experiences the generation creates certain political attitudes and world views which are in some ways particular to that generation" (Jeffries, 1974, p. 121). Or, as another investigator puts it, "Each generation has its own distinctive mark because it moves through life at the same period in history. In times of rapid change the generations become increasingly estranged, for each has developed its own special outlook on new events" (Rogers, 1977, p. 331). Thus, both a fast-changing society and a "shrinking world" ("shrinking" because the mass media are familiarizing people all over the globe with one another's cultures) have produced a widening gap between generations.

It shouldn't be surprising, then, that today's youth do not see eye to eye with their parents on many fundamental issues. These issues range from sex and sex roles to education, political convictions, and the importance of achievement striving. Some psychologists and sociologists have noted that there has been a shift in the younger generation away from the value placed on work or saving. Many young people are also unwilling to engage in delay of gratification (Havighurst, 1974).

It has been suggested that the attitudes of adults who are responsible for adolescents have changed substantially, and that the change has been in the direction of greater permissiveness. In fact, one opinion is that there is no longer any struggle, because adults put up no opposition to anything that adolescents choose to do. There is said to have been a breakdown of the family and of traditional values. The claim is made that the educational system is responsible and that it's failing.

Has the Educational System Failed? The ed-

summary

1. By late adolescence, physical and cognitive development are nearly complete. However, dramatic changes in the area of social development occur during the final years of adolescence.

2. Three important issues must be faced during the final phase of transition to adulthood: identity formation, selecting a mate, and choosing and preparing oneself for a career. As adolescents themselves realize, the decisions they make in these areas are likely to have life-long effects.

3. **Identity formation** is a gradual process that involves knowing what kind of person one wishes to be as an adult, and recognizing and accepting opposing forces in one's own personality. It is typically not achieved until late adolescence.

4. Self-esteem increases steadily during adolescence, due to (1) increased physical size; (2) increased access to adult roles, responsibilities, and privileges; and (3) a shift away from school as the central activity in one's life.

5. An adolescent may express or define his or her identity by becoming involved in a political cause, by becoming concerned with a

ucational system, in particular, has come under sharp fire as a cause of apathy among youth. Urie Bronfenbrenner, of Cornell University, has argued that adolescents feel hopeless, powerless, and apathetic because they have learned about society's ills but don't know how to cure them. Neither schools nor universities teach them how to use the public or private institutions of society in order to make social or political improvements. All our young people know about, says Bronfenbrenner (1972), is the simplistic solution: demand or destroy.

Harsh criticism of the prevailing educational system is to be expected in every age and in every generation. Nonetheless, the actual fact of a decline in achievement fuels the fire of concern. There *has* been a marked decline in the educational achievements of high school and college students, compared with earlier generations. The actual level of skill attained by individuals who are now becoming high school or college graduates appears to be considerably lower than 15 or 20 years ago. Nor is criticism limited just to schooling. College and universities have also changed character, making their own contribution to the shift in attitudes and values. Some people feel that older values of striving for achievement and excellence have

been seriously undermined and that a substantially different value system has taken its place.

> The counterculturists endorse a permissive academic atmosphere and commit themselves to their music, drug, and political sub-cultures without leaving the university. While the older faculty members become somewhat demoralized and grieve over the passing of the traditional university, many young teachers assist students in their battles with the establishment. (Rogers, 1977, p. 115)

Decline or Change? Concerns that the younger generation has declined in motivation, social consciousness, and level of achievement are as old as history. Indeed, it is perhaps inevitable that each generation sees its predecessors as naive and its successors as displaying a degeneration of values. This is particularly true in a world that experiences dramatic political, economic, and technological changes, from year to year and sometimes from week to week. Yet an ancient maxim states, Life is change. Perhaps it is reasonable, given the current state of the world, for schools and families to be less authoritarian and for young people to be less competitive or driven than their parents and grandparents. ∎

philosophical issue, or even by falling in love. As adolescents become more realistic, political concerns may give way to personal concerns.

6. According to Marcia, adolescents are on one of four levels of **identity status:** (1) **foreclosure,** a status in which the identity crisis has not yet been faced and anxiety is minimal; (2) **diffusion,** characterized by a lack of commitment and a general withdrawal from life; (3) **moratorium,** in which adolescents experience an ongoing identity crisis, put off making important decisions, and experience considerable anxiety; and (4) **achievement,** the status of ado-

lescents who have been through the identity crisis and who have made their commitments. Progress through these stages is not necessarily steady. An adolescent's status is related to the parenting style with which he or she was reared.

7. The aboriginals' *walkabout* is a **rite of passage** that marks the transition from childhood to adulthood. In our own society, rites of passage are absent and the transition is blurred. Can rites of passage be created for young people in our society? Should they be?

8. Dating, an activity that is oriented to the present, is distinguished from courtship, which has a permanent relationship as its goal.

9. At present, young people feel that the ideal male-female relationship should include the following: open communication, a willingness to reexamine gender-linked roles, a rejection of antisexuality, and a strong emphasis on empathy, love, intimacy, responsibility, authenticity, and mutual fulfillment. The great majority of adolescents and young adults still hold to the traditional ideal of a marriage in which the partners are faithful to each other.

10. Acceptance of sex before marriage has increased substantially. The level of a couple's relationship, rather than their parents' attitudes or their exposure to sex-education classes, seems to determine whether or not they will have intercourse.

11. Despite the easing of the "double standard," college women are still less likely to have had sexual intercourse than are college men. Also, young women tend to have had fewer sexual partners than young men.

12. "Living-together" arrangements are now common on college campuses. In the typical arrangement, the girl moves into the boy's room but keeps a nominal residence of her own, partly to keep her parents from finding out. Living-together arrangements tend to be quite intimate. Although the two people involved do not date others, they probably do not see their relationship as a "trial marriage." Only about half of the students who live together find it a successful experience.

13. There has been a drop in teenage marriages in recent years. The risk of an unsuccessful marriage is considerably greater for those who marry early.

14. The **lost adolescence syndrome** usually involves someone who has been in love with only one person—his or her spouse. The early years of such a marriage are generally happy, but later one or both partners begin to feel trapped and to regret the loss of the single adolescent life.

15. The understanding of occupational choice develops in three broad stages: (1) in the **fantasy period**, children perceive no limits on what they can do; (2) in the **tentative period**, they come to realize that jobs require specific training and abilities, and that education is costly; (3) in the **realistic period**, individuals choose a career after realistically considering all the relevant factors.

16. Although children no longer tend to "inherit" their parents' professions, they still tend to end up in occupations at the same socioeconomic level as their parents.

17. Achievement motivation plays an important role in career selection. Family background factors such as the parents' childrearing style, socioeconomic level, and family size all influence achievement motivation.

18. The high-school dropout rate has gone down in recent years. The rate is higher in big cities and among minority group members; dropouts are more likely than other adolescents to be involved in crime and delinquency. Efforts at dropout prevention have involved counseling, evening classes, and various forms of alternative education.

19. The weakening of the sexual stereotypes has led to more career opportunities for women, but also to more uncertainty for them. Some young women appear to have **fear of success**—concern that academic or career success may have negative social or personal consequences. This fear may develop by early adolescence and may thus influence girls' career decisions when they're still quite young.

20. Some young men are troubled by the thought that a woman may be their intellectual superior; a young woman may respond to this attitude by "playing dumb." Although most young men now say that their wives should be able to pursue a career, they also want their wives to take primary responsibility for the home and the children. Most young women seem to accept this traditional view, and expect that their careers will be secondary to those of their husbands.

21. **Androgyny** means the state or quality of having both masculine and feminine characteristics. Masculinity and femininity might not be opposites—it may be possible to become both more masculine (i.e., more competent) *and* more feminine (i.e., warmer and more expressive).

22. Today's youth differ from their parents on many fundamental issues. Are these differences due to a failure of the educational system, or are they just a natural result of a world that has changed so drastically and in so many ways?

Glossary

academic subculture. An adolescent subculture associated with a high interest in schoolwork and in going to college, and relatively little interest in dating.

accommodation. Piaget's term for the kind of adaptation that involves modifying a previously used action or idea to suit a new situation.

achievement motivation. The drive to be successful, to do well, to reach for relatively high goals.

achievement status. Marcia's term for the identity status of people who have been through the identity crisis and have made their commitments. People with this status tend to be achievement oriented and to enjoy high levels of intimacy in their personal relationships.

active sleep. A state of sleep in which the eyes can be seen moving beneath the closed lids, assumed (on the basis of work with adults) to be the state in which dreaming occurs.

adaptation. In Piaget's view, the process of change that results from having to deal with, and adjust to, the environment.

adopted child. A child who, through the process of legal adoption, has become a permanent member of his or her adoptive family.

adoption. A legal procedure that makes a child a permanent member of his or her adoptive family.

adoptive parent. A person who has adopted a child.

agemates. Children of approximately the same age.

aggression. Physical or verbal acts directed against people, animals, or things, and performed with the intention of hurting, damaging, or destroying.

altruism. The willingness to do something for others, possibly at inconvenience or danger to oneself, with no apparent selfish motive.

amblyopia. The failure to use one eye for vision, even though there is nothing wrong with the eye itself. Also called "lazy eye."

amniocentesis. A method used to check for birth defects in a developing fetus. A needle is inserted into the mother's uterus and some fluid, containing some of the fetus's cells, is withdrawn.

amnion. The protective, fluid-filled sac that encloses the developing baby during the prenatal period.

anal stage. In Freudian theory, the second stage of development, lasting from around age 1½ to 3. Pleasurable sensations are assumed to center around the anus (the opening through which bowel movements are made).

androgen. The male sex hormone. Often used in the plural to refer to several, closely related, male hormones.

androgynous. Having both masculine and feminine characteristics.

androgyny. The state or quality of having both masculine and feminine characteristics.

animism. Piaget's term for the belief, common in young children, that anything that moves (e.g., a river) or anything that does something (e.g., a gun that shoots) is alive.

anorectic. A person suffering from anorexia nervosa.

anorexia nervosa. An eating disorder most commonly found in adolescent girls. A person with this disorder restricts her food intake to the point where she is in danger of starving to death. (Usually just called *anorexia*.)

anoxia. The physical effects that occur when an organism is not getting enough oxygen.

antisocial behavior. A term applied to behavior that is contrary to the rules of our society—for example, harming people or property, lying, stealing, truancy, or drug abuse.

Apgar test. A test used to assess the physical condition of newborn babies, one minute and five minutes after birth.

argot. The characteristic vocabulary of slang words used by a particular group of people such as teenagers—often, as a way of excluding outsiders.

artificialism. Piaget's term for the belief, common in young children, that certain aspects of the natural environment (e.g., rivers and lakes, the sun and the moon) were constructed by people.

assimilation. Piaget's term for the kind of adaptation that involves applying an already known action or idea to a new object or situation.

associative play.   A type of interactive play that involves two or more children doing the same thing and doing it together, but with no attempt to organize the activity or to take turns.

attachment.   The bond of affection and dependency felt by a child for another person, which makes the child want to be near that other person and turn to him or her for comfort in times of stress.

authoritarian.   Baumrind's term for the parenting style that emphasizes strict enforcement of rules. Authoritarian parents view obedience as a virtue; their children are expected to do as they're told without argument.

authoritative.   Baumrind's term for the parenting style that uses firm enforcement of rules but allows verbal give-and-take between parents and children. Authoritative parents listen to their children's objections but retain the right to make the final decision; their children are encouraged to be independent.

autism.   A serious psychological disorder that is usually detected in late infancy or early childhood but is probably present from birth. Autistic children fail to form attachments to people, have speech and language difficulties, and tend to become upset if any change is made in their environment.

autonomy.   Self-determination, independence. The ability to decide for oneself what one is going to do.

autonomy versus shame and doubt.   In Erikson's view, the central issue of the second stage of development, toddlerhood. Toddlers are assumed to be engaged in a struggle for self-determination, while at the same time doubting their capabilities to achieve and to be "good."

Babinski reflex.   One of the reflexes of the newborn baby: when the sole of the foot is stroked, the big toe sticks up and the other toes fan outward.

basic trust versus mistrust.   In Erikson's theory, the central issue of the first stage of development, infancy. Babies are assumed to develop basic trust if they come to feel that their parents can be relied upon.

behavior modification.   The use of the principles of operant conditioning to change the behavior of an organism.

behaviorism.   The school of psychology that concerns itself with observable behavior, rather than "inner" things such as thoughts and feelings. Behaviorists stress the importance of the environment (rather than of hereditary factors) and study how organisms learn as a result of their experiences.

bell-and-pad device.   A device, used in the treatment of bed-wetting, that sounds an alarm if the child begins to urinate.

binocular cells.   Specialized neurons in the brain that receive inputs from the left eye and the right eye, and that are responsible for stereoscopic vision.

biological parent.   The biological parents of an adopted child are the woman who gave birth to the child and the man with whom she conceived the child.

biologically caused retardation.   Mental retardation due to an injury or abnormality of the brain, caused by accident, infection, or a genetic defect such as Down's syndrome.

birth parent.   Same as *biological parent.*

birthing center.   A part of a hospital or a separate facility in which a woman can give birth to her baby in a relaxed, homelike atmosphere.

blastula.   The hollow ball of cells formed in the first few days of prenatal development.

bone age.   The physical maturity of a child, judged by the appearance of the growing areas of the bones, as seen in X-rays. These areas harden when growth is complete, so if they haven't hardened yet, the child is still growing.

breech birth.   The delivery of a baby feet or buttocks first.

brightness constancy.   The visual mechanism that keeps black objects looking black and white objects looking white, despite the fact that a black object in bright sunshine is reflecting more light than a white object in dim illumination.

bulimia.   An eating disorder most commonly found in adolescent girls. A person with this disorder gorges herself with food and then uses laxatives or self-induced vomiting to rid herself of it.

carrier.   An individual who does not have a particular recessive trait, but whose chromosomes contain one gene for that trait, which can be passed on to his or her descendants.

case study.   A descriptive study that involves, in most cases, only a single subject—often one who is unusual in some way.

castration.   Amputation of the male genitals. In Freudian theory, the boy in the phallic stage has an unconscious fear of castration.

categorization.   A technique used in remembering a list of items: the items are grouped into categories.

catharsis. In Freudian theory, the reduction or elimination of a drive by giving expression to it, either symbolically or in reality.

center. To focus one's thought or attention on a single aspect of a situation.

central learning. Knowledge that is acquired intentionally, because one has been assigned the task of learning it. See *incidental learning*.

central nervous system. The brain and the spinal cord.

cervix. The entrance to the uterus, through which the baby passes during birth.

cesarean. The delivery of a baby through a surgical incision made through the mother's abdominal wall and the wall of her uterus.

childhood schizophrenia. A serious mental illness that is quite rare (the adult form is much more common). Children with this disorder might show strange mannerisms, abnormalities of speech, a lack of awareness of time and place, and self-destructiveness.

chromosomes. Large collections of genes strung together in a particular order. Every normal human cell (with the exception of egg and sperm cells) has 46 chromosomes.

chumship. Sullivan's term for a close, intimate friendship based on mutual concern.

circular reaction. Piaget's term for the repeated performance of an action that was at first performed at random, because of the interesting or pleasant results that the action produces.

class-inclusion problem. A problem that requires the comparison of two classes of things, one of which is included in the other. An example is the question, "Are there more roses or more flowers in this vase?"

classical conditioning. The conditioning of a simple, automatic, inborn response to a neutral stimulus, by pairing the neutral stimulus with a stimulus that already evokes the response. Eventually, the neutral stimulus alone is able to evoke the response.

cognitive behaviorism. A branch of social learning theory, which posits that reinforcements and punishments may be effective even if they're not experienced directly, but are only observed being given to another person (a model). These observed reinforcements and punishments are assumed to influence the observer's later behavior, through a learning process that is cognitive.

cognitive development. The development of the capacity to think, to reason, and to understand.

cognitive-developmental theory. Piaget's theory of cognitive development.

compensation. A principle used in solving a Piagetian conservation problem. If the problem involves, for example, liquid volume, the compensation principle would be the idea that the increase in the height of the liquid is balanced by a decrease in its diameter.

conception. The uniting of a sperm with an egg (or ovum).

concordance. A way of describing how similar (or dissimilar) twins are, in regard to a particular trait. Expressed as the percentage or proportion of twins in which both members of the pair are the same in that trait.

concrete operations, period of. In Piagetian theory, the period of development beginning around age 7 and ending around age 11. Children in this period can consider several aspects of a situation at once, but their understanding is tied to real (concrete) objects and events.

conditioned fear. Fear that can be evoked by a previously neutral stimulus, as a result of that stimulus having been paired with a stimulus that naturally produces fear.

conditioning. See *classical conditioning, operant conditioning*.

conservation. The principle that certain qualities, such as the volume of a given amount of liquid or the number of objects in a given set, are permanent and invariant. According to Piaget, preschoolers believe that a tall, thin container holds more liquid than a short, wide one because they lack the concept of the conservation of liquid volume.

contingent. Dependent upon. For instance, if a parent makes a particular response whenever a child performs a certain action, the parent's response is contingent on the child's action.

contrast effect. The tendency for twins or siblings to become less alike, due to their own efforts to carve out distinct personalities and to the fact that other family members tend to "typecast" them in contrasting ways.

controlled. A term applied to those factors that are held constant (not varied) in an experiment, generally so that the effects of one particular factor (which *is* varied) can be measured.

conventional moral reasoning. Kohlberg's term for a form of moral reasoning that focuses on upholding society's rules.

cooperative play. A type of interactive play in which two or more children cooperate in some kind of organized activity—e.g., "playing house," taking turns at something, or any kind of game involving rules.

correlation. A mathematical relationship between two sets of measurements, such that a knowledge of one set enables us to predict, with greater or lesser accuracy, the second set of measurements.

correlational study. A study designed to examine the relationship between two (or more) sets of measurements.

cortex. The outer surface of the brain. In humans, this heavily wrinkled layer controls the functions that distinguish us from other animals—the ability to use language, to think, to make plans, and so on.

critical period. A period during which some aspect of development must occur, if it is to occur at all.

cross-sectional study. A method of studying developmental changes by using subjects of different ages. See *longitudinal study*.

cross the placenta. To be transmitted from the mother's bloodstream to the bloodstream of the embryo or fetus, by way of the placenta. Many substances are capable of crossing the placenta, including disease-producing organisms and drugs or chemicals taken by the mother.

culture. The traditions, activities, beliefs, behaviors, values, and language shared by the members of a society.

decenter. To consider more than one aspect of a situation at the same time.

deferred imitation. The imitation of remembered actions—actions seen or heard at some time in the past.

delay of gratification. The period of time that elapses between when something is sought or desired, and when it is attained. The ability to accept a delay of gratification (and to resist the temptation of immediate gratification) is something that develops gradually as children get older.

delayed puberty. Unusually late development of sexual maturity.

delinquent subculture. An adolescent subculture associated with a high interest in dating, drinking, smoking, clothes, cars, and spending time away from home, and a low interest in schoolwork and going to college.

DES. Diethylstilbestrol, a synthetic hormone, used in the past to prevent miscarriage, that is now known to produce abnormalities of the reproductive system in young women whose mothers received the drug during pregnancy.

descriptive study. A way of doing research that primarily involves observing and recording what is observed.

development. The overall process that turns babies into children, children into adolescents, and adolescents into adults. Development includes changes in size and shape, in reasoning ability and knowledge, in motor ability, in the ability to communicate, and so on.

differentiation. The process that occurs when the cells of the blastula become specialized and begin serving different functions in the developing organism.

diffusion status. Marcia's term for an identity status in which the individual avoids making commitments or conscious decisions about the future, and may instead drop out. It is characterized by a lack of intimate relationships and a general withdrawal from life.

dilation. The first stage of labor, involving the widening of the opening of the cervix.

disadvantaged. Families or homes are referred to as disadvantaged when they are headed by individuals who are employed in unskilled, low-paying jobs or are unemployed, and who have relatively little education.

discipline. See *inductive discipline, power-assertive discipline*.

discrimination-shift problem. An experimental situation involving a discrimination task. The rules for determining which is the "correct" stimulus are suddenly changed, and the subject must learn to respond according to the new rules. See *reversal shift, nonreversal shift*.

discrimination task. An experimental situation in which the subject must learn to select the "correct" stimulus from two or more stimuli or classes of stimuli.

displaced. In Freudian theory, a displaced drive is one that is repressed because it is socially or psychologically unacceptable, and that reemerges in a different form or directed toward a different target.

displaced aggression. In Freudian theory, an aggressive urge that is directed toward a substitute person or even toward an animal, because its original target was a forbidden one.

doctrine of innate ideas. The belief that babies are born with their minds already furnished with the knowledge of such things as Truth, Beauty, and God.

dominant trait. A trait that will show up in an offspring if the gene for that trait is inherited from either parent, or from both parents. If a child inherits one gene for a dominant trait and one gene for the corresponding recessive trait, the dominant gene will win out—the child will have the dominant trait.

Down's syndrome. A birth defect, caused by an extra twenty-first chromosome, that produces mental retardation and a variety of distinctive physical characteristics. (Formerly known as *mongolism*.)

drive As used by Freud, a powerful instinctive desire.

drowsiness. One of the states of the newborn baby: a state between sleep and wakefulness, in which the baby lies quietly while his or her eyes open and close sleepily.

dyslexia. Reading disability. The inability to learn to read at anywhere near the normal level of competence, despite having normal intelligence and despite having been given the usual kind of instruction. This term is also applied to the *loss* of the ability to read, due to brain damage.

early adolescence. A period that begins when the individual is still looking and acting like a child, that includes the period of initial physical change and a noticeable growth spurt, and that ends with the individual looking and acting like an adolescent.

educable mentally retarded. A term used to refer to an individual who is mildly retarded (IQ in the 55 to 69 range). The majority of mentally retarded people fall into this category. Most learn to read and write; few are ever institutionalized.

ego. According to Freud, one of the three aspects of the human mind. The ego is the thinking, rational part.

ego growth. In Erikson's theory, the development of the personality, which includes the growth of autonomy, initiative, competence, and so on.

ego integrity. In Erikson's view, what people have achieved if they can look back on their lives and feel that it was worthwhile and that they did all right.

egocentric thought. In Piaget's view, the way preoperational children think, characterized by an inability to see things from someone else's point of view.

elaboration. A technique used to help in remembering something. Verbal ideas or visual images are thought up as memory aids, as a way of connecting two stimuli in paired-associate learning, for example.

Electra conflict. In Freudian theory, the female version of the Oedipal conflict. The phallic-stage girl is assumed to desire her father and have aggressive feelings toward her mother.

embryo. The developing human from 2 weeks after conception to 2 months.

empathy. The tendency to feel sad when another person is hurt or distressed, and to feel pleased when another person is happy. The ability to share in other people's feelings.

enactive representations. Bruner's term for mental representations based on previously performed motor responses.

encoding. The identification of stimuli (usually visual or auditory stimuli) by means of cognitive processes.

entry strategy. A technique used by an individual child to gain entry into a group of children.

enuresis. Lack of control over urination, especially during sleep. Bed-wetting.

environment. Any aspects of the world that a child experiences in any way, or that can affect the child in any way, are part of that child's environment.

enzyme. A substance, composed of protein, that is essential to the proper functioning of some bodily process. The human body contains a large number of different enzymes.

error of measurement. The difference between the score a person obtained on a particular test and his or her "true" score. The person's health and state of mind on the day of the test, errors made in administering or scoring the test, and other chance factors all contribute to error of measurement.

estrogen. The female sex hormone. Often used in the plural to refer to several, closely related female hormones.

ethological view. A theory of attachment that links attachment in human babies to attachment behavior in other species—e.g., imprinting in ducklings. According to this view, attachment is a built-in aspect of development, inherited because of its survival value.

ethology. A subfield of biology that focuses on the behavior of animals in their natural environment, with particular emphasis on species-specific behavior.

experimental method. A method for carrying out research that involves doing something—for example, treating a group of subjects in a particular way—and observing the results. Typically, that group of subjects is compared with a control group, who did not receive that treatment.

expressive jargon. A kind of "pretend speech" that

some babies produce shortly before they begin to speak in earnest. It has the rhythms and expressions of real speech, but it is unintelligible.

external locus of control. A person with an external locus of control feels that she has little control over the events of her life—she attributes her successes and failures to luck or to the attitudes and actions of other people. See *internal locus of control*.

externalizer. A person with an external locus of control.

extinction. In operant conditioning, the process that occurs when a response is no longer reinforced and eventually stops being made.

extinguish. To withhold reinforcement, making a previously reinforced response less likely to recur.

extrinsic motivation. The inclination to do something not because one wants to do it for its own sake, but because of the reward that one will get for doing it. See *intrinsic motivation*.

extrovert. A person who seeks and enjoys interactions with other people.

eye contact. What results when two people look at each other's eyes.

Fallopian tubes. The tube-like organs that extend from the uterus to the ovaries. Conception normally takes place in the Fallopian tubes.

familial retardation. Mental retardation (usually mild) that is not caused by brain abnormalities or injuries, but by a combination of genetic and environmental factors. Most children with familial retardation have parents who are of low normal intelligence or who are also retarded.

fantasy period. A period in the development of understanding about careers and occupations. During the fantasy period, which generally lasts until about age 11, the child perceives no limits on what he or she can potentially do. See *tentative period, realistic period*.

fear of success. Horner's term for the concern of some young women that academic, business, or professional success might lead to unfavorable social or personal consequences.

fetal alcohol syndrome. A group of characteristic physical and mental abnormalities sometimes found in the babies of alcoholic women.

fetus. The developing human from 2 months after conception to birth.

fixate. To point the eyes at something; to look at something without moving the eyes.

fixated. In Freudian theory, if things do not go well

during some stage of development, the person may become fixated, or "stuck," at that stage.

forceps delivery. The use of tongs, shaped to fit around a baby's head, to speed the birth of a baby.

foreclosure status. Marcia's term for an identity status in which the identity crisis has not yet been faced and anxiety is minimal. Adolescents with this status remain close to their parents, show little autonomy, and have a high need for social approval.

formal operations, period of. In Piagetian theory, the period of development that begins around age 11. It is characterized by the ability to reason abstractly and to test possible solutions to a problem in a systematic way.

formal teaching. A traditional teaching style: children are told where to sit and what to do; homework and tests are given and graded.

foster child. A child who is living temporarily in a foster home, either because a permanent adoptive home has not yet been found, or because his or her biological parents have not released the child for adoption.

foster parent. A person taking care of a foster child in his or her home. Foster parents usually receive a small salary to cover the expenses of caring for foster children.

fraternal twins. Twins who developed from two separate eggs, each fertilized by a different sperm. Genetically, they are no more alike than siblings born separately. Also known as *dizygotic* twins.

free association. A method devised by Freud and still used in psychoanalysis. The patient simply says whatever comes into his or her mind.

fun subculture. An adolescent subculture associated with an emphasis on being popular as a friend or a date, athletic ability, and participation in school activities.

fussiness One of the states of the newborn baby— the baby whimpers occasionally and there are movements of the arms, legs, and face.

gender identity. A person's knowledge that he is male, or that she is female, and the acceptance of that knowledge.

generalize. To transfer a learned response or concept to another stimulus or situation, similar (but not identical) to the one involved in the original learning.

genes. The biological units of heredity, composed of DNA.

genetic characteristics. Characteristics carried by

the genes. Inherited characteristics.

genetic parent. Same as *biological parent.*

genital herpes. A venereal disease caused by a virus. Although this virus cannot cross the placenta, it can infect a baby during its passage through the vagina.

genital stage. In Freudian theory, a stage of development that begins at adolescence and involves the reemergence of sexual feelings.

"gentle birth." Same as *Leboyer method.*

germinal stage. The first two weeks of prenatal development.

glial cells. The other kind of cell, besides neurons, found in the brain. Their function is to support and nourish the neurons.

grammatical morphemes. Words such as *in, on, is, are,* or *the,* and suffixes such as *-ing, -ed,* or *-s,* that tie together the other morphemes in a sentence and indicate how they are being used.

grasp reflex. One of the reflexes of the newborn baby: when a narrow object (such as a stick or an adult's finger) is placed in the baby's palm, his fingers close tightly around it.

habituate. To cease to respond to a stimulus after repeated or prolonged exposure to it, because it no longer arouses attention or interest.

habituation technique. A method for studying infant perception. The baby is habituated to one stimulus. If she then responds to a second stimulus, it is presumed that she can tell the first and the second apart.

hand-eye coordination. The ability to use information obtained through vision (in particular, visual feedback) to guide a sequence of hand movements.

heredity. A term used to refer to inherited or genetic characteristics—characteristics carried by the genes.

heritability. The proportion of the variation of a given trait, within a given population, that can be attributed to genetic factors.

hormones. Biochemical substances that are found in the blood in very small amounts and that influence the functioning of various body systems.

hyperactivity. A tendency to be extremely active and highly distractible. Hyperactive children "can't sit still"; they tend to do poorly in school because of their inability to focus their attention on something and keep it focused.

hysterical symptom. A disorder such as blindness, deafness, or numbness in a particular area of the body, due to psychological causes rather than to physical ones.

iconic representations. Bruner's term for mental representations that consist of visual images, or of mental images of things heard, tasted, smelled, or felt.

id. According to Freud, one of the three aspects of the human mind. The id is present from birth and is the home of powerful instinctive desires such as hunger, thirst, and the sexual urge.

identical twins. Twins who developed from a single fertilized egg, so that they have exactly the same genes. Also known as *monozygotic* twins.

identify. To take on another person's values, beliefs, behaviors, and so on. In Freudian theory, when the Oedipal or Electra conflicts are resolved, the child identifies with the same-sex parent.

identity. A principle used in solving a Piagetian conservation problem. If the problem involves, for example, liquid volume, the identity principle would be the idea that this is still the same water we started out with.

identity confusion. Erikson's term for the feelings of uncertainty and anxiety that the adolescent experiences if he or she has not yet established a firm sense of identity.

identity crisis. In Erikson's view, the important issue of adolescence—the "Who am I and where am I going?" issue.

identity formation. The gradual process, generally not completed until late adolescence, of developing a firm sense of identity—knowing what kind of person one is and what kind of person one wishes to become, and recognizing and accepting opposing forces in one's personality.

identity status. Marcia's term for the level of identity formation an adolescent has attained. See *achievement status, diffusion status, foreclosure status,* and *moratorium status.*

imaginary audience. A term used by Elkind to explain adolescents' self-consciousness, loudness, faddish dress, and other characteristic behavior. According to this view, adolescents act the way they do because they feel that they are playing to an imaginary audience.

imprinting. A phenomenon found in some species of birds, e.g., ducks. A newly hatched duckling will follow the first moving object it sees, will thereafter go to considerable trouble to remain near that object (which, in the usual case, is its mother), and will pay no particular attention to other moving things that appear later on.

impulsive. Kagan's term for children who respond quickly on the Matching Familiar Figures Test and who make a lot of errors. Such children tend to do less well in school than reflective children; they tend to jump to conclusions and to take risks.

inbred. A term applied to an animal that is the product of a number of generations of inbreeding. Inbred animals tend to be very similar to one another in genetic makeup.

inbreeding. A method of breeding animals that involves mating them with their close relatives— mothers to sons, sisters to brothers, and so on.

incidental learning. "Extra" knowledge that is acquired unintentionally, while one is engaged in learning something else. See central learning.

independence training. Parental encouragement or pressure to be self-reliant, to do things on one's own.

inductive discipline. A form of discipline that consists of explaining to the child the reasons and justifications for behaving in a particular way (or not behaving in a particular way).

industry versus inferiority. In Erikson's theory, the central issue during middle childhood. The conflict is between children's desire to learn the skills they will need as adults, and the fear of failure.

infancy. The period of development that starts at birth and ends when the infant becomes a toddler— when he or she begins to use walking as the chief means of getting from one place to another.

infantile autism. Same as autism.

informal teaching. A teaching style in which children are permitted a good deal of freedom to select their own activities. They are permitted to sit (or stand) where they wish; generally, grades are not given. Also known as the "open classroom."

information processing. The encoding and storage (in short-term memory) of sensory information.

initiative versus guilt. In Erikson's view, the central issue during the preschool period. Initiative arises as a result of the child's emerging ability to work toward a goal; guilt arises as a consequence of the development of the superego.

insecure attachment. A description of the quality of a child's relationship with another person, generally a parent. A child who is insecurely attached to his mother, for example, will not greet her with unmixed joy after being separated from her in the "strange situation." He may ignore her, act angry at her, or alternate between two conflicting kinds of behaviors.

instinct. An inborn pattern of behavior, nowadays more often called species-specific behavior.

intelligence quotient. Mental age divided by chronological (actual) age, multiplied by 100 to get rid of the decimal point.

interaction. An interaction between two people occurs when each person performs some action (or a series of actions) in regard to the other person. The actions can include speaking to the other person, kissing, hitting, or smiling at the other person, and so on.

internal locus of control. A person with an internal locus of control believes that she is responsible for her own successes and failures—that she is in control of the events in her life, rather than events controlling her. See external locus of control.

internalize. To take on (someone else's values or standards of behavior) as one's own; to believe in them.

internalizer. A person with an internal locus of control.

intrinsic motivation. The inclination to do something because one enjoys doing it and finds it interesting or gratifying, and not because of any reward that one will get for doing it. See extrinsic motivation.

introvert. A person who tends to avoid interactions with others and who often prefers being alone.

IQ. An abbreviation of intelligence quotient. Nowadays, however, a child's IQ is not calculated by dividing mental age by chronological age, but by comparing the child's performance on an IQ test with that of other children of the same age. The IQ score is presumed to be an indication of intellectual ability.

isolette. A completely enclosed crib, used for low-birthweight babies to maintain their body temperature and to guard them against infections.

juvenile delinquency. Violations of the law committed by underage individuals—16 or 18 is the cutoff age in most states.

karyotyping. A method used to check for

chromosomal abnormalities. A cell nucleus is photographed under a microscope, and the pictures of the individual chromosomes are cut out of the photograph and sorted out.

lanugo. The fine, downy hair often seen on the face or body of newborn babies. It falls out after a few weeks.

late adolescence. A period that begins when physical maturity is essentially complete, that ends when adulthood is reached, and that brings concerns about education, occupation, and marriage.

latency stage. In Freudian theory, a period of development (roughly 5½ to 12 years) during which sexual impulses remain submerged.

lateralization. Specialization of the two sides—for example, using the right and left sides of the brain, or the right and left hands, for different purposes.

learned helplessness. A failure to do anything to help oneself, resulting from repeated experiences in which one's actions have had no effect.

learning disability. A disorder that a child is presumed to have if his performance in school is considerably below what you'd expect from his IQ, and if the poor performance is not due to emotional or motivational difficulties, or to serious sensory or motor disabilities.

Leboyer method. A technique, also known as "gentle birth," designed to make the first moments of life as peaceful and pleasant as possible for the newborn baby.

locus of control. See *internal locus of control, external locus of control.*

long-term memory. "Permanent" memory, capable of retaining information for an indefinite length of time. Information stored in long-term memory must first have been in short-term memory, but not all the information in short-term memory enters long-term memory.

longitudinal study. A method of studying developmental changes by observing or testing a group of subjects repeatedly, over a period of time. See *cross-sectional study.*

lost adolescence syndrome. A term used to describe the experiences of people who become romantically attached to someone quite early in life, who marry that person, and who later come to regret that they married without gaining a wider range of personal experience with the opposite sex.

manipulation skill. An ability that involves acting upon something with the hands—e.g., using scissors, tying shoes.

Matching Familiar Figures Test. A test devised by Kagan and his associates, used to classify children as impulsive or reflective. For each item in the test, the children's task is to find the picture, in a set of several very similar pictures, that exactly matches the picture at the top.

maturation. Development—often physical or motor development—of a sort that is assumed to result from genetic preprogramming, or the gradual carrying out of a plan determined by the genes.

mean. The average of a group of measurements, determined by adding them up and dividing by the number of measurements.

mean length of utterance. The average length of a child's utterances, measured at a given age. The length of an utterance is calculated by counting the number of words it contains and adding the number of grammatical suffixes such as *-ing, -ed,* and *-s.*

memory retrieval. The process (or the results of the process) of remembering something that was stored in long-term memory.

memory span. The number of items that can be held in short-term memory. Memory span increases from about three items at age 3 to six or seven items in adulthood.

menarche. A girl's first menstrual period. (Pronounced muh-NAR-kee.)

mental age. How advanced a child is in his or her intellectual abilities and knowledge. For instance, an intellectually average 6-year-old would have a mental age of 6; a gifted one might have a mental age of 7 or 8.

mental retardation. Below-normal intellectual capacity. A score below 70 on an IQ test is generally taken as a criterion for mental retardation.

metacognition. The application of some cognitive process (e.g., understanding, paying attention to, and so on) to a cognitive process. Knowledge about the best ways to learn something, and understanding whether or not you are communicating successfully, are examples of metacognition.

mid-adolescence. A period that begins about 12 or 18 months after puberty (after the most noticeable changes in physical appearance have already occurred), that ends when physical maturity is essentially complete, and that is characterized by revolt mixed with conformity and by unpredictable mood swings.

middle childhood. The years from 6 to 12, or roughly from when a child enters first grade to when he or she graduates from sixth grade.

MLU. Same as *mean length of utterance.*

model. A person (e.g., an adult) who does something that another person (e.g., a child) might imitate.

modeling. Bandura's term for what a model does. An action performed by a model, possibly with the idea that an observer (e.g., a child) may imitate that action.

moratorium status. Marcia's term for the identity status of adolescents who are experiencing an ongoing identity crisis. Adolescents with this status put off making important personal decisions; they relate to their parents with guilt and ambivalence and experience considerable anxiety.

Moro reflex. One of the reflexes of the newborn baby: in response to a loud noise or a sudden loss of support, the baby's arms are flung wildly outward and then quickly brought toward the chest again.

morpheme. The smallest unit of meaning in a spoken or written language. A word with no prefixes or suffixes is one morpheme; a word with a prefix or a suffix is two morphemes.

motherese. A description of the language mothers (and other adults) tend to use when speaking to toddlers—sentences are short, simple, and repetitive, and easy words are used in place of ones that toddlers find difficult to pronounce.

motor development. The development of the ability to move and coordinate the parts of the body, as in crawling, walking, grasping things with the hands, and so on.

motor nerve. A nerve that carries neural signals from the brain or spinal cord to the muscles.

motor pattern. The basic sequence of movements involved in performing some action, for example walking or running.

motor skill. The ability to perform a motor pattern with some degree of smoothness and precision.

mutation. A change occurring in a gene, so that the ''instructions'' it contains are different from those it originally contained. Also, a characteristic produced by such a changed gene.

myelination. The process by which neurons in the nervous system are coated with a fatty substance called *myelin*. Myelination greatly speeds the transmission of neural signals and plays an important role in the maturation of the brain.

natural childbirth. A method of childbirth in which the mother receives little or no medication, and uses exercises and breathing techniques to deal with the pain of labor contractions.

nature. When used with *nurture,* nature is another word for heredity.

nature-nurture issue. The debate about whether various characteristics are primarily inherited or primarily the result of environmental influences.

need for achievement. Same as *achievement motivation.*

negative correlation. A correlation between two sets of measurements such that a high measurement in one set is likely to be associated with a low measurement in the second set.

neonate. A newborn human or animal baby.

nervous system. The brain, the spinal cord, and the sensory and motor nerves.

neuron. The basic cell of the nervous system, which carries information in the form of very small electrical pulses.

nonreversal shift. A kind of discrimination-shift problem. In the first part of the experiment, the subject must choose between stimuli that vary in two dimensions, of which only one dimension determines the correct stimulus. Then the rules are changed so that the correct stimulus is now determined by the other dimension.

norm. A mean or average—generally one that is based on a large, representative sample of subjects.

normal curve. A bell-shaped distribution of measurements—a curve of a particular shape and mathematical description.

normally distributed. A term applied to measurements that form a normal curve.

nuclear family. A family consisting of a husband, a wife, and their children.

nurture. A term used to refer to the way a child is reared, or (when contrasted with *nature*) to refer to environment in general.

object permanence. In Piagetian theory, the concept that things have a permanent existence in the world, even if they can't be seen at the moment.

observational learning. Learning that is acquired

through watching other people's behavior and through seeing the consequences that result from their behavior.

Oedipal conflict.   In Freudian theory, the struggle going on in the unconscious mind of the phallic-stage boy, between his desire for his mother and his fear of his father's wrath.

onlooker behavior.   The child who is engaged in this kind of behavior simply watches other children at play, perhaps making a comment or asking a question occasionally.

open classroom.   A classroom in which teaching is informal—children are allowed to select their own activities and to sit (or stand) wherever they wish. In many cases, walls between adjoining classrooms are removed, so that the children in a single open classroom may be from two or more grades.

operant conditioning.   Skinner's term for the process that occurs when an organism is reinforced for making a particular response. When a response is reinforced, it is more likely to be made again.

oral stage.   In Freudian theory, the first stage of development, lasting from birth to age 1 or 1½. Pleasurable sensations are assumed to center around the mouth.

organic retardation.   Same as *biologically caused retardation*.

organism.   A person or an animal. This term may also be used to refer to *any* living thing.

overextend.   To use a word for more things than the word can correctly be applied to. When a toddler sees an orange and says ''ball,'' that is an overextension.

overlearning.   The presumed effects of continued exposure to a learning situation after the desired response has already been learned. In the treatment of bedwetting, the overlearning method may be used after the child initially stops wetting the bed as a result of training with the bell-and-pad device. The child is given a quantity of fluid to drink before he goes to bed, so that he will either wet his bed again (thus setting off the alarm again) or get up and go to the bathroom.

ovum.   The egg of a mammal—a single cell, lacking a shell, that can just barely be seen with the naked eye.

paired-associate learning.   A memory task that involves learning an association between two stimuli such as words. The subject must learn to give the second stimulus in the pair, when he or she is presented with the first stimulus.

pairing.   In classical conditioning, the presenting of two stimuli simultaneously (or nearly simultaneously). Generally, a neutral stimulus is paired with one to which the organism has a built-in response.

parallel play.   When two (or more) children play side by side at the same activity, paying little or no attention to each other.

partial reinforcement.   Reinforcement of some responses but not all of them. Partial reinforcement may be given on an interval basis (e.g., a response is reinforced every 10 minutes or so), or on the basis of the number of responses made (e.g., every tenth response is reinforced).

peer group.   The group of children of roughly the same age with whom a child interacts at school or elsewhere, and who are presumed to share common values, standards of behavior, and so on.

peers.   A child's peers are other children of roughly the same age with whom he or she interacts in some way.

penis envy.   In Freudian theory, the unconscious desire, in little girls, to have a penis.

perceptual-motor skill.   An ability that uses sensory information (e.g., from visual or auditory stimuli) to regulate a pattern of motor responses.

period of concrete operations.   See *concrete operations, period of*.

period of formal operations.   See *formal operations, period of*.

period of gestation.   Same as *prenatal period*.

permissive.   Baumrind's term for the parenting style that uses as few restrictions as possible. Permissive parents behave in a kind, accepting way toward their children and demand very little.

personal fable.   A term used by Elkind to describe adolescents' belief in the uniqueness of their feelings and in their own invulnerability and immortality.

''person permanence.''   The concept that people continue to exist even when they can't be seen or heard.

phallic stage.   In Freudian theory, the third stage of development, lasting from about age 3 to 5½. Pleasurable sensations are assumed to center on the genitals. The Oedipal and Electra conflicts are assumed to occur in this stage.

phobia.   An irrational fear of something—a fear strong enough to interfere with one's day-to-day life.

phonics.   The correspondences between the sounds of spoken words and the letters of written words that exist in English (and in other languages written in alphabetic symbols). Children who are taught phonics when they're learning to read are taught to "sound out" written words.

pivot word. A word that can readily be combined with a variety of other words to produce simple two-word phrases—e.g., *it*, in "Get it" and "Tie it."

placenta. The organ, also known as the afterbirth, by which the embryo or fetus is attached to the wall of the uterus. Nutrients from the mother are transmitted to the developing child through the placenta.

plasticity. The quality of being flexible, capable of change. Used to refer to the fact that the structure of the nervous system is not entirely determined in advance, but can be influenced by what happens in the first months or years of life.

polygenic trait. A characteristic that is carried by more than one pair of genes.

position constancy. The visual mechanism that keeps objects looking stationary, despite movements of the viewer's eyes, head, or body.

positive correlation. A correlation between two sets of measurements such that a high measurement in one set is likely to be associated with a high measurement in the second set.

postconventional moral reasoning. Kohlberg's term for a form of moral reasoning that admits the possibility that some principles might be more important than upholding society's rules or laws.

power-assertive discipline. A form of discipline that consists of enforcing rules of behavior with threats and punishment.

precocious puberty. Unusually early development of sexual maturity.

preconventional moral reasoning. Kohlberg's term for a form of moral reasoning concerned only with the possibility of success or failure, where failure consists of "getting caught."

predisposition. An inborn tendency to develop a certain trait, given environmental conditions that favor that trait.

preferential-looking technique. A method for testing infants' visual perception. Two pictures (or other visual stimuli) are placed where the baby can see them, and the researcher records the amount of time the baby spends looking at each picture.

preformationism. The idea that a miniature adult is contained in the egg or sperm—a belief, dating from ancient times, that remained popular until the 1800s.

premature birth. Birth that occurs before prenatal development is complete—generally, at least two or three weeks before the end of the usual 38-week prenatal period.

prenatal. Before birth.

prenatal period. The period that begins at conception and ends at birth. In humans this period averages 266 days (38 weeks).

preoperational period. In Piagetian theory, the second major period of development—roughly from age 2 to age 7. The preoperational child, according to Piaget, can use mental representations but cannot adopt another person's point of view and cannot decenter.

prepared. Ready to learn something quickly, due to innate factors.

preparedness. The inborn tendency of an organism to learn certain things very readily (e.g., to become afraid of spiders after only one or two mildly scary incidents) and to learn other things much less readily.

preschool period. The period of development that begins around age 2½ and ends when the child enters first grade, usually around age 6.

preschooler. A child who is no longer a toddler but who is too young to enter first grade.

pretend play. Play that involves imagination. For example, a toddler may pretend to be asleep or to drink out of an empty cup; an older child may pretend that pebbles are food or that a box is a space capsule.

primary sex characteristics. The male and female reproductive organs—the penis and testes in males, the ovaries, uterus, and vagina in females.

private speech. "Thinking out loud," common in the preschool period.

production deficiency. A failure to use verbal mediators in situations in which verbal mediators would be helpful.

productive language. The words and grammatical constructions that a person uses in his or her speech or writing. (See *receptive language*.)

proprioception. The sense that keeps us informed of the positions (and locations in space) of the parts of our bodies, even when our eyes are closed.

prosocial. A term used to describe behaviors that benefit others—e.g., sharing, cooperating, and helping.

psychiatrist. A person who has been through medical school, gotten an M.D. degree, and then gone on to study human personality, with a particular emphasis on psychological problems. Most psychiatrists see patients and administer psychotherapy or drug treatment.

psychoactive drug. A drug that affects one's psychological state or mood, or one's psychological processes (such as perception).

psychoanalysis. A method of psychotherapy devised by Freud and based on his theories, that is still in use today.

psychoanalytic theory. A theory of human personality and development, originated by Sigmund Freud, which stresses the importance of unconscious motivations, particularly those of a sexual nature.

psycholinguist. A scientist who studies the use or the development of language.

psychologist. A person who studies human (or, in some cases, animal) behavior, or personality, or cognition, or learning, or memory, or sensation and perception, either from a scientific or a clinical viewpoint. Some administer psychotherapy. Most psychologists have Ph.D. degrees from the graduate divisions of university psychology departments.

psychosexual. A term applied to Freudian theory, acknowledging the important role that sexual drives play in this theory.

psychosis. A serious, and in many cases permanent, mental illness. Most psychoses involve some distortion of the perception of reality.

psychosocial. A term used to describe Erikson's theory (as opposed to Freud's, which is called *psychosexual*). Erikson puts more emphasis on social interactions, less on sexual matters.

psychotherapy. The treatment of emotional or personality problems by a psychologist or a psychiatrist, generally by means of conversation.

puberty. The attainment of sexual maturity. In girls, menarche; in boys, the discharge of semen containing live sperm.

punishment. The administration of something unpleasant, such as a stimulus that causes pain; or the removal of something pleasant, such as food.

quiet alertness. One of the states of the newborn baby. The baby lies quietly but fully alert, with eyes wide open and usually focused on something.

reaction formation. In Freudian theory, the process that occurs when an unacceptable impulse is repressed and the opposite kind of behavior emerges in its stead.

realistic period. The last period in the development of understanding about careers and occupations. During this period the individual chooses a career, after a realistic consideration of job requirements, opportunities for education or training, and his or her own abilities and personal values.

recall. When contrasted with *recognition,* a memory test that involves retrieving an item of information from memory—for instance, remembering someone's name or telephone number.

receptive language. The words and grammatical constructions that a person can understand, when he or she hears them (or sees them) in the speech (or writing) of others.

recessive trait. A trait that will not show up in an individual unless a gene for that trait is inherited from both parents. If only one gene for that trait is inherited, the individual will not have the trait but will be a carrier of it.

recognition. When contrasted with *recall,* a memory test that involves only a decision about whether a given stimulus is or isn't the correct one, or whether it has or hasn't been seen (or heard) before.

reflective. Kagan's term for children who respond slowly on the Matching Familiar Figures Test and who make few errors. Such children tend to do better in their schoolwork than impulsive children; they tend to be careful and analytical.

reflex. A simple, automatic, built-in response to a stimulus.

rehearsal. A method for retaining something (e.g., a number) in short-term memory, by saying it over and over to oneself.

reinforcement. The administration of a reinforcer.

reinforcer. Anything that an organism is willing to work for: for example, food (for a hungry organism), water (for a thirsty one), or a kind word or a pat on the head (for a child or a dog).

reliability. A test is said to have reliability when a child who takes it on Monday makes roughly the same score that she would have made if she had taken it on Friday. A reliable test, in other words, is one that is not very much affected by chance factors or day-to-day variations.

REM sleep. Rapid-eye-movement sleep—the same as *active sleep.*

representational thought. Mental processes that make use of representations.

representations. Mental images of things previously seen, heard, or otherwise experienced; or arbitrary symbols (such as words) used to think about actions or things.

representative sample. A sample of subjects that contains individuals from different racial and ethnic groups, from different socioeconomic levels, from different geographic locations, and so on, in approximately the same proportions as they occur in the population as a whole.

repressed. In Freudian theory, a repressed thought or desire is one that has been driven down into the unconscious mind.

response. An action—often, an action that occurs after exposure to a stimulus.

retention control training. A method used in the treatment of bed-wetting. The child is asked to postpone urinating as long as possible. The idea is to increase the capacity of the bladder and to strengthen the muscle used in holding back urination.

retrieval. See *memory retrieval.*

reversal shift. A kind of discrimination-shift problem. In the first part of the experiment, the subject must choose between stimuli that vary in two dimensions, of which only one dimension determines the correct stimulus. Then the rules are changed so that the correct stimulus is now the opposite one of the same dimension.

reversibility. A principle used in solving a Piagetian conservation problem. If the problem involves, for example, liquid volume, the reversibility principle would be the idea that we could pour the water back into the original container and it would look the same as it did at first.

rite of passage. A ceremony or ritual marking a person's transition from childhood to adulthood.

role model. An older person performing a given social or family role, whose behavior can serve as a model for a younger person to follow.

role-taking ability. The ability to imagine, or to be aware of, another person's thoughts, feelings, and motivations.

rooting. One of the reflexes of the newborn baby: a touch on the cheek causes the baby's head and lips to move in that direction.

rough-and-tumble play. A style of play quite common in preschool-age boys. It involves much running, jumping, and rolling around, as well as playful wrestling, shoving, and so on.

rubella. A viral disease, also known as *German measles,* capable of producing severe birth defects if a woman contracts it during the first trimester of pregnancy.

scheme. In Piagetian theory, a simple or complex pattern of action or thought that functions as a unit.

schizophrenia. See *childhood schizophrenia.*

secondary sex characteristics. Physical characteristics that distinguish men from women but are not directly related to reproduction—e.g., breast development in females, beard growth and deep voice in males. See *primary sex characteristics.*

secure attachment. A description of the quality of a child's relationship with another person, generally a parent. A child who is securely attached to his mother, for example, will greet her joyfully after having been separated from her in the "strange situation."

security of attachment. The quality of a child's attachment to a particular person, generally assessed in the "strange situation." See *secure attachment, insecure attachment.*

selective attention. The ability to focus attention on a particular stimulus, and to shut out, to a certain extent, less important stimuli.

self-fulfilling prophecy. A prediction that comes true because people expect it to come true; they expect it to come true because it was predicted.

sensitive period. A period during which some aspect of development can occur most readily.

sensorimotor period. In Piagetian theory, roughly the first two years of life. By the end of this period, the child has acquired object permanence and can use mental representations.

sensorimotor play. Piaget's term for the earliest type of play, which involves moving the body and, usually, doing something to an object or objects. Shaking a rattle and building a tower with blocks are examples.

sensory nerve. A nerve that carries neural signals to the brain or spinal cord from the sense organs, the skin, the muscles and joints, or the internal organs.

separation anxiety. Same as *separation distress.*

separation distress. The unhappiness experienced and expressed by a child when a person to whom that child is attached goes away from him or her.

serial monogamy. Being faithful to one partner in a romantic relationship, and then, when that relationship ends, being faithful to the next partner.

sex chromosomes. The pair of chromosomes that normally determine a person's sex. They are of two types, X and Y. Females have two X chromosomes; males have one X and one Y.

sex constancy. The understanding that maleness and femaleness depend on what kind of genitals a person was born with and not on clothing or hairstyle, and that people stay the same sex all through their lives.

sex difference. A significant difference, found in one study or in many studies, between girls' and boys' scores on some measurement.

sex identity. Same as *gender identity*.

sex-linked trait. A trait carried on the X chromosome. A boy with such a trait has inherited the gene that's responsible for it from his mother.

sex-typed behavior. Behavior that is considered typical for a particular sex, and not for the opposite sex.

sexual stereotypes. The ideas that people in a given society tend to hold about males and females—for example, that males are strong, brave, aggressive, and unemotional, and that females are weak, dependent, affectionate, and somewhat irrational.

shape constancy. The visual mechanism that keeps things looking constant in shape, despite differences in the angle they are viewed from.

shaping. Training an organism to make a new response, by reinforcing a response that has some features in common with the desired response, and then by gradually increasing the requirements for reinforcement.

short-term memory. Temporary memory, capable of holding a small number of items (such as numbers) for a short period of time, or for as long as they are retained by means of rehearsal. See *long-term memory*.

sibling. A brother or a sister.

SIDS. Same as *Sudden Infant Death Syndrome*.

significant. A result that is unlikely to have occurred merely by chance or coincidence is said to be significant.

significant difference. A difference between two sets of measurements that is unlikely to be the result of chance variations. In order to be significant, a difference does not necessarily have to be large, but it does have to be reasonably consistent.

size constancy. The visual mechanism that keeps things looking constant in size, despite the fact that a close object takes up more of the visual field than the same object seen from farther away.

skin senses. The senses that enable us to perceive pressure (or "touch"), heat, cold, and pain. The receptors for all of these senses are found in the skin.

Skinner box. A box containing some device with which an animal can make a response (usually a lever for a rat to press, or a lighted disk for a pigeon to peck), and another device that dispenses a reinforcer (usually food). Used in operant conditioning.

small for dates. A term used to describe a baby who weighs noticeably less than the expected weight, given the date of conception and the date of the baby's birth.

sociability. The aspect of a person's personality that determines the degree to which that person seeks and enjoys interactions with other people.

social learning theory. The view that children learn through observing others, as well as through the reinforcements and punishments that they themselves receive. See also *cognitive behaviorism*.

social punishment. An unpleasant reaction by one person to the behavior of another—for example, frowning, criticizing, hitting, ignoring, or taking something away from the other person.

social reinforcement. A pleasant reaction by one person to the behavior of another—for example, smiling, giving praise, showing affection, complying with a request, or simply paying attention to the other person.

socialization. The aspect of development that involves the child's learning to behave according to the rules of his or her society, and acquiring the attitudes, skills, and knowledge needed to get along in that society.

society. A group of people with a common culture.

sociodramatic play. Play in which two or more children adopt imaginary roles and take part in a game of make-believe. "Playing house" is a good example.

socioeconomic level. The socioeconomic level of a family is determined by the income, profession, education, and social status of its members.

sociometric measures. Measures of children's popularity with their peers, obtained by asking a group of children to name their best friends, or to name a certain number of children they particularly like, or to rate each of their classmates according to how well they like them.

sociometric status. How popular a child is with his or her peers, as determined by sociometric measures.

solitary play. Play that involves no interaction at all with other people.

space perception. The ability to localize objects in three-dimensional space. Stereoscopic vision is one way we can do this, but there are other ways, such as using the cues we get when we move around.

species-specific behavior. An inherited pattern of behavior. Examples are nest-building in many species of birds, washing the face and paws in cats, and mating rituals in all species of mammals.

stage. A period of development that is assumed to be qualitatively different from the previous or subsequent period. Stages are also assumed to occur in a particular order, though their timing can vary.

Stanford-Binet. A frequently used IQ test that can be given to children age 2 or over, and that is administered individually.

state. A term used by psychologists to describe the various types of sleep and wakefulness seen in newborn babies.

stepping reflex. Same as *walking reflex*.

stereoblind. Lacking stereoscopic vision. An estimated 2 percent of human adults are stereoblind.

stereoscopic vision. The aspect of visual perception that depends on the fact that the left eye's view is slightly different from the right eye's, and that enables us to see the world in three dimensions.

stereotyped movements. Movements consisting of one particular motor pattern—e.g., waving the hand—repeated again and again.

stimulus. Anything that can be seen or heard, or perceived through one of the other senses. This term is often applied to something (e.g., a picture, a sound) used in an experiment, particularly something that is expected to evoke a response.

"strange situation." An experimental procedure developed by Ainsworth and her associates, used to assess the quality of a child's attachment to his mother. During this procedure the mother twice leaves the child in an unfamiliar room—once leaving him with a stranger, and once leaving him alone.

strategy. A technique for doing something, especially one that is directed toward a particular goal. For instance, rehearsal is a metacognitive strategy for retaining words or numbers in short-term memory.

subject. A person participating in a study.

Sudden Infant Death Syndrome. The death of an infant due to causes that are still not completely understood, usually while he or she is sleeping. It is the leading killer of babies between 1 month and 12 months of age.

superego. According to Freud, one of the three aspects of the human mind. The superego is the equivalent of a conscience; it develops between the ages of 3 and 5½.

swaddling. Wrapping a baby tightly in a blanket or with strips of cloth—used in many societies because babies tend to cry less when they're swaddled.

swimming reflex. One of the reflexes of the newborn baby: when placed on her stomach, the baby may make rhythmic movements of her arms and legs, as though she were swimming.

symbolic representations. Bruner's term for mental representations that consist of symbols such as words.

synapse. A place where a neural message from one neuron is transmitted (by means of a substance known as a *neurotransmitter*) to another neuron.

syphilis. A veneral disease caused by a microorganism that can cross the placenta and harm a developing fetus.

tabula rasa. Literally, a blank slate. According to the philosopher John Locke, the mind of the newborn baby is like a slate with nothing written on it.

tadpole person. A typical drawing produced by a 3-year-old: a head without a body. The legs (and arms, if arms are included in the drawing) are connected directly to the head.

tag question. A question that is "tagged on" at the end of a sentence, turning a declarative sentence into an interrogative one. In the sentence, "You like candy, don't you?" the tag question is "don't you?"

telegraphese. Same as *telegraphic speech*.

telegraphic speech. A description of the speech of toddlers, whose utterances are still quite limited in length. They tend to leave out verb endings and unimportant words; as a result, their speech resembles the language used in telegrams.

temperament. The persistent aspects of a person's personality—for example, how adaptable, cheerful, active, and emotional that person is.

tentative period. A period in the development of understanding about careers and occupations, which generally begins at about age 11 and is eventually succeeded by the *realistic period*. The young adolescent in the tentative period realizes that jobs require specific training and abilities and that education is costly, but he or she has not yet made a definite decision about a career.

teratogen. Anything that can produce abnormalities

in a developing embryo or fetus.

thalidomide. A prescription drug, formerly used to quell nausea and vomiting, which produces serious birth defects when taken in early pregnancy. This drug was never sold in the United States.

toddlerhood. The period of development that starts when the child begins to use walking as his or her chief means of getting from one place to another, and that ends around the age of 2½.

tonic neck reflex. One of the reflexes of the newborn baby: when lying on his back the baby generally keeps his head turned to one side, with the arm on that side stretched out and the other arm bent, so that his fist is near the back of his head.

toxemia. A disorder of pregnancy, the cause of which is still unknown. If untreated, toxemia can be fatal to both mother and fetus. (Also known as *pre-eclampsia*.)

toxoplasmosis. A disease sometimes transmitted in cat droppings or raw meat. The microorganism that causes it is capable of crossing the placenta and harming a developing embryo or fetus.

transpose. To reverse or rotate something. In an experiment by Bruner, 5- and 6-year-olds were able to reproduce a display in its original orientation, but they were unable to transpose it—to reproduce it in a reversed or rotated orientation.

traumatic. A term applied to experiences that might have upsetting, or even injurious, effects.

trimester. A three-month period of pregnancy.

"true" score. The average score that a person would theoretically make on a test if he or she took the test over and over again, under optimum conditions.

trust versus mistrust. Same as *basic trust versus mistrust*.

umbilical cord. The rope-like structure, containing blood vessels, that connects the embryo or fetus to the placenta.

unconscious mind. In Freudian theory, the part of the mind that contains drives, feelings, memories, and thoughts that we are not aware of, but that nonetheless influence our behavior and our conscious thoughts.

underextend. To use a word for a smaller category of things than the word can correctly be used for. When a preschooler uses the word "bird" only for robins and bluejays and the like, and denies that turkeys and chickens are birds, that's an underextension.

uterus. A pear-shaped, hollow organ with muscular walls, located in a woman's abdomen. Also known as the womb.

utterance. A single word, or a phrase or a sentence spoken all in one piece (without pauses).

validity. A test is said to have validity if it accurately measures the quality or characteristic it was designed to measure.

variability. How widely the measurements in a set of measurements differ from each other.

verbal mediators. Words, either thought or spoken aloud, that come between a stimulus and a response. The stimulus evokes the verbal mediator and the verbal mediator directs the response.

vernix. A cheesy substance that coats the skin of the fetus and that is present on the skin of a newborn baby.

vicarious punishment. The result of seeing someone else punished for something he or she did.

vicarious reinforcement. The result of seeing someone else receive a reinforcement for something he or she did.

visual acuity. The sharpness or clarity of vision.

visual cliff. A device for testing depth perception in human or animal babies. It consists of a large table whose top is made of glass. A patterned surface can be seen directly under the glass on one side; on the other, the patterned surface is several feet below the glass.

visual constancies. Perceptual mechanisms that serve to produce a constant perception despite changes in the actual stimuli that reach the eyes. See *size, shape, position,* and *brightness constancy*.

visual feedback. The effects that are seen to occur as an immediate result of making a given movement.

visual-motor skill. An ability that uses information obtained through vision to regulate a pattern of motor responses.

visual-spatial ability. The ability to deal with mental representations of shapes and directions—to visualize relationships among them and the changes that would occur if these shapes or directions are moved around or rotated. An example would be visualizing how a diagram would look if it were turned upside down.

vocalize. To say a word or to make a speech-like sound. A baby's coos and babbles are considered vocalizations.

walking reflex. One of the reflexes of the newborn baby: when held upright with his feet touching a solid surface, the baby will make stepping movements similar to real walking.

whole-word method.   A method for teaching children to read that does not involve the teaching of phonics. Children are taught to recognize words as wholes, by their overall shape, instead of sounding them out letter by letter.

WISC.   The Wechsler Intelligence Scale for Children—an IQ test for school-age children, designed to be administered individually.

WPPSI.   The Wechsler Preschool and Primary Scale of Intelligence—an IQ test for 4- to 6-year-olds, designed to be administered individually.

X chromosome.   The larger of the two sex chromosomes, shaped roughly like an X. Everyone has at least one X chromosome—females have two, males have one (plus one Y chromosome).

Y chromosome.   The smaller of the two sex chromosomes, shaped roughly like a Y. Only males have a Y chromosome; they've inherited it from their fathers.

zygote.   A fertilized egg, containing (in the human) 46 chromosomes.

References

ABRAVANEL, E. (1982). Perceiving subjective contours during early childhood. *Journal of Experimental Child Psychology, 33,* 280–287.

ABELSON, H. I., & ATKINSON, R. B. (1975). *Public experience with psychoactive substances: A nationwide survey among adults and youth.* Princeton, N.J.: Response Corporation.

ADAMS, G. R., & JONES, J. M. (1983). Female adolescents' identity development: Age comparisons and perceived child-planning experiences. *Developmental Psychology, 19,* 249–256.

ADELSON, J. (1975). The development of ideology in adolescence. In S. E. Dragastin and G. H. Elder, Jr. (Eds.), *Adolescence in the life cycle.* Washington, D.C.: Hemisphere Publishing Corporation, 63–78.

ADELSON, J., & O'NEIL, R. (1966). The growth of political ideas in adolescence: The sense of community. *Journal of Personality and Social Psychology, 4,* 295–306.

AINSWORTH, M. D. S. (1977). Attachment theory and its utility in cross-cultural research. In P. H. Leiderman, S. R. Tulkin, & A. Rosenfeld (Eds.), *Culture and infancy: Variations in the human experience.* New York: Academic Press.

AINSWORTH, M. D. S., BLEHAR, M. C., WATERS, E., & WALL, S. (1978). *Patterns of attachment.* Hillsdale, N. J.: Erlbaum.

AITCHISON, J. (1977). *The articulate mammal: An introduction to psycholinguistics.* New York: Universe Books.

ALBERT, R. (1971). Cognitive development and parental loss among the gifted, the exceptionally gifted, and the creative. *Psychological Reports, 29,* 19–26.

ALLINGTON, R. L. (1982). The persistence of teacher beliefs in facets of the visual perceptual deficits hypothesis. *The Elementary School Journal, 82,* 351–359.

AMERICAN PSYCHOLOGICAL ASSOCIATION AD HOC COMMITTEE ON ETHICAL STANDARDS IN PSYCHOLOGICAL RESEARCH (1973). *Ethical principles in the conduct of research with human participants.* Washington, D.C.

AMSTERDAM, B. K. (1969). *Mirror behavior in children under two years of age.* Unpublished doctoral dissertation, University of North Carolina.

ANASTASI, A. (1976). *Psychological testing* (4th ed.) New York: Macmillan.

ANDERS, T. F. (1980). Night-waking in infants during the first year of life. In S. Chess & A. Thomas (Eds.), *Annual progress in child psychiatry and child development, 1980.* New York: Brunner/Mazel.

ANGLIN, J. M. (1977). *Word, object, and conceptual development.* New York: Norton.

ANNETT, M. (1974). Handedness in the children of two left-handed parents. *British Journal of Psychology, 65,* 129–131.

ANNIS, R. C., & FROST, B. (1973). Human visual ecology and orientation anisotropies in acuity. *Science, 182,* 729–731.

APGAR, Y., & BECK, J. (1972). *Is my baby all right?* New York: Trident Press.

ARONSON, E., & ROSENBLOOM, S. (1971). Space perception in early infancy: Perception within a common auditory-visual space. *Science, 172,* 1161–1163.

ASHER, S. R., & HYMEL, S. (1981). Children's social competence in peer relations: Sociometric and behavior assessment. In J. D. Wine & M. D. Smye (Eds.), *Social competence.* New York: Guilford Press.

ASHER, S. R., MARKELL, R. A., & HYMEL, S. (1981). Identifying children at risk in peer relations: A critique of the rate-of-interaction approach to assessment. *Child Development, 52,* 1239–1245.

ASHER, S. R., & RENSHAW, P. D. (1981). Children without friends: Social knowledge and social skill training. In S. R. Asher & J. M. Gottman (Eds.), *The development of children's friendships.* Cambridge: Cambridge University Press.

ASHMEAD, D. H. (1976). *Newborn attentional responses to vocal and nonvocal stimuli.* Unpublished honors thesis, Brown University.

ASHTON, P. T. (1978). The role of the attachment bond in effective parenting. In J. H. Stevens, Jr., & M. Mathews (Eds.), *Mother/child, father/child relationships.* Washington, D. C.: National Association for the Education of Young Children.

ASLIN, R. N., & DUMAIS, S. T. (1980). Binocular vision in infants: A review and theoretical framework. In H. W. Reese & L. P. Lipsitt (Eds.), *Advances in child development and behavior* (Vol. 15). New York: Academic Press.

ATWATER, E. (1983). *Adolescence.* Englewood Cliffs, N. J.: Prentice-Hall.

AZRIN, N. H., & THIENES, P. M. (1978). Rapid elimination of enuresis by intensive learning without a conditioning apparatus. *Behavior Therapy, 9,* 342–354.

BALL, W., & TRONICK, E. (1971). Infant responses to impending collision: Optical and real. *Science, 171,* 818–820.

BALLER, W. R. (1975). *Bed-wetting: Origins and treatment.* New York: Pergamon Press.

BANDURA, A. (1965). Influence of models' reinforcement contingencies on the acquisition of imitative responses. *Journal of Personality and Social Psychology, 1,* 589–595.

BANDURA, A., & MISCHEL, W. (1965). Modification of self-imposed delay of reward through exposure to live and symbolic models. *Journal of Personality and Social Psychology, 2,* 698–705.

BANDURA, A., ROSS, D., & ROSS, S. A. (1963a). Vicarious reinforcement and imitative learning. *Journal of Abnormal and Social Psychology, 67,* 601–607.

BANDURA, A., ROSS, D., & ROSS, S. A. (1963b). Imitation of film-mediated aggressive models. *Journal of Abnormal and Social Psychology, 66,* 3–11.

BANDURA, A., & WALTERS, R. H. (1959). *Adolescent aggression.* New York: Ronald Press.

BARBER, R. G., DEMBO, T., & LEWIN, K. (1943). Frustration and regression. In R. G. Barber, J. S. Kounin, & H. F. Wright (Eds.), *Child behavior and development.* New York: McGraw-Hill.

BARD, C., FLEURY, M., CARRIÈRE, L., & BELLEC, J. (1981). Components of the coincidence-anticipation behavior of children aged from 6 to 11 years. *Perceptual and Motor Skills, 52,* 547–556.

BARNES, A. B., COLTON, T., GINDERSEN, J., NOLLER, K. L., ZILLEY, B. C., STRAMA, T., TOWNSEND, D. E., HATAB, P., & O'BRIEN, P. C. (1980). *New England Journal of Medicine, 303* (5), 281.

BARNETT, M. A., HOWARD, J. A., MELTON, E. M., & DINO, G. A. (1982). Effect of inducing sadness about self or other on helping behavior in high- and low-empathic children. *Child Development, 53,* 920–923.

BARTON, J., CHASSIN, L., PRESSON, C. C., & SHERMAN, S. J. (1982). Social image factors as motivators of smoking initiation in early and middle adolescence. *Child Development, 53,* 1499–1511.

BATTELLE, P. (1981, Feb.). The triplets who found each other. *Good Housekeeping, 192* (2), 74–83.

BAUMRIND, D. (1967). Child-care practices anteceding three patterns of preschool behavior. *Genetic Psychology Monographs, 75,* 43–88.

BAUMRIND, D. (1975). *Early socialization and the discipline controversy.* Morristown, N.J.: General Learning Press.

BAYLEY, N. (1969). *Bayley scales of infant development.* New York: Psychological Corporation.

BECK, R. C. (1978). *Motivation: Theories and principles.* Englewood Cliffs, N.J.: Prentice-Hall.

BELL, R. Q. (1968). A reinterpretation of the direction of effects in studies of socialization. *Psychological Review, 75,* 81–95.

BELL, R. Q. (1974). Contributions of human infants to caregiving and social interaction. In M. Lewis & L. A. Rosenblum (Eds.), *The effect of the infant on its caregiver.* New York: John Wiley.

BELL, R. Q. (1979). Parent, child, and reciprocal influences. *American Psychologist, 34,* 821–826.

BELL, S. M. (1970). The development of the concept of object as related to infant-mother attachment. *Child Development, 41,* 291–311.

BELL, S. M., & AINSWORTH, M. D. S. (1972). Infant crying and maternal responsiveness. *Child Development, 43,* 1171–1190.

BELSKY, J., & STERNBERG, L. D. (1978). The effects of day care: A critical review. *Child Development, 49,* 920–949.

BERN, S. L. (1974). The measurement of psychological androgyny. *Journal of Consulting and Clinical Psychology, 42,* 155–162.

BENNETT, N. (1976). *Teaching styles and pupil progress.* Cambridge: Harvard University Press.

BERG, W. K., ADKINSON, C. D., & STROCK, B. L. (1973). Duration and periods of alertness in neonates. *Developmental Psychology, 9,* 434.

BERKO, J. (1958). The child's learning of English morphology. *Word, 14,* 150–177.

BERNDT, T. J. (1981). Effects of friendship on prosocial intentions and behavior. *Child Development, 52,* 636–643.

BERNDT, T. J. (1982). The features and effects of friendship in early adolescence. *Child Development, 53,* 1447–1460.

BETTELHEIM, B. (1976). *The uses of enchantment.* New York: Knopf.

BIBLOW, E. (1973). Imaginative play and the control of aggressive behavior. In J. L. Singer (Ed.), *The child's world of make-believe.* New York: Academic Press.

BIDDLE, B., BANK, B., ANDERSON, D. S., KEATS, J., & KEATS, D. (1981, April). The structure of idleness: In-school and dropout adolescent activities in the United States and Australia. *Sociology of Education,* pp. 106–119.

BIJOU, S. W., & BAER, D. M. (1965). *Child development* (Vol. 2). New York: Appleton-Century-Crofts.

BINDELGLAS, P. M., DEE, G. H., & ENOS, F. A. (1968). Medical and psychosocial factors in enuretic children treated with imipramine hydrochloride. *American Journal of Psychiatry, 124,* 125–130.

BJORKLUND, D. F., & HOCK, H. S. (1982). Age differences in the temporal locus of memory organization in children's recall. *Journal of Experimental Child Psychology, 33,* 347–362.

BLAKEMORE, C., & COOPER, G. F. (1970). Development of the brain depends on the visual environment. *Nature, 228,* 477–478.

BLEHAR, M. C., LIEBERMAN, A. F., & AINSWORTH, M. D. S. (1977). Early face-to-face interaction and its relation to later infant-mother attachment. *Child Development, 48,* 182–194.

BLOUNT, R., JR. (1981, December 20). When love is the best gift of all. *Parade,* pp. 4–6.

BORNSTEIN, M. (1975). Qualities of color vision in infancy. *Journal of Experimental Child Psychology, 19,* 401–419.

BOUCHARD, T. J., JR., & McGUE, M. (1981). Familial studies of intelligence: A review. *Science, 212,* 1055–1059.

BOURNE, E. (1978). The state of research on ego identity: A review and appraisal. *Journal of Youth and Adolescence, 7,* 223–251 and 371–392.

BOWER, T. G. R. (1975). Infant perception of the third dimension and object concept development. In L. B. Cohen & P. Salapatk (Eds.), *Infant perception: From sensation to cognition* (Vol. 2). New York: Academic Press.

BOWER, T. G. R. (1976, November). Repetitive processes in child development. *Scientific American,* pp. 38–47.

BOWER, T. G. R. (1977a). *The perceptual world of the child.* Cambridge: Harvard University Press.

BOWER, T. G. R. (1977b). *A primer of infant development.* San Francisco: W. H. Freeman & Company.

BOWER, T. G. R., BROUGHTON, J. M., & MOORE, M. K. (1970). Infant responses to approaching objects: An indicator of response to distal variables. *Perception and Psychophysics, 9,* 193–196.

BOWERMAN, C. E., & KINCH, J. W. (1969). Changes in family and peer orientation of children between the fourth and tenth grades. In M. Gold & E. Douvan (Eds.), *Adolescent development.* Boston: Allyn & Bacon.

BOWLBY, J. (1969). *Attachment and loss.* Vol. 1: *Attachment.* New York: Basic Books.

BRACKBILL, Y. (1973). Neonatal posture: Psychophysical effects. *Neuropädiatrie, 4,* 145–150.

BRACKBILL, Y., ADAMS, G., CROWELL, D. H., & GRAY, M. L. (1967). Arousal level in neonates and older infants under continuous auditory stimulation. In Y. Brackbill & G. G. Thompson (Eds.), *Behavior in infancy and early childhood*. New York: The Free Press.

BRAINE, M. D. S. (1963). The ontogeny of English phrase structure: The first phrase. *Language, 39,* 1–13.

BRAINERD, C. J. (1978). *Piaget's theory of intelligence*. Englewood Cliffs, N.J.: Prentice-Hall.

BRAUCHT, G. N., BRAKARSH, D., FOLLINGSTAD, D., & BERRY, K. L. (1973). Deviant drug use in adolescence: A review of psychosocial correlates. *Psychological Bulletin, 79,* 92–106.

BRAUNGART, R. G. (1974). The sociology of generations and student politics: A comparison of the functionalist and generational unit models. *Journal of Social Issues, 30,* 31–54.

BRAZELTON, T. B. (1961). Psychophysiologic reactions in the neonate. I. The value of observation of the neonate. *The Journal of Pediatrics, 58,* 508–512.

BRAZELTON, T. B. (1969). *Infants and mothers: Differences in development*. New York: Delacorte Press.

BRAZELTON, T. B. (1977). Implications of infant development among the Mayan Indians of Mexico. In P. H. Leiderman, S. R. Tulkin, & A. Rosenfeld (Eds.), *Culture and infancy: Variations in the human experience*. New York: Academic Press.

BRAZELTON, T. B., KOSLOWSKI, B., & MAIN, M. (1974). The origins of reciprocity: The early mother-infant interaction. In M. Lewis & L. A. Rosenblum (Eds.), *The effect of the infant on its caregiver*. New York: John Wiley.

BREGMAN, E. (1934). An attempt to modify the emotional attitude of infants by the conditioned response technique. *Journal of Genetic Psychology, 45,* 169–198.

BRODY, G. H., & SHAFFER, D. R. (1982). Contributions of parents and peers to children's moral socialization. *Developmental Review, 2,* 31–75.

BRONFENBRENNER, U. (1970). *Two worlds of childhood: U.S. and U.S.S.R.* New York: Russell Sage Foundation.

BRONFENBRENNER, U. (1972). The origins of alienation. In U. Bronfenbrenner & M. A. Mahoney (Eds.), *Influences on human development* (2nd Ed.). Hinsdale, Ill.: The Dryden Press.

BRONFENBRENNER, U. (1974). *Is early intervention effective? A report on longitudinal evaluations of preschool programs* (Vol. 2). Washington, D.C.: Office of Child Development, Department of Health, Education, and Welfare.

BRONSHTEIN, A. I., & PETROVA, E. P. (1967). The auditory analyzer in young infants. In Y. Brackbill & G. G. Thompson (Eds.), *Behavior in infancy and early childhood*. New York: The Free Press.

BROOK, J. S., WHITEMAN, M., & GORDON, A. S. (1983). Stages of drug use in adolescence: Personality, peers, and family conflicts. *Developmental Psychology, 19,* 269–277.

BROOKS, J., & LEWIS, M. (1976). Infants' responses to strangers: Midget, adult, and child. *Child Development, 47,* 323–332.

BROWN, J. L. (1964). States in newborn infants. *Merrill-Palmer Quarterly, 10,* 313–327.

BROWN, P., & ELLIOT, R. (1965). Control of aggression in a nursery school class. *Journal of Experimental Child Psychology, 2,* 103–107.

BROWN, R. (1958). How shall a thing be called? *Psychological Review, 65,* 14–21.

BROWN, R. (1973). *A first language: The early stages*. Cambridge: Harvard University Press.

BROWN, R., & BELLUGI, U. (1964). Three processes in the child's acquisition of syntax. In E. H. Lenneberg (Ed.), *New directions in the study of language*. Cambridge: MIT Press.

BROWN, R., CAZDEN, C., & BELLUGI-KLIMA, U. (1969). The child's grammar from I to III. In J. P. Hill (Ed.), *Minnesota Symposium on Child Psychology* (Vol. 2). Minneapolis: University of Minnesota Press.

BROWN, R., & HANLON, C. (1970). Derivational complexity and order of acquisition in child speech. In J. R. Hayes (Ed.), *Cognition and the development of language*. New York: John Wiley.

BROWN, R. T. (1982). A developmental analysis of visual and auditory sustained attention and reflection-impulsivity in hyperactive children. *Journal of Learning Disabilities, 15,* 614–618.

BRUNER, J. (1964). The course of cognitive growth. *American Psychologist, 19,* 1–15.

BRUNER, J. S. (1966). On cognitive growth. In J. S. Bruner, R. R. Olver, & P. M. Greenfield (Eds.), *Studies in cognitive growth*. New York: John Wiley.

BRUNER, J. S. (1973). The course of cognitive growth. In J. M. Anglin (Ed.), *Beyond the information given*. New York: Norton.

BRUNER, J. S., & KENNEY, H. (1966). The development of the concepts of order and proportion in children. In J. S. Bruner, R. R. Olver, & P. M. Greenfield (Eds.), *Studies in cognitive growth*. New York: John Wiley.

BRYANT, B. K., & CROCKENBERG, S. B. (1980). Correlates and dimensions of prosocial behavior: A study of female siblings with their mothers. *Child Development, 51,* 529–544.

BULLOCK, D., & MERRILL, L. (1980). The impact of personal preference on consistency through time: The case of childhood aggression. *Child Development, 51,* 808–814.

BURLINGHAM, D., & FREUD, A. (1967). Young children in wartime: Traumatic effects of separation from parents. In Y. Brackbill & G. G. Thompson (Eds.), *Behavior in infancy and early childhood*. New York: Free Press.

BURTON, R. V. (1976). Honesty and dishonesty. In T. Lickona (Ed.), *Moral development and behavior*. New York: Holt, Rinehart and Winston.

BURTON, R. V., MACCOBY, E. E., & ALLINSMITH, W. (1961). Antecedents of resistance to temptation in four-year-old children. *Child Development, 32,* 689–710.

BUTTERFIELD, E. C., & SIPERSTEIN, G. N. (1974). Influence of contingent auditory stimulation upon non-nutritional suckle. *Proceedings of the Third Symposium on Oral Sensation and Perception: The Mouth of the Infant*. Springfield, Ill.: Chas. C Thomas.

CALDWELL, B. M., BRADLEY, R. H., & ELARDO, R. (1975). Early stimulation. In J. Wortis (Ed.), *Mental retardation and developmental disabilities: An annual review*. New York: Brunner/Mazel.

CAMPOS, J. J., LANGER, A., & KROWITZ, A. (1970). Cardiac response on the visual cliff in prelocomotor human infants. *Science, 170,* 196–197.

CAPLAN, P. J., & KINSBOURNE, M. (1976). Baby drops the rattle: Asymmetry of duration of grasp by infants. *Child Development, 47,* 532–534.

CAREY, S. (1978). The child as word learner. In M. Halle, J. Bresnan, & G. A. Miller (Eds.), *Linguistic theory and psychological reality*. Cambridge: MIT Press.

CARMICHAEL, L. (1927). A further study of the development of behavior in vertebrates experimentally removed from the influence of external stimulation. *Psychological Review, 34*, 34–47.

CARPENTER, G. (1975). Mother's face and the newborn. In R. Lewin (Ed.), *Child alive*. New York: Doubleday.

CARRON, A. V., & BAILEY, D. A. (1974). Strength development in boys from 10 through 16 years. *Monographs of the Society for Research in Child Development, 39* (4, Serial No. 157), 1–37.

CASE, R., KURLAND, D. M., & GOLDBERG, J. (1982). Operational efficiency and the growth of short-term memory span. *Journal of Experimental Child Psychology, 33*, 386–404.

CAUWELS, J. M. (1983). *Bulimia*. Garden City, N.Y.: Doubleday and Co.

CHALL, J. S. (1964). *Learning to read: The great debate*. New York: McGraw-Hill.

CHARLESWORTH, R., & HARTUP, W. W. (1967). Positive social reinforcement in the nursery school peer group. *Child Development, 38*, 993–1003.

CHEYNE, J. A., & WALTERS, R. H. (1969). Intensity of punishment, timing of punishment, and cognitive structure as determinants of response inhibition. *Journal of Experimental Child Psychology, 7*, 231–244.

CHOMSKY, C. (1969). *The acquisition of syntax in children from 5 to 10*. Cambridge: MIT Press.

CHOMSKY, N. (1968). *Language and mind*. New York: Harcourt, Brace, & World.

CLARK, H. H., & CLARK, E. V. (1977). *Psychology and language*. New York: Harcourt Brace Jovanovich.

CLARKE, J. C., & WHITEHURST, G. J. (1974). Asymmetrical stimulus control and the mirror-image problem. *Journal of Experimental Child Psychology, 17*, 147–166.

CLARKE-STEWART, A. (1977). *Child care in the family: A review of research and some propositions for policy*. New York: Academic Press.

CLARKE-STEWART, K. A., & HEVEY, C. M. (1981). Longitudinal relations in repeated observations of mother-child interaction from 1 to 2½ years. *Developmental Psychology, 17*, 127–145.

CLORE, G. L., BRAY, R. M., ITKIN, S. M., & MURPHY, P. (1978). Interracial attitudes and behavior at a summer camp. *Journal of Personality and Social Psychology, 36*, 107–116.

CLOUTIER, R., & GOLDSCHMID, M. L. (1976). Individual differences in the development of formal reasoning. *Child Development, 47*, 1097–1102.

COHEN, J. (1979). High school subcultures and the adult world. *Adolescence, 14*, 491–502.

COHEN, R., SCHLESER, R., & MEYERS, A. (1981). Self-instructions: Effect of cognitive level and active rehearsal. *Journal of Experimental Child Psychology, 32*, 65–76.

COLEMAN, J. S., CAMPBELL, E. Q., HOBSON, C. J., MCPARTLAND, J., MOOD, A. M., WEINFELD, F. D., & YORK, R. L. (1966). *Equality of educational opportunity* (report from U.S. Office of Education). Washington, D.C.: U.S. Government Printing Office.

COLLINS, W. A. (1973). Effect of temporal separation between motivation, aggression, and consequences: A developmental study. *Developmental Psychology, 8*, 215–221.

COMER, J. P. (1982). Drugs and early adolescence. *Parents Magazine, 57*, 100.

THE COMMITTEE ON ADOLESCENCE, GROUP FOR THE ADVANCEMENT OF PSYCHIATRY (1968). *Normal adolescence*. New York: Scribner's.

CONDRY, J., & CONDRY, S. (1976). Sex differences: A study of the eye of the beholder. *Child Development, 47*, 812–819.

CONWAY, D., & LYTTON, H. (1975). *Language differences between twins and singletons—biological, environmental, or both?* Paper presented at the annual meeting of the Society for Research in Child Development, Denver.

CORBALLIS, M. C., & BEALE, I. L. (1976). *The psychology of left and right*. Hillsdale, N.J.: Erlbaum.

COREN, S., & GIRGUS, J. S. (1978). *Seeing is deceiving: The psychology of visual illusions*. Hillsdale, N.J.: Erlbaum.

COREN, S., PORAC, C., & DUNCAN, P. (1981). Lateral preference behaviors in preschool children and young adults. *Child Development, 52*, 443–450.

COREN, S., PORAC, C., & WARD, L. M. (1979). *Sensation and perception*. New York: Academic Press.

CORSARO, W.A. (1981). Friendship in the nursery school: Social organization in a peer environment. In S. R. Asher & J. M. Gottman (Eds.), *The development of children's friendships*. Cambridge, England: Cambridge University Press.

COSTANZO, P. R., & SHAW, M. E. (1966). Conformity as a function of age level. *Child Development, 37*, 967–975.

COWAN, W. M. (1979, September). The development of the brain. *Scientific American*, 112–133.

CRAIN, W. C. (1980). *Theories of development*. Englewood Cliffs, N.J.: Prentice-Hall.

CRANDALL, V. C. (1967). Achievement behavior in young children. In *The young child: Reviews of research*. Washington, D.C.: National Association for the Education of Young Children.

CRANDALL, V. C. (1973, August). *Differences in parental antecedents of internal-external control in children and in young adulthood*. Paper presented at the meeting of the American Psychological Association, Montreal.

CRANDALL, V. C., KATKOVSKY, W., & CRANDALL, V. J. (1965). Children's beliefs in their own control of reinforcements in intellectual-academic achievement situations. *Child Development, 36*, 91–109.

CRANDALL, V. J., KATKOVSKY, W., & PRESTON, A. (1962). Motivational and ability determinants of young children's intellectual achievement behaviors. *Child Development, 33*, 643–661.

CRATTY, B. (1979). *Perceptual and motor development in infants and children*. Englewood Cliffs, N.J.: Prentice-Hall.

CROOK, C. K. (1978). Taste perception in the newborn infant. *Infant Behavior and Development, 1*, 52–69.

CURTISS, S. R. (1977). *Genie: A linguistic study of a modern day "wild child."* New York: Academic Press.

DAMON, W., & HART, D. (1982). The development of self-understanding from infancy through adolescence. *Child Development, 53*, 841–864.

DAVIDOFF, J. B. (1975). *Differences in visual perception: The individual eye*. New York: Academic Press.

DAVIDSON, H. P. (1935). A study of the confusing letters B, D, P, and Q. *Journal of Genetic Psychology, 47,* 458.

DAVIS, R. (1979). Black suicide in the 70's: Current trends. *Suicide and Life-Threatening Behavior, 9,* 131–140.

DAY, R. H., & McKENZIE, B. H. (1973). Perceptual shape constancy in early infancy. *Perception, 2,* 315–321.

DAY, R. H., & McKENZIE, B. H. (1981). Infant perception of the invariant size of approaching and receding objects. *Developmental Psychology, 17,* 670–677.

DECI, E. L. (1971). Effects of externally mediated rewards on intrinsic motivation. *Journal of Personality and Social Psychology, 18,* 105–115.

deLISSOVOY, V. (1973). High school marriages: A longitudinal study. *Journal of Marriage and The Family, 35,* 244–255.

DEMENT, W. C. (1974). *Some must watch while some must sleep.* San Francisco: W. H. Freeman & Company.

DENNIS, M., SUGAR, J., & WHITAKER, H. A. (1982). The acquisition of tag questions. *Child Development, 53,* 1254–1257.

DENNIS, W. (1973). *Children of the crèche.* New York: Meredith Corporation.

DENNIS, W., & DENNIS, M. G. (1940). The effects of cradling practices upon the onset of walking in Hopi children. *Journal of Genetic Psychology, 56,* 77–86.

DE VILLIERS, P.A., & DE VILLIERS, J. G. (1979). *Early language.* Cambridge: Harvard University Press.

deVRIES, M. W., & deVRIES, M. R. (1977). Cultural relativity of toilet-training readiness: A perspective from East Africa. *Pediatrics, 60,* 170–177.

DiPIETRO, J. A. (1981). Rough and tumble play: A function of gender. *Developmental Psychology, 17,* 50–58.

DOLEYS, D. M. (1977). Behavioral treatments for nocturnal enuresis in children: A review of the recent literature. *Psychological Bulletin, 84,* 30–54.

DOLLARD, J., DOOB, L., MILLER, N. E., MOWRER, O., & SEARS, R. (1939). *Frustration and aggression.* New Haven: Yale University Press.

DOLLINGER, S. J., & THELEN,, M. H. (1978). Overjustification and children's intrinsic motivation: Comparative effects of four rewards. *Journal of Personality and Social Psychology, 36,* 1259–1269.

DONALDSON, M., & WALES, R. J. (1970). On the acquisition of some relational terms. In J. R. Hayes (Ed.), *Cognition and the development of language.* New York: John Wiley.

DOUGLAS, J. W. B., & BLOMFIELD, J. M. (1967). Bowel training and bed wetting. In Y. Brackbill & G. G. Thompson (Eds.), *Behavior in infancy and early childhood.* New York: The Free Press, (pp. 147–151.)

DUBERMAN, L. (1973). Step-kin relationships. *Journal of Marriage and The Family, 35,* 283–292.

DUNN, J., & KENDRICK, C. (1981). Social behavior of young siblings in the family context: Differences between same-sex and different-sex dyads. *Child Development, 52,* 1265–1273.

DWECK, C. S. (1981). Social-cognitive processes in children's friendships. In S. R. Asher & J. M. Gottman (Eds.), *The development of children's friendships.* Cambridge, England: Cambridge University Press.

ECKERMAN, C. O., WHATLEY, J. L., & KUTZ, S. L. (1975). Growth of social play with peers during the second year of life. *Developmental Psychology, 11,* 42–49.

EDWARDS, M., AND STEINNETT, N. (1974). Perceptions of college students concerning alternate life styles. *Journal of Psychology, 87,* 143–156.

EGELAND, B., & SROUFE, L. A. (1981). Attachment and early maltreatment. *Child Development, 52,* 44–52.

EICHORN, D. H. (1963). Biological correlates of behavior. In H. W. Stevenson (Ed.), *Child psychology* (Vol. 1). Chicago: University of Chicago Press.

EIDUSON, B. T., & WEISNER, T. S. (1978). Alternative family styles: Effects on young children. In J. H. Stevens, Jr., & M. Mathews (Eds.), *Mother/child, father/child relationships.* Washington, D.C.: National Association for the Education of Young Children.

EIMAS, P. D. (1975). Speech perception in early infancy. In L. B. Cohen & P. Salapatek (Eds.), *Infant perception: From sensation to cognition* (Vol. 2). New York: Academic Press.

EISENBERG, R. B. (1970). The organization of auditory behavior. *Journal of Speech and Hearing Research, 13,* 461–464.

EISENSTADT, J. M. (1978). Parental loss and genius. *American Psychologist, 33,* 211–223.

ELKIND, D. (1967). Egocentrism in adolescence. *Child Development, 38,* 1025–1034.

ELKIND, D. (1973). Giant in the nursery—Jean Piaget. In *Annual Editions: Readings in Psychology, '72–'73.* Guilford Conn.: Dushkin Publishing Group.

ENGEN, T., & LIPSITT, L. P. (1965). Decrement and recovery of responses to olfactory stimuli in the human neonate. *Journal of Comparative and Psychological Psychology, 59,* 312–316.

ENGLISH, H. B. (1929). Three cases of the "conditioned fear response." *Journal of Abnormal and Social Psychology, 34,* 221–225.

ERIKSON, E. H. (1959). *Identity and the life cycle.* New York: International Universities Press.

ERIKSON, E. H. (1963). *Childhood and society* (2nd ed.). New York: Norton.

ERON, L. D., LEFKOWITZ, M. M., HUESMANN, L. R., & WALDER, L. O. (1972). Does television violence cause aggression? *American Psychologist, 27,* 253–263.

ERON, L. D., WALDER, L. O., HUESMANN, L. R., & LEFKOWITZ, M. M. (1974). The convergence of laboratory and field studies of the development of aggression. In J. de Wit & W. W. Hartup (Eds.), *Determinants and origins of aggressive behavior.* The Hague: Monton.

ERVIN, S. M. (1964). Imitation and structural change in children's language. In E. H. Lenneberg (Ed.), *New directions in the study of language.* Cambridge: MIT Press.

ESLINGER, K. M., CLARKE, A. C., & DYNES, R. R. (1972). The principles of least interest, dating behavior, and family integration settings. *Journal of Marriage and the Family, 34,* 269–272.

EYFERTH, K. (1961). Leistungen verschiedner gruppen von besatzungskindern in Hamburg—Wechsler Intelligenztest für Kinder (HAWIK). *Archiv für die gesamte Psychologie, 113,* 222–241.

FAGAN, J. F. (1972). Infants' recognition memory for faces. *Journal of Experimental Child Psychology. 14,* 453–476.

FANTZ, R. L. (1958). Pattern vision in young infants. *Psychological Record, 8,* 43–47.

FANTZ, R. L., FAGAN, J. F., & MIRANDA, S. B. (1975). Early visual selectivity. In L. B. Cohen & P. Salapatek (Eds.), *Infant perception: From sensation to cognition* (Vol. 1). New York: Academic Press.

FARBER, S. (1981, January). Telltale behavior of twins. *Psychology Today*, pp. 58–62, 79–80.

FARNHAM-DIGGORY, S. (1978). *Learning disabilities*. Cambridge: Harvard University Press.

FEIN, G. G. (1981). Pretend play in childhood: An integrative review. *Child Development, 52*, 1095–1118.

FESHBACH, N. D., & FESHBACH, S. (1969). The relationship between empathy and aggression in two age groups. *Developmental Psychology, 1*, 102–107.

FESHBACH, S. (1956). The catharsis hypothesis and some consequences of interaction with aggressive and neutral play objects. *Journal of Personality, 24*, 449–461.

FIELD, D. (1981). Can preschool children really learn to conserve? *Child Development, 52*, 326–334.

FIELD, J., DIFRANCO, D., DODWELL, P., & MUIR, D. (1979). Auditory-visual coordination in 2½-month-old infants. *Infant Behavior and Development, 2*, 113–122.

FIELD, T. M. (1977). Effects of early separation, interactive deficits, and experimental manipulations on infant-mother face-to-face interaction. *Child Development, 48*, 763–771.

FIELDING, D. (1980). The response of day and night wetting children and children who wet only at night to retention control training and the enuresis alarm. *Behavior Research and Therapy, 18*, 305–317.

FINNEGAN, L. P., & FEHR, K. O. (1980). The effects of opiates, sedative-hypnotics, amphetamines, cannabis, and other psychoactive drugs on the fetus and newborn. In O. J. Kalant (Ed.), *Alcohol and drug problems in women: Research advances in alcohol and drug problems* (Vol. 5). New York: Plenum Press.

FLAVELL, J. H. (1977). *Cognitive development*. Englewood Cliffs, N.J.: Prentice-Hall.

FLAVELL, J. H. (1979). Metacognition and cognitive monitoring: A new area of cognitive-developmental inquiry. *American Psychologist, 34*, 906–911.

FLAVELL, J. H., BEACH, D. R., & CHINSKY, J. M. (1966). Spontaneous verbal rehearsal in memory task as a function of age. *Child Development, 37*, 283–299.

FLAVELL, J. H., FRIEDRICHS, A. G., & HOYT, J. D. (1970). Developmental changes in memorization processes. *Cognitive Psychology, 1*, 324–340.

FLAVELL, J. H., SHIPSTEAD, S. G., & CROFT, K. (1980). What young children think you see when their eyes are closed. *Cognition, 8*, 369–387.

FLAVELL, J. H., SPEER, J. R., GREEN, F. L., & AUGUST, D. L. (1981). The development of comprehension monitoring and knowledge about communication. *Monographs of the Society for Research in Child Development, 46*(5, Serial No. 192).

FLESCH, R. (1955). *Why Johnny can't read*. New York: Harper & Row.

FOLSTEIN, S., & RUTTER, M. (1978). Genetic influences and infantile autism. In S. Chess & A. Thomas (Eds.), *Annual progress in child psychiatry and child development: 1978*. New York: Brunner/Mazel.

FOX, H.E., STEINBRECHER, M., PESSEL, D., INGLES, J., MEDVID, L., & ANGEL, E. (1978). Maternal ethanol ingestion and the occurrence of human fetal breathing movements. *American Journal of Obstetrics and Gynecology, 132*, 354–358.

FOX, R., ASLIN, R. N., SHEA, S. L., & DUMAIS, S. T. (1980). Stereopsis in human infants. *Science, 207*, 323–324.

FRAIBERG, S. H. (1959). *The magic years*. New York: Scribner's.

FRAIBERG, S. (1977). *Insights from the blind: Comparative studies of blind and sighted infants*. New York: Basic Books.

FREEDMAN, D. G. (1979). *Human sociobiology*. New York: The Free Press.

FREEDMAN, D. G., & KELLER, B. (1963). Inheritance of behavior in infants. *Science, 140*, 196–198.

FREUD, A., & DANN, S. (1967). An experiment in group upbringing. In Y. Brackbill & G. G. Thompson (Eds.), *Behavior in infancy and early childhood*. New York: The Free Press.

FREUD, S. (1938). The history of the psychoanalytic movement. In A. A. Brill (Ed. and trans.), *The basic writings of Sigmund Freud*. New York: Modern Library.

FREUD, S. (1950). The analysis of a phobia in a five-year old boy. In *Collected Papers* (Vol. I). London: Hogarth. (Originally published in 1909.)

FREUD, S. (1965). *New introductory lectures in psychoanalysis* (J. Strachey, Ed. and trans.). New York: Norton. (Originally published in 1933.)

FRISCH, R. E., & REVELLE, R. (1970). Height and weight at menarche and a hypothesis of critical body weights and adolescent events. *Science, 169*, 397–399.

FRODI, A. M. (1981). Contribution of infant characteristics to child abuse. *American Journal of Mental Deficiency, 85*, 341–349.

FRY, P. S. (1975). Affect and resistance to temptation. *Developmental Psychology, 11*, 466–472.

FULLARD, W., & REILING, A. M. (1976). An investigation of Lorenz's "babyness." *Child Development, 47*, 1191–1193.

GALLUP, G. G. (1970). Chimpanzees: Self-recognition. *Science, 167*, 86–87.

GARDNER, B. T., & GARDNER, R. A. (1971). Two-way communication with an infant chimpanzee. In A. M. Schrier & F. Stollnitz (Eds.), *Behavior of Nonhuman Primates* (Vol. 4). New York: Academic Press.

GARDNER, H. (1980). *Artful scribbles: The significance of children's drawings*. New York: Basic Books.

GARDNER, L. I. (1972, January). Deprivation dwarfism. *Scientific American*, pp. 101–107.

GELMAN, R. (1978). Cognitive development. In L. W. Porter & M. R. Rosenzweig (Eds.), *Annual Review of Psychology* (Vol. 29). Palo Alto, Calif.: Annual Reviews.

GESELL, A., & AMES, L. B. (1947). The development of handedness. *Journal of Genetic Psychology, 70*, 155–175.

GESELL, A., & THOMPSON, H. (1929). Learning and growth in identical infant twins: An experimental study by the method of co-twin control. *Genetic Psychology Monographs, 6*, 1–125.

GESHWIND, N. (1979, September). Specializations of the human brain. *Scientific American, 241*(3), 180–199.

GEWIRTZ, J. L. (1972). Attachment, dependence, and a distinction in terms of stimulus control. In J. L. Gewirtz

(Ed.), *Attachment and dependency*. Washington, D.C.: Winston & Sons.

GIBBONS, M. (1974). Walkabout: Searching for the right passage from childhood and school. *Phi Delta Kappan, 55,* 596–602.

GIBSON, E. J., & WALK, R. D. (1960, April). The "visual cliff." *Scientific American,* pp. 64–71.

GINSBURG, H., & OPPER, S. (1969). *Piaget's theory of intellectual development: An introduction*. Englewood Cliffs, N.J.: Prentice-Hall.

GINSBURG, H. J., & MILLER, S. M. (1982). Sex differences in children's risk-taking behavior. *Child Development, 53,* 426–428.

GINZBERG, E. (1972). Toward a theory of occupational choice: A restatement. *Vocational Guidance Quarterly, 20,* 169–176.

GLASER, K. (1981). Psychopathologic patterns in depressed adolescents. *American Journal of Psychotherapy, 35,* 368–382.

GLEASON, J. B. (1967). Do children imitate? *Proceedings of the International Conference on Oral Education of the Deaf, 2,* 1441–1448.

GLEITMAN, H. (1981). *Psychology*. New York: Norton.

GLEITMAN, L. R., & GLEITMAN, H. (1981). Language. In H. Gleitman, *Psychology*. New York: Norton.

GLUCKSBERG, S., HAY, A., & DANKS, J. H. (1976). Words in utterance contexts: Young children do not confuse the meanings of *same* and *different*. *Child Development, 47,* 737–741.

GLUCKSBERG, S., & KRAUSS, R. M. (1967). What do people say after they have learned to talk? Studies of the development of referential communication. *Merrill-Palmer Quarterly, 13,* 309–316.

GLUCKSBERG, S., KRAUSS, R. M., & WEISBERG, R. (1966). Referential communication in nursery school children: Method and some preliminary findings. *Journal of Experimental Child Psychology, 3,* 333–342.

GLUECK, S., & GLUECK, E. (1950). *Unraveling juvenile delinquency*. Cambridge: Harvard University Press.

GLUECK, S., & GLUECK, E. (1974). *Of delinquency and crime*. Springfield, Ill.: Charles C. Thomas.

GOERTZEL, V., & GOERTZEL, M. G. (1962). *Cradles of eminence*. Boston: Little, Brown.

GOLDMAN, R. J., & GOLDMAN, J. D. G. (1982). How children perceive the origin of babies and the roles of mothers and fathers in procreation: A cross-national study. *Child Development, 53,* 491–504.

GOODMAN, S. H. (1981). The integration of verbal and motor behavior in preschool children. *Child Development, 52,* 280–289.

GOODNOW, J. (1977). *Children drawing*. Cambridge: Harvard University Press.

GORMAN, J. J., COGEN, D. G., & GELLIS, S. S. (1967). Testing the visual acuity of infants. In Y. Brackbill & G. G. Thompson (Eds.), *Behavior in infancy and early childhood*. New York: The Free Press.

GOSHEN-GOTTSTEIN, E. R. (1981). Differential maternal socialization of opposite-sexed twins, triplets, and quadruplets. *Child Development, 52,* 1255–1264.

GOTTMAN, J., GONSO, J., & RASMUSSEN, B. (1975). Social interaction, social competence, and friendship in children. *Child Development, 46,* 709–718.

GOULD, S. J. (1979, May). Mickey Mouse meets Konrad Lorenz. *Natural History,* pp. 30–36.

GRAHAM, P., RUTTER, M., & GEORGE, S. (1973). Temperamental characteristics as predictors of behavior disorders in children. *American Journal of Orthopsychiatry, 49,* 328–399.

GRATCH, G. (1975). Recent studies based on Piaget's view of object concept development. In L. B. Cohen & P. Salapatek (Eds.), *Infant perception: From sensation to cognition* (Vol. 2). New York: Academic Press.

GRAZIANO, W. G., MUSSER, L. M., ROSEN, S., & SHAFFER, D. R. (1982). The development of fair-play standards in same-race and mixed-race situations. *Child Development, 53,* 938–947.

GREEN, C. P. & LOWE, S. J. (1975). Teenage pregnancy: A major problem for minors. *Zero Population Growth National Reporter, 7,* 4–5.

GREEN, K. D., FOREHAND, R., BECK, S. J., & VOSK, B. (1980). An assessment of the relationship among measures of children's social competence and children's academic achievement. *Child Development, 51,* 1149–1156.

GREEN, M. G., BLAKE, B. F., CARBOY, G. J., & ZEHAUSEN, R. T. (1971). Personality characteristics of the middle class high school drug user. *Proceedings of the Annual Convention of the American Psychological Association, 6,* 559–560.

GREENFIELD, P. M. (1966). On culture and conservation. In J. S. Bruner, R. R. Olver, & P. M. Greenfield (Eds.), *Studies in cognitive growth*. New York: John Wiley.

GRIEVE, R., & GARTON, A. (1981). On the young child's comparison of sets. *Journal of Experimental Child Psychology, 32,* 443–458.

GRUSEC, J. E., & KUCZYNSKI, L. (1980). Direction of effect in socialization: A comparison of the parent's versus the child's behavior as determinants of disciplinary techniques. *Developmental Psychology, 16,* 1–9.

GUMPERZ, J. J., & TANNEN, D. (1979). Individual and social differences in language use. In C. J. Fillmore, D. Kempler, & W. S-Y. Wang (Eds.), *Individual differences in language ability and language behavior*. New York: Academic Press.

HALLER, A. O., OTTO, L. B., MEIER, R. F., & OHLENDORF, G. W. (1974). Level of occupational aspiration: An empirical analysis. *American Sociological Review, 39,* 113–121.

HALVERSON, C. F., JR., & WALDROP, M. F. (1976). Relations between preschool activity and aspects of intellectual and social behavior at age 7½. *Developmental Psychology, 12,* 107–112.

HANRATTY, M. A., LIEBERT, R. M., MORRIS, L. W., & FERNANDEZ, L. E. (1969). Imitation of film-mediated aggression against live and inanimate victims. *Proceedings of the 77th Annual Convention of the American Psychological Association, 4,* 457–458 (Abstract).

HANSEN, H., BELMONT, L., & STEIN, Z. (1980). Epidemiology. In J. Wortis (Ed.), *Mental retardation and developmental disabilities* (Vol. 2). New York: Brunner/Mazel.

HANSON, D. R., & GOTTESMAN, I. I. (1976). The genetics, if any, of infantile autism and childhood schizophrenia. *Journal of Autism and Childhood Schizophrenia, 6,* 209–234.

HANSON, J. W., STREISSGUTH, A. P., & SMITH, D. W. (1978).

The effects of moderate alcohol consumption during pregnancy on fetal growth and morphogenesis. *Journal of Pediatrics, 92,* 457–460.

HARDY-BROWN, K., PLOMIN, R., & DEFRIES, J. C. (1981). Genetic and environmental influences on the rate of communicative development in the first year of life. *Developmental Psychology, 17,* 704–717.

HARLOW, H. F. (1971). *Learning to love.* San Francisco: Albion.

HARLOW, H. F., & HARLOW, M. K. (1965). The affectional systems. In A. M. Schrier, H. F. Harlow, & F. Stollnitz (Eds.), *Behavior of nonhuman primates* (Vol. 2). New York: Academic Press.

HARLOW, H. F., & HARLOW, M. K. (1962, November). Social deprivation in monkeys. *Scientific American,* pp. 136–146.

HARPER, J., & COLLINS, J. K. (1972). The effects of early or late maturation on the prestige of the adolescent girl. *Australian and New Zealand Journal of Sociology, 8,* 83–88.

HARPER, L. V., & SANDERS, K. M. (1978). Preschool children's use of space: Sex differences in outdoor play. In M. S. Smart & R. C. Smart (Eds.), *Preschool children: Development and relationships.* New York: Macmillan.

HARPER, R. M., LEAKE, B., HOFFMAN, H., WALTER, D. O., HOPPENBROUWERS, T., HODGMAN, J., & STERMAN, M. B. (1981). Periodicity of sleep states is altered in infants at risk for the Sudden Infant Death Syndrome. *Science, 213,* 1030–1032.

HARRELL, T. W., & HARRELL, M. S. (1945). Army General Classification Test scores for civilian occupations. *Educational and Psychological Measurement, 5,* 229–239.

HARRIS, C. S. (1965). Perceptual adaptation to inverted, reversed, and displaced vision. *Psychological Review, 72,* 419–444.

HARRIS, C. S. (1980). Insight or out of sight? Two examples of perceptual plasticity in the human adult. In C. S. Harris (Ed.), *Visual coding and adaptability.* Hillsdale, N.J.: Erlbaum.

HARRIS, S. H. (1982). An evaluation of the Snijders-Oomen Nonverbal Intelligence Scale for Young Children. *Journal of Pediatric Psychology, 7,* 239–251.

HARTER, S. (1978). Pleasure derived from challenge and the effects of receiving grades on children's difficulty level choices. *Child Development, 49,* 788–799.

HARTER, S. (1982). The perceived competence scale for children. *Child Development, 53,* 87–97.

HARTSHORNE, H., & MAY, M. A. (1928). *Studies in the nature of character.* Vol. 1: *Studies in deceit.* New York: Macmillan.

HARVEY, A. (1975). Goal setting as a compensation for fear of success. *Adolescence, 10,* 137–142.

HASS, A. (1979). *Teenage sexuality,* New York: Macmillan.

HAVIGHURST, R. J. (1974). Youth in crisis. *School Review, 83,* 5–10.

HEBER, R. (1978). Research in prevention of socio-cultural mental retardation. In D. G. Forgays (Ed.), *Primary prevention of psychopathology.* Vol. 2, *Environmental influences.* Hanover, N.H.: University Press of New England.

HEBER, R., GARBER, H., HARRINGTON, S., HOFFMAN, C., & FALENDAR, C. (1972). *Rehabilitation of families at risk for mental retardation.* Madison: Rehabilitation Research and Training Center in Mental Retardation, University of Wisconsin.

HEIN, A. (1980). The development of visually guided behavior. In C. S. Harris (Ed.), *Visual coding and adaptability.* Hillsdale, N.J.: Erlbaum.

HEIN, A., & HELD, R. (1967). Dissociation of the visual placing response into elicited and guided components. *Science, 158,* 390–391.

HELD, R., & BAUER, J., JR. (1967). Visually guided reaching in infant monkeys after restricted rearing. *Science, 155,* 718–720.

HERKOWITZ, J. (1978). Sex-role expectations and motor behavior of the young child. In M. V. Ridenour (Ed.), *Motor development: Issues and applications.* Princeton, N.J.: Princeton Book Co.

HERRNSTEIN, R. J. (1973). *IQ in the meritocracy.* Boston: Atlantic Monthly Press.

HERRON, C. R., & JOHNSTON, D. (1975, August 24). There is less dropping out. *New York Times.*

HESS, E. H. (1970). The ethological approach to socialization. In R. A. Hoppe, G. A. Milton, & E. C. Simmel (Eds.), *Early experiences and the processes of socialization.* New York: Academic Press.

HESS, R. D., & SHIPMAN, V. C. (1965). Early experience and the socialization of cognitive modes in children. *Child Development, 36,* 869–886.

HESS, R. D., & SHIPMAN, V. C. (1968). Maternal attitudes toward the school and the role of the pupil: Some social class comparisons. In A. H. Passow (Ed.), *Developing programs for the educationally disadvantaged.* New York: Teachers College, Columbia University.

HETHERINGTON, E. M. (1979). Divorce: A child's perspective. *American Psychologist, 34,* 851–858.

HETHERINGTON, E. M., & MARTIN, B. (1979). Family interaction. In H. C. Quay & J. Werry (Eds.), *Psychological disorders of childhood* (2nd ed.). New York: John Wiley.

HICKS, R. E., & KINSBOURNE, M. (1977). Human handedness. In M. Kinsbourne (Ed.), *The asymmetrical function of the brain.* New York: Cambridge University Press.

HINDELANG, M. J., GOTTFREDSON, M. R., & FLANAGAN, T. J. (Eds.) (1981). *Sourcebook of criminal justice statistics—1980.* U.S. Department of Justice, Bureau of Justice Statistics. Washington, D.C.: U.S. Government Printing Office.

HINDELANG, M. J., HIRSCHI, T., AND WEIS, J. (1981). *Measuring delinquency.* Beverly Hills, Calif.: Sage Publications.

HOBSON, R. P. (1980). The question of egocentrism: The young child's competence in the coordination of perspectives. *Journal of Child Psychology and Psychiatry, 21,* 325–331.

HOCHBERG, J., & BROOKS, V. (1962). Pictorial recognition as an unlearned ability: A study of one child's performance. *American Journal of Psychology, 75,* 624–628.

HODAPP R. M., and MUELLER, E. (1982). Early social development in men. In B. B. Wolman, G. Stricker, S. J. Ellman, P. Keith-Spiegel, and D. S. Palermo (Eds.), *Handbook of developmental psychology.* Englewood Cliffs, N.J.: Prentice-Hall.

HOFFMAN, M. L. (1975a). Moral internalization, parental power, and the nature of parent-child interaction. *Developmental Psychology, 11,* 228–239.

HOFFMAN, M. L. (1975b). Developmental synthesis of affect

and cognition and its implications for altruistic motivation. *Developmental Psychology, 11,* 607–622.

HOFFMAN, M. L. (1977). Moral internalization: Current theory and research. In L. Berkowitz (Ed.), Advances in experimental social psychology (Vol. 10). New York: Academic Press.

HOFFMAN, L. W. (1979). Maternal employment: 1979. *American Psychologist, 34,* 859–865.

HOLDEN, C. (1979). Teenage pregnancies out of control. *Science, 204,* 597.

HOLSTEIN, C. B. (1976). Irreversible, stepwise sequence in the development of moral judgment: A longitudinal study of males and females. *Child Development, 47,* 51–61.

HORNER, M. S. (1969, November). A bright woman is caught in a double bind. *Psychology Today, 3,* 36–38.

HORNER, M. S. (1972). Toward an understanding of achievement-related conflicts in women. *Journal of Social Issues, 28,* 157–176.

HOROWITZ, F. D. (1980). Intervention program. In A. W. Brann & J. J. Volpe (Eds.), *Neonatal neurological assessment and outcome.* Report of the 77th Ross Conference on Pediatric Research. Columbus, Ohio: Ross Laboratories.

HOUTS, A. C., LIEBERT, R. M., & PADAWER, W. (1983). A delivery system for the treatment of primary enuresis. *Journal of Abnormal Child Psychology, 11,* 513–520.

HUBEL, D. H., & WIESEL, T. N. (1970). The period of susceptibility to the physiological effects of unilateral eye closure in kittens. *Journal of Physiology, 206,* 419–436.

HUDSON, L. M., FORMAN, E. A., & BRION-MEISELS, S. (1982). Role-taking as a predictor of prosocial behavior in cross-age tutors. *Child Development, 53,* 1320–1329.

HUDSON, W. (1960). Pictorial depth perception in subcultural groups in Africa. *Journal of Social Psychology, 52,* 183–208.

HULSEBUS, R. C. (1975). Latency of crying cessation measuring infants' discrimination of mothers' voices. Paper presented at meeting of Americal Psychological Association, Chicago.

HUNTINGTON, G. E. (1981, February). Children of the Hutterites. *Natural History,* pp. 34–47.

HYDE, J. S., & SCHUCK, J. R. (1977, September). The development of sex differences in aggression: A revised model. Paper presented at the annual meeting of the American Psychological Association, San Francisco.

HYMEL, S., & ASHER, S. R. (1977, March). Assessment and training of isolated children's social skills. Paper presented at the biennial meeting of the Society for Research in Child Development, New Orleans.

HYND, G. L., OBRZUT, J. E., & OBRZUT, A. (1981). Are lateral and perceptual asymmetries related to WISC-R and achievement test performance in normal and learning-disabled children? *Journal of Consulting and Clinical Psychology, 49,* 977–979.

INHELDER, B., & PIAGET, J. (1958). *The growth of logical thinking from childhood to adolescence.* New York: Basic Books.

INHELDER, B., & PIAGET, J. (1964). *The early growth of logic in the child.* New York: Norton.

ISAACS, C. (1981). A brief review of the characteristics of abuse-prone parents. *The Behavior Therapist, 4*(5), 5–8.

ISCOE, I., WILLIAMS, M., & HARVEY, J. (1963). Modification of children's judgment by a simulated group technique: A normative developmental study. *Child Development, 34,* 963–978.

JACKLIN, C. N. (1981). Methodological issues in the study of sex-related differences. *Developmental Review, 1,* 266–273.

JACKSON, J. F., & JACKSON, J. H. (1978). *Infant culture.* New York: Thomas Y. Crowell.

JACOBS, B. S., & MOSS, H. A. (1976). Birth order and sex of sibling as determinants of mother-infant interaction. *Child Development, 47,* 315–322.

JEFFREY, W. E. (1958). Variables in early discrimination learning. I. Motor responses in the training of a left-right discrimination. *Child Development, 29,* 269–275.

JEFFRIES, V. (1974). Political generations and the acceptance or rejection of nuclear warfare. *Journal of Social Issues, 30,* 119–136.

JENSEN, A. R. (1969). How much can we boost IQ and scholastic achievement? *Harvard Educational Review, 39,* 1–123.

JENSEN, A. R. (1974). How biased are culture-loaded tests? *Genetic Psychology Monographs, 90,* 185–244.

JENSEN, A. R. (1981). *Straight talk about mental tests.* New York: Free Press.

JESSOR, R., COSTA, F., JESSOR, L., DONOVAN, J. E. (1983). Time of first intercourse: A prospective study. *Journal of Personality and Social Psychology, 44,* 608–626.

JESSOR, R., & JESSOR, S. L. (1980). Adolescent development and the onset of drinking. In R. E. Muus (Ed.), *Adolescent behavior and society.* New York: Random House.

JOHNSON, C. J., PICK, H. L., Jr., SIEGEL, G. M., CICCIARELLI, A. W., & GARBER, S. R. (1981). Effects of interpersonal distance on children's vocal intensity. *Child Development, 52,* 721–723.

JOHNSON, J. E., & McGILLICUDDY-DELISI, A. (1983). Family environment factors and children's knowledge of rules and conventions. *Child Development, 54,* 218–226.

JONES, M. C. (1924). The elimination of children's fears. *Journal of Experimental Psychology, 7,* 383–390.

JUHASZ, A. M. (1976). Changing patterns of premarital sexual behavior. *Intellect, 104,* 511–514.

JULESZ, B. (1971). *Foundations of cyclopean perception.* Chicago: University of Chicago Press.

JURICH, A. P., & JURICH, J. A. (1975). The lost adolescence syndrome. *Family Coordinator, 24,* 357–361.

KAGAN, J. (1965). Impulsive and reflective children: Significance of conceptual tempo. In J. D. Krumboltz (Ed.), *Learning and the educational process.* Chicago: Rand McNally.

KAGAN, J. (1978, January). The baby's elastic mind. *Human Nature,* pp. 66–73.

KAGAN, J. (1979). Family experience and the child's development. *American Psychologist, 34,* 886–891.

KAGAN, J., & KOGAN, N. (1970). Individual variation in cognitive processes. In P. H. Mussen (Ed.), *Carmichael's manual of child psychology* (Vol. 1). New York: John Wiley.

KAGAN, J., KEARSLEY, R. B., & ZELAZO, P. R. (1978). *Infancy: Its place in human development.* Cambridge: Harvard University Press.

KAGAN, J., ROSMAN, B. L., DAY, D., ALBERT, J., & PHILLIPS, W.

(1964). Information processing in the child: Significance of analytic and reflective attitudes. *Psychological Monographs, 78* (1, Whole No. 578).

KAMIN, L. (1974). *The Science and politics of IQ.* Hillsdale, N.J.: Erlbaum.

KANDEL, D. B. (1980). Drug and drinking behavior among youth. *Annual Review of Sociology, 6*, 235–286.

KANNER, L. (1951). The conception of wholes and parts in early infantile autism. *American Journal of Psychiatry, 108*, 23–26.

KANNER, L. (1973). Early infantile autism revisited. In G. Usdin (Ed.), *The psychiatric forum.* New York: Brunner/Mazel.

KANTNER, J. (1974, September). Teenage sexual and reproductive behavior. Paper presented at meetings of the American Psychological Association, New Orleans.

KATCHADOURIAN, H. A. (1971). *The Biology of adolescence.* San Francisco: W. H. Freeman & Company.

KATCHADOURIAN, H. A. (1977). *The biology of adolescence.* San Francisco: W. H. Freeman.

KATKOVSKY, W., CRANDALL, V. C., & GOOD, S. (1967). Parental antecedents of children's beliefs in internal-external control of reinforcements in intellectual achievement situations. *Child Development, 38*, 765–776.

KATZ, R. B., SHANKWEILER, D., & LIBERMAN, I. Y. (1981). Memory for item order and phonetic recoding in the beginning reader. *Journal of Experimental Child Psychology, 32*, 474–484.

KAY, H. (1970). Analyzing motor skill performance. In K. Connolly (Ed.), *Mechanisms of motor skill development.* New York: Academic Press.

KEENEY, T. J., CANNIZZO, S. R., & FLAVELL, J. H. (1967). Spontaneous and induced verbal rehearsal in recall tasks. *Child Development, 38*, 953–966.

KELLER, A., FORD, L. H., JR., & MEACHAM, J. A. (1978). Dimensions of self-concept in preschool children. *Developmental Psychology, 14*, 483–489.

KELLER, B. B., & BELL, R. Q. (1979). Child effects on adult's method of eliciting altruistic behavior. *Child Development, 50*, 1004–1009.

KELLER, H. (1905). *The story of my life.* New York: Grosset & Dunlap.

KELLOGG, R. (1969). *Analyzing children's art.* Palo Alto, Calif.: National Press.

KEMPE, R. S., & KEMPE, C. H. (1978). *Child abuse.* Cambridge: Harvard University Press.

KENDLER, H. H., & KENDLER, T. S. (1962). Vertical and horizontal processes in problem solving. *Psychological Review, 69*, 1–16.

KENDLER, T. S. (1963). Development of mediating responses in children. In J. C. Wright & J. Kagan (Eds.), *Basic cognitive processes in children. Monographs of the Society for Research in Child Development, 28*(2), 38–52.

KENDLER, T. S. (1974). The effect of training and stimulus variables on the reversal-shift ontogeny. *Journal of Experimental Child Psychology, 17*, 87–106.

KENDLER, T. S., KENDLER, H. H., & LEARNARD, B. (1962). Mediated responses to size and brightness as a function of age. *American Journal of Psychology, 75*, 571–586.

KENISTON, K. (1975). Prologue: Youth as a stage of life. In National Society for the Study of Education, *Youth: The 74th Yearbook of the National Society for the Study of Education* (Part I). Chicago: University of Chicago Press.

KENISTON, K. (1965). *The Uncommitted.* New York: Delta.

KEOGH, J. (1973). Development in fundamental motor tasks. In C. B. Corbin (Ed.), *A Textbook of Motor Development.* Dubuque, Iowa: Brown.

KIMMEL, H. D., & KIMMEL, E. C. (1970). An instrumental conditioning method for the treatment of enuresis. *Journal of Behavior Therapy and Experimental Psychiatry, 1*, 121–123.

KINSBOURNE, M., & HISCOCK, M. (1977). Does cerebral dominance develop? In S. J. Segalowitz & F. Gruber (Eds.), *Language development and neurological theory.* New York: Academic Press.

KLAUS, M. H., & KENNELL, J. H. (1978). Parent-to-infant attachment. In J. H. Stevens, Jr., & M. Mathews (Eds.), *Mother/child, father/child relationships.* Washington, D.C.: National Association for the Education of Young Children.

KNOPF, I. J. (1979). *Childhood psychopathology: A developmental approach.* Englewood Cliffs, N.J.: Prentice-Hall.

KOHLBERG, L. (1966). A cognitive-developmental analysis of children's sex-role concepts and attitudes. In E. E. Maccoby (Ed.), *The development of sex differences.* Stanford: Stanford University Press.

KOHLBERG, L. (1968, April). The child as a moral philosopher. *Psychology Today, 2*, 25–30.

KOHLBERG, L. (1969). Stage and sequence: The cognitive-developmental approach to socialization. In D. A. Goslin (Ed.), *Handbook of socialization theory and research.* Chicago: Rand McNally.

KOHLBERG, L., & KRAMER, R. (1969). Continuities and discontinuities in childhood and adult moral development. *Human Development, 12*, 93–120.

KOLUCHOVÁ, J. (1972). Severe deprivation in twins: A case study. *Journal of Child Psychology and Psychiatry, 13*, 107–114.

KOLUCHOVÁ, J. (1976). The further development of twins after severe and prolonged deprivation: A second report. *Journal of Child Psychology and Psychiatry, 17*, 181–188.

KOMAROVSKY, M. (1973). Cultural contradictions and sex roles: The masculine case. *American Journal of Sociology, 78*, 873–884.

KOMPARA, D. R. (1980). Difficulties in the socialization process of stepparenting. *Family Relations, 29*, 69–73.

KONNER, M. (1977). Evolution of human behavior development. In P. H. Leiderman, S. R. Tulkin, & A. Rosenfeld (Eds.), *Culture and infancy: Variations in the human experience.* New York: Academic Press.

KONNER, M. (1977). Infancy among the Kalahari Desert San. In P. H. Leiderman, S. R. Tulkin, & A. Rosenfeld (Eds.), *Culture and infancy: Variations in the human experience.* New York: Academic Press.

KORNER, A. F. (1974). The effect of the infant's state, level of arousal, sex, and ontogenetic state on the caregiver. In M. Lewis & L. A. Rosenblum (Eds.), *The effect of the infant on its caregiver.* New York: John Wiley.

KOTELCHUCK, M. (1975, September). Father caretaking characteristics and their influence on infant-father interaction. Paper presented at the American Psychological Association meeting, Chicago.

KOTELCHUCK, M. (1976). The infant's relationship to the father: Experimental evidence. In M. E. Lamb (Ed.), *The* role of the father in child development. New York: Wiley.

KRATCOSKI, P. C., & KRATCOSKI, J. E. (1975). Changing patterns in the delinquent activities of boys and girls: A self-reported delinquency analysis. *Adolescence, 10,* 83–91.

KRAMER, P. E., KOFF, E., & LURIA, Z. (1972). The development of competence in an exceptional language structure in older children and young adults. *Child Development, 43,* 121–130.

KREBS, D., & GILLMORE, J. (1982). The relationship among the first stages of cognitive development, role-taking abilities, and moral development. *Child Development, 53,* 877–886.

KUCZYNSKI, L. (1983). Reasoning, prohibitions, and motivations for compliance. *Developmental Psychology, 19,* 126–134.

LADD, G. W., & ODEN, S. (1979). The relationship between peer acceptance and children's ideas about helpfulness. *Child Development, 50,* 402–408.

LAMB, M. (1977). Father-infant and mother-infant interactions in the first year of life. *Child Development, 48,* 167–181.

LAMB, M. E. (1978). The father's role in the infant's social world. In J. H. Stevens, Jr., & M. Mathews (Eds.), *Mother/child, father/child relationships.* Washington, D.C.: National Association for the Education of Young Children.

LAMBERT, W., & MEYERS, C. E. (1977, April). From California: Two views. *APA Monitor,* pp. 4–5, 180.

LANDAU, E. (1983). *Why are they starving themselves? Understanding anorexia nervosa and bulimia.* New York: Julian Messner.

LANE, H. (1976). *The wild boy of Aveyron.* Cambridge: Harvard University Press.

LANGLOIS, J. H., & DOWNS, A. C. (1979). Peer relations as a function of physical attractiveness: The eye of the beholder or behavioral reality? *Child Development, 50,* 409–418.

LASKY, R. E., KLEIN, R. E., YARBROUGH, C., ENGLE, P. L., LECHTIG, A., & MARTORELL, R. (1981). The relationship between physical growth and infant behavioral development in rural Guatemala. *Child Development, 52,* 219–226.

LEBLANC, A. F. (1969). Time orientation and time estimation: A function of age. *Journal of Genetic Psychology, 115,* 187–194.

LEFKOWITZ, M. M., ERON, L. D., WALDER, L. O., & HUESMANN, L. R. (1977). *Growing up to be violent.* New York: Pergamon Press.

LEMPERS, J. D., FLAVELL, E. R., & FLAVELL, J. H. (1977). The development in very young children of tacit knowledge concerning visual perception. *Genetic Psychology Monographs, 95,* 3–53.

LENNEBERG, E. H. (1964). A biological perspective of language. In E. H. Lenneberg (Ed.), *New directions in the study of language.* Cambridge: MIT Press.

LEPPER, M. R., GREENE, D., & NISBETT, R. E. (1973). Undermining children's intrinsic interest with extrinsic reward: A test of the "overjustification" hypothesis. *Journal of Personality and Social Psychology, 28,* 129–137.

LEVENSTEIN, P. (1970). Cognitive growth in preschoolers through verbal interaction with mothers. *American Journal of Orthopsychiatry, 40,* 426–432.

LEVINE, R. A. (1977). Child rearing as cultural adaptation. In P. H. Leiderman, S. R. Tulkin, & A. Rosenfeld (Eds.), *Culture and infancy: Variations in the human experience.* New York: Academic Press.

LEVINE, S. (1960, May). Stimulation in infancy. *Scientific American, 202*(5), 80–86.

LEVINE, S. (1971, January). Stress and behavior. *Scientific American, 224*(1), 26–31.

LEWIS, M., & BROOKS, J. (1975). Infants' social perception: A constructivist view. In L. B. Cohen & P. Salapatek (Eds.), *Infant perception: From sensation to cognition* (Vol. 2). New York: Academic Press.

LIBEN, L. S., & BELKNAP, B. (1981). Intellectual realism: Implications for investigations of perceptual perspective taking in young children. *Child Development, 52,* 921–924.

LIBERMAN, I. Y., SHANKWEILER, D., LIBERMAN, A. M., FOWLER, C., & FISCHER, F. W. (1977). Phonetic segmentation and recoding in the beginning reader. In A. S. Reber and D. S. Scarborough (Eds.), *Toward a psychology of reading.* Hillsdale, N.J.: Erlbaum.

LICKONA, T. (1976). Critical issues in the study of moral development and behavior. In T. Lickona (Ed.), *Moral development and behavior.* New York: Holt, Rinehart & Winston.

LIDZ, T. (1976). *The person: His and her development throughout the life cycle* (2nd ed.). New York: Basic Books.

LIEBERT, R. M., SPRAFKIN, J. N., & POULOS, R. W. (1975). Selling cooperation to children. In W. S. Hale (Ed.), *Proceedings of the 20th Annual Conference of the Advertising Research Foundation.* New York: Advertising Research Foundation, Inc.

LINTON, M. (1980). Information processing and developmental memory: An overview. In R. L. Ault (Ed.), *Developmental perspectives.* Santa Monica, Calif.: Goodyear Publishing Co.

LIPSITT, L. P. (1980). Taste, smell, and other pleasures of sensation. In A. W. Brann & J. J. Volpe (Eds.), *Neonatal neurological assessment and outcome.* Report of the 77th Ross Conference on Pediatric Research. Columbus, Ohio: Ross Laboratories.

LIPSITT, L. P., & LEVY, N. (1959). Electrotactual threshhold in the neonate. *Child Development, 30,* 547–554.

LOEBER, R. (1982). The stability of antisocial and delinquent child behavior: A review. *Child Development, 53,* 1431–1446.

LOEHLIN, J. C., & NICHOLS, R. C. (1976). *Heredity, environment and personality.* Austin: University of Texas Press.

LONDERVILLE, S., & MAIN, M. (1981). Security of attachment, compliance, and maternal training methods in the second year of life. *Developmental Psychology, 17,* 289–299.

LONGSTRETH, L. E. (1980). Human handedness: More evidence for genetic involvement. *Journal of Genetic Psychology, 137,* 275–283.

LONGSTRETH, L. E., LONGSTRETH, G. V., RAMIREZ, C., & FERNANDEZ, G. (1978). The ubiquity of big brother. In M. S. Smart & R. C. Smart (Eds.), *School-age children.* New York: Macmillan.

LORBER J. (1981, April). The disposable cortex. *Psychology Today*, p. 126.

LORENZ, K. (1971). *Studies in animal and human behaviour* (Vol. 2). Cambridge: Harvard University Press.

LOVELL, K. (1971). Some problems associated with formal thought and its assessment. In D. R. Green, M. P. Ford, and G. B. Flamer (Eds.), *Measurement and Piaget*. New York: McGraw-Hill.

LOWREY, G. H. (1978). Growth and development of children (7th ed.). Chicago: Year Book Medical Publishers.

LYTTON, H., CONWAY, D., & SAUVÉ, R. (1977). The impact of twinship on parent-child interaction. *Journal of Personality and Social Psychology, 35*, 97–107.

MACCOBY, E. E., & JACKLIN, C. N. (1974). *The psychology of sex differences*. Stanford: Stanford University Press.

MACCOBY, E. E., & JACKLIN, C. N. (1980). Sex differences in aggression: A rejoinder and reprise. *Child Development, 51*, 964–980.

MACFARLANE, J., ALLEN, L., & HONZIK, M. P. (1954). *A developmental study of the behavior problems of normal children between twenty-one months and fourteen years*. Berkeley: University of California Press.

MACKLIN, E. D. (1972). Heterosexual cohabitation among unmarried college students. *The Family Coordinator, 21*(4), 463–472.

MADDEN, J., LEVENSTEIN, P., & LEVENSTEIN, S. (1976). Longitudinal I.Q. outcomes of the mother-child home program. *Child Development, 47*, 1015–1025.

MADSEN, C. H., BECKER, W. C., THOMAS, D. R., KOSER, L., & PLAGER, E. (1968). An analysis of the reinforcing function of "sit-down" commands. In R. K. Parker (Ed.), *Readings in educational psychology*. Boston: Allyn and Bacon.

MADSEN, M. C. (1971). Developmental and cross-cultural differences in the cooperative and competitive behavior of young children. *Journal of Cross-Cultural Psychology, 2*, 365–371.

MALINA, R. M. (1982). Motor development in the early years. In S. Moore and C. R. Cooper (Eds.), *National Association for the Education of Young Children*. Washington, D.C., pp. 211–230.

MALINOWSKI, B. (1927). *Sex and repression in a savage society*. New York: Harcourt Brace Jovanovich.

MALLER, L., & DESOR, J. A. (1974). Effect of taste on ingestion by human newborns. In J. Bosma (Ed.), *Fourth symposium on oral sensation and perception: Development in the fetus and infant*. Washington, D.C.: U.S. Government Printing Office.

MANIS, F. R., & MORRISON, F. J. (1982). Processing of identity and position information in normal and disabled readers. *Journal of Experimental Child Psychology, 33*, 74–86.

MARCIA, J. E. (1966). Development and validation of ego identity status. *Journal of Personality and Social Psychology, 3*, 551–558.

MARCIA, J. E. (1976). Identity six years after: A follow-up study. *Journal of Youth and Adolescence, 15*, 150–153.

MASTERS, J. C., & FURMAN, W. (1981). Popularity, individual friendship selection, and specific peer interaction among children. *Developmental Psychology, 17*, 344–350.

MATAS, L., AREND, R., & SROUFE, L. A. (1979). Continuity of adaptation in the second year: The relationship between quality of attachment and later competence. *Child Development, 49*, 547–556.

MAURER, D. (1975). Infant visual perception: Methods of study. In L. B. Cohen & P. Salapatek (Eds.), *Infant perception: From sensation to cognition* (Vol. 1). New York: Academic Press.

MAURER, R. E. (1982). Dropout prevention: An intervention model for today's high schools. *Phi Delta Kappan, 63*, 470–471.

MCCALL, R. B. (1979). *Infants*. Cambridge: Harvard University Press.

MCCALL, R. B., APPELBAUM, M. I., & HOGARTY, P. S., (1973). Developmental changes in mental performance. *Monographs of the Society for Research in Child Development, 38*(3, Serial No. 150).

MCCALL, R. B., EICHORN, D. H., & HOGARTY, P. S. (1977). Transitions in early mental development. *Monographs of the Society for Research in Child Development, 42*(3, Serial No. 171).

MCCLELLAND, D. C. (1961). *The achieving society*. New York: The Free Press.

MCCLELLAND, D. C. (1971). *Motivational trends in society*. Morristown, N.J.: General Learning Press.

MCCLELLAND, D. C., ATKINSON, J. W., CLARK, R. A., & LOWELL, E. L. (1953). *The achievement motive*. New York: Appleton-Century-Crofts.

MCDAVID, J. W., & HARARI, H. (1966). Stereotyping of names and popularity in grade school children. *Child Development, 37*, 453–459.

MCGRATH, E. (1983, March 28). Confucian work ethic. *Time*, p. 52.

MCGRAW, M. B. (1967). Swimming behavior in the human infant. In Y. Brackbill & G. G. Thompson (Eds.), *Behavior in infancy and early childhood*. St. Louis: C. V. Mosby.

MCGUIRE, K. D., & WEISZ, J. R. (1982). Social cognition and behavior correlates of preadolescent chumship. *Child Development, 53*, 1478–1484.

MCKENZIE, B. E., & DAY, R. H. (1972). Object distance as a determinant of visual fixation in early infancy. *Science, 178*, 1108–1110.

MCNEILL, D. (1966). Developmental psycholinguistics. In F. Smith & G. A. Miller (Eds.), *The genesis of language: A psycholinguistic approach*. Cambridge: MIT Press.

MCSHANE, J. (1980). *Learning to talk*. Cambridge, England: Cambridge University Press.

MEAD, M. (1955). *Male and female*. New York: Mentor.

MEILMAN, P. N. (1979). Cross-sectional age changes in ego identity status during adolescence. *Developmental Psychology, 15*, 230–231.

MELTON, G. B. (1983, January). Toward "personhood" for adolescents. *American Psychologist*, 99–103.

MELTZOFF, A. N., & MOORE, M. K. (1977). Imitation of facial and manual gestures by human neonates. *Science, 198*, 75–78.

MENDELSON, M. J., & HAITH, M. M. (1976). The relation between audition and vision in the human newborn. *Monographs of the Society for Research in Child Development, 41* (Whole No. 4).

MEREDITH, H. V. (1978). Research between 1960 and 1970 on the standing height of young children in different parts of the world. In H. W. Reese and L. P. Lipsitt (Eds.), *Advances in child development and behavior* (Vol. 12). New York: Academic Press.

MEYER, B. (1980). The development of girls' sex-role attitudes. *Child Development, 51,* 508–514.

MICKLOS, J., JR. (1982). A look at reading achievement in the United States: The latest data. *Journal of Reading, 25,* 760–762.

MILLER, D. T., WEINSTEIN, S. M., & KARNIOL, R. (1978). Effects of age and self-verbalization on children's ability to delay gratification. *Developmental Psychology, 14,* 569–570.

MILLER, N. E., & DOLLARD, J. (1941). *Social learning and imitation.* New Haven: Yale University Press.

MILLER, P. H., KESSEL, F. S., and FLAVELL, J. H. (1970). Thinking about people thinking about people thinking about . . . : A study of social-cognitive development. *Child Development, 41,* 613–623.

MILLER, P. H., & WEISS, M. G. (1981). Children's attention allocation, understanding of attention, and performance on the incidental learning task. *Child Development, 52,* 1183–1190.

MILLER, P. H., & WEISS, M. G. (1982). Children's and adults' knowledge about what variables affect selective attention. *Child Development, 53,* 543–549.

MILLS, M., & MELHUISH, E. (1974). Recognition of mother's voice in early infancy. *Nature, 252,* 123–124.

MILNE, A. A. (1927). *Now we are six.* New York: Dutton.

MISCHEL, W. (1974). Processes in delay of gratification. In L. Berkowitz (Eds.), *Advances in experimental psychology* (Vol. 7). New York: Academic Press.

MISCHEL, W., & EBBESEN, E. (1970). Attention in delay of gratification. *Journal of Personality and Social Psychology, 16,* 329–337.

MISCHEL, W., & METZNER, R. (1962). Preference for a delayed reward as a function of age, intelligence, and length of delay interval. *Journal of Abnormal and Social Psychology, 64,* 425–431.

MISCHEL, W., & PATTERSON, C. J. (1976). Substantive and structural elements of effective plans for self-control. *Journal of Personality and Social Psychology, 34,* 942–950.

MITCHELL, D. E. (1980). The influence of early visual experience on visual perception. In C. S. Harris (Ed.), *Visual coding and adaptability.* Hillsdale, N.J.: Erlbaum.

MOELY, B. E., OLSON, F. A., HALWES, T. G., & FLAVELL, J. H. (1969). Production deficiency in young children's clustered recall. *Developmental Psychology, 1,* 26–34.

MOERK, E. L. (1975). Verbal interactions between children and their mothers during the preschool years. *Developmental Psychology, 11,* 788–794.

MOLFESE, D. L., FREEMAN, R. B., JR., & PALERMO, D. S. (1975). The ontogeny of brain lateralization for speech and nonspeech sounds. *Brain and Language, 2,* 356–368.

MONEY, J., & EHRHARDT, A. (1972). *Man and woman, boy and girl.* Baltimore: Johns Hopkins University Press.

MONTEMAYOR, R., and EISEN, M. (1978). The development of self-perceptions in children and adolescents. In M. S. Smart & R. C. Smart (Eds.), *Adolescents: Development and relationships.* New York: Macmillan.

Monthly Vital Statistics Report (1979). *Final Mortality Statistics (1977),* Nos. 79–1120. Hyattsville, Maryland: National Center for Health Statistics, Health Education, and Welfare.

MONTOUR, K. (1977, April). William James Sidis, the broken twig. *American Psychologist, 32,* 265–279.

MOODY, P. A. (1975). *Genetics of man* (2nd ed.). New York: Norton.

MOORE, B. S., UNDERWOOD, B., & ROSENHAN, D. L. (1973). Affect and altruism. *Developmental Psychology, 8,* 99–104.

MORRIS, J. (1974). *Conundrum.* New York: Harcourt Brace Jovanovich.

MOSS, H. A., & JONES, S. J. (1977). Relations between maternal attitudes and maternal behavior as a function of social class. In P. H. Leiderman, S. R. Tulkin, & A. Rosenfeld (Eds.), *Culture and infancy: Variations in the human experience.* New York: Academic Press.

MOWRER, O. H., & MOWRER, W. M. (1938). Enuresis, a method for its study and treatment. *American Journal of Orthopsychiatry, 8,* 436–459.

MUIR, D., & FIELD, J. (1979). Newborn infants orient to sounds. *Child Development, 50,* 431–436.

MULHERN, R. K., JR., & PASSMAN, R. H. (1981). Parental discipline as affected by sex of the parent, sex of the child, and the child's apparent responsiveness to discipline. *Developmental Psychology, 17,* 604–613.

MUNRO, G., & ADAMS, G. R. (1977). Identity formation in college students and working youth. *Developmental Psychology, 13,* 523–524.

NAEYE, R. L. (1980, April). Sudden infant death. *Scientific American,* pp. 56–62.

NEALE, J. M., & LIEBERT, R. M. (1969). Reinforcement therapy using aides and patients as behavioral technicians: A case report of a mute psychotic. *Perceptual and Motor Skills, 28,* 835–839.

NELSON, K. (1973). Structure and strategy in learning to talk. *Monographs of the Society for Research in Child Development, 38* (1–2, Serial No. 149).

NELSON, K. (1981). Individual differences in language development: Implications for development and language. *Developmental Psychology, 17,* 170–187.

NELSON, L., & MADSEN, M. C. (1969). Cooperation and competition in four-year-olds as a function of reward contingency and subculture. *Developmental Psychology, 1,* 340–344.

NYHAN, W. L. (1976). *The heredity factor.* New York: Grosset & Dunlap.

ODEN, S., & ASHER, S. R. (1977). Coaching children in social skills for friendship making. *Child Development, 48,* 495–506.

O'LEARY, K. D., O'LEARY, S., & BECKER, W. C. (1969). Modification of a deviant sibling interaction pattern in the home. In B. G. Guerney, Jr. (Ed.), *Psychotherapeutic agents: New roles for nonprofessionals, parents, and teachers.* New York: Holt, Rinehart & Winston.

O'LEARY, K. D., PELHAM, W. E., ROSENBAUM, A., & PRICE, G. H. (1976). Behavioral treatment of hyperkinetic children: An experimental evaluation of its usefulness. *Clinical Pediatrics, 15,* 510–515.

OLEJNIK, A. B. (1980). Adult's moral reasoning with children. *Child Development, 51,* 1285–1288.

OSOFSKY, J. D. (1976). Neonatal characteristics and mother-infant interaction in two observational situations. *Child Development, 47,* 1138–1147.

OTTO, H. (Ed.) (1971). *The new sexuality.* Palo Alto, Calif.: Science and Behavior Books.

PARK, C. C. (1967). *The siege.* New York: Harcourt, Brace, & World.

PARKE, R. D. (1970). The role of punishment in the socialization process. In R. A. Hoppe, G. A. Milton, & E. C. Simmel (Eds.), *Early experiences and the processes of socialization.* New York: Academic Press.

PARKE, R. D. (1979). Perspectives on the father-infant interaction. In J. D. Osofsky (Ed.), *Handbook of infant development.* New York: John Wiley.

PARKE, R. D. & SAWIN, D. B. (1976). The father's role in infancy: A re-evaluation. *The Family Coordinator, 25,* 365–371.

PARKE, R. D., & SAWIN, D. B. (1977, March). The family in early infancy: Social interaction and attitudinal analyses. In F. A. Pederson (Chair), *The family system: networks of interactions among mother, father and infant.* Symposium presented at the meeting of the Society for Research in Child Development, New Orleans.

PARSONS, J. E., ADLER, T. F., & KACZALA, C. M. (1982). Socialization of achievement attitudes and beliefs: Parental influences. *Child Development, 53,* 310–321.

PARTEN, M. B. (1932). Social participation among pre-school children. *Journal of Abnormal and Social Psychology, 27,* 243–269.

PASTOR, D. (1981). The quality of mother-infant attachment and its relationship to toddlers' initial sociability with peers. *Developmental Psychology, 17,* 326–335.

PATTERSON, G. R. (1976). The aggressive child: Victim and architect of a coercive system. In E. J. Mash, L. A. Hamerlynck, & L. C. Handy (Eds.), *Behavior modification and families.* New York: Brunner/Mazel.

PATTERSON, G. R. (1979). A performance theory for coercive family interaction. In R. R. Cairns (Ed.), *Social interaction: Analysis and illustration.* Hillsdale, N. J.: Erlbaum.

PATTERSON, G. R., LITTMAN, R. A., & BRICKER, W. (1967). Assertive behavior in children: A step toward a theory of aggression. *Monographs of the Society for Research in Child Development, 32* (5, Serial No. 113).

PAYNE, F. D. (1980). Children's prosocial conduct in structured situations as viewed by others: Consistency, convergence, and relationships with person variables. *Child Development, 51,* 1252–1259.

PEDERSEN, E., FAUCHER, T. A., & EATON, W. W. (1978). A new perspective on the effects of first-grade teachers on children's subsequent adult status. *Harvard Educational Review, 48,* 1–31.

PERRY, D. G., & PERRY, L. C. (1974). Denial of suffering in the victim as a stimulus to violence in aggressive boys. *Child Development, 45,* 55–62.

PERRY, D. G., PERRY, L. C., BUSSEY, K., ENGLISH, D., & ARNOLD, G. (1980). Processes of attribution and children's self-punishment following misbehavior. *Child Development, 51,* 545–551.

PERRY, F. L., JR., & SHWEDEL, A. (1979). Interaction of visual information, verbal information, and linguistic competence in the preschool-aged child. *Journal of Psycholinguistic Research, 8,* 559–566.

PETZEL, S. R., & CLINE, D. W. (1978). Adolescent suicide: epidemiological and biological aspects. *Adolescent Psychiatry, 6,* 239–266.

PHILLIPS, J. L., JR. (1975). *The origins of intellect: Piaget's theory* (2nd ed.). San Francisco: W. H. Freeman & Company.

PIAGET, J. (1926). *The language and thought of the child* (M. Worden, trans.). New York: Harcourt, Brace.

PIAGET, J. (1928). *Judgment and reasoning in the child* (M. Worden, trans.). London: Routledge & Kegan Paul.

PIAGET, J. (1929). *The child's conception of the world* (J. & A. Tomlinson, trans.). New York: Harcourt, Brace.

PIAGET, J. (1932). *The moral judgment of the child.* (M. Worden, trans.). New York: Harcourt, Brace.

PIAGET, J. (1952). *The origins of intelligence in children* (M. Cook, trans.). New York: International Universities Press.

PIAGET, J. (1954). *The construction of reality in the child.* (M. Cook, trans.). New York: Basic Books.

PIAGET, J. (1962). *Play, dreams, and imitation in childhood* (C. Gattegno & F. M. Hodgson, trans.). New York: Norton.

PIAGET, J. (1965). *The child's conception of number.* (C. Gattegno & F. M. Hodgson, trans.). New York: Norton.

PIAGET, J. (1977). The first year of life of the child. In H. E. Gruber & J. J. Vonèche (Eds. and trans.), *The essential Piaget.* New York: Basic Books. (Originally published in 1927.)

PIAGET, J., & INHELDER, B. (1941). *Le développement des quantités chez l'enfant.* Neuchâtel: Delachaux & Niestle.

PIAGET, J., & INHELDER, B. (1956). *The child's conception of space* (F. J. Langdon & J. L. Lunzer, trans.). London: Routledge & Kegan Paul.

PIAGET, J., & INHELDER, B. (1969). *The psychology of the child* (H. Weaver, trans.). New York: Basic Books.

PIAGET, J., & INHELDER, B. (1977). Intellectual operations and their development. In H. E. Gruber & J. J. Vonèche (Eds.), *The essential Piaget.* New York: Basic Books. (Originally published in 1963.)

PINES, M. (1981, September). The civilizing of Genie. *Psychology Today,* pp. 28–34.

PLOMIN, R., & DEFRIES, J. C. (1980). Genetics and intelligence: Recent data. *Intelligence, 4,* 15–24.

PLOMIN, R., & FOCH, T. T. (1981). Sex differences and individual differences. *Child Development, 52,* 383–385.

PLOMIN, R., & ROWE, D. C. (1977). A twin study of temperament in young children. *Journal of Psychology, 97,* 197–213.

POLIT, D. F., NUTTALL, R. L., & NUTTALL, E. V. (1980). An only child grows up: A look at some characteristics of adult only children. *Family Relations, 29,* 99–106. POLLITT, E., MUELLER, W., & Leibel, R. L. (1982). The relation of growth to cognition in a well-nourished preschool population. *Child Development, 53,* 1157–1163.

PRESSLEY, M. (1982). Elaboration and memory development. *Child Development, 53,* 296–309.

PROVENCE, S., & LIPTON, R. C. (1962). *Infants in institutions.* New York: International Universities Press.

PUTALLAZ, M., & GOTTMAN, J. M. (1981). Social skills and group acceptance. In S. R. Asher & J. M. Gottman (Eds.), *The development of children's friendships.* Cambridge, England: Cambridge University Press.

QUINN, L. (1981). Reading skills of hearing and congenitally deaf children. *Journal of Experimental Child Psychology, 32,* 139–161.

RARING, R. H. (1975). *Crib death.* Hicksville, N.Y.: Exposition Press.

REINISCH, J. M. (1977). Prenatal exposure of human foetuses to synthetic progestin and estrogen affects personality. *Nature, 266,* 561–562.

RHEINGOLD, H. L. (1961). The effect of environmental stimulation upon social and exploratory behavior in the human infant. In B. M. Foss (Ed.), *Determinants of infant behavior* (Vol. 1). London: Methuen.

RHEINGOLD, H. L. (1976). Some visual determinants of smiling in infants. Unpublished Ph. D. dissertation, University of North Carolina, Chapel Hill.

RICHARDS, M. P. M. (1977). An ecological study of infant development in an urban setting in Britain. In P. H. Leiderman, S. R. Tulkin, & A. Rosenfeld (Eds.), *Culture and infancy: Variations in the human experience*. New York: Academic Press.

RIDENOUR, M. V. (1978). Programs to optimize infant motor development. In M. V. Ridenour (Ed.), *Motor development: Issues and applications*. Princeton, N.J.: Princeton Book Co.

RIFE, D. C. (1940). Handedness, with special reference to twins. *Genetics, 25,* 178–186.

RIMLAND, B. (1964). *Infantile autism: The syndrome and its implications for a neural theory of behavior*. New York: Meredith Publishing Co.

ROBINSON, N. M., & ROBINSON, H. B. (1976). *The mentally retarded child* (2nd ed.). New York: McGraw-Hill.

ROBSON, K. (1968). The role of eye-to-eye contact in maternal-infant attachment. In S. Chess & A. Thomas (Eds.), *Annual progress in child psychiatry and child development*. New York: Brunner/Mazel.

ROCHE, A. F. (1979). Secular trends in stature, weight, and maturation. In A. F. Roche (Ed.), Secular trends in human growth, maturation, and development. *Monographs of the Society for Research in Child Development, 44* (Serial No. 179).

RODE, S. S., CHANG, P.-N., FISCH, R. O., & SROUFE, L. A. (1981). Attachment patterns of infants separated at birth. *Developmental Psychology, 17,* 188–191.

ROEDELL, W. C., & SLABY, R. G. (1977). The role of distal and proximal interaction in infant social preference formation. *Developmental Psychology, 13,* 266–273.

ROFFWARG, H. P., MUZIO, J. N., & DEMENT, W. C. (1966). Ontogenetic development of the human sleep-dream cycle. *Science, 152,* 604–619.

ROGERS, D. (1977). *The psychology of adolescence*. Englewood Cliffs, N.J.: Prentice-Hall.

ROGERS, D. (1979). *The adult years: An introduction to aging*. Englewood Cliffs, N.J.: Prentice-Hall.

ROSCH, E., & MERVIS, C. B. (1978). Children's sorting: A reinterpretation based on the nature of abstraction in natural categories. In M. S. Smart & R. C. Smart (Eds.), *Preschool children*. New York: Macmillan.

ROSEN, B. C. (1961). Family structure and achievement motivation. *American Sociological Review, 26,* 574–585.

ROSEN, B. C., & D'ANDRADE, R. (1975). The psycho-social origins of achievement motivation. In U. Bronfenbrenner & M. A. Mahoney (Eds.), *Influences on human development* (2nd ed.). Hinsdale, Ill.: Holt, Rinehart & Winston.

ROSENHAN, D. L., & WHITE, G. M. (1967). Observation and rehearsal as determinants of prosocial behavior. *Journal of Personality and Social Psychology, 5,* 424–431.

ROSENKOETTER, L. I. (1973). Resistance to temptation: Inhibitory and disinhibitory effects of models. *Developmental Psychology, 8,* 80–84.

ROSENTHAL, R., & JACOBSON, L. (1968). *Pygmalion in the classroom*. New York: Holt, Rinehart & Winston.

ROSENZWEIG, M. R. (1966). Environmental complexity, cerebral change, and behavior. *American Psychologist, 21,* 321–332.

ROSINSKI, R. R. (1977). *The development of visual perception*. Santa Monica, Calif.: Goodyear Publishing.

ROSS, A. O. (1980). *Psychological disorders of children: A behavioral approach to theory, research, and therapy* (2nd ed.). New York: McGraw-Hill.

ROSS, D. M., & ROSS, S. A. (1976). *Hyperactivity: Research, theory, action*. New York: John Wiley.

ROSS, G., KAGAN, J., ZELAZO, P., & KOTELCHUCK, M. (1975). Separation protest in infants in home and laboratory. *Developmental Psychology, 11,* 256–257.

ROWE, D. C. (1981). Environmental and genetic influences on dimensions of perceived parenting: A twin study. *Developmental Psychology, 17,* 203–208.

ROZIN, P., & GLEITMAN, L. R. (1977). The structure and acquisition of reading. II.: The reading process and the acquisition of the alphabetic principle. In A. S. Reber & D. S. Scarborough (Eds.), *Toward a psychology of reading*. Hillsdale, N.J.: Erlbaum.

ROZIN, P., PORITSKY, S., & SOTSKY, R. (1971). American children with reading problems can easily learn to read English represented by Chinese characters. *Science, 171,* 1264–1267.

RUBIN, Z. (1980). *Children's friendships*. Cambridge: Harvard University Press.

RUFF, H. A., & HALTON, A. (1978). Is there directed reaching in the human neonate? *Developmental Psychology, 14,* 425–426.

RUSSELL, M. J. (1976). Human olfactory communication. *Nature, 260,* 520–522.

RUTTER, M. (1974). *The qualities of mothering: Maternal deprivation reassessed*. New York: Jason Aronson.

RUTTER, M. (1978). Diagnosis and definition of childhood autism. *Journal of Autism and Childhood Schizophrenia, 8,* 139–161.

RUTTER, M. (1979). Maternal deprivation, 1972–1978: New findings, new concepts, new approaches. *Child Development, 50,* 283–305.

RUTTER, M. (1983). School effects on pupil progress: Research findings and policy implications. *Child Development, 54,* 1–29.

RUTTER, M., & BARTAK, L. (1971). Causes of infantile autism: Some considerations from recent research. *Journal of Autism and Childhood Schizophrenia, 1,* 20–32.

RUTTER, M., YULE, W., & GRAHAM, P. (1973). Enuresis and behavioral deviance: Some epidemiological considerations. In I. Kolvin, R. C. MacKeith, & S. R. Meadow (Eds.), *Bladder control and enuresis*. Philadelphia: Lippincott.

SACHS, J., & DEVIN, J. (1976). Young children's use of age-appropriate speech styles in social interaction and role-playing. *Journal of Child Language, 3,* 81–98.

SACKER, I. M., & NEWHOFF, S. D. (1982). Medical and psychosocial risk factors in the pregnant adolescent. In I. R. Stuart & C. F. Wells (Eds.), *Pregnancy in adolescence*. New York: Van Nostrand Reinhold.

SALAPATEK, P. (1975). Pattern perception in early infancy. In L. B. Cohen & P. Salapatek (Eds.), *Infant perception: From sensation to cognition* (Vol. 1). New York: Academic Press.

SALGUERO, C. (1980). Adolescent pregnancy: A report on

ACYF-funded research and demonstration projects. *Children Today, 9,* 10–11.

SALK, L. (1962). Mother's heartbeat as an imprinting stimulus. *Transactions of the New York Academy of Sciences, 24,* 753–763.

SAXE, G. B., & SICILIAN, S. (1981). Children's interpretation of their counting accuracy: A developmental analysis. *Child Development, 52,* 1330–1332.

SCARR, S. (1969). Social introversion-extroversion as a heritable response. *Child Development, 40,* 823–832.

SCARR, S., & MCCARTNEY, K. (1983). How people make their own environments: A theory of genotype → environment effects. *Child Development, 54,* 424–435.

SCARR, S., & WEINBERG, R. A., (1976). IQ test performance of black children adopted by white families. *American Psychologist, 31,* 726–739.

SCARR, S., & WEINBERG, R. A. (1978). The influence of "family background" on intellectual attainment. *American Sociological Review, 43,* 674–692.

SCHAEFER, A. E., & JOHNSON, O. C. (1969). Are we well fed? The search is for an answer. *Nutrition Today, 41,* 2–11.

SCHAEFER, C. E. (1969). Imaginary companions and creative adolescents. *Developmental Psychology, 1,* 747–749.

SCHAEFER, H. R., & EMERSON, P. E. (1964). Patterns of response to physical contact in early human development. *Journal of Child Psychology and Psychiatry, 5,* 1–13.

SCHAIE, K. W., LABOUVIE, G., & BUECH, B. V. (1973). Generational and cohort-specific differences in adult cognitive functioning: A fourteen-year study of independent samples. *Developmental Psychology, 9,* 151–166.

SCHOFIELD, J. W. (1981). Complementary and conflicting identities: Images and interaction in an interracial school. In S. R. Asher & J. M. Gottman (Eds.), *The development of children's friendships.* Cambridge, England: Cambridge University Press.

SCHWEICKART, R., & WARSHALL, P. (1980). Urination and defecation in zero-g: There ain't no graceful way. In S. Brand (Ed.), *The next whole earth catalog.* Sausalito, Calif.: Point.

SEARS, R. R. (1963). Dependency motivation. In M. Jones (Ed.), *Nebraska Symposium on motivation* (Vol. 11). Lincoln: University of Nebraska Press.

SEARS, R. R., MACCOBY, E. E., & LEVIN, H. (1957). *Patterns of child rearing.* Evanston, Ill.: Row, Peterson.

SEAVER, W. B. (1973). Effects of naturally induced teacher expectancies. *Journal of Personality and Social Psychology, 28,* 333–342.

SECORD, P., & PEEVERS, B. (1974). The development and attribution of person concepts. In T. Mischel (Ed.), *Understanding other persons.* Oxford: Blackwell.

SEIDEN, R. H. (1969). *Suicide among youth: A review of the literature, 1900–1967.* Chevy Chase, Maryland: National Clearing House for Mental Health Information.

SELIGMAN, M. E. P. (1972). Phobias and preparedness. In M. E. P. Seligman & J. L. Hager (Eds.), *Biological boundaries of learning.* New York: Appleton-Century-Crofts.

SELIGMAN, M. E. P. (1975). *Helplessness: On depression, development, and death.* San Francisco: W. H. Freeman & Company.

SELMAN, R. (1981). The child as friendship philosopher. In S. R. Asher & J. M. Gottman (Eds.), *The development of children's friendships.* Cambridge, England: Cambridge University Press.

SERBIN, L. A., O'LEARY, K. D., KENT, R. N., & TONICK, I. J. (1973). A comparison of teacher response to the pre-academic and problem behavior of boys and girls. *Child Development, 44,* 796–804.

SHAFFER, D. R. (1979). *Social and personality development.* Monterey, Calif.: Brooks/Cole.

SHAH, F., ZELNIK, M., & KANTNER, J. (1975). Unexpected intercourse among young unwed teenagers. *Family Planning Perspectives, 7,* 39–44.

SHAPIRA, A., & MADSEN, M. C. (1974). Between- and within-group cooperation and competition among kibbutz and nonkibbutz children. *Developmental Psychology, 10,* 140–145.

SHARABANY, R., GERSHONI, R., & HOFMAN, J. E. (1981). Girl-friend, boyfriend: Age and sex differences in intimate friendship. *Developmental Psychology, 17,* 800–808.

SHATZ, M., & GELMAN, R. (1973). The development of communication skills. *Monographs of the Society for Research in Child Development, 38*(3, Serial No. 152).

SHINN, M. (1978). Father absence and children's cognitive development. *Psychological Bulletin, 85,* 295–324.

SHIRLEY, M. M. (1933). *The first two years: A study of twenty-five babies* (Vol. 2). Institute of Child Welfare Monograph No. 7. Minneapolis: University of Minnesota Press.

SIEGEL, E. (1982, December 12). How children make friends. *The Boston Globe Magazine,* pp. 12–15, 42, 49–52.

SIEGLER, R. S., LIEBERT, D. E., & LIEBERT, R. M. (1973). Inhelder and Piaget's pendulum problem: Teaching preadolescents to act as scientists. *Developmental Psychology, 9,* 97–101.

SIEGLER, R. S., & LIEBERT, R. M. (1975). Acquisition of formal scientific reasoning by 10- and 13-year-olds: Designing a factorial experiment. *Developmental Psychology, 11,* 401–402.

SIMNER, M. L. (1971). Newborn's response to the cry of another infant. *Developmental Psychology, 5,* 136–150.

SINGER, J. L., & SINGER, D. G. (1981). *Television, imagination, and aggression: A study of preschoolers.* Hillsdale, N.J.: Erlbaum.

SINGLETON, L. C., & ASHER, S. R. (1979). Racial integration and children's peer preferences: An investigation of developmental and cohort differences. *Child Development, 50,* 936–941.

SKEELS, H. M. (1966). Adult status of children with contrasting early life experiences: A follow-up study. *Monographs of the Society for Research in Child Development, 31,* (No. 3).

SKINNER, B. F. (1957). *Verbal behavior.* Englewood Cliffs, N.J.: Prentice-Hall.

SKINNER, B. F. (1979). *The shaping of a behaviorist.* New York: Knopf.

SKLAR, J., & BERKOR, B. (1974). Teenage family formation in postwar America. *Family Planning Perspectives, 6,* 80–90.

SLABY, R. G. (1975). Verbal regulation of aggression and altruism. In W. Hartup & J. De Wit (Eds.), *Determinants and origins of aggressive behavior.* The Hague: Mouton.

SLABY, R. G., & FREY, K. S. (1975). Development of gender constancy and selective attention to same-sex models. *Child Development, 46,* 849–856.

SLOBIN, D. I. (1971). *Psycholinguistics.* Glenview, Ill.: Scott, Foresman.

SMART, M. S., & SMART, R. C. (1978). *Adolescents: Development and relationships* (2nd ed.). New York: Macmillan.

SMART, M. S., & SMART, R. C. (1978). *School-age children* (2nd ed.). New York: Macmillan.

SMART, M. S., & SMART, R. C. (1978). *Infants: Development and relationships*. New York: Macmillan.

SNOW, C. E. (1977). The development of conversation between mothers and babies. *Journal of Child Language, 4,* 1–22.

SNYDER, J. J. (1977). Reinforcement analysis of interaction in problem and nonproblem families. *Journal of Abnormal Psychology, 86,* 528–535.

SOLOMON, R. W., & WAHLER, R. G. (1977). Peer reinforcement control of classroom problem behavior. In K. D. O'Leary & S. G. O'Leary, *Classroom management* (2nd ed.). New York: Pergamon Press.

SOPHIAN, C., & STIGLER, J. W. (1981). Does recognition memory improve with age? *Journal of Experimental Child Psychology, 32,* 343–353.

SORENSEN, R. (1973). *Adolescent sexuality in contemporary America: Personal values and sexual behavior, ages 13–19.* New York: World Publishers.

SOROKA, S. M., CORTER, C. M., & ABRAMOVITCH, R. (1979). Infants' tactual discrimination of novel and familiar tactual stimuli. *Child Development, 50,* 1251–1253.

SOSA, R., KENNELL, J., KLAUS, M., ROBERTSON, S., & URRUTIA, J. (1980). The effect of a supportive companion on prenatal problems, length of labor, and mother-infant interaction. *New England Journal of Medicine, 303*(11), 597–600.

SPANIER, G. B. (1975). Sexualization and premarital sexual behavior. *Family Coordinator, 24,* 33–41.

SPENCE, J. T., & HELMREICH, R. L. (1978). *Masculinity and femininity: Their psychological dimensions, correlates, and antecedents.* Austin: University of Texas Press.

SPERLING, G. (1963). A model for visual memory tasks. *Human Factors, 5,* 19–31.

SPIKER, C. C., GERJUOY, I. R., & SHEPARD, W. O. (1956). Children's concept of middle sizedness and performance on the intermediate size problem. *Journal of Comparative and Physiological Psychology, 49,* 416–419.

SPITZ, R. A., & WOLF, K. M. (1946). Anaclitic depression: An inquiry into the genesis of psychiatric conditions in early childhood. *The Psychoanalytic Study of the Child* (Vol. 2). 313–342. New York: International Universities Press.

SROUFE, L. A. (1977). Wariness of strangers and the study of infant development. *Child Development, 48,* 731–746.

SROUFE, L. A. (1978, October). Attachment and the roots of competence. *Human Nature,* pp. 50–57.

STALLINGS, J. (1975). Implementation and child effects of teaching practices in follow through classrooms. *Monographs of the Society for Research in Child Development, 40,* (7–8, Serial No. 163).

STANOVICH, K. E. (1982). Individual differences in the cognitive processes of reading: I. Word decoding. *Journal of Learning Disabilities, 15,* 485–493.

STAUB, E. (1974). Helping a distressed person: Social, personality, and stimulus determinants. In L. Berkowitz (Ed.), *Advances in experimental social psychology* (Vol. 7). New York: Academic Press.

STECHLER, G. & HALTON, A. (1982). Prenatal influences on human development. In B. B. Wollman, G. Stricker, S.

J. Ellman, P. Keith-Spiegel, & D. S. Palermo, (Eds.), *Handbook of developmental psychology.* Englewood Cliffs, N.J.: Prentice-Hall.

STEELE, B. F., & POLLOCK, C. B. (1974). A psychiatric study of parents who abuse infants and small children. In R. E. Helfer & C. H. Kempe (Eds.), *The battered child* (2nd ed.). Chicago: The University of Chicago Press.

STEIN, Z. A., SUSSER, M. W., SAENGER, G., & MAROLLA, F. (1975). *Famine and human development: The Dutch hunger winter, 1944–1945.* New York: Oxford University Press.

STEINBERG, L. D., & HILL, J. P. (1978). Patterns of family interaction as a function of age, the onset of puberty, and formal thinking. *Developmental Psychology, 14,* 683–684.

STEINER, J. E. (1974). Discussion paper: Innate discriminative human facial expressions to taste and smell stimulation. *Annals of the New York Academy of Sciences, 237,* 229–233.

STERN, D. N. (1974). Mother and infant at play: The dyadic interaction involving facial, vocal, and gaze behaviors. In M. Lewis & L. A. Rosenblum (Eds.), *The effect of the infant on its caregiver.* New York: John Wiley.

STERN, D. (1977). *The first relationship.* Cambridge: Harvard University Press.

STEVENSON, H. W. (1972). *Children's learning.* New York: Appleton-Century-Crofts.

STOTT, D. H., & COTCHFORD, S. A. (1976). Prenatal antecedents of child health, development, and behavior: An epidemiological report of incidence and association. *Journal of the American Academy of Child Psychiatry, 15,* 161–191.

STRICKBERGER, M. W. (1968). *Genetics.* New York: Macmillan.

SULLIVAN, H. S. (1953). *The interpersonal theory of psychiatry.* New York: Norton.

SUOMI, S. J., & HARLOW, H. F. (1972). Social rehabilitation of isolate-reared monkeys. *Developmental Psychology, 6,* 487–496.

SUOMI, S. J., & HARLOW, H. F. (1975). The role and reason of peer relationships in rhesus monkeys. In M. Lewis & L. A. Rosenbaum (Eds.), *Friendships and peer relationships.* New York: Wiley.

TANNER, J. M. (1974). Variability of growth and maturity in newborn infants. In M. Lewis & L. A. Rosenblum (Eds.), *The effect of the infant on its caregiver.* New York: John Wiley.

TANNER, J. M. (1978). *Foetus into man: physical growth from conception to maturity.* Cambridge: Harvard University Press.

TAUBER, M. A. (1979). Sex differences in parent-child interaction styles during a free-play session. *Child Development, 50,* 981–988.

TAYLOR, M., & BACHARACH, V. R. (1981). The development of drawing rules: Metaknowledge about drawing influences performance on nondrawing tasks. *Child Development, 52,* 373–375.

TEEPLE, J. (1978). Physical growth and maturation. In M. V. Ridenour (Ed.), *Motor development: Issues and applications.* Princeton, N.J.: Princeton Book Co.

TELLER, D. Y., PEEPLES, D. R., & SEKEL, M. (1978). Discrimination of chromatic from white light by two-month-old human infants. *Vision Research, 18,* 41–48.

TERMAN, L. M. (1954a). The discovery and encouragement

of exceptional talent. *American Psychologist, 9*, 221–230.

TERMAN, L. M. (1954b). Scientists and nonscientists in a group of 800 gifted men. *Psychological Monographs, 68*, 1–44.

TERRACE, H. S. (1979). *Nim.* New York: Knopf.

THELEN, E. (1981). Rhythmical behavior in infancy: An ethological perspective. *Developmental Psychology, 17*, 237–257.

THOMAS, A., & CHESS, S. (1977). *Temperament and development.* New York: Brunner/Mazel.

THOMAS, A., CHESS, S., & BIRCH, H. G. (1968). *Temperament and behavior disorders in children.* New York: New York University Press.

THOMPSON, W. R. (1954). The inheritance and development of intelligence. *Research Publications of the Association for Research in Nervous and Mental Disease, 33*, 209–331.

TISHLER, C., MCKENRY, P. C., & MORGAN, K. C. (1981). Adolescent suicide attempts: Some significant factors. *Suicide and Life-Threatening Behavior, 11*, 86–92.

TONER, I. J., MOORE, L. P., & EMMONS, B. A. (1980). The effect of being labeled on subsequent self-control in children. *Child Development, 51*, 618–621.

TONER, I. J., & SMITH, R. A. (1977). Age and verbalization in delay maintenance behavior in children. *Journal of Experimental Child Psychology, 24*, 123–128.

TOUBIN, A. (1978). Cerebral dysfunctions related to prenatal organic damage: Clinical neuropathological correlations. *Journal of Abnormal Psychology, 87*, 617–635.

TUCKER, J., STEVENS, L. J., & YSSELDYKE, J. E. (1983). Learning disabilities: The experts speak out. *Journal of Learning Disabilities, 16*, 6–14.

TULKIN, S. R. (1977). Social class differences in maternal and infant behavior. In P. H. Leiderman, S. R. Tulkin, & A. Rosenfeld (Eds.), *Culture and infancy: Variations in the human experience.* New York: Academic Press.

TURNER, J. S. & HELMS, D. B. (1979). *Life span development.* Philadelphia: W. B. Saunders.

UTECH, D. A., & HOVING, K. L. (1969). Parents and peers as competing influences in the decisions of children of differing ages. *Journal of Social Psychology. 78*, 267–274.

VASTA, R. (1982). Physical child abuse: A dual-component analysis. *Developmental Review, 2*, 125–149.

VASTA, R., & COPITCH, P. (1981). Simulating conditions of child abuse in the laboratory. *Child Development, 52*, 164–170.

VENTURA, S. J. (1977). Teenage childbearing: United States, 1966–1975. *Monthly Vital Statistics Reports.* Washington, D.C.: National Center For Health Statistics, 26 (No. 5, Supp.).

VEROFF, J. (1965). Theoretical background for studying the origins of human motivational dispositions. *Merrill-Palmer Quarterly, 11*, 3–18.

VISHER, E. B., & VISHER, J. S. (1979). *Step families: A guide to working with stepparents and stepchildren.* New York: Brunner/Mazel.

VREELAND, R. S. (1972). Is it true what they say about Harvard boys? *Psychology Today, 5*, 65–68.

VYGOTSKY, L. S. (1962). *Thought and language.* Cambridge: MIT Press.

WALK, R. D., & GIBSON, E. J. (1961). A comparative and analytical study of visual depth perception. *Psychological Monographs, 75*(15, Whole No. 519).

WALLACH, M. A., & WALLACH, L. (1976). *Teaching all children to read.* Chicago: University of Chicago Press.

WALLERSTEIN, J. S., & KELLY, J. B. (1980). *Surviving the breakup: How children and parents cope with divorce.* New York: Basic Books.

WALTERS, R. H., & BROWN, M. (1963). Studies of reinforcement of aggression. Part III: Transfer of responses to an interpersonal situation. *Child Development, 34*, 563–572.

WALTERS, R. H., & BROWN, M. (1964). A test of the high-magnitude theory of aggression. *Journal of Experimental Child Psychology, 1*, 376–387.

WARDEN, C. J. (1931). *Animal motivation: Experimental studies on the albino rat.* New York: Columbia University Press.

WATERS, E., VAUGHN, B. E., & EGELAND, B. R. (1980). Individual differences in infant-mother attachment relationships at age one: Antecedents in neonatal behavior in an urban, economically disadvantaged sample. *Child Development, 51*, 208–216.

WATSON, E. S., & ENGLE, R. W. (1982). Is it lateralization, processing strategies, or both that distinguishes good and poor readers? *Journal of Experimental Child Psychology, 34*, 1–19.

WATSON, J. B. (1930). *Behaviorism* (2nd ed.). Chicago: University of Chicago Press.

WATSON, J. S. (1972). Smiling, cooing, and "the game." *Merrill-Palmer Quarterly of Behavior and Development, 18*, 323–339.

WATSON, J. B., & RAYNER, M. (1920). Conditioned emotional reactions. *Journal of Experimental Psychology, 3*, 1–14.

WEINRAUB, M. (1978). Fatherhood: The myth of the second-class parent. In J. H. Stevens, Jr., & M. Mathews (Eds.), *Mother/child, father/child relationships.* Washington, D.C.: National Association for the Education of Young Children.

WEISFELD, C. C., WEISFELD, G. E., & CALLAGHAN, J. W. (1982). Female inhibition in mixed-sex competition among young adolescents. *Ethology and Sociobiology, 3*, 29–42.

WERTHEIMER, M. (1961). Psycho-motor coordination of auditory-visual space at birth. *Science, 134*, 1692.

WHITE, B. L., CASTLE, P., & HELD, R. (1964). Observations on the development of visually-directed reaching. *Child Development, 35*, 349–364.

WHITE, T. G. (1982). Naming practices, typicality, and underextension in child language. *Journal of Experimental Child Psychology, 33*, 324–346.

WHITING, B., & EDWARDS, C. P. (1973). A cross-cultural analysis of sex-differences in the behavior of children aged three through eleven. *Journal of Social Psychology, 91*, 171–188.

WHITING, J. W. M., & CHILD, I. L. (1953). *Child training and personality: A cross-cultural study.* New Haven: Yale University Press.

WHITING, J. W. M., LANDAUER, T. K., & JONES, T. M. (1968). Infantile immunization and adult stature. *Child Development, 39*, 59–68.

WICHERN, F., & NOWICKI, S. (1976). Independence training practices and locus of control orientation in children and adolescents. *Developmental Psychology, 12,* 77.

WIESEL, T. N. (1975, May). Monkey visual cortex. II. Modifications induced by visual deprivation. Friedenwald Lecture presented at Association for Research in Vision and Ophthalmology, Sarasota, Florida.

WILKINSON, A. C. (1981). Growth functions for rapid remembering. *Journal of Experimental Child Psychology, 32,* 354–371.

WILLERMAN, L. (1973). Activity level and hyperactivity in twins. *Child Development, 44,* 288–293.

WILLERMAN, L. (1977). *The psychology of individual and group differences.* San Francisco: W. H. Freeman and Company.

WILLERMAN, L., & FIEDLER, M. F. (1974). Infant performance and intellectual precocity. *Child Development, 45,* 483–486.

WILLERMAN, L., NAYLOR, A. F., & MYRIANTHOPOULOS, N. C. (1974). Intellectual development of children from interracial matings: Performance in infancy and at 4 years. *Behavior Genetics, 4,* 83–90.

WILLERMAN, L., & PLOMIN, R. (1973). Activity level in children and their parents. *Child Development, 44,* 854–858.

WILLIAMS, J. E., BENNETT, S. M., & BEST, D. L. (1975). Awareness and expression of sex stereotypes in young children. *Developmental Psychology, 11,* 635–642.

WINICK, M. (1968). Nutrition and cell growth. *Nutrition Reviews, 26,* 195–197.

WINICK, M. (1980, December). The web of hunger. *Natural History,* pp. 6–13.

WINTERBOTTOM, M. R. (1953). The relation of need for achievement to learning experiences in independence and mastery. In J. W. Atkinson (Ed.), *Motives in fantasy, action, and society.* Princeton, N.J.: Van Nostrand.

WOLFENSTEIN, M. (1967). Trends in infant care. In Y. Brackbill & G. G. Thompson (Eds.), *Behavior in infancy and early childhood.* New York: The Free Press.

YAFFE, E. (1982). More sacred than motherhood. *Phi Delta Kappan, 63,* 469–472.

YANDO, R.M., & KAGAN, J. (1968). The effect of teacher tempo on the child. *Child Development, 39,* 27–34.

YARROW, M. R., SCOTT, P. M., & WAXLER, C. Z. (1973). Learning concern for others. *Developmental Psychology, 8,* 240–260.

YATES, G. C. R., LIPPETT, M. K., & YATES, S. M. (1981). The effects of age, positive affect induction, and instructions on children's delay of gratification. *Journal of Experimental Child Psychology, 32,* 169–180.

YONAS, A. (1979). Studies of space perception in infancy. In A. D. Pick (Ed.), *Perception and its development: A tribute to Eleanor J. Gibson.* Hillsdale, N.J.: Erlbaum.

YOUNG, G. C., & MORGAN, R. T. T. (1972). Overlearning in the conditioning treatment of enuresis. *Behavior Research and Therapy, 10,* 147–151.

YOUNG, W. C., GOY, R. W., & PHOENIX, C. H. (1964). Hormones and sexual behavior. *Science, 143,* 212–218.

ZAHN-WAXLER, C., RADKE-YARROW, M., & KING, R. A. (1979). Child rearing and children's prosocial initiations toward victims of distress. *Child Development, 50,* 319–330.

ZAJONC, R. B. (1976). Family configuration and intelligence. *Science, 192,* 227–236.

ZAJONC, R. B., & MARKUS, G. B. (1975). Birth order and intellectual development. *Psychological Review, 82,* 74–88.

ZELAZO, P., KOTELCHUCK, M., BARBER, L., & DAVID, J. (1977, March). The experimental facilitation of attachment behaviors. Paper presented at the Society for Research in Child Development meeting, New Orleans.

ZELAZO, P. R., ZELAZO, N. A., & KOLB, S. (1972). "Walking" in the newborn. *Science, 176,* 314–315.

ZELNIK, M. (1979). Sex education and knowledge of pregnancy risk among U.S. teenage women. *Family Planning Perspectives, 11,* 355–357.

ZELNIK, M., & CANTNOR, J. F. (1980). Sexual activity, contraceptive use and pregnancy among the metropolitan-area teenager, 1971–1979. *Family Planning Perspectives, 12,* 230–237.

ZELSON, C. (1973). Infant of the addicted mother. *New England Journal of Medicine, 288,* 1383–1385.

ZIGLER, E. (1973). Project Head Start: Success or failure? *Learning, 1,* 43–47.

Name Index

James, W., 149
Jeffrey, W. E., 269
Jeffries, V., 514
Jensen, A. R., 69–70, 333, 384, 387, 389
Jessor, R., 479, 483
Jessor, S. L., 479, 483
Johnson, C. J., 323
Johnson, J. E., 426
Johnson, O. E., 256
Johnston, D., 508
Jones, J. M., 502
Jones, M. C., 109
Jones, S. J., 187
Jones, T. M., 309
Juhasz, A. M., 504, 506
Julesz, B., 155
Jung, C. G., 87
Jurich, A. P., 506
Jurich, J. A., 506

K

Kaczala, C. M., 548
Kagan, J., 32, 33, 43, 189, 190, 191, 229, 401
    on impulsive/reflective children, 393–94
    vs. Piaget on babies' cognitive development, 222
Kamin, L., 69
Kandel, D. B., 478
Kanner, L., 313
Karniol, R., 293
Katchadourian, H., 462, 486
Katkovsky, W., 397, 398
Katz, R. B., 417
Kay, H., 358
Kearsley, R. B., 43
Keats, D., 508
Keats, J., 508
Keeney, T. J., 371
Keller, A., 434
Keller, B., 71
Keller, B. B., 426
Keller, H., 234–35
Kellogg, R., 275
Kelly, J. B., 46
Kempe, C. H., 41, 42
Kempe, R. S., 41, 42
Kendler, H. H., 368–70
Kendler, T. S., 368–70
Kendrick, C., 314
Keniston, K., 497

Kennell, J. H., 131, 198
Kenney, H., 366–67
Kent, R. N., 298
Keogh, J., 354
Kessel, F. S., 469
Kimmel, E. C., 359
Kimmel, H. D., 359
Kinch, J. W., 472
King, R. A., 291
Kinsbourne, M., 265, 266
Klaus, M. H., 131, 198
Klein, R. E., 257
Knopf, I. J., 385t
Koff, E., 496
Kogan, N., 394
Kohlberg, L., 99–100, 301, 426, 452–55
Kolb, S., 147, 161
Koluchová, J., 230
Komarovsky, M., 511
Kompara, D. R., 48
Konner, M., 144, 175
Korner, A. F., 186
Koser, L., 424
Koslowski, B., 175
Kotelchuck, M., 190
Kramer, P. E., 496
Kramer, R., 100
Kratcoski, J. E., 475
Kratcoski, P. C., 475
Krauss, R. M., 345, 373
Krebs, D., 455
Krowitz, A., 153
Kuczynski, L., 73, 427
Kurland, D. M., 375
Kutz, S. L., 203

L

Labouvie, G., 13
Ladd, G. W., 441
Lamb, M. E., 187, 190, 191
Lambert, W., 387
Landau, E., 467
Landauer, T. K., 309
Lane, H., 245
Langer, A., 153
Langlois, J. H., 314
Lasky, R. E., 257
Latchford, S. A., 128
Learnard, B., 370
LeBlanc, A. F., 468

Leboyer, F., 131–33, 134
Lechtig, A., 257
Lefkowitz, M. M., 19, 297, 454
Leibel, R. L., 258
Lempers, J. D., 323
Lenneberg, E. H., 245, 265
Lepper, M. R., 408
Levenstein, P., 334
Levenstein, S., 334
Levin, H., 73, 287
LeVine, R. A., 188
Levine, S., 308, 309
Levy, N., 158
Lewin, K., 294
Lewis, M., 190, 226, 227, 228
Liben, L. S., 323
Liberman, A. M., 412, 416
Liberman, I. Y., 412, 416, 417
Lickona, T., 455
Lidz, T., 460, 484, 496
Lieberman, A. F., 196
Liebert, D. E., 362
Liebert, R. M., 104, 291, 296, 359, 362, 469
Linton, M., 375
Lippett, M. K., 451
Lipsitt, L. P., 151, 157, 158
Lipton, R. C., 179
Littman, R. A., 295, 453
Locke, J., 83–84
Loeber, R., 454
Loehlin, J. C., 65, 70, 71
Londerville, S., 196, 199
Longstreth, G. V., 425
Longstreth, L. E., 265, 425
Lorber, J., 231
Lorenz, K., 167–68, 193
Lovell, K., 469
Lowell, E. L., 395
Lowrey, G. H., 258
Luria, Z., 496
Lytton, H., 346

M

Maccoby, E. E., 73, 286, 287, 297, 298, 299–300, 302, 391
Macfarlane, J., 310
Macklin, E. D., 505
Madden, J., 334
Madsen, C. H., 424
Madsen, M. C., 390, 291f

Main, M., 175, 196, 199
Malina, R. M., 261
Malinowski, B., 90
Maller, L., 157
Manis, F. R., 417
Marcia, J. E., 500
Markell, R. A., 444, 446
Markus, G. B., 44
Marolla, F., 231
Martin, B., 46, 47
Martorell, R., 257
Masters, J. C., 313, 314
Matas, L., 199
Maurer, D., 149
Maurer, R. E., 509
May, M. A., 100
McCall, R. B., 148, 150, 179, 227, 240, 332
McCartney, K., 74
McClelland, D. C., 394–95, 480
McDavid, J. W., 440
McGillicuddy-Delisi, A., 426
McGrath, E., 395
McGraw, M. B., 25–26
McGue, M., 64, 66, 68–69
McGuire, K. D., 437, 442
McKenry, P. C., 488, 489
McKenzie, B. E., 153, 270
McNeill, D., 242
McPartland, J., 398
McShane, J., 233–34
Meacham, J. A., 434
Mead, M., 134
Meier, R. I., 508
Meilman, P. N., 497, 502
Melhuish, E., 156
Melton, E. M., 449–50
Melton, G. B., 473
Meltzoff, A. N., 148
Mendel, G., 50
Mendelson, M. J., 156
Meredith, H. V., 257
Merrill, L., 454
Mervis, C. B., 342
Metzner, R., 293
Meyer, B., 427
Meyers, A., 394
Meyers, C. F., 387
Micklos, J., Jr., 411
Miller, D. T., 293
Miller, N. E., 104, 294
Miller, P. H., 373, 377, 469

Miller, S. M., 298
Mills, M., 156
Milne, A. A., 309
Miranda, S. B., 153
Mischel, W., 107, 292–93
Mitchell, D. E., 155, 156
Moely, B. E., 372
Moerk, E. L., 344
Molfese, D. L., 265
Money, J., 120, 302–3
Montemayor, R., 469
Montour, K., 391–92
Mood, A. M., 398
Moody, P. A., 51, 52
Moore, B. S., 449
Moore, L. P., 451
Moore, M. K., 148, 153
Morgan, K. C., 488, 489
Morgan, R. T. T., 359
Morris, J., 303
Morris, L. W., 296
Morrison, F. J., 417
Moss, H. A., 187, 346
Mowrer, O. H., 294, 359
Mowrer, W. M., 359
Mueller, W., 258
Muir, D., 20–23, 156
Mulhern, B. K., Jr., 73
Munro, G., 497
Murphy, P., 431
Musser, L. M., 432
Muzio, J. N., 141
Myrianthopoulos, N. C., 387

N

Naeye, R. L., 165
Naylor, A. F., 387–88
Neale, J. M., 104
Nelson, K., 233, 241
Nelson, L., 290
Neuhoff, S. D., 490
Nichols, R. C., 65, 70, 71
Nisbett, R. E., 408
Nowicki, S., 398
Nuttall, E. V., 45
Nuttall, R. L., 45
Nyhan, W. L., 125

O

Obrzut, A., 414
Obrzut, J. E., 414

Oden, S., 441, 442, 444–45
Ohlendorf, G. W., 508
O'Leary, K. D., 105, 298, 415
O'Leary, S., 105
Olejnik, A. B., 426
Olson, F. A., 372
O'Malley, P. M., 498
O'Neil, R., 470
Opper, S., 219
Osofsky, J. D., 196
Otto, H., 502
Otto, L. B., 508

P

Padawer, W., 359
Palermo, R. S., 265
Park, C. C., 312
Parke, R. D., 44, 186, 190, 287
Parsons, J. E., 548
Parten, M. B., 305
Passman, R. H., 73
Pastor, D., 204
Patterson, C. J., 293
Patterson, G. R., 295, 297, 453
Pavlov, I. P., 101
Payne, F. D., 439
Pedersen, E., 404–5
Peeples, D. R., 154
Peevers, B., 434
Pelham, W. E., 415
Perry, D. G., 452, 453
Perry, F. L., Jr., 344
Perry, L. C., 452, 453
Petrova, E. P., 151
Petzel, S. R., 488
Phillips, J. L., Jr., 221
Phillips, W., 393
Phoenix, C. H., 299
Piaget, J., 94–98, 94t, 99
    on adolescents (period of formal operations), 98,
        466–68, 470
    on babies (sensorimotor period), 95–96, 210–25,
        212, 226
    conservation experiments, 95–96, 324, 325, 360–61
    on egocentrism:
        in adolescents, 470
        in middle childhood, 429, 446
        in preschoolers, 95–96, 322–23, 345
    on friendship, 446
    on language, 234, 321

on mental representations, 95, 218–19, 224, 225

on middle childhood (period of concrete operations), 97, 360, 362–63, 364–65, 373, 429, 446

on moral development, 98, 452, 453

on object permanence, 95, 219–25, 224t

on play, 306–7

on preschoolers (preoperational period), 96, 322–23, 324, 325, 345

on self-recognition, 228

on sexual reproduction, children's theories of, 364–65

"three mountains" experiment, 322

on training, limitations of, 361, 362–63

Pick, H. L., 323

Pines, M., 245

Plager, E., 424

Plomin, R., 64, 70, 71, 73, 240, 298

Polit, D. F., 45

Politt, E., 258

Pollack, C. B., 42

Porac, C., 265, 270f

Poritsky, S., 413

Poulos, R. W., 291

Pressley, M., 373

Presson, C. C., 479

Preston, A., 398

Price, G. H., 415

Provence, S., 179

Putallaz, M., 442

Q

Quinn, L., 416

R

Radke-Yarrow, M., 291. *See also* Yarrow, M. R.

Ramirez, C., 425

Raring, R. H., 164–65

Rasmussen, B., 441, 442

Rayner, M., 101

Reiling, A. M., 168

Reinisch, J. M., 127

Renshaw, P. D., 445

Revelle, R., 463

Rheingold, H. L., 192, 228

Richards, M. P. M., 183

Ridenour, M. V., 161

Rife, P. C., 265

Rimland, B., 312, 313

Robinson, H. B., 384

Robinson, N. M., 384

Robson, K., 175

Roche, A. F., 56

Rode, S. S., 198

Roedell, W. C., 192

Roffwarg, H. P., 141

Rogel, M. J., 490

Rogers, O., 473, 475, 483, 503, 511

Rosch, E., 342

Rosen, B. C., 396

Rosen, S., 432

Rosenbaum, A., 415

Rosenbloom, S., 157

Rosenhan, D. L., 448, 449

Rosenkoetter, L. I., 452

Rosenthal, R., 402

Rosenzweig, M. R., 62

Rosinski, R. R., 270

Rosman, B. L., 393

Ross, A. O., 386

Ross, D., 296, 454

Ross, D. M., 415

Ross, G., 190

Ross, S. A., 296, 415, 454

Rousseau, J.-J., 84–85, 403

Rowe, D. C., 65, 71

Rozin, P., 412, 413, 416

Rubin, Z., 430, 438–39

Ruff, H. A., 147

Russell, M. J., 157

Rutter, M., 75, 199, 200, 201, 229, 313, 358, 399–402

S

Sachs, J., 324

Sacker, I. M., 490

Saenger, M. W., 231

Salapatek, P., 154

Salguero, C., 488, 490

Salk, L., 156

Sanders, K. M., 263

Sauvé, R., 346

Sawin, D. B., 186

Saxe, G. B., 373

Scarr, S., 70, 71, 74, 388

Schaefer, A. E., 256

Schaefer, C. E., 310

Schaffer, H. R., 184–85

Schaie, K. W., 13

Schleser, R., 394

Schofield, J. W., 428, 430–31

Thompson, W. R., 62
Thorndike, E. L., 100
Tishler, C., 488, 489
Toner, I. J., 293, 451
Tonick, I. J., 298
Tronick, E., 153
Tucker, J., 414
Tulkin, S. R., 38, 188
Turner, J. G., 482

U

Underwood, B., 449
Utech, D. A., 431

V

Vasta, R., 41, 42
Vaughn, B. E., 196
Ventura, S. J., 486
Veroff, J., 508
Visher, E. B., 47
Visher, J. S., 47
Vosk, B., 440
Vreeland, R. S., 503
Vygotsky, L. S., 321

W

Wahler, R. G., 432
Walder, L. O., 19, 297, 454
Waldrop, M. F., 387
Wales, R. J., 345
Walk, R. D., 152–53
Wall, S., 195
Wallach, L., 412, 413
Wallach, M. A., 412, 413
Wallerstein, J. S., 46
Walters, R. H., 287, 295, 297
Ward, L. M., 270f
Warden, C. J., 167
Waters, E., 195, 196
Watson, E. S., 414
Watson, J. B., 99–101, 108–9
Watson, J. S., 215
Waxler, C. Z., 292. *See also* Zahn-Waxler, C.
Weinberg, R .A., 70, 388
Weinfeld, F. D., 398
Weintraub, M., 187
Weinstein, S. M., 293
Weis, J., 475
Weisberg, P., 345

Weisfeld, C. C., 356
Weisfeld, G. E., 356
Weisner, T. S., 175
Weiss, M. G., 373, 377
Weisz, J. R., 437, 442
Wertheimer, M., 156
Whatley, J. L., 203
Whitaker, H. A., 339
White, B. L., 162, 164
White, G. M., 448
White, T. G., 343
Whitehurst, G. J., 269
Whiteman, M., 478
Whiting, B., 297
Whiting, J. W. M., 200, 309
Wichern, F., 398
Wiesel, T. N., 155
Wilkinson, A. C., 375
Willerman, L., 73, 227, 387–88, 415
Williams, J. E., 427
Williams, M., 473
Winick, M., 230
Winterbottom, M. R., 395
Wolf, K. M., 179
Wolfenstein, M., 201

Y

Yaffe, E., 509
Yando, R. M., 401
Yarbrough, C., 257
Yarrow, M. R., 292. *See also* Radke-Yarrow, M.
Yates, S. M., 451
Yates, G. C. R., 451
Yonas, A., 272
York, R. L., 398
Young, G. C., 359
Young, W. C., 299
Ysseldyke, J. E., 414
Yule, W., 358

Z

Zahn-Waxler, C., 291. *See also* Waxler, C. Z.
Zajonc, R. B., 44
Zelazo, N. A., 147
Zelazo, P. R., 43, 147, 161, 190, 191
Zelnik, M., 487, 488
Zelson, C., 127
Zigler, E., 333
Zuehlki, M. E., 490

Subject Index

A

Abortion:
  after amniocentesis, 59, 124
  and teenage pregnancy, 490
Accidents, 354
Achievement, academic, 392–409
  impulsiveness vs. reflectiveness, 393–94
  intrinsic vs. extrinsic motivation, 407–9
  and locus of control, 396–97
  motivation, 394–96
  and popularity, 440
  and school's influence, 399–409
Activity level
  and environment, 74
  and heredity, 72–73
  and intelligence, 387
Adolescence:
  cognitive development in, 466–71, 496, 497
  cultural differences and, 464
  drug use in, 477–82
  eating disorders in, 466–67
  egocentrism in, 470, 490
  friendship in, 472, 475–77
  identity formation in, 497–502
  and ideology, 470–71, 498–500
  intolerance in, 477
  juvenile delinquency, 473–75
  language development in, 496
  marriage in, 506–7
  motherhood in, 490
  occupational choice in, 507–12
  and parents, 472–73, 483, 484–85, 502, 514
  physical development in, 460–64, 463t, 496
  political involvement in, 498–500, 498–99t
  pregnancy in, 486–90
  pressures in, 496–97
  puberty, 462–64
  rebellion in, 472–73, 514–15
  and rites of passage, 501
  school dropouts, 508–9
  self-esteem, growth of, 497–98
  sexuality, 482–90, 502–7
    awakening of sexual interest, 482–83

    dating, 483, 502
    homosexuality, attitudes toward, 485–86
    living together, 504–6
    masturbation, 485
    and parents, 483, 484–85
    premarital sex, attitudes toward, 504
    psychoanalytic perspective on, 484–85
    sexual activity, early and late, 483–84
  subcultures of, 472, 473
  suicide, 488–89
  suicide-prevention, strategies for parents, 489
Adoption:
  and attachment, 198
  and foster care, 68
  and genetic counseling, 59
  interracial, 388
  and teenage pregnancy, 490
Adoption studies:
  of intelligence, 68–69, 229, 333, 388
  of language development, 240
  of twins and triplets, 65–68
Aggression:
  and fantasy play, 307–8
  in middle childhood, 453–54
  in preschoolers, 293–97
  sex differences in, 297–99
Albinism, 51–52
Alcohol:
  and prenatal development, 127–28
  use in adolescence, 477, 478, 479–80
Altruism, 446–50
  and modeling, 448
  and mood, 449–50
  and role-taking ability, 446–48
American Psychological Association guidelines, 25–26
Amniocentesis, 54–55, 57, 59, 124
Androgyny, 304, 512
Animal studies:
  of attachment, 40, 193–95, 202–3
  of intelligence and heredity, 62
  of language, 245–47
  of proprioception, 163–64
  of reinforcement, 102–3

beginnings, 203–4
correlated with unselfish behavior, 437
in middle childhood, 435–46
in preschoolers, 310–14
sex differences in, 438–40, 475, 476
theories of, 435–37
    Piaget, 429, 437
    Selman, 435–37, 436t
    Sullivan, 437

G

Games, in preschool period, 259
Gender identity. *See also* Sex-role development
    case of Jan Morris, 303
    case of opposite-sex identical twins, 302–3
Generational change, 514–15
Genes, 48
    and heredity, 49–53
    mutation of, 52–53
    polygenic traits, 55–58
    and schizophrenia, 76
Genetic counseling, 56–59
Gifted children, 389–91
    child geniuses usually boys, 391
    enrichment programs for, 392
    Sidis, William, 390–91, 391–92
    skipping grades, effects of, 392
    Terman study, 389–90, 392
    Wiener, Norbert, 391

H

Handedness, 265–67
    brain damage theory of left handedness, 266
    famous left-handed people, 267
    and heredity, 266–67
    and intelligence, 266
    and lateralization of the brain, 266
    and left-right confusions, 268–69
Head Start. *See* Operation Head Start
Heredity, 48–58
    and activity level, 72–73
    and bedwetting, 358
    and childhood schizophrenia, 76
    dominant and recessive traits, 50–52
    and dyslexia, 415
    and eye color, 51, 64–65
    genetic abnormalities, 51–53
        Huntington's chorea, 52
        mental retardation, 51

        sickle-cell anemia, 59
        Tay-Sachs disease, 56–59
        thalassemia, 59
    genetic predispositions, 67
    and handedness, 265, 266–67
    and inbreeding, 52
    and intelligence, 69–70, 333
    and language, 240, 346
    and learning disabilities, 415
    and motor development, 261–62
    and sociability, 71
    and temperament, 71
Homosexuality, adolescent attitudes to, 485–86
Hormones, 119–20
    and aggression, 299
    and stress, 309
Hyperactivity, 415

I

Idealism, in adolescence, 470–71, 498–500
Identity crisis, 92
Identity formation, 497–502
Identity status, Marcia's levels of, 500–502
Infants. *See* Babies; Babies, newborn; Parent-infant
        interactions
Inoculation, 309
Institutionalized children, development of, 39–40
Intelligence. *See also* Gifted children; IQ tests
    and academic achievement, 383–91
    and activity level, 387
    adoption studies of, 68–69, 229
    and aggressiveness, 453
    and class differences, 387
    correlation between parents' and children's IQs,
        68–69
    decline in later years, 13
    and deprivation, 229–31
    and divorce, 46–47
    enrichment programs, effects on, 333–34
    and family size, 387
    and handedness, 266
    heritability of, 69–70
    and language acquisition, 240
    and moral development, 452–55
    and nearsightedness, 389
    and nutrition, 230, 257–58
    and physical growth, 257–58, 387
    and prenatal malnutrition, 229–30
    in preschoolers, 328–35
    racial and ethnic differences in IQ scores, 387–89

Acknowledgments

CHAPTER OPENING PHOTO CREDITS

(left to right)

1 Richard Frieman, Photo Researchers, Inc.; Jerry Cranham, Photo Researchers, Inc.; Nancy Hayes, Monkmeyer

2 UNICEF Photo by William Campbell; Ken Karp; Richard Frieman, Photo Researchers, Inc.

3 Terri Leigh Stratford; Alice Kandell, Photo Researchers, Inc.; Alice Kandell, Photo Researchers, Inc.

4 WHO Photo by E. Mandelman; Neil Goldstein

5 Terri Leigh Stratford; Suzanne Szasz, Photo Researchers, Inc.; UNICEF Photo by Tom Marotta

6 Erika, Photo Researchers, Inc.; Laimute E. Druskis; Suzanne Szasz, Photo Researchers, Inc.

7 Erika Stone; Laimute E. Druskis; Neil Goldstein

8 Ken Karp; Neil Goldstein; Charles Gatewood

9 Ken Karp; Charles Gatewood; David M. Grossman, Photo Researchers, Inc.

10 Hanna W. Schreiber, Rapho/Photo Researchers, Inc.; Michael C. Hayman, Photo Researchers, Inc.

11 Alice Kandell, Rapho/Photo Researchers, Inc.; Carmine L. Galasso; Laimute E. Druskis

12 Children's Bureau, Dept. of Health and Human Services; Ken Karp

13 Christa Armstrong, Rapho/Photo Researchers, Inc.; Laimute E. Druskis; Ken Karp

14 Ken Karp; Marc P. Anderson; Ken Karp

15 Ken Karp; Ken Karp; Ken Karp

TEXT PHOTOS

pages 4 & 5 David Strickler, Monkmeyer **12** Georg Gerster, Photo Researchers, Inc. **26** Mimi Forsyth, Monkmeyer **30** Paul Conklin, Monkmeyer **33** © Abraham Menaske, Photo Researchers, Inc. **34** Craig Aurness, Woodfin Camp and Associates **36** Jerry Cooke, Photo Researchers, Inc. **37** Hella Hammid, Photo Researchers, Inc. **40** Univ. of Wisconsin, Primate Laboratory **42** UPI **43** Van Bucher, Photo Researchers, Inc. **46** Erika Stone, Photo Researchers, Inc. **49 & 54** OMIKRON, Photo Researchers, Inc. **55** Bruce Roberts, Photo Researchers, Inc. **57 & 58** Laimute E. Druskis **63** Alice Kandell, Photo Researchers, Inc. **67** Karen Epstein/Camera 5 **74** Neil Goldstein **83** Ernest Nash, Monkmeyer (left); The Bettmann Archive, Inc. (right) **84 & 86** The Bettmann Archive, Inc. **91** Jon Erikson **93** Wayne Behling **97** Mimi Forsyth, Monkmeyer **101** The Bettmann Archive, Inc. **106** Bandura, A., Ross, D., and Ross, S.A. Imitation of film-mediated aggressive models, *Journal of Abnormal and Social Psychology,* 1963, 66, p. 8. **114** Inger McCabe, Photo Researchers, Inc. **116** UPI **118** Dr. Landrum B. Shettles **121** Illustrations from *The Development of the Brain* by Maxwell Cowan. *Scientific American,* Sept. 1979. **125** UPI **132** Irene Bayer, Monkmeyer **141** Ed Lettau, Photo Researchers, Inc. **143** Suzanne Szasz, Photo Researchers, Inc. **146** From H.F.R. Prechtl, *The Neurological Study of Newborn Infants* (2nd ed.) London: SIMP/Heineman Medical; Philadelphia: Lippincott, 1977. (top, left & right). Ken Karp (bottom). **147** Photos by Jane Dunkeld. First published in *A Primer of Infant Development,* T.G.R. Bower, San Francisco: W.H. Freeman, 1977. **150** Photo courtesy of David Linton, *Scientific American,* May 1961, p. 66 **152** William Vandivert/*Scientific American* **161** Doris Pinney, Monkmeyer **162** Ed Lettau, Photo Researchers, Inc. **163** From "Dissociation of the Visual Placing Response into Elicited and Guided Components," Hein, A. and Held, R., *Science,* Vol. 158, pp. 390–391, 20 October 1967. **174** Doris Pinney, Monkmeyer **176** Mimi Forsyth, Monkmeyer **180** Nikki Salter, Photo Researchers, Inc. **182** Freda Leinwand, Monkmeyer **186** Erika Stone, Photo Researchers, Inc. **189** Suzanne Szasz, Photo Researchers, Inc. **191** Mimi Forsyth, Monkmeyer **193** Thomas McEvoy, Time-Life Picture Agency © 1955 Time Inc. **197** Inger McAbe, Photo Researchers, Inc.

201 M.W. deVries from *Pediatrics,* Vol. 60, No. 2, 1977. **203** Photo courtesy of Gordon Coster, *Scientific American,* Nov. 1962, p. 144.
213 Suzanne Szasz, Photo Researchers, Inc.
216 Lew Merrim, Monkmeyer **218** Alice Kandell, Photo Researchers, Inc. **220** George Zimbel, Monkmeyer **223** Photos by Jennifer G. Wishart. First published in *A Primer of Infant Development,* T.G.R. Bower, San Francisco: W.H. Freeman, 1977.
227 Lew Merrim, Monkmeyer **232** Alice Kandell, Photo Researchers, Inc. **237** Marilyn M. Pfaltz, Taurus Photos **246** Photo courtesy of H.S. Terrace
255 Erika Stone, Peter Arnold, Inc. **257** Peter G. Aitken, Photo Researchers, Inc. **259** Nancy J. Pierce, Photo Researchers, Inc. **262** Marion Faller, Monkmeyer **264** OMIKRON, Photo Researchers, Inc. **289** Alice Kandell, Photo Researchers, Inc.
292 Ken Karp **295** Sybil Shelton, Monkmeyer **301** Yan Lucas, Photo Researchers, Inc. **306** Alice Kandell, Photo Researchers, Inc. **311** Neil Goldstein **323** Erika Stone, © Peter Arnold, Inc.
325 The Psychological Corporation **331** Ann Zane Shanks, Photo Researchers, Inc. **334** UNICEF Photo by Tom Marotta **343** Ken Karp **353** Stan Goldblatt, Photo Researchers, Inc. **355** Freda Leinwand, Monkmeyer **357** David S. Strickler, Monkmeyer **365** Mimi Forsyth, Monkmeyer **372** Michael Kagan, Monkmeyer **377** Carmine L. Galasso **382** Ken Karp **390** Ken Karp **397** Ken Karp **401** Chuck Iossi **403** Ken Karp **407** Freda Leinwand, Monkmeyer **411** Mimi Forsyth, Monkmeyer
422 Library of Congress **425** Sybil Shackman, Monkmeyer **428** Anita Duncan **433** Carl Weese, Rapho/Photo Researchers, Inc. **438** Freda Leinwand, Monkmeyer **439** Eric Brown, Monkmeyer
441 Steve Kagan, Photo Researchers, Inc. **447** Alice Kandell, Photo Researchers, Inc. **451** Mimi Forsyth, Monkmeyer **454** John Engh, Photo Researchers, Inc. **465** Mimi Forsyth, Monkmeyer **471** Mimi Forsyth, Monkmeyer **475** Richard Hutchings, Photo Researchers, Inc. **476** Ken Karp **480** Paul S. Conklin, Monkmeyer **484** Joseph Szabo, Photo Researchers, Inc. **487** Erika Stone, Photo Researchers, Inc. **500** Ken Karp **503** Chester Higgins, Jr., Rapho/Photo Researchers, Inc.
513 Suzanne Szasz, Photo Researchers, Inc.

FIGURES, TABLES, TEXT

Fig. 1-1 M.M. Shirley (1933). *The first two years: A study of twenty-five babies,* Vol. 2. Institute of Child Welfare Monograph No. 7. Minneapolis: University of Minnesota Press. **Table 1-1** Adapted from D. Muir & J. Field (1979). Newborn infants orient to sounds. *Child Development,* 50, p. 433. **P. 25** M.B. McGraw (1967). Swimming behavior in the human infant. In Y. Brackbill & G.G. Thompson (eds.), *Behavior in Infancy and Early Childhood.* St. Louis: C.V. Mosby. **P. 93** J. Piaget (1952). *The origins of intelligence in children* (M. Cook, trans.) New York: International Universities Press. **Pp. 95, 96, 221** From THE CONSTRUCTION OF REALITY IN THE CHILD, by J. Piaget, translated by Margaret Cook. © 1954 by Basic Books, Inc. Publishers. **Fig. 5-1** Data from W.K. Berg, C.D. Adkinson, B.L. Strock (1973). Duration and periods of alertness in neonates. *Developmental Psychology,* 9, 434 and H.P. Roffwarg, J.N. Muzio, & W.C. Dement (1966). Onotogenic development of the human sleep-dream cycle. *Science,* 152, 604–619. **Table 5-1** From the Bayley Scales of Infant Development. Copyright © 1969 by the Psychological Corporation. All rights reserved. Reproduced by permission. **Fig. 5-2** Adapted from H.M. Halverson (1931). An experimental study of prehension in infants by means of systematic cinema records. *Genetic Psychology Monographs, 10,* p. 107. **P. 201** M.W. deVries & M.R. deVries (Aug. 1977). PEDIATRICS, Volume 60, Number 2, pages 170–117. Copyright American Academy of Pediatrics 1977. **Table 7-3** M. Lewis & J. Brooks (1975). Infant's social perception: A constructivist view. In L.B. Cohen & P. Salapatek (eds.), *Infant perception: From sensation to cognition,* (vol. 2). New York: Academic Press, p. 124. **Table 7-4** R. Brown & U. Bellugi (1964). Three processes in the child's acquisition of syntax. In E.H. Lenneberg (Ed.), *New directions in the study of language.* Cambridge: MIT Press and S.M. Ervin (1964). Imitation and structural change in children's language. In E.H. Lenneberg (Ed.), *New directions in the study of language.* Cambridge: MIT Press. **Fig. 7-1** Adapted from R. Brown (1973). *A first language: The early stages.* Cambridge: Harvard University Press, p. 55. **Table 7-5** From PSYCHOLINGUISTICS, 2nd edition by Dan Isaac Slobin. Copyright © 1979, 1974, 1971 by Scott, Foresman & Co. Reprinted by permission. **Fig. 8-1** From M.V. Ridenour (1978). Programs to optimize infant motor development. In M.V. Ridenour (Ed.), *Motor development: Issues and applications.* Princeton, N.J.: Princeton Book Co. **Fig. 8-2** S. Coren, C. Porac, & L.M. Ward (1979). *Sensation and perception.* New York:

Academic Press, p. 337. **Fig. 8-3** Adapted from J. Hochberg, & V. Brooks (1962). Pictorial recognition as an unlearned ability: A study of one child's performance. *American Journal of Psychology, 75,* 626. **Fig. 8-4** Adapted from W. Hudson (1960). Pictorial depth perception in sub-cultural groups in Africa. *Journal of Social Psychology, 52,* 186. **Fig. 8-5** From THE DEVELOPMENT OF VISUAL PERCEPTION by Richard R. Rosinski. Copyright © 1977 by Scott, Foresman and Co. Reprinted by permission. **Fig. 8-7** E. Abravanel (1982). Perceiving subjective contours during early childhood. *Journal of Experimental Child Psychology, 33,* 282. **Figs. 8-9a; 8-12** J. Goodnow (1977). *Children drawing.* Cambridge: Harvard University Press, p. 54, 45. **Figs. 8-9a, b; 8-11** M. Taylor & V.R. Bacharach (1981). The development of drawing rules: Metaknowledge about drawing influences performance on nondrawing tasks. *Child Development, 52,* pp. 374, 375. **Fig. 9-1** M.C. Madsen (1971). Developmental and cross-cultural differences in the cooperative and competitive behavior of young children. *Journal of Cross-Cultural Psychology, 2.* **P. 340-41** Reprinted from WORD, OBJECT, AND CONCEPTUAL DEVELOPMENT by Jeremy M. Anglin, by permission of W. W. Norton & Company, Inc., Copyright © 1977 by W. W. Norton & Company, Inc. **Fig. 10-1** Adapted from J. Berko (1958). The child's learning of English morphology. *Word, 14,* 150–177. **Fig. 11-1** J.S. Bruner (1973). The course of cognitive growth. In J.M. Anglin (Ed.), *Beyond the information given.* New York: Norton. **Figs. 11-3; 11-4** Adapted from H.H. Kendler & T.S. Kendler (1962). Vertical and horizontal processes in problem solving. *Psychological Review 69.* **Table 12-1** I.J. Knopf (1979). *Childhood psychopathology; A developmental approach.* Englewood Cliffs, N.J.: Prentice-Hall and A.O. Ross (1980). *Psychological disorders of children: A Behavioral approach to theory, research, and therapy.* (2nd ed.). New York: McGraw-Hill. **P. 384** N.M. Robinson & H.B. Robinson (1976). *The mentally retarded child.* (2nd ed.) New York: McGraw-Hill. **Fig. 12-1** R.M. Liebert & R. Wicks-Nelson (1974). *Developmental Psychology* (3rd ed.) Englewood Cliffs, N.J.: Prentice-Hall, p. 292. **Fig. 12-2** J. Kagan, B.L. Rosman, D. Day, J. Albert, & W. Phillips (1964). Information processing in the child: Significance of analytic and reflective attitudes. *Psychological Monographs, 78,* (1, Whole No. 578). **Table 12-2** V.C. Crandall, W. Katkovsky, & V.J. Crandall. Children's beliefs in their own control of reinforcements in intellectual-academic achievements situations. *Child Development,* 1965, *36.* Courtesy of Virginia Crandall.

Fig. 12-3 P. Rozin, S. Poritsky, & R. Sotsky (March 26, 1971). American children with reading problems can easily learn to read English represented by Chinese characters. SCIENCE, *171,* 1264–1267. **Fig. 13-1** Reprinted by permission of Macmillan Publishing from M.S. Smart & R.C. Smart (1977). *Children: Development and relationships,* (3rd ed.) New York: Macmillan. Copyright © 1977 by Macmillan Publishing Co., Inc. **Fig. 13-2** L.C. Singleton & S.R. Asher (1979). Racial integration and children's peer preferences: An investigation of developmental and cohort differences. *Child Development, 50,* 936–941. **Table 13-1** From S. Harter (1982). The perceived competence scale for children. *Child Development, 53,* 89. **Table 13-2** Based on R. Selman (1981). The child as friendship philosopher. In S.R. Asher & J.M. Gottman (Eds.), *The Development of Children's Friendships.* Cambridge: Cambridge University Press. **Fig. 13-3** Based on data from B.S. Moore, B. Underwood, & D.L. Rosenhan (1973). Affect and altruism. *Development Psychology, 8,* 99–104. **Fig. 14-1** Adapted from J.M. Tanner (1970). In P.H. Mussen (Ed.), Carmichael's *Manual of Child Psychology* (3rd ed.) *1,* New York: John Wiley. **Fig. 14-2** From data in Vital and Health Statistics (1973). Series 11, No. 124. Rockville, Md.: Dept. of Health, Education, and Welfare. **Fig. 14-3** Data from C.E. Bowerman & J.W. Kinch (1969). Changes in family and peer orientation of children between the fourth and tenth grades. In M. Gold & E. Douvan (Eds.), *Adolescent development.* Boston: Allyn & Bacon. **Table 15-1** From R.G. Braungart (1974). The sociology of generations and student politics: A comparison of the functionalist and generational unit models. *Journal of Social Issues, 30,* 31–54.

About the Authors

Bob Liebert and Judy Harris

For **Judy Harris,** co-authoring this book combined two of her major interests: an interest in the clear communication of ideas, and an interest in children. Her interest in child development began in a somewhat roundabout way; her graduate training (at Harvard University, where she studied under B. F. Skinner and S. S. Stevens) did little to advance it. "In those days," Harris explains, "the field wasn't nearly as interesting as it is today. It really took off in the early 1970s." By then, she was in the middle of a ten-year period that she devoted to rearing her own two children, Nomi, now 18, and Elaine, 14. During this time, she started to read and think about the factors that affect the way children behave, and those that are involved in differences in intelligence and personality. These concerns eventually led to her work on this book. Harris has also co-authored a number of journal articles on perception, information processing, and computer-aided instruction.

To the collaboration that resulted in this text, **Bob Liebert** brings a background that serves as a complement to Harris's. Liebert received his doctorate at Stanford University under Walter Mischel; he was also influenced by Albert Bandura, E. A. Bilodeau, and E. R. Hilgard. Internationally respected for his work on the effects of TV violence on children, Liebert has published papers on many other aspects of child development—cognitive development, moral development, social learning processes, the development of altruism, test anxiety in adolescents, fears in preschool children, and so on. His previous books include *Science and Behavior* and *The Early Window*. Since 1974, Liebert has been Professor of Psychology and Psychiatry at the State University of New York at Stony Brook.

In writing this book, Harris and Liebert had two important goals. First, they wanted to give an accurate, up-to-date, and useful summary of what is currently known about child development. And second, they wanted it to be highly readable.